AGRICULTURAL LAW
Principles and Cases

Donald L. Uchtmann, M.A., J.D.
Associate Professor of Agricultural Law
College of Agriculture
University of Illinois

J. W. Looney, M.S., J.D.
Associate Professor of Law
School of Law
University of Arkansas

N. G. P. Krausz, J.D.
Professor of Agricultural Law, Emeritus
College of Agriculture
University of Illinois

H. W. Hannah, J.D.
Professor of Agricultural Law, Emeritus
College of Agriculture
University of Illinois

McGraw-Hill Book Company

New York   St. Louis   San Francisco   Auckland   Bogotá   Hamburg
Johannesburg   London   Madrid   Mexico   Montreal   New Delhi
Panama   Paris   São Paulo   Singapore   Sydney   Tokyo   Toronto

AGRICULTURAL LAW: Principles and Cases

234567890 DODO 898765432

This book was set in Century by Publication Services.
The editors were David A. Damstra and Susan Hazlett;
the designer was Joseph Gillians; the production
supervisor was Diane Renda.
R. R. Donnelley & Sons Company was printer and
binder.

Library of Congress Cataloging in Publication Data

Main entry under title:

Agricultural law.

    Includes bibliographical references and index.
    1. Agricultural laws and legislation—United States
—Cases. I. Uchtmann, Donald L.
KF1682.A4A34   343.73'076   80–39851
ISBN 0-07-065746-7

*To Nancy
and Era*

Contents

Table of Cases

Names of cases reprinted are marked with an asterisk (*).

Preface

Agricultural Law: Principles and Cases has been developed to meet the growing need for classroom and reference materials addressing broad contemporary legal issues of practical concern to agriculture. The text is quite comprehensive, ranging from basic contract, tort, and property law to the regulation of agricultural employment; from a variety of natural resources issues to provisions in the Uniform Commercial Code of special concern to agriculture; from legal issues surrounding alternative forms of business organizations to a basic discussion of federal estate, gift, and income taxation.

The general principles of agricultural law have been organized into chapters that focus primarily on typical agricultural activities—the acquisition of real estate, the use of land and water, the management of livestock, the sale of agricultural products, the creation of landlord-tenant relationships, the organization of farm businesses, and the ever-present need for tax planning—rather than on traditional divisions of law. The early chapters represent an exception to this organizational pattern because they deal with general principles of contract, tort, and property law which cut across almost all agricultural activities. These early chapters, an invaluable starting point for the reader who has not been exposed to the study of law, may be covered lightly or even skipped where the reader has had previous law courses.

The book includes many cases that have been edited at the discretion of the authors. The book also contains significant textual discussions and numerous footnotes. *Agricultural Law: Principles and Cases* is thus a "hybrid" product, falling somewhere between a more traditional casebook and a treatise of law. The cases provide the undergraduate student with an exposure to the case method of studying law and the law student with a valuable opportunity to learn much about agriculture as well as agricultural law. The inclusion of significant textual material allows the book to be more comprehensive as well as more valuable as a reference for use outside the classroom. The division of content between text and footnotes is designed to make the book more readable by keeping practical information in the text and information of more concern to the legal researcher in the footnotes.

The organization of *Agricultural Law: Principles and Cases* facilitates a variety of uses. The book has been written primarily for students in their final year of undergraduate study but can be adapted for use in junior colleges or, by omitting the material treated in the early chapters, for use in law school courses. In addition the book is intended as a reference for agricultural producers, suppliers, lenders, and those who market agricultural products.

The book is ideally suited as a textbook for a four semester-hour or six quarter-hour agricultural law course, but can be adapted for a shorter course. For example, the materials discussed in Chapter 14 and those that follow—the discussion of alternative business organizations and federal taxation—may be included or excluded depending on the coverage of these subjects in other courses. Also, chapters dealing with particular agricultural activities, such as activities involving farm animals, can be omitted in states where those particular activities are not agriculturally significant.

The authors are indebted to many people for their assistance and support. First, and foremost are the authors' families, whose lives were disrupted by the tremendous amount of time demanded for the preparation of this text. The authors also are indebted to several very capable research assistants who helped in the development of the manuscript, including Ms. Helen Hartnell and Mr. Keith Parr; and to numerous colleagues, including Professor Stephen Matthews of the University of Missouri at Columbia and John Davidson of the University of South Dakota School of Law, who provided helpful suggestions regarding content. Finally, the authors wish to acknowledge the dedicated typing assistance of Mrs. Ruth Sharpton and especially of Mrs. Dorothy Sullivan.

Donald L. Uchtmann

J. W. Looney

1

Introduction—Law and Agricultural Law

The study of agricultural law is a most interesting endeavor. It is both exciting and challenging. It will produce moments of discouragement because of a strange, new vocabulary, complex ideas, and subtle distinctions, but as this study progresses, the legal jargon will seem less foreign and the practical legal principles will be more understandable. When this study of agricultural law is finally completed, one will undoubtedly look back with great satisfaction. But now the task is to look ahead.

1.1 THE DEFINITION AND MEANING OF LAW AND AGRICULTURAL LAW

The Concept of Law

What is this subject of agricultural law? Perhaps this question can best be answered by examining the very concept of law. Law is a deliberate system of enforceable rules intended to coincide with generally accepted concepts of right and wrong. Certainly law implies sanctions, for unless a person can be forced to comply with a legal standard, or at least be held accountable for failure to do so, the purported requirement is not law.

It is the objective of law to give validity and effect to those principles of economic, social, and moral behavior conducive to the welfare of the majority of the people. Justice Holmes said, "Just so far as the aid of the public force is given a man, he has a legal right, and this right is the same whether his claim is founded in righteousness or iniquity." It has been truly said that law follows rather than precedes the social and economic desires of people. This is necessarily true if laws are to be practical. At the same time, however, they must not lag too far behind evident needs.

The range of subject matter dealt with by the law comprehends the whole of human activity and extends from such minute details as the temperature at which milk should be pasteurized to the establishment of broad and sweeping social programs such as medicare and urban renewal. More concretely, law is a constitutional principle, a statute, a legislative enactment, a city ordinance, a park district regulation—in short, the whole body or system of rules of conduct emanating from court decisions and legislative acts.

American farmers or ranchers are governed by laws from all of these sources. There are many local ordinances and regulations that affect their daily activity. A city milk ordinance or a township highway ordinance may have more direct application to them than many of the agricultural laws at the state or federal level.

Agricultural Law

Law is like other social sciences and the humanities in that it touches people in many ways. The selection of those ways which should be organized and discussed under the heading of "agricultural law" is not easy nor will it ever be done with finality. In a *theoretical* sense, agricultural law could be defined as law which is *unique* to agriculture. Such a definition would include subject matter ranging from the organization of the U.S. Department of Agriculture to specific tax laws of concern only to agriculturalists. In a *practical* sense *agricultural law* can be defined as that body of law that is of significance to the everyday business and family lives of agricultural producers. To the extent that such legal issues often involve agricultural producers *and* those who supply agricultural credit, provide other inputs into the production process, and transport or market agricultural products, such a definition includes legal principles that are of practical concern to the entire agribusiness community.

As is apparent from a review of the table of contents, this book utilizes the latter, practical definition of agricultural law. The selection of subject matter to be addressed in the chapters that follow has been

based on the authors' conception of those legal principles of *use* to farmers and ranchers and to the agribusiness community in general. Many of these legal principles, such as basic contract law, have significance outside the agricultural sector as well as within. Nevertheless, since these principles are to be discussed in an agricultural law course, they will be illustrated with cases containing agricultural fact patterns.

A Brief Historical View. It is not surprising that the earliest written laws, such as the Code of Hammurabi (about 2200 B.C.), the Greek Farmer's Law (about 1000 B.C.), the Ecolga (a later Greek code applying to agriculture), and the Mosaic Code, should all contain many provisions regarding farmers. The Code of Hammurabi contained several statements about the rental of farmland and the responsibilities of both landlord and tenant. Many good husbandry requirements were incorporated into the law. One interesting section in the code provided that if a tenant failed to till a field properly, he was required to give to the owner the same amount of grain that his neighbor produced, to plow and harrow the field properly, and then to give the field back to the owner.

The Greek Farmer's Law, even more extensive than the Code of Hammurabi, contained provisions on the preservation of farm boundaries, exchanges of farms, ownership controversies, share renting, cultivation of woodlands, payment of taxes by farmers, thefts of agricultural implements, dealings with cattle, animal trespasses, killing of sheep dogs, and trespasses in vineyards and fig yards, among a number of other subjects.

The Ecolga, a later Greek law, reflected the Roman influence and contained a number of harsh punishments. For example, one who wrongfully drove away the animals belonging to another for a first offense was subjected to a beating, for a second offense to banishment, and for a third offense to having a hand cut off.

Early English law, since it was the foundation of the common-law system adopted in the American states, furnishes much background and many precedents on which our current law is built. Certain laws in England are more comprehensive than ours and have been developed over a longer period of time—those laws relating to land tenure and the rights of landlords and tenants, for example. In the decade 1930–1940, when there was much concern in America about the percentage of land operated by farm tenants, the English Agricultural Holdings Act was studied assiduously by many scholars, and numerous recommendations were made to our state legislatures to incorporate some of its provisions. In our own country, while the trend has been toward an increase in the statutory and regulatory laws concerning agriculture, the common law nevertheless plays an important role, and frequently its historical bases need to be examined.

Selecting Law of Use to Agriculturalists.   If the famous maxim "Ignorance of the law excuses no one" were given a literal application, all of us would be in trouble. But there is another saying popular with the legal profession: "A little learning is a dangerous thing." It is argued that a lay person briefly exposed to legal learning tends to couple this exposure with imagination and when confronted with a legal problem produces a solution which, say some members of the profession, is invariably wrong.

Obviously, the correct approach to legal learning is represented by neither of these adages. It is impossible for anyone to learn and keep abreast of all the laws which affect a person and a person's business. In a sense lawyers themselves have only a smattering of law, farmers only a smattering of the science of soil maintenance and improvement, and ministers only a smattering of the theology which will make bad people good. If we accept the proposition that partial learning is all that is possible in any field, we might be willing to accept the conclusion that successful use of this partial learning depends at least as much on the judgment and acumen of particular individuals as it does on any measured amount of factual knowledge possessed by them. Belief in this conclusion is necessary if we intend to support an educational program in agricultural law—or in soil physics or farm management or beekeeping.

Farmers and ranchers want and need certain facts at certain times. Only during periods of extreme leisure will some of the more inquisitive and persistent seek general learning for its own sake. In that respect farmers are like most other people. Some facts which farmers need to know are a necessary part of their daily decisions, others are called out intermittently, and still others may arise infrequently or not at all. Only a few principles of legal learning fall into the first category, many such principles fall into the second, and still more fall into the third. It would not be profitable for a farmer to spend hours learning the details of eminent domain procedure in his or her state against the time when the county might condemn a strip of the farmer's land for a highway. But it would be profitable and necessary for farmers or ranchers to know the details of applicable labor regulations if they employ agricultural labor—and a knowledge of the fence laws of the state would seem desirable since they maintain their fences all the days of the year.

The impression should not be gained that a farmer's activities are hedged about by legal restraints. Such is not the case. It is true that farmers are touched much more by law than they were several decades ago, and regardless of how much significance the famous maxim "Ignorance of the law excuses no one" may have had in the past, it has more today. This is true not only because there are more laws, but because the individual farmer or rancher circulates in a wider medium.

Resulting Organization of Text

The general principles of agricultural law selected for discussion have been organized into chapters that focus primarily upon typical agricultural activities rather than traditional divisions of law. Such an organization is appropriate when dealing with agricultural law in a practical rather than a theoretical sense. Exceptions to this method of organization can be found in the early chapters wherein broad legal principles cutting across almost all agricultural activities are developed.

As we move through the first five chapters, we will take a "hop, skip, and a jump" through basic principles of contract, tort, and property law, pausing briefly in the chapter "Agricultural Labor, Independent Contractors, and Agents" to discuss some rather specific labor-related laws as well as broad tort concepts such as vicarious liability and the common-law defenses to a negligence action. As we move into Chapter 6 and the remaining chapters, we will shift from an overview of legal principles with widespread application to the consideration of legal principles collected into chapters dealing with typical agricultural activities, such as the acquisition of real estate, the use of land and water, the raising of animals, the sale of agricultural products, the creation of landlord-tenant relationships, the organization of farm businesses, and the ever-present need for tax planning.

1.2 WRITTEN LAW AND COMMON LAW

In a sense, all law is written law. Even the common law is found and determined by reading what judges wrote in the reports of their decisions. But the common law is not written in the sense that a constitution is written, or a body with authority, such as a legislature or a city council or Congress, expresses in written-form commands, prohibitions, or requirements which then become the duty—or the right—of those to whom they apply.

Written Law

In the United States the written law exists at many levels. The federal Constitution is our most important written document. Many of the fundamental rights and duties of citizens of the United States stem from it. The U.S. Constitution is the supreme law of the land. The powers of our federal government arise from it, and it also limits the power of the federal and state governments to interfere with the rights of private citizens. Federal or state legislation that violates basic constitutional principles is invalid. While court interpretation may give meaning to the U.S. Constitution which the average reader could not suspect, these interpretations nevertheless must be based on words in the Constitution.

International agreements and treaties likewise represent an important segment of our written law. Once agreed to, they become binding and their language becomes all-important. Acts of Congress and the published regulations of federal agencies, such as the Departments of Agriculture, Labor, and the Treasury, also are examples of written federal law.

Each state has a written constitution which sets the pattern for many important activities in the state—education and taxation, for example—but, which from the standpoint of political theory, is not the origin of the state's power. State constitutions should be viewed more as limitations or guides to the use of the state's authority, whereas the federal Constitution is the source of federal authority.

Perhaps the single most important source of written law for the farmer and for agriculture generally is the state legislature. State agencies, such as a state environmental protection agency or department of agriculture, likewise must promulgate written rules and regulations to further interpret state laws. Such rules and regulations generally have the force and effect of law. States and agencies within states vary considerably in their policies regarding the publishing and dissemination of these rules and regulations. There has been much improvement in recent years partly as a result of developing legal principles of due process or fairness. At the local level, many bodies, such as municipalities and even townships, engage in legislative and rule-making functions. These local ordinances and rules also must be written and published in some manner to be valid.

The Common Law

Since court interpretations of rules of law are as much a part of the law as the rules themselves, one must look to the opinions of courts to discover how various rules have been applied to particular facts. Thus, court decisions are used as a primary source for discovering the actual substance of our law. These court decisions are called *case law* or *the common law*.

The common law has its roots in the middle ages of England and has slowly grown and evolved. Since the time when court opinions and decisions were first recorded, subsequent courts have looked at the records of preceding decisions and used them as guidance for their own decisions. By the late nineteenth century courts began to view previous holdings as binding on that court or an inferior court if similar facts were present. This doctrine of authoritative precedent is sometimes referred to as *stare decisis*, which literally means "to stand by the decisions." In its modern application *stare decisis* is not absolute; courts are only bound to previous holdings in the absence of good reasons not to follow the precedent. In the decades since the Great Depression courts have tended to view precedent as less binding because the philosophical, economic, and social settings have changed so much over time.[1] Nevertheless, many of today's decisions are still based in part upon the law as laid down by English courts as far back as the twelfth century. These decisions were based entirely on personal feelings of justice and on the decisions that had been handed down before. To many the common law means "written reason," and there is a feeling that through refinement and understanding it could be made to approach absolute justice.

Common law had its beginning in social usage and custom which became law through recognition and enforcement by the courts. This is why common law is frequently referred to as "judge-made law." The influence of the common law is widespread within the United States. For example, most states originally adopted some version of the English common law.[2] The common law of many states today is the English law as modified by more recent American court decisions and statutes.[3]

---

[1] *See* H. J. BERMAN AND W.R. GREINER, THE NATURE AND FUNCTIONS OF LAW § 28.4 (Foundation Press 4th ed. 1980).
[2] *E.g.*, ILL. REV. STAT. ch. 27, § 1. (1979). Illinois adopted the English common law as it existed in 1607—"prior to the fourth year of James the First."
[3] ARTHUR R. HOGUE, ORIGINS OF THE COMMON LAW 3-4 (Indiana University Press 1966). "Rules of common law touch a farmer's property rights in a crop of wheat planted in a rented field or the right to use a public roadway. Nor is the common law a stranger in the market place; the fishmonger as well as the banker may invoke its protection. The bond, then, between law and society is close and intimate; the history of the common law is matter-of-fact and rests ultimately on the relationships of people who have taken their differences before a court for settlement...the common law

Both the written law and the common law vary somewhat from state to state. The chapters which follow present the *more typical and representative rules* of contract, tort, property, and other law. The reader must be aware that *any particular state or jurisdiction may have developed rules which vary slightly or even extensively* from the typical rules illustrated in the chapters which follow.

1.3 ENFORCING THE LAW—LAWYERS AND THE LEGAL SYSTEM

The best source of advice about specific legal problems arising in the farm business is a lawyer. If lawyers were consulted sooner about some things which ripen into first-rate controversies, they could often give sound legal information which, if followed, might avert the controversy or prevent it from reaching dangerous proportions. When it is used frequently and at the right time, legal service is not as expensive as many people imagine. A small amount of litigation is more costly than a great deal of paid legal service and advice. Furthermore, it is likely to be more traumatic.

Lawyers and Their Role as Advisers

The law in most states provides that plaintiffs may prosecute and defendants defend suits themselves. Very few people, however, choose to depend on their own knowledge of law and court procedure. They would rather employ a lawyer, and in this, they are wise. It is the lawyer's business to protect their clients or to procure for clients what they demand, providing lawyers can do so without violating their own conscience and the ethics of the profession. If it is obvious that a client does not have a cause of action, it is the lawyer's duty to so inform the client and not take the case to court.

To become a lawyer in most states, one must complete 7 years of collegiate training, including 3 years in law school, and pass the examination given by the Board of Bar Examiners. In a sense, lawyers are considered as "officers of the court"; that is, they have a duty not only to promote the cause of their client, but to promote the cause of justice and to help the court arrive at a fair decision.

When any farm or other agricultural enterprise achieves a size or complexity which involves a considerable amount of paperwork and the use of many forms, the services of a lawyer are probably required. Certainly a lawyer who understands the farm business and who has had past dealings with an owner can be of more help to the owner when a controversy arises. Though in many states there is no formal recognition of specialization in the law, many lawyers do nevertheless tend to specialize. Some, for example, will handle primarily insurance and corporation cases; others will handle personal injury actions, even to the extent of being only plaintiffs' or defendants' attorneys. If one needs the continuing services of a lawyer, it is well to become acquainted with the specialization patterns of the lawyers in one's community and find an attorney who is willing to deal with and who understands the problems of a farmer.

Lawyers have a high standard of professional conduct that is required by their own professional code of responsibility. Generally lawyers do a pretty good job of living up to these standards, but occasionally an attorney may become delinquent. State bar associations have machinery to investigate cases of unprofessional, unethi-

---

has grown, now rapidly, now reluctantly, to keep pace with changes in the social order, from which, again, it is inseparable." *Id.*

cal, or illegal conduct, and the courts have the power to impose sanctions, such as temporary or permanent suspension of the right to practice law. However, in order for this system of discipline to function, unprofessional conduct must be brought to the attention of the state bar association. On the rare occasion that the high standards of professional conduct, including good faith, reasonable care, and full disclosure, are not met by the lawyer, the client should first advise the attorney, and if the matter cannot be adequately explained, the state bar association should then be consulted.

The American Court System

In America there are two distinct systems of courts—the federal courts and the state courts. The main business of the federal courts is to consider controversies involving federal law or controversies between the citizens of different states. Many of the federal cases which are appealed to higher courts involve constitutional questions. The final authority in the federal court system is the Supreme Court of the United States. The state courts consider all cases not falling under federal jurisdiction. The final authority in these cases is ordinarily the supreme court of the state, though there are some cases which may be appealed from the state supreme court to the Supreme Court of the United States.

Federal Court System. Generally speaking, the federal system has three types of courts: courts of original jurisdiction called *district courts*, in which lawsuits are commenced; eleven circuit courts of appeals, which settle large numbers of controversies appealed from the district courts, the U.S. Tax Court, and various administrative agencies; and the Supreme Court, or "court of last

resort." Figure 1.1 shows how these three types of courts are organized.

State Court Systems.   State court systems are often organized much like the federal system.[4] All state constitutions provide for one court of final review with the exception of New Hampshire, where the highest court was established by the legislature in conformity with its constitutional authority. In most of the states this court is called the supreme court. The name *court of appeals* is employed in Kentucky, Maryland, and New York. In Maine and Massachusetts, this court is called the *supreme judicial court*. In Virginia, the highest court is designated as the *supreme court*, although it was previously known as *the supreme court of appeals*. The courts of last resort hear appeals from designated state courts, either the lower state trial courts or courts of intermediate appeal, usually without regard to the amount of money involved in the controversy.

Supreme court justices are elected in about one-half of the various states. In a few states, such as Delaware, Hawaii, New Jersey, Massachusetts, Maine, and New Hampshire, justices are appointed by the governor with the approval of the state senate or the executive council. In other states, such as Vermont, Rhode Island, South Carolina, and Virginia, final selection is made by the legislature. Many states are adopting a nonpartisan system of judicial selection known as the Missouri or American Bar Association Plan. The major thrust of this plan is the appointment of judges from a list of qualified candidates nominated by a nonpolitical commission. After a period of probationary service, these judges stand for election on the basis of their records, rather than in a contest against other candidates.

[4] F.J. KLEIN, FEDERAL AND STATE COURT SYSTEMS 7–11 (1977).

Figure 1-1   The United States Court System

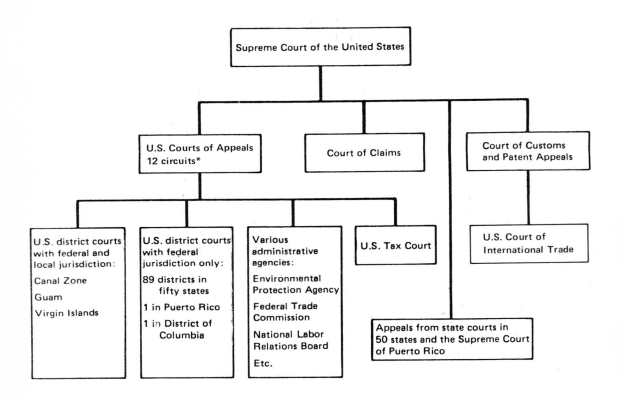

*District of Columbia Circuit, Washington, D.C. (District of Columbia); 1st Circuit, Boston, Mass. (Maine, Massachusetts, New Hampshire, Rhode Island, and Puerto Rico); 2nd Circuit, New York, N.Y. (Connecticut, New York, and Vermont); 3rd Circuit, Philadelphia, Pa. (Delaware, New Jersey, Pennsylvania, and the Virgin Islands); 4th Circuit, Richmond, Va. (Maryland, North Carolina, South Carolina, Virginia, and West Virginia); 5th Circuit, New Orleans, La. (Louisiana, Mississippi, Texas, and the Canal Zone); 6th Circuit, Cincinnati, Ohio (Kentucky, Michigan, Ohio and Tennessee); 7th Circuit, Chicago, Ill. (Illinois, Indiana, and Wisconsin); 8th Circuit, St. Louis, Mo. (Arkansas, Iowa, Minnesota, Missouri, Nebraska, North Dakota, and South Dakota); 9th Circuit, San Francisco, Cal. (Alaska, Arizona, California, Hawaii, Idaho, Montana, Nevada, Oregon, Washington, and Guam); 10th Circuit, Denver, Colo. (Colorado, Kansas, New Mexico, Oklahoma, Utah, and Wyoming); 11th Circuit, Atlanta, Ga. (Alabama, Florida, and Georgia).

About half of the states have established intermediate appellate courts. Ordinarily, these courts are called courts of appeal. The name *appellate court* is employed in Illinois and Indiana, and in Pennsylvania the intermediate appellate court is called the *state superior court*. Intermediate appellate jurisdiction is given to the appellate divisions of the New Jersey Superior Court and the New York Supreme Court. Arkansas has authorized the creation of intermediate appellate courts in the event its Supreme Court becomes too heavily burdened. There is little uniformity in the jurisdiction exercised by intermediate appellate courts. Some of them are given original jurisdiction in special cases. Generally, however, they exercise appellate jurisdiction.

The state trial courts or courts of original jurisdiction may handle civil, criminal, equity, and probate cases. Some states, e.g., South Carolina, maintain separate criminal and civil divisions. Other states, e.g., New York, Massachusetts, and Michigan, maintain separate probate courts to handle estate matters. Most states have abolished procedural distinctions between law and equity, although some states, such as Arkansas and Mississippi, continue to maintain equity courts. In an earlier time, many states provided for special courts to dispose of petty cases. Such "justice of the peace" courts were administered by elected officials who were compensated by the amount of fees collected and did not have to be attorneys. Most states have now abolished such courts in favor of trial courts of broader jurisdiction.

Many states have established special trial courts to hear and determine relatively minor controversies.[5] These courts, often known as *small claims courts* and occasionally referred to as "debtors' courts," typically allow persons to present and argue their cases personally rather than forcing them to rely on legal counsel. The court proceedings are often less formal with no jury, the judge acting as trier of fact. Generally, small claims courts have jurisdictional limits such as $500, $1000, or $1500, and their power is limited to a determination of dollar amounts that must be paid to the aggrieved party. The small claims courts are often appropriate and available for a variety of agriculturally related claims and other personal claims.

Usually judges of the trial courts are selected by the same process as judges of the highest state court. The geographic location of trial courts is usually set by statute, and in most states sessions are held in the county seats.

For the most part, the state judicial systems operate in the same manner in both urban and rural areas. Some differences between the administration of justice in urban and rural areas have been suggested, however.[6]

1.4 THE CASE METHOD OF STUDYING LAW

What to Look For

The approach of the following chapters is to utilize the case method. This method is employed in most law schools across the country as well as in many undergraduate classrooms, and has been adopted by the authors as a most effective way of teaching agricultural law to both graduate and undergraduate students. Law in the abstract is very difficult to remember and even more difficult to comprehend. By studying

---

[5] *See, e.g.,* ILL. REV. STAT. ch. 110A § 291 (1979).
[6] *See, e.g.,* E.K. STOTT, JR., RURAL COURTS THE EFFECT OF SPACE AND DISTANCE ON THE AD-

MINISTRATION OF JUSTICE (a publication of the National Center for State Courts, 1660 Lincoln St., Denver, CO, 1977).

the way courts and administrative bodies have applied the law to actual situations, the student will be in a much better position to understand the law and to appreciate the kind of fact situations that are likely to develop into legal problems. The student should read each case taking note of the underlying facts, the legal principles illustrated, and the policy reflected in each legal principle. The student should also recognize that many of the cases have been appealed on procedural grounds. For example, the party that lost in the trial court may appeal on the grounds that the jury verdict was not supported by the evidence or that the trial judge committed an error of law in disregarding the jury verdict and entering a judgment notwithstanding the verdict (judgment n.o.v.). The student should not be overly concerned about such procedural issues but should concentrate on the "substantive" law illustrated in the case.

Outline of a Civil Action

Civil actions can be distinguished from *criminal actions* in that the former are lawsuits in which disputes between *individuals* are adjudicated while the latter are cases in which the *state* prosecutes an individual accused of having committed a crime. The following is a brief description of the stages in a typical civil action in an American court.[7]

A has been injured by some act of B. A consults an attorney who advises that on the basis of the facts reported by A, B is legally obligated to compensate A for the injury. At A's request a suit against B is initiated by the attorney, who files a written complaint in a court stating that A

has been wronged by B and that A desires the court to entertain the suit and award a judgment against B. B is informed of this complaint. He too enlists the aid of an attorney and is advised that he may have a valid defense against A's claim. At B's request his attorney undertakes the defense. B's attorney informs the court, in writing, of B's intention to defend the suit and the grounds of B's defense. A, now referred to as the plaintiff, has entered a plea for legal redress, and B, now referred to as the defendant, has entered his plea that the court deny the claim. A and B are now parties to a civil action, the case of A versus B.

A number of further preliminary steps will now be taken by the attorneys for A and B. These steps are primarily concerned with developing more detailed information regarding the case so that after the pleading and the preliminary preparation has been completed the nature of the dispute between the parties will be more clearly delineated. During this preliminary process questions may arise regarding the events and circumstances which support the claim of A and the defenses of B. These events and circumstances are "the facts" of the case. They relate to the question, "Who did what to whom when, how, and why?" Questions may also arise regarding the legal significance of the facts. For example, if it is assumed that the facts as stated by the plaintiff (or defendant) are correct, do those facts give rise to a good claim for relief or a good defense under the rules of law relevant to the decision of the case? These questions of fact and questions of law will then be resolved by a trial. (Note that it is not always necessary to have a trial to dispose of a lawsuit. The parties may agree to a settlement prior to trial. Or the

[7] H.J. BERMAN AND W.R. GREINER, THE NATURE AND FUNCTIONS OF LAW § 1 (Foundation Press 4th ed. 1980).

preliminary preparation of the case may provide a basis for judicial resolution of the dispute prior to trial.)

The trial is a hearing at which the parties are given an opportunity to present their respective sides of the matter to an impartial tribunal. This presentation is divided into two parts: (a) the plaintiff's case and (b) the defendant's case.

(a) The plaintiff, through his attorney, will introduce evidence which tends to support his allegations concerning the facts on which his suit is based. His attorney will also present an argument regarding the legal principles which he believes will support a judgment for A. At the close of the plaintiff's case the defendant may ask that the suit be dismissed. For example, he may argue that the plaintiff has failed to introduce evidence sufficient to substantiate his claim or that the plaintiff has failed to show that the law provides for the relief which the plaintiff seeks. If this request (motion) is granted the trial ends; otherwise it will proceed and the defendant will be allowed to present his case.

(b) The defendant, through his attorney, may then present evidence which tends to substantiate his view of the facts or contradict the evidence presented by the plaintiff. Similarly, the defense may present an argument which tends to refute the legal argument advanced on behalf of the plaintiff and which substantiates the defendant's claim that judgment should be entered in his favor. Thus the opposing sides are responsible for developing the information regarding fact and law on which the court's decision is predicated.

The basic responsibility of the court is to hear opposing sides, decide the disputed issues of fact or law, and render judgment in accord with the facts and law as found.

The chief officer of the court is the judge. Sometimes he will hear cases sitting alone; at other times he may have the assistance of a jury, usually consisting of twelve persons drawn from the community at large. When the judge sits alone he must decide both the facts and the law and render judgment accordingly. When the judge sits with a jury there is a division of function. The judge (often referred to as "the court") decides what law is applicable to the case and informs ("instructs") the jury what that law is. The jurors then must determine what are the facts and what result (verdict) should follow from applying to those facts the law which the judge has given to them. Usually the jury verdict is in a "general" form, e.g., "We find for the plaintiff in the sum of $7,500." or "We find for the defendant." The judge will then—in most cases—render a judgment based on the jury verdict. The judgment in a civil case is a formal declaration of the outcome of the suit and an announcement of the remedy (if any) to which the winner is entitled. This terminates the trial phase of the litigation but is not necessarily the end of the judicial proceedings.

Either or both of the parties may not be satisfied that the judgment of the court is proper. If this is so, there may be an appeal from the decision of the trial court. The appeal will be made to an appellate court, a tribunal established expressly for the purpose of reviewing the decisions of lower courts, such as the trial court.

The function of the appellate court is to review decisions of lower courts to determine if substantial error has been committed in those courts. If an error has been committed which, in the opinion of the appellate court, actually or potentially led to a judgment adverse to the party who appealed (appellant), then the appellate court may act to correct this error. Such action will be taken only in those instances where the error was of a type which the appellate court is competent to review. We may label these errors as errors of law. For example, where a trial judge finds that rule X is applicable to a particular point in a case and the appellate court finds instead that rule Y is the appropriate rule, we may say that an error of law has been committed and the appellate court may correct this error. On the other hand, claims that a jury has erred in making findings of fact are not generally a sound basis for appeal, for the finding of fact is the special province of the trial court and appellate courts are reluctant to disturb such findings. However, if the record of the case makes it abundantly clear that the facts found by the jury (or judge) were not supported by the evidence presented in the trial, the appellate court may reverse the decision, for a gross misreading of the evidence is considered an "error of law."

The party who wishes to appeal must complain to the appellate court that error has been committed and must take the necessary steps to present his case to the reviewing court. Upon such request an appellate hearing will be held. This hearing affords the appellant (sometimes referred to as the petitioner, or the plaintiff in error) and the other party (variously referred to as the appellee, the respondent, or the defendant in error) an opportunity to make argument to the court. The appellate court consists of a panel of three or more judges who sit to hear counsel present arguments and then to decide the appeal by vote (majority rule). No new evidence is presented since the appellate court is not competent to make new findings of fact; rather the court bases its decision on the verbatim record of the trial court proceedings, on the argument of the attorneys in the appellate proceeding, and on its own understanding of the applicable law.

The oral argument in the appellate hearing is a discussion between lawyers at the bar (the attorneys) and lawyers on the bench (the judges) as to the correct legal principles which govern the case at hand. (In addition to hearing oral arguments, the appellate court receives "briefs"— written arguments—from the attorneys.) If the record and the argument disclose substantial error, the appellate court may then take steps to correct the error by reversing the judgment and finding for the appellant or by sending the case back for a new trial (these are the most common but not the sole remedies afforded in the appellate court). The appellate court's decision is, in most cases, announced through a written opinion prepared by one of the judges.

When a final judgment is pronounced in a court action the issues in the case are said to be *res judicata*—"the matter is adjudged" —and will not be reexamined by the courts. This rule has exceptions but for the most part the courts adopt a policy which favors the termination of litigation between parties once they have had a full and fair hearing of their case and a judgment thereon.

This is but a rough outline of the procedure through which a civil action—a case involving the competing claims of individual parties—passes on its way to judicial resolution. It is not a totally accurate or perfect description of the process but for our purposes it provides basic information sufficient to facilitate a better understanding of the cases which follow.

STUDY QUESTIONS

1. What are some of the earliest laws pertaining to agriculture and what kinds of issues did they address?

2. From what sources does our current body of law arise? Are these written or unwritten?

3. In your locality where can you find the written and unwritten law? What are the names of the references containing the written law?

4. How does the concept of law differ from religious or ethical mores?

5. What is *stare decisis*?

6. What are the two parallel court systems that exist in the United States?

7. What kinds of controversies can be heard in federal courts?

8. What are the three levels of courts in the federal court system?

9. How many levels of courts are in your state court system? What are they?

10. What is the difference between a civil court action and a criminal court action?

11. What are small claims courts?

12. What steps are likely to occur in a civil action before the controversy actually goes to trial?

13. What are the relative roles of a judge and jury in a civil trial?

14. What is the function of an appellate court? What is an error of law?

15. What is the meaning of the latin phrase *res judicata* and what is its practical significance?

2
Contracts

Individuals may govern conduct among themselves by mutual agreements, validly made and consistent with law and public policy. Such agreements—really self-imposed rules—are called *contracts*. Simply defined, a contract is an agreement between two or more parties consisting of a promise or a set of promises which the law will enforce or the performance of which the law in some way recognizes as a duty.[1]

Contractual obligations are applicable only to the parties agreeing to them. These rights or obligations are created by words, or sometimes by conduct, that demonstrate an intention of the parties involved to exchange certain rights with a concurrent exchange of duties.

Most people make numerous contracts in the course of daily living, many of which are simple oral agreements which express the intent of the parties. Certainly, the operation of a business involves contracts on a regular basis. The buying and selling of supplies and products, real estate transactions, employment agreements, leases of land or machinery, and numerous other ordinary business transactions involve rules of contract law.

The following pages will discuss principles of contract law applicable to almost all contractual settings. Such principles include the meaning and elements of express and implied contracts, the instances when contracts are required to be in writing, the insignificance of prior oral promises or statements once a contract is reduced to writing, and potential remedies when a contract is breached. Additional contract

---

[1] 1 S. WILLISTON, TREATISE ON THE LAW OF CONTRACTS § 1 (3d ed. 1957).

principles of particular importance to certain transactions such as the purchase of real estate and the sale of agricultural products will be developed in later chapters.

2.1 THE ELEMENTS AND NATURE OF CONTRACT

Express Contracts

Certain elements are necessary for a valid contract: (1) legally competent parties, (2) proper subject matter, (3) offer, (4) acceptance, and (5) consideration.[2] If any one of these elements is absent, there is no contract. In addition to the above, certain contracts must be in writing to be enforceable.

The requirement of legal capacity is especially important when one prospective party to an agreement is a minor or of deficient mental capacity. The age of majority was 21 at common law, but an increasing number of states have lowered the age to 18. Generally persons under the age of majority lack capacity to enter into contracts binding upon themselves. Such agreements are said to be "voidable" by the infant but binding upon the other party. Some exceptions exist, however, including contracts for necessities or, in some states, student loans.

Whether a party to a contract has sufficient mental capacity to be a legally competent party is a more difficult issue. Generally, one whose mental capacity is so deficient that he or she is incapable of understanding the significance of a contract may disaffirm it during a lucid moment or through his or her legal representative. Deficient mental capacity can arise

from mental illness or even intoxication. As in the case of minors, mental incompetents can still be held liable for necessities.

A contract may lack proper subject matter if the agreement involves illegal activity. Thus, agreements in restraint of trade, gambling contracts, murder contracts, and the like are not enforceable in the courts because the element of proper subject matter is missing.

A mutual understanding or a "meeting of the minds" must be present before a contract can exist. Such agreement is usually reached through a process of offer and acceptance, oftentimes including counteroffers and much altering of conditions before an agreement is finally reached. Questions which concern delivery, quantity, weight, price, quality, payment, or any other things that may affect the agreement should be settled.

To be enforceable, a contract must provide consideration; i.e., the parties must exchange something of value. The thing of value may consist of money, labor, goods, or a promise to do or not to do some specific thing. A contract may come into existence when each party has promised something of value to the other, or when one party actually performs part of the agreement in return for a promise from the other.

If one party fails to carry out its terms, the other may sue for damages or, in some instances, force the party who is not carrying out the terms to perform them. Forcing the performance of the terms is called *specific performance*.

Creating Express Contracts. The following cases illustrate the elements of a contract and how a contract is created.

---

[2] *See* RESTATEMENT (SECOND) OF CONTRACTS §§ 18, 22, 24, 52, 75 (1973).

CONTRACT OFFER

LUCY v. ZEHMER
Supreme Court of Appeals of Virginia, 1956
196 Va. 493, 84 S.E.2d 516

This suit was instituted by the Lucys, complainants, against the Zehmers, defendants, concerning the validity of an alleged contract by which the Zehmers sold to the Lucys a tract of land owned by A.H. Zehmer in Dinwiddie County containing 471 acres, more or less, known as the Ferguson farm, for $50,000.

The instrument sought to be enforced was written by A.H. Zehmer on December 20, 1952, in these words: "We hereby agree to sell to W.O. Lucy the Ferguson Farm complete for $50,000, title satisfactory to buyer," and signed by the defendants, A.H. Zehmer and Ida S. Zehmer.

The answer of A.H. Zehmer admitted that at the time mentioned Lucy suggested a sale of the farm for $50,000 cash, but that he, Zehmer, considered that the suggestion was made in jest; that so thinking, and both he and Lucy having had several drinks, he wrote out "the memorandum" quoted above and induced his wife to sign it; that he did not deliver the memorandum to Lucy, but that Lucy picked it up, read it, put it in his pocket, attempted to offer Zehmer $5 to bind the bargain, which Zehmer refused to accept, and realizing for the first time that Lucy was serious, Zehmer assured him that he had no intention of offering to sell the farm and that the whole matter was a joke. Lucy left the premises insisting that he had purchased the farm.

The defendants insist that the evidence was ample to support their contention that the writing sought to be enforced was prepared as a bluff or dare to force Lucy to admit that he did not have $50,000; that the whole matter was a joke; that the writing was not delivered to Lucy and no binding contract was ever made between the parties.

In his testimony Zehmer claimed that he "was high as a Georgia pine," and that the transaction "was just a bunch of two doggoned drunks bluffing to see who could talk the biggest and say the most." That claim is inconsistent with his attempt to testify in great detail as to what was said and what was done. The record is convincing that Zehmer was not intoxicated to the extent of being unable to comprehend the nature and consequences of the instrument he executed, and hence that instrument is not to be invalidated on that ground. It was in fact conceded by defendants' counsel in oral argument that under the evidence Zehmer was not too drunk to make a valid contract.

[An offer creates a power of acceptance in the offeree and a corresponding liability on the part of the offerer. For statements to constitute an offer, they must create a reasonable expectation in the offeree that the person making the offer is willing to enter into a contract. In order to create such a reasonable expectation the offer must express an intention to enter into a contracted commitment, it must provide certainty and definiteness as to the essential terms of the contract, and it must be communicated to the offeree.]

In the field of contracts, as generally elsewhere, "[W]e must look to the outward expression of a person as manifesting his intention rather than to his secret and unexpressed intention." An agreement of mutual assent is of course essential to a valid contract but the law imputes to a person an intention corresponding to the reasonable meaning of his words and acts. If his words and acts, judged by a reasonable standard, manifest an intention to agree, it is immaterial what may be the real but unexpressed state of his mind. A person cannot set up that he was merely jesting when his conduct and words would warrant a reasonable person in believing that he intended a real agreement.

The appearance of the contract, the fact that it was under discussion for forty minutes or more before it was signed; Lucy's objection to the first draft because it was written in the singular, and he wanted Mrs. Zehmer to sign it also; the rewriting to meet that objection and the signing by Mrs. Zehmer; the discussion of what was to be included in the sale, the provision for the examination of the title, the completeness of the instrument that was executed, the taking possession of it by Lucy with no request or suggestion by either of the defendants that he give it back, are facts which furnish persuasive evidence that the execution of the contract was a serious business transaction rather than a casual, jesting matter as defendants now contend....

The complainants are entitled to have specific performance of the contract sued on. The decree appealed from is therefore reversed and the cause is remanded for the entry of a proper decree requiring the defendants to perform the contract in accordance with the prayer of the bill.

CONTRACT ACCEPTANCE

BRAUN v. CAMAS PRAIRIE R. CO.
Supreme Court of Idaho, 1951
72 Idaho 83, 237 P. 2d 604

Plaintiff claimed that defendant negligently killed his registered Milking Shorthorn cow with her sucking calf, and one heifer, of the reasonable value of $1,100.00 on December 5, 1946.

Questioning the asserted value of the animals, negotiations were carried on between plaintiff, and in later stages, his attorney, and defendant's claim agents, culminating in defendant's grudging letter of February 10, 1949 containing nevertheless the complete and definite offer to pay $400.00. The letter was as follows.

Lewiston, Idaho, Feb. 10, 1949

Mr. Samuel Swayne, Attorney
Orofino, Idaho

Re: Carl P. Braun vs. Camas Prairie RR.

Dear Sir:

Sorry to have kept you waiting so long but in the meantime, Mr. Rolland Little has been contacted and more data received on the case.

It is true that Mr. Braun purchased two pedigreed animals from Mr. Little, but, also the only way animals can be definitely identified is by the branding marks, which in this case seemed badly mixed up.

In case of court procedure, it might be extremely difficult and doubtful for your client to have his contention sustained, that the particular animal claim is made for, is the same animal killed. You must remember that your client is making a claim for a cow tattooed [*sic*] LE 50, whereas the cow that was killed was tattooed [*sic*] LE 20. I do not doubt that your client is honest in his opinion that it is one and the same cow, but the doubt remains.

Even with this doubt existing, I am willing to compromise if your client is, and in the interest of good will, the offer of $400.00 is made with the understanding that this amount covers all animals included in his claim.

Please inform me of your decision.

Yours truly,

(s) J.M. McBride
Claim Agent

On March 4 of the same year, plaintiff's attorney, by what the authorities deem a grumbling or complaining letter, accepted the offer:

March 4, 1949

Mr. J.M. McBride,
Claims Agent,
Camas Prairie Railroad,
Lewiston, Idaho

Re: Carl Braun

Dear Mr. McBride:

At my insistance Mr. Carl Braun will accept the four hundred dollars ($400.00) as settlement for the destruction of his cattle by your locomotive.

However, I wish you would reconsider and at least split the difference with him for the following reasons:

There is no doubt as to the identity of this animal, and I believe it could be established by Affidavits of fifteen or twenty persons. I happen to live next door to Mr. Little and am personally acquainted with many of the facts of this case. I also raise Registered Shorthorn Cattle and in my judgment, the compensation is inadequate for the animal, not to mention others that were killed with it.

I also have personally tattooed these animals, and am not so sure there is any discrepancy in the identity. If you will examine the enclosed piece of paper it will illustrate my point. I have placed the number fifty (50) and twenty(20) on the paper with the X beside the twenty (20) hold it up to the light and read it through the paper and you will understand how a five could appear as a two if read from the opposite side of the ear, which might easily happen if the punch penetrates clear through the ear, as frequently is the case.

If you have the ears in your possession, I suggest that you examine and see if this is not what happened.

I repeat that I think under the circumstances that Five hundred Dollars ($500.00) is very fair to you and wholly inadequate to Mr. Braun. Nevertheless under the duress of bundlesome litigation, Mr. Braun, at my insistance [sic] will accept the Four Hundred Dollars ($400.00).

Yours very truly,

(s) Samuel F. Swayne

March 10, 1949, the claim agent, in a letter to plaintiff's attorney, attempted to revoke the offer:

Lewiston, Idaho, Mar. 10, 1949

Mr. Samuel Swayne,
Attorney,
Orofino, Idaho

Re: Carl Braun

Dear Sir:

This letter is to advise you that the offer of settlement in the Carl Braun claim, on the date of February 10, 1949 is withdrawn.

As you are no doubt aware the Idaho statute limits the time of action to eighteen (18) months, where animals are killed on the Railroad right-of-way and I doubt very much if any grounds remain on which to base the payment to Mr. Braun.

(s) J.M. McBride

Claim Agent

Defendant refused to pay and suit was instituted. At the trial defendant sought to place in evidence all of the prior and subsequent correspondence between the parties. Plaintiff objected and the objection was sustained on the ground that the offer and acceptance letters constituted a complete contract. Verdict was directed for plaintiff for $400.00. Defendant appeals.

The sole question involved is whether the letter of plaintiff's attorney of March 4, 1949 constituted a definite acceptance, defendant contending it was conditional and contemplated further negotiations. The majority of the decided cases hold that an acceptance must be absolute, unqualified, and unconditional, and that one who has the power of acceptance utilize a valid mode for communicating the acceptance. An express and definite acceptance is not conditional because the acceptor expresses dissatisfaction with the offer or seeks as a favor modification of the offer, but does not present such a request as a condition of acceptance. In a Michigan case, the court held that an acceptance was definite and final when made in the following language:

"We think you ought to pay us $3,333.33, but if you will not pay that sum we will take $2,500.00, which please send."

The letter herein, though indicating that $500.00 would be fair to defendant and inadequate to Braun, concluded: "Nevertheless under the duress of burdensome litigation, Mr. Braun, at my insistence, will accept the four hundred dollars ($400.00)." The letter constituted a sufficient acceptance to make a completed contract.

The cases indicate that for an acceptance to be effective, it must contain a specific condition and one which the acceptor offers as a definite alternative to or in lieu of the offering, and not merely grumbling or complaining. None of the correspondence rejected by the trial court when it was offered by defendant, or the evidence presented, was sufficient to annul the contract offer and acceptance made complete by the letter of plaintiff's attorney. Judgement, therefore, is affirmed.

For a meeting of the minds to occur, the acceptance must be effective before the offer expires or is revoked. An offer can expire by its own terms or after the passage of reasonable time. An offer can be revoked by operation of law if the subject matter of the contract is destroyed, if a new legal prohibition arises, or if the person making the offer dies or becomes insane. An offer also can be revoked by an express communication to that effect made before the offer is accepted.

As a general rule, offers, acceptances and revocations of offers are effective when the communication is received by the other party.[3] The "mailbox rule" is an exception to the general rule, but the "mailbox rule" exception applies only to *acceptances*. The rule states that where use of the mails is a reasonable method of accepting an offer, the acceptance is deemed effective when posted. This rule does not apply to offers or revocations.

The Contracts of Married Persons.   By common law, when a man and woman married, they became as one. The "one" was the husband. He controlled his wife's person and property rights, was entitled to any money she might earn from outside employment, and represented her in lawsuits.

In most states, these common-law principles have been replaced by statutes giving women equal property rights with men. These statutes typically give a married woman the right to own, purchase, sell, mortgage, or otherwise deal with her own personal and real property; to sue and to be sued without joining her husband with her; to defend in her own right if she and her husband are sued together; to prosecute or defend in her husband's name if she is deserted by her husband, any actions he might have prosecuted or defended; to be immune from her husband's creditors except insofar as his obligations are for family expenses and the education of their children; to enter into contracts; to receive, use, and possess her own earnings, and to sue for them in her own name, free from the interference of her husband or his creditors.[4]

Often states limit the right of husband and wife to contract *with each other* by

---

[3] See RESTATEMENT (SECOND) OF CONTRACTS §§ 41, 64, 69 (1973).

[4] E.g., ILL. REV. STAT. ch. 40, §§ 1001–1021 (1979).

providing that neither husband nor wife shall be entitled to recover any compensation for any labor performed or services rendered for the other, whether in the management of property or otherwise. In interpreting such laws, the courts have held that a wife is not entitled to compensation for nursing her husband during illness, nor is the husband entitled to compensation for labor performed on his wife's farm.

Implied Contracts

Most contracts are formed by express language as seen in the previous cases, although sometimes a contract can be implied. For example, suppose farmer A contracts for the painting of A's barn. The painter makes an honest mistake and paints farmer B's barn instead. If B was present and sat idly by (perhaps thinking how wonderful it was to have the barn painted free!), B would be in for a surprise. Where one knows or should have known that another party is making a mistake, one's conduct in failing to advise of the mistake can be construed by the courts as an implied promise to pay for the service at the intended contract price. Such a contract is *implied in fact*.

Alternatively, suppose B was on vacation when the contractor mistakingly painted B's barn. Since B could not have known of the mistake, B's failure to tell the contractor of the mistake does not give rise to a contract implied in fact. Nevertheless, a court could find that a contract was *implied in law*.[5] Both B and the painter are innocent parties. However, B has a newly painted barn, and as a result has been "unjustly enriched." A court would probably require B to compensate the mistaken painter by an amount representing B's increased property value.

Note that in both examples of implied contracts, the mistake was honest. If the painter was working his or her way through college by intentionally painting every barn in sight, he or she could not seek redress through the courts because the requirement of an honest mistake would be lacking.

2.2 WRITTEN AND ORAL CONTRACTS

When a Written Instrument Is Required— The Statute of Frauds

All states have adopted some version of the statute for the prevention of frauds and perjuries enacted by the English Parliament in 1677. This statute contained twenty-five sections, one of which declared that the following types of oral promises should not be enforceable unless some written note or memorandum evidencing the agreement had been signed by the party to be charged:

1. Promises of an executor or administrator to pay any debt or damages out of his or her own estate
2. Promises of any defendant to pay for the debts, defaults, or miscarriages of another person
3. Promises made in exchange for marriage
4. Promises that cannot be performed within 1 year of the date of the promise
5. Promises concerning the sale of land

Another section of the English statute required a similar written memorandum for the sale of any goods if the selling price was "ten pounds sterling" or upward. Most states have updated this provision by adopting Sec. 2–201 of the Uniform Commercial Code (UCC). The UCC sets forth the

---

[5] RESTATEMENT (SECOND) OF CONTRACTS §§ 57, 72 (1973); 1 S. WILLISTON, *supra* note 1, at § 3; G.C. GRISMORE, PRINCIPLES OF THE LAW OF CONTRACTS § 8 (rev. ed. J.E. Murray, Jr. 1965).

general rule that contracts for the sale of goods for $500 or more must be evidenced by a writing signed by the party against whom enforcement is sought.[6]

At least three of the provisions noted above are of particular importance to farmers and ranchers: (1) transfers of real estate, (2) contracts that cannot be performed within 1 year after they are made, and (3) contracts to sell goods for $500 or more.

Whether or not a written contract should be prepared is likely to be more a question of business procedure than one of law. A well-prepared written contract can take care of many questions which might arise later—questions regarding such things as number, place of delivery, time of delivery, price, quality, and other essential elements of the agreement which, if not settled in advance, may cause controversy. While the courts will recognize customs regarding delivery, establishment of price, and other elements of the agreement, the court cannot "make" a contract for the parties when their own agreement fails to reduce to sufficiently definite determination an essential condition without which there cannot be a contract. The courts, however, do recognize the principle that partial performance of an agreement which would otherwise be void may make it a valid agreement. This is one of the principal ways in which an oral agreement may become enforceable even though at the time of agreement it was void under the statute of frauds. Cases which follow illustrate the importance of the statute of frauds and the impact which it still has in the field of contract.

Required Contents of the Memorandum

STATUTE OF FRAUDS—SUFFICIENCY OF MEMORANDUM

CALLAGHAN v. MILLER
Supreme Court of Illinois, 1959
17 Ill. 2d 595, 162 N.E. 2d 422

Defendant Wilma Martin Miller, executrix of the estate of Altha G. Martin, deceased, appeals from a decree of the circuit court of Kane County, compelling specific performance of an alleged real-estate contract and ordering the defendant to execute a real-estate deed for same to the plaintiffs, Charles Callaghan and Sylvia Callaghan. From this decree, defendant appeals directly to this court, a freehold necessarily being involved.

On July 17, 1957, Mrs. Altha G. Martin engaged Mrs. Ida Tank, a realtor, to sell a certain five-acre tract of land north of Batavia, Illinois, and owned

---

[6] UCC § 2-105 defines goods as follows: 1)"'Goods' means all things, including specially manufactured goods, which are movable at the time of identification to the contract for sale other than the money in which the price is to be paid, investment securities (Article 8) and things in action. 'Goods' also includes the unborn young of animals and growing crops and other identified things attached to realty as described in the section on goods to be severed from realty (Section 2-107). 2) "Goods must be both existing and identified before any interest in them can pass. Goods which are not both existing and identified are 'future' goods. A purported present sale of future goods or of any interest therein operates as a contract to sell."

Some states differentiate goods and other personal property. For example, Virginia generally requires that contracts for the sale of goods exceeding $500 be in writing and that contracts for the sale of other personal property exceeding $5000 be in writing.

by her. The property was improved by a residence and used as a trailer court. Mrs. Tank obtained a 60-day exclusive contract to sell the realty for $52,000 at 5 per cent commission. The plaintiffs contacted Mrs. Tank in regard to a possible purchase of the same, and later inspected the property in company with Mrs. Martin, Mrs. Tank and Ralph Johnson. On September 9 the plaintiffs offered to purchase the property for $47,500 and tendered and deposited the sum of $1,000. Mrs. Tank communicated the offer to Mrs. Martin and drew up a receipt for plaintiffs which Mrs. Martin signed as approved. The receipt or memorandum was as follows:

Room 26, Sept. 9, 1957

Ida M. Tank, Real Estate
123 W. Front Street, Wheaton, Illinois

Received of Charles Callaghan and Sylvia Callaghan his wife, One Thousand Dollars ($1,000), being deposited as earnest money for purchase of the Altha Martin property located on Route 25, north of the City of Batavia, Illinois (not in corporation). This area comprises five acres more or less. The space now occupied by 20 trailers is properly licensed and zoned by the State of Illinois and Kane County Zoning Dept. (non-conforming use).

Above deposit is made on offer to purchase of the Altha Martin property for $47,500 with 1/3 cash at time of transfer of title to buyer, balance evidenced by amortizing mortgage with $200 or more to be paid each month thereafter, plus interest at 5 per cent per annum paid monthly on the unpaid balance.

Subject to approval by owner.

Possession to be given 30 days after closing of above deal.

Sgnd/Ida M. Tank,
Realtor

Approved
Altha G. Martin/Sgnd/.

In the presence of Mrs. Tank and Ralph Johnson, Mrs. Altha G. Martin signed the receipt or memorandum "approved" and signed her name. Mrs. Tank placed the $1,000 in her special account in the Gary-Wheaton Bank, and delivered a copy of this receipt to the plaintiffs.

Thereafter, Mrs. Tank called Richard D. Shearer, the attorney for Mrs. Martin, and requested that he draft a contract setting forth the detailed terms of the purchase and sale. On September 17, 1957, Shearer prepared a contract, and the plaintiffs appeared in his office and signed it. They were then informed that Mrs. Martin was ill in the hospital.

About four days later Mrs. Martin died without having signed the contract. Mrs. Wilma Miller, a daughter of Mrs. Martin and the executrix of her estate refused to convey the property to the plaintiffs, and they brought this proceeding for specific performance to require the executrix to convey the realty to them. The court found the memorandum met the requirements of the Statute of Frauds, and decreed specific performance. A freehold being involved the defendant executrix appeals directly to this court, contending that the receipt or memorandum on its face does not spell out the terms with sufficient certainty and clarity for the court to enforce the same.

The memorandum is sufficient to satisfy the Statute of Frauds if it contains upon its face the names of the vendor and the vendee, a description of the property sufficiently definite to identify the same as the subject matter of the contract, the price, terms and conditions of the sale, and the signature of the party to be charged. The names of both vendees, Charles Callaghan and Sylvia Callaghan, and the name of the vendor, Altha Martin, appear upon the face of the memorandum.

The subject matter of the contract is "the Altha Martin property located on Route 25, north of the city of Batavia, Illinois (not in corporation). This area comprises five acres more or less. The space now occupied by 20 trailers is properly licensed and zoned by the State of Illinois and Kane County Zoning Dept. (non-conforming use)." The plaintiffs, Ralph Johnson, Mrs. Tank, and even the defendant have all identified the property. The property is thus sufficiently and clearly identified.

The price, terms and conditions are definite and certain. They are stated as $47,500 with 1/3 cash at time of transfer of title to buyer, balance evidenced by amortizing mortgage with $200 or more to be paid each month thereafter, plus interest at 5% per annum paid monthly on the unpaid balance."

The memorandum bears the signature of Altha G. Martin as approving the memorandum and offer of purchase. The Statute of Frauds is thus clearly satisfied.

Defendant executrix urges, in addition, that the memorandum of September 9, 1957, is merely a contract to make a contract, and is thus too indefinite to be specifically enforced. Defendant bases her assertion upon the fact that decedent's attorney prepared a contract embodying all of the details of the memorandum, spelled out in more specific terms. However, in this case, even though decedent's attorney did prepare a detailed contract which Mrs. Martin was never able to execute, the terms are sufficiently definite and certain in the memorandum to be specifically enforced. As in the case of *Welsh v. Jakstas*, 401 Ill. 288, cited to us by defendant, this memorandum did not constitute a contract under which the parties were to negotiate and agree upon the terms of another contract to be entered into when the terms had been ascertained and determined. The memorandum, containing the proposal of purchase, itself constituted an adequate memorandum of the agreement of the parties when approved by the decedent. The memorandum itself then constituted a contract of sale in sufficiently clear and unambiguous language to be specifically enforced. It is not rendered indefinite or void because an additional contract was thereafter prepared.

The decree of the circuit court of Kane County is affirmed.

Exceptions to the Writing Requirement

The purpose of the English statute of frauds and its contemporary counterparts was to prevent the perpetration of fraud by those who were able to obtain perjured testimony. By simply refusing to enforce oral contracts in those situations that were especially troublesome (e.g., promises to answer for the debt of another) or significant (e.g., contracts for the sale of land), Parliament hoped to achieve this purpose. Unfortunately, what was gained in the prevention of fraud came at the expense of permitting persons who had in fact made oral promises "to break those promises with impunity and to cause loss and disappointment to honest men."[7] As a result courts have often interpreted the statute of frauds very narrowly.

For example, in the Iowa case of *Bader v. Hiscox*, 188 Iowa 986, 174 N.W. 565 (1919), a farmer's son seduced a 17-year-old girl. After becoming pregnant, she brought civil and criminal proceedings against the farmer's son. The farmer orally promised to deed a farm to her if she would marry the son and dismiss the proceedings. The girl married the son and dismissed her suit but the farmer refused to convey the land. When the girl sued to collect the value of the farmland, the farmer set forth the statute of frauds as a defense, arguing that his promise was for the sale of real estate, was a promise to answer for the default of another, and was a promise based upon the consideration of marriage. The trial court dismissed the case but the Iowa Supreme Court disagreed, holding that the statute of frauds did not apply.

The court sidestepped the marriage provision of the statute by concluding that marriage was not the "end to be attained" but was a mere necessary "incident"; it sidestepped the provision dealing with promises to pay for the debt or default of another by concluding that the father did not promise to serve the son's potential jail sentence or pay any civil judgment against the son; it sidestepped the provision dealing with the sale of lands by concluding that full performance of a contractual obligation by one party was a recognized exception that took the case out of the statute of frauds.

Partial Performance and Estoppel. Several common situations where oral contracts are enforced even though the statute of frauds would generally require a writing are illustrated in the following cases.

---

[7] A. CORBIN, CORBIN ON CONTRACT 372 (1 vol. ed. 1952).

PARTIAL PERFORMANCE

WURTH v. HOSMANN
Supreme Court of Illinois, 1952
410 Ill. 567, 102 N.E. 2d 800

Mr. Justice Fulton delivered the opinion of the court:

Fred Wurth, the appellee, brought this suit in the circuit court of Cook County, seeking specific performance of a contract to convey a farm of approximately 56 acres under an agreement with his uncle, Fred Hosmann. It is claimed that the uncle promised to leave the farm to his nephew, Fred Wurth, if the nephew would stay on the farm and help his uncle until the latter's death. The suit was brought against Lottie Irene Hosmann, wife of Fred Hosmann, to whom the property was conveyed on October 12, 1943. The circuit court entered a decree for the plaintiff. An appeal has been taken to this court, a freehold being involved.

The complaint filed by appellee alleges that his uncle, Fred Hosmann, entered into an agreement with the plaintiff that if plaintiff would stay and work on the farm with him, the said Fred Hosmann would devise and bequeath to the plaintiff, by his last will and testament, his farm property, together with the farm house, farm buildings, furniture, household goods and effects, consumable stores and provisions, crops, livestock, poultry, tools, implements, and other property belonging to the said farm upon the death of the said Fred Hosmann.

The complaint further stated that plaintiff accepted the same and completely performed his part of the contract; that on November 21, 1936, Fred Hosmann made and executed an instrument purporting to be his last will and testament devising and bequeathing all of said property to the plaintiff; that on October 9, 1943, Fred Hosmann married the defendant, Lottie Irene Hosmann, and on October 12, 1943, he conveyed the said real estate to one Nettie D. Phillips, who in turn, on the same date, conveyed the real estate to Fred Hosmann and Lottie Irene Hosmann jointly.

The answer of the defendant denied the material allegations of the complaint and particularly denied that any such contract had been entered into or that plaintiff had worked on said farm without adequate remuneration. She further alleged that she and Fred Hosmann occupied the farm as their homestead from the date of their marriage until the date of Hosmann's death and that she is still in possession of said premises as the surviving joint tenant.

Briefly, the evidence of plaintiff, Fred Wurth, shows that in June, 1912, shortly after the death of his mother, he went to live on the Hosmann farm with his maternal grandmother and two bachelor uncles, Henry and Fred Hosmann; that he graduated from grammar school in 1917; that he continued to live and work on the farm but never received any pay for his work until 1920; that his father died previous to 1920 and up until that time his father had bought all his clothes and furnished him with spending money; that his uncles then began to pay him $12 a month for his service on the farm and he purchased his own necessities from that salary. After two years he told his uncles he needed more money so they paid him $15 a month. At the time they began paying him $15 a month, the plaintiff was about 20 years of age and they continued paying him this salary until 1925; that during the year 1925 the Hosmann brothers sold twenty acres of the farm for $20,000 cash. After that they gave him $25 a month until 1928. Plaintiff then asked his uncles for more money and after two or three days' deliberation they told him they had decided to pay him $30 per month, but they couldn't give him any more at that time and that "they were going to take care of me later on, as the farm would be mine."

Plaintiff was paid $30 a month until June, 1936. In the meantime, Henry Hosmann had died and plaintiff told his uncle, Fred Hosmann, that he had twice as much work to do since Henry was gone; that he was then 33 years of age and had prospects of better jobs that would pay him more money; that Fred Hosmann replied to this statement by saying that he knew he was not paying plaintiff enough money, but he said, "If you will stay with me and we will run the farm the same as we did before, I agree right now to leave you the farm and all the implements, livestock, and household goods after I die." Plaintiff replied that he would like to see that in writing and Hosmann said he would make arrangements to have it put in writing. Later Hosmann showed plaintiff a will he had executed on November 21, 1936, and stated, "Fred, I have made my will and I want you to read it." After reading it, Hosmann asked plaintiff if he was satisfied and plaintiff replied that he was.

By the terms of his will, Fred Hosmann devised and bequeathed to his nephew, Fred Wurth, by legal description, the farm of 55 acres and all of the personal property located on the premises. The will was prepared by Thomas W. Winton, Hosmann's lawyer, duly signed and sealed by Hosmann and properly attested by three witnesses. At that time plaintiff was 33 years of age and unmarried. After that date he continued to live on the farm and received for his services $30 per month until 1940. During the year 1940 he did not receive any money and from 1940 on, plaintiff furnished most of the money for running the farm, the food, repairs, etc. Five years later in May, 1945, Lottie Irene Hosmann told him she now owned the farm and ordered him off.

The plaintiff was corroborated by substantial witnesses. Thomas W. Winton, a lawyer of standing, William J. Narten, a reputable licensed real-estate broker, and Mildred Reinke, all of whom testified that frequently and repeatedly they asked the Hosmann brothers and Fred Hosmann why they did not pay Fred Wurth higher wages, and that each time they received the same reply, "Well, he is going to get the farm anyhow. One of us will see that he gets the farm." "Oh, Fred is all right, he knows that everything we have is his if he stays with us and works the farm."

We are in accord with the statement of defendant that the proof which will justify a court in decreeing specific performance of a parol contract must be clear and conclusive and there must be no reasonable doubt that the contract was made and all of its terms clearly proved. In *Weidler v. Seibert*, 405 Ill. 477, we said, "that where an oral contract to convey or devise real estate is claimed, the evidence must be clear and convincing, and that it should be scrutinized carefully by the court, if it appears to be contrary to the provisions of a will; that evidence establishing the contract must be sufficiently definite to show the property involved, and the promise upon which the conveyance or devise was to be made." It was further stated in that case, "And where a promisor makes a will disposing of the property involved in a manner other than promised, it will be considered but does not prevent enforcement of the contract."

In the present case, the evidence is conclusive that the contract was made, and the plaintiff, over a long period of years, was devoted to performing his part of the contract, working for extremely small wages and sacrificing any opportunity to better himself through other employment. The corroborative testimony is practically undisputed and there can be no doubt about the credibility of plaintiff's witnesses. The services performed by plaintiff were satisfactorily proved. "Courts of equity grant relief in such cases on the theory that the parties cannot be placed in status quo or damages awarded which would be full compensation."

The decree of the circuit court of Cook County is, therefore, affirmed.

ESTOPPEL

OZIER v. HAINES
Supreme Court of Illinois, 1952
411 Ill. 160, 103 N.E. 2d 485

Plaintiffs, the operators of a grain elevator, brought this suit in the circuit court of Piatt County to recover $4,450 damages which allegedly resulted when the defendant, George Haines, breached an oral contract whereby he sold 5,000 bushels of corn to plaintiffs. Defendant filed a motion to dismiss the complaint, setting up the Statute of Frauds as a defense. The trial court allowed the motion and when plaintiffs elected to stand by their pleading, final judgment was entered for defendant. An appeal followed in which the judgment of the trial court was affirmed by the Appellate Court. The latter court has granted plaintiffs' petition for leave to appeal to this court, certifying that important questions of law are involved in the cause.

In substance, the complaint alleged that defendant came to plaintiffs' elevator on February 11, 1947, and verbally sold them 5,000 bushels of corn at $1.24 per bushel; that, relying on said contract of sale, plaintiffs immediately resold the corn to a broker in Decatur by telephone while defendant was still in their offices, and that defendant knew the grain had been resold in reliance upon his agreement, thereby estopping him to defend against his act, representations and contract. The complaint further alleged that it was the custom of the trade, and of plaintiffs' elevator, to buy and sell grain upon verbal contracts, and for the purchasing elevator, immediately after the verbal sale had been made, to resell to a grain broker, which customs were well known to all parties here and relied upon by them. The complaint continued that defendant thereafter refused to deliver the corn making it necessary for plaintiffs to purchase corn on the open market, at a higher price, to fulfill their obligation to the broker, and necessitating this suit to recover $4,450, the difference in price at which corn was purchased on the open market and the price at which defendant had agreed to sell to plaintiffs.

The defendant's position is that the oral contract is unenforceable because of the Statute of Frauds pertaining to sales of personal property valued in excess of $500. Plaintiffs counter that the doctrine of equitable estoppel prevents defendant from relying on such a defense and, in addition, that the effect of existing trade customs, known to the parties, is to create an enforceable contract despite the Statute of Frauds. The Appellate Court found that there were insufficient grounds upon which the doctrine of equitable estoppel could be invoked, and that custom could not render the statute nugatory.

In the case of *Lowenberg v. Booth*, 330 Ill. 548, it is stated that six elements must appear in order to invoke the doctrine of equitable *estoppel:*

(1) Words or conduct by the party against whom the estoppel is alleged, amounting to a misrepresentation or concealment of material facts; (2) the party against whom the estoppel is alleged must have knowledge, either actual or implied, at the time the representations were made, that they were untrue; (3) the truth respecting the representations so made must be unknown to the party claiming the benefit of the estoppel at the time they were made and at the time they were acted on by him; (4) the party estopped must intend or expect that his conduct or representations will be acted on by the party asserting the estoppel or by the public generally; (5) the representations or conduct must have been relied and acted on by the party claiming the benefit of the estoppel; and (6) the party claiming the benefit of the estoppel must have so acted, because of such representations or conduct, that he would be prejudiced if the first party is permitted to deny the truth thereof.

The Appellate Court denied relief to plaintiffs in this cause because of the nonexistence of the first element, namely, words or conduct amounting to the misrepresentation or concealment of existing facts.

It is true that harsh results, or moral fraud, as plaintiffs choose to term it, may occur where one has changed his position in reliance on the oral promise of another, but it is a result which is invited and risked when the agreement is not reduced to writing in the manner prescribed by law. The present case is a patent example, for although the parties were in each other's presence and in a business office, no attempt was made to reduce their agreement to the simplest writing.

The doctrine of equitable estoppel and that of the Statute of Frauds have developed side by side in the law, each for the ultimate purpose of preventing fraud and injustice. Despite this, as one writer points out, the one may be a modification and regulation of the other. We believe, however, that each doctrine must be given a field of operation and that neither should be allowed to completely efface the other. To withdraw the first element of the *Lowenberg* case where equitable estoppel is urged against one asserting the Statute of Frauds, as plaintiffs urge, would allow either party to circumvent the Statute of Frauds at will.

It is true that a fraudulent intention or purpose is not essential to the doctrine of estoppel, but in cases involving oral contracts the estoppel must be based on misrepresentation or concealment if the Statute of Frauds is to be given effect at all. This is the point of counterbalance between the two doctrines and the factor for determining which shall apply. When the parties here entered the disputed oral contract, each knew, or is deemed to have known, that they had entered into an unenforceable agreement. Both had all knowledge in reference to the transaction, and neither side had information that the other did not have. What either side did thereafter in reference to the subject matter would not take their agreement out of the Statute of Frauds, unless they were induced to take the action by some misrepresentation or fraud of the other. In the absence of fraud or misrepresentation, the party changing his position must be said to have acted solely upon his own judgment and at his own risk, and he is not entitled to an application of the estoppel doctrine.

Plaintiffs further contend that if the defendant heard plaintiff's manager telephone the broker and resell the corn, he was guilty of a fraudulent act when he did not then state that he had no intention to perform his agreement. Such speculation need not be answered in this opinion, for the facts pleaded do not attribute such knowledge to defendant. The complaint states only that the corn was resold to the broker over the telephone while defendant was still in plaintiff's "offices." It is next contended that defendant's knowledge of the customs of the trade, admitted by his pleading, make him guilty of a wrongdoing in not keeping his oral agreement, sufficient to form a basis for the application of the doctrine of equitable estoppel. The customs of trade relied upon are, first, the custom of buying and selling grain by oral contract and, second, the custom of the purchasing elevator to resell the grain rather than to hold it for speculative purposes. While there are many instances where custom and usage have been used to interpret an enforceable contract, we know of no case, and none has been brought to our attention, where custom and usage have been held to create an enforceable contract.

Plaintiffs point to the many businesses in which similar customs prevail and state that if the practices are to be changed, this court should expressly so declare. Again, they state that it would be unfortunate if the practices and customs were modified suddenly by a decision of this court. No decision by this court is necessary or can be forthcoming on the issue raised, for the legislature has already prescribed the manner in which such sales should be consummated if they are to become enforceable in the eyes of the law. This court has no authority to give license to a custom or usage which is outside the methods established by rule of law. We can only say that those who pursue other methods operate at their risk, and if the enforcement of the law creates a peril to our business structure, the remedy lies with the legislature, not with the courts.

In conclusion, plaintiffs urge that title to the corn passed to them on February 11, 1947, and that defendant's delivery elsewhere constituted a conversion. In view of our conclusion that the Statute of Frauds was not satisfied, there can be no merit to this contention. In addition, it is our further conclusion that plaintiff's complaint does not support such a theory.

Some courts have been more generous in applying estoppel principles. The case of *Warder & Lee Elevator, Inc.* v. *Britten*, 274 N.W. 2d 339 (Iowa 1979) involved facts very similar to *Ozier*. Applying the doctrine of *promissory estoppel*, the Supreme Court of Iowa found for the elevator noting that an oral promise which a farmer should reasonably expect to induce action on the part of an elevator and which does induce such action is enforcable in spite of the statute of frauds if injustice can be avoided only by enforcement of the promise.

The Merchant's Exception of the Uniform Commercial Code. Another exception to the statute of frauds can arise if the parties to the oral contract are merchants. In such a case if one merchant sends a written confirmation of the oral agreement to the other merchant within a reasonable time and the other merchant does not object within 10 days, the oral agreement is enforceable in the courts. Specific details of this rule and the extent to which a farmer or rancher is considered to be a merchant are discussed in Chapter 12 dealing with the sale of agricultural products.

Oral Promises Omitted from a Written Contract—The Parol Evidence Rule

Questions often arise as to whether a written contract is "complete" or whether other evidence should be admitted to show that the written contract is not a complete statement of the parties' intention. The parol evidence rule applies in such circumstances and generally provides as follows: If an agreement is reduced to writing, that writing is the agreement and constitutes the only evidence of it. All prior or contemporary negotiations and agreements are merged into the written agreement. Other evidence is not admissible to add to, detract from, or alter the agreement as written.[8]

Several exceptions to this rule do exist.[9] One of these exceptions applies where there is uncertainty or ambiguity in the written contract's terms or a dispute as to the meaning of those terms. In such cases additional evidence can be received to aid the court in interpreting the agreement. However, if the meaning of the agreement is clear, such extrinsic evidence is not admissible.

The parol evidence rule is an important rule for farmers, ranchers, and other members of the agribusiness community. In effect, the rule says that oral statements or promises that are made during the contract negotiations carry no weight unless these statements are incorporated into the written document.

---

[8] RESTATEMENT (SECOND) OF CONTRACTS § 239 (1973).

[9] For a further discussion *see id.* at §§ 240–241.

PAROL EVIDENCE RULE

ZUMMO CATTLE COMPANY v. MILLARD
Court of Civil Appeals of Texas, 1972
482 S.W. 2d 17

Appellant Zummo Cattle Company, hereinafter called "Zummo," brought suit against George H. Millard, Jr. and George H. Millard, Sr., dba Millard Feed Lots, hereinafter called "Millard," on a written feed lot contract whereby Millard fed cattle for Zummo. Paragraph 8 of the contract read as follows:

All death losses and mysterious disappearance of cattle will be at the expense of the feedlot. If the cattle are not being cared for in a satisfactory animal husbandry program, Zummo Cattle Company has the option of removing the cattle from feedlot before expiration of 75 days.

Zummo sued for loss of profits, failure of Millard to use medication, for loss of unaccounted for cattle, and claimed such losses were caused by mixed lots of cattle, refusal to allow Zummo to remove cattle in an orderly manner, and failure to properly care for cattle. Zummo further claimed that such acts by Millard disrupted Zummo's business operation and caused Zummo to have to buy cattle on the open market and put many of the cattle in other feed lots.

Millard, by way of counter-claim, alleged that Paragraph 8 of the contract was not the agreement of the parties, but that it should be the normal 3% loss which was claimed to be standard in the cattle feeding industry, and that [prior] to the execution of the contract the parties agreed to change Paragraph 8 to the effect that Millard would be responsible for death and mysterious disappearance of cattle not to exceed 3%.

George Millard, Jr. testified that he received the contract in the mail from Zummo, and that before he (Millard) signed it he called John Zummo by telephone and told him that he, Millard, could not take that kind of risk involving about 3,000 head of cattle and a possible loss of a quarter of a million dollars. Millard further testified that John Zummo told him he could take the normal death losses and mysterious disappearances up to 3% and that he, Millard, agreed to that arrangement, and that he, Millard, thereafter signed the contract, and the Paragraph 8 was left in the contract because John Zummo said it would help him with his banker. Millard also testified he never intended to be bound nor did he agree to Paragraph 8 of the contract. Zummo denied there was any alteration, modification or side agreement of any kind pertaining to Paragraph 8.

Zummo objected that the testimony of Millard was a violation of the parol evidence rule, and such objection was overruled by the trial court. The judgment of the trial court limited Millard's liability to 3% of the 407 cattle lost by death and mysterious disappearance.

Zummo appeals contending that the trial court erred (1) by not charging Millard with all losses from death or mysterious disappearance of cattle under the terms of the contract; and (2) by permitting George Millard, Jr. to testify, in violation of the parol evidence rule, that he and John Zummo prior to the execution of the contract made an agreement relating to the death and mysterious disappearance losses of cattle which was contrary to the written provisions in Paragraph 8 of the contract, there being no allegation of fraud, accident or mistake alleged in the execution of the contract.

The parol evidence rule is the rule which, "upon the establishment of the existence of a writing intended as a completed memorial of a legal transaction denies efficacy to any prior to contemporary expressions of the parties relating to the same subject-matter as that to which the written memorial relates." It is our opinion that it was a violation of such parol evidence rule to permit the witness Millard to testify about expressions or agreements between the parties occurring before or at the time of execution of the contract.

There were 407 cattle lost by death or mysterious disappearance, and at the average purchase price of $92.39 the value of the cattle lost would be $37,602.73. The judgment of the trial court is reformed so that Millard is liable for this entire loss.

2.3 REMEDIES FOR BREACH OF CONTRACT

Excused Performance or Breach of Contract

Whether or not a party has failed to live up to the terms of the contract is generally a question of fact. For example, in *Puterbaugh v. Winchester*, 29 Ill. 194 (1862), Puterbaugh sold to Winchester six mules which had escaped from his pasture for $300, and Winchester was to capture the mules. One mule could not be found, so Winchester sued Puterbaugh for the purchase price of one mule, claiming there had been a breach of contract. The Supreme Court of Illinois denied recovery, saying there had not been a breach of contract since the risk of capturing all the mules was on the purchaser and the lesser price for which he had been able to buy them recognized this fact. Minor deviations in performance are not likely to constitute such a breach as to destroy the contract, but obviously parties differ in their view about what constitutes a minor deviation. This is what gives rise to many lawsuits.

Impossibility of performance arising after the contract has been entered will generally excuse one from performing contractual duties also, but not always. For example, a farmer contracts to sell a buyer a *particular* bull but the bull dies before it can be delivered. Since the specific subject matter has been destroyed, the farmer is excused from performing his duty under the contract. Of course, the farmer would be required to refund any of the purchase price already advanced. In contrast, if the farmer had contracted to deliver 1000 bushels of corn at $2.50 per bushel, but the farmer's corn was destroyed by fire or flood before the time of delivery, the farmer would still be required to deliver 1000 bushels. The farmer's performance is not impossible because the farmer can purchase corn elsewhere. Supervening illegality or the physical incapacity or death of the person whose particular personal services were the subject of the contract are additional examples of impossibility.

Some courts excuse contractual duties where the performance, although theoretically possible, has become *impractical* or where the purpose of the contract has been frustrated. To be impractical the performance must result in extreme and unreasonable difficulty not otherwise anticipated. For example, a farmer contracts with an applicator to aerially spray an insecticide. The applicator's plane is destroyed in a storm and the applicator would incur extreme additional expense in acquiring a substitute plane. A court would probably excuse the applicator's promise because of the unanticipated extreme difficulty.

Where the *purpose of the contract has been frustrated*, courts also will excuse the performance of duties. For example, a farmer contracts with an aerial applicator for the spraying of alfalfa. In the meantime, the alfalfa is destroyed by a flood. Spraying the drowned alfalfa is not impossible, nor is it extremely difficult. The problem, of course, is that spraying is no longer necessary or useful. The farmer's promise to hire the aerial applicator is discharged because the purpose of contract has been frustrated.

The above rules are somewhat technical and difficult to apply to particular circumstances.[10] Perhaps a synthesis of the technical rules would be more useful. Generally, the duties of all parties to a contract are excused when the circumstances affecting a party's performance have so changed that the parties would not have entered into the contract if they had known of the new circumstances. Even this general rule is subject to exceptions. Hence, we return to our original statement that whether or not there has been a breach of contract is primarily a question of fact and how the jury and court feel about it.

Various Remedies for Breach of Contract

If there is a valid contract and one party fails or refuses to perform, the other party may seek one or a combination of several remedies. These remedies include damages, specific performance, and rescission and restitution.

Damages. One remedy for breach of contract is money damages sufficient to make the injured party "whole." For example, in sales contracts the amount of such damages generally can be determined by reference to the difference between the fair market value and the contract price of items covered by the contract.[11] Here again, the amount of damages recoverable is primarily a question of fact. Arbitrary amounts such as those arrived at by taking

---

[10] It has been held, for example, that the flooding of agricultural land resulting in total inability to plant and raise a crop did not excuse the lessee from liability on promissory notes given as payment of rent on the land. Likewise, in *United Sales Co. v. Curtis Peanut Co.* 302 S.W. 2d 763 (Tex. Civ. App. 1957), the court held that drought and adverse weather conditions resulting in a short peanut crop did not excuse the seller from delivering the thirteen carloads of peanuts which had been contracted. The court said there was no language in the contract indicating that this would be an excuse for performance and that it did not appear that it was impossible to obtain the peanuts elsewhere to fulfill the terms of the contract. To the contrary, however, are *Matousek v. Galligan,* 104 Neb. 731, 178 N.W. 510 (1920), holding that the seller was excused from delivering 60 tons of good, #1 merchantable hay where unusual storms and rainfall made it impossible to bale and deliver such hay; and *Pearce-Young-Angel Co. v. Charles R. Allen, Inc.,* 213 S.C. 578, 50 S.E. 2d 698 (1948), where the court held that torrential rains destroying a crop of blackeye peas excused the seller from delivery.

[11] For example, in *Hurt v. Earnhart,* 539 S.W. 2d 133 (1976), a producer contracted to deliver 10,000 bushels of soybeans to the Hurt Seed Company for $3.25 per bushel. The producer did not deliver the full 10,000 bushels and Hurt sued for damages.

an average of all the opinions of all the jurors (quotient verdicts) are not proper determinations and will be rejected by the court.

Generally, a jury's verdict regarding the amount will not be disturbed if it falls within some reasonable range. Likewise, the jury may be relied upon to decide upon the facts which determine the amount of damages. For example, in *Frambers v. Risk*, 2 Ill. App. 499 (1877), where there was an alleged mistake in weighing hogs, the court held that a witness should have been permitted to testify as to the weight of hogs of the age and type of those sold by the plaintiff when fed in the described manner. In *Devine v. Edwards*, 101 Ill. 138 (1881), where both seller and purchaser were mistaken in the contents of a container used to measure milk, the court held that the seller was liable for the value of the amount of milk represented by the difference between the container which the parties thought they were using and that which they were actually using. Obviously values are more easily established for items that have a standard price per unit—wheat and corn, for example—but even so, controversies can arise over the quality and amount of grain and over any extra damages to the injured party caused by failure to perform at the time specified in the contract.

Stipulated or Liquidated Damages.   Sometimes the parties to a contract will specify in the contract the amount of damages that are to be paid in the event of a breach. For example, in *National Farmers Organization v. J.O. Smith*,[12] a farmer entered into a contract with the National Farmers Organization (NFO) whereby the farmer agreed to sell to the NFO a certain quantity of milo. The agreement contained a liquidated damages provision:

For failure to deliver under the contract, member agrees that such act will damage NFO in an amount that is and will be impracticable and very difficult to determine and fix and, therefore, the member agrees to pay NFO 25 percent of the gross value of the production so committed as liquidated damages for all the production that is disposed of contrary to this agreement.

Whether such a provision is enforceable by the courts depends on whether the provision is an excessive penalty designed to coerce performance or an honest estimate of probable loss. If it is an excessive penalty, courts generally disregard the stipulation and assess damages as if the contract were silent on this issue. If the provision appears to be a reasonable estimate of probable loss likely to be caused by the breach, courts generally award the stipulated amount regardless of the actual damages suffered by the breach.[13] In *National Farmers Organization*, noted above, the court implicitly determined that the liquidated damages provision was reasonable and allowed liquidated damages of $12,600 for the farmer's failure to sell his grain to the NFO.[14]

The court awarded damages of $2396.94. The award was based on 46 cents per undelivered bushel—the difference between the contract price and the market price of beans when Hurt first learned that the producer was not going to deliver the remainder of the beans due under the contract.

[12] 526 S.W. 2d 759 (Tex. Civ. App. 1975).

[13] G.C. GRISMORE (rev. ed. J.E. Murray, Jr.), *supra* note 5, at § 205.

[14] The farmer had contracted to sell the milo to the NFO for $3 per hundredweight. When the market price rose dramatically, the farmer intentionally breached the NFO agreement and sold the milo for $4.20 to another party. The farmer had hoped that the "25 percent of gross production" liquidated damages provision would be based on the $3 contract price. The court, however, applied the 25 percent provision to the $4.20 sale price. Interestingly, the farmer still came out ahead, but not as far ahead as he had hoped.

When are stipulated damages excessive penalties and when are they reasonable estimates? Several factors have an important bearing on this question. If it was difficult to foresee actual damages, the tendency is to treat the provision as a reasonable estimate rather than as an excessive penalty. If a single sum is to be the liquidated damages for breach of each of a variety of different obligations and if the actual losses would vary greatly depending on which obligation was breached, the tendency is to treat the provision as a penalty. Whether the amount fixed to be paid is called "liquidated damages" or a "penalty" in the actual contract is irrelevant.[15]

Specific Performance. Whether or not the injured party asks for damages, that party may seek to have the contract performed as agreed. When, for example, the contract is for land, for a breeding animal, or for something the purchaser is particularly desirous of having—or that the seller is particularly desirous of selling—it may be felt that the best remedy is to compel a transfer of the land or personal property involved. Thus, in many such instances when it is still possible to do so, the courts will order specific performance by the defaulting party. However, the remedy of specific performance is usually not available if damages can adequately compensate the plaintiff. As a general rule specific performance will be available only in those situations where the subject matter of the contract is in some way unique, such as in contracts for the sale of land.

Rescission and Restitution. In some situations the injured party may be damaged more by accepting performance of the contract in the manner proposed by the defaulting party than by asking for relief from the terms of the contract and for damages. In such situations the court will permit the injured party to rescind and ask for restitution. *Rescission* has been described by the courts as the cancellation, avoidance, unmaking, or termination of a contract. It is in effect an equitable remedy under which the contract is canceled and the injured party made whole—for example, through *restitution*, which is the payment for any benefits already transferred.

The Importance of Prompt Action— The Statute of Limitations

Does one who has been injured, by a breach of contract or otherwise, need to take prompt action to assure a right of recovery? At common law, one who was injured and did not attempt to enforce his or her rights within a reasonable time was barred from enforcing that right by a doctrine known as *laches*. In effect, if a person "sat on his rights" too long, the person could lose those rights.

Most states have adopted this general concept in specific statutes called *statutes of limitations*. Failure to file a cause of action within the statutory time limit bars the action. The specific time limits vary from state to state and also depend on the kind of actions. In Illinois, for example, the time limit for libel and slander is 1 year, for many unwritten contracts is 5 years, and for many written contracts is 10 years.[16]

---

[15] G.C. GRISMORE (rev. ed. J.E. Murray, Jr.,), *supra* note 5, at § 205, note 95.

[16] ILL. REV. STAT. ch. 83, §§ 14, 16, 17 (1979). The UNIFORM COMMERCIAL CODE § 2-725 provides: 1) "An action for breach of any contract for sale must be commenced within 4 years after the cause of action has accrued. By the original agreement the parties may reduce the period of limitation to not less than one year but may not extend it. 2) "A cause of action accrues when the breach occurs, regardless of the aggrieved party's lack of knowledge of the breach. A breach of warranty occurs when tender of delivery is made, except that where a warranty explicitly extends to

STUDY QUESTIONS

1. What is a contract? What elements are required for a valid contract? What is the meaning of each of these elements?

2. Why might a person lack legal capacity to form a contract?

3. What is the status of contracts entered into by minors? At what age does one cease to be a minor?

4. Does current state law differentiate between the right of a man or woman to contract?

5. What are implied contracts and when may they come into existence?

6. What kinds of contracts are generally required to be in writing? What is the history and rationale for this rule? What should be the contents of the writing?

7. When will a court enforce oral contracts normally required to be in writing?

8. What is the meaning and significance of the parol evidence rule?

9. When is the failure to perform a contractual duty excused?

10. What is the most typical remedy for breach of contract awarded by the courts?

11. If a contract is breached, will a court enforce a contractual stipulation concerning the damages to be awarded?

12. What is specific performance and when is a court likely to grant this remedy?

13. When are rescission and restitution appropriate remedies?

14. How does one differentiate between a joking contract offer and a serious contract offer?

15. What are statutes of limitations?

16. Carlton Johnson wrote Sam Williamson on January 2, as follows:

"Dear Mr. Williamson: I would like to buy your 160-acre farm in Texas Township, DeWitt County, Illinois, and I am willing to pay $380,000 cash for it.

Signed, Carlton Johnson."

Sam called Carlton and said, "Fine, it's a deal. I will sell for $380,000. I will draw up the necessary papers and I will see you in a few days." Later that same day Sam wrote to Carlton offering to sell his tractor for $2000. Nothing was said in this letter about how the offer might be accepted. Carlton received the letter the following day, and he mailed his acceptance that afternoon. Two days later, Carlton phoned Sam to tell him he was not going through with the purchase of the farm. Angered, Sam stated he was withdrawing the offer for the tractor. (He had not yet received Carlton's written acceptance.)

Can Sam hold Carlton to a binding contract for the sale of the farm? Is there a binding contract for the sale of the tractor?

---

future performance of the goods and discovery of the breach must await the time of such perform-

ance the cause of action accrues when the breach is or should have been discovered."

3

Torts

3.1 NATURE AND MEANING OF TORT

Where no contract exists to cover a particular situation, conduct is governed by the law of torts. A *tort* is a personal or civil wrong inflicted upon one person by another for which the law allows redress. The word itself derived from the Latin means "twisted" and describes conduct that is twisted, or crooked, conduct other than straight.

The law of torts consists of rules of conduct based on the doctrine that every individual has certain legal rights and duties. An invasion of a legal right or a failure to perform a legal duty results in a tort, and the injured party is entitled to recover damages to the extent of injury. In certain cases the injured party may have the cause of the injury abated or may sometimes obtain an order from the court (called an *injunction*) commanding the offending party to act or not to act, as the occasion requires.

A tort may arise as the result of an intentional or willful act, negligent conduct, or the willful or negligent omission to act. In some situations, acts ordinarily tortious may be privileged. In other situations, lawful acts may be tortious depending on the manner in which they are performed.

Modern tort law is governed by both statutes and common law.

In *Dawson v. Ellis*, 151 Ill. App. 92 (1909), the court quoted Sir Frederick Pollock in giving a good definition of tort:

Tort is an act or omission (not being merely the breach of duty arising out of a personal relation or undertaken by contract) which is related to harm suffered by a determinate person in one of the following ways: (a) It may be an act which, without lawful justification or excuse, is intended by the agent to cause harm, and does cause the harm complained of. (b) It may be an act in itself contrary to law, or an omission of specific legal duty, which causes harm not intended by the person so acting or omitting. (c) It may be an act or omission causing harm which the person so acting or omitting did not intend to cause, but might and should with due diligence have foreseen and prevented. (d) It may, in special cases, consist merely in not avoiding or preventing harm which the party was bound absolutely, or within limits, to avoid or prevent.

In *Gindele v. Corrigan*, 129 Ill. 582, 22 N.E. 516 (1889), a tort is defined "to be an injury or wrong committed, with or without force, to the person or property of another, and such injury may arise by either nonfeasance, malfeasance or misfeasance of the wrongdoer.'' Actual fraud or intent to inflict the injury occasioned by the wrongful act is not necessary to constitute a tort. The actionable wrong may be purely a legal wrong unmixed with any element of fraud or intent on the part of the wrongdoer.

Tortious acts may damage us personally or they may damage our property or business. Personal damages may be of a physical nature or they may involve our reputation or sensibilities. Assault, battery, and mayhem, for example, are intentional wrongs which injure us physically. Slander and libel damage our reputation, and nuisances of many kinds may affect our sensibilities—a sewage disposal plant next door, for example. The most common type of injury to property is trespass.

Some tortious acts are prohibited by law and subject the wrongdoer to criminal prosecution. This fact has nothing to do with the right of an injured party to recover in a civil suit based on the tort or negligence theory. One may recover damages for the wrongful act even though the state fails to make its case in attempting to prosecute the wrongdoer. For example, a trespass on posted farm premises constitutes a misdemeanor for which the trespasser can be prosecuted in many states. However, the right of the landowner or tenant to recover damages for the trespass or to perhaps get an injunction against continuing trespass does not depend on the status of the act as a misdemeanor.

3.2 NEGLIGENCE

The General Concept

Although farmers and ranchers occasionally become involved in intentional torts such as assault or intentional trespass, negligence is of much greater significance and will be the focus of our study. *Negligence* may be simply defined as want of due care under the circumstances, but a more technical description includes the following elements.[1]

1. The defendant owed the plaintiff a duty to exercise reasonable care under the circumstances. This duty may arise from our common-law duty to conduct our affairs in such a manner as to protect others from unreasonable risks of injury, or it might arise from a particular statute, e.g., a speed limit.
2. The defendant breached this duty by failing to conform to the specified standard.
3. The breach of duty was the proximate cause of the plaintiff's injury. In almost all situations there may be more than one contributing factor to the damage. In some situations there are many, and it is very difficult to identify the one thing without which the injury would not have occurred. Legal theorists have tried to arrive at an answer through the concept of "proximate cause." Webster defines *proximate cause* as "a cause which directly or with no mediate agency produces an effect or a specific result." *Ballentine's Law Dictionary* defines it as "a cause of which the injury is a natural and a probable consequence." It has been pointed out that

---

[1] W.L. Prosser, Law of Torts § 30 (4th ed. 1971).

proximate cause is not that which necessarily stands closest to the event in time or space, but that which stands closest in causal relation.

Its determination is a mixture of fact and law. In *Gorris v. Scott*, Law Reports, 9 Exchequer 125 (1874), a defendant shipowner had not constructed pens on his ship which were required to keep animals segregated for disease prevention purposes. During a storm at sea, many of the plaintiff's cattle were swept overboard. He sued the shipowner, claiming that if the pens had been constructed they would have prevented his cattle from being swept overboard. The court held for the defendant shipowner, saying that the cattle were not lost by reason of the hazard which the pens were supposed to prevent.

4. Damage to the plaintiff's person or property.

With very few exceptions, proof of negligence is necessary before one can be held responsible for any kind of injury to another person. However, under the doctrine of *respondeat superior* an employer may be held liable for the negligent acts of employees or agents. The law views an employee or an agent as an extension of the arm of the employer, and hence their negligence becomes the employer's negligence. A farmer's liability is likely to arise from one of five sources: (1) personal actions, (2) trespass or injury by livestock, (3) the negligent acts of employees in the course of their employment resulting in injury to others, (4) the condition of the premises, (5) injury to employees arising from personal actions, defective machinery or equipment, dangerous animals, or defective conditions in the premises.

NEGLIGENCE

EVANS v. STUART
Supreme Court of Utah, 1966
17 Utah 2d 308, 410 P. 2d 999

The plaintiffs, surviving widow and children of Hugh Alva Evans, sued for damages resulting from his wrongful death caused by defendant's negligence in connection with a fire on the latter's farm in Davis County. Upon trial to the court judgment was entered for the plaintiffs for $9,000 general and $870.55 special damages. Defendant appeals.

Defendant's attack upon the judgment follows a pattern which is not unusual in such cases. He contends, *inter alia*, that the evidence does not support the finding that he was negligent.

Defendant, Glen Stuart, has a dairy farm a couple miles west of Kaysville. Deceased was 67 years of age and was retired. The defendant hired him from time to time to help with odd jobs on the farm. On March 7, 1963, the defendant told him to start a fire to burn up weeds and growth to clean out an irrigation ditch. The preceding winter months had been unusually dry. Adjacent to the ditch there was flammable wheat and alfalfa stubble. When the defendant told the deceased to start the fire the latter called attention to the fact that there was a little breeze blowing. Both men realized that the wind was variable at that time of the year. The deceased went back to work on the fence and the defendant undertook to watch the fire.

The wind did increase and the fire began to spread. Defendant got his small tractor scraper to fight the fire and keep it from extending in the stubble. The tractor ran out of gas and despite the efforts of defendant and another hired man, Rex Terkelson, the fire continued to spread toward some gas tanks and around the area of the home. Continuing their efforts where they were, defendant sent the deceased over to watch the fire which was working toward a pile of lumber.

When deceased called for help defendant went to aid him, but by then he was on fire and rolling in the dirt. He was so severely burned that he was taken to a hospital where he languished for a month and five days and died.

The primary question confronted, and the most serious one in this case, is whether the evidence will support the finding of the defendant's negligence. The foundational concept of negligence is sometimes stated as conduct which a person should realize exposes others to an unreasonable risk of harm. This reference to conduct which is "unreasonable" ties back to the time-honored definition of negligence: The failure to exercise the degree of care which an ordinary, reasonable and prudent person would use under similar circumstances. It must be appreciated that there is some lack of precision in the word, "reasonable." But neither its use nor the lack of certainty implicit in it can be avoided. And when there is uncertainty as to whether conduct falls within its ambit, the question must be resolved by the "reasonable" mind of the court or jury as to what conforms within the bounds of propriety as fashioned by the customs and the conscience of society. It is with these principles in mind that we consider the problems here involved.

The defendant is charged with knowing, and unquestionably did know, that which accords with the common knowledge and experience of mankind; that a fire in an area which abounds with dry and flammable materials is a dangerous instrumentality; and that when the wind was already blowing and was gusty and likely to change, the fire might spread and get out of control. He did not have his tractor-scraper, which he appears to have had as a means of emergency control of the fire, prepared for the emergency when it arose. He knew that the deceased was a man 67 years of age and therefore would be somewhat limited in ability to cope with such a fire. He nevertheless directed the deceased to go to "watch" the fire approaching the woodpile.

It is urged that this was all deceased was told to do and that he went beyond this direction in fighting the fire. Reasonable inferences can be drawn, and it certainly could be taken to mean that he was to attempt to control the fire, not simply to stand by and watch it work its destruction. When deceased called for help his first two calls went unheeded. It may well be that under this evidence some reasonable minds might have concluded that the defendant used reasonable care for deceased's safety. But it is our opinion that there is also a reasonable basis in the evidence upon which the trial court could believe and find as it did that the defendant failed to exercise the standard of reasonable care the law required of him set forth herein.

The decision of the trial court is affirmed.

The "reasonable person" standard of care noted above requires that a defendant's conduct be measured against what the conduct of a reasonable, ordinary, and prudent person would be under similar circumstances. What physical characteristics, mental ability, and knowledge does this mystical "reasonable person" possess?

Generally, he or she is considered to have the same physical characteristics as the defendant, but to have average mental ability and to have knowledge of things known by the average member of the community. The following case illustrates the kind of knowledge that a jury might require of a defendant.

NEGLIGENCE IN TURNING COW INTO SALES RING

GARDNER v. KOENIG
Supreme Court of Kansas, 1961
188 Kan. 135, 360 P. 2d 1107

This is an action for damages in which the plaintiff seeks to recover for personal injuries as a result of the alleged negligence of the defendants in turning a nervous and unruly cow into a sales ring unescorted and unattended.

The plaintiff, Mr. Gardner, took some hogs to the Koenig sales barn on May 15, 1958. Plaintiff was directed by an employee of Koenig to take vaccination certificates to the auctioneer at the south end of the show ring. Adjoining the southeast corner of the show ring was a cattle pen containing a "nervous and unruly cow...weighing about 900 to 1,000 pounds." Plaintiff alleges that Lester Oherhelman, an employee of Koenig, "suddenly and without warning" opened the gate between the cattle pen and the cattle show ring. The cow immediately ran into the plaintiff who was standing six feet from the gate with his back to the gate talking to the auctioneer about the vaccination certificates. Plaintiff was knocked to the ground and injured.

The defendants rely on the general rule of law that the owner of a domestic animal not naturally vicious is not liable for injury done by it when it is in place where it has a right to be, unless it is known by the owner to be vicious. The foregoing rule may be conceded, but it does not control the facts alleged in the third amended petition. In the first place, this suit is not against the owner of the animal but against the proprietor of a public sales barn.

The third amended petition alleges facts concerning the public nature of the defendants' business as a community sale, and the attendance of the plaintiff as a customer and patron in his legal status as an invitee. The plaintiff seeks to recover under the rule that an operator of a business or storekeeper, while not an insurer of the safety of his customers, is liable for injuries resulting from negligence on his part.

From the allegations in the third amended petition it is clear the cow was not led into the show ring with a halter, but was released from the pen and permitted to enter the ring unescorted, while the plaintiff was standing therein only six feet away with his back turned.

In *Porter v. Thompson*, 74 Cal. App. 2d 474, 169 P. 2d 40, the plaintiff was a prospective purchaser of cattle at an auction sale being conducted by the defendant, and it was held the defendant had a duty to exercise reasonable care to maintain supervision, a reasonably safe enclosure, and seats for customers so they would not be injured by cattle attempting to escape the enclosure. In the opinion the court said:

> The question to be determined is, what would a reasonably prudent person be required to do, under such circumstances, for the protection of his invited customers. The fact that the defendants did not actually know that the particular cow in question was fractious, nervous or dangerous does not necessarily acquit them of negligence on that score....

In *Thompson v. Yellowstone Livestock Comm.*, 133 Mont. 403, 324 P. 2d 412, the plaintiff brought an action for injuries sustained when struck by an unruly cow which climbed a barricade and fell upon the plaintiff as an invitee. The court held the complaint stated a cause of action where the allegations established a legal duty by the defendant to the plaintiff, failure to perform such duty, and damages proximately resulting in injury to the plaintiff from such failure. The court said it was the duty of the defendant to maintain such barrier of sufficient strength and height as to prevent animals, which had occasion to become frightened, from jumping over the fence and upon the patrons.

The Restatement of Law, Torts, 518, Comment g, states the following rule:

> One who keeps a domestic animal which possesses only those dangerous propensities which are normal to its class is required to know its normal habits and tendencies. He is, therefore, required to realize that even ordinarily gentle animals are likely to be dangerous under particular circumstances and to exercise reasonable care to prevent foreseeable harm....

We adopt the foregoing statement of the rule as sound law and controlling of the decision herein. It is not unreasonable to assume that the defendants should have anticipated some cows would become nervous, uncontrollable and resort to dangerous behavior when driven into a small enclosure, such as a sales ring, in the presence of numerous spectators where unfamiliar noises, commotion and confusion are encountered.

The judgment of the trial court is affirmed.

A decision in accord with that in the above case was reached in *Anderson v. Welty*, 334 S.W.2d 132 (Mo. App. 1960), in which the plaintiff recovered for personal injuries sustained when he was struck by cattle which were being driven through an alley in the defendant's sales barn. The Court of Appeals upheld the judgment of the lower court, saying that the evidence presented a question for the jury as to whether defendants were negligent in that their employees drove cattle into and through an alley in which the plaintiff and others were standing without any proper warning.

Common-Law Defenses

As a practical matter, even when an injured person can prove the four elements of negligence, that injured person may not be able to recover damages from the negligent party. At common law, a variety of additional defenses existed that would provide a barrier to recovery by the injured party. These defenses, including contributory negligence and other defenses, will be developed in greater detail in the following chapter, but some discussion is appropriate here.

Contributory Negligence. The foundation of the contributory negligence defense is the common-law notion that one has a duty to exercise reasonable care for the safety of *one's own person or property* as well as for the person or property of others. If the injury or damage suffered by a person resulted not only from the negligence of another, but also because of the negligence of the injured or damaged person, that injured or damaged person could not recover from the other person who was also negligent. The negligence of the injured or damaged party, called *contributory negligence*, constituted a complete bar to recovery at common law.

Comparative Negligence and Last Clear Chance. Dissatisfaction with the doctrine that contributory negligence would completely bar recovery was widespread. Some states have adopted comparative negligence statutes which divide the damages between the two parties. In 1910, Mississippi became the first state to adopt a general comparative negligence statute.[2] Nebraska, Wisconsin, South Dakota, Arkansas, Minnesota, and other states followed this lead. An example can illustrate the application of such statutes. If the defendant's fault is found to be twice as great as that of the plaintiff, only two-thirds of the damages will be recovered by the plaintiff, who will have to bear the remainder of the loss alone.[3]

Comparative negligence statutes could not solve all the difficulties in the troublesome area, however, because comparative negligence has its own set of problems. Application of the concept is relatively easy where only two parties are involved, but the application is complicated significantly if multiple plaintiffs and defendants are involved. Furthermore, the interaction of comparative negligence and the doctrine of last clear chance can be problematic.

The doctrine of last clear chance is a more commonly accepted modification of the strict rule that contributory negligence constitutes a complete defense. Under this doctrine, if the defendant has the last clear opportunity to avoid the harm, the injured plaintiff's own carelessness is not a proximate cause of the result. Thus, the injured plaintiff's carelessness does not constitute contributory negligence because the element of proximate cause is missing. Most jurisdictions recognize some form of the doctrine, at least in special circumstances.[4]

The doctrine of last clear chance can be criticized from a policy standpoint because it theoretically encourages negligent conduct. For example, if A drives down the highway with eyes closed, A could never

[2] *See* Shell and Bufkin, COMPARATIVE NEGLIGENCE IN MISSISSIPPI, 27 MISS. L. REV. 105 (1956).

[3] The application of the comparative negligence concept varies tremendously from state to state.

See W.L. PROSSER, LAW OF TORTS § 67 (4th ed. 1971).

[4] *See generally* W.L. PROSSER, LAW OF TORTS § 66 (4th ed. 1971).

have the last clear chance to prevent an accident. If a collision occurred and the other driver, B, were also negligent, B could not recover in some jurisdictions because B had the last clear chance to avoid the accident.

Burdens of Proof

As a general rule the plaintiff must prove the elements of negligence by a preponderance of the evidence. This same burden of proof is found in practically all civil actions. In order to prove the elements, the plaintiff must introduce evidence tending to prove that the elements are present.

Occasionally an injury occurs through no fault of the injured party, but one which ordinarily does not occur without negligence on someone's part. If a second party has complete control over the situation and is the only one who knows the facts, the injured party may be able to recover damages from the second party even though no actual proof of the second party's negligence can be established. In such cases a rule of *res ipsa loquitur*, Latin for "the thing speaks for itself," applies. For example, suppose a passerby on a sidewalk is injured by a beer barrel that falls from a second-floor window of a brewery. Such an event does not ordinarily occur without negligence. Although the passerby was not negligent, proof of the brewery's negligence cannot be shown because only the brewery knows the facts in this situation. Under *res ipsa loquitur* the law will presume the brewery was negligent, unless it can be shown otherwise, and will allow the injured party to recover. The injured party is not required to offer additional evidence that the brewery was negligent in order to recover for the injuries. It should be noted that a defendant can rebut the presumption created by *res ipsa loquitur* by offering evidence tending to show the defendant was not negligent.[5]

The doctrine of *res ipsa loquitur* is illustrated in the case of *Jirik v. General Mills, Inc.*, 122 Ill. App.2d 111, 251 N.E.2d 353 (1969), where the trailer of a semitrailer truck was lifted on a grain hoist at the elevator to unload the grain. After the trailer was unloaded and as the hoist was descending, it stopped with a jerk, and the trailer fell off backward damaging it. Prior to this the truck had been unloaded seventy-five times without accident. The court held *res ipsa loquitur* to apply, noting that it was no fault of the truck owner and that the hoist and truck were under the control of an employee of the elevator. Not every accident, the court said, will support the presumption of negligence, but when the truck owner showed all probable causes were negligence on the part of the elevator, recovery would be allowed. The lower court verdict for the truck owner was upheld.

3.3 LIABILITY WITHOUT FAULT

For intentional torts and negligence, liability is based upon some conception of fault. A few exceptions to the general rule that fault is a prerequisite of liability have developed at common law, and others are emerging by legislative enactment.

---

[5] *See* W.L. PROSSER, LAW OF TORTS § § 39, 40 (4th ed. 1971). The conditions usually stated as necessary for the application of *res ipsa loquitur* are as follows: (1) the event must be of a kind which ordinarily does not occur in the absence of someone's negligence; (2) it must be caused by an agency or instrumentality within the exclusive control of the defendant; (3) it must not have been due to any voluntary action or contribution on the part of the plaintiff. Some courts have at least suggested a fourth condition, that evidence as to the true explanation of the event must be more readily accessible to the defendant than to the plaintiff. *Id.* § 39.

In some instances the owner of an animal may be held liable for damage or injury caused by that animal even though the owner neither intentionally nor negligently allowed the animal to cause harm. For example, the owner or custodian of a wild animal generally considered to be dangerous to human beings (e.g., a wild boar or tiger) is automatically liable for any injury occasioned by the animal.[6] In some cases, the owner of domesticated farm animals may be held automatically liable for damage caused by such animals. The particular rules will be discussed in Chapter 10 dealing with farm animals. Blasting activities or the aerial application of pesticides are more typical examples where liability without fault is likely to be invoked.[7]

STRICT LIABILITY—BLASTING

RICHARD v. KAUFMAN
U.S. District Court, Eastern District of Pennsylvania, 1942
47 F. Supp. 337

Defendants filed motions to set aside the verdict and judgment thereon for plaintiff and to enter judgment in their favor or be granted a new trial.

The action was brought by the plaintiff to recover damages for depreciation in the value of a farm owned by her in Carbon County, Pennsylvania, because of a diminution of water in a spring thereon as a result of blasting operations conducted by the defendants on neighboring property. The defendants denied that their blasting operations, which were incidental to the construction of a tunnel, were the cause of diminishing the water in plaintiff's spring.

The case was tried before a jury, which rendered a verdict for the plaintiff in the amount of $1,200. Defendants thereupon filed the present motions to set aside the verdict and judgment thereon and to enter judgment in their favor or be granted a new trial.

Defendants' first argument is directed against the sufficiency of the evidence to show any basis of liability in the absence of any allegation or proof

---

[6] *E.g.,* King v. Blue Mountain Forest Association, 100 N.H. 212, 123 A.2d 151 (1956).

[7] Generally strict liability is imposed where a person is injured by "ultrahazardous activities" or "abnormally dangerous activities." The RESTATE-MENT (SECOND) OF TORTS § 519 (1976) provides as follows: "(1) One who carries on an abnormally dangerous activity is subject to liability for harm to the person, land or chattels of another resulting from the activity, although he has exercised the utmost care to prevent such harm. (2) This strict liability is limited to the kind of harm the possibility of which makes the activity abnormally dangerous." Section 520 lists the factors to be used when determining what constitutes an abnormal-ly dangerous activity: In determining whether an activity is abnormally dangerous, the following factors are to be considered: a) Whether the activity involves a high degree of risk of some harm to the person, land or chattels of others; b) Whether the gravity of the harm which may result from it is likely to be great; c) Whether the risk cannot be eliminated by the exercise of reasonable care; d) Whether the activity is not a matter of common usage; e) Whether the activity is inappropriate to the place where it is carried on; and f) The value of the activity to the community. Whether an activity is abnormally dangerous is a question of law for the court to decide.

of negligence. Under the law of Pennsylvania, which is controlling in this case, a person who conducts an ultrahazardous activity, such as blasting, is responsible for damages directly resulting therefrom, even in the absence of negligence or fault. Restatement of the Law of Torts, § 519. The fact that the damage is claimed to have resulted from vibrations in the ground, rather than from the propulsion of debris or other objects through the air, does not make the trespass any the less direct.

The principal contention of the defendants is that there is no credible evidence that the decrease in the flow of the spring was the result of the blasting. Defendants adduced considerable evidence tending to show that, because of the geological formations, the blasting could not have affected plaintiff's spring, and that any diminution which occurred was the result of extraordinary droughts. This evidence was for the jury however, and the sole question now presented is the sufficiency of plaintiff's evidence as to causation. This evidence consisted of testimony as to the temporary stoppage of flow of water from the spring at the time of the blasting and the marked decrease in the flow existing since then from that which existed prior thereto; testimony as to tremors in the ground at plaintiff's farm which were felt at the time of the blasting, as well as vibrations in the farmhouse and the rattling of windows, and the opinion of an expert witness whose qualifications defendants challenge. This testimony was sufficient to present a jury question.

ULTRAHAZARDOUS ACTIVITIES

GOTREAUX v. GARY
Supreme Court of Louisiana, 1957
232 La. 373, 94 So. 2d 293

Julian Gotreaux instituted this suit for damages in the sum of $2,405.75. It is alleged that Welsh Flying Service, Inc., sprayed 2,4-D poisoning on the rice crop grown on Roy Gary's tenant farm on July 2, 1953, and that the wind carried the herbicide to plaintiff's crop—approximately 13.3 acres of cotton and 3 acres of peas—causing the destruction of all but one bale of cotton.

Defendants denied liability and plead lack of negligence by the use of due and reasonable care, relying on Act 502 of 1952, LSA-R.S. 3:1621, and the regulations of the Louisiana Department of Agriculture and Immigration.[8]

The trial court held defendant free from any negligence and dismissed plaintiff's action. Plaintiff's appeal to the Court of Appeal, First Circuit, was transferred to this Court.

---

[8] Section 8—Regulation Covering the Use of 2,4-D and Related Herbicides, Louisiana Department of Agriculture and Immigration, Promulgated in Accordance With the Provisions of Act 502 of 1952. "No spraying shall be carried out when wind velocity exceeds six (6) miles per hour except in isolated areas by special permit from the Commissioner."

The record discloses that Defendant Gary employed Welsh Flying Service, Inc., to spray a tenant rice crop of 240 acres on July 2, 1953. Spraying operations were commenced before 8:30 a.m., and after that hour the pilot determined that the wind was too high to continue. Gary's farm lands were located some 3 1/4 miles south of plaintiff's farm, and the wind was blowing from the south on July 2, 1953. There is a dispute as to the wind's velocity at the time of the spraying; however, after the spraying, the wind reached a velocity higher than that permitted by the regulations.

In the case of Fontenot v. Magnolia Petroleum Co., 227 La. 866, 80 So. 2d 845, 848, the defendants were free of negligence. There we held that plaintiffs, whose residences were damaged by blasting operations carried on by defendants, were entitled to recover damages as a result of an invasion of their privacy of their respective homes, inconvenience occasioned them, and mental anguish suffered as a result of property damages.

In the instant matter, it is true that the Legislature consented to the use of herbicides, but this did not entitle defendants to injure plaintiff's crops. Although the use of the spraying operation was lawful, it was carried out in such a manner as to unreasonably inconvenience plaintiff and deprive him of the liberty of enjoying his farm.

We adopt the following ruling made in the case of *Fontenot v. Magnolia Petroleum Co.*, supra:

We are unwilling to follow any rule which rejects the doctrine of absolute liability in cases of this nature [ultra-hazardous activities] and prefer to base our holding on the doctrine that negligence or fault, in these instances, is not a requisite to liability, irrespective of the fact that the activities resulting in damages are conducted with assumed reasonable care and in accordance with modern and accepted methods.

We believe that there is adequate proof in the record to substantiate the amount of damages alleged to have been suffered by plaintiff. While there is some dispute as to the value of the pea crop, we do not believe that defendants have sufficiently controverted the loss alleged by plaintiff.

For the reasons assigned, the judgment of the trial court is annulled and set aside, and plaintiff is allowed judgment against the defendants in the sum of $2,405.75, together with legal interest from demand until paid; all costs to be paid by the defendants.[9]

3.4 INSURING THE LIABILITY RISK

Farmers and ranchers can reduce the risk associated with tort liability in two ways.

Because liability is generally based upon fault, the most obvious way of reducing liability risk is to exercise reasonable care in one's daily operations. By taking steps

---

[9] The application of strict liability for damages resulting from the aerial application of other pesticides is probably the minority view. For a more detailed analysis, see the discussion Liability for Pesticide Application in Section 7.4 of Chapter 7.

to assure that one's premise is safe, that one's machinery is properly maintained, and that employees and visitors are warned of dangers that cannot be prevented, and by cultivating a "safety consciousness," the probability of an accident causing injury or property damage can be reduced but not eliminated entirely. Thus, farmers and ranchers also must carry adequate insurance to protect themselves and their assets from the risk of tort liability.

Some insurance coverage is usually required by state law. For example, owners of motor vehicles are typically required to have some minimum level of liability coverage. Also, some farmers and ranchers may be required to carry special workers' compensation insurance. In other areas of potential tort liability, the nature and amount of insurance coverage is generally a matter of individual discretion. There is almost no limit to the hazards for which a liability policy may be obtained.

Liability insurance policies typically have a provision that the company will defend and pay all sums that the insured becomes legally obligated to pay if the injury or damage is covered by the policy. Such policies refer to legal obligations, not moral obligations. A *legal obligation* is one resulting from a court judgment, or one from which the company believes the insured would be liable. A *moral obligation*

is one which an individual feels should be paid, but for which the individual is not legally responsible.

A popular liability policy is called *farmers' comprehensive liability policy*. Such a policy provides payment for personal injuries and property damage to third persons to whom the farmer is legally liable as well as medical payments to injured persons regardless of legal liability.

Farmers' comprehensive personal liability policies generally provide extremely broad coverage.[10] The farmer or rancher is protected from legal liability resulting from occurrences involving farm machinery on or off the premises, injuries caused by employees, and damage or injury caused by livestock. The policy protects against claims made by guests, salespeople, deliverers, and trespassers who are injured on the premises. Farmers and their families are covered if they injure someone while hunting, fishing, camping, or engaging in any other sport or recreational activity. They are also typically protected against suits for injuries to independent contractors or their employees while they are working on the premises. Because of the extensive coverage provided by the comprehensive policy, farmers and ranchers should generally have this kind of insurance protection.[11] A landlord who does not actively participate in the farm business

[10] Even comprehensive policies have exceptions, however. Such policies often do not cover liabilities arising out of a business other than farming. Also, protection is usually extended only to property described in the policy. If someone is injured in a dwelling owned by the farmer but not mentioned in the policy, the farmer is not protected. Typically, coverage does extend to property acquired after the policy is taken out, but all new property must be reported when the policy is renewed for another term. Farmers' comprehensive policies usually do not cover injuries to others off the farm that involve the farmer's autos or trucks. Intentional injuries caused by or at the direction of the farmer are usually excluded from coverage. For example, if a farmer or an employee

punches a salesperson in the nose, the farmer usually is not protected. The farmer is protected, however, for intentional injuries caused by the farmer's employees in the course of their employment and committed on their own accord. Many policies also omit coverage for accidents resulting from custom farm work unless there is a special endorsement on the policy, and almost all policies exclude coverage for liability arising out of dusting and spraying operations from an airplane. Obviously, great care must be taken to assure a farmer or rancher that adequate insurance protection has been obtained.

[11] *See* Annot., 8 A.L.R.3d 916–924 (1966) for a summary of cases involving questions of coverage by farmers' comprehensive personal liability insur-

can usually obtain a policy of his or her own at a very modest rate.

The kinds of liability risks that farmers and ranchers encounter in their business operations will be more apparent in the following chapters. In addition to liability insurance, other forms of insurance protection are desirable. Such insurance includes fire and windstorm protection; health and sickness insurance; accidental death, dismemberment, and disability protection; injury and illness protection; crop insurance; and life insurance. Insurance representatives are happy to discuss these additional kinds of insurance as well as liability insurance.

STUDY QUESTIONS

1. What is a tort? What are some examples of tortious acts?

2. Is tortious conduct necessarily criminal conduct? Can tortious conduct be criminal conduct?

3. Define negligence in general terms. What are the technical elements of negligence and what is the meaning of each element?

4. What kinds of agricultural activities are likely to create liability arising from torts?

5. What physical characteristics, mental ability, and knowledge does the mystical "reasonable person" possess?

6. What is the meaning of contributory negligence, and what is the practical effect of its presence in most jurisdictions?

7. How do comparative negligence statutes generally deal with liability for injuries where the injured party was also partly at fault? Does your state have a comparative negligence statute?

8. What is the doctrine of last clear chance?

9. Who has the burden of proof in civil actions? What level of proof is required?

10. What is the doctrine of *res ipsa loquitur*?

11. What is strict liability, and to what activities is this concept likely to be applied?

12. Where strict liability applies, is it still necessary to prove causation between the ultrahazardous activity and the damage?

13. Frank Farmer drove his pickup truck down a blacktop road at 55 miles per hour, knowing that the brakes were faulty. As Frank approached a two-way sign, he took his foot off the gas pedal intending to coast to a stop. Instead, Frank Farmer coasted past the stop sign and onto the two-lane highway, where the pickup truck was hit by Doug Driver, who was unable to avoid the collision. The front of Driver's car was "banged up" in the accident. Driver sues Farmer, seeking to recover damages based upon Farmer's negligence. What four elements must Driver prove to win his case? What is the meaning of each element, and is it present in this case?

14. Why do farmers and ranchers need liability insurance? Does the insurance company typically initiate and defend liability suits?

ance. *See* Annot., 29 A.L.R.2d 790–810 (1953) for a good discussion of animal or livestock insurance: risks and losses covered.

4

Agricultural Labor, Independent Contractors, and Agents

The subject of agricultural labor law has become an increasingly complex dimension of agricultural law. Much of the applicable law is still based upon the common law. The nature of the employer-employee relationship, the master-servant doctrine, the doctrine of *respondeat superior*, and the common-law liability of a farmer for the injuries of an employee have their origins in the common law and have undergone little change in this century.

Other aspects of agricultural labor law are governed by state and federal legislation which has expanded or modified common-law rules. These statutory aspects of agricultural labor law have undergone enormous change in the twentieth century,

largely as a result of the changing structure of agricultural labor and changing socio-economic philosophies. For example, agricultural production has become much more capital-intensive and much less labor-intensive, particularly in the Prairie and Great Plains states. Public attitudes have also changed regarding the extent and nature of compensation to be provided injured workers.

Initially, state and federal labor legislation was aimed at the industrial and mining sectors of our economy. Many of these laws contained broad exemptions for agricultural workers. However, many of these exemptions have been dramatically reduced in recent years. Any treatment of contemporary agricultural labor law must include a study of workers' compensation laws, child labor laws, occupational safety and health acts, unemployment compensation laws, laws pertaining to migrant workers, and numerous others. Many of these statutory aspects of agricultural labor law have been in a state of flux and make the study of agricultural labor law a dynamic study.

4.1 THE EMPLOYER–EMPLOYEE RELATIONSHIP

When a farmer hires a person to do work on a farm, a legal relationship is established. Depending upon the type of work to be performed and the agreement, the relationship may be that of master-servant, principal-agent, or farmer-independent contractor.

An important question which arises from the master-servant relationship is that of liability if the hired hand is injured. Many farm employer-employee relationships are controlled by the common law. Under the common law, the employer was liable for injuries to an employee if the employer was negligent and the employee was not negligent, and if the employee did not knowingly assume the risk of the thing which caused the injury. However, if a farmer engages in a business other than farming or hires a sufficient amount of labor, the farmer may be liable under the Workmen's Compensation Act which simplifies an employee's recovery for an injury by removing many of the common-law obstacles. A farmer may gain protection from either risk by carrying insurance.

Vicarious Liability

In addition to a farmer's liability for injuries to employees, liability also may be imposed for injuries by them to others. The negligent acts of a farmer's employee are imputed to the farmer by the common-law master-servant doctrine. Liability in any of these cases depends on whether or not the employee was acting within the scope of employment. The employee also is potentially liable for negligent acts, regardless of the employer's vicarious liability.

MASTER AND SERVANT[1]

EVANS v. DAVIDSON
Court of Appeals of Maryland, 1879
53 Md. 245, 36 A. 400

It appears in proof that the defendant was a farmer, and that his farm adjoined that of one Boulden; that he had employed on his farm one Lewis, and two other hands, and that they were employed for a period of nine months to do general farm work on the farm; that on the day the plaintiff's cow was killed, the defendant was away from home, and that the three servants or hirelings were at work in the corn field cultivating the corn, when a herd of cattle, consisting of about thirty head, among which was the plaintiff's cow, broke into the defendant's cornfield, where his hirelings were at work, from

[1] See W. Prosser, Handbook of the Law of Torts §§ 70, 80 (4th ed. 1971).

the adjoining farm belonging to Boulden; and that, upon discovering the cattle among the corn, the servants "immediately started to drive them out, and in doing so the said Lewis negligently struck the plaintiff's cow with a stone, and killed her before she had left the field." There was also proof on the part of the defendant that he had given no orders in regard to driving cattle out of the field, and that he did not know that the cattle were in the corn until after the cow had been killed.

There is no question as to whether the relation of master and servant existed between the defendant and the party doing the wrongful act complained of; that is conceded. But the question is whether the act of driving the cow out of the cornfield was within the scope of the servant's employment, under the circumstances of the case.

If that act was, either expressly or by fair implication, embraced within the employment to do general farm work on the defendant's farm, then, it is clear, the latter is liable for any wrong or negligence committed by the servant in doing the act authorized to be done. In one sense, where there is no express command by the master, all wrongful acts done by the servant may be said to be beyond the scope of the authority given; but the liability of the master is not determined upon any such restricted interpretation of the authority and duty of the servant. If the servant be acting at the time in the course of his master's service and for his master's benefit, within the scope of his employment, then his act, though wrongful or negligent, is to be treated as that of the master, although no express command or privity of the master be shown.

Therefore the fact that the master gave no express direction in regard to driving the cattle out of the cornfield and did not know of their being in it until after the doing of the injury complained of, will not avail to exonerate the master, if the servant was acting in the course of his employment.

Was, then, the servant acting in the course of his employment? What is embraced, as commonly understood, in general farm work? In the very nature of the employment there must be some implied authority and duties belonging to it; and this as well for the protection of the master as third parties. If, for instance, a servant thus employed should see a gate open or a panel of fence down, through which a herd of cattle might or would likely enter and destroy his master's grain, we suppose all would say that it would be the positive duty of the servant to close the gate or put up the fence to prevent destruction of the grain; and if he should pass by and willfully neglect such duty, it would constitute cause and a sufficient justification for the discharge of the servant. If that be so, how much more imperative the duty, where, as in this case, in the absence of the master, the servant being in the field at work, and seeing a herd of cattle break into the field, and in the act of destroying the corn, to drive out the cattle and thus to save the corn from destruction? To do such act, for the preservation of the growing crops, must be regarded as ordinary farm work, and such as every farmer employing a servant to do general farm work would reasonably contemplate and have a right to expect as a matter of duty from the servant. The servant, therefore, was acting in the course of his employment in driving out the cattle, and if he did, while driving them out, commit the wrong complained of, the master is liable therefore.

Farm Wage Contracts and Bonus Plans

The thoroughness with which farm employers and farm laborers discuss the terms of employment varies considerably. From a legal standpoint such agreements have at least two important characteristics: (1) nearly all of them are oral, and (2) many do not specify the length of time the laborer is to work.

If a wage contract specifies an indefinite term of employment or a term that will end within a year from the time the contract is made, the contract is valid whether it is in writing or not. But if the term of employment agreed upon is for a year or more, the statute of frauds requires the agreement to be in writing and signed by the employer and employee.

Courts have held that when a person is employed for an indefinite time, the agreement constitutes a hiring at will. Many decisions indicate that if the employee is hired at will, he or she may quit or be discharged at any time without incurring any liability or acquiring any rights because of the quitting or the discharge.

The application of this rule has sometimes been unjust to farm laborers, because it has forced them to move out of their homes without sufficient notice. A simple written wage contract that states the length of time for which a person is hired and provides that notice to quit be given a definite time in advance of the end of the contract would give a farm laborer the protection needed. When, however, a definite term has thus been agreed upon in writing, it is binding upon both employer and employee.

When a farm laborer is employed at no specific wage, the prevailing rate in the community for the kind of work the laborer is employed for will apply. However, the state minimum wage law and the federal Fair Labor Standards Act may be applicable. Farmers using more than 500 worker-days of labor during any calendar quarter of the preceding calendar year are subject to the federal law.

Many employers of farm labor are interested in wage-bonus plans. They wish to set up arrangements that will cause employees to take a greater interest in their work, that will pay them for doing a superior job, that will attract and keep skilled, dependable labor on the farm, and that will result in greater production of crops and livestock.

Obviously no one plan fits every farm equally well. Some farms have specialized hog enterprises and can base incentive payments on the hog enterprise; others are grain farms and can offer payments on production or income from grain; many are general farms and can make payments on several enterprises.

Following are some items which should be considered in establishing a bonus plan:

1. The employee should receive the going wage in the community plus a bonus on the production or gross income from one or more principal products. Because of accounting problems and other complications, a bonus based on net farm income is usually not satisfactory except between close relatives such as father and son.
2. The employee should have a good, comfortable, and pleasant place to live. No plan can be satisfactory unless both the employee and the employee's family are reasonably happy and content with their living arrangements.
3. The kind and size of bonus should

depend on size of business, type of farming, ability of the employee and length of
tenure, among other factors.

4. The bonus plan should be simple. If
the plan is too complicated to state in
simple, understandable language, it should
not be used.

5. The agreement should be in writing.

6. Several bonus payments during the year
are better than one payment at the end
of the year—for example, one based on

monthly dairy sales in contrast to one
based on net farm returns for the year.

Besides containing a bonus plan, a farm
wage contract which will be competitive
with other kinds of employment should
complement social security benefits with
contributions to insurance or a retirement
program, should guarantee a minimum
wage, and should provide for arbitration
of differences, among other fringe benefits.

FARM LABOR—SPECIAL CONTRACTS

ROBINSON v. WEBB
Appellate Court of Illinois, Third District, 1897
73 Ill. App. 569

On the sixth of March, 1893, plaintiff-appellee began working as a farm
hand for defendant-appellant at $20 per month and continued to work for
him at that rate for four years, when his wages were changed to $18 per month
and so continued until the employment terminated on the twentieth of May,
1897. Appellant is an extensive stock farmer in Logan County, and during
the course of the employment appellee performed some work on Sundays,
such as milking cows and feeding stock. An account was kept during the
entire time by appellant and frequent settlements were made by it. On the
twentieth of May, 1897, at the time the employment terminated, a final settlement was had between the parties, and appellee accepted a bank check for
$24.35, which recited that it was in full payment for work to date. It has
never been claimed by appellee that he has not been fully paid for the stipulated monthly wages of $20 and $18 per month. This suit was brought to
recover for work done Sundays, however, and in the Circuit Court a judgment
was rendered in his favor for $52.50.

Where a man enters the employment of a farmer as a farm hand at a stipulated rate per month, knowing that work in the nature of "choring" will
be required of him on Sundays, the law will not imply a promise to pay additional wages for such work, and before a recovery could be had for it, it
would develop upon the plaintiff to show that there was a special agreement
on the part of the employer to pay extra...[for such work].

In this case appellee swears that appellant made a special promise to pay
for work done on Sundays over and above the stipulated monthly wage. He
is contradicted by appellant, and several witnesses, some of whom worked
with him, testified that appellee told them he was to receive nothing extra
for Sunday work. The testimony of appellee is unreasonable and unworthy
of belief. If there was such an agreement as he contends for, it is not reason-

able to believe that in the frequent settlements had during the course of the four years' employment he would not have insisted upon compensation for Sunday work being included. Nor can we think that he would have accepted a check for $24.35 when the employment terminated, which recited that it was in full for all work, if at that time appellant owed him for what he had done on Sundays. Where parties have a settlement of their accounts and a check for the amount found due from one to the other, which recites that it is in full, is accepted and afterward paid, the presumption of fact is strong that all items properly chargeable at the time are embraced in the settlement.

We are forced to say that the jury in this case either misconceived the evidence or were actuated by prejudice. The facts are so clearly against appellee that judgment in his favor for any amount should not be permitted to stand. The one rendered will be reversed, but the case will not be remanded. Judgment reversed.

Common-Law Liability for Employee's Injury and Defenses[2]

Where workers' compensation laws do not apply, the liability of a farmer for injuries to farm laborers will generally be governed by common-law principles. At common law, if an employee could establish that injury was due to the employer's negligence, the employer might be liable for the damages. However, even where the employer had been negligent, the worker still could not recover if the worker was guilty of contributory negligence, if the worker assumed the risks resulting in the injury, or if the injury was due to the negligence of fellow employees. Obtaining compensation under common-law principles was difficult, at best, for an injured worker.

DEFENSES: CONTRIBUTORY NEGLIGENCE[3]

WILLS v. PAUL
Appellate Court of Illinois, Third District, 1960
24 Ill. App. 2d 417, 164 N.E. 2d 631

This is an action for damages resulting from personal injuries sustained by plaintiff while working as a farmhand for the defendant.

In the complaint it is alleged that on December 15, 1955, plaintiff, at the request of and as an employee of the defendant, was operating a corn picker; that while plaintiff was removing a corn stalk which had become lodged in said corn picker his right hand was injured; that said injury was due solely to the negligence of defendant in that he directed and ordered plaintiff to operate a corn picker which he knew had a defective gear and because of said defective gear the corn stalk became lodged in the corn picker. Defendant's

---

[2] *See generally* 3 N. HARL, AGRICULTURAL LAW § 20.04.

[3] *See* W. PROSSER, HANDBOOK OF THE LAW OF TORTS § 80 (4th ed. 1971).

answer consisted of a general denial of the complaint allegations. A trial by jury resulted in a verdict for plaintiff assessing his damages at $10,000. The trial court allowed defendant's post-trial motion and entered judgment notwithstanding the verdict in his favor on the grounds that the farmworker was guilty of contributory negligence, as a matter of law.

There is no substantial conflict in the evidence, which discloses that at the time of his injury plaintiff was 44 years of age; that he had worked as a farm laborer all his life; that he had worked for defendant for about 12 years and was well acquainted with the operation of farm machinery including corn pickers; that while the program of farm operation was prescribed by defendant, the crops were planted and harvested by the plaintiff; that plaintiff also looked after the farm machinery and if it needed repair he reported such fact to the defendant; that the corn picker in which plaintiff was injured was a used machine purchased in 1954; that it was equipped with a power take-off device which enables the operator to stop the picker by shutting off all power from the tractor; that although requiring repairs on numerous occasions, it was used by plaintiff to pick all but 2 1/2 acres of the 1955 corn crop of about 55 acres; and that a new gear for the machine had been ordered but had not arrived at the time of the accident.

In arguing that he was not guilty of contributory negligence as a matter of law, plaintiff relies principally on the testimony of Robert Brown, a defense witness, who on cross-examination, stated it was common practice for farm employees to remove a corn stalk while the picker was running. It is pointed out that since what plaintiff did was not an uncommon or unusual practice in farm operation, his action in striking the corn stalk was involuntary and the natural and probable act of a reasonable person. There is no merit in such argument. In determining whether the particular acts of a plaintiff constitute negligence, the test is not the frequency with which other men commit such acts but whether the plaintiff at the time of the occurrence, used that degree of care which an ordinary careful person would have used for his own safety under like circumstances. In substance, the evidence as to the actual occurrence is that with the power take-off on, plaintiff removed his glove and placed his hand where it became enmeshed in the machine's revolving rollers. We think all reasonable men would agree that these undisputed facts fail to establish due care on the part of plaintiff.

For the reasons indicated, we are of the opinion that the trial court did not err in entering judgment for defendant notwithstanding the verdict of the jury.

Affirmed.

ASSUMPTION OF RISK[4]

CONBOY v. CROFOOT
Supreme Court of Kansas, 1964
194 Kan. 46, 397 P. 2d 326

This appeal is from an order of the district court sustaining the defendants' demurrer to the plaintiff's amended petition.

Peter J. Conboy, Jr., was employed by the defendants. On December 20, 1960, the defendants were preparing a shipment of cattle to be removed from the feeding lots and during this operation the plaintiff was ordered by the defendants to stand in the center of a sorting alley, directing the cattle as they came toward him individually into one pen if they were ready for the market and into another pen if they were not yet ready for the market, under the supervision of John Crofoot. The portion of the feeding lot in which the plaintiff was ordered to stand was extremely wet and muddy due to the snow, sleet, and rain which had fallen prior to and on December 19, 1960, but was partially due to the fact that a large number of cattle were being kept within the area of the feeding lots.

On the day in question, the plaintiff was wearing ordinary work boots which were sufficient to protect his feet from the elements during the performance of his regular duties. The temperature on the morning of December 20, 1960, was from 21 to 22 degrees and to carry out the orders and commands of his employer, the plaintiff was forced to stand in mud continuously for a period lasting from two to two and a half hours.

One of the risks incident to long, continued outdoor employment in the wintertime is that one's hands and feet will become cold and may be injured by freezing, is so clearly within the rule of assumption of risk on the part of the servant as to require no argument. When a person is capable of and intelligent enough to understand the physical effects of heat and cold upon his body, he assumes the risk for a continuance in service, and cannot recover for the suffering and inconvenience directly due or caused by the exposure to the heat and cold.

In occupations involving no extraordinary hazard, in which an employee engages voluntarily, without compulsion or emergency, he is conclusively presumed to have assumed such risks as are ordinarily incidental thereto, not due to the employer's negligence or violation of law.

We find no merit to appellant's contention that his evidence presented a question for determination by the jury. Under the existing facts, conditions and circumstances the all-decisive question was one for determination by the trial court. In *Blackmore v. Auer*, supra, we said:

The assumption of the usual risks of an employment is not ordinarily a jury question. It is a matter of law. It is only where the risk is or may be unusual that a jury question can arise; and even in such cases, if the risk though

---

[4] *Id.* § 69.

unusual is obvious, such as an ordinarily prudent man could appreciate and understand, the workman who persists in the employment assumes the risk of it. Lively v. Chicago, R. I & P. Railway Co., 115 Kan. 784, 225 P. 103 and authorities cited therein.   [187 Kan. pp. 444, 445, 357 P. 2d p. 773.]

What has been heretofore stated and held compels a conclusion that the trial court did not err in sustaining appellee's demurrer to appellant's evidence and that its judgment must be affirmed.

In discussing the doctrine of assumption of risk in the context of a machinery-related accident, an Illinois court noted the importance of appreciating danger in *Fox v. Beall*, 314 Ill. App. 144, 41 N.E.2d 126 (1942). The court stated that, in many jurisdictions, it is essential to the operation of the principle of assumed risk incident to the use of defective machinery that the servant not only know of such defect but also know and appreciate the danger and risk connected therewith. Although an employee may have knowledge of the defective condition of an appliance, by reason of which the employee sustains an injury, it does not thereby follow that the employee must be held to have appreciated the danger to which he or she was thereby exposed. An apprehension of the danger is the factor that established responsibility, not mere knowledge of the defect or condition by which the danger is created.

The distinctions between contributory negligence and assumption of risk recognized in many states are stated in the case of *Clubb v. Main*, 65 Ill. App.2d 461, 213 N.E.2d 63 (1965), in which the decedent fell from an allegedly defective tractor seat. The court noted that under Illinois law, while plaintiffs must prove themselves free of contributory negligence, the proof of assumption of risk is the defendant's burden. This Illinois rule represents a minority view, most states placing upon the defendant the duty of raising the contributory negligence defense. The court also noted that the standard to be applied

on the issue of assumption of risk is a subjective one, of what the particular plaintiff sees, knows, understands, and appreciates. On the other hand, in determining the issue of contributory negligence, the conduct of the plaintiff is measured against the objective standard of what a reasonably careful person would do under the same or similar circumstances.

Further insights into contributory negligence and assumption of risk are described in *Brown v. McColl*, 36 Ill. App.2d 215, 183 N.E.2d 541 (1962), wherein one of the plaintiffs, Robert Brown, a boy of 16 years, hitched the defendant's farm tractor to a rack, placed his collie dog thereon, and went down the road to get some pea vines. The road was high-crowned and blacktop, with sloping grass ditches, and on that morning, dry and devoid of traffic. He proceeded at top speed—10 to 12 miles per hour—in spite of the fact that he knew the left brake was defective. A bit down the road, his dog spied a rabbit and began to bark, as dogs will. Robert looked back, as boys will, to see what the dog was barking about. At that instant, the tractor began to leave the blacktop. In attempting to regain the road, he turned the wheel and went through the motions of applying the brake. The brake didn't hold; the tractor turned over, pinning him beneath. The jury awarded him $1000, and his father $5500 for his expenses. With regard to the brake condition, the same had existed for several months before the accident. Robert, while knowing of the condition, continued to operate the farm tractor, but did call it to the attention of defendant on a number of occasions.

In discussing the standard of care required of youth, the court noted that "boys of sixteen are expected to exercise the care and caution of boys of that age." The court's view was in accord with the majority view that a child is required to conform to the standard of care of a child of like age, education, intelligence, and experience. This standard is more subjective than the "reasonable person" standard applied to adults.

The court's discussion of assumption of risk was also enlightening. Excerpts from that discussion appear in the following paragraphs.

Assumption of risk cases are getting to be a rarity nowadays. One area where they still persist is on the farm. The doctrine finds its parentage in the law of contracts, while contributory neglience was conceived in the law of torts. The rule, more simply put than the quotation above, says that when one assumes a known risk, he cannot complain when he loses. This is a fairly understandable concept and consonant with conditions necessarily imposed by being alive. As Mr. Justice Cardozo once remarked, "The timorous may stay at home," meaning that once you go outside, you assume certain risks.

Take the word "risk." To assume a risk means knowledge of the risk. One cannot assume a risk he knows nothing about. All men would agree that there is a risk implicit in bad brakes. Robert did have knowledge of the brake condition, but we judge the extent of his knowledge of the risk in the light of his youth. The risk to him might not be as clearly perceived as by one older and more experienced. Sixteen year old boys are different from twelve year olds, and both are different from adults. Indeed, sixteen year old boys can and do differ. One may have had experience with tractors, another not. With the former the assumption of risk is greater, with the latter, much less, if at all.

A further ramification or facet obtrudes itself. What is meant by the word "assumption." One might be said to have, or be charged with having, a sufficient knowledge of a given risk, and still not be charged with having assumed it if he had no choice. Obviously, if one is ordered to do something, and he has absolutely no choice but to do it, it cannot be said that there has been any true assumption of any risk of whether he knew about them or not. On the contrary, in the context of the doctrine, he has assumed nothing. Without getting too abstract, assumption presupposes choice, and choice presupposes free will, or at least some degree of volition. Not in an absolute sense, of course, but reasonably related to the circumstances. At sixteen, he may have believed that he had no choice. Youth to age does bow, even where there may be no contractual relationship.

FELLOW SERVANT RULE[5]

PALMER v. WILTSE
Supreme Court of Minnesota, 1953
239 Minn. 130, 57 N.W. 2d 812

Plaintiff, William Palmer, was injured while employed by defendant, Merle Wiltse, as a farm hand. A fellow employee dropped two bales of hay

[5] *Id.* § 80.

down a hay chute onto plaintiff while he was engaged in preparing to feed a span of horses in defendant's barn. At the conclusion of plaintiff's evidence, the trial court granted defendant's motion for dismissal. Subsequently, the court denied plaintiff's motion for a new trial, and judgment was entered in favor of defendant. This appeal is from that judgment.

It appears that plaintiff was working about defendant's barn with another employee, Carl Nelson. They were both engaged in preparing to feed stock. Nelson was getting hay down from the mow into the alley between the horse stalls and the cow stanchions. Plaintiff was putting a pail of corn in a manger near the horses, preparatory to feeding them later. In so doing, plaintiff passed near or under the hay chute. Nelson threw two bales of hay through the hay chute; one of them struck plaintiff and caused his injuries.

Defendant had instructed his men to break up the bales before throwing them down the chute, but Nelson apparently did not always follow instructions in this regard and usually shouted, "Timber," when throwing down an unbroken bale. On the occasion on which plaintiff was hurt, he failed to warn plaintiff. Defendant was not present when the bale struck plaintiff.

In a personal injury action by a servant against a master, where there is no evidence that the injuries were due to unsafe working conditions to which the servant was exposed, and the injuries to plaintiff were due solely to the negligence of a fellow servant which did not involve a breach of any nondelegable duty, the master is not liable.

The decision of the trial court is affirmed.

SIMPLE TOOL RULE

FIELDS v. JOHNSON
Mississippi Supreme Court, 1965
252 Miss. 705, 173 So. 2d 428

Plaintiff below, appellant here, filed suit against defendant below, appellee here, for personal injuries. The court sustained a demurrer to the declaration and dismissed the suit. Plaintiff appealed to this Court.

For the purposes of this opinion the facts are stated as charged in the declaration and considered as true. Plaintiff was an employee on the farm of defendant. In the early spring of 1962 defendant was in a hurry to complete work of tearing down houses on the farm, putting up fences, and making repairs before the farming season arrived. In order to construct a fence along the creek bank, it was necessary to cut the underbrush and trees, and on the date charged in the declaration, plaintiff was clearing the creek bank of underbrush. Defendant's son and agent brought an extremely dull ax to the place where plaintiff was working. The ax had been used to wreck houses and cut tin and had not thereafter been sharpened. The defendant was in a hurry to complete the work of clearing the creek bank and building the fences because of the nearness of the farming season. Plaintiff was required and commanded to cut the underbrush with the extremely dull ax, and was required to cut a pecan tree or bush about one inch in diameter, and when he attempted to do so the ax failed to cut the sapling and the top of it sprang back and struck and injured his eye.

At common law, an employee was deemed to be just as capable of finding defects in simple tools as the employer. Thus, under the simple tool rule, an employer would generally not be held liable for injuries to an employee occasioned by use of a simple tool like a hammer, a ladder, or an ax. An exception to this rule applies where the employer ordered the worker to use the defective tool. Plaintiff argued that he should be able to recover because of the affirmative command.

In arguing this contention, plaintiff relies on the rule firmly established in this jurisdiction that an employee is bound to obey the direct order of the master or risk being discharged for insubordination, and if the master orders the employee to use a defective tool or appliance, even a simple tool, over the protest of the employee, the employee is not held to assume the risk incident to the use of such tool and may recover if injured thereby. Plaintiff contends that the affirmative command of the defendant, through his agent, to plaintiff requiring him to perform an unsafe act raises a question of negligence for the jury.

We have carefully considered this argument and in doing so find that the declaration does not charge that the defendant's agent commanded or ordered plaintiff to cut the particular pecan sapling with the dull ax. What the declaration does is charge that "plaintiff was required and commanded to cut the underbrush with an extremely dull and dangerous ax." It does not charge that defendant's agent gave a direct command to use the dull ax on the particular sapling or to cut the sapling in any particular manner.

The decision of the trial court to sustain the demurrer is affirmed.

Although the previous discussion of the various defenses to a negligence action appears quite confusing at first, a unifying thread can be found. The very concept of negligence and the various defenses all focus upon "fault." Unfortunately, when the principle of fault is applied by various judges and juries, the results are very difficult to predict. The following decisions by Illinois courts illustrate the uncertainty involved with common-law recovery.

Holdings in Other Cases Involving Farm Machinery.[6] In *McDaniel v. Hulva*, 34 Ill. App. 2d 388, 181 N.E.2d 364 (1962), a farmhand did not recover when he drove a tractor into some tree limbs while reaching back to engage a plough. In *Pennewell v. Magnelia*, 2 Ill. App. 2d 290, 119 N.E.2d 511 (1954), the court sustained a directed verdict for the defendant where a 17-year-old farmhand lost his leg in an elevator auger while kicking at the latch on an endgate, though a safety bar which fitted over the auger was not in place at the time of the accident. In *Kelley v. Fletcher—Merna Co-op Grain Co.*, 29 Ill. App. 2d 419, 173 N.E.2d 855(1961), the court

---

[6] Annot., 67 A.L.R.2d 1120–1237 (1959).

held that the plaintiff had assumed the risk when he caught his foot in the defendant's auger equipment while transferring corn from a government bin to the defendant's bin. In *Brownback v. Thomas*, 101 Ill. App. 81 (1901), a farmer was instructed to wait at the dump with his load of oats until he could get help. He attempted to operate the dump himself and was injured. The court held that he had assumed the risk and there was no recovery. In *Black v. White*, 13 Ill. App.2d 134, 140 N.E.2d 736 (1957), the plaintiff recovered when a tractor wouldn't stop because of a defective clutch which the defendant had been aware of. In *Ferguson v. Lounsberry*, 58 Ill. App.2d 456, 207 N.E.2d 309 (1965), the court reversed a trial court judgment for the plaintiff when he was injured because his clothes became entangled in the mechanism of a power-driven corn elevator on his employer's farm. The court held that since the manner and method of doing the job rested in the sole judgment of the plaintiff and he was aware that the square shaft and knuckle revolving at a rate in excess of 500 revolutions per minute presented an area of danger, his recovery was barred by contributory negligence. In *Fosen v. Odell Grain & Coal Company*, 70 Ill. App.2d 384, 217 N.E.2d 126 (1966), the court held that where the plaintiff was injured at the defendants' elevator while unloading corn for his neighbor with whom he exchanged labor, the relationship of master and servant did not exist between the plaintiff and the elevator and therefore the latter could not use the defense of assumption of risk in an action for injury caused when the plaintiff's hand was caught in an auger being used to unload the corn.

Liability to Farm Workers Injured Other than by Farm Machinery.[7] Obviously all farm accidents are not caused by machinery. Some of the other items which have given rise to suits by employee against employer are farm animals, explosives, wagons and other implements, tools, condition of the premises, ladders, hay chutes, and icy floors. Employees falling off loads and having undue exposure to the elements are also causes of suits by employee against employer. Following are some examples:

An employee fell through a hole in the haymow at a time when he was not required to be in the haymow. The court held for the defendant.

An employee fell from a wagon when the wire broke on a bale of hay. The court held for the defendant.

An employee was thrown from an unbroken mule which he was trying to ride during off-duty hours. The court held that this came under the heading of recreation. There was no recovery.

The plaintiff was injured when thirty-five brood sows weighing between 400 and 600 pounds rushed him at feeding time and pushed loose feed troughs against him. The court held for the plaintiff.

The court allowed recovery in an action for wrongful death where the plaintiff employee was killed by a bull which he was trying to handle only with a halter even though the bull had a ring in its nose and the plaintiff had not fastened the strap in it.

A sheepherder hired by the defendant was injured by exposure to snow and cold when the defendant's camp mover, whom the facts disclosed was frequently drunken and neglectful, moved camp without telling the herder. Recovery was allowed.

Statutory Liability: Workers' Compensation Laws[8]

At common law, the ability of an injured worker to recover damages from the

---

[7] Annot, 9 A.L.R.3d 1061–1140 (1966).

[8] *See generally* 3 N. HARL, AGRICULTURAL LAW § 20.01 *et seq.* (1980).

employer was limited. As noted earlier, the worker not only had to establish negligence on the part of the employer, but also had to overcome contributory negligence or assumption of risk. As the industrial revolution progressed, public dissatisfaction with the common-law principles of liability became more widespread. Most workers' compensation laws came into effect in the early twentieth century. Generally, these acts provide for automatic compensation, regardless of fault, when a worker is injured or killed as a result of a work-related accident. Thus, where workers' compensation acts are applicable, the common-law principles of negligence, contributory negligence, and assumption of risk are irrelevant to the issue of liability.

Agricultural Exemptions. Agricultural employment was initially exempt from the provisions of many state workers' compensation acts. For example, the 1915 workers' compensation statute in Illinois contained a sweeping exclusion of farmers, their employees, tenant farmers, and stock raisers. Kansas passed a statute in 1911 excluding workers in agricultural pursuits, and Georgia enacted a similar exclusion in 1920.[9]

More recently, various state legislatures have established a trend toward broader agricultural coverage of workers' compensation laws. In 1915 the Montana legislature enacted a statute allowing contributory negligence, assumption of the risk, and negligence of a fellow servant as defenses to liability in cases involving injury to farm employees and not to other employees.[10] A 1973 amendment repealed this provision and placed agricultural laborers on the same level with other employees.[11] The blanket agricultural exemption enacted by the Illinois legislature in 1915 has been reduced to a 500 worker-day per calendar quarter exemption which excludes work performed by members of the farm employer's immediate family.[12] In some states, such as California, Ohio, and Montana, the agricultural worker has been totally integrated into the general coverage of industrial employees and thus receives equal treatment with nonagricultural workers.[13] In 1974 the National Commission on State Workmen's Compensation Laws recommended that state acts be amended to cover all employees, including agricultural workers.[14] The Commission recognized that there had never been a federal workers' compensation statute and that individual state acts, more so than in any other area of labor law, lacked uniformity. For the most part, the states have continued to exercise their independence in formulating coverage of agriculture, ignoring to a large extent the commission's recommendations for uniform inclusive coverage of agricultural labor.

---

[9] 1920 Ga. Laws, p. 177.

[10] 1915 Mont. Laws ch. 96, § 3.

[11] 1973 Mont. Laws ch. 492. § 2.

[12] ILL. REV. STAT. ch. 48, § 138.3(19) (1979).

[13] CAL. LAB. CODE § 3351 (West Supp. 1977); OHIO REV. CODE ANN. § 4123.01 (Page 1973).

[14] Moore, *Workmen's Compensation—An Introduction to Changes in the Kansas Statute*, 24 KAN. L. REV. 603 (1976).

CONSTITUTIONALITY OF MICHIGAN'S AGRICULTURAL EXEMPTION

GALLEGOS v. GLASER CRANDELL COMPANY
Supreme Court of Michigan, 1972
388 Mich. 654, 202 N.W. 2d 786

ADAMS, Justice.

Plaintiff Frank Gallegos is a Mexican-American, thirty-eight years old. On August 2, 1967, while in the employ of defendant Glaser Crandell, Gallegos fell and sustained a fractured wrist on defendant's property. Plaintiff Mary Gutierrez, also in the employ of Glaser Crandell, sustained a fall on the same property on August 13, 1967. She received injuries to her left leg and back. Both plaintiffs are agricultural workers whom defendant employed on a seasonal basis.

After defendant refused to pay workmen's compensation benefits voluntarily, plaintiffs filed an application with the Bureau of Workmen's Compensation and asked for a hearing. Both plaintiffs and defendant requested a ruling on the constitutionality of certain portions of the Workmen's Compensation Act.

Plaintiffs argue that the exclusion from workmen's compensation benefits of those agricultural workers who are paid on a piecework basis and those agricultural workers who do not work thirty-five or more hours per week for the same employer for thirteen or more consecutive weeks denies those workers the equal protection of the laws. They claim that the exceptions set forth in the statute result in the establishment of a class and the invidious discrimination against the members of that class.

In *Fox v. Employment Security Commission*, 379 Mich. 579, 589, 153 N.W. 2d 644, 648 (1967), it was said:

Legislation which, in carrying out a public purpose for the common good, is limited by reasonable and justifiable differentiation to a distinct type or class of persons is not for that reason unconstitutional, because class legislation, if germane to the object of the enactment and made uniform in its operation upon all persons of the class to which it naturally applies; but if it fails to include and affect alike all persons of the same class, and extends immunities or privileges to one portion and denies them to others of like kind, by unreasonable or arbitrary subclassification, it comes within the constitutional prohibition against class legislation.

Turning back to the present case, from an examination of the definition of "agricultural employer" it will readily be seen that it includes all possible kinds of work "on a farm," such as plowing, planting, harvesting, maintenance of machinery, bookkeeping, processing, canning, raising cattle or other livestock. The work can vary from the most menial (digging ditches) to the most exacting (expert cross-pollination of plants or flowers) as long as it is "on a farm."

There is no basis for distinguishing the work of a laborer who drives a truck at a factory from a laborer who drives one on the farm or for any one of numerous other labor activities "on the farm" as distinguished from the same activity in industry, wholesaling, retailing, or building. There is no basis for a special definition of "weekly wage" for farm labor as distinguished from any other type of labor. "All private employers" come under the act if they regularly employ 3 or more employees at one time. On the other hand, only "agricultural employers" who employ 3 or more employees, not on piece work, 35 or more hours per week by the same employer for 13 or more weeks during the preceding 52 weeks come under the act.

From the above, it will be seen that while Justice Kavanagh posits the reasonableness of the agricultural classification, in order to consider the propriety of the subclassification of "agricultural workers" which results from the exclusion of certain of them from coverage, my difficulty is with the classification of agricultural employers. Agricultural employers, regardless of the skills of their employees or the activities engaged in, are accorded a special treatment and classification of their employees not accorded any other private or public employer. Such treatment is impermissible, clearly discriminatory and has no rational basis.

I vote to reverse and remand to the Workmen's Compensation Commission for determination of plaintiffs' claims.

I would award costs to plaintiffs.

T.M. KAVANAGH, C.J., and BLACK and SWAINSON, JJ., concur.
T.G. KAVANAGH, Justice.

Justice Adams' opinion concludes that on its face M.C.L.A. § 418.115(d); M.S.A. § 17.237(115)(d), denies equal protection of the laws to those persons thereby excluded from coverage under Michgan's Workmen's Compensation law. He writes "such treatment is impermissible, clearly discriminatory. We concur in the decision to "reverse and remand to the Workmen's Compensation Commission for determination of plaintiffs' claims."

Our vote to reverse and remand, however, is based upon our persuasion that there is a rational basis for the distinction drawn by the statute between agricultural and other employees, but the distinguishing provisions are otherwise invalid under the United States and Michigan Constitutions.

We are not here concerned with the division of workers into "industrial" and "agricultural" classes. We posit the reasonableness of such classification in order to consider the propriety of the subclassification of "agricultural" workers which results from the exclusion of certain of them from coverage. We note that the exceptions contained in the statute do establish two separate subclasses—those agricultural workers covered by the act and those not covered by the act on account of such exceptions. It is not disputed that this latter group are seasonally employed and we will hereafter refer to them as "seasonal workers."

When classification is alleged to deny an individual equal protection of the law, such classification, as a general rule, must be shown to be unreasonable. In determining reasonableness courts usually express as a standard the equivalent of: "A distinction in legislation is not arbitrary, if any state of facts reasonably can be conceived that would sustain it." However, if the class affected is one limited by race, religious creed, or political beliefs, the classification is considered to be "inherently suspect" and a compelling gov-- ernmental interest must be shown.

Seasonal agricultural workers comprise one of the poorest segments of our society. The majority of these workers have earnings which are below the poverty level. Indeed such earnings are often less than would be received if the workers went on welfare. While a classification based on wealth alone has never been held to be "inherently suspect," wealth is a factor which is given great weight in determining whether there has been a denial of equal protection.

We conclude that no compelling state interest has been shown. There- fore, those portions of the statute excepting piecework employees, and those excepting persons not employed thirty-five hours a week for 13 con- secutive weeks for the same employer are in violation of U.S. Const., AM. XIV and Const. 1963, art. 1, § 2. Therefore, these sections are stricken from the statute.

Reversed and remanded to the Workmen's Compensation Commission for determination of the claim.

No costs, a matter of public interest.

BRENNAN, Justice (dissenting).

I dissent.

The problem of providing workmen's compensation for migrant farm workers was considered by the legislature in the general revision of 1969. 1969 P.A. 317.

The categories established do not discriminate against migrant farm work- ers. Indeed, subsection 115(e) provides a special remedy for migrant farm workers which is not provided for non-agricultural workers.

It is obvious that the legislature has attempted to draw a line between small farms (subsection 115[e]) and big farms (subsection 115[d]). Big farms are treated exactly like any other employer—agricultural or non- agricultural. Little farms, unlike little gas stations, little stores or casual residential employers, are required to carry medical insurance under section 315.

Thus, if I employ a handyman to work around my house for six weeks, I am not subject to the workmen's compensation act. (Section 118[2]). If a farmer puts on a hired hand for the same length of time, medical and hospi- tal coverage must be provided. Where is the discrimination?

Farm employers not exempt from the state workers' compensation act must purchase a special workers' compensation insurance policy. Some states, such as

Illinois, allow an alternative in which the employer can be approved as a self-insurer. Failure to take one step or the other is unlawful and subjects the farmer to possible fine and the very real risk that the existing insurance coverage will not pay a workers' compensation claim.

Farm employers who are exempt from the mandatory coverage of the act may be allowed to elect workers' compensation coverage. Although somewhat costly, the purchasing of workers' compensation insurance may assure injured workers of prompt and dependable compensation for work-related injuries.

Generally, workers' compensation acts represent a complete departure from common law and substitute a new system of rights, remedies, and procedures where work-related injury or death occurs. The primary purpose of these laws is to give improved financial protection to workers and their families by providing prompt, sure, and definite compensation. A further purpose is to require that the cost of such injuries or death be borne by the industry itself.

Although workers' compensation laws may be an improvement over common-law rules, such laws certainly fall short of a perfect solution. In certain states, such as Illinois, the workers' compensation laws are severely criticized by some who suggest the benefits are excessive and the costs of the insurance prohibitive. In other states, workers' compensation laws are criticized because of delays in administration and because of benefits that lag behind actual medical costs. Largely because of such criticism, in 1978 Missouri, for example, repealed the provision requiring mandatory coverage of agricultural workers.

The amount of compensation in workers' compensation claims is usually based upon medical expenses plus the salary of the worker and the nature of the worker's injury. Such often litigated matters as damages for pain and suffering are not included in the statutory formula. Workers' compensation acts, where applicable, are often the exclusive remedy of an injured worker, thus precluding any other common-law or statutory recovery.

WORKERS' COMPENSATION—A SUBSTITUTE FOR COMMON-LAW LIABILITY

LOPEZ v. GALEENER
Illinois Appellate Court, 1975
34 Ill. App. 2d 815, 341 N.E. 2d 59

The defendants, Gibson Galeener and Lawrence Hess, appeal from a judgment of the circuit court of Madison County which was entered upon a jury verdict that was rendered in favor of the plaintiffs, Richard Schuette and Douglas Lopez's estate. The defendants request a judgment notwithstanding the verdict, or in the alternative, a new trial.

The critical issue in this appeal is whether Richard Schuette and Douglas Lopez were engaged in the line of their duty as employees of Gibson Galeener when they were injured in an automobile accident, so that they were precluded from recovering from the defendants on the theory of common law tort liability by section 5(a) of the Workmen's Compensation Act, which states in pertinent part:

No common law or statutory right to recover damages from the employer... for injury or death sustained by any employee while engaged in the line of his duty as such employee, other than the compensation herein provided, is available to any employee who is covered by the provisions of this Act....

The facts were as follows. Gibson Galeener operated a feed store in St. Jacob, Illinois, and a poultry farm which was about one and one-half miles north of St. Jacob. Galeener employed one or two young men steadily to help him in the operation of his feed store and poultry farm. Lawrence Hess was one of Galeener's steady employees.

In April of 1970, Galeener gave part-time jobs to Douglas Lopez and Richard Schuette. Lopez and Schuette were hired to shovel the droppings from beneath the chicken cages on Galeener's poultry farm. At his feed store in town, Galeener provides a shower room where the young men who did this kind of work could change their clothes. On the afternoon of April 14, 1970, Lopez and Schuette went to Galeener's feed store after school. They arrived at the feed store about 2:45. Lopez and Schuette changed their clothes, and Hess (another employee) loaded Galeener's station wagon with sacks of feed. Hess, Lopez, and Schuette left together in the station wagon and headed for Galeener's poultry farm north of town.

On the way to the poultry farm, the young men stopped at Bloomer's Cafe in St. Jacob. They remained in the cafe about 20 minutes, drinking soda and talking with their friends. After they left the cafe, Hess drove the station wagon on the road that led north out of town. Schuette rode in the middle of the front seat, and Lopez sat on the right in the front seat of the automobile. Hess drove the station wagon into an intersection, where it was hit by an automobile traveling west on U.S. 49. Lopez was killed in the collision and Schuette was injured. These facts were not disputed.

Schuette and Lopez's estate sued Hess on the theory that Hess had negligently caused the collision of the automobiles. Because Hess was Gibson Galeener's employee, Schuette and Lopez's estate sued Gibson Galeener on the theory of *respondeat superior*. The defense raised by Galeener and Hess was that Schuette and Lopez were injured in the line of their duty as employees of Galeener, and that they were therefore prevented by section 5(a) of the Workmen's Compensation Act from recovering from the defendants on a theory of common law tort liability.

A special interrogatory was submitted to the jury which required the jury to state whether Schuette and Lopez were in the line of their duty as employees of Gibson Galeener at the time of the accident. The jury answered the special interrogatory "No" and awarded damages against Galeener and Hess to both Schuette and the administrator of Douglas Lopez's estate. A judgment was entered in accordance with the jury's verdict.

Galeener and Hess appeal from the circuit court's denial of their post-trial motion and ask for a judgment notwithstanding the verdict on the ground that they had a valid defense based upon section 5(a) of the Workmen's Compensation Act.

A general rule has been developed in workmen's compensation cases that accidents that occur while an employee is going to or from his place of employment do not arise out of and in the course of his employment and are, therefore, not compensable. The reason is that the employee's trip to and from work is the product of his own decision as to where he wants to live, a matter in which his employer ordinarily has no interest. An exception to this rule has been recognized by the Illinois Supreme Court, which is that an employee will be considered to have been engaged in the line of duty even while going to or coming from work if the course or method of his travel was determined by the demands or exigencies of his job rather than by his own personal preferences as to where he desired to live. The defendants, Galeener and Hess, have argued that the travel of Schuette and Lopez from the feed store to the poultry farm was occasioned by the demands or exigencies of their employment with Galeener. The evidence, when viewed most favorably to plaintiffs shows they were not required by their employment to go to the feed store, and that they were not required by their employment to travel from the feed store to the poultry farm. The most that can be said about the relationship of Schuette and Lopez to the feed store is that Schuette and Lopez could go to the feed store to change their clothes if they desired to do so. The verdict of the jury that Schuette and Lopez were not engaged in the line of their duty at the time of the accident was, therefore, supported by the evidence. The defendants, Galeener and Hess, are not entitled to a judgment notwithstanding the verdict.

Judgment affirmed.

What would have happened in the above case if the injuries had occurred while Schuette and Lopez were "on the job," assuming Galeener's farming operations were not exempt from the Workmen's Compensation Act?

As to Lopez's widow, the determination would probably be simple. The widow would request compensation according to the statutory formula from Galeener or his insurer. The widow and children would be entitled to weekly compensation based upon a statutory percent of Lopez's weekly wage. Such compensation would continue until the death of the widow or until the youngest child reached age 18, whichever would come later.

Schuette would be entitled to his medical expenses, a statutory percent of his salary for any period of temporary total incapacity, and stipulated amounts for partial incapacity and permanent injury. If Schuette and Galeener (or his insurer) could not agree on the nature of Schuette's injuries, the Illinois Industrial Commission would appoint an arbitrator to settle this dispute. If either party was dissatisfied with the decision of the arbitrator, that party could petition the Industrial Commission to review the arbitrator's decision. In some instances, the decision of the Industrial Commission can be appealed.

Occupational Diseases. Workers' compensation laws did much to improve the plight of workers who became disabled because of work-related accidents. Other legislation was needed, however, to provide the same protection to workers from the hardships of work-related diseases. This additional protection came in the form of occupational diseases laws, which generally provide for automatic compensation to workers who contract a disease out of and in the course of their employment. The compensation generally is based upon the same formulas present in workers' compensation laws; i.e., base salary is an important variable.

The public policy underlying those laws was the same as for workers' compensation. Agriculture has also been exempt from those laws. For example, agriculture was initially exempt from the Illinois Occupational Diseases Law. However, in 1975 the law was amended so that agricultural employment within the scope of the Workmen's Compensation Law also came within the scope of the Occupational Diseases Law.

It is difficult to determine the kinds of claims that might arise from agricultural employees under occupational diseases laws. Some diseases can be transmitted from livestock. Other diseases might be caused by frequent exposure to dust conditions often found in agriculture. Exposure to agricultural chemicals might, someday, be found to cause diseases.

Employment of Minors—Child Labor Laws Applicable to Agriculture[15]

A Historical Perspective. Historically, children have worked. In earlier times they hunted, fished, and cared for crops and livestock as members of tribes or separate families. In medieval Europe young boys were indentured to masters to learn trades and girls served as domestic workers. Yet even these tasks tended to educate young people to fill adult roles in that society. As the industrial revolution emerged in England and later in the United States, the employment of children took a more oppressive course.[16]

Industrialization moved the working children from the home or small shop to the factory. Children were employed extensively in the cotton, silk, hat, and ribbon trades at ages as young as 5 or 6. In the coal mines, some children started working at age 8 or 9, but even younger children could be used effectively to pull coal through the low shafts of an underground mine. Even in the United States, children were employed extensively in textile mills and other manufacturing establishments. The profitability of this cheap source of labor, the influx of aliens including immigrant children, and the laissez faire political and economic philosophy all contributed to the rise of child labor as an institution.

In the late eighteenth and early nineteenth centuries, the attack on the institution of child labor gained momentum in the United States, primarily because of the educational deprivation that resulted but also because of deplorable working conditions. In the ensuing decades authors, political parties, fledgling labor unions, and women's clubs all joined in denouncing the institution of child labor. These efforts bore fruit. In 1867 Massachusetts began the nation's first factory inspection program. Prohibitions on the nighttime employment of children soon followed in Massachusetts and many other states. Protective legislation continued to evolve, initially at the state level and finally at the federal level.

The general tenor of contemporary child labor legislation is to outlaw the employment of young persons under the age of 16 in virtually all occupations and to outlaw the employment of young persons between

---

[15] *See generally* 3 N. HARL, AGRICULTURAL LAW § 17.04. (1980).

[16] *See generally* W. TRATTNER, CRUSADE FOR THE CHILDREN (Quadrangle Books 1970):

the ages of 16 and 18 in selected occupations deemed to be particularly hazardous.[17] Some exemptions are present, such as employment by a parent or guardian, and special rules apply to agriculture. The discussion which follows applies to agricultural employment of minors.

Agricultural employment of minors is regulated by legislation at both the federal and state levels. The federal legislation is contained in the federal Fair Labor Standards Act. Some highlights follow.

Work by Family Members. Members of a farmer's immediate family who live with the farmer are exempt from virtually all federal and state child labor regulations while employed by the farmer.

Nonfamily Minors 16 Years of Age and Older. Minors 16 years of age or older can be employed in any agricultural occupation at any time.

Nonfamily Minors under 16 Years of Age—Hazardous Occupations. Minors under 16 may not be employed at any time in an agricultural occupation declared hazardous by the Secretary of Labor. The Secretary has declared the following activities as hazardous agricultural occupations in the Code of Federal Regulations, Title 29, Sec. 570.71:

1. Operating a tractor of over 20 PTO horsepower, or connecting or disconnecting an implement or any of its parts to or from such a tractor.

2. Operating or assisting to operate (including starting, stopping, adjusting, feeding, or any other activity involving physical contact with the operating) any of the following machines:
    a. Corn picker, cotton picker, grain combine, hay mower, forage harvester, hay baler, potato digger, or mobile pea viner;
    b. Feed grinder, crop dryer, forage blower, auger conveyer, or the mechanism of a nongravity-type self-unloading wagon or trailer;
    c. Power post-hole digger, power post drive, or nonwalking type rotary tiller.

3. Operating or assisting to operate (including starting, stopping, adjusting, feeding, or any other activity involving physical contact associated with the operation) any of the following machines:
    a. Trencher or earthmoving equipment;
    b. Fork lift;
    c. Potato combine; or
    d. Power-driven circular, band, or chain saw.

4. Working on a farm in a yard, pen, or stall occupied by a:
    a. Bull, boar, or stud horse maintained for breeding purposes; or
    b. Sow with suckling pigs, or cow with newborn calf (with umbilical cord present).

5. Felling, buckling, skidding, loading, or unloading timber with butt diameter of more than 6 inches.

6. Working from a ladder or scaffold (painting, repairing, or building structures, pruning trees, picking fruit, etc.) at a height of over 20 feet.

7. Driving a bus, truck, or automobile when transporting passengers, or riding on a tractor as a passenger or helper.

8. Working inside:
    a. A fruit, forage, or grain storage designed to retain an oxygen deficient or toxic atmosphere;
    b. An upright silo within 2 weeks after silage has been added or when a top loading device is in operating position;

---

[17] 29 U.S.C. § 203(1).

c. A manure pit; or

d. A horizontal silo while operating a tractor for packing purposes.

9. Handling or applying (including cleaning or decontaminating equipment, disposal or return of empty containers, or serving as a flagman for aircraft applying) agricultural chemicals classified under the Federal Insecticide, Fungicide, and Rodenticide Act (7 U.S.C. 135 *et seq.*) as Category I of toxicity, identified by the word "poison" and the "skull and crossbones" on the label; of Category II of toxicity, identified by the word "warning" on the label;

10. Handling or using a blasting agent, including but not limited to, dynamite, black powder, sensitized ammonium nitrate, blasting caps, and primer cord; or

11. Transporting, transferring, or applying anhydrous ammonia.

Persons age 14 or older who have completed the applicable training programs can obtain approval for employment in occupations 1 or 2, above. Such special training programs include the 4-H tractor operation program, the 4-H machine operation program, or a tractor and machine operation program. Also, vocational agriculture student-learners can obtain approval for employment in occupations 1 through 6, above.

Some states have adopted additional regulations concerning the employment of minors in hazardous occupations. The Ohio Revised Code, for example, prohibits minors under 18 from working in certain agricultural jobs. Often family members of the farmer are exempt from such regulations.

Nonfamily Minors under 16 Years of Age— Nonhazardous Occupations.[18]   Minors under 16 years of age cannot be employed even in nonhazardous agricultural occupations during normal school hours for the school district where the child is living. Therefore, the employment of minors under 16 is normally lawful only before or after school hours, on the weekends, on other school holidays, and during summer vacation. If the child is under 14, parental consent usually is required. If the child is under 12, the child cannot work on a farm employing 500 worker-days of labor or more per quarter. Generally a nonfamily minor under age 10 cannot work in agriculture at any time.

For each violation of the child labor provisions of the Fair Labor Standards Act, employers may be subject to a civil money penalty of up to $100. Willful violation and offenses after conviction for a similar offense can result in fines up to $10,000, up to 6 months' imprisonment, or both. Individual states have enacted additional restrictions.[19] Under Illinois law, for example, no minor under 10 years of age (other than members of the farmer's immediate family residing with the farmer) can be employed in agriculture at any time.

Violation of federal or state child labor laws may also result in other serious consequences. If an illegally employed child is injured, a negligence action against the employer may be present because of the statutory violation. Furthermore, the defenses of contributory negligence or assumption of risk may not be allowed.[20]

---

[18] *See* 29 U.S.C. § 213(c)(1).

[19] *See* 3 N. Harl, Agricultural Law § 23.06. (1980).

[20] *See* Boyles v. Hamilton, 235 Cal App. 2d 492, 45 Cal. Rptr. 399 (1965). A paperboy was injured. The defenses of assumption of risk and contributory negligence were disallowed because of the violation of child labor statute.

Minimum Wage Laws

Federal Law. Minimum wage is one area in which agricultural laborers receive treatment most like that of their industrial counterparts. The federal Fair Labor Standards Act (FLSA) provides that as of December 31, 1977, agricultural employees were to receive a minimum wage not less than the minimum wage for employees in general—$3.10 an hour beginning in 1980 and $3.35 an hour in 1981.[21] This degree of equality of treatment with industrial workers has not always been present in the FLSA. From its enactment in the 1930s until the amendments of 1966, the FLSA totally exempted agricultural employees from protection under the minimum wage provisions. The 1966 amendments to the FLSA granted protection to about 500,000 agricultural employees, or to workers on 2% of the nation's farms, but imposed a lower minimum wage for agricultural workers than for industrial workers. Agricultural workers received a minimum wage that was 40 cents below that of the industrial workers in 1961 and 45 cents below that of the industrial workers in 1969. This difference widened to 50 cents in 1975 and 1976, but was eliminated by the end of 1977. Actually, the statement that agricultural employees receive equal treatment under the FLSA is misleading because the FLSA does not cover all agricultural workers, although it goes much farther in that direction than most other labor laws.

The way in which the FLSA's basically broad coverage of employees is qualified in the case of agricultural employees is best described by examining a few of the FLSA's definitional and numerical provisions. The definition of agriculture in the FLSA is well developed, more so than in the other labor laws. Agriculture in the FLSA encompasses:

farming in all its branches and among other things includes the cultivation and tillage of the soil, dairying, the production, cultivation, growing, and harvesting of any agricultural or horticultural commodities (including commodities defined as agricultural commodities in section 1141j(g) of Title 12), the raising of livestock, bees, fur-bearing animals, or poultry, and any practices including any forestry or lumbering operations performed by a farmer or on a farm as an incident to or in conjunction with such farming operations, including preparation for market, delivery to storage or to market or to carriers for transportation to market.[22]

Despite this all-inclusive definition, there are some agricultural workers whom the FLSA does not cover: (1) workers who are employed by farmers who use 500 or less *worker-days* (defined as any day during which an employee works at least one hour) of labor during *each* quarter of the year, and (2) certain hand harvest workers and workers under 16 who are paid on a piece rate basis at the same rate as workers over 16, and who are employed on the same farm as their parents. The FLSA also excludes the child, parent, or spouse of the employer. (29 U.S.C.A. § 213 (a) (6).)

Since its inception, the FLSA has moved gradually toward inclusive coverage of agricultural workers. The 1966 amendments introduced the coverage of agricultural employees. The amendments, however, contained the 500 worker-day floor which still remains as a limitation on the coverage

---

[21] 29 U.S.C.A. § 213 (a) (6).

[22] The lead case in interpreting this definition is *Farmers Reservoir & Irrigation Co. v. McComb,* 337 U.S. 755 (1949), wherein the U.S. Supreme Court elaborated on the primary and secondary classification of agriculture.

of agricultural workers. The 1966 FLSA also excluded those seasonal hand harvest laborers paid on a piece rate basis who were working less than 13 weeks a year and commuting to the place of work. When this second limitation was removed by the 1974 amendments to the FLSA, the prohibition on counting the hand harvest workers for purposes of calculating the 500 worker-days was also lifted.

The 1974 amendments broadened the inclusion of agricultural employees in another way. It extended coverage to employees of the employer who was controlled or supported by a large parent business, even when the employer used fewer than 500 worker-days. Despite the consistent broadening of the coverage of the agricultural worker under the FLSA, workers on about 98 percent of U.S. farms may not be covered.[23]

Even the FLSA contains disparity in treatment between agricultural and non-agricultural workers for overtime pay. Nonagricultural workers are to receive a minimum of 1½ times the minimum hourly wage for each hour of work in excess of 40 hours a week, whereas agricultural workers are exempt from this provision.[24]

State Law.[25]   The states are free to regulate workers not regulated by the FLSA or to provide regulation not inconsistent with the FLSA. If any trend is developing in the minimum wage laws of the states, it is toward even more inclusive coverage of agricultural workers than in the FLSA.

Texas, New York, and Montana have enacted state minimum wage laws that include a larger class of agricultural workers than the FLSA. Texas, for example, has copied the all-inclusive definition of agriculture provided in the FLSA. In addition, Texas has extended coverage to all employees whose employer uses more than 300 worker-days of agricultural labor during any quarter of the preceding year. The Texas law also extends coverage by a piece rate minimum wage to hand harvest pieceworkers and provides minimum wage protection for the spouse, parent, or children of the employer as long as they live off the premises of the employer.[26]

Montana and New York also extend minimum wage protection for agricultural workers farther than the FLSA does. Both states' statutes define agriculture broadly and eliminate all coverage limitations on the worker-days used by the employer. In addition, Montana provides a minimum wage, either hourly or monthly, for seasonal workers whose workday fluctuates. New York specifically excludes from coverage only the parent, spouse, or a child of the employer and hand harvest workers under 17 years of age who work on the same farm as their parents and who are paid by the piece rate at a rate equal to that of workers over 17.[27]

Some states have not followed the trend toward more inclusive state minimum wage laws. Illinois provides virtually a carbon copy of the federal coverage of agricultural workers.[28] The coverages for farm workers

---

[23] Scher and Catz, *Farmworker Litigation under the Fair Labor Standard Act: Establishing Joint Employer Liability and Related Problems*, 10 HARV. C.R.—C.L.L. REV. 577 at n. 17 (1975), suggests that over 700,000 farm employees were not covered by the minimum wage provisions as of the 1966 amendments. The 500 worker-day requirement is, according to Scher's research, primarily responsible.

[24] 29 U.S.C. § 213 (b)(12).

[25] *See* 3 N. HARL, AGRICULTURAL LAW § 23.02. (1980).

[26] TEX. LAB. CODE ANN. tit. 5159d, § 3(f) *et. seq.* (Vernon 1971).

[27] MONT. REV. CODES ANN. § 41-2302 *et. seq.* (Cum. Supp. 1977); N.Y. LAB. LAW § 670 *et seq.* (McKinney).

[28] ILL. REV. STAT. ch. 48, § 1003(d) (1971).

in other states are even more narrow. California keys its minimum wage law to the FLSA, but it covers only agricultural workers covered by FLSA as of February 1967.[29] Thus, coverage under California's minimum wage law does not extend to hand harvest workers. Kansas exempts agricultural workers entirely from its minimum wage protection, whereas Georgia relieves farm owners, sharecroppers, and land renters from the duty to pay minimum wages.[30]

Although under federal law the minimum wage for agricultural and nonagricultural workers is the same, the same equality of wage standards is not present in many of the state minimum wage laws. Montana and Illinois, for example, provide the same minimum wage to agricultural and nonagricultural employees, while New York provides a lower minimum wage for agricultural workers.[31]

Occupational Safety and Health

OSHA Standards. At the national level, the federal Occupational Safety and Health Act (OSHA) provides for specific standards designed to reduce the number of work-related injuries occurring in the United States and a general duty clause requiring employers to furnish a workplace free from recognized hazards.[32] Unless exempt, any farmer employing labor must comply with applicable standards. Initially, these standards have concerned temporary labor camps,[33] storage and handling of anhydrous ammonia,[34] pulpwood logging,[35] slow-moving vehicles,[36] roll-over protective structures (ROPS) for agricultural tractors,[37] and safety shields for farm equipment.[38]

States also have become involved in regulating workplace safety.[39] Nothing in the federal act prevents any state agency or court from asserting jurisdiction under state law over any issue on occupational safety or health for which no federal standard is in effect. The OSHA also provides for procedures whereby states can assume responsibility for development and enforcement of federal occupational and health standards. Several of these federal standards are summarized below.

Anhydrous Ammonia. This is largely an equipment standard. Dealers supply most of the anhydrous ammonia application equipment, and farmers are responsible to comply with this standard when employees are using application equipment. Farmers should ask suppliers to verify that their equipment meets OSHA standards. A supplier with application equipment that does not meet OSHA standards appears to be somewhat negligent by providing substandard equipment for use by farmers. Farmers should find a supplier who has equipment that meets OSHA standards. Equipment owned by farmers should meet OSHA standards. If it does, employees can use it. If it does not meet standards, it must be

---

[29] Cal. Lab. Code § 1182 (Cum. Supp. 1980).

[30] Kan. Stat. Ann. § 44-1202 (Cum. Supp. 1979); Ga. Code Ann. § 54-1202 (1974).

[31] Mont. Rev. Codes Ann. § 41-2303(2) (Cum. Supp. 1977) and Ill. Rev. Stat. ch. 48, § 1004 (1979). Compare N.Y. Lab. Law § 652(1) (g) with § 673(1) (McKinney 1977).

[32] *See* 3 N. Harl, Agricultural Law § 18.01 *et. seq.* (1980).

[33] 29. C.F.R. § 1910.142.

[34] *Id.* § 1910.111(a), (b).

[35] *Id.* § 1910.266.

[36] *Id.* § 1910.145.

[37] *Id.* § 1928.51.

[38] *Id.* § 1928.57.

[39] *See* 3 N. Harl, Agricultural Law § 23.04. (1980).

brought up to standard or used only by the farm operator. Key points to consider are quality and condition of hoses and valves. Personal protective equipment must be used by employees who handle anhydrous ammonia. This includes approved gloves and goggles, in addition to 5 gallons of water mounted on equipment and recommended squeeze bottle for personal use.

Pulpwood Logging. This standard is directed toward those who hire employees to work specifically in this type of work. The standard covers both protective equipment and working practices. The standard is both detailed and specific to this industry. Persons involved in pulpwood logging employment should secure the appropriate OSHA regulations and interpret them for their specific situation.

Roll-over Protective Structures (ROPS) for Farm Tractors. This federal standard requires that all employee-operated tractors of over 20 horsepower manufactured after October 25, 1976, must be equipped with a seat belt and cab or protective frame meeting crush resistance requirements specified in the standard. Frames and cabs that meet this standard are equipped with a label stating they meet OSHA regulations. Employees must use seat belts when operating a tractor equipped with such frames or cabs. Selected "low-profile" tractors for use in orchards and other special situations are exempt from the ROPS standard only if used exclusively in low-profile situations.

Every employee who operates an agricultural tractor shall be informed of the following operating practices and any other practices dictated by the particular job. Such information is to be provided at the time of initial assignment and at least annually thereafter.

1. Securely fasten your seat belt if the tractor has a ROPS.

2. Where possible, avoid operating the tractor near ditches, embankments, and holes.
3. Reduce speed when turning or crossing slopes and on rough, slick, or muddy surfaces.
4. Stay off slopes too steep for safe operation.
5. Watch where you are going, especially at row ends, on roads, and around trees.
6. Do not permit others to ride.
7. Operate the tractor smoothly—no jerky turns, starts, or stops.
8. Hitch only to the drawbar and hitch points recommended by tractor manufacturers.
9. When tractor is stopped, set brakes securely and use park lock if available.
10. Employer must inform you of any other operating practices dictated by the work environment.

Machinery Guarding and Shielding. This standard is to protect employees from hazards associated with moving farm machinery parts. The standard includes farm field equipment, such as tractors and field implements, and self-propelled equipment in addition to farmstead equipment normally considered to be stationary. The stationary equipment includes augers, elevators, self-unloading equipment, and bunker feeders. The examples cited in the preceding statements are only a few of those pieces of equipment covered by the standard. It is safe to assume that any piece of farmstead or field equipment, stationary or otherwise, with moving parts is included. Generally, this standard requires that all power takeoff drives be guarded, all equipment have shielding and guarding devices, all electrically powered farmstead equipment meet specific disconnect and lockout requirements, and all employees receive specified training.

The General Duty Clause. The general duty clause is a "catchall" provision that requires an employer such as a farmer or rancher to furnish workers with "employment and a place of employment ... free from recognized hazards that are causing or are likely to cause death or serious physical harm."[40] Courts have held that the duty extends only to hazards that feasibly can be eliminated; that recognized hazards should be broadly defined; and that the likelihood of death or serious physical harm be plausible, not necessarily probable.

Record-Keeping Requirements. Employers are required to keep OSHA records of work-related accidents, injuries, illnesses, and days off the job only if they employed eleven or more employees on any 1 day during the calendar year. A summary of such records, if required, is to be posted during the month of February each year.[41] Employers with fewer than eleven employees are only required to report fatalities, multiple hospital accidents, and other specially requested reports.

Agricultural Inspection Exemption. The federal Occupational Safety and Health Act of 1970 provided broad coverage for workers. In 1976, the U.S. Department of Labor estimated that the act applied to 5 million workplaces and 65 million employees. A ruling appearing in the Code of Federal Regulations interpreted the act to cover any person engaged in agricultural activity employing one or more employees. A Program Directive states, however, that members of the employer's immediate family are not employees.[42] Also, in *Five Migrant Farm Workers v. Hoffman*, decided under the OSHA in 1975, a New Jersey court held that the act of 1970 encompassed the "entire gamut of migrant farmworker protection."[43]

Had this statutory scheme remained in effect in its original form, it would have provided the most inclusive coverage of agricultural workers found in any of the labor laws considered in this chapter. In 1976, however, the Labor Department introduced an agricultural inspection exemption which limited substantially the inclusion of agricultural workers in the OSHA. The temporary exemption appeared in the 1977 HEW Appropriations Bill[44] and has reappeared in subsequent bills. The exemption was effected by refusing to appropriate funds for the inspection of small *farming operations* with ten or fewer employees during the past year. The exemption applied to virtually all kinds of farming operations and related activities, but its continued existence depends on continued spending limitations in future appropriations. In effect, the exemption lives from appropriation to appropriation. If and when the temporary exemption is lifted by removing the spending limitation from the annual appropriation, the OSHA will once again have the most inclusive agricultural coverage of the federal labor statutes.

The general duty clause and safety standards should not be taken lightly, however. Violation of these provisions may constitute the breach of duty necessary for a negligence action against the employer. Furthermore, it is possible that a farm employer's potential defenses of contributory negligence or assumption of risk

---

[40] 29 U.S.C. § 654(a) (1).

[41] *See Recordkeeping Requirements*, OSHA Leaflet 0-570-326.

[42] OSHA Program Directive 76-9 (November 26, 1976). *See* 29 C.F.R. § 1975.4 (b) (2).

[43] 136 N.J. Super. 242, 345 A.2d 378 (Sup. Ct. Law Div. 1975).

[44] P.L. 94-439.

would not be allowed because of the statutory violation, although the likelihood is
not as great as it would be for a violation
of child labor laws.[45]

UNCONSTITUTIONALITY OF WARRANTLESS OSHA INSPECTIONS[46]

MARSHALL v. BARLOWS, INC.
Supreme Court of the United States, 1978
436 U.S. 307

Mr. Justice White delivered the opinion of the Court. Section 8(a) of the
Occupational Safety and Health Act of 1970 (OSHA) empowers agents of
the Secretary of Labor (the Secretary) to search the work area of any employment facility within the Act's jurisdiction. The purpose of the search is
to inspect for safety hazards and violations of OSHA regulations. No search
warrant or other process is expressly required under the Act.

II

The Secretary nevertheless stoutly argues that the enforcement scheme of
the Act requires warrantless searches, and that the restrictions on search
discretion contained in the Act and its regulations already protect as much
privacy as a warrant would. The Secretary thereby asserts the actual reasonableness of OSHA searches, whatever the general rule against warrantless
searches might be. Because "reasonableness is still the ultimate standard,"
the Secretary suggests that the Court decide whether a warrant is needed by
arriving at a sensible balance between the administrative necessities of
OSHA inspections and the incremental protection of privacy of business
owners a warrant would afford. He suggests that only a decision exempting
OSHA inspections from the Warrant Clause would give "full recognition to
the competing public and private interests here at stake."

For purposes of an administrative search such as this, probable cause justifying the issuance of a warrant may be based not only on specific evidence
of an existing violation but also on a showing that "reasonable legislative or
administrative standards for conducting an...inspection are satisfied with respect to a particular [establishment]." A warrant showing that a specific
business has been chosen for an OSHA search on the basis of a general administrative plan for the enforcement of the Act derived from neutral sources
such as, for example, dispersion of employees in various types of industries
across a given area, and the desired frequency of searches in any of the
lesser divisions of the area, would protect an employer's Fourth Amendment

---

[45] See Boyles v. Hamilton, 235 Cal. App. 2d
492, 45 Cal. Rptr. 399 (1965). Paperboy injured;
defenses of assumption of risk and contributory
negligence were disallowed where child labor
statute had been violated.

[46] This case has been substantially edited. Such a
process is especially difficult for Supreme Court
decisions which typically have quite profound
policy issues under review. For a deeper appreciation of the issues and a thorough discussion of the
arguments, the student should seek out the entire
opinion.

rights. We doubt that the consumption of enforcement energies in the obtaining of such warrants will exceed manageable proportions.

Nor do we agree that the incremental protections afforded the employer's privacy by a warrant are so marginal that they fail to justify the administrative burdens that may be entailed. The authority to make warrantless searches devolves almost unbridled discretion upon executive and administrative officers, particularly those in the field, as to when to search and whom to search. A warrant, by contrast, would provide assurances from a neutral officer that the inspection is reasonable under the Constitution, is authorized by statute, and is pursuant to an administrative plan containing specific neutral criteria. Also, a warrant would then and there advise the owner of the scope and objects of the search, beyond which limits the inspector is not expected to proceed:

III

We hold that Barlow was entitled to a declaratory judgment that the Act is unconstitutional insofar as it purports to authorize inspections without warrant or its equivalent and to an injunction enjoining the Act's enforcement to that extent. The judgment of the District Court is therefore affirmed.

MR. JUSTICE STEVENS, with whom MR. JUSTICE BLACKMUN and MR. JUSTICE REHNQUIST join, dissenting.

Congress enacted the Occupational Safety and Health Act to safeguard employees against hazards in the work areas of businesses subject to the Act. To ensure compliance, Congress authorized the Secretary of Labor to conduct routine, non-consensual inspections. Today the Court holds that the Fourth Amendment prohibits such inspections without a warrant. The Court also holds that the constitutionally required warrant may be issued without any showing of probable cause. I disagree with both of these holdings.

The Fourth Amendment contains two separate clauses, each flatly prohibiting a category of governmental conduct:

The right of the people to be secure in their persons, houses, papers, and effects, against unreasonable searches and seizures, shall not be violated....
....and no Warrants shall issue, but upon probable cause, supported by Oath or affirmation, and particularly describing the place to be searched, and the persons or things to be seized.

Because of the acknowledged importance and reasonableness of routine inspections in the enforcement of federal regulatory statutes such as OSHA, the Court recognizes that requiring full compliance with the Warrant Clause would invalidate all such inspection programs. Yet, rather than simply analyzing such programs under the "reasonableness" clause of the Fourth Amendment, the Court holds the OSHA program invalid under the Warrant Clause and then avoids a blanket prohibition on all routine, regulatory inspections by relying on the notion that the "probable cause" requirement in the Warrant Clause may be relaxed whenever the Court believes that the governmental need to conduct a category of "searches" outweighs the intrusion on interests protected by the Fourth Amendment.

The Court's approach disregards the plain language of the Warrant Clause and is unfaithful to the balance struck by the Framers of the Fourth Amendment—"the one procedural safeguard in the Constitution that grew directly out of the events which immediately preceded with England." [Landynski, Search and Seizure and the Supreme Court, 19 (1966).]

[O]ur constitutional fathers were not concerned about warrantless searches, but about overreaching warrants. It is perhaps too much to say that they feared the warrant more than the search, but it is plain enough that the warrant was the prime object of their concern. Far from looking at the warrant as a protection against unreasonable searches, they saw it as an authority for unreasonable and oppressive searches.... [Taylor, Two Studies in Constitutional Interpretation, 41 (1969).]

The essential function of the traditional warrant requirement is the interposition of a neutral magistrate between the citizen and the presumably zealous law enforcement officer so that there might be an objective determination of probable cause. But this purpose is not served by the new-fangled inspection warrant. As the Court acknowledges, the inspector's

entitlement to inspect will not depend on his demonstrating probable cause to believe that conditions in violation of OSHA exist on the premises.... For purposes of an administrative search such as this, probable cause justifying the issuance of a warrant may be based...on a showing that "reasonable legislative or administrative standards for conducting an...inspection are satisfied with respect to a particular [establishment]."

To obtain a warrant, the inspector need only show that "a specific business has been chosen for an OSHA search on the basis of a general administrative plan for the enforcement of the Act derived from neutral sources...." Thus, the only question for the magistrate's consideration is whether the contemplated inspection deviates from an inspection schedule drawn up by higher-level agency officials.

Fidelity to the original understanding of the Fourth Amendment, therefore, leads to the conclusion that the Warrant Clause has no application to routine, regulatory inspections of commercial premises. If such inspections are valid, it is because they comport with the ultimate reasonableness standard of the Fourth Amendment. If the Court were correct in its view that such inspections, if undertaken without a warrant, are unreasonable in the constitutional sense, the issuance of a "new-fangled warrant"—to use Mr. Justice Clark's characteristically expressive term—without any true showing of particularized probable cause would not be sufficient to validate them.

I respectfully dissent.

Other Laws Affecting Agricultural Labor

Migrant Labor. Numerous federal and state laws affect farmers and ranchers who employ migrant labor. Many states have promulgated migrant labor camp regulations which often provide for licensing, inspections by state or local health officials, and proper maintenance of migrant labor camps. In addition to this state regulation, agricultural employers using the interstate worker recruitment service of the U.S. Department of Labor must have housing approved by the Department. Inspection of labor camps for the Department of Labor is based on federal regulations. These regulations specify standards for the housing site; water supply; condition of housing and space provided; screening; heating; electricity and lighting; toilets; bathing, laundry, and hand washing; cooking and eating facilities; garbage and other refuse disposal; insect and rodent control; sleeping facilities; and fire, safety, and first aid. The OSHA temporary labor camp regulations also apply, although there is no licensing procedure under these regulations. Labor camp inspections are made on a random basis and in response to employee complaints or following a report of a fatality.

Persons who transport migrant farm workers a total distance exceeding 75 miles *and* across a state line are subject to the federal Motor Carrier Safety Regulations. These regulations do not apply to employers transporting workers solely within a given state, nor do they apply if fewer than three workers are transported at any one time or if a station wagon or passenger car is used. The regulations pertain to qualifications of drivers or operators, the driving of motor vehicles, parts and accessories necessary for safe operation, hours of service by drivers, maximum driving time, and inspection and maintenance of motor vehicles. There are detailed provisions under each of these categories. Regulations promulgated under the federal Farm Labor Contractor Registration Act may also apply.[47] Generally, farm operators who deal directly with a labor contractor must determine that the contractor is properly registered with the U.S. Department of Labor and must maintain payroll records as well.

Alien Workers. An alien is a foreign-born resident in the United States who has not become naturalized. Alien farm workers may be legal or illegal aliens. A certified alien farm worker is one who is legally in the country through a certification program administered by the U.S. Department of Labor. An illegal alien (undocumented alien) is not certified by the Department of Labor, and the illegal alien's presence in the United States is in violation of the Immigration and Nationality Act.

Employers may request admission of aliens into the United States for temporary farm work. Such admission is possible only if the Department of Labor certifies that qualified Americans are not available and that the employment of an alien would not adversely affect the wages and working conditions of similarly employed workers in the United States. Department of Labor regulations set forth the fact-finding process for granting or denial of temporary labor certification. These regulations also set forth the responsibilities of employers wishing to employ aliens in temporary farm work.

---

[47] 7 U.S.C. § 2041 *et. seq.* See generally 3 N. HARL, AGRICULTURAL LAW § 19.01 *et seq.* (1980).

Employers wishing to hire certified aliens must demonstrate that they have attempted to recruit U.S. workers through advertising, through the public employment service, and by other specified means. These recruitment efforts must assure that there has been an adequate test of the availability of U.S. workers.

Unemployment Compensation.   Historically, agricultural labor has been exempt from state and federal laws establishing the unemployment insurance system in the United States. That system is financed through an excise tax on employers based upon the amount of wages paid. However, in 1974 Congress passed emergency federal legislation to help alleviate the hardships of unemployment created by the recession. Generally, that emergency legislation expanded the time period for which unemployment compensation benefits would be paid to workers traditionally covered by the insurance program. Other provisions of the legislation temporarily made unemployment benefits available to employees who had not traditionally been protected, such as farm workers.

In 1976 Congress amended the Unemployment Compensation Act to bring certain agricultural employment within the *permanent* coverage of the act (26 U.S.C. § 3306). Under the new provision, agricultural employment will be subject to the act if:

1.   Labor is performed for a farmer who pays cash wages of $20,000 or more to employees during any *calendar quarter* of the current or preceding calendar years, *or*
2.   the farmer employs ten or more individual employees on at least 1 day during each of 20 different calendar weeks.

Farm employers who meet either of the above tests will be required to pay a tax based upon the amount of wages paid.[48]

Withholding Federal Income Tax.   In contrast to nonagricultural employers, farmers are not required to withhold federal income tax on agricultural wages. However, the farmer and the farmer's employee can voluntarily agree that the employer will withhold income tax.

Social Security Taxes.   Generally, farmers and ranchers must withhold the employee's portion of social security taxes and forward it to the Internal Revenue Service along with the employer's portion of the tax. These social security taxes are often referred to as FICA (Federal Insurance Contributions Act) taxes. Farmers who pay less than $150 in annual cash wages to each employee *and* employ each worker less than 20 days each year for cash wages computed on a time basis are exempt from the withholding requirements. Also, the employer's child under 21 years of age and the employer's spouse are not covered by social security.

Unionization of Agricultural Labor.   The intensive use of farm labor in agricultural production varies tremendously from region to region within the United States. For some regions of the country, union organizing efforts have a long history, while in other regions the union is a relatively new phenomenon. The most well-known union organizing effort was initiated in the 1960s by Caesar Chavez and what is now known as the United Farm Workers Union of America, AFL-CIO. The United Farm Workers Union now has substantial activities in Florida, Arizona, and, of course, California. The Farm Labor Organizing Committee in the midwest and the

---

[48] 26 U.S.C. § 3306.

efforts of other groups in the northeast represent further union organizing activities. One can expect efforts to organize agricultural workers to be an ongoing process in the years ahead.

A farmer may learn that his or her employees are the subject of a labor union organizing campaign, or the farmer may be confronted with a demand from a person claiming to represent a majority of the employees, asking that the farmer recognize a union as the bargaining agent of the employees and sign a collective bargaining contract with that union. Faced with either of those events, the farmer and rancher must recognize that there is no federal statute setting out ground rules for labor union organization, recognition, and bargaining that applies to the farmer and the farmer's employees.

Employees engaged in agriculture are exempted from coverage under the National Labor Management Relations Act (NLRA). In 1945 and 1947, riders to the bills enacting the Taft-Hartley Act specified that the agricultural labor exemption be based upon the definitions of agricultural labor contained in the federal Fair Labor Standards Act. More recently, Congress has attempted to amend the NLRA agricultural exemption. In 1973 the House Subcommittee on Labor received two bills designed to govern farm labor. One would have amended the NLRA's definition of employee, eliminating the exemption of agricultural labor. The other would have established a National Labor Relations Board for farm labor. Neither bill was adopted, but further legislation narrowing the agricultural exemption is quite possible in the future.

Although federal law does not apply, unionization activity may be regulated by state law.[49] California, Idaho, Arizona,[50] and Kansas, for example, have adopted labor relations acts which specifically include some agricultural labor. Despite its limitation on coverage of agriculture workers according to the size of the employer's operation, the Kansas statute provides rather broad and inclusive coverage for agricultural workers. Few other states have followed suit. Illinois, Georgia, Montana, and Texas have no state unionization laws and New York's law exempts farm laborers completely.

Agricultural employers from states without unionization laws applying to agricultural workers are left to their own resources in dealing with a union organization campaign. Some things that a farmer might or might not do in such a situation are noted below.

1. If the farmer receives a demand to recognize a union as the bargaining agent for his or her farm employees, the farmer should try to obtain an agreement for a secret ballot election among the employees to determine whether or not a majority of them want that union to act as their bargaining agent.
2. The person presenting the demand may show the farmer cards that some or all of the farmer's employees have signed for membership in the union. The farmer may look at the cards, but should make no statement concerning the validity of the cards or that the cards indicate that the union has or has not obtained a majority of the employees as members.

[49] See N. HARL, AGRICULTURAL LAW § 22.01 et seq. (1980).
[50] In Babbitt v. United Farm Workers National Union, 442 U.S. 936 (1979), the Supreme Court considered the argument that the election scheme in the Arizona Agricultural Employment Relations Act was unconstitutional. More specifically, the

United Farm Workers contended that delays and limitations on voting in union elections severely curtailed freedom of association. The Court concluded that complaints about ineffective election procedures are matters for state legislatures and not the federal courts.

3.   The farmer or rancher should contact legal counsel as soon as possible and may attempt to persuade the person demanding recognition of the union that the fair way to determine whether the employees want this union to represent them is to hold a secret ballot election among them. Because such unionization activity is unregulated by state law, there is no legal provision for such an election. Demanding such an election may cause the union to call the workers out on strike if it is true that the union has been successful in organizing a majority of the employees.

4.   If the first demand upon the farmer is for both recognition of a union and the execution of a collective bargaining agreement, the farmer should pursue the above recommended course in regard to the demand for recognition and should politely refuse to execute a collective bargaining agreement until after the results of the election are known and until the farmer's attorney has an opportunity to review the proposed collective bargaining agreement.

A good personnel program and good employer-employee communication are perhaps more important than any statutory provision in determining a farmer's success with farm labor relations. Because of the perishable nature of some farm commodities and seasonality of almost all farming operations, a farmer will be reacting under extreme pressure if a union attempts to organize the farmer's employees. How much better it would be if the farmer developed sound personnel programs long before union organizers appeared and problems reached a crisis stage. Such a program would include providing wages and benefits equal to the prevailing community standards, providing safe and healthy working conditions, developing procedures to resolve employee complaints, adopting fair and consistent disciplinary procedures, and initiating a system for recognizing and rewarding good performance.

4.2 INDEPENDENT CONTRACTORS

The employment of "custom operators" in agriculture is a practice of long standing. Threshing machines and hay balers were among the early devices which lent themselves to use by custom operators. For the most part, custom operators would be classed as independent contractors. Other types of custom operators which we could add to the list would be feed grinders, spray operators, contract feeders, and most of the people hired to construct and repair farm improvements—painters, builders, electricians, well drillers, tilers, and plumbers, among others.

Black's Law Dictionary defines an *independent contractor* as "one who, exercising an independent employment, contracts to do a piece of work according to his own methods and without being subject to the control of his employer except as to the result of the work." The right to control the method of doing the job is the prime test of whether the one employed is an independent contractor or a farm laborer. If the employee is subject to direction and control by the employer, the employee is not an independent contractor. For example, the farm employer does not tell custom spray operators how to handle their equipment, or custom shellers how to adjust their shellers. It is true of course that skilled farm laborers may know a great deal more about many farm jobs than their employer, but their employer still has the right to have them do the job wrong if that is what the employer desires.

Liability Issues

There is a general rule that when someone (a farmer or rancher, for example) employs an independent contractor to do a job, the farmer or rancher is not liable for injury to the contractor's workers or to third parties who may be injured by the contractor's negligence. In effect, the doctrine of *respondeat superior* does not apply because an employer-employee relationship is not present. There seem to be two general exceptions to this rule: when the employer is the negligent one, and when the job performed by the independent contractor is inherently dangerous. This latter exception has been invoked, for example, to hold liable the employer of a custom spray applicator when the operation damages any adjoining crops or livestock. Some courts say spraying or dusting are "inherently dangerous" and that anyone employing an independent contractor can expect that damage may result. The independent contractor may also be held liable.

Negligence on the part of an employer which might be sufficient for liability to be imposed even though an independent contractor is employed could consist in failure to warn about dangerous conditions of the premises, failure to warn about animals to which the contractor and the contractor's workers must be exposed, loaning the contractor defective equipment, or perhaps selecting a contractor known to operate in an unsafe manner.

Contracts between the employer and independent contractor should make the contractor answerable for any damage caused the employer and should recite that adequate liability insurance is carried by the contractor to pay legitimate damage claims of injured third parties.

SPRAYING BY AIRPLANE—DAMAGE TO BEES

S.A. GERRARD CO. v. FRICKER
Arizona Supreme Court, 1933
42 Ariz. 503, 27 P. 2d 678

The Gerrard Company appeals from a judgment against it for damages to Fricker's apiary. We shall refer to the parties as plaintiff and defendant.

The plaintiff's apiary is located near Chandler in Maricopa County, and adjacent thereto the defendant was growing 105 acres of lettuce. In the process of spraying an insecticide called Dutox No. 20 on defendant's lettuce field to rid the field of worms, the spray fell upon, or was blown upon, the plaintiff's apiary, with the result that his bee business was damaged. The spraying was done from an airplane flying over the lettuce field and, as plaintiff claims, over his apiary and releasing the dust or spray. The defendant did not itself operate the airplane, but it employed the Hawks Crop Dusting Company to do the spraying. This corporation was engaged in that particular kind of work. It furnished its own pilots and airplanes and in the operation was not under the control or direction of the defendant. This powder or dust was fatal to lettuce worms, and to bees, judging from what happened in this case. The spraying was done October 11, 1931, between 8 and 9 o'clock in the morning and consumed about twenty-five minutes. At 4 o'clock in the afternoon the bees were flying around, buzzing, and dropping; some were dying. They were scattered all over the yard. The death rate was greatest for about four days, but continued for nine days. Most of the workers were killed. Some of the brood died because there were not enough workers to keep the brood warm. Many queens died, and all of them quit laying.

The trial was before a jury and resulted in a verdict and judgment for plaintiff for $2,000.

Defendant's assignments of error raise four questions of law. It contends: (1) that the Hawks Crop Dusting Company was an independent contractor, and that therefore defendant was not liable for any damage suffered by the plaintiff; (2) that, since plaintiff alleged that his bees were poisoned, he must show that the substance that killed them was poisonous, which he has failed to do; (3) that the instructions were erroneous in assuming that the Dutox dust or powder was in fact a poison; and (4) that the verdict was excessive in that the greatest loss proved did not exceed 75 colonies at $7.50 per colony.

As a general rule the employer is not liable for the negligence of an independent contractor. There are, however, certain exceptions to this general rule. One of such exceptions is that the law will not allow one who has a piece of work to be done that is necessarily or inherently dangerous to escape liability to persons or property negligently injured in its performance by another to whom he has contracted such work. This is especially true where the agency or means employed to do the work, if not confined and carefully guarded, is liable to invade adjacent property, or the property of others, and destroy or damage it. The defendant was within its legal rights in depositing the insecticide on its lettuce field for the purpose of ridding it of the worms with which it was infested, and it could do this work itself or it could contract it, but, because of the very great likelihood of the poisonous dust or spray spreading to adjoining or nearby premises and damaging or destroying valuable property thereon, it could not delegate this work to an independent contractor and thus avoid liability.

There is nothing to defendant's second point, as we see it. The plaintiff alleged that the Dutox spray or dust was poisonous, and that the poison killed and damaged his bees. The evidence that it was poisonous was very meager aside from the fact that it killed most of the bees that it contacted. If it killed the bees, it was because they inhaled it. It was poisonous to them.

The damages plaintiff suffered are under the evidence fairly susceptible of computation. We should bear in mind that a colony or hive consists of the box that houses it, the worker bees, the drones and the queen. The workers are the most numerous and are the ones that collect honey, honeycomb and bee bread. A few are nurses or guards and attend or wait on the queen. The drones are for mating with the queen, and only one of them may enjoy that privilege. The queen lays the eggs for the colony and in doing so measures the needs of the colony with an accuracy something like the accuracy that mercury gauges heat and cold. If there is a good flow of honey in prospect the queen by a bountiful crop of eggs supplies the needed workers to gather it, but if the flow is poor or the prospect not promising she retrenches in the egg crop. The colony is a unit. The worker bees, the drones and queen together are valuable, but separate them and they are valueless. So a colony or hive must be thought of and treated as a unit, just as a cow or sheep is thought of and treated as a unit.

As the owner may recover damages for the breaking of his cow's or sheep's leg, so may the beekeeper recover damages to his colony or hive caused by the killing or weakening of his bees. The killing or destroying of a few bees of a hive or the major portion thereof is an injury to the colony. Damages would be to the colony and not for the value of the bees as separate entities. We think the true measure of damages as applied to the facts is the difference between the market value of the colonies at the time they were damaged and their value after they were rebuilt, together with the reasonable expenses incurred by plaintiff in an effort to mitigate or keep down the loss as much as possible.

The verdict was not excessive. The amount found as plaintiff's damages is well within the proof after excluding increase and honey lost.

Liens

Most states have enacted mechanic's lien statutes whereby those who furnish materials, labor, or skilled service for the construction of buildings have a claim against such buildings for payment; this claim extends not only to the building but to the owner's interest in any land connected with the building. The lien is based on the theory that since the labor and materials involved become a part of the real estate, those furnishing the labor or materials should have a prior claim against the real estate. Lumber dealers, material suppliers, architects, carpenters, painters, contractors, subcontractors, and their laborers are examples of persons entitled to the lien.

The lien typically attaches to the property on the date of the contract for service or materials. The existence of a contract is necessary as a basis for the lien, but the contract may be either express or implied and does not have to be in writing. To be effective against other creditors, this lien must be either foreclosed or filed with the clerk of the circuit court within a specified time. Any property against which a me-

chanic's lien has been foreclosed may be redeemed within the same period allowed for redeeming real estate, often 12 months, by paying for the services of materials plus costs and interest.

It is important that a farm buyer find out if any unsettled mechanic's liens exist against the house, barn, or other farm buildings. If such claims exist, and if the seller does not pay them, the buyer will either have to pay them or suffer a foreclosure against the buyer's property. Also, persons who make improvements to real estate should obtain mechanic's lien waivers from the general contractors and subcontractors upon making payment. Failure to do so could result in paying for the improvements twice—once to the general contractor who might abscond or go bankrupt without paying the subcontractors, and again when the unhappy subcontractors foreclose their mechanics' liens against the improved property.

Many state legislatures have created liens for other persons who furnish certain services. Because of their nature, some of these statutory liens have been designated as agricultural and exist for the benefit of independent contractors and others rendering a service. There are several such liens. Examples include stable keepers or persons keeping, yarding, feeding, or pasturing domestic animals for others with a lien against the animals for feed and labor; threshers, clover hullers, corn shellers, and hay balers with a lien against the crop threshed, hulled, shelled, or baled; and the owners of stallions, jacks, or bulls with a lien for the service fee against the mare, jennet, or the cow and the progeny. Often to secure the benefit of these liens, the independent contractor must file a claim for lien in writing and under oath with the appropriate county official.

In *Washakie Livestock Loan Co. v. Meigh*, 50 Wyo. 480, 62 P.2d 523 (1936), a herdsman filed a counterclaim for wages when his employer was sued by the chattel mortgagee of the sheep. His counterclaim was based on the Wyoming Agisters Law. The court ruled against him, holding that employees have no lien under the agisters lien statute.[51] Similar decisions have been reached in other states (Utah and Washington, for example), but in Oregon, after the court held adversely on the claim of a cattle herder, the legislature passed a special lien law for herders.

4.3 AGENTS

Farmers and ranchers may create a principal-agent relationship with another party whereby the agent is authorized to represent the principal in business dealings with third parties. Limited or special "powers of attorney" and farm management contracts are examples of principal-agent relationships.

The most important aspect of this relationship is that the principal is contractually liable for the actions of the agent performed within the scope of the agent's authority. The authority may be expressly stated within the "four corners" of the agency agreement. For example, a farm management agreement may provide that the manager has authority "to collect rentals." The authority also may be implied. A farm manager given the express authority to "manage" a particular farm would have the implied authority to arrange for normal maintenance and repair of farm buildings.

Sometimes principals can be contractually liable for the actions of other persons because the other person has apparent authority. For example, suppose that Jones, in the presence of Farmer, tells Smith that she (Jones) is Farmer's agent. If Farmer remains silent, he can be contractually liable for Jones's business actions because of apparent authority. Also, a principal can be contractually liable if the actions of another taken without any authority whatsoever are somehow ratified. Suppose a barn painter asks a part-time employee if the barn should be painted. The part-time employee has no authority to bind the farmer-employer contractually but, nevertheless, says OK. The farmer sees the barn being painted and says OK or just remains silent. The farmer's express affirmation or mysterious silence could be construed as ratification giving rise to a contractual duty to pay the price agreed upon by the painter and the part-time employee.

Agents have whatever duties are expressly stated in the agreement creating the agency. In the absence of contrary provisions in the agreement, agents also have three duties implied by law: reasonable

---

[51] *See* Annot., 107 A.L.R. 1072-1080 (1937) for a discussion of agister's lien laws.

care, obedience, and loyalty. Principals generally have the duty to provide reasonable compensation to the agent, unless the agent has agreed to act gratuitously, and to indemnify the agent for all expenses or losses reasonably incurred in performing authorized activities.

DUTY OF LOYALTY

RAYMOND v. DAVIES
Supreme Judicial Court of Massachusetts, 1936
293 Mass. 117, 199 N.E. 321

This is an action of contract to recover salary due and money lent. It appears from the facts found by the auditor that the plaintiff had been employed by the defendant as manager of her farm, known as Carver Hill Farm, in Natick in the Commonwealth; that he hired the employees and paid them and the bills generally; that he kept a bank account under the name of "Carver Hill Orchard," drew checks on the account, and made purchases of supplies for the farm, the checks being signed by him as manager.

The auditor found that the plaintiff made purchases on behalf of the defendant from a corporation in which he was a stockholder, and that because of such purchases he received a commission of seven shares of stock from that corporation. He did not inform the defendant of the receipt of these shares of stock. This constituted a "secret" profit for which he never accounted to the defendant.

As manager of the defendant's farm the plaintiff was required to exercise the utmost good faith in his dealing with her.

If the agent does not conduct himself with fidelity towards his principal, but is guilty of taking a secret profit or commission in regard to the matter in which he is employed, he loses his right to compensation on the grounds that he has taken a position wholly inconsistent with that of agent for his employer, and which gives his employer, upon discovering it, the right to treat him so far as compensation, at least, is concerned, as if no agency had existed. This may operate to give the principal the benefit of valuable services rendered by the agent, but the agent has only himself to blame for that result. Little v. Phipps, 208 Mass. 331, 333–334.

As the plaintiff was guilty of taking a bonus in the form of shares of stock in a corporation in which he was a stockholder, by reason of his purchases from that corporation on behalf of his employer, he is barred from the recovery of salary or wages.

Exceptions overruled.

STUDY QUESTIONS

1. When is an employer liable for the torts of an employee?

2. Can the contributory negligence of an injured employee bar recovery against the employer? What if the employee had assumed the risk?

3. What is the difference between contributory negligence and assumption of risk?

4. What is the meaning of the fellow servant rule? The simple tool rule?

5. What criticisms can be made against the common-law system of tort recovery as that system applies to agricultural employees injured on the job?

6. How do workers' compensation laws work? Are agricultural employees typically covered by such laws?

7. Do workers' compensation laws preclude common-law recovery from the employer? Do they preclude common-law recovery from others such as manufacturers of unsafe equipment or persons exercising control over unsafe premises?

8. What is the typical nature of occupational diseases laws?

9. What are the general rules regarding the employment of minors?

10. What common activities have been designed as hazardous by the Secretary of Labor?

11. What are the regulations regarding the employment of persons under 16 in nonhazardous occupations?

12. When does the federal minimum wage law apply to agricultural employees?

13. Are nonexempt agricultural workers entitled to overtime pay under the FLSA?

14. What is the trend regarding the inclusion of agricultural workers under state minimum wage laws?

15. What OSHA standards apply to agriculture?

16. Are agricultural employers likely to be inspected under the federal Occupational Safety and Health Act?

17. What laws apply to migrant agricultural laborers or alien agricultural workers?

18. To what extent does the federal Unemployment Compensation Act apply to agricultural employment? Are workers entitled to benefits? Are agricultural employers required to pay into the system?

19. What payroll taxes apply to agricultural employment?

20. Is the unionization of agricultural labor regulated by federal law? By state law?

21. How does an independent contractor differ from an employee? Are farmers and ranchers vicariously liable for the negligence of independent contractors?

22. What are mechanic's liens?

23. What are the implied duties in a principal-agent relationship?

24. What is the most important aspect of a principal-agent relationship?

25. What is the meaning of "within the scope of the agent's authority"?

26. Frank Farmer operated a large dairy and grain farm. He employed eight persons (A, B, and six other persons) to help with the milking. All of the employees worked 6 days a week and 52 weeks out of the year. Worker A was 15 years of age. One day Frank Farmer asked A to finish plowing the south forty instead of doing the milking. Frank said he really wanted the plowing finished and would pay A $2 per hour instead of the $1.50 he usually paid. Frank thought he could justify the extra pay because A would be more productive plowing with an 80 horsepower tractor than she would be assisting with the milking. While A was plowing, she turned too fast at the end of the field. A and her tractor left the field, careened down a road embankment, and flipped over on a highway. A was injured as a result.

Meanwhile, B, also an employee of Frank Farmer, was speeding down the highway because he was late for work. He was also very sleepy because he had gone to bed at 3:00 a.m. He had slept through his 5:00 a.m. alarm but, fortunately, was awakened by a nightmare—the unmilked cows, angry at his failure to arrive at work on time, were about to trample him in his bed! Suddenly B saw the overturned tractor in the road. Because of his speed and lack of alertness, he was unable to stop in time. Rather than ram the overturned tractor, he "hit the ditch." B was injured and his car was damaged. Frank Farmer saw the series of events and called an ambulance and a tow truck. While the tow truck was towing the tractor to the shop, the driver of the truck negligently ran over Pedestrian.

What laws, if any, has Frank Farmer violated? Discuss.

What rights does A have for damages or compensation for her injuries?

Discuss the rights of B to recover for his personal injury and property damage. Your discussion should identify the persons potentially liable, the theory of recovery, why a statutorily prescribed system of recovery was used or not used, and the presence or absence of potential barriers to recovery.

Is Frank Farmer liable for the negligence of the tow truck driver in running over Pedestrian?

5

Nature and Meaning of Property

Concepts of property are of critical importance to farmers and ranchers, for agriculture, literally, has its roots in property. This and the next two chapters are devoted to a discussion of property. This chapter deals with the definition and meaning of property, including the various property interests that are recognized within the United States. Subsequent chapters will deal with the transfer of property and the rights and duties of those who control property.

At the onset it should be noted that a very close relationship exists between property and law. Without the law to define our rights in property and to provide sanctions to those who violate these rights, no meaningful concept of property could exist. Property exists only to the extent that law will provide for its existence and will protect the rights of the holder.

Property has often been referred to as a "bundle of rights." The nature of the particular property right depends upon how many sticks are in the bundle. Property can be possessed without being owned and owned without being possessed. Ownership is not essential to enjoyment. A person may have a portion of the total bundle of rights in the form of a leasehold, a bailment, or a loan which gives a right of enjoyment without giving what would generally be regarded as the ownership of the property.[1]

5.1 REAL AND PERSONAL PROPERTY DISTINGUISHED

Occasionally real property and personal property must be distinguished.[2] For example, different rules may govern the distribution of real and personal property at the death of the owner. In some states real property may be subject to an annual tax, while personal property is not; and

---

[1] *See generally* 1 G. THOMPSON, COMMENTARIES ON THE MODERN LAW OF REAL PROPERTY § 5 (1964).

[2] *Id.* § § 18–19.

contracts for the sale of real estate must usually be in writing, while no such requirement exists for many contracts involving the sale of personal property.

Generally speaking, *real property* is immovable property consisting of such things as land, things fixed to land such as buildings, and other things incidental or appurtenant to land. *Personal property*, on the other hand, is generally movable, but technically includes every kind of property that is not realty. In addition to tangible personal property, such as tractors, cows, and household goods, there are all kinds of representations of property under the heading of intangibles. Stocks, bonds, bills, notes, checks, bills of lading, warehouse receipts, promises to pay, obligations under a contract, and judgments of a court are all intangibles, but at the same time they are personal property. The rules for distinguishing real and personal property are easily stated, but application is sometimes difficult. Controversies often arise over improvements to land and over minerals, trees, crops, and even manure. An example of a more technical holding is as follows: when turpentine oozes down the side of a tree, it is considered real estate, but when it drips into a container, it becomes personalty.

TREES AS REAL ESTATE

NEW RIVER LUMBER CO. v. BLUE RIDGE LUMBER COMPANY
Supreme Court of Tennessee, 1921
146 Tenn. 181

In 1903 C.J. Sawyer and others were the owners in fee of certain tracts of land. They executed a deed for the lumber growing on this land to the New River Lumber Company. The deed stated that Sawyer and his associates were conveying 4235 previously marked trees on particularly described land. The deed also stated that the New River Lumber Company had the right to cut and remove the timber at any time.

In 1906 C.J. Sawyer and his associates conveyed by deed the fee of the tracts of land to the Blue Ridge Lumber Company, but this deed excepted all of the lumber previously sold to the New River Lumber Company. The New River Lumber Company's right to remove the timber was in no way restricted until 1911 when the Blue Ridge Company addressed a notice to the New River Lumber Company stating, in substance, that as no time for the removal of the timber had been specified in said deed of May 23, 1903, it must be removed within a reasonable time, and that Blue Ridge thought it had had a reasonable time in which to cut and remove said timber, and stated that the timber branded should be removed from the land, and notified the New River Lumber Company to proceed to cut and remove the same.

In 1920 Blue Ridge Lumber Company began cutting and removing said timber, and the present bill was filed on April 15, 1920, by the New River Lumber Company for the purpose of setting up title in it to said timber by virtue of said deed of May 23, 1903, which it insists vested it with the title to said trees, with the perpetual and unrestricted right to enter upon said lands and cut and remove said marked timber therefrom.

The defendant answered the bill and amendment, setting up its title to said timber, and claiming under its 1906 deed from Sawyer and his associates. Its answer averred that the deed by which complainant acquired said trees, properly interpreted, only gave it a reasonable time in which to cut and remove said timber from said lands, and that such reasonable time had expired. The answer further denied that, by the conveyance from Fowler and Sawyer and their associates of May 23, 1903, it was intended to create in complainant an estate in perpetuity in said timber.

The rule is well established in this State and elsewhere that standing trees must be regarded as part of the realty on which they stand; and, inasmuch as they are the natural and permanent growth of the soil they cannot be regarded as partaking of the character of emblements or *fructus industriales*, and therefore a sale, conveyance, or mortgage of land carries with it the trees growing upon the land. They cannot be levied upon or sold as chattels while standing, but trees as soon as they are severed from the land lose their character as realty and become personalty.

It is generally recognized that standing timber may be transferred by a deed, grant or reservation, and constitute an estate separate from the land itself. When so separated it retains its character so long as it remains uncut, but when severed it becomes personal property.

Where the owner of land grants the trees growing thereon to another and his heirs, with liberty to cut and carry them away at his pleasure forever, the grantee acquires an estate in fee in the trees, with an interest in the soil sufficient for their growth, while the fee in the soil itself remains in the grantor.

We are of the opinion that the deed under consideration, when construed in the light of the situation, circumstances and surroundings of the parties at the time of its execution, must be held to convey a right in perpetuity in the trees therein described, and that complainant has the unrestricted right to enter upon said lands and cut and remove said trees at its pleasure or convenience.

In *French v. Freeman*, 43 Vt. 93 (1869), the court noted that manure is not necessarily real estate; it may be real or personal according to the circumstances under which it is placed. When lying without severance upon the soil where it was first dropped, it is a part of the soil, like a clod of earth, loose stones, or fallen and decaying vegetation, and is real estate. When severed from the soil, gathered up, and secured for use elsewhere, it is merely a personal chattel. A similar sentiment regarding crops was expressed in *Bagley v. Columbus S.R. Co.*, 98 Ga. 626, 25 S.E. 638 (1896). The court said the only deduction to be drawn from the mystic maze of uncertainty and contradiction in which the law governing growing crops has become involved is that a growing crop is a sort of legal species of chameleon, constantly changing color to meet the emergency in each particular class or case in which it arises. Perhaps the situation is not quite this hopeless, but controversies do arise over the character of a growing crop.

Although the distinctions between real and personal property include many shades of gray, as illustrated by the cases appearing above, some general principles can be stated, at least as far as crops are concerned. Crops which grow spontaneously on the land, such as trees, bushes, or grass, are described as *fructus naturalis* and are considered to be a part of the land until severed.[3] Crops which are the result of annual planting and cultivation, such as corn, wheat, or vegetables, are described as *fructus industriales* and are considered personalty.[4]

5.2 FEE SIMPLE AND OTHER FEE ESTATES

Ownership of real property in the United States has its origins in the feudal system of England which developed after the Norman Conquest in 1066. This early system of landownership may be graphically pictured as a pyramid. At the top was the king (or in some cases, the church) as the final owner of the land. The king granted large tracts to his friends and allies. They, in turn, dealt out parcels to their most faithful followers. The land was held primarily by what is known as "military tenure." That is, the people to whom the king granted the land supplied soldiers to help him fight his wars. The titles of English nobility as we now know them were applied to those who held varying-sized parcels of land which the king had granted. The person at the bottom of this pyra-

midal structure, the person who actually tilled the soil, had few rights which resemble modern ownership.

As time passed, there was an insistence that the person on the land, and, for that matter, others in the pyramidal structure, have more rights in the land and greater freedom of disposition. Eventually, through acts of Parliament and the cooperation of the courts in hearing cases and establishing precedent, the pyramidal structure was effectually broken, and ownership very much as we recognize it now in the United States was established. These great changes took place before the colonies in America were established, so the tenure pattern we inherited from England recognized the right to inherit and the right to transfer land. For the most part, the system of *primogeniture*—the right of the oldest son to inherit—which existed in England was not established in the colonies and did not become a part of the American common-law tradition. Retention by the government of the right to tax land and the right to acquire interests in land for public purposes (known as the *right of eminent domain*) are sometimes pointed to as vestiges of the feudal system under which the king or government had all the right in the land.

The concept of an "estate" in land is one of the most flexible concepts in Anglo-American property law. *Estates* are interests in land which are presently possessory or which will entitle the owner to possession at some future time when intervening estates have ended. Estates are simply a way of expressing ownership rights measured in terms of duration. They are to be distinguished from other interests which are nonpossessory, such as easements.

---

[3] *Id.* § § 95–106.
[4] *Id.* § § 115–124.

Estates are often further divided into leasehold and freehold estates. The *leasehold estate* refers to one of the lesser estates under which a lessee is given the possessory right and use of the land for some limited or determinable periods of time—an apartment lease, for example. *Freehold estates*, on the other hand, have potentially infinite duration or an unpredictable length.

Freehold estates can be divided into fee estates and lifehold estates. The most common fee estate is the one known as the *fee simple*. It represents the highest type of ownership, is inheritable and transferable, and is capable of being divided into many kinds of lesser estates under our system of law. A *life estate* gives the holder virtually the same rights as a fee simple except that the interest is only for life; therefore, the holder cannot convey the land acting alone or pass on anything by inheritance. The life estate is discussed more fully in a subsequent section. The fee simple and other fee estates are discussed more fully in the following paragraphs.

The *fee simple absolute* is often referred to as the fee simple or fee. It is a common estate and encompasses what is typically thought of as full ownership.[5] The fee simple can be transferred by either sale, gift, or inheritance to any person. If the owner dies without a will, the estate will pass to the decedent's heirs at law. Thus, the fee simple absolute is an estate of potentially infinite duration. Most jurisdictions have enacted statutes whereby every estate in land is presumed to be a fee simple absolute unless a lesser estate is indicated by the grantor.

There are other kinds of fees. The *fee tail* grew up in the English tenure system as a means of keeping the land in the family indefinitely. In effect, fee tail was a series of life estates limited to either the heirs generally or to male or female heirs.[6] Such a limitation was felt by the legislatures of the American states to be too restrictive; hence, the fee tail has been, in effect, outlawed by statute. In several states, an attempt to create such a limitation results in a life estate in the first taker; after that, however, the heirs take a fee simple rather than another life estate. In other states, the attempt to create a fee tail limitation is disregarded, and so the first taker receives a fee simple absolute.

Several other kinds of fee estates are of potentially infinite duration, but may be terminated on the happening of a specified event. One such estate is the *fee simple determinable*, which automatically terminates upon the happening of a stated event.[7] For example, if a landowner transferred title to a railroad for as long as the railroad used the property for railroad purposes, the railroad would have a fee simple determinable; if a landowner transferred title to an agricultural producer for as long as the property was used for agricultural purposes, the producer would have a fee simple determinable. In both examples, the landowner started with a fee simple absolute but transferred a fee simple determinable. If the railroad ceases to use the property for railroad purposes (or the farmer for agricultural purposes), title to the property would automatically revert to the landowner. The landowner has retained a future interest known as a *possibility of reverter*.

An estate rather similar to the fee simple determinable is the *fee simple subject to a condition subsequent*, which, when created,

---

[5] 2 R. POWELL, THE LAW OF REAL PROPERTY ¶ 190 (1977); 4 G. THOMPSON, *supra* note 1, at § § 1864, 1970 (1979).

[6] 2 R. POWELL, *supra* note 5, at ¶ ¶ 196–198; 4 G. THOMPSON, *supra* note 1, at § 1866 (1979).
[7] 2 R. POWELL, *supra* note 5, at ¶ 187.

contains language giving the grantor the power to terminate the estate on the happening of a specified event.[8] Suppose that a landowner transfers land to a railroad (or farmer) using the following language: "provided, however, that if you cease to use the land for railroad (agricultural) purposes, I or my successor have the right to reenter and retake the property." If the railroad (or the farmer) ceases to use the premises for railroad uses (or agricultural purposes), the fee simple conditional does not automatically end. It continues until the landowner or the landowner's successors reenter and retake the property. This future interest of the landowner is called a *right of entry for condition broken* or a *power of termination.*

5.3 LIFE ESTATES, REVERSIONS, AND REMAINDERS

When one's right in a farm or other real property exists only for the lifetime of the holder, the interest is referred to as an *ordinary* life estate. If one has an interest measured by the life of another, as would occur where one life tenant transfers all the life interest to some third party, the interest is said to be a life estate *pur autra vie.*[9]

Though the life tenant has the possessory right and use of the property and in nearly all respects is like a fee simple owner, such a person does not have the legal title; hence, this tenant does not have an inheritable estate. The legal title is vested in persons known as "reversioners" or "remaindermen." Technically they are known as *reversioners* if no disposition was made of the fee at the time the life estate was created. In such a case, on termination of the life estate, the right to possession and use reverts to the grantor or to the grantor's heirs who have all along held the fee interest. In case the person creating the life estate designated the persons who are to take possession after the life estate ends, these persons are technically known as *remaindermen.* When the life estate terminates, they will take the possessory right and use of the property. They already have the fee or title. Life estates are ordinarily created either by deed or by will.

In most cases the purpose of a life estate is to ensure possession, use, and income for a surviving spouse during his or her lifetime with an assurance that the property will go to the children following the death of the life tenant. While there is certainty in this regard, the separation of legal rights created by the establishment of a life estate and a class of reversioners or remain-

---

[8] *Id.* ¶ 188. In many ways the apparent difference between the possibility of reverter and the right of entry for condition broken (power of termination) is a distinction without a difference. For example, state statutes which have limited the duration of these future interests (*e.g.*, Illinois) or statutes which require periodic re-recording to perpetuate the future interests (*e.g.*, New York) generally do not make a distinction. Similarly, continued possession by the holder of the fee simple determinable or fee simple conditional after the stated event has occurred generally starts the period of adverse possession. Adverse possession will be discussed

more fully in the next chapter. Perhaps the only practical difference between the possibility of reverter and the right of entry for condition broken (power of termination) concerns who is entitled to the profits (*e.g.*, rents from the land) between the happening of the stated event and the actual repossession by the holder of the future interest. The holder of a possibility of reverter would be entitled to these interim profits, while the holder of a right of entry for condition broken (power of termination) would not.

[9] *Id.* ¶¶ 201–203.

dermen can lead to controversies between these parties and to an exhaustive and depletive use of the farm by the life tenant. As can be seen from the case which follows, there is not much legal encouragement for the life tenant to make improvements on the land.

IMPROVEMENTS BY LIFE TENANT

CARTER v. CARTER
Supreme Court of Illinois, 1908
234 Ill. 507, 85 N.E. 292

In 1866 William G. Carter departed this life testate.... The first paragraph of his will began as follows:

First, I give and bequeath to my wife, Mary Jane, the full use and control of the following described real estate situated in Champaign County, in the state of Illinois, to wit (describing the 260 acres in controversy in this case) during her natural life, to use and occupy as she sees fit....

His wife, Mary Jane, died December 30, 1905, and at the May term, 1906, of the circuit court of Vermilion County, Plaintiffs, children of deceased, filed a bill claiming that they, while occupying the farm as tenants of their mother, erected dwelling houses, barns, and other structures, and made other improvements thereon, at their own expense, which have increased the value of the premises $12,000, which increase rightfully belongs to plaintiffs as against the other children (defendants herein).

Upon a hearing, the court entered a decree dismissing the bill for want of equity, decreeing partition on the cross-bill in accordance with the interests as therein set forth, and refusing plaintiffs any compensation for their improvement of the premises, from which decree they appeal to this court.

The question arising on the record is:... Are plaintiffs entitled to an allowance for their improvements?

The improvements placed upon the lands by the plaintiffs were placed there during the life of their mother, who was entitled to the possession of the land as life tenant. Their possession was not that of co-tenants with the other owners, but was exclusive under the life tenant. Their right was no greater than hers, and the rule is that a life tenant cannot, by placing permanent improvements on land, however much they may enhance its value, create a charge against the remainderman. Such improvements will be deemed to have been made for the life tenant's own benefit during the existence of his own estate, and upon its termination, being part of the realty, they will go to the remainderman, who will take them without any liability to reimburse the life tenant.

As a practical matter, the lack of incentive to make improvement can easily be overcome if the life tenant and remaindermen have a good working relationship. Nothing prevents the life tenant and remaindermen from reaching agreement about how the costs of improvements, such as confinement livestock facilities, silos, or drainage tiles, should be shared. Presumably, such improvements will generate an increase in income accruing to the benefit of the life tenant and an increase in the value of the property which will someday benefit the remaindermen. As a starting point for reaching agreement about the sharing of costs, the parties might consider that interest should be paid by the life tenant and principal payments paid by the remaindermen. A variety of variations are possible. The expected life of the life tenant and of the improvement will be important considerations.

Although a life tenant may not have much incentive to make improvements to real estate, the life tenant does have a common-law duty to protect and preserve the property. This duty is sometimes referred to as the duty to avoid waste.[10] A life tenant may not, for example, exploit the timber, minerals, oil, or other natural resources on the property. Some exceptions to this rule exist, such as where the natural resources are taken in reasonable amounts for repair and maintenance, where the right to exploit was expressly provided for in the grant of the life estate, or where the right to exploit is implied because the land is only suitable for such exploitation or because exploitation was under way when the grant was made.

Life tenants also have the duty to make and pay for repairs necessary to maintain structures in a reasonable state of repair, to pay interest on any encumbrances such as a mortgage, and to pay all ordinary taxes on the land.[11] All of these duties are generally limited to an expenditure of funds up to the actual income derived from the land or to the reasonable rental value of the land.

It should also be noted that a life tenant is under no common-law duty to insure the property for the benefit of remaindermen. Both the life tenant and remaindermen have insurable interests, however, and each should insure that respective interest as a general rule. If the life tenant is insuring the entire property interest, the remaindermen should reimburse the life tenant for the remaindermen's proportionate part. If the property is damaged, some courts have held that where the insurance proceeds exceed the value of the life tenant's interest, the excess should be used to rebuild or repair or should be paid to the remaindermen. The issue of proper insurance coverage is an important one and should be discussed with a knowledgeable insurance representative. That representative should be on notice that the property interests are divided between a life tenant and remaindermen.

5.4 CO-OWNERSHIP: TENANCY IN COMMON, JOINT TENANCY, TENANCY BY THE ENTIRETY, AND COMMUNITY PROPERTY

Each of the estates in land discussed in the preceding section can be held by just one person or by several persons concurrently. Several different types of concurrent ownerships are recognized by the courts. Some of the distinctive features of each are noted in the paragraphs that follow.

---

[10] 5 *id.* ¶ 640 (1979); 4A G. THOMPSON, *supra* note 1, at § 1900 (1979).

[11] *See, e.g.,* Fonda v. Miller, 411 Ill. 74, 103 N.E. 2d 98 (1952).

Tenancy in Common

Tenancy in common is a widespread form of co-ownership.[12] In many states tenancy in common is presumed when property is transferred to co-owners without specifying which particular form of concurrent ownership is intended. Probably most tenancies in common are created when property is transferred at death, either by applying the presumption to bequests in a will or to the laws of descent which govern the distribution of property when there is no will.

The interests of each tenant in common may or may not be equal. Nevertheless, each tenant in common has the right to use the whole of the premises subject to the rights of other co-tenants. On the death of one of the tenants in common, that person's interests pass to his or her heirs or grantees as tenants in common with the other tenants. In other words, the undivided and undesignated share owned by a tenant in common is nevertheless a transferable and inheritable right in the property. It should be noted that the word "tenant" as used in describing kinds of concurrent ownership in fact means an "owner" rather than a "lessee" of land, the more commonly understood meaning of the term.

A tenancy in common may be terminated in any of several ways: (1) by sale of the property to a third party and a division of the proceeds among the tenants in common, (2) by a transfer to one tenant in common of the interests of all the other tenants in common, (3) by voluntary division and an exchange of deeds among the tenants in common, (4) by partition.

When tenants in common continue to hold farmland undivided, there should be cooperative agreement among them which will permit proper management and use of the land. In the absence of special agreement, they should share income from the farm in accordance with their fractional interests in the tenancy in common. If one tenant in common operates the farm as operator, that person should be entitled to the usual tenant's share or such share as the lease between the tenants in common specifies. If tenants in common are cooperative, many different kinds of arrangements are possible. One may farm the land as a tenant. If there is sufficient land, more than one may operate the land as a tenant; if none of them wish to farm the land, they may appoint one tenant in common to act as manager for the others. If all of them are either disinterested in or not experienced in managing farmland, they may cooperate in hiring a professional farm manager.

Joint Tenancy

Joint tenancy is a common method of holding property by husband and wife. The primary and most important difference between a tenancy in common and a joint tenancy is that the latter provides a right of survivorship.[13] The tenants, whether two or more, hold undivided *equal* shares. These shares must be the same kind of holding in the property and must give each tenant an equal possessory interest. Upon the death of one co-tenant, that person's interest automatically vests in the surviving tenants. When all tenants but one are deceased, the survivor holds the entire interest in the property. Obviously one's undivided interest as a joint tenant is not inheritable because if a co-tenant dies, the

---

[12] *See generally* 4 A.R. POWELL, *supra* note 5, at ¶¶ 602–608 (1979).

[13] *Id.* ¶¶ 615–618.

interest of that person is already limited to go to the survivor or survivors. The final survivor, of course, takes a property interest which is inheritable, but the joint tenancy has then run its course and no longer exists.

At common law, to create a joint tenancy a conveyance had to be made from a third party. It was impossible for an owner of land to convey it directly to himself or herself and another as joint tenants with the right of survivorship. Thus, if an owner of property wished to create a joint tenancy with his or her spouse, this result could only be obtained by making a conveyance to a disinterested third party and having that party instantly convey the property back to the desired parties as joint tenants and not tenants in common. Many states have eliminated this requirement by statute and permit the creation of a joint tenancy by any parties including the owner. However, the requirement that the language used in creating the joint tenancy must expressly negate the idea that it is a tenancy in common is still operative. The usual language used is "to A and B as joint tenants with a right of survivorship and not as tenants in common."

The timing and manner of death may affect the survivorship nature of joint tenancy. Many states have enacted the Uniform Simultaneous Death Act, which provides generally that

where there is no sufficient evidence that two joint tenants have died otherwise than simultaneously, the property so held shall be distributed one-half as if one had survived and one-half as if the other had survived. If there are more than two joint tenants and and all of them have so died, the property thus distributed shall be in the proportion that one bears to the whole number of joint tenants.

In effect, this means that when it cannot satisfactorily be determined that one joint tenant survived the others, the joint tenancy will be converted to a tenancy in common and the heirs or devisees of each joint tenant shall take his or her undivided share.[14]

As a general rule, one joint tenant cannot acquire the jointly held property through survivorship by murdering the other joint tenant. For example, in *Bradley v. Fox*, 7 Ill.2d 106 (1955), the court said that "One of the implied conditions of the joint tenancy contract is that neither party will acquire the interest of the other by murder." The court compelled the murderer to hold the entire interest for the benefit of the estate of his co-tenant except that the murderer was entitled to one-half the income for life. In effect, the court decreed a remedy by which the heirs of the murder victim would be treated as the surviving joint tenant.

CONVEYANCE BY ONE OF THREE JOINT TENANTS

JACKSON v. O'CONNELL
Supreme Court of Illinois, 1961
23 Ill. 2d 52, 177 N.E.2d 194

This appeal from a decree for partition entered by the circuit court of Cook County presents the question whether a conveyance by one of three

---

[14] *See, e.g.*, ILL. REV. STAT. ch. 3, § 41c.

joint tenants of real estate to another of the joint tenants destroyed the joint tenancy in its entirety or merely severed the joint tenancy with respect to the undivided third interest so conveyed, leaving the joint tenancy in force and effect as to the remaining two-thirds interest.

The controlling facts, as we viewed the case, are simple and uncontroverted. The various parcels of real estate in question are situated in Cook County and were formerly owned by Neil P. Duffy. The latter died testate in 1936 and by his will he devised the properties to his three sisters, Nellie Duffy, Anna Duffy, and Katherine O'Connell, as joint tenants. Thereafter Nellie Duffy, a spinster, by quitclaim deed dated July 21, 1948, conveyed and quitclaimed all her interest in the properties to Anna Duffy. The deed was in statutory form. It was duly delivered and recorded. Nellie Duffy died in 1949.

Some eight years later, in May 1957, Anna Duffy died testate. By her will she devised whatever interest she had in the real estate in question to four nieces, Beatrice Jackson, Eileen O'Barski, Catherine Young and Margaret Miller, plaintiffs herein.

Following the death of Anna Duffy, the plaintiffs commenced this suit against Katherine O'Connell (hereafter referred to as the defendant) and others to partition the real estate. Their suit is predicated on the theory that Nellie Duffy's quitclaim deed, dated July 21, 1948, to Anna Duffy severed in its entirety the joint tenancies existing between Nellie Duffy, Anna Duffy, and the defendant; that as a result, Anna Duffy became the owner of an undivided two-thirds interest and defendant an undivided one-third interest in the various parcels of real estate, as tenants in common; that plaintiffs, as successors in interest to Anna Duffy, accordingly each own an undivided one-sixth and defendant an undivided one-third interest as tenants in common. The defendant answered and filed a counterclaim on the theory that Nellie Duffy's quitclaim deed of July 21, 1948, to Anna Duffy severed the joint tenancies only so far as the grantor's one-third interest was concerned; that the joint tenancies between Anna Duffy and defendant continued in full force and effect as to the remaining two thirds; that upon Anna Duffy's death in 1957, defendant succeeded to that two-thirds interest as surviving joint tenant; and that plaintiffs are each entitled to one-twelfth interest only, as devisees of the one-third interest which passed to Anna Duffy by reason of Nellie Duffy's quitclaim deed.

The cause was referred to a master who found the interests in accordance with defendant's contentions. The decree for partition appealed from confirmed the master's conclusions.

The problem resolves itself down to the effect of Nellie Duffy's quitclaim deed upon the joint tenancy as a matter of law. The question appears to be one of first impression in Illinois.

The estate of joint tenancy comes down to us from the early English law and while the rules applicable to it have been modified in some particulars by statute in Illinois, most of the principles governing joint tenancies today are those which existed at common law. For example, it has been held from the earliest times that four co-existing unities are necessary and requisite to the creation and continuance of a joint tenancy; namely, unity of interest, unity of title, unity of time, and unity of possession. Any act of a joint tenant which destroys any of these unities operates as a severance of the joint tenancy and extinguishes the right of survivorship.

It appears to have been well settled at common law that where there were three joint tenants and one conveyed his interest to a third party, the joint tenancy was only severed as to the part conveyed; the third party grantee became a tenant in common with the other two joint tenants, but the latter still held the remaining two thirds as joint tenants with right of survivorship therein.

Modern-day writers support the same view. In American Law of Property, vol. II, sec. 6.2, it is said:

Where one joint tenant conveys to one of his cotenants, where there are more than two, the cotenant grantee holds the share conveyed as a tenant in common, taking it at a different time by a different title, while his original share is held with the remaining cotenants as a joint tenancy, the unity continuing to that extent.

Other writers lay down the same rule.

With respect to the contention that Nellie Duffy's quitclaim deed destroyed the joint tenancies in their entirety because as a result of that deed the undivided interests of the grantee, Anna Duffy, and the defendant in the various properties were rendered unequal, it is to be noted that their interests in the undivided two-thirds, which formed the subject matter of the joint tenancies here in question, remained the same. It is settled in Illinois that a valid joint tenancy may exist with respect to the undivided interest which forms the subject matter of the joint tenancy.

The decree of the circuit court of Cook County was right and is affirmed.

JOINT TENANCY—UNITY OF INTEREST

PALUSZEK v. WOHLRAB
Supreme Court of Illinois, 1953
1 Ill. 2d 363, 115 N.E. 2d 764

The plaintiff, Mary Paluszek, brought this action in the Superior Court of Cook County against her sister, Elizabeth E. Wohlrab, to establish a resulting trust in property which had been jointly purchased by the defendant and John Dumovic, who was the brother of the plaintiff and the defendant. The property in question, an improved parcel of real estate, was purchased on July 30, 1948, for $12,000. Of the purchase price, Mrs. Wohlrab paid $6,318.50 and her brother paid $5,681.50. The property was conveyed to the two grantees as joint tenants by a warranty deed which satisfied the requirements of section I of the statute concerning joint rights and obligations. Defendant and her brother occupied the property as their home from September, 1948, until the brother's death on October 20, 1949. The defendant has since continued to live there. Dumovic died intestate. He was survived by his two sisters, the defendant and the plaintiff, who are his only heirs-at-law.

There are no disputed issues of fact. The evidence established the joint purchase of the property by the defendant and her brother, their respective contributions to the purchase price, the conveyance to them "not in tenancy in common, but in joint tenancy," and occupancy of the property by them until the brother's death. Upon this evidence the master found that a true joint tenancy existed between defendant and her brother, and that upon the brother's death title to the property vested solely in the defendant. Exceptions to the report were overruled, and a decree was entered approving the master's report and dismissing plaintiff's amended complaint. Plaintiff appeals directly, a freehold being involved.

In order to reach this result, the plaintiff first argues that because the co-tenants did not make equal contributions to the purchase price, there is lacking the unity of interest requisite to a joint tenancy. This argument is without foundation. The unity of interest required for the creation of a joint tenancy refers to equality among the co-tenants only as to their interest in the estate. Thus a deed granting one tenant an estate for life and the other an estate for years cannot create a joint tenancy. Nor can one tenant be granted a one-fourth interest and the other a three-fourths interest. So, also, when a joint tenancy has been established, each tenant is regarded as having an equal interest in the entire estate. In neither case does unity of interest relate to an equality in the contribution of purchase money. Affirmed for the defendant.

JOINT BANK ACCOUNT

MURGIC v. GRANITE CITY TRUST & SAV. BK.
Supreme Court of Illinois, 1964
34 Ill. 2d 587, 202 N.E. 2d 470

This case again involves the effect to be given joint tenancy bank accounts. Plaintiff, Peter A. Murgic, the surviving joint tenant, brought this action against the depositary bank for the proceeds of a savings account in his name and one Mike Yurkovich. Illinois State Trust Company, administrator of Yurkovich's estate, interpleaded and appealed to the Appellate Court, Fifth District, from a judgment on the jury's verdict in favor of Murgic. The Appellate Court reversed and we granted leave to appeal.

Yurkovich and Murgic went to the bank to open a joint account. A bank official explained the nature and effect of such an account stating that either could draw on it and that upon the death of either the then balance would go to the survivor. In the course of the conversation Yurkovich said that he had no relatives in this country, that in the past he had sent funds, food and other things to relatives in Croatia but after a trip to visit them he felt they were not deserving of further consideration, that Murgic was his closest friend, and that he wanted him to have the funds. Thereupon Yurkovich deposited $12,500 in their joint names and they both signed a joint account agreement. After passing the pass book back and forth and having some discussion as to who should hold the book, Yurkovich retained it. Yurkovich later deposited $13,500 additional in the account without Murgic's knowledge.

Since there seems to be some difference of opinion among the courts of the State on the degree and burden of proof required of a claimant adverse to the deposit agreement, we will, therefore, give further consideration to this issue.

A prima facie presumption of donative intent exists where the proof shows that the making of the deposit and the execution of the contract is in conformity with the statute. As we stated in recognizing the increased use of joint tenancy accounts and legislative relaxation of rules pertaining to them: "Public policy would seem to require the adoption by the courts of a more liberal and practical view of these common transactions." The legislative policy to treat the joint account as a useful technique for transferring intangibles dictates that the estate or other person claiming against the survivor should have the burden of disproving intent on the part of the decedent, and the degree of proof required to void the presumption should be clear and convincing. This would add certainty to the law and at the same time protect a depositor's estate where the joint account was created without donative intent, for example where the account was opened for the convenience of the depositor. To hold that a lesser degree is required or that the burden shifted would tend to make every joint tenancy account suspect would promote instability rather than stability of ownership. A personal representative of a deceased joint tenant should not be constantly faced with the risk of charges of mismanagement for failure to litigate each joint account to which it or his decedent was a party.

We hold that an instrument creating a joint account under the statutes presumably speaks the whole truth; and, in order to go behind the terms of the agreement, the one claiming adversely thereto has the burden of establishing by clear and convincing evidence that a gift was not intended. This burden does not shift to the party claiming under the agreement.

The proof established that the account was understandingly created, that Yurkovich knew the funds could be drawn by either, and that the balance in the account would go to Murgic if he (Yurkovich) died first.

The judgment of the Appellate Court, Fifth Judicial District, is reversed and the judgment of the circuit court of Madison County is affirmed.

Persons will often ask whether joint tenancy or tenancy in common is preferred. Unfortunately, the answer is that "it depends." Joint tenancy offers a simple way of transferring interest to another at death. As long as the joint tenancy is not destroyed, it has the effect of immediately vesting all interests in the property in the survivor at the moment of death, without even the need for probate. Consequently, joint tenancy ownership has been referred to as "the poor man's will."

Many farmers and ranchers, however, are no longer poor. The rising value of farmland, in particular, has increased the net worth of many landowners. Because of this increased wealth, federal estate tax considerations are of much greater importance than they were a few decades ago. Generally, large holdings of joint tenancy property in more typical agricultural estates create *severe* estate tax problems. If taxation is an important factor in planning an estate, the owner should obtain counsel before placing property in joint tenancy or converting joint tenancy to tenancies in common. The problems are technical and the tax picture may be a complicated one. Among the factors to consider are whether termination of the joint tenancy involves a gift tax, what the amount of the capital gains tax is likely to be if the survivor sells the property, and whether there is a possibility of "double taxation," particularly when the survivor lives only a few years after the death of the other joint tenant.

PARTITION

HELDT v. HELDT
Supreme Court of Illinois, 1963
29 Ill. 2d 61, 193 N.E. 2d 7

This is an appeal from a decree of partition entered by the circuit court of Henry County. A freehold is involved.

John Heldt, the defendant, and Betty Heldt, the plaintiff, are husband and wife and are the parents of three teenage children. Some six years ago the parties acquired the property in question as joint tenants and built a residence wherein the family still resides. In December, 1961, plaintiff filed a complaint to partition the premises, and on a date not entirely clear from the record presented defendant filed a separate complaint for divorce. The latter action, however, was voluntarily dismissed by defendant after the action for partition had gone against him and shortly after this appeal had been filed. Defendant's initial response to the partition complaint was a motion to dismiss which, in substance, alleged as grounds that partition would work irreparable hardship on defendant and the children, that plaintiff's motive for filing the suit was to force defendant to give her a divorce, and that plaintiff had been guilty of infidelity. When the motion to dismiss was denied, defendant filed an answer alleging by way of affirmative defenses, first, that there was an implied agreement between the parties not to partition, and, second, that defendant was entitled to homestead in the premises. After a hearing the circuit court resolved the issues for the plaintiff, the decree of partition expressly finding that homestead would not be set off in favor of either party.

The defendant has appealed, contending that the lower court erred both in denying the motion to dismiss and in granting partition. For the most part basic and well established principles of law are involved, and the issue presented is largely whether we should extend them to the unprecedented extremes urged by defendant and thus deny to plaintiff the right to partition.

Generally, in the absence of special equities, one owning land in common with another, such as a tenant in common or a joint tenant, has an absolute right to partition. It is well settled that when a husband and wife are joint tenants, either may maintain a successful action in partition against the other regardless of the effect on the tenancy. At the same time, however, we have stated on many occasions that a court of chancery will not permit a partition proceeding to be used to circumvent established principles of law or public policy and will, in the exercise of equitable jurisdiction, control the proceedings to protect the rights of all the parties.

Defendant suggests, without citation of authority or extended argument, that equity requires that the right of partition be denied plaintiff in this case because she had an improper motive in bringing the action, because partition will work irreparable hardship on defendant and the children and because plaintiff had been guilty of adultery. Apart from the fact that these grounds, stated in the motion to dismiss, are largely conclusions of the pleader, they afford no basis for the result the defendant seeks. It has been consistently held that motive for partition is immaterial, and that the absolute right to partition yields to no consideration of hardship, inconvenience or difficulty. Nor, in the absence of fraud or coercion attending the creation of the tenancy between the husband and wife, (and none has been alleged or shown here,) will subsequent acts of misconduct by either spouse be looked upon by equity as a basis for denying relief.

Next, and principally, defendant urges that we should declare it against public policy for either spouse, holding as a joint tenant, to partition premises being used as a home for both the husband and wife and their minor children. Stated otherwise, it is defendant's position that the absolute right to partition should be excepted when it involves a family home with minor children. While such an argument may at first blush have a certain amount of surface appeal, it comes to us without citation of authority or a cogent argument of legal or logical reasons for its acceptance.

We are not disposed to promulgate a sweeping rule of law which would in effect hold that the bonds of matrimony coupled with having children will deprive both parents of full rights and benefits in their property, and of the remedies provided by law with respect thereto. Apart from the arbitrary and discriminatory aspects of the rule contended for, we feel, as counsel for plaintiff aptly states in his brief, that "The hopes, aspirations and best intentions of a married couple in building a home to raise a family are not tantamount in law with an implied agreement not to partition, when hopes, aspirations and intentions falter."

The decree of the circuit court of Henry County is affirmed.

In most states the right of any co-tenant to petition the court for partition is a near absolute right based on the policy that no person should be a co-owner of property against his or her will. In a partition action, the court will divide the property into separately owned tracts if this is practical. Otherwise, the court will order the property sold and the proceeds of sale divided among the co-owners. Of course, co-tenants may voluntarily agree on how to convert undivided interests into separate, divided interests without court intervention. The right to bring a court action for partition provides a strong incentive for voluntary partition.[15]

Tenancy by the Entirety

Many jurisdictions recognize the co-ownership arrangement referred to as *tenancy by the entirety*, which comes into being when property is transferred to a husband and wife.

Tenancy by the entirety is similar to joint tenancy in that the right of survivorship is present. It differs from joint tenancy and other forms of co-ownership, however, in that neither tenant can terminate the estate without the consent of the other. Thus, the right to partition is not present. Generally, a tenancy by the entirety can be terminated only by the death of either spouse (which leaves the survivor as the owner of the fee), by divorce (which leaves the parties as tenants in common), by court action of a joint creditor of both husband and wife, or by mutual agreement.

Today the concurrent estate of tenancy by the entirety varies widely from state to state.[16] In some states it retains much of its common-law heritage, while in other states the concept has been modified. The estate has no significance at all in more than half of the states where a conveyance to a husband and wife creates a tenancy in common or a joint tenancy, rather than a tenancy by the entirety.[17] But in those states that recognize tenancy by the entirety, the particular concept should be understood.

Community Property

Although property law in the United States has been influenced most heavily by the English tradition, the concept of community property is a product of Spanish influence. The underlying principle of *community property* is that husband and wife should share equally in the property acquired through their joint efforts during marriage. The general principle is rather straightforward, but the application of this principle varies widely in the community property states of Arizona, California, Idaho, Louisiana, Nevada, New Mexico, Texas, and Washington.

Generally, all property acquired by a spouse before marriage, property acquired after marriage by will, inheritance, or gift, and the income from such property is separate property to which the other spouse has no claim. All other property is community property to which the other spouse has equal rights. Where there is no

---

[15] 4A R. POWELL, *supra* note 5, at ¶¶ 609–613.
[16] Tenancy by the entireties exists in some form in Arkansas, Delaware, District of Columbia, Florida, Indiana, Kentucky, Maryland, Massachusetts, Michigan, Missouri, New Jersey, New York, North Carolina, Oregon, Pennsylvania, Rhode Island, Tennessee, Vermont, Virginia, and Wyoming. 4 G. THOMPSON, *supra* note 1, at § 1784.
[17] 4A R. POWELL, *supra* note 5, at ¶¶ 620–624.1; 4 G. THOMPSON, *supra* note 1, at §§ 1771–1773 (1979).

clear evidence that particular property is separate property, most of the community property states have a presumption in favor of community property.[18]

5.5 TRUSTS

Generally

A *trust* is a fiduciary relationship between a trustee and beneficiaries whereby the trustee holds legal title to specific property under a duty to deal with the property for the benefit of the beneficiaries. The trust is a variation on the co-ownership forms of ownership discussed in the preceding section. In tenancy in common, for example, legal title is held by several persons in undivided interests. In most trusts the trustee is said to hold legal title and the beneficiaries are said to hold equitable title.[19]

Most trusts are created by express written agreement in which an owner of property (the seller) transfers his or her title to a trustee for the benefit of the beneficiaries. Such trusts are often created for estate planning reasons. Thus, the discussion of express trusts appears in Chapter 17, "Estate Planning." Other trusts may be implied or constructive trusts.

Implied Trusts and Constructive Trusts Distinguished

Trusts may sometimes be implied or constructive. Both are determined by law to exist when equity seems to demand that rights be protected.[20] The *constructive* trust is a *remedy* created by the courts to obtain title from a person who ought not to have it and force a conveyance to the one who should have it. It has been said that the constructive trust is not "intent-enforcing," but rather "fraud-rectifying." The *implied*, or resulting, trust, on the other hand, is very much like an express trust except the intention to create the trust is inferred.

IMPLIED TRUST—PURCHASE MONEY RESULTING TRUST

HANLEY v. HANLEY
Supreme Court of Illinois, 1958
14 Ill. 2d 566, 152 N.E. 2d 879

This action was brought in the circuit court of McLean County by Marie B. Hanley, plaintiff, to eject her husband, Edward V. Hanley, defendant, from an 80-acre farm they had occupied as husband and wife prior to their separation in 1955, and for an accounting of profits received by the defendant therefrom. In answer to the complaint, defendant admitted that record title to the farm property was taken in the plaintiff's name in 1936 and had so remained. However, he alleged by way of affirmative defense that this was done "as a matter of convenience" because he was then "plagued by many creditors" and "in great financial distress;" that he was the equitable owner

---

[18] 4 A.R. POWELL, *supra* note 5, at ¶¶ 624.2–628 (1979).

[19] 5 *id.* §§ 2330–2337 (1979).
[20] *Id.* §§ 2361–2367.

of the farm; and that the deed was issued to plaintiff to secure money advanced by her and should be treated as a mortgage. The cause was referred to a master in chancery, who recommended that an order be entered granting plaintiff possession of the premises, and that an accounting be made.

Plaintiff testified before the master that she paid the purchase price of $18,300 for the farm from the proceeds of Federal loans and from about $2,500 of her individual funds; that in addition, she compromised other liens upon the property and borrowed $4,000 from her family which she expended for this purpose; that when an 80-acre tract was sold in 1938, the family loan was repaid and the balance applied upon the existing mortgages; that farm-loan installments and taxes were paid by amounts received from the farming operation; that she never promised to convey an interest in the property to defendant; and that no accounting had ever been made to her for crops produced on the premises.

Defendant testified that he and plaintiff each contributed $2,500 toward the initial purchase price of the farm upon the understanding that when all their bills were paid plaintiff would place title to the land in both their names as joint tenants. Although he claimed that his share of the purchase money was paid by check, it was later stipulated that plaintiff would testify that, upon examination of bank records and cancelled checks, no evidence of any such payment was found. Defendant stated that he managed the farm from the time of its purchase; used the proceeds therefrom to pay taxes, mortgage installments, and living expenses and was never asked by plaintiff for an accounting until the commencement of this litigation; that title to the farm was taken in plaintiff's name because he then had outstanding judgment creditors; and that the final mortgage payment of $5,000 was made by him from his individual funds.

Defendant's contentions as raised by the pleadings were that title to the farm was placed in plaintiff's name for convenience only, and defendant is the equitable owner thereof; that the deed to the plaintiff was for security purposes and should be considered as a mortgage; that plaintiff orally agreed to convey a joint tenancy interest in the premises to him; and that a trust arose from his contributions to the purchase price of the farm. However, in the brief filed herein, defendant has argued only that the alleged oral promise should be enforced, or a resulting or constructive trust declared.

Since record title to the land is in the name of the plaintiff, she is entitled to possession unless the defendant can show equitable ownership by reason of a constructive trust, a resulting trust, or an oral agreement to convey. The burden of proof in these respects is upon him, and since both the master and lower court have found for the plaintiff, their decision will be disturbed by this court only if against the manifest weight of the evidence.

From defendant's argument it is not clear whether he is contending that the facts establish a constructive or a resulting trust. To justify the declaration of a constructive trust, defendant must plead and prove either actual fraud or the abuse of a confidential relationship. We find no evidence in this record of actual fraud on the part of plaintiff, or that she abused a confidential relationship, and therefore defendant cannot prevail on this theory.

A resulting trust arises by operation of law and is founded on the presumed intent of the parties ascertained from their acts and attendant facts and circumstances, and usually comes into existence where one person furnishes the consideration, or an aliquot part thereof, for the purchase of property while the title is taken in the name of another, and it arises, if at all, at the instant legal title is taken and vests. Acts of the alleged trustee or equitable owner subsequent to the taking of title, have no bearing upon the question of whether a resulting trust was raised. Moreover, when payment is made by a husband and title taken in the name of the wife, it is presumed that the initial contributions were gifts to the wife, and while such presumption is rebuttable, it "is not to be frittered away by mere refinement." To justify the declaration of such trust, the evidence must be clear, convincing and unmistakable.

In the case at bar, the only evidence of an initial contribution by defendant was his assertion that he contributed $2,500 toward the purchase price of the farm, which was denied by plaintiff, and defendant produced no corroborative cancelled checks or other records. Nor is there any substantial evidence to rebut the presumption of a gift. Although defendant may have contributed some of his own funds to pay principal and interest on the mortgages, taxes and other expenses, such matters are not material to this issue. Consequently, the trial court did not err in refusing to declare a resulting trust.

For the reasons stated, the order of the trial court will be affirmed.

The above case states that when a husband purchases property and places it in the name of the wife, a rebuttable presumption arises that the transfer was a gift. The same is true if a father pays for property and takes title in the name of a child. However, if a wife purchases property and places it in the name of a husband, or a child purchases property and places it in the name of a parent, the law assumes that the intent of the wife or child was to create a trust for the benefit of the purchaser. Thus, a purchase money resulting trust is presumed.

STUDY QUESTIONS

1. What is the difference between real and personal property? How are they treated differently?

2. What is meant by an "estate in land"? How do leasehold and freehold estates differ?

3. What are the various kinds of fee estates, and how do they differ from life-hold estates?

4. What rights and duties does the holder of a life estate have? By whose life is a life estate measured?

5. What is the difference between a reversion and a remainder interest?

6. What is meant by co-ownership? What are the various types of co-ownership, and how do they differ?

7. What kind of co-ownership is presumed?

8. Describe the right of partition? What may be the result of a partition action?

9. What is a trust? What is the difference between an express trust, an implied trust, and a constructive trust?

10. D died leaving a will that included the following provision: "Fourth, I bequeath my farm, specifically described as the N½, Sec. 1, T. 6 N., R. 10 E. of the Third Principal Meridian, to L, for the rest of her natural life, then to my dear unrelated friends, A and B."

What "estate in land" does L acquire in the farm, assuming the will is given effect? What benefits of the land can be enjoyed by L as a result of her "estate in land?" Are A and B remaindermen or reversioners? L dies and A and B take possession of the property. Are A and B "joint tenants," "tenants by the entirety," or "tenants in common"? A demands that peanuts be grown on the property and B demands that grass be grown. The conflict is irreconcilable. They cannot reach voluntary agreement on how to divide the property. What civil action may either party bring to resolve this stalemate?

6

Acquiring and Disposing of Real Property

Most people are likely to become involved in some form of real estate transaction—either voluntarily as buyers or sellers of farmland, homes, or condominiums, or perhaps involuntarily through foreclosure or eminent domain. Certainly some basic knowledge of real estate transactions, deeds, legal descriptions, and ways of guaranteeing good title will be of value in buying or selling real estate. An understanding of the laws that govern the potential taking of property through eminent domain or adverse possession can give greater insight into how to protect property when confronted with these situations.

6.1 BRINGING BUYER AND SELLER TOGETHER

There are several methods by which a buyer and a seller of land can be brought together to complete a voluntary sale of farmland. The four most common methods are by private agreement, through a broker, by auction, and by sealed bid. These methods have varying applicability to transfers of farmland, differing legal characteristics, and unique methods of determining the selling price. Nevertheless, the four methods also have some similarities.

Private sales and brokerage sales appear to be the most popular methods, although there is a variation from region to region. A survey conducted in Illinois and published in 1973 indicated that private sales of farmland accounted for approximately 24 percent of the total farm sales in Illinois; brokerage sales, for some 58 percent; auction sales, for about 15 percent; sealed-bid sales and other methods, approximately 3 percent.[1]

Private Agreement

Perhaps the simplest method of selling land is to do so by private agreement. This method utilizes a contract between two individuals, usually without the intervention of a third party. A sale by private agreement is commonly used when the seller wants his or her land to go to a particular buyer, such as a sale from father to son, or when a particular buyer has a special interest in a certain parcel of land, such as where a development project is under way or where one neighbor is in the best position to merge the new land into an existing farming operation. In such situations, the potential buyer and seller are identified; the only unanswered questions are whether there will actually be a sale and, if so, at what price per acre.

The price-determining mechanism for the sale by private treaty is rather simple. It is basically a "take it or leave it" mechanism, with some room for bargaining. The buyer is pitted against seller, for they must decide on a price that is mutually acceptable. This procedure is in contrast to most other methods of selling land in which buyers are pitted against each other in some form of competitive bidding.

Since the market forces of a competitive bidding system are not available to help determine a market price in sales by private agreement, the buyer and the seller must rely on other techniques to determine a "fair" selling price. An appraisal based on expected returns from the land and on recent sales of similar properties is commonly used.

Through a Broker

Another method of transferring farmland is to sell it through a licensed broker. Selling farmland through a broker is an appropriate method in most situations. This is true when the present owner and the owner's broker have good information about the value of the property and when the property does not have to be sold by a particular date. Selling through a broker is similar to a sale by private agreement in that the sale price is determined by the buyer and seller rather than by competitive bidding, as is the case in a sale by auction or sealed bid. The broker method differs, however, in that numerous persons may look at the property and several offers from different persons may be made. Selling through a broker also differs from

---

[1] *Farm and Land Realtor*, Vol 25, No. 5 (May 1973).

other methods in that the broker is available to advise the seller as to what might be a reasonable sale price.

In most states, the real estate broker and the real estate salesperson are licensed. The licensing is done to help ensure the competency of those engaged in the real estate business. In most states, every person applying for a real estate license must pass an examination covering an understanding of deeds, mortgages, market prices, land contracts of sale, leases, and the legal obligation between principal and agent. The broker must act on the seller's behalf in good faith, with reasonable care, and with full disclosure of all relevant information.[2] Where a landowner learns that a broker is violating these duties, the landowner should advise the state licensing authority or the local board of realtors or both.

Since the broker will be acting as the agent of the seller and since the laws of many states require that such authority must be in writing when land is concerned, the contract (listing) between seller and broker should always be in writing. Such a writing also serves as a good record of all aspects of the agreement, including the type of listing to be used. There are four different ways to list real property with a broker: the open listing, the exclusive-agency listing, the exclusive-right-to-sell listing, and the multiple listing.

The *open listing* is one which typically states that the broker will be paid a commission when he finds a buyer who is ready, willing, and able to pay the price being

asked. The seller is allowed to use other brokers at the same time or to sell the property alone. Because of broker resistance, this type of listing is being used less and less.

The *exclusive-agency listing* is a contract by which only one broker is authorized to sell the property. That broker is protected as the sole agent of the seller, although the commission may be split with another broker who actually sells the property. It is important to note, however, that the owner retains the right to sell the property. A sale by the owner avoids any responsibility to pay a commission to the exclusive broker.

The *exclusive-right-to-sell listing* is generally sought by the broker. Under this procedure, the exclusive broker is entitled to the commission if the property is sold by anyone (that broker, another broker, or the owner) at the specified terms and within the specified time period covered by the listing.

The *multiple listing* is a pooling of exclusive-agency listings or exclusive-right-to-sell listings. Multiple-listing services are generally operated by real estate boards, subject to prior agreement among the participating brokers. That agreement describes how the commission will be divided between the listing broker and the one actually selling the property, if the property is sold.

The real estate broker earns a livelihood by the commission. For farm sales, the commission rates are usually between 3

---

[2] In *Duffy v. Setchell*, 38 Ill. App. 3d 146, 347 N.E. 2d 415 (1976), a broker acted as agent for both the buyer and the seller of a farm without disclosing this fact to the parties. The broker brought suit for his commission; the seller brought a third-party complaint, alleging the sale was void. In disallowing the broker's commission and in voiding the sale, the court stated: "If a buyer requests a broker's assistance in obtaining particular property, the broker may be held to be the buyer's agent for that transaction, even though the broker is only paid by the seller. If the broker also becomes the seller's agent, the broker has conflicting duties and will not be able to act for both without the knowledge and consent of both. A contract negotiated by an agent for both parties is voidable by a principal who did not have knowledge of the double agency."

and 6 percent of the selling price depending on the circumstance—size of tract, amount of improvements, and the like. In order to earn the commission, it is generally sufficient if the broker finds a potential buyer who is ready, willing, and able to purchase the property according to the terms specified in the original brokerage agreement and within the time period covered by the listing. As long as these conditions are met, the broker is generally entitled to the commission even though the seller refuses to sell to the particular buyer for some personal reason.[3]

Auction

By definition, an *auction* is a public sale of property to the highest bidder. This method is familiar to most persons because of the public notices circulated in preparation for an auction. The type of auction generally used in the United States is the ascending-bid auction. However, other forms of auctions do exist. The Dutch auction, for example, is a public offer of property in which the auctioneer starts the bidding at a price considerably higher than the reasonable value of the property and offers to sell at successively lower bids until one of the prospective buyers accepts. The Japanese auction is still another form. In that type of auction, all bids are made simultaneously, and the highest bid wins. The Japanese system is used in the sale of fish in Japan, where the bidding is done by simultaneous hand signs. The system has some similarity to the American sealed-bid system, which will be discussed later.

Whether the owner of land should sell property at auction rather than by some other method depends largely on the circumstances. The auction seems appropriate when competition for the particular property already exists, when the sale must be made by a certain date (such as a fixed date by which executors hope to close an estate), or when the value of the land is not known and the auction will be used as the determining mechanism. Using an auction is probably not appropriate when the landowner has an exaggerated view of the property's value or when the owner is not necessarily committed to selling the property. In such situations, an auction would probably result in an aborted sale.

An auction may be accomplished with or without reserve. If the auction is with reserve, the seller has the right either to "bid in" the property if dissatisfied with the highest bid or to establish a price below which the property is not to be sold. If the property is being sold without reserve, the seller must sell the property to the highest bidder no matter how dissatisfied the seller is with the price. Although it may be safer to sell property with reserve, it can be argued that an auction without reserve will attract more bidders and may result in a higher sale price.

Auctions are subject to regulation by the state. Many states require that auctioneers be licensed and that they post a bond. Other states have passed legislation allowing the individual municipality to license auctioneers. In either case, the right of the state or the municipality to regulate auctions is based on the state's inherent power to prevent fraud and abuse.

---

[3] In *Garrett v. Babb*, 24 Ill. App. 3d 941 (1975), a broker sued for his commission, even though the purchaser whom the broker had obtained did not purchase the farm. In a decision favorable to the broker the court noted: "Where a broker is employed to sell property by the owner, if he produces a purchaser within the time limited by his authority who is ready, willing and able to purchase the property upon the terms proposed by the seller he is entitled to his commission, even though the seller refuses to perform the contract...."

Several other principles of law have evolved regarding auctions. The courts have generally held, for example, that use of a puffer will not be condoned by the law. A *puffer* is a person employed by the seller to raise the price by making fictitious bids. The puffer is protected by a secret understanding with the seller to the effect that the puffer will not be bound by bids made. On the other hand, price-depressing activities by potential buyers are also illegal.

In one case, the property of a deceased person was being sold at public auction. The son of the deceased man was hired by a private party to act as the private party's agent. Sympathetic people who wanted to buy the property did not want to bid against the son, who appeared to be buying back the family property. Because the private party who employed the son used this "chilling" tactic for his own gain, the court found that it was a case of restricting the bidding.

The fees charged for auctioning real property are usually a percentage of the sale price. In some instances, a different rate is applied for improved property than for unimproved property. The size of the tract is also an important consideration. The fee usually ranges from 3 to 6 percent, as with the use of a broker.

The role played by the auctioneer can vary. The auctioneer may actually have the power to complete the sale and to bind the seller with the fall of the hammer. In that case, the auctioneer is also likely to be a licensed real estate broker, as would be required by many states. On the other hand, the auctioneer may simply have the task of finding the person who is willing to pay the highest price. Once the high bidder is found, that person and the seller's attorney are brought together to complete the contract for sale. The auctioneer does not actually sell the property, but merely brings the highest bidder and the seller together face to face. Since the auctioneer does not actually sell the property, some courts have held that a license is not necessary.

Sealed Bid

A final method of bringing the buyer and seller together is by sealed bids. The primary difference between a sale by sealed bids and by auction is that with the sealed-bid method the potential buyers can bid only once and without knowledge of competitors' bids. Thus, the bidders are, for the most part, in an information vacuum. As a result, many prospective buyers do not like this method.

In some local areas a "hybrid" method of sealed bidding has developed. Initially, this method resembles the usual sealed-bid procedure. However, once the sealed bids are opened the persons submitting bids are allowed to make oral bids, just as if an auction sale were being conducted. In effect, this hybrid method is identical to the auction method except that a person must have submitted a sealed bid in order to become part of the auction.

In conclusion, from the standpoint of price determination, selling farmland by auction and by sealed bid are similar in the sense that under both methods, numerous prospective buyers are competing against one another. Selling through a broker and selling by private agreement are similar in that both employ a price-determining mechanism through which one buyer and one seller try to reach agreement between themselves.

From the legal standpoint, the character of the various methods can vary. For example, both brokers and auctioneers are generally subject to regulation by the state. In addition, both may have certain duties of acting in good faith with the seller, acting with reasonable care on the seller's behalf, and fully disclosing all relevant information.

All four methods also have a number of similarities. Most states require the actual contract for sale to be in writing and signed by both parties if that contract is to be enforceable in the courts against either party. Also, regardless of the method, the property must ultimately be deeded from the seller to the buyer in a manner employing all of the typical formalities—a writing delivered to the buyer containing the names of both parties, the signature of the seller, the words of transfer, and a legal description of the property.

An attorney should be retained by each party to a real estate transaction to provide appropriate legal advice and to prepare and review all formal legal documents. The importance of the attorney in real estate transactions will be more apparent in the following sections and in later chapters on income and estate tax management.

6.2 SHORT-TERM REAL ESTATE CONTRACTS

Real estate contracts can be divided into (1) short-term contracts, typically of several months' duration, which will culminate in a transfer of legal title and possession at some future date; and (2) long-term contracts, under which the buyer takes possession but the seller retains title, typically for many years, until the final installment payment is made. This section deals primarily with the short-term contract. The long-term contract, or installment contract, will be discussed in Chapter 11 as a method of financing the purchase of farmland.

A *contract of sale* is an agreement to acquire or to dispose of property at some specified date. Both parties to the contract are bound by its terms. If one fails to perform, the other has a right of action, for either damages or specific performance, or both. Under the statute of frauds, con-

tracts for the sale of real estate must be in writing to be enforceable. Frequently the real estate agent prepares a simple memorandum containing all the essential facts. This may serve to make the agreement binding, but is not likely to settle all the questions which should be settled between buyer and seller before final agreement is reached. While such a brief memorandum may sometimes work to the advantage of one or the other of the parties by making the agreement binding, it may limit the ability of either buyer or seller (usually the buyer) to insist on conditions and agreements which would further clarify the transfer and more clearly delineate the rights of the parties.

Besides the usual elements necessary for creation of the contractual relation, a contract for the sale of farm real estate should contain the following items:

1. The purchase price and when and how it is to be paid
2. The date of possession
3. A complete and accurate legal description
4. A statement regarding any right reserved by the seller (such as minerals or growing crops)
5. How taxes, assessments, and insurance are to be apportioned
6. How rental payment shall be divided if there is a tenant on the land, and an agreement either to end the tenancy in time to give possession by the date agreed or agreement by the purchaser to accept the tenancy
7. How government payments which may be due shall be apportioned
8. Agreement by the seller to furnish an abstract and permit sufficient time for the purchaser to examine it and notify the seller of title defects which should be cured
9. An agreement about any improvements which may cause doubt (temporary

fencing or a movable brooder house, for example)

10. A statement regarding any easements which may exist in the property, particularly easements of way or drainage

11. A statement regarding escrow arrangements if escrow is involved

Escrow Arrangements

An *escrow* is a deed or other document deposited with a third person, to be delivered upon the happening of an event. The deed or other instrument itself imposes the obligations or conditions that must be met before delivery of the deed or instrument. The third person serving as a depositary is called the *escrow agent*.

Escrows are used most commonly in the purchase of real estate. After the seller and buyer have entered into a contract for sale and the buyer has made a deposit on the purchase price, some time elapses before the transaction is closed by payment of the full price and transfer of title. This time is needed to bring the abstract to date, to have it examined for defects, and to have these defects corrected. Also, time may elapse while the buyer secures a loan to cover the purchase price. During this time several things—such as death, marriage, or divorce of the seller—can occur, which might adversely affect the transaction and make it difficult, if not impossible, to complete. By using an escrow, the parties protect themselves against happenings that could affect the title and completion of the deal. This is especially true from the standpoint of the buyer.

Basically, escrow works in this way: The seller deposits a warranty deed and a copy of the contract of sale with the escrow agent. The escrow agent may record the deed from the seller to the buyer immediately—allowing the buyer to secure a purchase money mortgage—or recording

may be delayed. In either case, when the terms of the escrow agreement indicate that all conditions have been met, the buyer receives the deed and other documents and the seller gets the purchase money.

Option Contracts

An *option contract* is one by which the owner of property agrees with another person that the latter shall have the right to buy the former's property at a fixed price within a certain time. The owner sells the right or privilege to buy at the option of the other party. The second party gets the right to buy the land at the price specified, but is not obligated to do so.

Usual Steps Involved in Purchase of Real Estate

Table 6.1 summarizes the numerous steps typically involved in the purchase of real estate by cash sale, loan and mortgage, or conditional or installment sale.

Real Estate Contract Problems

The following cases deal with some of the issues that can arise in contracts for the sale of real estate. The first issue discussed is whether a purchaser of real estate can obtain specific performance as a remedy when only one of several co-owners has executed the contract.

Damages are a more typical remedy in contract law, but a court can decree specific performance in cases where damages cannot make the plaintiff whole, such as where unique parcels of real estate are involved. Other cases deal with situations of whether growing crops follow the land in a sale of real estate and whether one who contracts to purchase real estate may or may not be entitled to a refund of the down payment after having a "change of heart."

Table 6.1   Usual Steps Involved in Purchase of Real Estate

Cash Sale	Loan and Mortgage	Conditional Sale of Installment
Negotiation for sale	Negotiation for sale	Negotiation for sale
	Negotiation for loan	
Contract of sale and down payment (there may be an escrow arrangement)	Contract of sale and down payment (there may be an escrow arrangement)	Contract of sale (there may or may not be a down payment); escrow agreement
Abstract or title insurance commitment furnished	Abstract or title insurance commitment furnished	Abstract or title insurance commitment furnished
Abstract or title insurance commitment examined	Abstract or title insurance commitment examined	Abstract or title insurance commitment examined
Title opinion or opinion regarding commitment	Title opinion or opinion regarding commitment	Title opinion or opinion regarding commitment
(Title cleared)	(Title cleared)	(Title cleared)
(Prior claims paid and released)	(Prior claims paid and released)	(Prior claims paid and released)
(Title guaranty policy—if desired or contracted for)	(Title guaranty policy—if desired or contracted for) Mortgage and note executed	(Title guaranty policy—if desired or contracted for)
Warranty deed delivered and balance of price paid	Warranty deed delivered and any additional down payment paid	Warranty deed placed in escrow Installments paid Warranty deed delivered after last installment or a specified amount is paid
Deed recorded	Deed and mortgage recorded	Deed recorded
	Loan paid	Note: If deed is delivered before the full amount is paid, a note and mortgage is usually given as security to the seller.
	Mortgage released	

UNDIVIDED INTEREST—SPECIFIC PERFORMANCE

ENNIS v. JOHNSON
Supreme Court of Illinois, 1954
3 Ill. 2d 383, 121 N.E. 2d 480

This is a direct appeal by defendant, Ernest Johnson, from a decree of the circuit court of Cook County ordering him to convey his undivided half interest in certain improved real property, held in joint tenancy with his wife, to plaintiff, John Ennis, pursuant to an alleged contract for the sale of the entire premises.

The cause presents for our determination the issue of whether the purchaser is entitled to specific performance to the extent of the vendor's undivided half interest in certain improved real property held in joint tenancy, where the alleged contract is for the sale of the entire property, but signed only by one joint tenant.

Defendant urges that the circuit court erred in decreeing specific performance, inasmuch as a contract may be specifically enforced according to its terms or not at all, and that the remedy will not be granted as to a one-half interest in property held in joint tenancy where the contract was for the entire premises and would have to be substantially reformed by the court to give effect to the various equities between the parties.

Plaintiff, however, argues that specific performance of a contract to convey real estate may be granted as to whatever title the vendor may have in the property, with a proportionate abatement of the purchase price.

We find no authority that supports defendant in his position that he cannot be compelled to convey his interest in the property to the vendee. There is no doubt that plaintiff contemplated the purchase of the entire property held in joint tenancy by Ernest and Olga Johnson. For aught that appears, Ernest Johnson, at the time he executed the contract, thought that his wife would join him in the conveyance. The fact that Ernest Johnson failed to perform in accordance with the terms of his written agreement should not provide him with an excuse for not doing that which was within his power to do.

In the case of *Moore v. Gariglietti*, 228 Ill. 143, there was a contract by Marian Moore to sell twenty acres of land when at the time she was the owner of only a two-fifths interest. The owners of the remaining interest did not join in the contract to sell. It was there contended that if the contract was one for a conveyance of the whole tract, it was erroneous for the court to decree the conveyance of the title to an undivided part of the premises. The court, rejecting this contention, said, "An agreement by one tenant in common to convey the whole of the joint property cannot be enforced against his co-tenants, but may be enforced as to his interest in the premises."

A joint tenancy, even though the joint tenants are husband and wife, is severed when one joint tenant conveys his or her interest to a stranger. We fail to find any merit in appellant's contention that the contract under consideration was so vague, incomplete and ambiguous that it was incapable of being enforced. The purchase price was $21,000. There was a mortgage indebtedness, tax items, and rental adjustments. The process of prorating and making computations was a matter of simple arithmetic. There was nothing indefinite about the contract that left to the chancellor a remaking of the agreement based on guess and conjecture. Specific performance of a contract to convey real estate may be granted as to whatever title the vendor may have in the property, with a proportionate abatement of the purchase price commensurate with the interest of the vendor in the whole.

In the light of the foregoing analysis, the decree entered herein should be and is affirmed.

Could one defend a suit for specific performance on the grounds that the money paid was too low? In *Hotze v. Schlanser*, 410 Ill. 265, 102 N.E.2d 131 (1951), plaintiffs sought specific performance of a contract for the sale of real estate by the defendant to the plaintiff. The defendant contended that the purchase price was much less than the land was worth. The court held for the plaintiff. "It is the general rule that inadequacy of consideration, exorbitance of price, or improvidence in a contract will not, in the absence of fraud, constitute a defense for specific performance."

GROWING CROPS

FIREBAUGH v. DIVAN
Supreme Court of Illinois, 1904
207 Ill. 287, 69 N.E. 924

This is an action begun in the circuit court of Champaign County by the appellant, against the appellee. The complaint alleged that on the 21st day of October, 1902, the plaintiff sold and delivered to the defendant a certain piece of real estate, and conveyed the same to him by warranty; that at the time of said sale the plaintiff had standing upon said land the corn that was grown thereon that year; that while said corn was still undetached from the soil, it was, nevertheless, fully matured and ready for gathering and cribbing at the time of said sale; that said corn was not reserved or mentioned in said deed; that a few days after said deed was delivered plaintiff sought to remove the corn but was prevented from so doing by the defendant; that the defendant gathered the corn and converted the same to his own use, to the damage of the plaintiff of the sum of $300. Judgment was rendered in favor of the defendant. The plaintiff appealed to the Appellate Court for the Third District, where the judgment was affirmed, and a certificate of importance having been granted by the Appellate Court, a further appeal has been made to this court.

John J. Rea, attorney, arguing for appellant:

A conveyance of land, either by voluntary deed or judicial sale, without reservation, carries all growing crops with the title to the land. This rule only applies to crops which are immature and have not ceased to draw nutriment from the soil at the time of the sale, and is not applicable to crops that are ripe and ready for harvest. This distinction has been carefully recognized in all the cases where the subject was considered.

Crops ripe for the harvest are personal property. They pass to the executor, and not to the heir. They are liable to be seized on execution, and the officer may enter, cut down, seize and sell the same as other personal estate.

A conveyance of realty carries the annual crops, but crops that are ripe and ready for harvest will not, being unmentioned in the deed, pass thereby as realty.

F.M Green and Son, attorneys, arguing for appellee:

Matured crops, if severed from the soil, become personalty, and do not pass by a deed; but crops not severed, whether ripe or unripe, pass to the vendee by the deed, as being annexed to and forming a part of the freehold.

The general rule of the common law is, that growing crops form a part of the real estate to which they are attached and from which they draw nourishment, and unless there has been a constructive severance of them from the land they follow the title thereto.

Mr. Chief Justice Hand delivered the opinion of the court:

The law in this State is well settled that, as between vendor and vendee, growing crops produced by annual planting and cultivation are real estate, and pass to the vendee unless they are reserved in the deed or by other writing executed simultaneously with the deed. This is conceded by the appellant to be the general rule, but it is contended where the crops are fully matured at the time of the execution of the deed and are ready to be severed from the soil they do not pass to the vendee, but that the title thereto remains in the vendor, and he may afterwards enter upon the land and remove the same, and if they are gathered by the vendee and converted to his use he is liable to the vendor for their value. We do not agree with such contention, but are of the opinion, upon principle and authority, that there is no distinction in this particular between crops, whether mature or immature, standing upon the land at the time of the conveyance. A deed, when delivered, transfers to the grantee all the interest of the grantor in the land not reserved and entitles the grantee to possession. The title to the crops then standing upon the land, not severed from the soil, whether ripe or unripe, passes to the vendee as a part of the land. By the delivery of the deed the vendor loses all dominion over the land.

The judgment of the Appellate Court will be affirmed.

Growing annual crops are actually personal property, but title to the crops follows the real estate if nothing is stated in the contract regarding this issue. It should be noted that the above case does not involve crops planted by a tenant. The tenant is the owner of the crops planted on rented land. Such crops belong to neither the buyer nor the seller of the real estate.

TIMELINESS OF PERFORMANCE

CHRISTOPHER v. WEST
Supreme Court of Illinois, 1951
409 Ill. 131, 98 N.E. 2d 722

Christopher sued West in the circuit court of Sangamon County for the return of a down payment made as earnest money on the purchase of certain real estate. For convenience and to avoid confusion we shall refer to the parties as Christopher and West, or as "purchaser" and "seller."

The trial court directed a verdict in favor of the purchaser and against the seller. On appeal to the Appellate Court, that court reversed the circuit court without remanding, *on the sole ground that a tender was necessary* from the purchaser to the seller (which was not made), of the balance of the purchase price, coupled with a demand for performance as a condition precedent to instituting suit. We granted leave to appeal.

West was a resident of Iroquois County and the land, situated there, was sold at public sale on February 22, 1946, at the courthouse in Ford County. Christopher was a resident of Sangamon County. Immediately following the sale a written contract was entered into, whereby West agreed to convey by good and sufficient warranty deed the land contracted for and to furnish an abstract of title and allow second party reasonable time to have same examined. It was further provided that after the examination was made, the seller should within a reasonable time correct any defects in the title "and shall make such abstract show a merchantable title." The purchaser agreed to pay in all $27,076.50, and down payment of $4,061.47 was paid as earnest money.

Time was of the essence and the covenants extended to their heirs, executors, administrators and assigns. The contract was dated February 22, 1946. Christopher entered into possession soon thereafter, and on May 15 West delivered to him an abstract under date of May 8. On May 20, a "preliminary" opinion of title was sent to West, claiming title was unmerchantable. The main objection concerned a failure to serve sufficient notice of the petition to probate the will on one Logan A. Gridley, deceased, who appeared in the chain of title. West proposed certain measures to cure the objections, which were not acceptable to Christopher. On July 2, the latter advised West by registered mail of his rescission of the agreement and demanded return of the down payment, interest thereon, and expenses incurred. The basis of this rescission was that West had not within a reasonable time made the title merchantable as specified in the preliminary opinion, and that he could not do so within a reasonable time. *Possession was relinquished about August 1.*

On August 13, West instituted suit in Iroquois County, where the land is situated, to quiet and confirm title in him, and a decree to that effect was entered on November 15. Shortly thereafter, on November 22, the parties at the request of West met with their respective attorneys in Springfield, and West tendered a warranty deed, signed by himself and wife, and an abstract of title continued to November 18, showing the quiet-title proceedings and decree. This tender Christopher refused, on the ground the same was not tendered within a reasonable time as contemplated by the agreement. He insisted the title was not merchantable at the time of the examination, and West did not make it so within a reasonable time after the expiration of the ninety days and the tender of November 22 was beyond the expiration of a reasonable time. This suit was started in January, 1947.

Under the agreement, West was obligated to convey fee-simple title by warranty deed. He contracted only to deliver an abstract of title to afford the purchaser an opportunity to ascertain the condition of the title and to enable the seller to correct any defects therein within a reasonable time. Payment was to be made, it is true, within ninety days and time was declared, by the contract, to be of the essence thereof. Christopher erroneously construes the contract as though West had agreed to deliver an abstract showing merchantable title within the time fixed for payment. An analysis of the contract discloses this was not the expressed agreement of the parties. West under the terms thereof was to warrant only that title the abstract ultimately had to show, namely, a merchantable title. Such title need not necessarily be a perfect record title without fault, defect or omission. Differences of opinion as to the merchantability may, and frequently do, arise among attorneys astute in title matters; but whenever the abstract, together with explanatory affidavits, evidences an indefeasible title in fee simple, whether had by deed, devise or by the Statute of Limitations, there is a merchantable title.

Aside from the question of merchantability or non-merchantability of this particular title at the time the same was raised by the "preliminary" opinion of Christopher, and even assuming the objections were well taken, West still had a right to be definitely advised as to their nature and whether or not the purchaser desired to waive some or even all of the objections, as he had a right to do. Under the circumstances here, neither party made a tender of performance within the ninety-day period set for the payment of the full purchase price, and such nonaction constituted a waiver and a mutual negation of the requirement that time of payment as specified thereunder was of the essence of the agreement. Acts and statements of the two show they both considered the agreement to have otherwise retained all of its vitality subsequent to that date, and that the transaction was to be fully closed within a reasonable time thereafter. The purported letter or rescission of July 2 at least confirmed West in the belief the defects complained of were of sufficient import to cause the purchaser to refuse title if the same were not cured. He immediately, or at least within a reasonable time, proceeded to correct these defects by bill to quiet title, and accomplished this result as soon thereafter as could reasonably be expected.

Judgment for seller.

FRAUD

MCMEEN v. WHIPPLE
Supreme Court of Illinois, 1961
23 Ill. 2d 352, 178 N.E. 2d 351

Plaintiffs contend that they were induced to make an exchange of real estate by false representations of Whipple and were thereby defrauded. The alleged false statements were: that the farm had a market value of $20,000 to $22,000 invested in the farm when in fact his investment was less than

$10,000; that he misrepresented the amount of the landlord's share of crops; and that there was a means of access to the farm by a public highway or roadway, whereas there is none.

The defendants maintain that valuation statements were mere "puffing." They further say that plaintiffs inspected the farm, had the duty to ascertain the means of access, and that the doctrine of caveat emptor applies.

While there is some dispute, a fair reading of the record discloses the following facts. The parties arrived at the farm late in the afternoon on Thanksgiving day. They drove onto the land a few car lengths, reaching it from the north by driving down an adjacent owner's lane over a rickety bridge and through a gate. When asked if that was the only way in, Whipple told them that there was a public highway or roadway on the south side of the farm across the creek which ran through the land, and that they had used a short cut. The creek was impassable by automobile. The women stayed near the car and the men walked out onto the farm a short distance. The parties remained only a short time and plaintiffs' inspection was cursory because of impending darkness. They were never shown the public highway or road which Whipple indicated furnished access to the land from the south.

There is no public highway or public road adjacent to the subject land. In fact, there is neither proof of the location of the nearest public road nor the exact location of even a private road which would furnish access. The land in question was originally the northerly part of a farm owned by one Daniel Yeoman. It was separated from the remainder by deed dated December 10, 1927, to a predecessor in title, which deed was silent as to access. On the same day the remainder of the original farm was conveyed and that deed recited: "There shall be free ingress and egress to the land adjoining on the north that was part of the Dan Yeoman Estate at the date of this deed, providing gates are kept closed."

The question presented at the outset is whether defendant Whipple's untrue representation that a public highway or road furnished access to the land constitutes fraud which would justify rescission. Under the decisions a false representation of a material existing fact, made with the intention to deceive, either knowing it to be false or making it in culpable ignorance of its truth or falsity, which was believed and justifiably relied upon by the other party to his injury, is actionable. The representation was false, since the only access was over the land of another with the burden of passing through and keeping gates closed. It involved a material fact. Its purpose was to misinform and deceive. It is not certain that Whipple knew the representation to be false since he testified that he had never seen the road. However, he had owned the land for two years and should have known that the statement was false. Plaintiffs suffered injury, since it is a matter of common knowledge that land without an outlet to a public way is less valuable. That the representation was believed and relied upon by plaintiffs is evidenced by the fact that they entered into the exchange without examining the premises until the day following such exchange.

The remaining problem is whether plaintiffs were justified in relying upon the statement without attempting to ascertain its truth. "In determining this question, the representations must be viewed in the light of all the facts of which the plaintiff had actual notice, and also for such as he might have availed himself by the exercise of ordinary prudence." Here, plaintiffs had done business with Whipple before and he had given them no reason to distrust him. Because of approaching darkness, they apparently did not have time to drive around to check for a public road. They lived a long distance from the farm and from each other. Defendant Whipple was pressing for an early closing and succeeded in getting an exchange just four days later. Under such circumstances we are of the opinion plaintiffs were justified in relying upon Whipple's word and that they were not negligent in failing to make a further independent investigation.

We find no error, and accordingly the decree of the circuit court of Bureau County granting rescission is affirmed in all respects.

6.3 DEEDS AND WARRANTIES

A *deed* is an instrument used to transfer legal title to real estate from the grantor to the grantee. Compared to real estate contracts, the deed appears to be much simpler, as is illustrated by the short-form warranty deed in use in Illinois shown in Figure 6.1.[4]

The four parts of a deed can also be seen in the form. The *premises* contains the names of the grantor and grantee, the operative words of conveyance, a recital of consideration, and a legal description of the land. The *habendum* describes the estate to be taken by the grantee, such as a life estate or a fee simple, and often is inserted after the legal description. If a description of the estate is omitted, most states presume a fee simple has been granted. The *executur* contains the date and signature of the grantor. The seal of the grantor and the signatures of witnesses were required at common law, but generally are not required today. The *acknowledgment* contains the attestation of a notary public or other public official and is required for the recordation of the deed.

The statutes of many states provide additional requirements for recordation to facilitate tax collection and other matters. Such statutes may require that any deed or instrument of conveyance that requires recording shall have printed or typed beside or below all signatures the names of all parties signing each instrument; that the name and address of the person to whom the tax bill shall be sent shall appear on a new deed or instrument of conveyance; that the name and address of the person preparing the document appear on the face of the document; that a newly executed instrument of conveyance which describes the property by metes and bounds have a general description locating the property in the proper quarter section or lot, or lot and block, preceding the metes and bounds description.[5] Typically, failure to comply

---

[4] ILL. REV. STAT. ch. 30, § 8 (1979).

[5] *See, e.g.,* ILL. REV. STAT. ch. 115, §§ 9.2, 9.3 (1979).

DOCUMENT NO. ________________

For Recorder's Certificate Only

WARRANTY DEED

THE GRANTOR__, Mary M. Rancher, a widow not since remarried,

of the city of Philo, in the County of Champaign, and State of Illinois, for and in consideration of Ten Dollars ($10.00) and other good and valuable consideration in hand paid, **CONVEY**S AND **WARRANT**S *to* the **GRANTEE**S, Timothy T. Farmer and Sharon R. Farmer, husband and wife

of the city of Urbana, County of Champaign, and State of Illinois, the following described real estate:

The Northwest Quarter (NW 1/4) of the Southwest Quarter (SW 1/4) of Section Five (5), Township Seven (7) South, Range Five (5) West of the 3rd Principal Meridian, Randolph County, Illinois, containing forty (40) acres more or less.

Subject to: **(1) Real estate taxes for the year 1980 and subsequent years;**
(2) Covenants, conditions, restrictions and easements apparent or of record;
(3) All applicable zoning laws and ordinances;

hereby releasing and waiving all rights under and by virtue of the Homestead Exemption Laws of the State of Illinois.

Dated this 15th day of January, 1981.

/s/ Mary M. Rancher

Mary M. Rancher

STATE OF ILLINOIS }
CHAMPAIGN COUNTY } SS

I, the undersigned, a Notary Public in and for said County and State aforesaid, **DO HEREBY CERTIFY**, that Mary M. Rancher personally known to me to be the same person__ whose name__ is subscribed to the foregoing instrument, appeared before me this day in person and acknowledged that She signed, sealed and delivered the said instrument as her free and voluntary act, for the uses and purposes therein set forth, including the waiver of the right of homestead.

Given under my hand and Notarial Seal, this 15th day of January, A.D. 1981.

(SEAL)

/s/ Donald L. Uchtmann Notary Public

Figure 6–1 Warranty Deed

with any of these special provisions will not invalidate the instrument.

Warranty and Quitclaim Deeds

Warranty Deeds.   In a warranty deed, such as the one illustrated, certain warranties or covenants are implied. The exact nature of these covenants may vary slightly from state to state, but the following covenants are typical:

1.   At the time the deed was delivered the seller had an *indefeasible estate* (estate free of claims), in fee simple, with the right and power to convey (that is, to transfer) the real estate described.

2.   The property was at that time free from encumbrances (claims or liens), except as noted in the instrument.

3.   The buyer will have quiet and peaceable possession, and the seller will defend the title against all persons lawfully claiming it.

Quitclaim Deeds.   The warranties or covenants noted above are implied in a warranty deed only. Such warranties are not present in a quitclaim deed, which is used primarily to clear titles. All who have even a remote interest in the property—often an interest too minor to be of any value—relinquish it by making a quitclaim deed to one person. That person then holds, if all interests are thus transferred to him or her, a clear title to the property.

The quitclaim deed is effective to transfer whatever interest the grantor held in the property. Thus, one can acquire legal title through a quitclaim deed if the grantor had legal title. However, if the grantor did not have legal title, the grantee cannot collect from the grantor on the basis of the implied warranties, because such warranties are absent in a quitclaim deed. Also,

the quitclaim deed generally does not convey any rights acquired by the grantor after the execution of the deed unless the deed specifically so states.

The form for a quitclaim deed is almost identical to the warranty deed, except the former uses the language "conveys and quitclaims" instead of "conveys and warrants."

Recording Deeds

Each state designates some county official to act as recorder of deeds. This function may be performed by a county or circuit clerk, along with other duties, or by an official whose only function is to maintain records of deeds, mortgages, and other documents affecting real estate. These officials—often called the *recorders of deeds*—have the duty of keeping a permanent record of deeds and other eligible legal instruments offered for recording. At one time these documents were copied at length, either by hand or by typewriter. The copies were then filed for record. Modern science has assisted the recorder in performing this task, and now it is permissible for the recorder to make photocopies of all or parts of instruments if the copies are complete and intelligible.

Recorders often are required by law to keep certain books. These may include (1) an entry book showing the names of the parties appearing on each instrument, the month, hour, and year of receipt, and a brief description of the premises; (2) a grantor's index showing the name of each grantor in alphabetical order, the date and type of instrument, and other details; (3) a grantee index; (4) an index to each book of record; and (5) an index to recorded maps, plats, and subdivisions. In addition, the recorder may be required to keep a "tract index" showing a true chain of title to each tract of land as shown by the records.

The general public is entitled to examine the records and to make notes or memoranda at any time during the hours the recorder's office is open. However, the recorder usually is not required to assist persons in making notes nor to make duplicates or copies of instruments, unless it is done for a uniform fee as part of routine business.

All deeds—whether warranty, quitclaim, trust, or mortgage—and all. mortgage or trust deed releases must be recorded to protect the purchaser, grantee, or releasee.

Deeds of Gift and Deeds Effective at Death

Deeds of Gift.   Passing farmland on to the next generation is one of the privileges given by law to farm owners in the United States. Most property owners are familiar in a general way with the law of descent and the possibility of disposing of property by making a will. But few have considered the desirability of making lifetime transfers that will fix the title to their property long before they die.

There are several situations in which a lifetime transfer should be considered: when there is only one heir and the owner is financially able to make a conveyance; when there are several heirs and they agree on a family settlement in advance of the owner's death; when one heir agrees to remain at home and support the parents, and they wish for that reason to convey title to that person; and in cases where death taxes would be substantially reduced by making a lifetime gift. Also, when an owner is able to convey property during the owner's lifetime, it gives the heir an earlier interest in the property and may help the heir much more than a gift of the farm effective at the death of the owner.

This same reasoning applies to the transfer of personal property.

To accomplish a lifetime disposition, a deed rather than a will is the appropriate instrument. Either personal property or real estate may be transferred by a "deed of gift," and no money payment has to be made to make the deed binding. A deed to transfer personal property can be an informal instrument and need not be acknowledged and recorded like a deed to real estate.

When there are several heirs and the parents wish to convey the farm to one son or daughter, they may have a deed prepared that will give the son or daughter an heir's interest but will require the other heirs to be paid some amount specified in the deed. Or the parents may make an installment contract to sell the farm to a son or daughter, using the installments to make equalizing gifts to the other children. Such arrangements can usually be worked out more equitably than those made at the time of the owner's death, and they tend toward greater family interest and continuity with regard to the land itself.

Certainly in all situations where the owner promises the farm to an heir in return for care and support and there are other heirs in the family, a deed is one option for accomplishing the transfer. Federal gift tax consequences should be considered along with other legal ramifications of such transfers.

Deeds Effective at Death.   Persons sometimes execute warranty deeds during their lives in an attempt to transfer real estate at the time of their death. The deed or deeds are placed in a safety deposit box or kept at home with a notation "to be given to my son John (or daughter Mary) at my death." Occasionally a deed is given to a friend with directions that the deed be given to John or Mary at the owner's death, unless the deed is recalled by the owner.

Many times a deed effective at death will convey the property as intended, simply because no one contests its validity. But some deeds of this kind are challenged, and the courts often hold them invalid. When a deed effective at death is held invalid, the property passes to the heirs according to the laws of descent—unless the deceased had a will, in which case it may pass according to the terms of the will. In either case it is possible that the property will not go to the persons intended by the deceased.

The reason that these deeds often fail is because the person is trying to evade the law, which sets forth in considerable detail the method for transferring property at death. The necessary instrument is a will. If a will is not used, then the attempted transfer to take effect at death is likely to fail. Since a will must be executed in accordance with statutory requirements (witnesses are usually necessary), a deed is ineffective to do the same job. A deed is signed and acknowledged but usually not witnessed.

However, it is possible to transfer real estate effective at death using a lifetime deed. One way is to convey a remainder interest by deed reserving a life estate. This method allows the owner to use the property and take the income during the owner's life. At death of the owner, the property goes to the holder of the remainder interest. Another way is to place a warranty deed in the hands of an uninterested party with written directions covering disposition. If the deed cannot be recalled, it is considered a present transfer with possession retained by the owner for life.

DEEDS—MINOR

SHEPHERD v. SHEPHERD
Supreme Court of Illinois, 1951
408 Ill. 364, 97 N.E. 2d 273

On December 3, 1946, Robert Shepherd presented a quit claim deed to his mother and requested her to execute the deed reconveying to him the interest in the farm which he had conveyed to her on June 8, 1942. Late the same day, at his attorney's office, Robert handed his mother a written document, notifying her that he had rescinded and declared void the deed of June 8, 1942, conveying to her a life estate, demanded cancellation of the deed, a reconveyance, and an accounting to him of all rents, issues, profits and income received by her from the property since the day named. The next day, December 4, 1946, Robert Shepherd and his son, Robert Eugene Shepherd, Jr., by his father and next friend, brought an action in the circuit court of Sangamon County against the defendants, Helen B. Shepherd and Minnie S. Shepherd.

The master-in-chancery to whom the cause was referred made his revised report, finding that Robert Shepherd, upon attaining twenty-one years of age, was vested with an undivided one-half interest in the property, subject to the life estate of his mother; that, having conveyed a life estate during minority, Robert had the right to rescind his action; that "This was done"; that the deed to his mother, insofar as it affects the interest of Robert conveyed to her for life, had, by his rescission, been avoided, and that she should reconvey an undivided one-half of her life interest to him and account to him for one-half of the rents since his repudiation of the deed on December 3, 1946. The chancellor sustained objections to the master's report, and entered a decree adjudging that the mother held a life estate in the property by virtue of the deed from her son.

A deed executed by a minor is not void but voidable only, and becomes valid and effective if ratified by him after he attains his majority. A minor may disaffirm a contract made by him during minority within a reasonable time after reaching his majority or he may, by acts recognizing the contract after becoming of legal age, ratify it. In particular, if a minor, after becoming of age, does any distinct and decisive act clearly showing an intention to affirm a deed made by him during his minority, he will be deemed to have ratified the deed and cannot thereafter avoid it. A ratification made by a person of sound mind, upon arriving at his majority, is valid if untainted with fraud or undue influence, although the party making it is not at the time aware that it bound him in law. In other words, it is not necessary to a binding ratification that the party sought to be charged knew at the time of the act that he had the legal right to avoid the contract. "Ignorance of the party ratifying that his infancy gives him a legal defense is generally and rightly held to be immaterial in the more recent decisions."

The chancellor also found that Robert Shepherd did not repudiate the deed promptly after becoming twenty-one years of age. The right of a minor to disaffirm must be exercised within a reasonable time after reaching his majority. Some states have adopted, as a maximum reasonable time, arbitrary periods, for example, the time fixed by the Statute of Limitations, when ratification is conclusively presumed, but what is a reasonable time is generally a question of fact dependent upon the circumstances of the particular case. Robert took no affirmative action to disaffirm until December 3, seven months after attaining his majority. During this period, his mother had no right to possession of the farm except by virtue of the deed of June 8, 1942. Robert recognized and acquiesced in her control and management of the land and ratified her action by working as her employee on the farm after May 2, 1946, his twenty-first birthday.

The situation presented is that of a minor who, for all practical purposes, recognized the life interest of his mother in the property involved when he continued in her employment after becoming twenty-one years of age, thereby ratifying the deed; did not disaffirm within a reasonable time, considering the facts and circumstances described, particularly when the evidence discloses that he suggested to his mother she rent the property to a tenant and, four months before disaffirmance, requested his sister-in-law to join with him in asserting his alleged right to rescind, and, in addition, received substantial benefits under the deed which cannot be returned because of the passing of time.

The fact that Robert may not have known of his rights under the law when he became twenty-one is immaterial. It is his actual inclination and desire to abide by the deed, apart from his legal rights, which control. The privilege of minority, it has frequently been stated, is to be used as a shield and not as a sword. A minor's right to disaffirm upon coming of age, like the right to disaffirm in any other case, should be exercised with some regard to the rights of others, certainly with as much regard to those rights as is fairly consistent with adequate protection of the right of the minor himself. The equities are clearly with the mother rather than the son in the present case.

The decree of the Circuit Court of Sangamon County is right, and it is affirmed.

DEEDS—DELIVERY

SHROYER v. SHROYER
Supreme Court of Missouri, Division No. 1, 1968
425 S.W. 2d 214

Bill in equity to cancel a warranty deed on the ground of nondelivery. Plaintiff is Jessie Shroyer, mother of the defendants J. Wesley and Wayne Shroyer. The trial chancellor cancelled the deed. Defendants appealed.

The common source of title is Jennie Peters, a widow, who acquired the farm by deed in 1935. Jennie's brother, Virgil Shroyer, helped her run the farm for many years, until his death in July, 1960. At the time of Virgil's death Jennie's family consisted of her brother George Shroyer and his wife Beulah; Virgil's widow (Jessie Shroyer, plaintiff herein), and Jessie's five daughters and two sons (Wayne and Wesley, defendants herein).

On October 15, 1960, Jennie made and executed a will, properly witnessed, leaving the 80-acre farm to Virgil's widow, Jessie Shroyer, reciting that Virgil had kept up the farm for 30 years and that Jessie, his wife, "has been more than a sister to me in that time and all without compensation of any kind." (At that time Jessie owned or had an interest in farms totaling 663 acres, and a house in Mercer, subject to a mortgage of between $10,000 and $11,000, facts of which Jennie was aware.)

After executing the will dated October 15, 1960, Jennie turned it over to her niece Betty Daily with the request that Betty put it in her bank box and "not ever say anything about it." Jennie said she thought it would "keep down trouble in the family" if nobody knew about it. The will remained in Betty's safety deposit box in Peoples Bank of Mercer until Jennie died. After giving Betty possession of the will Jennie did not thereafter discuss the will with Betty, or request of Betty that she return the will or destroy it.

Robert and Rachel Jones were close neighbors with whom Jennie had almost daily discussions about her business. Jennie discussed with the Joneses the deeding of the 80-acre farm to Wayne and Wesley Shroyer. She stated that she wanted to deed the property to them; that "she wanted Wayne and Wesley to have the farm and that was her intentions." Robert Jones suggested that Jennie get a lawyer to prepare the deed but she wanted him to prepare it, so finally he "gave up" and he and his wife prepared the deed. Jennie made it known to Jones that the purpose of preparing the deed was "to pass title before she died so it wouldn't be probated as a part of her estate."

The deed to Wesley and Wayne bears date December 1, 1964. It was notarized on December 8, 1964. When the notary first saw the paper to be notarized it was lying on a table in the kitchen. Jennie asked the notary if she would notarize her signature "on that." Jennie folded it so that the notary could not see whose names were on the deed. Jennie did not identify the grantee. Only Jennie and the notary were in the room when the paper was notarized. Wayne was in another part of the house. The deed was not handed to Wayne in the notary's presence. It was lying on the table when the notary left.

Jennie died in a hospital October 3, 1966. Two or three weeks before her death, just before going to the hospital for her final illness, Jennie obtained her "papers" from a bank box. At Jennie's instance the Joneses bought a metal strongbox for Jennie. Jennie put her papers in it and handed the box to Robert Jones, asking him to keep it while she was in the hospital. Jones refused to take the key to the strongbox, preferring not to have access to the box. Jennie did not give Jones instructions as to what to do with the metal box other than to keep it—she did not instruct him to deliver it to anyone else. Specifically, she did not tell the Joneses to give the deed to defendants in case she died.

The only question is whether there was a delivery of the deed. The controlling element in determining this question is the intention of the parties, particularly the intention of the grantor. The vital inquiry with respect to the grantor is whether she intended a complete transfer; whether she parted with dominion over the instrument with the intention of relinquishing all dominion and control over the conveyance and of making it presently effective and operative as a conveyance of the title to the land. It is not necessary, in order to constitute a delivery of a deed, that the instrument actually be handed over to the grantee, or to another person for the grantee. There may be a delivery notwithstanding the deed remains in the custody of the grantor. A valid delivery once having taken place is not rendered ineffectual by the act of the grantee in giving the deed into the custody of the grantor for safekeeping. It is all a question of the intention of the parties, which may be manifested by words or acts or both.

In the state of Missouri, the burden of proof of nondelivery of a deed is upon the party who seeks to invalidate the conveyance on the ground of nondelivery. In this case plaintiff, Jessie Shroyer, has the burden of proof of nondelivery.

We find that Jennie, under the false impression that her will of October 15, 1960, had been destroyed, made a warranty deed on December 1, 1964, and executed it one week later, by which she intended and undertook to convey her 80-acre homeplace to her nephews Wesley and Wayne Shroyer, but that she did not deliver, or intend to deliver, the deed to Wayne with the intention of relinquishing all dominion and control over the conveyance or of transferring title to Wesley and Wayne *in praesenti;* that in December, 1964, she wanted her nephews to eventually become the owners of the farm; that her attempts to effect such a transfer of title by the deed in question were ineffective for lack of delivery; that the deed never became operative and was properly cancelled and set aside by the chancellor.

We are impelled to these findings by all of the evidence considered in its totality, being especially persuaded by the following facts: The deed did not reserve a life estate to Jennie. Such a reservation would have raised a strong presumption that she intended that title should immediately vest in the grantees. Grantor retained possession of the deed until the date of her death. Grantees had no access to and no permission from grantor to take possession of the deed. It was found in her strongbox, which she had placed in the temporary custody of her trusted friends and neighbors, Robert and Rachel Jones. Grantor retained the keys and had the right to call for the return of the strongbox and its contents, including the deed in question, at any time. Grantor did not place the deed in the possession of her banker, the notary, the Joneses, her brother George (in whom she confided in business matters), or anyone else, with directions to deliver the deed to the grantees. Grantor had a penchant for changing her mind about the disposition of her property, and frequently did so. Nondelivery would make it possible for her to destroy the deed and otherwise dispose of the farm if she later decided to do so. The secrecy employed in the transaction is consistent with nondelivery and retention of control over the deed. Nondelivery would make it less likely that the transaction would come to the attention of the other members of the family than delivery. When the deed was found, after grantor's death, it had not been recorded. Grantor's retention of the unrecorded deed, in a place under her control, was consistent with her previous history of change in the disposition of her property. The significance grantor's manual handing of the deed to Wayne (if this actually happened) might otherwise have had is overcome by the fact that the deed was never recorded. The failure to record is consistent with the conclusion that grantor did not intend to pass to the grantees any present title, and no title at all until her death.

The judgment is affirmed.

Deed Delivered to Escrow

Where a grantor delivers a deed of conveyance to a third person to be delivered to the grantee after the death of the grantor, certain questions of law and fact are presented. The effect of the delivery of the deed depends upon the intention of the grantor at the time the deed was delivered to the custodian. To be a valid and complete delivery the grantor must at that instant surrender all dominion over the deed. Where the grantor intended to part with all control over the deed, a subsequent change of intention can have no effect upon the delivery. Where the deed is placed in the hands of a third party merely for safekeeping and as a convenient place of deposit, the deed is not validly delivered and conveys no title.

The question of delivery is one of facts which must be gathered from all of the surrounding circumstances established by the evidence. The intent to deliver may be shown by direct evidence or presumed from acts and declarations of the parties, and, in like manner, presumptions of delivery may be rebutted or overcome by proof or presumption of a contrary intention. In some states, a grantee claiming under a deed not in the grantee's possession at the death of the grantor has the burden of proving delivery, and it is incumbent upon the grantee to overcome the prima facie case against delivery by showing the terms and conditions of the escrow and their complete performance. The execution of the deed with the formality required by law, the consultation with an attorney at the time of making it, and the subsequent acts of the grantor recognizing the title in the grantee may all be considered as an indication that the grantor intended the deed to take effect immediately upon its execution, and that the grantor delivered it with such thought in mind.[6]

6.4 LEGAL DESCRIPTIONS

Adequate legal descriptions are essential in many types of legal instruments—for instance in deeds, wills, contracts to sell real estate, and mortgages. A deed to land without an adequate legal description is valueless. In fact, the courts have held that a legally sufficient description is equally as important as a grantor and a grantee. For this reason, the use of a uniform system of description is highly important.

What is an adequate description? Some courts have said it is simply one that will enable a surveyor to locate the land involved. The courts have been faced with many problems involving descriptions of land and are often confronted with accepting or rejecting ambiguous or erroneous descriptions. Most court cases involving legal descriptions come about through the use of what are known as "common descriptions." Some such descriptions have been upheld, while others have not. In one case, the grantor described the property as "my lands in Sections 16 and 17, Auburn Township, Sangamon County, Illinois, commonly known as the Barr farm." The court upheld this description as legally sufficient since "my lands" could be readily located on the basis of the description. In another case involving the construction of a will, the description of "my house and lot in the town of Patoka, Illinois," was upheld as sufficient. At no time had the grantor ever owned any other house and lot in Patoka. In a third case, the description "the southwest part of the northeast fractional quarter of Section 36" was held void, since there was no specification of quantity. In still another case, a description reading "the South ½ of the Northeast ¼ of the Southeast ½ of Section Nineteen" was held void because of uncertainty.

Although descriptions of varying form and completeness have been upheld by the courts, as the above examples demonstrate, a uniform system of legal description that would make locating land easy and accurate obviates many court hearings and costly litigation.

---

[6] Calcutt v. Gaylord, 415 Ill. 390, 114 N.E. 2d 340 (1953).

The Government Survey System

The system most frequently used to describe land for legal purposes in most of the Midwest and West is based on the rectangular survey system used in the government survey. Land in Illinois, for example, was surveyed by government surveyors during the years 1808–1855, the major part of the work being done between 1815 and 1835. In the rectangular survey system, land is described according to its distance from two fixed lines, one at right angles to the other. One line is a true north-south line and is called the *principal meridian*. The other line, an east-west line, is called the *base line*.

Meridians. The Third Principal Meridian, which roughly cuts Illinois in two, is located about 9 miles west of the eighty-ninth geographic meridian. It was established as a line running true north from the point of confluence of the Ohio and Mississippi rivers. Its exact location is 89°10′30″ west of Greenwich, England. Greenwich is the starting point for all longitudinal measurements since longitude 0° passes through it.

The Fourth Principal Meridian was established for surveying lands located between the Illinois and Mississippi rivers. It begins at a point near Beardstown and is along a line straight north from the mouth of the Illinois river near Grafton. The longitudinal reading of this line is 90°20′45″ west.

The Second Principal Meridian, used in descriptions of some land in Illinois, is located in Indiana. Its reading is 86°28′0″ west. Not all principal meridians are numbered. Some, such as the Michigan and Louisiana Meridians, are named for the state in which they are located. Others are named for territorial features; for example, the Indian Meridian in Oklahoma and the Salt Lake Meridian in Utah. There are over thirty principal meridians in the United States.

Principal Meridians do not always extend from one state to another. The Third Principal Meridian is located entirely within Illinois; the Fourth Principal Meridian, however, extends into Wisconsin and is the reference line for all land descriptions in Wisconsin and for some in northeast Minnesota.

Base Lines. The true east-west line under the rectangular survey system is called a base line. Like the principal meridians, the base lines were arbitrarily established by the government surveyors. There is at least one base line for each meridian. The base line for the Second and Third Principal Meridians is the same. It is a latitudinal line with a reading of 38°28′20″ north of the equator. It intersects the Third Principal Meridian at a point near Centralia, Illinois. The base line for the Fourth Principal Meridian runs straight west from the beginning of the Meridian near Beardstown. The geographical location of this line is 40°0′30″ north. The Fourth Principal Meridian has a second base line used for describing land in Wisconsin and parts of Minnesota. The base line coincides with the Wisconsin-Illinois border.

Correction Lines. Because of the curvature of the earth's surface, the meridians, if extended, would converge at the North Pole. Therefore, to keep their measurements accurate, government surveyors established correction lines at various distances from the principal meridians and base lines. In Illinois these lines are irregularly located, but in areas surveyed later they occur every 24 miles. Surveyors worked from one correction line to the next, and as a result, sections located on opposite sides of a correction line will not have corresponding corners. The evidence of this exists today in the form of "jogs" in township roads. Correction lines for base lines are called *standard parallels* and those for principal meridians are called *guide meridians.* There are no guide meridians in Illinois. Correction lines for base lines were established to take care of mechanical errors.

Townships.   A *township*, as the term is used here, means a regular unit of 36 square miles. This is the so-called Land Office or Congressional Township and is not to be confused with civil townships of greater or less size. Because the township is a political subdivision in many states and because county lines do not always coincide with Land Office township lines and range lines, a named civil township may or may not contain 36 square miles. In legal descriptions, only Land Office or Congressional Townships are used.

In the rectangular survey system, lines were established every 6 miles from the base line and from the meridian. The east-west lines are called *township lines* and form the northern and southern boundaries for individual townships. The north-south lines established every 6 miles are called *range lines* and form the eastern and western boundaries of townships. The townships thus established are 6 miles on each side and are described according to their distance from the meridian and base lines in terms of the township and range lines. For example, townships between the meridian and the first range line east of the meridian are said to be in Range 1 East, while those located between the third and fourth township lines north of the base line are described as Township 4 North.

To locate a single township, both the township and range readings are used. Thus a township located between the first and second township lines north of the base line and between the third and fourth range lines east of the meridian is described as Township 2 North, Range 4 East. A township located between the second and third township lines south of the base line and between the second and third range lines west of the meridian is described as Town-

ship 3 South, Range 3 West. The principal meridian involved must be included in the description. Thus if the Third Principal Meridian is involved, the latter part of the description of the second township in the example above would be Township 3 South, Range 3 West of the Third Principal Meridian. The county and state should also be given.

Sections.   Each township is divided into thirty-six sections of 1 square mile each. To locate and describe land within a township, it is necessary to identify the section in which it is located. Federal law established the numbering system used to differentiate sections. Sections are numbered consecutively, 1 through 36, beginning with Section 1 in the northeast corner of the township and proceeding west to Section 6. Section 7 is located immediately below or south of Section 6. The numbering then goes back and forth until it reaches Section 36 in the southeast corner of the township.

A section theoretically contains 640 acres. But because of the convergence of lines and surveying errors, many sections do not contain this amount. To avoid having small errors in all sections of a township, it was determined that all shortages or surpluses would be assigned to sections on the north and west sides of a township. Thus all shortages or surpluses in north and south measurements will appear in the northern tier of sections (1 to 6). Shortages or surpluses in east and west measurements will appear in the west tier of sections (6, 7, 18, 19, 30, and 31). In general, surveyors were directed to assign the irregularities to the outer half of the sections. Although the procedure used varies, the assignments were generally made by subdividing all sections on the north and west sides of a township, except Section 6, into two regular quarter sections and two regular half-quarter sections. The remaining four fractional quarter sections of about 40 acres each are commonly called *government lots*. In Section 6, there are seven government lots along the north and west edges of the section.

Subsections.   Since most tracts of land that are the subject of a description are smaller than a full section, it is nearly always necessary to describe land within a section. In the government survey, each section was divided into regular quarter sections of 160 acres each. Under a law passed in 1805, markers were established at each quarter-section corner of every section, except at the center of the section. Each quarter section thus established is described according to its geographical position as the Northeast, Northwest, Southwest, or Southeast quarter. Tracts smaller than a quarter section are ordinarily described according to their fractional part of a quarter section and their location within the quarter. The square 40-acre tract in the southwest corner of a section would be described as the Southwest quarter of the Southwest quarter of the section, or in abbreviated form, the SW ¼ of the SW ¼.

Plat Acts.   When tracts of land are subdivided into small parcels, a state's Plat Act may be applicable. In Illinois, for example, the Plat Act specifies that when the owner of land subdivides it into two or more parts, any one of which is less than 5 acres in area, the owner must have the land surveyed and a plat made.

Metes and Bounds System

Many tracts are described either partially or wholly under a much older system known as the *metes and bounds system*. This system described the land according to its boundaries and their measurements. It is frequently necessary or desirable to use metes and bounds descriptions in combination with the rectangular survey system, especially when rivers, lakes, and in some instances highways form a part of the boundary.

Starting Point.   Any description according to the metes and bounds system must have a point of reference or starting place. The

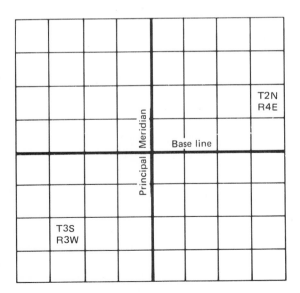

Figure 6-2   Description of Townships According to Township and Range Lines

6	5	4	3	2	1
7	8	9	10	11	12
18	17	16	15	14	13
19	20	21	22	23	24
30	29	28	27	26	25
31	32	33	34	35	36

Figure 6-3   Section Numbering in a Township

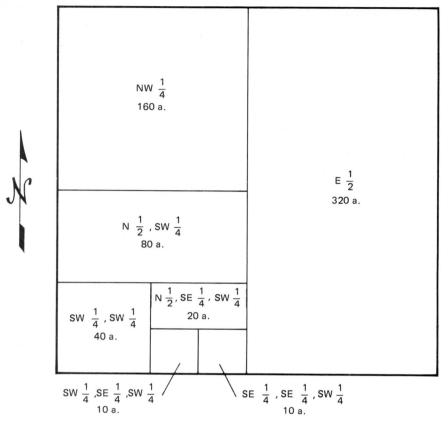

NW $\frac{1}{4}$
160 a.

E $\frac{1}{2}$
320 a.

N $\frac{1}{2}$, SW $\frac{1}{4}$
80 a.

N $\frac{1}{2}$, SE $\frac{1}{4}$, SW $\frac{1}{4}$
20 a.

SW $\frac{1}{4}$, SW $\frac{1}{4}$
40 a.

SW $\frac{1}{4}$,SE $\frac{1}{4}$,SW $\frac{1}{4}$
10 a.

SE $\frac{1}{4}$, SE $\frac{1}{4}$,SW $\frac{1}{4}$
10 a.

Figure 6-4   Descriptions Used in Fractional Sections

description then continues specified distances along lines called *courses* until the tract has been circumscribed and the starting point reached. It is necessary that the "calls" or recitals of distance and direction describe an enclosed tract. If they do, the description is said "to close."

The starting point of metes and bounds descriptions may be the quarter-section corners of the government survey. These points may be ascertained by reference to the original or restored corner markers. Metes and bounds descriptions sometimes involve topographic features as a point of reference or starting point. Trees, stones, rivers, or lakes referred to in this connection are called *natural monuments*.

Government survey corner markers, fences, and highways are called *artificial monuments*. A disadvantage in using monuments, natural or artificial, in descriptions is that they may be moved, destroyed, or obliterated.

Courses and Distances.   Courses are lines identified by their direction. *Distances* are linear measurements along these lines. There are many ways used to describe a course. Some involve the use of monuments. A description of this type might read in part: "Starting at the big oak tree, thence 317 feet to the maple tree...." A course, however, is generally described in terms of its angular relation to a point of reference. The point of reference ordinarily used is a meridian, or true north and south line. The course is given in terms of angular measurement to the meridian. Such a course is also called the *bearing of the line*.

A circle is composed of 360 divisions, called *degrees*. A degree is made up of 60 minutes of 60 seconds each. Thus a true east direction forms an angle of 90° and no minutes, with a true north-south line. In describing an angular course, the angle formed with the meridian and the point of reference is given. A course in a northeast direction would be described as N45°E, meaning that the course is 45° east of the true north-south line.

Many units of measurement are used to describe distances along a line. Miles, feet, and rods are the most commonly used, though chains are also frequently used. A *chain* is 66 feet long and is composed of 100 links of 7.92 inches. Actual chains having 50 links were used in much of the surveying of land. These chains, called *two-pole chains*, are half as long as the legal chain. The following is a table of commonly used measurements and their equivalents:

Measurement	Equivalents
1 mile	5280 feet; 320 rods; 8 furlongs; 80 chains
1 rod*	16 1/2 feet; 25 links
1 furlong	660 feet; 1/8 mile; 40 rods; 10 chains
1 chain	66 feet; 4 rods; 100 links
1 link	7.92 inches; 1/100 chain

Irregular Boundaries. Not all tracts of land have regular rectangular boundaries. Lands bordering on lakes or rivers are in this category. Descriptions of land bordering on such irregular boundaries are likely to include phrases such as "to X river, thence along X river...." As a general rule in many states, unless the deed expressly states otherwise, the description will be interpreted to mean a tract with one boundary at the center line or thread of the stream. This means that the boundary is the middle line between the shores regardless of the location of the channel. In the case of navigable rivers or streams, the ownership of the stream bed is burdened with the right to navigation on behalf of the public.

Lake boundaries are in a somewhat different class from river boundaries. Title to the beds of lakes which are navigable and meandered is in the state in trust for the people.[7] In other natural lakes, owners of property abutting the lake own to the center of the lake. Ownership of the beds of artificial lakes depends upon the words of conveyance used in transferring shoreline properties. There is no presumption that the conveyance includes any part of the bed to such lakes.

Highways and streets are sometimes used as boundaries in legal descriptions, especially if the highway forming the boundary is curved or irregular. Descriptions of land abutting public highways often will be interpreted to include a portion of the right-of-way unless the wording makes it clear that ownership does not include such a portion. This rule does not apply, however, where the public owns the right-of-way in fee simple absolute (complete title), nor when a city street is involved. For example, in many states when the plat for city property is recorded, title to the streets shown on such plats vests in the city.

---

*Also called a perch or pole. The term "rod" is derived from the use of a pole 16½ feet long as a measuring device.

[7] A meandered lake is one shown on the government surveys by meander or traverse lines run along the water's edge to show the area of the water. Meander lines do not constitute boundaries.

MISSING LEGAL DESCRIPTION

DEULEN v. WILKINSON
Supreme Court of Missouri, Division No. 1, 1971
473 S.W. 2d 357

Action by purchasers for reformation of contract covering sale of farm and for specific performance. The Circuit Court, Greene County, Jack A. Powell, J., granted specific performance and vendors appeal.

Around December 20, 1968, Mr. Funkhouser took Mr. Deulen and Mr. and Mrs. Toben out to the farm. Both Wilkinsons were present. They inspected the farm and house, and inquired about hay crops and dairy facilities. After leaving plaintiffs authorized Mr. Funkhouser to offer $60,000 for the 80 acres and equipment.

Mr. Funkhouser, acting as go-between, relayed the offers, rejections, and counteroffers between the parties; and, on January 2, 1969, plaintiffs, the Wilkinsons, and Mr. Funkhouser assembled in the barn on the 80 acres to discuss the various propositions. During the negotiations Mr. Funkhouser accompanied the Wilkinsons to their kitchen to discuss the sale and, in the course of such discussion, Mr. Funkhouser agreed to cut his commission so that the Wilkinsons would net $57,000 in the event they agreed to sell for $60,000.

They went back to the barn and an agreement was reached whereby the Wilkinsons would sell their farm, including attached improvements, for $60,000, with possession to be given March 31, 1969. In the course of reducing the agreement to writing, Mr. Funkhouser stated he did not have the legal description. Everyone was cold and in a hurry and agreed to his supplying the legal description in lieu of "80 acres more or less & all attached improvements thereon."

Wilkinsons were satisfied with the contract price but were unwilling to complete the sale because they had not found any place they wished to go.

As appellants, the Wilkinsons contend the court erred in reforming the contract "as such contract was voidable under the statute of frauds...as there was no legal description of any kind or any description from which a legal description or location could in any way be determined in the contract."

Appellants' argument is that there is no designation of state, county, township, range, or reference from which a complete description could be obtained, and therefore the court created a contract in place of reforming a contract.

Secondly, they argue that without a contract subject to reformation the court could not decree specific performance.

Accordingly, the decisive question is whether the writings construed with other evidence sufficiently describe and identify the real estate in question to satisfy the statute of frauds and thus give life and form to a contract so that it may be reformed and, as reformed, ordered performed.

[1] Contrary to appellants' argument, a description deficient in respects similar to those noted by appellants is not fatally defective under the statute

of frauds if the available writings are a guide to external matters from which the property can be identified with certainty. As stated in *Ray v. Wooster*, Mo., 270 S.W. 2d 743, 750[4],

such omission is not fatal, under the statute, if the location in any manner otherwise appears from the writing, or, if the property can be identified with reasonable certainty with the aid of the data supplied by the instruments and a consideration of the attending circumstances.

The written contract in evidence described the property in question as "80 acres more or less and all improvements." The Wilkinsons, named as sellers and, inferentially, owners, were shown as residing at Republic, Missouri, which is in Greene County, and they lived on subject farm. The contract further noted the presence of a dairy barn and dairy equipment, showing the contract to relate to a dairy farm. Admittedly, the Wilkinsons owned no real estate other than subject 80-acre dairy farm in Greene County, Missouri, and the contract was executed with all parties present on subject farm at the time of execution and agreeing that the exact legal description could be supplied later by the real estate agent. There is no dispute with respect to price and it and mode of payment are shown by the contract. These factors were sufficient to enable plaintiffs to ascertain the exact description from Wilkinsons' abstract of title in possession of their mortgagee.

[2] So, given the vendors, names, county of location, exact acreage, type of farm, all ascertainable from the face of the written sales contract, there is no problem under the surrounding circumstances in further identifying such property with certainty sufficient to satisfy the statute of frauds for purposes of reformation of subject contract. And since the contract was properly reformed, the court also properly decreed specific performance of the contract as reformed.

Judgment affirmed.

6.5 GUARANTEEING GOOD TITLE

The purchase of real estate invariably involves the expenditure of large sums of money or other consideration. Certainly one who purchases real property wants to be sure that he or she is getting good title. Several methods may be used to be reasonably certain that good title is being obtained.

Abstract and Attorney's Opinion of Title

An *abstract* may be defined as a chronological arrangement of the essential facts from documents of record affecting the title to a tract of land. Abstracts do not guarantee title; they simply afford a competent examiner the basis for determining whether or not a title is merchantable. "Merchantability" itself is a relative term since no title is likely to be perfect in the eyes of everyone who might examine it. Courts have said that a *merchantable title* is one which a person of reasonable prudence is willing to accept and one which such a person would be willing to pay full value for the land.

Ordinarily a contract for the sale of land provides that the seller shall furnish an abstract and that the purchaser shall have an opportunity to examine it and raise any questions about the title which may be disclosed by such examination. In many states, abstracts are prepared by private companies which charge for such preparation and also charge for making copies and for bringing abstracts up to date.

Since an abstract is not a guarantee of title, what is the responsibility of the company preparing an abstract? There have been a number of court decisions involving claims against abstract companies. Following is a summary of the holdings from these decisions: (1) The abstract should be complete; that is, the company is responsible for finding all documents of record which should be a part of the abstract, (2) If the abstractor fails to note that a tax sale has occurred, the abstractor can be held liable for the amount necessary to remove the cloud cast on the title by such tax sale, (3) The copy of a bad abstract, even though made by a reputable abstractor, does not render the copyist liable for anything other than the correctness of copy unless the copyist specifically assumes liability for the quality of the whole abstract, (4) It is the abstractor's duty, when finding that a complete and reliable abstract cannot be furnished, to give the party notice of that fact, (5) Persons engaged in the business of making abstracts of title are held to a strict responsibility in the exercise of the trust and confidence reposed in them. They must use due care in the performance of their duties, and for failure in this respect, an injured party is entitled to recover.

Though the abstract itself has nothing to do with the quality of one's title, it is nevertheless an essential document when all or a portion of the property is to be conveyed. It should be up-to-date through the last transaction affecting the land and should be certified by the abstractor and kept in a lockbox or other safe place.

The attorney examining the certified abstract has the responsibility of analyzing the chronological arrangements of essential facts in the abstract and rendering an opinion as to whether title is merchantable and, if not, what steps need to be taken to correct the defects or clouds on title.

What kind of defects might the examination of an abstract by an attorney disclose? Following are some which frequently occur:

1. Failure of all necessary parties to sign a deed or other instrument conveying property
2. Faulty description of the property
3. Parties incorrectly named or designated
4. An incorrect proof of heirship at the death of an owner
5. Failure to establish heirship
6. Failure of a married person to convey dower and homestead
7. No releases of record for mortgage, mechanic's lien, trust deed, or other encumbrance of record
8. Unsatisfied tax and judgment liens
9. Minors and incompetents improperly represented in a legal proceeding involving the land

Many such defects can easily be corrected once discovered. Some may require a suit to quiet title, and occasionally a defect may be so material as to completely negate any claim of title or right by the current holder.

The rendering of opinions of title is an important task fraught with potential liability for the attorney. If the attorney fails to properly analyze the abstract (for example, by failing to realize that a mortgage has not been released even though the mortgage is included in the abstract), the attorney is liable in a malpractice sense to the client for any damage caused by this erroneous opinion of title.

In summary, the abstract company is liable for failing to get a recorded document summarized into the abstract. The attorney is liable for failing to properly analyze the chain of title appearing in the abstract.

Title Insurance

A title insurance policy provides the purchaser of land with security against imperfections in the purchaser's title. The policy is usually issued for a single premium and remains in effect until the title is transferred to another. The amount of the policy ordinarily covers the price paid for the property. If, however, unimproved land is purchased and improvements are to be made, the policy may be designed to include the cost of such improvements. Also, some title insurance companies issue policies that increase the coverage annually based upon some index of land or residence appreciation.

Typically, a title insurance policy may be obtained from any of several companies operating in a state. The purchaser may apply for title insurance at any time after taking title to real property, or may request that the seller furnish a title policy as a condition in the contract of sale.

A major function and primary expense of a title insurance company is not the cost of claims but the cost of maintaining records and a skilled staff to search for defects in titles, so encumbrances on property can be reported and cleared up before an owner or mortgage lender makes an investment. In effect then, the title insurance company maintains its own private title registration system built up over time through the examination of abstracts and other documents and transactions having to do with the title of lands it insures. A

title insurance company will not issue a policy on a title until it has made a title examination.

The Torrens System

The Torrens System of title registration is a plan under which a public registrar of deeds theoretically supplants the abstract and title examination system. Under this system, a proceeding is instituted in court somewhat like a quiet title proceeding to make an initial registration of each tract of land. Once this has been accomplished, transfers can then be evidenced by getting a certificate of title from the public registrar. A record of all conveyances, releases, and other documents affecting the title to land is kept by the registrar.

Experts are divided on the advantages of the Torrens System. Some feel it is an economical, simple way of handling land titles and should replace the present system; others feel that there would be no advantages gained in adopting it. Those who favor it maintain that issuing certificates of title to land by an appropriate officer of the government is a service to which the public is entitled. Use of the Torrens System is not widespread. In Illinois, for example, only Cook County (Chicago) has adopted the system.

6.6 EMINENT DOMAIN

Eminent domain is the right of the public to take private property for public use through condemnation proceedings. A government could not exist without the right to take such land as it needs for public purposes. The agencies by which we are governed and served must have room in which to operate. A state without grounds for a statehouse, a county without a public square for the courthouse, or a power company with no path across the country for its towers and lines could not function.

Eminent domain is of great importance to farmers and ranchers because these people collectively own much of the real estate in this country. Farmers and ranchers are often defendants in condemnation proceedings as the power of eminent domain is used to acquire land for miles of new highways, public buildings, water supply systems, parks, and dozens of other public uses. In future years, the use of eminent domain is likely to be more closely related to our energy needs. For example, in 1977, the pipeline industry planned or began construction of 20,442 miles of pipeline in the United States, over 40 percent of which was for the transportation of natural gas.[8] With the increasing need to depend on domestic coal reserves, electric utilities are hoping to use slurry pipelines to transport coal. Also, public utilities are carefully planning the construction of new electric transmission lines and the acquisition of rights-of-way for these lines.

Entities with the Power of Eminent Domain

Specific laws regulating the power of eminent domain vary somewhat from state to state. Thus, entities with the power of eminent domain, condemnation procedures, and the defenses to condemnation actions will vary slightly from state to state. Nevertheless, the concept of eminent domain in each of the states is generally the same.

In most states the following entities have the power of eminent domain:

1. The federal government or any of its agencies
2. The state government or any of its agencies
3. Political subdivisions of the state (counties and townships)
4. Municipalities
5. Public corporations (school districts, drainage districts, fire-protection districts
6. Public utilities, public-service corporations, or quasi-public corporations (power, light, gas, gas storage, electric, telephone, telegraph, water, or pipeline companies)

Private corporations and individuals generally do not have the power of eminent domain, though sometimes a right of necessity may be granted to one individual in the land of another. For example, in Missouri an owner of landlocked property has a right to acquire or condemn an easement of way of up to 40 feet across adjacent property in order to gain access from a public road.

The Prerequisite of Public Purpose

The constitutions of the United States and individual states restrict the right to take private property by saying that private property can only be condemned for *public use*.[9] The court or commission hearing the condemnation action will make an independent determination as to whether the property is being acquired for public use, but it should be noted that public use has been broadly defined by various courts.

Farmers and ranchers should also recognize that a variety of issues related to public use are often debated long before condemnation proceedings are filed with the court. Farmers and ranchers who wait until the condemnation proceeding to voice their arguments on issues related to public use may well find that the "ball game is over before they came to bat." For example,

---

[8] PIPELINE AND GAS J., Jan. 1977, at 17.

[9] U.S. CONST. amend. V; *e.g.*, ILL. CONST. art. 1, § 15.

in Illinois a public utility must generally obtain a certificate of public convenience and necessity and an order authorizing the construction of the power line or pipeline before it can construct a new utility line or exercise the power of eminent domain. The utility company applying for a certificate of public convenience and necessity must prove that the utility line is in the public interest and that the utility line route location is reasonable, considering the particular features and uses of the lands that will be affected. A landowner may challenge the utility company's proof that the utility line is in the public interest, or that the route is reasonable. The landowner may also attempt to prove that the utility company did not act in good faith during negotiations for the right-of-way contract.

The findings of a state's commerce commission or public utilities commission will be very persuasive in any condemnation proceeding to follow. It is unlikely that a court would find public use lacking or that the amount of property to be condemned is beyond the amount required for public use if a public commission has reached an opposite finding after extensive public debate.[10]   Therefore, interested parties should participate in the public hearings that are technically independent of, but often precede, many condemnation actions.

The Requirement of Just Compensation

The constitutions of the United States and most individual states also place a second limitation on the power of eminent domain—just compensation *must be paid* to all those owning rights in the property.[11]

For What Must Compensation Be Paid? Broadly speaking, an owner is not entitled to compensation simply because use of the property is curtailed by laws or regulations. For example, a zoning law may restrict the type of structure which an owner may build on the land. A railroad may be required to fence its right-of-way. Dumping garbage into a stream may be declared a public nuisance. None of these restrictions is a taking of property within the meaning of the constitutional guarantee. Also, destroying property in an emergency—to prevent the spread of fire, for example—may be justified without compensation. Owners do have legal remedies for unauthorized or unreasonable regulations imposed by the police power or for unwarranted destruction under the guise of an emergency.

Before an owner is entitled to compensation, some *possessory interest in the property* must have passed to the agency involved. The courts have held that the term "private property" as used in the Constitution and the eminent domain act includes both real and personal property and also includes

---

[10] *See, e.g., Fortenberry the Exercise of Eminent Domain by Private Bodies for Public Purposes,* 1966 U. ILL. L.F. 131, 151–152. Also in *Department of Public Works and Buildings v. McNeal,* 33 Ill. 2d 248, 211 N.E. 2d 266 (1956), the Supreme Court of Illinois held that where the Department of Public Works and Buildings condemned a strip of the defendant's land for the purpose of widening an existing public highway, the trial court's modification of the department's specifications in regard to point of limited access and the size of an underpass violates the separation of powers provision of Article III of the Constitution. The court held that

where the right and reasonable necessity for the exercise of the power of eminent domain exists, the matter of engineering design is not a proper subject for judicial interference. And in *Department of Public Works and Buildings v. Farina,* 29 Ill. 2d 474, 194 N.E. 2d 209 (1963), the court stated that the authority of the Department of Public Works and Buildings in establishing, maintaining, and improving highways is broad and plenary, and only in exceptional cases will the courts interfere with decisions to condemn land for such purposes.

[11] U.S. CONST. amend. V; *e.g.,* ILL. CONST. art. 1, § 15.

the right of using and enjoying property.[12] It is well established that every person with an interest, whether partial, temporary, permanent, or absolute, has a right to compensation in proportion to the injury received. Also the condemning agency cannot be made to pay more than would be necessary if one person had a complete and perfect title to the property. This is sometimes called the *unit rule*, meaning that the property must be evaluated as a whole. As a general rule, the compensation for property interests taken is the fair market value of the property at its highest and best use.

When may an owner be compensated for *property not taken*? The theory of compensation when private property is taken by the public is that the owner shall be left "whole," or in as good a position as before the property was taken. Often the owner must be paid for something in addition to the value of the property actually taken. This additional payment is called compensation for damage to property not taken. In order to receive compensation for property damaged but not taken, the damaged property must be closely associated with the property taken. For example, land must be physically joined or be inseparably connected in use with the land taken. For agricultural lands, where large rectangular tracts are desirable, damages

to land not taken often include *severance damages* based upon the theory that a smaller tract is not worth as much per acre as a larger tract. Also, if the remaining tract is not rectangular, some diminution in value is present because the odd-shaped tract is more difficult and costs more to farm.

Special benefits such as an improved road also may be considered, and if they equal damages, the owner does not receive any compensation in some jurisdictions. If there is no damage beyond the loss of property, there is, of course, no additional compensation.

Damage to property not taken is generally measured by its depreciation in value. For example, when a drainage district takes land to widen a ditch and places the excavated earth on the banks, the property owner is entitled to one recovery—the difference in cash value of the farm before and after the improvement. If it is worth as much as it was originally, there are no damages. However, all past, present, and future damages which may reasonably be attributed to the improvement may be considered. Expert testimony may be brought in when needed (to render an opinion on danger from power lines, for example).[13]

When the owner conveys land by deed as a result of agreement with the public agency it is assumed that the purchase

---

[12] A landowner must be paid, the courts have ruled, for the loss of any of these property interests:

1.   Land and permanent improvements, including fences, drainage systems, orchards, crops, woodlands, and structures.
2.   Riparian rights, at least in Illinois courts (where a stream channel is altered, for example).
3.   Trees and shrubbery, springs and wells, minerals, underground waters.
4.   Natural drainage rights (if natural drainage is altered, damages may be due the landowner).
5.   Right of access to an existing highway.
6.   Easements (a right-of-way across the con-

demned land, for example). Covenants and contractual rights are not compensable—there must be an interest in the land itself.
7.   An additional use of a right previously acquired by the public (for example, erecting a telephone pole on a right-of-way previously acquired for use as a highway).

[13] Some of the items which may depreciate property not taken, and for which the courts have said that an owner is entitled to damages, are:

1.   Power, telephone, or telegraph lines running over a strip of land. (The only property taken is that necessary for poles or towers).

price includes damage to land not taken. The owner cannot, therefore, claim a separate allowance for such damages. Also, some damages and inconveniences have been deemed too speculative or remote. Such consequential damages as the danger to an owner in crossing a new highway have not been allowed.[14]

How Can Value Be Established?   The courts have agreed that *just compensation* means the full and perfect equivalent in money of the property taken. The owner is to be placed in as good a position financially as the owner would have been in had the property not been taken. Values are to be set as of the time the petition is filed. Regarding value, the courts have said:

The *fair cash market value* is the test. This is frequently defined as the amount a willing buyer will pay a willing seller. The value of the land for the highest, best, and most profitable use to which it could be put, either now or later, may be shown. Special value to the owner is admissible, but with limitations. Rental value is an important test but not the only one. Buildings, minerals, and timber are to be considered, though the land must be valued as a whole. Improvements not permanently "affixed" so they become a part of the real estate are not to be considered.

Typical Condemnation Procedure
General Steps.   The following paragraphs de-

---

2.   Gas or pipelines running through a strip of land. (The surface is not taken, but the owner's use may be affected.)

3.   Lines damaging trees.

4.   Cutting land off from water supply.

5.   Shrinkage in farming area. This is sometimes called "severance damage," and is regarded by some as an exception to the rule that "consequential" damages cannot be allowed.

6.   Division of farming area or change in shape of the area.

7.   Obstruction of drainage when a road is built, forcing water onto one's land.

8.   Changes in the grade of a road, affecting access to property.

9.   Removal of lateral support.

10.   Cost of new fencing, resulting from a new road or drainage works.

11.   Necessary cost of moving buildings.

12.   Weeds and insects around the base of towers.

13.   Damage to crops and livestock.

14.   Loss of time in plowing, cultivating, and reaping.

15.   Inconvenience, danger, and depreciation in value of land not taken when it is necessary to drive livestock back and forth across a highway. (The danger of loss must be clear and the evidence specific.)

16.   Damage to business and income.

17.   Any special damages that an owner can prove and that most other owners may not have (increase in insurance rates, for example).

[14] Other alleged damages for which the courts have refused to allow compensation include:

1.   The vacating of a road by the public (special damage must be shown).

2.   Damages caused by the taking of adjoining property belonging to another. (If damages actually result, there are legal remedies outside the eminent domain act.)

3.   "Mere conjecture, speculation, fancy, or imagination" (damage must be real).

4.   Fear of danger from a power line.

5.   Danger of fire or explosion of gas line not located near buildings or on land not suitable for residential use.

6.   Remote possibility that there will be trespass, danger, a need for fencing, or other inconveniences.

7.   Possibility of having undesirable callers due to the nearness of a highway.

8.   Possible difficulty of settling future claims.

9.   Future loss of profits.

10.   Possible loss of good will.

11.   Loss of aesthetic or sentimental value (removal of trees or shrubs).

12.   Unsightliness of poles and lines.

13.   Expense of removing personal property.

14.   Dust, fumes, noise, traffic, and annoyance from a highway or railroad.

15.   Loss of business during the progress of work.

16.   Necessity of more costly fencing around towers.

scribe general steps often encountered in a condemnation action.

When Is the Right of Eminent Domain Exercised? Agencies needing rights in private property first try to get them through agreement with the owner. If the owner is willing to donate the right, or will accept what is offered and transfer the right, nothing needs to be done beyond completing the formalities of transfer. If the owner refuses to convey the right, the agency may begin an eminent domain proceeding (sometimes referred to as a "condemnation" proceeding). Also, when an owner is for some reason not able to consent, when an owner is not a resident of the state, or when an owner's residence is unknown, eminent domain may be used.

Where Are Proceedings Conducted? An eminent domain proceeding is a suit at law and must be conducted in a court. If the federal government is involved, the suit is conducted in a federal district court; otherwise the suit is in the circuit court of the county in which all or part of the property is located.

What Are the Rights of the Property Owner? The purpose of the eminent domain procedure is to make sure that the property owner is fairly treated and that the public gets the rights it needs. An owner may bring in evidence to establish the value of the property that is being taken and to show how much the owner will be damaged. Depending on state law, a judge, jury, or group of commissioners hears the evidence and decides the amount of compensation the owner is to receive. The owner or the party bringing suit may ask the jury (if a jury is used) to go upon the property and examine it before making a decision. Appeals may be taken from the circuit court to state appellate courts and

from the federal district court to the court of appeals.

In court the landowner may challenge the right of the petitioner to take property by stating that it is not being taken for a public purpose. The petitioner must show that the property is needed for a public purpose.

How Is a Proceeding Conducted in State Courts? The agency wanting to take private property begins by filing a petition with the clerk of the circuit court. This petition must show the authority of the agency to take by eminent domain, the purpose for which the property is wanted, a description of the property, the names of all known owners of the property, and a listing of other parties interested in the property. After the petition is filed, a summons is served on the defendant and notice of the hearing is published. The law requires that the hearing be set a specified number of days after the summons is served on the defendant or after the notice is published. The court may permit amendments of the petition and may bring in parties not named in the petition.

Any person not included as a party to an eminent domain proceeding may become a party by filing a cross-petition stating that he or she is an owner or has an interest in the property which will be taken. The court must then determine the cross-petitioner's rights and give them full consideration.

Under the law of many states, any number of separately owned tracts in the same county may be included in one petition. The compensation for each may be decided in the same or in different trials, or by the same or different juries (if a jury is used), as decided by the court.

Appearance in Court. A statement that the agency has the right to take private property must appear on the face of the petition. If the owner wishes to challenge the right of the petitioner to take all or any portion of the land described in the petition, a motion to dismiss must be filed. Then the court can hear evidence from both parties in determining whether the motion should be sustained. If the owner feels that the petition has not been properly filled out—if, for instance, the reason for taking the property is not stated or the description of it is inaccurate—a motion to dismiss should be filed. Such a motion is not a challenge to the right to take the land, but an allegation that the case has not been properly presented and the court cannot legally proceed.

Defenses Available to a Landowner. With the help of the attorney, a landowner may make the following moves to defend the property:

1. Challenge the right to take the property.
2. Challenge the necessity of taking the land requested. This may be based on the theory that more property is requested than is necessary. An owner will need clear and convincing proof to back up such a challenge, for the courts have given public agencies wide leeway in deciding how much land they need. For example, a strip of land ½ rod wide for a telegraph line and enough land to eliminate a right-angle turn in a highway have been held necessary and reasonable.
3. Challenge the sufficiency of the petition.
4. Show that the petitioner did not try to reach an agreement with the landowner on the price for the land and that therefore the petitioner has no right under the law to begin an eminent domain proceeding. The petitioner cannot answer such an objection by saying that the owner did not ask for

compensation because the law does not require an owner to make a claim to protect the constitutional rights.
5. File a cross-petition asking for damages to land not taken.
6. Demand a jury. In most states, both the landowner and the agency wanting land have the right to ask a jury to go upon the land and examine it. After seeing the land and hearing the proof offered by both parties, the jury will make a report to the court stating what compensation is fair. The impaneling of the jury, challenging, and other procedures are often conducted as in other civil suits.

Costs, Expenses, and Fees. Usually the petitioner pays the costs of an eminent domain proceeding, but the landowner pays his or her own attorney's fees.

Interest. Interest on an award is ordinarily payable from the time the judgment is given until the award is paid.

Appeals. If the landowner or the petitioner is not satisfied with the decision of the circuit court, either party may appeal to an appellate court. When a petition includes several owners, each owner is entitled to a separate appeal. An appeal may be based on alleged errors of the court or an alleged inadequate compensation. An award will not be changed unless the appellate court feels that the jury acted without considering the evidence or that the lower court allowed substantial error to creep in. When the evidence is conflicting, the appellate court prefers to rely on the judgment of the jury that heard the case.

When Must an Owner Yield Possession? The general rule in many states is that the owner does not have to give up the property until payment has been made. There are some exceptions to this rule. If the case is appealed by the owner, the petitioner may give bond guaranteeing payment and take possession. Also if the owner is not known, or for some reason cannot receive payment, the amount may be paid to the county treasurer, and the petitioner may take the property.

In certain cases both the state and federal governments have statutory authority to take possession of property before the condemnation proceeding is concluded. Such statutes are known as "quick-take" laws. The federal law is used to acquire property for military purposes or for defense highways. The law in Illinois, for example, may be used for highways, airports, sanitary districts, and certain installations relating to coal and energy.

What Rights Does the Owner Retain? When the public acquires farmland, it may take either the fee or title interest or an easement giving it the needed rights. When the complete interest is taken, as is usually the case when land is taken for highways, the owner has no further rights in the property except as a member of the public or perhaps as an adjoining owner. But when the agency takes only an easement, the owner may use the property in any manner not interfering with the public use. For example, the land under which pipes are laid or over which lines are placed may be farmed.

Where land is taken for today's modern highways, the owner retains very few rights. For example, the owner probably will not have the right of immediate access and may be prevented from crossing the highway with machinery and livestock.

Particular Problems Illustrated

EMINENT DOMAIN—ADEQUACY OF AWARD

STATE HIGHWAY COMMISSIONER v. FRAZIER
Supreme Court of Virginia, 1974
214 Va. 556, 203 S.E. 2d 350

The sole assignment of error on this appeal granted the appellant, State Highway Commissioner of Virginia, in an eminent domain proceeding, is that the trial court erred in setting aside, on the ground of gross inadequacy, the award of the commissioners and ordering a rehearing of the case before a new panel of commissioners.

On August 12, 1971, appellant filed a petition to condemn a .77-acre parcel of land owned by the defendants, Lyle E. Frazier and Iva V. Frazier, for use in a highway construction project on Route 15 in Culpeper County. The regularly appointed commissioners, after viewing the property and hearing evidence, filed their report awarding $6,350 for the land taken and $500 for damages to the residue, or a total of $6,850.

Counsel for the landowners then moved the court to set aside the award on the ground of inadequacy and filed his exceptions to the report. On a later date, the trial judge set aside the award on the ground that it shocked his conscience, and, over the objections of the appellant, ordered another hearing before new commissioners.

At the hearing before the first commissioners, an expert witness for the appellant testified that the best use of the property taken was for residential purposes. He valued the land taken at $5,766 and damages to the residue in the amount of $235, or a total value of $6,001. The landowners' two witnesses estimated the value of the land for commercial use. One valued the take at $11,792 and damages at $5,575, and the other fixed the value of the land at $12,192 and damages at $6,690. The landowners placed the value of the take at $10,000 and damages at an equal amount.

At a rehearing before the new commissioners, the testimony was the same as that at the first hearing. The commissioners returned an award for $12,500, without allowing any damages to the residue. At a subsequent date, the trial court entered its order awarding $6,250 for the take and an equal amount for damages to the residue. Appellant noted his exception to the award and the action of the trial court.

We have many times held that in the trial of a civil action the trial judge may not set aside a jury verdict simply because he disagrees with the amount of the verdict. If a fair and impartial jury reached a verdict which is supported by sufficient evidence, it is not to be disturbed.

The same principles apply with respect to the power of a trial judge over the awards of commissioners in eminent domain proceedings.

We have repeatedly said that in an eminent domain proceeding the report of the commissioners is entitled to great weight, is *prima facie* correct, and must be confirmed unless 'good cause be shown against it.' Where there is a conflict of evidence before the commissioners, neither the trial court nor this court can set aside the award unless it be shown that the commissioners proceeded upon erroneous principles, or unless the amount allowed is so grossly inadequate as to show prejudice or corruption on their part. This is because the commissioners may base their finding largely upon facts obtained by their own view of the property which do not appear in the record.

There is nothing in the record in this case to show that in arriving at the first award the commissioners acted upon erroneous principles. The exceptions were taken to the instructions which set out the applicable legal principles. Nor was there any suggestion that the award of the commissioners was the result of prejudice or corruption on their part. Indeed, the only reasons given by the trial judge in setting aside the award was that he thought it was wholly inadequate and that it shocked his conscience.

The amount of the first award was within the range of value shown by the evidence. Thus, there was sufficient evidence to support the award, and the trial judge erred in setting it aside merely because it seemed to him to be inadequate.

For the reasons stated, the order appealed from is reversed and the cause is remanded with directions to reinstate the first award and make proper order for the disposition of the funds.

EMINENT DOMAIN—DAMAGE BY PIPELINE TO LAND NOT TAKEN

TRUNKLINE GAS COMPANY v. O'BRYAN
Supreme Court of Illinois, 1960
21 Ill. 2d 95, 171 N.E. 2d 45

Plaintiff, the Trunkline Gas Company, filed four separate petitions in the circuit court of Champaign County seeking to condemn, for a pipe-line right of way, an easement strip extending across farm lands owned by the respective defendants. In each instance, defendants filed a cross petition for damages to land not taken and the causes were thereafter consolidated for purposes of trial. After trial by a jury, which viewed the premises, defendants recovered verdicts and judgments totaling $3,865.50 for 6.5 acres lying within the easement strip. As to the cross petitions, however, the court directed verdicts for the plaintiff and it is from this action of the court that defendants appeal. The sole issue raised is whether the court properly excluded the testimony by which defendants sought to prove damages to land lying outside the easement strip.

Before looking to the disputed testimony, a better understanding of the issue involved requires a brief explanation of the project to be undertaken by the plaintiff. The allegations of the petition, which are binding on the condemnor, show that the easement strip will be 66 feet wide, that a 26-inch pipe will be buried therein at a minimum of 30 inches below the surface of the earth, that the strip will not be fenced, that plaintiff does not require or seek to obtain the exclusive use and occupancy of any portion of the strip, and that the owners of the land, while not permitted to build structures thereon, will have the right to cultivate the strip over the top of the line, or to make such other use of it as will not interfere with the operation of the pipe line. The petitions further set forth that, as an element of the easement, plaintiff requires authority to remove from the strip trees, shrubs, crops, fences and tile, insofar as may be necessary to the construction, operation and maintenance of the line, but that plaintiff will repair and replace all fence and tile damaged or removed.

To sustain their burden of proving damage to land not taken defendants sought to introduce the testimony of five witnesses who were of the opinion that the taking of the easement strip for pipe-line purposes would reduce the value of the remaining lands from $55 to $60 an acre. In each instance, however, on either or both grounds, the trial court sustained objections that the witnesses were not qualified by experience to give such opinions, or that the opinions were based upon remote, speculative or other improper elements of damage.

In the matter of agricultural lands, permanent interference with farming caused by an improvement, as distinguished from temporary interference or inconvenience, has at various times been held to be a proper element of damage to land not taken. Comparing favorably in some respects to evidence present in the decisions last cited, the witnesses in this case, based upon estimates that the ridge would not subside for a period of two to five years, testified the improvement would make it necessary to farm the land in two tracts, thus affecting crop rotation and requiring the farm to be cultivated in point rows, a more costly and time-consuming process than would otherwise be required. Because of these evidential similarities, defendants assert that the interferences testified to must likewise be considered as a proper element of damage in this case. We do not agree that such a conclusion follows. It has long been settled that temporary consequential interference with the use of property occasioned by the construction of a public improvement is not a proper element of damage. Moreover, in the instant case, the testimony of defendants' witnesses is predicated upon a contingency that farm equipment will not be able to pass over the pipe-line ridge for a period of two to five years. In view of the evidence that the 36-inch ridge of loose soil will have a maximum height of but 6 to 8 inches, and in the absence of any proof that subsidence of the ridge would produce deep or dangerous depressions, it is our opinion that the contingency indulged in is extremely remote and speculative. The measure of damages in the case of land not taken is the difference between the value of the property unaffected by the improvement, and its value as affected by it. When that test is applied here, we cannot say that the temporary interference with farming which will result is a proper element of damage.

Two witnesses speculated that the improvement would affect the surface drainage upon the lands not taken, but made no explanation as to why this was so, and two witnesses likewise stated their opinions were based on the possibility that the line would interfere with tiling, if any should be needed. On the state of the record, these elements are not only speculative, but also overlook that plaintiff bound itself by its petitions to restore all drain tile to the condition in which it existed before the improvement.

The majority of the witnesses testified that the danger of fire and explosion attending a leakage of gas from the line would depreciate the value of the land not taken. While we are of the opinion such element of damage would be entirely proper where a high pressure gas line is situated in close proximity to buildings or habitations or, where there is some showing that the highest and best use of the land not taken is for residential or factory purposes neither of these circumstances were shown to exist in the present case. Absent some proximity to real danger, we have held in the case of high tension lines that the law cannot regard the mere fear of the presence of such instrumentality as an element of depreciation resting on a substantial basis, and we think that the same reasoning is applicable here.

Without the discussion of other elements relied upon by the witnesses which we deem improper, we conclude, on the basis of the particular record before us, that the testimony of defendants' witnesses was properly excluded. Accordingly, the judgment of the circuit court of Champaign County is affirmed.

Judgment affirmed.

Property Taken under Federally Financed Programs

In January 1971 the Uniform Relocation Assistance and Land Acquisition Policies Act of 1970 was enacted.[15] The purpose of this act was "to provide for uniform and equitable treatment of persons displaced from their homes, businesses, or farms by Federal and federally assisted programs and to establish uniform and equitable land acquisitions policies for Federal and federally assisted programs." Rights-of-way for power transmission and gas lines are examples of takings where the taking agency is likely to be a private company without federal funding. However, highways, parks, and many other projects for public benefit are likely to be partially or totally federally funded.

The policies adopted by the act include policies designed to expeditiously acquire real estate by negotiation through the use of open and fair appraisal procedures and written offers documenting the basis for establishing that amount. Coercive actions are to be avoided, and landowners are to be reimbursed for reasonable costs associated with the transaction.[16]

Also, when persons are displaced as a result of federal or federally assisted programs, such displaced persons are to receive payment for reasonable expenses incurred in moving themselves, their families, their business or farm operation—including expenses incurred in searching for a replacement farm or business—and other personal property. Additional relocation assistance is also to be available.[17]

Many states also provide relocation assistance similar to that provided by federal law,[18] and some states, such as Indiana, have amended their eminent domain statutes to require *written* offers before a condemnation action can be filed.

6.7 ADVERSE POSSESSION

Although the public has the right to take private property through the exercise of eminent domain, private citizens can take legal title to property from other persons through adverse possession. The analogy is by no means perfect, however, because adverse possession does not require the payment of compensation. It is more in the nature of a forfeiture.

The following common-law rule has been well recognized in all jurisdictions. If one person held and used the land of another for a long period, the person so holding would after a period of years acquire title to such property so long as the possession was open, actual, notorious, adverse or hostile, continuous, and exclusive under a claim of right.[19] This rule is the essence of adverse possession. To many this seems to be an unfair rule, but there are at least two good reasons why it is used: to encourage the definite utilization and improvement of land, and to aid in clearing title which might otherwise entail endless research.

Real estate titles are, at best, difficult to preserve accurately. Many agreements affecting the land are not written or re-

---

[15] P.L. No. 91–646, 84 Stat. 1894 (codified at 42 U.S.C. §§ 1415, 2473, 3307, 4601, 4602, 4621–4638, 4651–4655; 49 U.S.C. § 1606).
[16] 42 U.S.C.A. § 4651 (West 1977).
[17] 42 U.S.C.A. § 4622 *et seq.* (West 1977).
[18] For example, § 3–107.1 of the Illinois Highway Code was amended authorizing payments for mov-

ing expenses, for losses of personal property resulting from moving, and for reasonable expenses in searching for a replacement farm. There are limits on the amount of payment for each kind of loss.
[19] *See, e.g.,* Massey v. Price, 252 Ark. 617, 480 S.W. 2d 377 (1972).

corded; easements may be created, mistakes may creep into written instruments, and other things may arise which make the tracing of titles an uncertain process. To prevent some of the confusion which might otherwise exist, state legislatures have established periods of limitation during which claims to land may be made but after which certain claims are not enforceable. In the absence of such a statute the common-law period of 20 years is generally applicable.

Required Duration of Adverse Possession

At common law, the required period of adverse possession was 20 years. Many states, however, have by statute altered the common-law rule. Periods of 15 years or longer prevail in nearly two-thirds of the states (most of which are east of the Mississippi), while most of the states west of the Mississippi have periods of 10 years or less. Table 6.2 shows some of the periods of adverse possession for selected states.

Adverse possession not only clears the record of many old claims, but it frequently results in the passing of land from the record title holder to one who has used and claimed the land for many years. A frequent example of the latter exists in the case of misplaced line fences. In most states if an owner occupies land up to a fence line, claiming it as his or her own, the owner

will acquire the land up to the fence after years of adverse possession, even though the fence line is not properly located and is on the land of the adjoining owner.[20]

The concept of *tacking* is important in determining whether the period of adverse possession has been satisfied. As a general rule, the years of adverse possession by one occupant can be "tacked" on to the uninterrupted years of adverse possession by prior occupants. A later case will provide an excellent example of this concept.

The legal capacity of the person holding legal title is also important. Generally, periods during which the holder of legal title suffers from a disability (such as being a minor or being insane) do not count in determining the period of total adverse possession by an occupant. Jurisdictions are divided, however, as to whether the count begins where it left off once the disability has ended, or whether the count must start all over again. The latter approach could seem to afford too much protection to the legal title holder and be inconsistent with the policy considerations justifying adverse possession in the first place.

Shorter Periods: Color of Title, Payment of Taxes, Purchase at Tax Sale

Most states have provisions for shorter periods of adverse possession where taxes are paid by the person claiming adverse possession, where he or she has possession under color of title, or where property

---

[20] Some states, such as Arkansas, apply a similar doctrine known as the *theory of acquiesence.* Under this doctrine, the basic question is one of intention. Did the adjoining landowners mean to recognize the fence as the boundary? The controlling distinction was clearly stated by Justice Bohlinger in *Carney v. Barnes*, 235 Ark. 887, 363 S.W. 2d 417 (1962): "The case hinges on whether or not the old fence and the fence row was an agreed line between the two pieces of property. While the construction and maintenance of a division fence, when mutually regarded as a boundary, may constitute recognition and acquiescence, mere existence of a fence between adjoining land owners is not of itself sufficient. There must, therefore, be a mutual recognition of the fence as the dividing line." *See also* Fish v. Bush, 253 Ark 27, 484 S.W. 2d 525 (1972).

Table 6.2   General Adverse Possession Periods of Selected States

State	No. of Years	State	No. of Years
Alabama	10	Nebraska	10
Alaska	7	Nevada	5
Arizona	10	New Mexico	10
Arkansas	7	New York	10
California	5	North Carolina	20
Colorado	18	North Dakota	20
Florida	7	Ohio	21
Idaho	5	Oklahoma	15
Illinois	20	Oregon	10
Indiana	15	South Carolina	10
Iowa	10	South Dakota	20
Kansas	15	Tennessee	7
Kentucky	15	Texas	10
Maryland	20	Utah	7
Michigan	15	Virginia	15
Minnesota	15	Washington	10
Mississippi	10	West Virginia	10
Missouri	10	Wyoming	10
Montana	5		

Source: Derived from information contained in 7 R. POWELL, THE LAW OF REAL PROPERTY ¶ 1019 (1979).

was purchased at a tax sale. For example, Illinois law provides that every person

in the actual possession of lands or tenements, under claim and color of title, made in good faith, and who shall for seven successive years, continue in such possession, and shall also, during said time, pay all taxes legally assessed on such lands or tenements, shall be held and adjudged to be the legal owner of said lands or tenements, to the extent and according to the purport of his or her paper title[21]

Color of title is not a claim of ownership that is defective for some technical reason, nor is it meant to be something just short of absolute title. Rather, *color of title* is

an instrument or a record that in fact does not convey title but appears to have the effect of claimed ownership by the grantee. It need be only some semblance of title, however invalid may be that claim.

A forged deed, when taken in good faith, may constitute color of title if at the time of the purchase of the deed the grantee believed it to be genuine.[22]

The Definition of Adverse

Whether or not possession has been "adverse" is often a very difficult question to settle. Tests employed by the court relate to the nature and extent of the adverse possession—whether or not it is "open, notorious, uninterrupted, without

[21] ILL. REV. STAT. ch. 83, § 6 (1979). *See generally* 5 G. THOMPSON, COMMENTARIES ON THE MODERN LAW OF REAL PROPERTY § 2552 (1979). This reference provides an excellent summary of the

special rules in each state.
[22] Burgensen v. Clauss, 15 Ill. 2d 337, 155 N.E. 2d 20 (1958).

consent." When the issue arises in a lawsuit, it is generally left to the jury to decide. Fencing, cultivating, employing good timber management practices including thinning timber, and posting of "No Trespassing" signs would be important factors to consider. The fundamental issue is whether the property has been used in a manner in which an average owner would use it.

The use of land on which a claim of adverse possession is based must be more than casual. The extent of the use will depend somewhat on the nature of the land. In *Cagle v. Valter*, 20 Ill.2d 589, 170 N.E.2d 593 (1960), the court held that vague testimony about cutting brush and sprouts on bottomland does not show a sufficient dominion to support adverse possession. Likewise, clearing a small area in a large tract is not likely to support a claim of adverse possession to the whole tract except under most unusual circumstances.

There are some situations under which the period of adverse possession does not run. For example, generally one cannot claim by adverse possession against the public, i.e., federal or state governments or their subdivisions. Adverse possession does not run in favor of tenants who remain after their lease has expired; it does not run when land is divided and parties agree to the line, even though the line is mislocated; it does not run during the period of ownership of a life tenant against the reversioners or remaindermen.[23]

ADVERSE POSSESSION

WALTER v. JONES
Supreme Court of Illinois, 1958
15 Ill. 2d 220, 154 N.E. 2d 250

Ray Walter brought an action in ejectment against Violet Clark Jones and others in the circuit court of Christian County. The complaint alleged that plaintiff holds legal title to the south 57 acres of the west 71 acres of the north half of the southwest quarter of section 9, township 12 north, range 2 west of the third principal meridian; that defendant Violet Clark Jones is the owner of the north 14 acres of said west 71 acres; and that defendants are wrongfully in possession of a strip of land about 80 feet in width immediately south of said 14 acres, which strip is a part of plaintiff's land. Defendant Jones filed an answer alleging ownership of the strip of land by adverse possession. The cause was heard by the court without a jury, at the conclusion of which hearing judgment was rendered for the defendant. Plaintiff appeals, contending the evidence is not of sufficient weight to warrant a finding that title was acquired by adverse possession. Since a freehold is involved the cause is properly before this court on direct appeal.

There is no dispute as to the record title. On and prior to December 5, 1925, the entire 71-acre tract was owned by one John B. Colegrove. On that

---

[23] *See generally* 7 R. POWELL, THE LAW OF REAL PROPERTY ¶ 1012 *et seq.* (1979); 5 G. THOMPSON, COMMENTARIES ON THE MODERN LAW OF REAL PROPERTY § 2540 *et seq.* (1979).

date he conveyed the north 14 acres to Jennie Seibert. She and her husband occupied it until 1929, when she reconveyed to Colegrove. Edward and Millie Kenetz acquired title in 1932, and they conveyed to defendant in 1941. On October 1, 1955, defendant deeded the 14 acres to Albert and Donna Gherardini, who reconveyed to her in 1957. The Gherardinis remained in possession as tenants. The remaining 57-acre tract owned by John B. Colegrove was sold at a foreclosure sale in 1931, and after various conveyances it was purchased by the plaintiff on April 2, 1943. Prior to that date he had farmed the land as tenant of Colegrove.

The property in dispute measures 80 feet in width from north to south, and 2,090 feet in length east and west. It comprises about four acres in area, of which only about one-half acre is suitable for cultivation. The east three-fourths of the strip is sloping and covered with brush patches. The west portion has some trees. In 1927, after the Seiberts acquired the north 14 acres, they erected a fence 20 inches high and about 200 feet long, for a hog lot, in about the same place where the defendant now claims the boundary to be. At that time Seibert asked Colegrove, the owner of the property to the south, whether he wanted a survey made to determine the boundary line. Colegrove replied that he did not, and told Seibert to build the fence at his own judgment. Seibert testified he farmed the land north of the fence with Colegrove's permission.

When Kenetz took possession in 1932, the 200-foot section of fence was still standing. Neither Kenetz nor his wife was living at the time of the trial. According to the testimony of a neighbor, Kenetz farmed and pastured the land in question and threatened to shoot any cattle that broke through his fence line, which then extended clear through. In 1939 the defendant, Violet Jones, became interested in buying the 14-acre tract and examined the property. She testified that the fence then extended the entire length of the tract and that the wire was old and brittle and the posts rotten or decayed. She further testified that Kenetz stated the property ran from the north fence to the south fence. She occupied the tract, including the disputed strip, until 1955. During that period she farmed the one-half acre of the disputed strip that was farmable, used part for pasture and planted some trees thereon. She also built a garage, with the plaintiff's assistance, which extended into the disputed area. Violet Jones testified further that during the period of her occupancy she maintained the fence on the south, replacing worn out wire and posts from time to time but never changing its location; that when plaintiff's cows came through the fence she told him he had better fix it, and he put up another strand of wire; and that at no time did he make any assertion of ownership to the property north of the fence.

In 1946 the plaintiff married the daughter of Violet Jones, and a friendly and normal family relationship existed between them. He was permitted to let his cattle in through the south fence to pasture on portions of the property north of the fence which were not farmed, and defendant's sheep were allowed to pasture on plaintiff's land. There was no dispute as to the boundary until after Gheradini purchased the 14 acre tract in 1955. The plaintiff began to remove the fence, whereupon Gherardini objected, claiming ownership of the land north of it. The plaintiff then obtained a survey of his tract, which disclosed that the Gherardinis were in possession of a portion of land belonging to the 57-acre tract. They continued to occupy the north 14 acres, including the disputed strip, at the time the present action was brought, although they had reconveyed the property to Violet Jones in November, 1957.

The plaintiff testified that when defendant acquired the 14 acres there was very little fence, if any; that there were a few posts at the east end without any wire; and that he set posts and put on barbed wire. He built about a quarter-mile of fence from a point near the east line, so as to enclose some corn stalk ground for pasturing purposes. He testified that the fence was not intended as a division fence but was put there temporarily as a stock fence; and that he pastured on both sides of it every year except the last two years.

The plaintiff contends the evidence is insufficient to establish the defense of adverse possession; that any possession of the disputed strip by defendant and her predecessors prior to 1955 was permissive rather than adverse or hostile; and that in any event proof of adverse possession was not clear and unequivocal with respect to the boundary of the area claimed. The rules of law applicable in cases of this kind are well established. Where the plaintiff in an action of ejectment has proved a connected title from the United States, the presumption is that such title is valid, and that possession of the real estate is subservient to the rights of the owner of the record title. The burden of producing evidence to overcome the presumption is on the defendant; and the proof to establish title by adverse possession must be clear, positive and unequivocal. It must show a definitely defined tract; that the possession thereof was hostile, actual, visible, notorious and exclusive; and that such possession was continuous for twenty years or more under claim of ownership. Where the original possession is permissive and consistent with the title of the true owner, it will not become adverse, so as to start the running of the Statute of Limitations, until the party in possession has done some act equivalent, under the circumstances of the case, to a repudiation of the permissive character of the possession.

To constitute a bar under the statute, however, it is not necessary that the possession be accompanied by an express declaration or claim of title. It is sufficient if the proof shows that the party in possession has acted so as to clearly indicate he did claim title; and that he has been in actual, visible, and exclusive possession for 20 years with acts of ownership during that period. The acts required to accomplish adverse possession may vary, depending upon the nature of the property itself and the uses to which it is adaptable. The possession is not required to be more full than the character of the land admits. A fence is notice of actual occupancy; and such acts of dominion over land as will indicate to persons residing in the immediate neighborhood who has the exclusive management and control of the land are sufficient to constitute possession.

Applying the foregoing rules to the evidence in this record we think the trial court was justified in its conclusion. While the initial possession by the Seiberts in 1925 may have been permissive in character it is evident that

Kenetz, who purchased in 1932, claimed ownership to the fence line. His conduct, as testified to by neighbors, is entirely inconsistent with a permissive occupancy. It is also clear that the defendant, who bought in 1941, as well as her subsequent grantees, understood that the fence marked the southern boundary of the tract. She maintained and rebuilt it, and used the land for the only purposes for which it was suitable. She farmed a small portion, planted trees and pastured livestock thereon. The land is hilly, largely covered with brush patches, and not suitable for general farming. It appears that little more could have been done by defendant and her predecessor in title to show their intention to exercise dominion over it. The fence was visible for a considerable distance from the road which runs north and south along the west line of the tracts involved here, and indicated to plaintiff and other persons residing in the neighborhood that it was the boundary separating the two tracts. While the plaintiff occasionally pastured his livestock on property north of it, the testimony indicates this was done with permission of defendant Violet Jones, and not with a claim or right. Not until the survey was made did the plaintiff make any assertion of ownership to property north of the fence. Prior to that time neither plaintiff was aware of the fact that the fence encroached upon his land. Under such circumstances it is highly unlikely that defendant's possession could have been permissive.

We conclude that the judgment of the circuit court is supported by the evidence, and no error has been shown therein. The judgment will therefore be affirmed.

STUDY QUESTIONS

1. Compare and contrast the various mechanisms for bringing a buyer and a seller of real estate together.

2. What kinds of questions should be answered in a contract for the sale of agricultural real estate?

3. How does an escrow arrangement work?

4. What is an option contract?

5. What are the usual steps involved in the purchase of real estate?

6. What kinds of real estate contract problems were discussed in the cases of this chapter? How might those problems have been avoided?

7. What is the purpose of a deed?

8. What is the difference between a warranty deed and a quitclaim deed? Can good title be acquired with a quitclaim deed?

9. Why should deeds be recorded?

10. Can a deed be used to effect a death transfer?

11. What is the effect of a deed executed by a minor? An undelivered deed? A deed with a missing legal description?

12. Describe the various systems used to measure land.

13. Compare and contrast the different ways of guaranteeing good title.

14. What is the nature of eminent domain?

15. What prerequisites are necessary before the power of eminent domain can be exercised?

16. Describe the kinds of damages for which a landowner may be compensated in a condemnation proceeding.

17. Generally, when must an owner yield possession of condemned land?

18. What conditions are necessary before adverse possession can apply? What is the rationale for adverse possession?

19. To what extent must one claiming under adverse possession have used the property?

20. Can periods of adverse use by prior occupants be taken into account in determining the duration of adverse possession?

21. To what extent is infancy or insanity on the part of the holder of title important in determining whether adverse possession is present?

22. Is the time period for adverse possession less if the occupant has been paying real estate taxes?

23. Steve Thompson and Paul Williams were neighbors. Some years ago they built a fence on an agreed boundary line. Actually, the fence was placed 25 feet inside Thompson's land. Williams cultivated up to the fence for 10 years without knowing of the mistake. Then he sold his farm to Jim Brewster, who had a survey made. The surveyor told Brewster of the mistake, but Brewster did nothing about it. He continued to cultivate up to the fence for another 10 years. When Thompson finally learned of the mistake, he immediately demanded that the fence be moved to the true line.

Does he have a legal right to do this? Please explain. Would the answer be different if Thompson had been legally insane for the previous 5 years?

24. Your neighbor tells you that the county has filed a petition to condemn 40 acres of her farm so that Disney Productions can build a Disney World in the heart of your state. She further informs you that this is the first time she has ever heard of the plan. She asks you if there is anything she can do to prevent the action. Please reply, discussing all possible defenses to this eminent domain proceeding.

7

Rights and Limitations in the Use and Ownership of Agricultural Property

It has been stated that the use of agricultural land for agricultural purposes may be a natural right. As a general statement, this is acceptable, but in the sections which follow in this chapter, it will become apparent that even the agricultural use of land is conditioned by many statutory and common-law rules. Some of these rules operate as limitations and some operate to enlarge and to protect the rights of use.

The concept of rights in the use of land is a relative consideration based upon the rights of others who own adjoining land or who in some way may be affected by use of land. Sometimes these rights and limitations are divided into two major categories, one dealing with the rights of an owner in the use of his or her own land and a second dealing with rights and limitations with regard to adjacent land.

Regulation of land use, including agricultural land use, is accomplished by a variety of legal rules. These include the laws of easement, nuisance, lateral and subjacent support, trespass, boundaries, and many others. The federal, state, and local governments and certain other local political units have authority to impose reasonable regulations and limitations upon an owner's use of land through exercise of police power. This is done directly by means of city and county zoning ordinances and indirectly through taxation, use of the power of eminent domain, grants-in-aid, and certain voluntary programs of government containing monetary inducements. Many factors influence lawmaking bodies and the courts in enacting laws and regulations and arriving at decisions regarding relative rights in the use of land. As far as the future is concerned, several trends can be expected to be of material significance in determinations of rights and limitations in using farm property.

1. Controls will increase. Economic and social pressures and the demand for space itself will increase, and more judgments will have to be made about the merits of different kinds of usage. The conflicts may be more intense, but the level of conflict will be different—it will be centered more on alternative kinds of control than on control versus no control. This is not a new problem—the courts have made some policy headway in zoning cases and in "balancing the equities" in nuisance cases.

2. Land as a factor in agricultural production is becoming more important once again because of the increasing costs of fertilizer and of energy in particular. This will change value judgments regarding the use of agricultural land.

3. More planning will be done. The growth of urbanization and the location of more industry in "parks" and model towns are factors making planning imperative.

4. The zoning activity of local bodies—counties and municipalities—will eventually lead to more legislation aimed at more uniform and effective control of those activities which evolve as common problems in all zoning efforts.

5. The planning for land use and governmental decisions based on this planning will have to more and more consider judgments about the values in our society, because the merits of different kinds of use can be weighed only in light of the weigher's feelings about values to be preserved.

6. The federal government will become more and more insistent that states step up their planning activity if they are to qualify for various kinds of federal aid. This will induce states to take the planning function more seriously, which will in turn lend impetus and direction to local planning bodies—planning and zoning commissions, municipalities, watershed organizations, and conservancy districts, for example.

7. Universities will, of necessity, expand their research and public service facilities in the area of land use planning and control.

8. The need for private controls through contract, covenant, and mutual agreements will remain, but the subject matter of such controls will change since more current values will be protected both by a public planning and zoning effort through the establishment of more local public bodies and by additional legislation.

7.1 EASEMENTS AND COVENANTS RUNNING WITH THE LAND

Every owner of land has, by virtue of ownership, certain rights in the land of adjoining owners, in waters that come within the boundaries, and in the use of the premises. These rights are spoken of generally as "rights in land" and for the most part consist of rules which have developed as a result of the close physical association of properties and the policy of allowing owners certain privileges with respect to the property of others in order that they may make a reasonable use of their own. One of the most important rights which one may have in the lands of another is an easement. An *easement* has been defined as the right of one property owner to use the land of another for some specific purpose. Such tracts are usually adjacent but need not be. The most common example is a right-of-way across the land of another, spoken of as an "easement of way." Other examples of easements which may be acquired are the right to flood the land of an upper owner, to change the flow of surface waters onto the land of lower owners, and to maintain a drain across the land of another.[1] One purchasing land should ascertain whether or not the land will be subject to an easement of any kind in adjacent landowners.

Generally, easements pass to subsequent owners of the land and can be lost only by nonuse—when such nonuse amounts to an abandonment of the use formerly made— or by specific conveyance. As a matter of terminology, the land in which a right exists is called a *dominant tenement*, and the land which is burdened is called a *servient tenement*. Easements may be conveyed by lease, will, quitclaim, or warranty deed. Also, easements cease to exist when the dominant and servient ownerships are "merged" or held by the same person. When a public easement, such as one for road or school purposes, terminates, the original owner or the owner's heirs or assigns may have the right to repossess, unless barred by a statute of limitations.

Creation of Easements[2]

An easement can be created by any of four methods: express grant, reservation, prescription, or implication. The *express grant or reservation* is stated in a deed. For example, the owner of tract A could execute an easement deed to the owner of tract B, whereby owner A creates an easement of way across the property so that owner B will have more convenient access. Alternatively, the easement could have been created by reservation in a deed. For example, owner B might have originally owned tracts A and B. When owner B deeded tract A to another person, owner B could have reserved an easement of way across tract A.

The creation of an *easement by prescription* is illustrated in the case of *Wiley v. Lamprecht*, 400 Ill. 587, 81 N.E.2d 459 (1948), wherein the court noted

the main question in the case is whether or not the proof establishes use of the cartway for more than 20 years. In order to establish a way by prescription, public or private, the use must be adverse, uninterrupted, ... continuous and under a claim of right. The burden of establishing such a right rests on the party pleading it. Where a way

---

[1] When the easement right benefits the holder in the holder's physical use and enjoyment of another tract of land, an *easement appurtenant* is said to exist. Easements of way fit into this category. The easement can be enjoyed by anyone possessing the "dominant tenement." *Easements in gross* comprise a second category of easements. In such easements, the holder's enjoyment of an adjacent tract of land is not enhanced. In fact, there is no dominant tenement. A right-of-way for a utility line is an example of the easement in gross.

[2] *See generally* 3 R. POWELL, THE LAW OF REAL PROPERTY ¶¶ 404 *et seq.* (1979).

has been used openly, uninterruptedly, [and] continuously...for more than a period of 20 years, origin of the way not being shown, there is a presumption of a right or grant from the long acquiescence of the party upon whose land the way is located.

Drainage cases provide another class of examples in which easements are often created by prescription. Such cases will be discussed in more detail in a subsequent chapter. In most states the required period of prescription is identical to the period required for acquisition of land by adverse possession. A table showing these periods for selected states appeared in the previous chapter.

Implied easements arise in situations where a conveyance of property has been made with no express reservation of an easement, but where the underlying circumstances imply an intention to create an easement. In effect, the courts protect the parties from their lack of forethought by assuming an unarticulated intention. For an easement by implication to exist, a separation of title must occur—adjacent lands must be initially owned by a single owner and subsequently sold so that there is more than one owner.

Some courts recognize the common-law distinction between implied easements of absolute necessity and implied easements of reasonable necessity. Implied easements of absolute necessity arise, for example, when the owner of a tract of land sells part of the tract that has *no* outlet to a public road except over the remaining lands of the seller. An implied easement of reasonable necessity would be created if some other access was possible but would result in great hardship. For the implied easement of reasonable necessity to be recognized, prior, continuous, and obvious use of the right-of-way must exist in addition to the separation of title and the reasonable necessity.

IMPLIED EASEMENT OF REASONABLE NECESSITY

WALKER v. WITT
Supreme Court of Illinois, 1953
4 Ill. 2d 16, 122 N.E. 2d 175

This is an appeal from two judgment orders of the circuit court of Sangamon County. The first order, entered on July 9, 1953, pursuant to plaintiff's motion for judgment on the pleadings, found the defendant, Ambrose Witt, guilty of trespass on the lands and crops of the plaintiffs and ordered that a jury be impaneled for the purpose of determining damages. The second order, entered on January 29, 1954, after a jury had been waived, awarded the plaintiffs actual damages in the amount of $34 and exemplary damages in the amount of $315.

The dispute which occasioned the suit concerned the use made by the defendant of a fifteen-foot strip of land belonging to the plaintiffs as a means of ingress and egress for the purpose of cultivating and farming an adjacent tract of land owned by the defendant. The existence of an easement being in issue, a freehold is involved and this court has jurisdiction on direct appeal.

The plaintiffs own a tract of farmland in Sangamon County, containing 20 acres. Along the west side of this land, which we refer to as tract A, runs a public road. The defendant owns 80 acres of land which adjoins the plaintiffs' said land on the east. This land, which will be referred to as tract B, is completely landlocked, it not being adjacent to any public road. However, the defendant claims an easement by implication over the north fifteen feet of tract A in order to have an ingress and egress to tract B.

In 1942 the United States of America acquired title to all of section 23, which included both of said tracts. On January 3, 1946, the United States conveyed tract A to the plaintiffs' predecessors in title, and on that date the United States still owned different sides of said section. Eleven days later, on January 14, 1946, the United States conveyed tract B to defendant's predecessor in title, still owning other land in said section which bordered upon two public highways.

On June 20, 1952, and on other occasions prior thereto, the defendant drove a farm tractor and other farm machinery over said fifteen-foot strip on tract A for the purpose of getting to and from tract B, destroying crops of the plaintiffs planted in said strip and for which the plaintiffs brought this instant suit for damages. The plaintiffs claimed said acts constituted trespasses, and the trial court sustained their position. The defendant contends he was not trespassing but had an easement by implication over said land. In support thereof he alleges the following: that at the time the government of the United States acquired title to tract B, and for more than forty years prior thereto, the owner or owners of said tract used said fifteen-foot strip of land as a means of ingress and egress to tract B; that at all times prior to the time the United States acquired title and during the time the United States held title to tract B, the said fifteen-foot strip of land was a permanent, open, visible, and apparent means of ingress and egress to tract B; that at the time the defendant purchased tract B no other land or roadway was then used or available as a means of ingress and egress to said tract, and said land or roadway over the fifteen-foot strip was then and is now necessary to the enjoyment and use of said tract; that no other means of ingress or egress is presently available to tract B.

The defendant argues on this appeal that he acquired an easement on the fifteen-foot strip of land by implied grant and that judgment on the pleadings was not proper. The plaintiffs contend that even if such an easement as claimed by the defendant existed prior to the time title to both tracts merged in the government, such merger destroyed the easement, and when the government sold the land such easement was not revived nor did it pass by implication.

As has been stated, from July, 1942, to January, 1946, the United States owned both of the tracts of land in question. Since it is fundamental that one cannot have an easement in his own land, an easement of one part with respect to another does not arise, if at all, until there is a severance of ownership. Therefore, whether an easement was created by implication in tract A (the alleged servient estate) must be determined as of the time it was severed from the other land of the grantor, which was January 3, 1946.

Thus, in order to sustain his position, the defendant's allegations must show that as of January 3, 1946, the United States had an easement by implication in tract A entitling it to use the north fifteen feet thereof for purposes of ingress and egress to their land.

The essential elements which must exist to create an [implied easement of reasonable necessity] are as follows: "(1) there must be a separation of title; (2) before the separation occurs, the use which would give rise to an easement must have been so long continued, obvious or manifest to that degree which will show the use was meant to be permanent; and (3) it is necesary that the use of the claimed easement be essential to the beneficial enjoyment of the land granted or retained."

In this case it is clear that the first two of the enumerated elements are satisfied, but it is not alleged by the defendant that as of January 3, 1946, the use of the claimed easement was [reasonably necessary] for the beneficial enjoyment of the land retained by the United States. On the contrary, the defendant admits that at the time the United States sold tract A to the plaintiffs' predecessors in title, the government still had other land in the section which was adjacent to and bordered by public highways on two different sides of the section. Actually, the admitted facts establish that, as of the time tract A was conveyed by the government to plaintiffs' predecessors in title, the government still owned the entire remainder of the south half of said section. Moreover, there were public highways running along both the east and west sides of said section. Such being the case, the government had easy access to the land described as tract B over other land in said half section. It cannot, therefore, be said that the use of said fifteen-foot strip of land in tract A was essential or necessary to beneficial enjoyment of the land which it retained.

It is to be noted that the attempt here is to establish an easement by implied reservation, rather than by implied grant. While the cases, particularly the later ones, have not always distinguished between the two types of cases, still there are many decisions wherein courts have taken the position that a grantor should not be permitted to claim an easement by implied reservation and thus derogate from his grant in the absence of showing a real necessity therefore. This distinction does not prevail in the Illinois cases, and, as aforesaid, the degree of necessity required is not so strict, it being necessary only that "the use of the claimed easement be essential to the beneficial enjoyment of the land granted or retained." However, as we have pointed out, the defendant has not even shown this more liberal requirement to be satisfied, since it is undisputed that the government at the time it conveyed the alleged servient estate had easy and convenient access to the alleged dominant estate over other land which it owned in the section. This court has said that if available alternatives affording reasonable means of ingress and egress are shown to exist, an easement of implication is not sanctioned.

While there can be no question but that a person whose land is landlocked must be accorded an access to a public road, still, the defendant has not alleged facts showing a right to look to the plaintiffs for such access, especially in view of the fact that, where an owner of land conveys a parcel thereof which has no outlet to a highway except over the remaining land of the grantor or over the land of strangers, a way of necessity exists over the remaining lands of the grantor.

We conclude, therefore, that the trial court was correct in allowing plaintiffs' motion for judgment on the pleadings, and inasmuch as the defendant does not argue that the determination of damages was in error unless the court was incorrect in holding the defendant did not have an easement in said fifteen-foot strip, both judgment orders are correct and are accordingly affirmed.

The easement of way is probably the most common example of an easement. Such a right may be acquired by a grant or reservation in a deed, by long-continued use (as specified by state law), or by "necessity"[3] when an owner must cross the land of others to reach a highway. Also, the public may acquire an easement of way in less than the prescriptive period.

An easement cannot be used more heavily after acquisition than before if such use will result in damage to the servient tenement. The person using an easement of way is responsible for its upkeep, and the owner of the servient tenement is not responsible for damage to it unless the damage is caused negligently or willfully. For example, one having an easement across a neighbor's pasture cannot complain of damage to the land by the neighbor's livestock if the neighbor has been in the habit of pasturing the field and the owner of the easement has not fenced it off.

Covenants Running with the Land[4]

Parties conveying land often make certain agreements concerning its use. These conditions may be written into the deed and become binding upon subsequent owners acquiring the land through the regular chain of title. Such binding agreements are called "covenants running with the land." One of the most familiar examples is the well-known restrictive covenant used to control the type of houses constructed in a residential area or subdivision. The courts have set up certain standards which aid in defining and classifying covenants.

There are two general classifications: express covenants and implied covenants. An *express covenant* is one that is expli-

---

[3] Where property is landlocked, many states utilize the concept of an implied easement to create an easement of way. Other states have been more direct, giving the owner of landlocked property a right tantamount to a right of private condemnation. Missouri, for example, allows an owner of landlocked land to petition the circuit court for establishment of a private road. The circuit court appoints three disinterested residents as commissioners to view the premises, mark off the road, and assess damages. Where no objections are raised, the circuit court orders the establishment of the road and the payment of damages in accordance with the commissioners' report. If an objection is filed by the person across whose land the private road would pass, that person is entitled to a determination of damages by a jury trial. The landowner whose land is taken for the road can have a reasonable time not to exceed 6 months to erect fences or gather growing crops. *See* Mo. Ann. Stat. § 228.34 *et seq.* (Vernon 1952).

[4] *See generally* 5 R. Powell, The Law of Real Property ¶¶ 670 *et seq.*; 7 G. Thompson, Commentaries on the Modern Law of Property §§ 3150 *et seq.* (1962).

citly stated in a deed. As one would suppose, an *implied covenant* is not stated in writing but is implied from the language of the deed and existing conditions. For example, if a purchaser buys land with full knowledge that a tenant is in possession, an agreement to accept the tenant's possession will be inferred. With respect to covenants which run with the land, the courts have said that they must concern the land itself and refer to the thing granted or demised. An agreement to drink a quart of milk every day would not run with the land and bind subsequent grantees, because it does not concern the land, but a covenant for the quiet enjoyment of the land or a covenant that the grantor has a clear title would run with the land because it directly concerns it.

Covenants for the repair of fences or those creating charges and liens on the land will run with the land. Frequently an owner will convey a farm to a child interested in farming, subject to fixed payments or charges in favor of other children. Generally speaking, any party in interest injured by the breach of such a covenant may enforce it or collect damages for its breach.

A covenant running with land may confer a burden or a benefit on the owner of the land to which it attaches, depending upon its terms. A covenant of quiet enjoy-ment from the grantor is a benefit to the owners of land, whereas a covenant to keep all of a division fence in repair would be a burden.

Enforcing the Covenants. Generally, only the owner of land benefited by a restrictive covenant or someone else expressly intended to be benefited has standing to enforce a restrictive covenant. Possible remedies for breach of the restrictive covenant include damages, injunction, or specific enforcement.

Duration. As a general rule restrictive covenants can be enforced for as long a period as the original parties intended. Where the original writing does not specify a duration, some states statutorily limit the duration to 20 or 30 years. Of course, the parties themselves may terminate the covenant before the intended period has passed.

Termination. Conduct of the parties can terminate the restrictive covenant. Examples of such conduct include a breach of the promise followed by acquiescence, merger, an express release or rescission, or conduct indicating an intent not to enforce the right followed by reliance on the part of the other party. Sometimes courts will terminate a covenant because of changing circumstances, e.g., the changing character of the geographic area.

UNCONSTITUTIONAL RESTRICTIVE COVENANTS

WEST HILL BAPTIST CHURCH v. ABBATE
Court of Common Pleas of Ohio, Summit County, 1969
24 Ohio Misc. 66, 261 N.E. 2d 196

Cramer, J. The plaintiff seeks a declaratory judgment declaring that certain restrictive covenants appearing in the chain of title of its real estate be declared invalid and unenforceable. United in interest with the plaintiff and seeking the same relief as does plaintiff, but seeking it by way of cross-petition and joined as defendants here, are Adath Israel Anshe Sfard (hereinafter referred to as Anshe Sfard) and the Maronite Club of Akron, Ohio. These latter defendants are owners.

There are two sets of covenants affecting the lands in question, one herein referred to as the Wright restrictions—recorded May 29, 1952, and the other herein referred to as the Vaughn restrictions.

The Wright restrictions seem to limit the use of land located therein to residential and agricultural and the Vaughn restrictions purport to limit the use of land located therein to agricultural and single family residential use. Both sets of restrictions contain provisions as to lot sizes, frontage, building setbacks and minimum structure size.

The pleadings and the evidence raise the issue as to whether the plaintiff, The Maronite Club and Anshe Sfard, as property owners and religious organizations, have the right to construct and operate their respective churches and synagogue thereon notwithstanding the existence of two sets of restrictive covenants which prohibit the use of their property for other than single family residence purposes.

It is urged that those who seek the enforcement of the restrictive covenants, and their predecessors, have for a long period of time, acquiesced in the violation of the restrictions and are, therefore, estopped from seeking their enforcement.

It is asserted that the erection of the two churches in the area having been assented to, the defendants are in no position to complain respecting the erection of additional churches and are, therefore, estopped from the enforcement of the covenant restricting the building of any structure for a use other than residential [or agricultural]. In this connection, it is asserted—with some justification under the evidence—that the existence of these churches in the area not only lulled the parties into feeling safe in purchasing their lands on which to erect churches and a synagogue but, in a sense, motivated them so to do.

It cannot in actuality be said that an estoppel occurred, because the churches were built only after litigation and not with the consent of the complaining defendants and their predecessors. Their failure to make a defense to those actions and allowing the judgments therein to be taken by default cannot be considered in the nature of either consent or acquiescence.

It is further claimed that conditions have so changed since the inception of the covenants so as to render them of no value, invalid and, therefore, unenforceable.

It is our opinion that the evidence shows that the restrictive covenants are still of substantial value to those for whose benefit the covenants operate.

[But] ...it would appear that before this particular claim [for a declaratory judgment] can be said to have been sustained it must be shown that a *radical* change has rendered the restrictions inoperative. This we cannot find from the evidence.

We come now to a consideration of the claim that the restrictions are, as they relate to houses of worship, violative of the Constitutions of the United States and of Ohio.

Zoning is the exercise of police power regulating and controlling the uses of real property. Restrictive covenants, with which we are here dealing, and which, of course, purport to control the use of real property are in the nature of private zoning or zoning by contract.

It would follow, however, that if a zoning ordinance is, in its operation, unconstitutional, a restrictive covenant in the same area having the same effect would likewise be unconstitutional.

The courts have considered that the private enjoyment of surrounding property and maintenance of its economic value are not considered important enough to require exclusion of religious uses.

It has also been held that a zoning ordinance which prohibits the use of certain residential land for church purposes does not bear any substantial relation to public health, safety, morals and general welfare. and, therefore, is violative of constitutional rights.

Thus, it seems to us, that covenants such as those here in issue, which seek to limit an area to residential use only, thereby barring churches, would be unconstitutional as to houses of worship if they were in the form of zoning ordinances or resolutions rather than covenants.

Our question then is: Are such *restrictive covenants* which bar churches and synagogues from areas unconstitutional as to such institutions?

In *Shelley v. Kraemer*, 334 U.S. 1, the court declared:

"That the action of state courts and of judicial officers in their official capacities is to be regarded as action of the state, within the meaning of the Fourteenth Amendment...."

Therefore, if this court were to enforce (by declaratory judgment) the restrictive covenants here we would be engaging in state action.

In *Kraemer, supra*, the United States Supreme Court held that judicial enforcement by a state court of a restrictive covenant excluding persons from purchasing real property because of their race or color was unconstitutional as state action within the prohibition of the Fourteenth Amendment and thereby violated due process and equal protection of law.

It would thus appear that the rationale of *Kraemer, supra*, applies with equal force here.

It is our conclusion that the enforcement of these covenants which would result in prohibiting the use by the plaintiff and the cross-petitioners of their property for the erection thereon of houses of worship, would constitute state action (through this court) violative of the free exercise of religion provision of the First Amendment of the Constitution of the United States and of comparable provisions of the Constitution of Ohio and against public policy, and that such action bears no reasonable relationship to the public health, safety, morals and general welfare.

We, therefore, declare that such restrictive covenants are not enforceable, so as to prevent the use of the properties of plaintiff and cross-petitioners to which they seek to put them, namely, the erection and maintenance of churches and a synagogue and all structures necessary to be used in connection therewith.

Judgment for plaintiffs.

7.2 AIR RIGHTS, SOLAR RIGHTS, RIGHTS TO LATERAL AND SUBJACENT SUPPORT, AND RIGHTS AGAINST TRESPASSERS

Additional rights of landowners include certain rights for air and light, the right to lateral and subjacent support, and rights against trespassers. Rights to water are also present, but will be discussed in a subsequent chapter.

Of all these rights, a landowner's rights in the air above are probably the least significant. Generally, the landowner's rights to airspace are not exclusive, though they do include the right to be free from excessive noise and unreasonable transit of aircraft.

Similarly, a landowner has only limited rights for light. As a general rule, when one acquires property from another, courts do not recognize an implicit grant of light over the grantor's remaining land. Also, courts generally do not recognize a right to acquire an easement for light and air by prescription. Interestingly, the Missouri legislature preferred not to rely on these general rules when it passed legislation preventing the acquisition of solar easements by prescription.[5]

Lateral and Subjacent Support

When an owner of land makes an excavation near his or her property line and causes the land of another to cave in, the injured owner is entitled to be paid for the destruction of "lateral support." When a coal company tunnels under farmland and causes it to subside or sink, the owner of the land is entitled to damages for the loss of "subjacent support." *Lateral support* is the right to have land supported by the land which lies next to it. *Subjacent support* is the right to have land supported by the land which lies under it.

A farm owner has a right to lateral support against all owners with adjoining land, even when part of the adjoining land is a road owned by the public. To what extent the idea of lateral support would apply to damage caused by unchecked erosion on adjoining land is an unsettled question. The right of lateral support is effective against positive acts such as excavation or the cutting of grades by road officials. Sometimes the damages recoverable are very small, but when a large area is affected or buildings which have stood for a long time near the property line are caused to fall, substantial damages may be recovered.[6] Among the several states there is a division

---

[5] H.B. No. 71, 80th Gen. Assembly [Codified at Mo. ANN. STAT. § 442.012 (Vernon)]. The act reads as follows: "SECTION 1.   1. The right to utilize solar energy is a property right but eminent domain may not be used to obtain such property right.   2. Any easements obtained for the purpose of construction, reconstruction, remodeling or acquisition of a solar energy device shall only be created in writing and shall be subject to the same conveyancing and instrument recording requirements as other easements. Any instrument creating a solar easement shall include, but not be limited to: The vertical and horizontal angles, expressed in degrees, at which the solar easement extends over the real property subject to the solar easement and any terms or conditions or both

under which the solar easement is granted or will be terminated. Easements for solar light shall be considered a negative easement and cannot be acquired by prescription but must be negotiated expressly." *See generally* 1A G. THOMPSON, COMMENTARIES ON THE MODERN LAW OF REAL PROPERTY § § 235 *et seq.* (1980).

[6] In Korogodsky v. Chimberoff, 256 Ill. App. 255 (1930), plaintiffs wished to build on their lot, and in excavating were required to shore defendant's adjoining property to keep it from caving in on them. Plaintiff sued to recover for the expense of shoring the property. The court held for the defendant. "The owner of real estate is entitled to have his soil sustained in its natural state, when necessary, by the lateral support of the adjacent soil of the

of authority as to whether damage to buildings is recoverable. The right to lateral support for buildings and other improvements may be reserved, of course, when an owner conveys a part of the property.

The common law of lateral support has been further developed by statute in many states. These statutes typically prescribe the duty of an owner or an occupant of land on which excavations are made to furnish lateral and subjacent support to adjoining lands and structures. Illinois, for example, has a statute for the protection of adjacent landowners.[7] Excerpts from the law follow.

Each adjacent owner is entitled to the continuous lateral and subjacent support which his land receives from the adjoining land, subject to the right of the owner of the adjoining land to make proper and usual excavations on the same for purposes of construction or improvements, under the following conditions: ...

Any owner or possessor of land intending to make or to permit an excavation to be made on his land shall give due and reasonable notice in writing to the owner or owners of adjoining lands and adjoining buildings and other structures.... In making any excavation, reasonable care and precautions shall be taken to sustain the adjoining land as such, without regard to any building or other structure which may be thereon, and there is no liability for damage done to any building or other structure by reason of the excavation

except as herein provided or otherwise provided or allowed by law.... If the excavation is intended to be or is deeper than the standard depth of foundations as herein defined, then the owner of the land on which the excavation is being made, if given the necessary license to enter on adjoining land, and not otherwise, shall protect the said adjoining land and any building or other structure thereon, without cost to the owner thereof, by furnishing lateral and subjacent support to said adjoining land and all buildings and structures thereon, in such a manner as to protect the same from any damage by reason of the excavation and shall be liable to the owner of such property for any damages to the land or to any buildings or other structures thereon.

The right to subjacent support is important in agricultural areas where underground mining is carried on. Generally, a landowner is entitled to have his or her land supported in its natural state from beneath. Thus, if a mining company damages land in its natural state, the company is *absolutely* liable. If the land is improved by buildings and subsidence results in damage to the buildings as well as to the surface, the mining company also is *absolutely* liable for the damage to buildings only if the land would have collapsed in its natural state. If the subsidence would not have occurred except for the weight of the buildings, the mining company is *still* liable for the buildings if the mining was performed negligently.

---

adjoining owner. Moreover, a person owning such land and in the act of excavating is required to use reasonable skill and care in view of the character of the work being done and the nature of the soil so as to avoid doing unnecessary injury to the adjoining property. The one making the improvement has a common law right to go upon the premises of the other for the purpose of shoring

such building in order to protect property, when it is necessary, to prevent damage by reason of an excavation, but this done at his own expense and cost."

[7] ILL. REV. STAT. ch. 17 1/2, § 51. For a discussion of lateral support in Illinois see *The Doctrine of Lateral Support in Illinois*, 1956 ILL. LAW F. 646.

Rights to lateral and subjacent support can be waived in a deed or lease. One granting mineral rights to another should not waive such rights and should make adequate provision for subjacent support to protect the agricultural use of the surface.

Some states have enacted legislation to provide for a sharing of subsidence risk. Illinois, for example, has a law that encourages landowners to include a "subsidence clause" in their insurance policies.[8] Insurance companies must automatically offer the state subsidized subsidence insurance as a part of their standard policies in all counties where subsidence is a potential problem. A separate premium must be stated. The subsidence insurance protection will be effective unless expressly waived by the landowner. In its initial form, protection was limited to *structures* on real estate and specifically excluded land, trees, plants, and crops.

SUBJACENT SUPPORT

WILMS v. JESS
Supreme Court of Illinois, 1880
94 Ill. 464

Plaintiff-appellee brought an action against defendants in the circuit court of Sangamon County, for injuries to his premises, caused by the removal by the defendant of the underlying strata of coal, without leaving sufficient support for the surface.

The entire title to the lot of ground involved in the litigation was originally in Jacob Bunn; but, on the 20th day of March, 1870, he leased to the assignor of appellants and his co-defendants "the sole and exclusive right of boring, digging and otherwise prospecting for coal," in a large body of land, including this lot, and of "taking out and working the said coal, together with the right of way and surface of so much of the track as may be necessary for the economical use of the same." The lease contained, among others, this clause:

It is further understood and agreed, that the said party of the second part shall mine the coal in a workmanlike manner, no pillars to be withdrawn within six hundred (600) feet of the shaft, and that the entries giving access to the coal not mined at the termination of this lease shall be turned over to the party of the first part in as good condition as the nature of the mine will admit.

On the 5th day of October, 1877, Bunn, having previously sold, conveyed this lot to appellee, making this exception in the deed: "Except all coals and minerals of every description under the surface of said premises (which is hereby expressly reserved), and the right to take therefrom all coals and minerals, with the privilege of extending entries thereunder."

---

[8]ILL. REV. STAT. ch. 73, § 1065.401 *et seq.*

Appellee at once took possession of the lot and soon thereafter commenced making improvements thereon, and had dug a well, constructed a cistern, begun the erection of a house which was estimated to cost some $5,500 and progressed therewith until the brick work was completed, the frame work raised and sheeted ready for weather-boarding, and the roof and cupola completed, when the surface of the underlying soil suddenly subsided for the distance of some three feet, and thereby seriously damaged the house and destroyed the well and cistern.

This was caused by defendants' mining and removing the strata of coal underlying the lot.

The gist of the action is the mining and removal of the coal without leaving sufficient support for the surface.

Defendants pleaded not guilty. The cause was submitted to a jury who returned a verdict finding the defendants guilty, and assessing the plaintiff's damages at $1000. The circuit court, after overruling motions for new trial and in arrest of judgment, rendered judgment, upon this verdict—and appellant took the case, by appeal, to the Appellate Court for the Third District, where the judgment of the circuit court was affirmed.

The present appeal is from that judgment of affirmance.

Where the surface of land belongs to one and the minerals to another, no evidence of title appearing to regulate or qualify their rights of enjoyment, the owner of the minerals cannot remove them without leaving support sufficient to maintain the surface in its natural state.

But it is contended, defendants were exonerated from protecting the surface, because the lease here stipulates that "no pillars shall be withdrawn within six hundred feet of the shaft," upon the principle that, "having expressed *some*, the parties have expressed *all* the conditions by which they intend to be bound under that instrument."

By looking to the lease we think it quite clear this stipulation has relation to the mine only, and no reference whatever to the superincumbent soil. The whole clause relates to the manner of working the mine and the condition in which it shall be left. It requires that the mining shall be done in a workmanlike manner, that no pillars shall be withdrawn within six hundred feet of the shaft, and that the entries giving access to the coal not mined at the termination of the lease, shall be turned over, etc., in good condition, etc.—all for the obvious purpose of preserving that shaft and access to coal not mined.

The rule is well settled, when one owning the whole fee grants the minerals, reserving the surface to himself, his grantee is entitled only to so much of the minerals as he can get without injury to the superincumbent soil.

And it is held, where a land owner sells the surface, reserving to himself the minerals with power to get them, he must, if he intends to have power to get them in a way which will destroy the surface, frame the reservation in such a way as to show clearly that he is intended to have that power.

But, it is contended, this obligation to protect the superincumbent soil only extends to the soil in its natural state, and that no obligation rests on the owner of the subjacent strata to support additional buildings, in the absence of express stipulation to that effect. This is, doubtless, true, but "the mere prescence of a building or other structure upon the surface does not prevent a recovery for injuries to the surface, unless it is shown that the subsidence would not have occurred except for the presence of the buildings. Where the injury would have resulted from the act if no buildings existed upon the surface, the act creating the subsidence is wrongful and renders the owners of the mines liable for all damages that result therefrom, as well to the buildings as to the land itself.

The act of removing all support from the superincumbent soil is, prima facie, the cause of its subsequently subsiding, but if the subsiding is, in fact, caused by the weight of buildings erected subsequent to the execution of the lease of the mine, this is in the nature of contributive negligence, and may be proved in defense. The authorities do not require that plaintiff's proofs shall exclude that hypothesis in the first instance.

The judgment of the Appellate Court is affirmed.

Trespassers

Civil Trespass. The mere entry on another's property without permission is a technical trespass even when no damage is done, and a recovery at law may be had though the compensation may be only nominal. This right of recovery, whether or not actual damage is suffered, is considered vital to the preservation of the concept of absolute ownership.

The law has declared numerous acts to constitute a trespass. The mere overhanging of the branches of a tree or the shooting of a gun across an individual's land constitutes trespass. Hunting, driving animals, injuring buildings, fences, or improvements, injuring crops, and damaging the soil itself in any unauthorized way all may constitute a trespass.

Since one is presumed to own a column of air to the sky, invasion of this column of air may also amount to a trespass. Some concession, however, had to be made to the flying of planes. Even so, the operators of aircraft may be liable to the owner of the column of air if they violate rights and cause damage. In this connection the courts have recognized the possibility of damage by cloud seeding, and in a Texas case a temporary injunction was granted against a company carrying on cloud seeding (artificial nucleation), pending a final hearing and determination of causes.

The right to maintain an action for trespass to land rests with the lawful possessor of the land. If farmland is rented to a tenant, the owner may become a trespasser unless the owner enters the premises for purposes of inspection, collection of rent, or repair of permanent improvements, or enters under particular rights of entry specified in a written lease. In *Westcott v. Arbuckle*, 12 Ill. App. 577 (1883), the court said

The owner of real estate has a right to enter upon and enjoy his property if he can do so without a forcible disturbance of the possession of another, but such entry, if forcible and against the will of the occupant, is unlawful and being unlawful, is a trespass for which an action will lie.

In the absence of a special statute, trespass is a civil wrong for which recovery may be had in a civil action. If the trespass is of a continuing nature for which damages are not an adequate remedy, an injunction may be granted.

Criminal Trespass. Some kinds of trespass are also forbidden by statute, in which case they constitute a criminal act or misdemeanor.[9] Fines or jail sentences typically may be imposed by the courts for criminal trespass. Interestingly, Missouri divides criminal trespass into two categories—with a harsher penalty available for the more serious trespass in the first degree.[10]

In most states a criminal trespass will occur if one enters property that is reasonably posted with "no trespassing" or some equivalent language, or if an entrant refuses to leave when asked by the occupant. Where a criminal trespass has occurred, the occupant may call upon the sheriff, the sheriff's deputies, or other law enforcement officers to arrest the trespasser. Prosecution will take place through the criminal justice system rather than through the civil courts.

Trespassing Hunters. No one has a right to hunt on property without the permission of the owner or tenant. If the owner is not the operator and the land is leased, the hunter must obtain permission from the tenant. Even the landlord may not hunt on rented farms without permission from the tenant, unless this right was reserved in the lease.

One who hunts without permission may be held liable for trespassing. This means that the occupant of the land may recover money damages for any harm caused by the trespasser, whether it be an animal killed, livestock frightened, or crops or fences trampled down. And the trespasser may be liable even though the property is not fenced or posted.

In addition, the trespasser also may be held criminally liable in many states if entry is made onto farm premises with firearms or if the person enters or remains on land after receiving notice from the owner or tenant that such entry is forbidden. A person has received the required notice if notified personally, either orally or in writing, or, in some states, if a printed or written notice forbidding such entry has been conspicuously posted at the main entrance to the land.

A person who hunts on land with proper consent generally is called a "licensee," although that person may be viewed as an "invitee" if the person intends to share the game with the landowner or occupant. The "license" (or permission) to hunt there may be revoked anytime and for any reason. If the hunter's license is revoked, liability may be imposed for trespass if

---

[9] For example, The Illinois Criminal Code, ILL. REV. STAT. ch. 38, § 21–3 (1979) provided that "(a) Whoever enters upon the land or any part thereof of another, after receiving, immediately prior to such entry, notice from the owner or occupant that such entry is forbidden, or remains upon the land of another after receiving notice from the owner or occupant to depart, shall be fined not to exceed $500 or imprisoned in a penal institution other than the penitentiary not to exceed 30 days. (b) A person has received notice from the owner or occupant within the meaning of Subsection (a) if he has been notified personally, either orally or in writing, or if a printed or written notice forbid-

ding such entry has been conspicuously posted or exhibited at the main entrance to such land or the forbidden part thereof."

If the property is properly posted, the trespasser may be found guilty of violating this Illinois law even though the trespasser did not see the sign. The penalty is a fine of not more than $500 or imprisonment not exceeding 30 days. This criminal law strengthens the law of trespass and gives farmers considerably more protection from negligent hunters than they would have if only a civil remedy for damages were provided.

[10] MO. REV. STAT. §§ 569.140, 569.150 (1979).

the person refuses to leave. Even though a person has permission to hunt, liability may still be imposed for any damages caused on the property by negligence.

7.3 DUTY TO PROTECT THOSE ENTERING AGRICULTURAL LAND AND POTENTIAL LIABILITY FOR INJURIES

General Rules[11]

Farmers or ranchers are not liable just because someone is injured on their premises. Their must be some showing of negligence on their part. However, the duty which a farmer owes to one on the premises depends in part on the status of the person injured. Three general categories are recognized: trespassers, licensees, and invitees. The duty owed to *trespassers* is slight. Basically it consists in not maliciously injuring trespassers and in not using more force than is reasonably necessary to eject them from the premises in case this becomes necessary after a request that they leave. However, if one knows that trespassers are on the property and that some dangerous situation exists which may result in injury to them, there would probably be some duty to warn them of the danger.

Anyone may become a trespasser after being requested by the owner to leave, even though the trespasser may have been a licensee or invitee prior to such request. Ordinarily, force should not be used to eject a trespasser from the property. The courts have said that the safety of human life may not be unnecessarily endangered

in the protection of property and that no greater force than is necessary is justified in repelling invasion of one's private property. There is more justification, naturally, if a criminal act is being committed or threatened.

The duty owed to *licensees* is somewhat higher. A licensee is a person who enters the property of another with permission, for his or her own purpose or business rather than for the landowner's or tenant's benefit. Social guests and insurance salespeople are examples of licensees. The additional duty to the licensee would consist primarily in warning of any dangerous condition or dangerous animal which might be encountered while on the premises. If one permits hunters to use the property, there is probably a duty to warn them if other hunters are already on the premises. Whether or not such a duty exists is a question of fact—if the terrain is open so all the hunters can readily see each other, then there would probably be no such duty. Some states have enacted special legislation regarding the duty of landowners and land occupiers toward licensees who are on their property for recreational purposes.

The duty owed an *invitee* is higher than that owed a licensee. An invitee is someone on the property for a purpose related to the occupant's business. Examples would include a deliverer or a customer at a U-Pick orchard. The invitee has a right to expect that the premises are reasonably safe and that warnings will be given about any conditions which cannot be made safe by the owner or tenant. This is particularly true if a farmer operates a business which

---

[11] *See generally* 1 N. HARL, AGRICULTURAL LAW § § 4.01 *et seq.* (1980).

brings many people to the premises—selling milk, eggs, or other farm products on the farm, for example, or conducting a sizable purebred or seed business. Generally, a landowner or occupant also has a duty to invitees to make reasonable inspections for hidden dangers. Contributory negligence and assumption of risk may be good defenses in actions brought by invitees or licensees. A person in the purebred business, for example, would be presumed to know something about the habits of animals and be expected to exercise some precaution when on farm premises.

Trends. A *trend* toward a view that an occupier's liability to one injured upon the premises is governed simply by a standard of reasonable care under the circumstances rather than by common-law distinctions among entrants has been developing in recent years. Alaska, New Hampshire, Louisiana, New York, Rhode Island, Iowa, Colorado, Hawaii, and California have abandoned the use of all these common-law categories as the sole method of determining the degree of care owed.[12] For example, in the leading California case of *Rowland v. Christian*, 62 Cal.2d 108, 443 P.2d 561 (1968), the court imposed a duty of rea-

sonable care in favor of all entrants whose presence was immediately foreseeable. The court developed a test of liability which involved the following considerations: (1) The foreseeability of harm to plaintiff, (2) The closeness of the connection between the defendant's conduct and the injury, (3) the moral blame attached to defendant's conduct, (4) the extent of the burden to defendant, (5) the consequences to the community of imposing a duty with resulting liability for breach, and (6) the availability, cost, and prevalence of insurance for the risk involved.

North Dakota, Wisconsin, Massachusetts, Minnesota, and Connecticut have abolished the distinctions between licensees and invitees.[13] Other jurisdictions have redefined the status of a social guest by considering the guest as invitee or by establishing special standards of care for protection.[14] Nevertheless, in determining premises liability, most states still follow the common-law distinctions between trespassers, licensees, and invitees that have been described above and applied in the cases which follow.

Trespassers. As will be apparent below, the duty owed to a trespasser is slight.

---

[12] Webb v. City of Sitka, 561 P. 2d 731 (Ala. 1977); Ouelette v. Blanchard, 364 A. 2d 631 (N.H. 1976); Cates v. Beauregard Elec. Cooperative, Inc., 328 So. 2d 367 (La. 1976); Scurti v. City of New York, 40 N.Y. 2d 433, 354 N.E. 2d 794 (1976); Mariorenzi v. Joseph Di Ponte, Inc., 141 R.I. 294, 333 A. 2d 127 (1975); Rosenau v. City of Esterville, 199 N.W. 2d 125 (Iowa 1972); Mile High Fence Co. v. Radovick, 175 Colo. 537, 489 P. 2d 308 (1971); Pickard v. City and County of Honolulu, 51 Haw. 134, 452 P. 2d 445 (1969); Rowland v. Christian, 69 Cal. 2d 108, 443 P. 2d 561 (1968).

[13] O'Leary v. Coenen, 251 N.W. 2d 746 (N.D. 1977); Antoniewicz v. Reszcynski, 70 Wisc. 2d 836, 236 N.W. 2d 1 (1975); Mounsey v. Ellard, 363 Mass. 693, 297 N.E. 2d 43 (1973); Peterson v. Balach, 294 Minn. 161, 199 N.W. 2d 639 (1972); CONN. GEN. STAT. § 52–557a.

[14] *E.g.*, Scheibel v. Hillis, 531 S.W. 2d 285 (Mo. 1976); Memel v. Reimer, 85 Wash. 2d 685, 538 P. 2d 517 (1975); Hardin v. Harris, 507 S.W. 2d 172 (Ky. 1974).

DUTY AND LIABILITY TO TRESPASSER

KATKO v. BRINEY
Supreme Court of Iowa, 1971
183 N.W. 2d 657

MOORE, Chief Justice.

The primary issue presented here is whether an owner may protect personal property in an unoccupied boarded-up farm house against trespassers and thieves by a spring gun capable of inflicting death or serious injury.

We are not here concerned with a man's right to protect his home and members of his family. Defendants' home was several miles from the scene of the incident to which we refer infra.

Plaintiff's action is for damages resulting from serious injury caused by a shot from a 20-gauge spring shotgun set by defendants in a bedroom of an old farm house which had been uninhabited for several years. Plaintiff and his companion, Marvin McDonough, had broken and entered the house to find and steal old bottles and dated fruit jars which they considered antiques.

At defendants' request plaintiff's action was tried to a jury consisting of residents of the community where defendants' property was located. The jury returned a verdict for plaintiff and against defendants for $20,000 actual and $10,000 punitive damages.

After careful consideration of defendants' motions for judgment notwithstanding the verdict and for new trial, the experienced and capable trial judge overruled them and entered judgment on the verdict. Thus we have this appeal by defendants.

Most of the facts are not disputed. In 1957 defendant Bertha L. Briney inherited her parents' farm land including an 80-acre tract in southwest Mahaska County where her grandparents and parents had lived. No one occupied the house thereafter. Her husband, Edward, attempted to care for the land. He kept no farm machinery thereon. The outbuildings became dilapidated.

For about 10 years, 1957 to 1967, there occurred a series of trespassing and housebreaking events with loss of some household items, the breaking of windows and "messing up of the property in general." The latest occurred June 8, 1967, prior to the event on July 16, 1967, herein involved.

Defendants through the years boarded up the windows and doors in an attempt to stop the intrusions. They had posted "no trespass" signs on the land several years before 1967. The nearest one was 35 feet from the house. On June 11, 1967, defendants set "a shotgun trap" in the north bedroom. After Mr. Briney cleaned and oiled his 20-gauge shotgun, the power of which he was well aware, defendants took it to the old house where they secured it to an iron bed with the barrel pointed at the bedroom door. It was rigged with wire from the door knob to the gun's trigger so it would fire when the door was opened. Briney first pointed the gun so an intruder would be hit in the stomach but at Mrs. Briney's suggestion it was lowered to hit the legs. He admitted he did so "because I was mad and tired of being tormented" but "he did not intend to injure anyone." He gave no explanation of why he used a loaded shell and set it to hit a person already in the house. Tin was nailed over the bedroom window. The spring gun could not be seen from the outside. No warning of its presence was posted.

Plaintiff lived with his wife and worked regularly as a gasoline station attendant in Eddyville, seven miles from the old house. Prior to July 16, 1967, plaintiff and McDonough had been to the premises and found several old bottles and fruit jars which they took and added to their collection of antiques. About 9:30 p.m. they made a second trip to the Briney property. They entered the old house by removing a board from a porch window which was without glass. While McDonough was looking around the kitchen area plaintiff went to another part of the house. As he started to open the north bedroom door the shotgun went off striking him in the right leg above the ankle bone. Much of his leg, including part of the tibia, was blown away. Only by McDonough's assistance was plaintiff able to get out of the house and after crawling some distance was put in his vehicle and rushed to a doctor and then to a hospital. He remained in the hospital 40 days.

Plaintiff's doctor testified he seriously considered amputation but eventually the healing process was successful. Some weeks after his release from the hospital plaintiff returned to work on crutches. He was required to keep the injured leg in a cast for approximately a year and wear a special brace for another year. He continued to suffer pain during this period.

There was undenied medical testimony plaintiff had a permanent deformity, a loss of tissue, and a shortening of the leg.

The record discloses plaintiff to trial time had incurred $710 medical expense, $2,056.85 for hospital service, $61.80 for orthopedic service and $750 as loss of earnings. In addition thereto the trial court submitted to the jury the question of damages for pain and suffering and for future disability.

Plaintiff testified he knew he had no right to break and enter the house with intent to steal bottles and fruit jars therefrom. He further testified he had entered a plea of guilty to larceny in the nighttime of property of less than $20 value from a private building. He stated he had been fined $50 and costs and paroled during good behavior from a 60-day jail sentence. Other than minor traffic charges this was plaintiff's first brush with the law. On this civil case appeal it is not our prerogative to review the disposition made of the criminal charge against him.

The main thrust of defendants' defense in the trial court and on this appeal is that "the law permits use of a spring gun in a dwelling or warehouse for the purpose of preventing the unlawful entry of a burglar or thief." They repeated this contention in their exceptions to the trial court's instructions 2, 5, and 6.

In instruction 2 the court referred to the early case history of the use of spring guns and stated under the law their use was prohibited except to prevent the commission of felonies of violence and where human life is in danger. The instruction included a statement that breaking and entering is not a felony of violence.

Instruction 5 stated:

You are hereby instructed that one may use reasonable force in the protection of his property, but such right is subject to the qualification that one may not use such means of force as will take human life or inflict great bodily injury. Such is the rule even though the injured party is a trespasser and is in violation of the law himself.

Instruction 6 stated:

An owner of premises is prohibited from willfully or intentionally injuring a trespasser by means of force that either takes life or inflicts great bodily injury; and therefore a person owning a premise is prohibited from setting out "spring guns" and like dangerous devices which will likely take life or inflict great bodily injury, for the purpose of harming trespassers. The fact that the trespasser may be acting in violation of the law does not change the rule. The only time when such conduct of setting a "spring gun" or a like dangerous device is justified would be when the trespasser was commiting a felony of violence or a felony punishable by death, or where the trespasser was endangering human life by his act.

The overwhelming weight of authority, both textbook and case law, supports the trial court's statement of the applicable principles of law.

Prosser on Torts, Third Edition, pages 116–118, states:

the law has always placed a higher value upon human safety than upon mere rights in property, it is the accepted rule that there is no privilege to use any force calculated to cause death or serious bodily injury to repel the threat to land or chattels, unless there is also such a threat to the defendant's personal safety as to justify a self-defense....Spring guns and other man-killing devices are not justifiable against a mere trespasser, or even a petty thief. They are privileged only against those upon whom the landowner, if he were present in person would be free to inflict injury of the same kind.

Restatement of Torts, section 85, page 180, states:

The value of human life and limb, not only to the individual concerned but also to society, so outweighs the interest of a possessor of land in excluding from it those whom he is not willing to admit thereto that a possessor of land has, as is stated in § 79, no privilege to use force intended or likely to cause death or serious harm against another whom the possessor sees about to enter his premises or meddle with his chattel, unless the intrusion threatens death or serious bodily harm to the occupiers or users of the premises....A possessor of land cannot do indirectly and by a mechanical device that which, were he present, he could not do immediately and in person. Therefore, he cannot gain a privilege to install, for the purpose of protecting his land from intrusions harmless to the lives and limbs of the occupiers or users of it, a mechanical device whose only purpose is to inflict death or serious harm upon such as may intrude, by giving notice of his intention to inflict, by mechanical means and indirectly, harm which he could not, even after request, inflict directly were he present.

   The legal principles stated by the trial court in instructions 2, 5, and 6 are well established and supported by the authorities cited and quoted supra. There is no merit in defendants' objections and exceptions thereto. Defendants' various motions based on the same reasons stated in exceptions to instructions were properly overruled.

   Plaintiff's claim and the jury's allowance of punitive damages, under the trial court's instructions relating thereto, were not at any time or in any manner challenged by defendants in the trial court as not allowable. We therefore are not presented with the problem of whether the $10,000 award should be allowed to stand.

   We express no opinion as to whether punitive damages are allowable in this type of case. If defendants' attorneys wanted that issue decided it was their duty to raise it in the trial court.

   Affirmed.

   All Justices concur except Larson, J., who dissents.

Larson, Justice.

   I respectfully dissent, first, because the majority wrongfully assumes that by installing a spring gun in the bedroom of their unoccupied house the defendants intended to shoot any intruder who attempted to enter the room. Under the record presented here, that was a fact question. Unless it is held that these property owners are liable for any injury to an intruder from such a device regardless of the intent with which it is installed, liability under these pleadings must rest upon two definite issues of fact, i.e., did the defendants intend to shoot the invader, and if so, did they employ unnecessary and unreasonable force against him?

   It appears to me that the learned trial court was and the majority is now confused as to the basis of liability under the circumstance revealed. Certainly, the trial court's instructions did nothing to clarify the law in this jurisdiction for the jury. Timely objections to Instructions Nos. 2, 5, and 6 were made by the defendants, and thereafter the court should have been aware of the questions of liability left unresolved, i.e., whether in this jurisdiction we by judicial declaration bar the use in an unoccupied building of spring guns or other devices capable of inflicting serious injury or death on an intruder regardless of the intent with which they are installed, or whether such an intent is a vital element which must be proven in order to establish liability for an injury inflicted upon a criminal invader.

Although the court told the jury the plaintiff had the burden to prove "That the force used by defendants was in excess of that force reasonably necessary and which persons are entitled to use in the protection of their property," it utterly failed to tell the jury it could find the installation was not made with the intent or purpose of striking or injuring the plaintiff. There was considerable evidence to that effect. As I shall point out, both defendants stated the installation was made for the purpose of scaring or frightening away any inturder, not to seriously injure him. It may be that the evidence would support a finding of an intent to injure the intruder, but obviously that important issue was never adequately or clearly submitted to the jury.

Unless, then, we hold for the first time that liability for death or injury in such cases is absolute, the matter should be remanded for a jury determination of defendant's intent in installing the device under instruction usually given to a jury on the issue of intent.

My second reason for this dissent is the allowance of an award of punitive damages herein. Plaintiff claimed a remedy which our law does not allow, and the trial court should not have submitted that issue to the jury. Like the law establishing liability for installing a spring gun or other similar device, the law recognizing and allowing punitive or exemplary damages is court-made law, not statutory law. As to the property owner's liability for exemplary damages where one is engaged in a serious criminal offense at the time of his injury, we also have a case of first impression. We have never extended this right to such a claimant, and I would not do so now. Unless we do, or there is a compelling reason or authority for such a right, which I fail to find, the trial court erred in submitting that issue to the jury. Like the case where a judgment is entered without jurisdiction of the subject matter, I would hold the award of $10,000 to plaintiff is void.

Cases in many other jurisdictions are in accord with Iowa.

The facts in *Allison v. Fiscus*, 156 Ohio 120, 100 N.E.2d 237, 44 A.L.R.2d 369, decided in 1951, are very similar to the case above. There plaintiff's right to damages was recognized for injuries received when he feloniously broke a door latch and started to enter defendant's warehouse with intent to steal. As he entered, a trap of two sticks of dynamite buried under the doorway by defendant owner was set off and plaintiff was seriously injured. The court held the question of whether a particular trap was justified as a use of reasonable and necessary force against a trespasser engaged in the commission of a felony

should have been submitted to the jury. The Ohio Supreme Court recognized plaintiff's right to recover punitive or exemplary damages in addition to compensatory damages.

In *Starkey v. Dameron*, 96 Colo. 459, 45 P.2d 172 (1935) plaintiff was allowed to recover compensatory and punitive damages for injuries received from a spring gun, which defendant filling-station operator had concealed in an automatic gasoline pump as protection against thieves.

In *Wilder v. Gardner*, 39 Ga. App. 608, 147 S.E. 911 (1929) a judgment for plaintiff for injuries received from a spring gun which defendant had set, the court said: "A person in control of premises may be responsible even to a trespasser for injuries caused by pitfalls, mantraps, or other like contrivances so dangerous in character as to imply a disregard of consequences or a willingness to inflict injury."

In *Phelps v. Hamlett*, Tex. Civ. App., 207 W.W. 425 (1918) defendant rigged a bomb inside his outdoor theatre so that if anyone came through the door the bomb would explode. The court reversed plaintiff's recovery because of an incorrect instruction, but at page 426 said: "While the law authorizes an owner to protect his property by such reasonable means as he may find to be necessary, yet considerations of humanity preclude him from setting out, even on his own property, traps and devices dangerous to the life and limb of those whose appearance and presence may be reasonably anticipated, even though they may be trespassers."

In *United Zinc & Chemical Co. v. Britt*, 258 U.S. 268, 275, 42 S.Ct. 299, 66 L.Ed. 615, 617 (1922) the court states: "The liability for spring guns and mantraps arises from the fact that the defendant has expected the trespasser and prepared an injury that is no more justified than if he had held the gun and fired it."

In addition to civil liability, many jurisdictions hold a landowner criminally liable for serious injuries or homicide caused by spring guns or other set devices. See in these cases: *State v. Childers*, 133 Ohio 508, 14 N.E.2d 767 (1938) (melon thief shot by spring gun); *Pierce v. Commonwealth*, 135 Va. 635, 115 S.E. 686 (1923) (policeman killed by spring gun when he opened unlocked front door of defendant's shoe repair shop); *State v. Marfaudille*, 48 Wash. 117, 92 P.939 (1907) (murder conviction for death from spring gun set in a trunk); *State v. Beckham*, 306 Mo. 566, 267 S.W. 817 (1924) (person killed by spring gun attached to window of defendant's chili stand); *State v. Green*, 118 S.C. 279, 110 S.E. 145, 19 A.L.R. 1431 (1921) (intruder

shot by spring gun when he broke and entered vacant house. Manslaughter conviction of owner affirmed); *State v. Barr*, 11 Wash. 481, 39 P. 1080 (1895) (murder conviction affirmed for death of an intruder into a boarded-up cabin in which owner had set a spring gun).

For cases apparently holding that dangerous force may be used to ward off and prevent a trespasser from breaking and entering into an inhabited dwelling, see *State v. Vance*, 17 Iowa 138 (1864); *Grant v. Hass*, 31 Tex. Civ. App. 688, 75 S.W. 342 (1903); *Scheuermann v. Scharfenberg*, 163 Ala. 337, 50 So. 335 (1909); *Simpson v. State*, 59 Ala. 1, 31 Am. Rep. 1. (1877); *State v. Childers*, 133 Ohio 508, 14 N.E.2d 767 (1938); *Gramlich v. Wurst*, 86 Pa. 74, 80 (1878). Also for cases considering the devices a property owner is apparently privileged to use where there is no threat to human life or safety, see *Allison v. Fiscus*, 156 Ohio St. 120, 100 N.E.2d 237 (1951); *State v. Barr*, 11 Wash. 481, 39 P. 1080 (1895); *State v. Childers, supra; Weis v. Allen*, 147 Or. 670, 35 P.2d 478 (1934); *Pierce v. Commonwealth*, 135 Va. 635, 115 S.E. 686 (1923); *Johnson v. Patterson*, 14 Conn. 1 (1940); *Marquis v. Benfer*, 298 S.W.2d 601 (Tex. Civ. App. 1956).

Attractive Nuisance: A Special Rule for Trespassing Youth. The owners or tenants in possession of farmland may be held liable for injury to trespassing children when they would not have been held liable for injury to trespassing adults. This theory is based on the notion that children do not have the judgment of adults and that many things attract them so strongly that they will answer an urge to explore and satisfy their curiosity. Farm ponds (some states distinguish between natural and artificial bodies of water, and many states do not apply the attractive nuisance doctrine to any bodies of water), animals (especially young animals), and farm machinery may, under certain circumstances, constitute attractive nuisances. Though the courts have gone pretty far in holding owners liable under the attractive nuisance theory, they have not said that there is liability without fault. The fault or negligence may be slight; it may simply consist of failure to foresee what a reasonably prudent person should have foreseen with respect to the likelihood that children would be attracted.

The steps which an owner should take to prevent unauthorized entry by children onto the owner's premises are not always easily determined and may not make the owner popular in the community. But if there is a farm pond or other potentially dangerous situation, the least that the owner could do would be to warn the children themselves and their parents, put up appropriate signs, and, where feasible, enclose the dangerous premises with fencing. These steps might still not be enough, but they would go a long way in showing that the owner was not negligent.

ATTRACTIVE NUISANCE

ANDERSON v. CAHILL
Supreme Court of Missouri, Division No. 2, 1972
485 S.W. 2d 76

In this action for personal injuries, the trial court sustained defendant's Motion for Directed Verdict at the close of plaintiff's case and plaintiff appeals. Plaintiff was injured when he fell into a ten foot deep excavation on the premises of St. Mary's Church in Independence, Mo. At the time of his injury, October 13, 1962, plaintiff was four years ten months of age.

Defendant Cahill had entered into a construction contract with the church diocese to build an addition to the church. Construction commenced on September 5, 1962. Thereafter, defendant Perry, at the direction of defendant Cahill, dug the rough excavation for the foundation wall footings. The depth of the excavation pit was approximately ten feet, the space between the foundation wall and the side of the excavation approximately two feet.

Plaintiff contends he made a submissible case under Section 339, Restatement of the Law, Torts, First (1934), and that the trial court erred in directing a verdict for defendants at the conclusion of his case. Missouri has adopted Section 339, which reads as follows:

A possessor of land is subject to liability for bodily harm to young children trespassing thereon caused by a structure or other artificial condition which he maintains upon the land, if

(a) the place where the condition is maintained is one upon which the possessor knows or should know that such children are likely to trespass, and

(b) the condition is one of which the possessor knows or should know and which he realizes or should realize as involving an unreasonable risk of death or serious bodily harm to such children, and

(c) the children because of their youth do not discover the condition or realize the risk involved in intermeddling in it or in coming within the area made dangerous by it, and

(d) the utility to the possessor of maintaining the condition is slight as compared to the risk to young children involved therein.

In overruling plaintiff's Motion for New Trial, the trial judge held Section 339 not applicable, noting a lack of evidence as to how the children got onto the premises, the magnetism of activities at construction sites in attracting children and others, the impracticability of sealing such sites against small children, and the ability of children of any age, including plaintiff, to realize and appreciate the risk involved in falling from high places. In addition, defendant contends plaintiff's evidence failed on each element of Section 339.

In the Comment (p. 920) on Clause (a) the Restatement says:

It is not necessary that the defendant should know that the condition which he maintains upon his land is likely to attract the trespasses of children or that the children's trespasses shall be due to the attractiveness of the condition. It is sufficient to satisfy the conditions stated in Clause (a) that the possessor knows or should know that children are likely to trespass upon a part of the land upon which he maintains a condition which is likely to be dangerous to them because of their childish propensities to intermeddle or otherwise. Therefore, the possessor is subject to liability to children who after entering the land are attracted into dangerous intermeddling by such a condition maintained by him although they were ignorant of its existence until after they had entered the land, if he knows or should know that the place is one upon which children are likely to trespass and that the condition is one with which they are likely to meddle.

[1]   The construction site was located in a residential area on premises occupied by a high school with an enrollment of 200 to 250 students and an elementary school with an enrollment of approximately 400 students. A jury could reasonably find that defendant should have anticipated the presence of children in the area and the possibility that one of them might find his way into the construction site.

[2]   Defendant also argues that the passageway between the high school and construction sheds was a distance of 100 to 150 feet from the playground area and a distance of 240 to 260 feet from Liberty Street, with no part of the excavation site visible from that opening. This, of course, would have precluded recovery prior to the adoption of Section 339, when a possessor of land was liable only if the condition causing the injury enticed or lured the child into exposing himself to the danger. Adoption of Section 339, however, eliminated the element of allurement and enticement. This constitutes the fundamental difference between the Restatement rule and Missouri's earlier attractive nuisance doctrine. The distances from the playground and Liberty Street to the construction site may now be considered, along with other evidence, only in determining the foreseeability of trespassing children.

Defendant further contends that a court would be justified in ruling as a matter of law that a normal child four years and ten months old has sufficient mental development to appreciate the risk of falling into an excavation, and that defendant would not, therefore, be liable for any injury sustained in such a fall.

In the Comment (p. 923) on Clause (b) the Restatement says:

An artificial condition may be peculiarly dangerous to children because of their tendency to intermeddle with things which are notoriously attractive to them, but this is not the only childish characteristic which may make an artificial condition, which involves no serious risk to an adult, highly dangerous to children. Children are notoriously inattentive to their surroundings, and this characteristic may make it unlikely that children will discover a condition which would be obvious to an adult. The lack of experience and judgment normal to young children may prevent them from realizing that a condition observed by them is dangerous or, although they realize that it is dangerous, may prevent them from appreciating the full extent of the risk.

In overruling plaintiff's Motion for New Trial, the trial judge noted that such construction sites "held magnetism to children and others." Such a construction site with its accompanying sand, rock and material piles, might certainly be distracting to trespassing children and a jury could find it so distracting that this young plaintiff, while playing within such an area, would not discover or appreciate the risk of falling into the excavation located therein.

[3]   A prima facie case was made under Section 339. The trial court erred in sustaining defendant Cahill's Motion for Directed Verdict.

[4]   The order of the trial court in directing a verdict in favor of defendant Perry at the close of plaintiff's case is affirmed. Plaintiff failed to establish any control of the premises by defendant Perry, whose only participation in the construction was in digging the excavation for the foundation. This work was done at the direction of defendant Cahill. Defendant Perry was never in possession of the premises.

It should be noted that *The Restatement (Second) of Torts* § 339 adds a fifth condition to the applicability of the attractive nuisance doctrine: "The possessor fails to exercise reasonable care to eliminate the danger or otherwise to protect children."

There is a trend away from attractive nuisance concepts. Several states (Ohio, Illinois, Vermont, Maryland, and Massachusetts) have entirely repudiated the attractive nuisance doctrine, preferring to impose the more general rule that one must exercise reasonable care under the circumstances.[15]

Licensees and Invitees. The following case il-

lustrates the duties owed to licensees and invitees.

LIABILITY TO INVITEE

CIAGLO v. CIAGLO
Illinois Appellate Court, 1959
20 Ill. App. 2d 360, 156 N.E. 2d 376

While picking plums on a farm in Wisconsin during a visit to her son who operated the farm, plaintiff fell from a ladder and was injured. She sued Walter Kansteiner, the owner, her son and one Majesz, an assistant manager, who was never served with process. At the close of all the evidence, the court instructed the jury to find defendants not guilty. Plaintiff appeals from an order denying her motion for a new trial and from the judgment entered on the verdicts.

The principal question presented, one of law and fact, is whether plaintiff was an invitee or a licensee, and involves the degree of care that defendants owed her under the attendant circumstances. There is substantially no dispute as to the salient facts.

Plaintiff testified that at breakfast on September 15, 1954, the day of the accident, her son told her: "You go, Ma, help Florence pick up the plums"; he added that he was going to take the plums to town and sell them. She stated that her son had not agreed to pay her any money; plum picking was evidently one among a number of chores that she was performing. Accordingly, following breakfast, plaintiff, accompanied by her daughter-in-law Florence, went out to pick plums. Plaintiff reached the plums by ladder, and after she had filled a small basket, she would descend from the ladder

---

[15] Brown v. Rechel, 108 Ohio App. 347, 161 N.E. 2d 638 (1959); Kahn v. James Barton Co., 5 Ill. 2d 614, 126 N.E. 2d 836 (1955); Trudo v. Lazarus, 116 Vt. 221, 73 A. 2d 306 (1950); State v. Baltimore Fidelity Warehouse Co., 176 Md. 341, 4 A. 2d 739 (1939); Urban v. Central Mass Elec. Co., 301 Mass. 519, 17 N.E. 2d 718 (1933).

In *Skaggs v. Junis*, 27 Ill. App. 2d 25, 169 N.E. 2d 684 (1960), a 16-year-old boy became paralyzed from the neck down as a result of diving into an artificial pond on defendant John Junis's farmland, where the boy allegedly struck his head on a submerged stump hidden from view beneath the water. In discussing attractive nuisance, the court noted that general negligence concepts apply.

Foreseeability of harm to a child is the true basis of liability, and the element of attraction is important only in that it indicates that the trespass should have been anticipated by the landowner. In *McIntire v. McIntire*, 558 S.W. 2d 836 (1977), the Supreme Court of Tennessee considered the application of the attractive nuisance doctrine where a 14-year-old boy was injured while driving a motorcycle on the defendant's unimproved rolling land. The court held for the defendant landowner, noting that a minor is often held to an adult standard of care when operating a motor vehicle for which a license is required and that the doctrine is usually applied to artificial conditions not present in the case.

and place the plums on the ground. She stated that there were two ladders in the immediate vicinity of the trees, that she used one approximately eight or ten feet high, while her daughter-in-law took the smaller of the two ladders. In the morning the two women worked within five to seven feet of each other, but in the afternoon, after lunch, plaintiff worked alone. Her son had had his silo-filler on loan to a neighboring farmer, and that day he had spent all the forenoon and part of the afternoon dismantling the filler so that he could bring it back to his own farm. About two-thirty he returned momentarily to his own farm prior to setting out to pick up his children at school; at that time he glimpsed his mother in the orchard "picking the plums off of the ground." When, about four o'clock, he returned with his silo-filler, he heard a yell, ran to the enclosure, and found plaintiff against a tree in a sitting position. According to Ciaglo, she told him that she had fallen off the ladder. Plaintiff testified that immediately prior to the accident she saw one of the yearlings with its head against the ladder on which she was standing, causing it to shake; she became frightened, caught hold of a tree branch which broke, and fell to the ground. A doctor was called, and on his arrival plaintiff was taken to a hospital.

The controlling question with respect to Ciaglo is one of law and fact. The trial judge, in arriving at his decision for a directed verdict of not guilty, considered the pleadings, the facts and the legal questions involved, as indicated by his oral opinion at the conclusion of all the evidence. He found that plaintiff was a social guest, or licensee, and not an invitee or employee, and indicated that he had also considered the relationship of the plaintiff to her son. He found from the evidence that Ciaglo owed his mother only ordinary, reasonable, care.

Minor services performed by the guest for the host during the visit will not be sufficient to alter his status as guest. A social guest in the position of plaintiff cannot recover without a showing of active negligence. Incidental tasks performed for the benefit of the host do not change the status of the guest from the position of licensee to one of invitee. In the course of its opinion the court found the law to be "well settled that a social guest is treated as a licensee and not an invitee and therefore must prove wilful and wanton misconduct in order to recover against the possessor of the land."

There is no evidence to sustain the additional contention of plaintiff that her son was guilty of either active or passive negligence. There was a total failure on the part of plaintiff to produce evidence of any negligence or liability on the part of Ciaglo which proximately caused the injuries of which plaintiff complains. She admitted that she fell from the ladder and stated unconditionally that she "did not see the little cows at any time before" she "fell off the ladder," and that her son came to the pasture after the accident. "No one was around" when she fell from the ladder.

To sustain her contention that Ciaglo was guilty of negligence, plaintiff argues that he knew the propensities of young cattle to butt into fence posts, trees and other upright objects, and that, although knowing these facts, he nevertheless directed her at the breakfast table to enter the pasture for the purpose of picking plums for the market. An attempt was made to show, through an expert who was engaged in cattle breeding, the habits of yearlings. He stated that, like all young animals, they have a great deal of pep and energy; that they are curious but hesitant and careful—they would not run up to a strange object immediately but would come up, stand around and investigate. There is lacking in the testimony, however, any suggestion that the yearlings on Ciaglo's farm had vicious, malicious or mischievous propensities. Under the substantive law of Wisconsin it has been held that "If risk of harm cannot be foreseen by a reasonably prudent and intelligent man, the risk is not unreasonable, hence there is no negligence, consequently no liability." Plaintiff had been born on a farm in Poland, on which her father kept two cows; she testified both that she had spent the first seven years of her life, and also the first seventeen years of her life, there—the discrepancy in her testimony can be attributed, in all likelihood, to plaintiff's lack of fluency in English; she testified in part through an interpreter. In any event, although she stated that she had "never learned anything about the habits of cows when" she "was in Poland," she could not have been entirely unfamiliar with the activities of cows, as a citybred person would be; and it is undisputed that she had fed the yearlings on her son's farm before the accident. Under the circumstances it would seem that her son could realistically assume that she had some familiarity with bovine characteristics.

Unless it be shown that an animal has a mischievous propensity to commit injury and that the owner had notice thereof, or that the injury was attributable to some other negligence on his part, he cannot be charged with negligence. In this respect the rule of law in Wisconsin and in Illinois is in accord.

The court properly found that if the case of Ciaglo fell, of necessity the case of Kansteiner must also fall, since he had no part whatever in the operation of the farm, and there is no evidence charging either him or Ciaglo with negligence.

Based on the evidence, there was no question of fact for the jury to consider, and we think the court was correct in directing verdicts in favor of both defendants; accordingly, the judgment of the Circuit Court is affirmed.

Judgment affirmed.

Recreational Use of Agricultural Land

An increasing number of farmers and ranchers are finding ways and means of making their enterprise available as a recreational outlet for their city brethren. There are many economic, managerial, and sociological considerations in establishing and operating such an enterprise. In addition, there are some important legal considerations which, while not unique to an agricultural recreational enterprise, do nevertheless become pertinent because of the varied kinds of activities which may be included.

General Liability. Since those who pay to use rural recreational facilities are business invitees, a higher duty is owed for their safety than is owed to a trespasser or a mere licensee. Among such duties would be adherence to laws and regulations on the providing of safe facilities for swimming and boating or on the carrying on of other enterprises which involve special hazards and for which there are particular state laws and regulations; protecting patrons from dangerous conditions of the premises; providing safe equipment; giving proper instructions or warning about anything which might cause harm; controlling poisonous or irritating plants such as poison ivy; publishing some basic rules of conduct for patrons to avoid the chance of liability for injury of one patron by another; providing safe parking facilities; providing safe and adequate egress and ingress from the recreational areas; providing adequate custody of property (clothing deposited in a bathhouse, for example); meeting statutory and regulatory requirements for the safe preparation, handling, and dispensing of food and drink, if this is involved; and taking special precautions where necessary to protect young children in order that the attractive nuisance doctrine may not apply.

A number of states have enacted protective statutes which limit the liability of a possessor of land to licensees who are on the premises for recreational purposes without charge.[16] The Kansas statute, for example, provides as follows:

[A]n owner of land who either directly or indirectly invites or permits without charge any person to use such property for recreational purposes does not thereby:
(a) Extend any assurance that the premises are safe for any purpose.
(b) Confer upon such person the legal status of an invitee or licensee to whom a duty of care is owned.

(c) Assume responsibility for or incur liability for any injury to person or property caused by an act of omission of such persons.[17]

Under the Kansas statute, recreational uses include, but are not limited to, hunting, fishing, camping, picnicking, hiking, pleasure driving, nature study, swimming, boating, waterskiing, and other water sports and viewing or enjoying archaeological, scenic, or scientific sites.[18]

Though one may conduct rural recreational activities within the law and make the premises safe for users, the owner may nevertheless, because of noise, dust, and heavy traffic or for other reasons, create a nuisance which would give adjoining property owners a right to take action.

In 8 ALR 2d, pages 1254–1315, is the following statement about the liability of resort owners:

It is said to be well settled that the owners of resorts to which people generally are expressly or by implication invited to come are legally bound to exercise ordinary care and prudence in the maintenance and management of such resorts to the end of making them reasonably safe for visitors, and that when the business is that of keeping or carrying on a bathing resort, the proprietors or owners thereof are not only required to exercise that same degree of care and prudence with respect to keeping the premises in a reasonably safe condition which the law imposes on keepers of public resorts generally for the protection of their patrons, but the law imposes upon them the additional duty, when the character and conditions of the resort are such that

---

[16] *E.g.*, ILL. REV. STAT. ch. 70, §§ 31–37; VA. CODE § 8-654.2.

[17] KANS. STAT. ANN. § 58-3204.
[18] KANS. STAT. ANN. § 58-3202.

because of deep water or the rising of sudden storms or other causes the bathers may get into danger, of having in attendance some suitable person with the necessary appliances to effect rescues and save those who may meet with accidents, and that it is not only the duty of such owners to be so prepared to rescue those who may get into danger while bathing, but it is their duty to act with promptness and to make every reasonable effort to search for, and if possible, recover those who are known to be missing.

Laws and Regulations. Reference has already been made to certain laws and regulations having to do with swimming, boating, and food service. There may be others. These should be ascertained and studied thoroughly by one contemplating a rural recreational enterprise so that one can conform to the law and thereby reduce the likelihood of liability to patrons. If there is a county zoning ordinance in effect, one who contemplates establishing a rural recreational enterprise should ascertain the status of the enterprise in the contemplated area. If zoning prohibits such a business, a variance or special use permit may be sought.

The operation of some enterprises in a rural recreational area—a food service, for example—may require a license. This should be ascertained and the necessary licenses procured.

Some rural recreational enterprises may be taxable. Also, if food and drink are supplied, a sales tax may be involved. Besides the possibility of both local and state taxes, there may even be federal taxes on some kinds of amusement.

If the federal government or the state department of conservation stocks a fish pond, then the owner will be subject to certain regulations regarding protection of the fish and fishing rights.

7.4 SPRAYING AND DUSTING

The use of herbicides and insecticides has become of great importance to agriculture. The intensification of cropping patterns, the increasing size of agricultural units, the continuing substitution of capital for labor in the production process, and the phenomenal development of the chemical industry have combined to make the use of pesticides an essential part of modern-day agricultural production. Nevertheless, a number of legal issues surround the use of pesticides by farmers, ranchers, and those they hire. Two of the most important of these focus on the regulation of pesticides and the potential liability for their use.

Federal Pesticide Regulations

Historical Background. As early as 1910, the distribution and use of chemical pesticides reached a level which required federal regulations for the protection of users, consumers, and the general public. Federal regulation of pesticides began with the enactment of the Federal Insecticide Act of 1910, although state regulation was undertaken in some states at an even earlier date. The Federal Insecticide Act of 1910 prevented the manufacture, sale, or transportation of adulterated or misbranded insecticides and fungicides.

In June 1947, the Federal Insecticide Act of 1910 was repealed and replaced by the Federal Insecticide, Fungicide and Rodenticide Act. By this time great changes had occurred in the field of chemical pesticides, or economic poisons. New plant materials and synthetic chemicals developed through both private and publicly financed research had greatly increased the number of pesticides available and widened the scope of their usefulness. DDT and herbicides were becoming increasingly important. Included in the 1947 act were a number of regulatory requirements including registration of chemical pesticides prior to sale or interstate shipment, the coloring of dangerous white-powdered insecticides to prevent them from being mistaken for foodstuffs, and the inclusion of appropriate warnings and instructions on labels.

In 1954 pesticide regulations were expanded further by an amendment to the Food and Drug Act authorizing its administrator to set tolerance limits for the residues of pesticides on foods. This provision, known as the "Miller amendment," required the pretesting of a chemical pesticide before it could be used on food crops. As a result, data on the usefulness of a chemical to agriculture, the residue levels that would remain on food crops after application, and the toxicity of a chemical to warm-blooded animals were made available to the FDA.

After 1947, several new types of agricultural chemicals, generally referred to as nematocides, defoliants, desiccants, and plant regulators, were developed and acquired widespread commercial use. Nematocides were used to control nematodes, or very small eelworms, which attack the roots of plants. Defoliants were found useful in making leaves drop from plants to facilitate mechanical harvesting of the crop. Desiccants also were found useful in drying plant tissues to facilitate harvesting of the crop. And, plant regulators were found useful under some conditions in regulating the growth processes of plants. In 1959 the act was again amended to include these products under the general regulatory provisions for economic poisons on chemical pesticides.

In the early 1960s increasing public concern regarding the longer-run public health and ecological effects of some of the chemical pesticides led to the creation of a Presidential Scientific Advisory Committee, which made a number of recommendations in its 1963 report.

It concluded among other things that

1. Monitoring programs to obtain systematic data on pesticide residues should be expanded.
2. Federal research programs concerned with pesticides should be expanded and coordinated.
3. A broad educational program emphasizing the hazards in the use of pesticides should be undertaken.

It was the consensus of that committee that people must continue to fight insects and other pests in the most efficient manner possible, and that an integrated program involving chemicals was absolutely necessary.

The 1964 amendments to the Federal Insecticides, Fungicide and Rodenticide Act incorporated many of these recommendations and expedited procedures for suspending the marketing of previously registered pesticides found to be unsafe. Six years later the Environmental Protection Agency was created, and the pesticide and pure-food regulatory staffs located in the Departments of Agriculture, of the Interior, and of Health, Education and Welfare were transferred to this new agency.

Finally, the Federal Environmental Pesticide Control Act of 1972[19] completely revised the Federal Insecticide, Fungicide and Rodenticide Act. Among the provisions of most direct significance to farmers and ranchers were those requiring pesticides to be classified for general or restricted use and those providing for the certification of applicators by the various states

---

[19] 7 U.S.C. § 136 (1972).

under a program approved by the administrator of the Environmental Protection Agency (EPA). Additional revisions were made in the Federal Pesticide Act of 1978.[20]

Classification of Pesticides. All pesticides in the channels of U.S. trade must be registered with the EPA. The EPA must approve the registration if the pesticides warrant the claims made for them, if their labeling meets certain requirements, and if they will not have substantial adverse effects on the environment when properly used. The burden of proof is on the applicant to substantiate the claims for the pesticide by test data and otherwise to support the registration of the pesticide.

As part of the registration procedure, pesticides must be classified for general use, for restricted use, or for both. A *general use pesticide* is one which will not cause substantial adverse effects on the environment when applied in accordance with its directions for use or in accordance with a commonly recognized practice.

A *restricted use pesticide* is one which could cause substantial adverse effects on the environment without additional regulatory restrictions. Generally, all restricted use pesticides must be used under the supervision of a certified applicator.

Certification of Applicators. Applicator certification is accomplished through a state program in those states that have submitted a certification plan and obtained EPA approval of that plan. A certification program is administered by the EPA for those states without approved plans.

Federal regulations set forth requirements to be met before a state certification plan can be approved.[21] These requirements provide for the certification of private applicators and commercial applicators.

Private applicators are certified applicators who use restricted use pesticides for producing agricultural commodities on property owned or rented by their employers, or on the property of another person if applied without compensation other than the trading of personal services between agricultural producers. The term *commercial applicators* refers to all other certified applicators. The regulations also provide that subcategories of commercial applicators can be established, such as "animal control" and "forest pest control."

As a minimum requirement for certification as a private applicator, one must demonstrate that one possesses a practical knowledge of the pest problems and pest control practices associated with one's agricultural operations; these include proper storage, use, handling, and disposal of the pesticides and containers and the related legal responsibility. To be approved, a state certification system must also employ a written or oral testing procedure.

As a minimum requirement for certification as a commercial applicator, one must demonstrate competency in the following areas: label and labeling comprehension, safety, the potential environmental consequences of pesticide use, pest identification, knowledge of pesticides and application techniques, and knowledge of applicable state and federal laws and regulations. Additional areas of competency may be defined for subcategories of commercial applicators. Competency in all these areas is to be determined on the basis of written examinations and performance testing, as appropriate.

Worker Protection Standards. Other regulations establish occupational safety and health standards for the protection of agricultural workers performing hand-labor

---

[20] Pub. L. No. 95–396, 92 Stat. 819 (1978).
[21] EPA Certification of Pesticide Applicators, 40 C.F.R. § 171 (1979).

operations in fields after pesticides have been applied.[22] Generally, these regulations provide that an area being treated must be vacated by unprotected employees and that no application of a pesticide shall be made if workers can be exposed directly or through drift. The regulations also specify that workers without protective clothing shall not subsequently be permitted to enter a treated area until sprays have dried or dusts have settled. Pesticides containing certain specified ingredients have specific minimum reentry times, typically of 1 or 2 days.

State Regulations

Some states have approved applicator certification programs that predate the federal requirements and have more exacting standards. For example, in order to obtain a license or certification in some states, one must provide satisfactory proof of bond or liability insurance coverage in addition to demonstrating competency.[23]

Many states also regulate the use of specific chemicals. California has an extensive pesticide regulation program which requires a person desiring to use a restricted pesticide to first obtain a use permit from the local county agricultural commissioner. The commissioner must consider a number of factors relating to the protection of public health and the environment before issuing the permit, and is proscribed from issuing the permit if there is a reasonably effective alternative less restrictive to the environment.[24]

Liability for Pesticide Application

The spraying of pesticides can result in damage beyond the destruction of the target pest. Persons who apply pesticides or persons hiring the applicator may be held liable for such additional damage on a variety of theories. Sprayers themselves may be liable on the basis of negligence,[25] trespass,[26] or strict liability.[27] Those who hire the sprayers may be vicariously liable for sprayers' negligence on the grounds that spraying is inherently dangerous, or they may be held strictly liable along with the sprayers on the basis that the spraying was an ultrahazardous activity.[28] Certainly, great care must be taken in selecting and mixing the pesticide and in calibrating and operating the spraying equipment. Also, adequate insurance protection is a must.

---

[22] EPA Worker Protection Standards for Agricultural Pesticides, 40 C.F.R. § 170.

[23] E.g., ILL. REV. STAT. ch. 5, § 810(3). California has a similar requirement.

[24] CAL. FOOD & AGRIC. CODE § 14006.5 (West Supp. 1980).

[25] See, e.g., Sanders v. Beckwith, 79 Ariz. 67, 283 P. 2d 235 (1955); W.B. Bynum Cooperage Co. v. Coulter, 219 Ark. 818, 244 S.W. 2d 955 (1952); Nizzi v. Laverty, Inc., 259 Iowa 112, 143 N.W. 2d 312 (1966). See generally Annot. Liability for injury caused by spraying or dusting crops, 37 A.L.R. 3d 833 (1971).

[26] See, e.g., Alm v. Johnson, 75 Idaho 521, 275 P. 2d 959 (1954); Wall v. Trogdon, 249 N.C. 747, 107 S.E. 2d 757 (1959).

[27] See, e.g., Gotreaux v. Gary, 232 La. 373, 94 So. 2d 293 (1957) (aerial application of pesticide). Young v. Darter, 363 P. 2d 829 (Okla. 1961) (landowner held liable for ground application of 2, 4-D). Some states have enacted legislation which makes a custom applicator automatically liable for personal injury or property damage caused by application of pesticides.

[28] See, e.g., Gotreaux v. Gary, 232 La. 373, 94 So. 2d 293 (1957).

LIABILITY BASED ON NEGLIGENCE

SUN PIPELINE CO., INC. v. KIRCKPATRICK
Court of Civil Appeals of Texas, 1974
514 S.W. 2d 789

Defendants appeal from an adverse judgment wherein plaintiff recovered for damage done to his growing timber and to his fences. Plaintiff owned a large tract of land in Montgomery County with Sun Pipe Line Company having an easement approximately 30 feet in width across the northern boundary thereof. Limbs growing upon trees on plaintiff's land obscured the surface of the easement and prevented the use of airplanes to patrol and inspect the pipeline for leaks. Sun engaged the defendant, Mobley Co., Inc., to spray these overhanging limbs with a chemical spray. Mobley sprayed the right-of-way and plaintiff testified that a large number of his trees were killed; others, weakened by the spray, became infested with beetles and died; that the trees which were killed fell across his fences causing further damage.

The jury found that the chemical drifted onto plaintiff's land and caused the trees to become weak and damaged, but failed to find any negligence in the application of the chemical by Mobley Co., Inc.

Under our law it is clearly required, in a case such as the present, before an injured suitor may recover, that he obtain fact findings of actionable negligence. In the absence of these, he is not entitled to judgment. A finding of injury is not enough. *Vrazel v. Bieri*, 294 S.W. 2d 148, 152.

The trial court's rejection of the requirement of negligence in this case and the adoption of the trespass theory is based on his finding that the spraying operation was *inherently dangerous*. We readily accept the proposition that the employer of an independent contractor may not escape liability for the acts of the contractor which are "intrinsically dangerous." However, the record does not show *conclusively* that either Sun or Mobley: (a) did the spraying "recklessly or negligently," or (b) that the damage was "a result of an *abnormally* dangerous activity."

Reversed and rendered.

CUSTOM SPRAYING—STRICT LIABILITY[29]

LOE v. LENHARDT
Supreme Court of Oregon, 1961
277 Or. 242, 362 P. 2d 312

Goodwin, Justice.

The plaintiffs, who raise seed crops on their farm near Silverton, appeal from judgments entered in favor of two defendants in an action of trespass for crop damage resulting from the spraying of chemicals by airplane.

The defendant Lenhardt operated the aircraft which applied the chemicals. The defendant Schnider owned the lands adjacent to the plaintiffs' farm and hired the services of Lenhardt. Upon the conclusion of the plaintiffs' case, Schnider moved for and was granted a judgment of involuntary nonsuit. Upon the conclusion of all the evidence, Lenhardt moved for and was granted a directed verdict.

On the issues thus made up we have for decision the question whether an unintentional trespass causing crop damage imposes liability upon the perpetrators of the damage without a pleading or proof of fault upon their part. Specifically, upon what theory, if any, is one liable for the miscarriage of aerial spraying activity, and what effect, if any, is to be given the relationship between the defendant independent contractor and the defendant landowner? The case is one of first impression in this court.

Damage from crop dusting has been a fruitful source of litigation elsewhere. It will be found from an examination of the cases that liability frequently has been imposed on the basis of fault, either a finding of lack of due care in spraying or a finding that the activity was unreasonable at the time and place. In some cases, it is difficult to detect what theory the court was following. Only in Louisiana, where the court was applying civil-law principles, have we found a direct holding for the plaintiff without a pleading or proof of negligence. Gotreaux v. Gary, 232 La. 373, 94 So. 2d 293.

The plaintiff tried the case on the theory that the activity being conducted over Schnider's land was an inherently dangerous activity within the rule found in Chapter 15, Restatement, 2 Torts 1099, §§ 416, 426, and 427, that one who employs a contractor to carry on such an activity cannot thereby insulate himself from liability. While Restatement, 2 Torts 1147, § 427, is limited in its present form to cases involving "bodily harm," a number of cases have applied the principle stated therein to property damage where negligence was shown.

The authorities are practically uniform in holding that crop dusting is an activity sufficiently freighted with danger to impose liability upon the land-

---

[29] *See generally* 1 N. Harl, Agricultural Law § 2.03 (1980).

owner having the work done if negligence is proven, even though the fault, if any, is that of an independent contractor. However, with one exception, each of the cases we have examined found sufficient evidence of negligence on the part of the person applying the chemicals to support a verdict based upon negligence.

The foregoing discussion of "inherently dangerous activity" in negligence cases, however, is instructive only in a secondary way in the case at bar. The plaintiffs have not sought to prove negligence, but seek to impose liability upon the basis of damage flowing from an "innocent" trespass.

A trespass, once established, carries with it liability for resulting harm. The plaintiff here seeks to establish a trespass and a remedy therefor whether the trespass had its origin in conduct that was intentional, careless, or indeed innocent but fraught with a high degree of danger.

It is true that at common law every unauthorized entry upon the soil of another was a trespass. Prosser, Torts (2d Ed., 1955) 54. But the Restatement of Torts takes the position that liability will be imposed in the case of an unintentional intrusion only when it arises out of negligence or the carrying on of an extrahazardous activity. Restatement, 1 Torts 359, § 158, and 390, § 165. (The rationale of the Restatement in limiting liability for unintended invasions of land to actual damages flowing from negligent or extra hazardous conduct commends itself to this court and is consistent with our own cases.)

However common may be the practice of spraying chemicals by airplane, the prevalence of the practice does not justify treating the sprayer and the "sprayee" as the law of negligence treats motorists, leaving each to fend for himself unless one can prove negligence against the other. We think the better principle was stated for this court by Mr. Justice LUSH, who concluded a careful study of the application of strict liability to damages caused by shock waves from nonnegligent dynamite blasting:

Basic to the problem is an adjustment of conflicting interests of the right of the blaster, on the one hand, to pursue a lawful occupation and the right of an owner of land, on the other, to its peaceful enjoyment and possession. Where damage is sustained by the latter through the nonculpable activities of the former, who should bear the loss—the man who caused it or a "third person," as Judge Hand says, "who has no relation to the explosion, other than that of injury"?

We need only substitute the words "sprayer" for "blaster" and "spraying" for "explosion," and the principle applies with equal force to the facts of the case at bar.

Under the facts of this case, where a farmer hired a contractor to spray chemicals from an airplane, the activity was one capable of inflicting damage upon neighboring crops notwithstanding the exercise of the utmost care by the applicator. Under the circumstances, the damage which resulted was within the scope of the risk that droplets of spray cast into the air could, and probably would, drift onto the adjoining field. In such a case, it is the voluntary taking of the risk, Restatement, 1 Torts 390, §165, rather than the intention to invade the plaintiffs' land, Restatement, 1 Torts 359, §158, which imposes liability.

It follows that the landowner who hires the contractor is liable for the resulting harm. To this extent, the rule of nondelegability followed in the so-called inherently dangerous activity negligence cases, Restatement, 2 Torts 1147, §427, applies with equal or greater force to the conduct of extra hazardous activity. It was, accordingly, error to release the defendant Schnider by a judgment of involuntary nonsuit against the plaintiffs.

Procedures for Obtaining Damages. Some states, such as Oregon, Arizona, and California, have statutes specifying particular procedures for obtaining damages arising from the application of pesticides by a commercial applicator. Frequently, such statutes require that a report of loss be filed with the state department of agriculture within a certain time period. Would a commercial applicator be absolved of liability if such reports were not properly filed?

A second issue addressed in *Loe v. Lenhardt* involved just such an argument. Although Loe had filed the report loss in time, it was not properly verified. The court noted that in the field of negligence actions against municipal corporations, where a verified claim is commonly made a condition precedent to the bringing of the action, the right to sue the governmental unit at all is a creation of the legislature and is thus clearly subject to legislative restrictions. But when an attempt is made in good faith to comply with a statute which purports to limit a constitutional right to redress for property damage caused by a private party, minor defects should not bar a meritorious action. The court adopted a liberal construction of the filing require-ment and held the custom applicator liable.

Damages to Crops and Livestock from Spraying Highway. Farmers and ranchers may experience damage caused by the spraying of pesticides on highway rights-of-way. Can a government be held liable for the damage? In two Illinois Court of Claims cases, *Frega v. State*, 22 Ill. Ct. Cl. 399 (1959), and *Swets v. State*, 22 Ill. Ct. Cl. 651 (1958), claims were allowed for damage to tomatoes and other vegetables. The court found the Division of Highways negligent in the manner in which 2, 4-D was applied. But in *Pitts v. State*, 22 Ill. Ct. Cl. 258 (1956), the court did not allow a claim for the loss of two steers, a loss claimed to have been caused by the spraying of 2, 4-D by the Division of Highways. After the appearance of many witnesses and the introduction of much testimony, the court said: "We are of the opinion that claimant has failed to prove his claim by a preponderance or greater weight of the evidence, by which we could reach the conclusion that the steers did not die from some cause other than the spraying of the weeds." The court also expressed the view that the state has no duty to notify adjoining landowners that certain spraying operations are going to take place at a particular time. It should be noted, however, that full compliance with procedural requirements for actions against the state is essential.

7.5 NUISANCE

In using their property, individuals often create conditions which are obnoxious to their neighbors. The nuisance itself may interfere with free movement, curtail the profits from an investment, offend the senses of smell, hearing, and sight, or merely cause bodily discomfort or mental distress. In any of these instances, if the disturbance is great enough or a sufficient number of persons are affected, it can usually be stopped, or at least modified.

Municipalities, factories, and other users of land may create conditions which invade the rights of farmers and hence amount to nuisances. Likewise, the farmer may engage in activities which are offensive to nearby property owners and be held liable for creating a nuisance. In any case, facts and circumstances are important in determining whether or not a nuisance exists. Some activities are so obviously harmful that they are classified as *nuisances per se*, or nuisances "on their face." Throwing a dead animal in a stream or leaving dead animals unburied would be examples.

A nuisance may be either private or public depending on its nature, how many people it affects, and whether or not there are any statutory provisions concerning it. State legislatures have determined that several specified activities are nuisances. Some which have been so specified are: permitting the carcass of an animal or any other filthy substance to remain unburied or undisposed of to the prejudice of others;

throwing or depositing offal or offensive matter or the carcass of a dead animal in a watercourse, lake, pond, spring, well, street, or public highway; rendering impure the water of any spring, river, stream, or pond to the injury of others; obstructing a public highway; dumping garbage, rubbish, or trash along a public highway or upon the land of another; obstructing an open drain with trash; depositing trash or rubbish on the ice of any lake, river, stream, pond, or canal; failing to fence junkyard areas in accordance with provisions in the statutes;[30] using any building or other place for the exercise of a trade or employment which occasions noxious exhalations or offensive smells, or otherwise endangers the health of individuals or of the public.[31]

Livestock Problems

Of particular interest to farmers is the trend of court decisions which have considered the nuisance character of livestock activities. Many such cases have been brought before the courts. In some cases the livestock or poultry activity has been enjoined; in others, it has not. Critical factors are the proximity of residential property, the size and nature of the livestock enterprise, and the manner in which it is conducted. The courts have varied in their opinions about the nuisance potential of particular kinds of enterprises. For example, in *Pendoley v. Ferreira*, 345 Mass 309, 187 N.E.2d 142 (1963), the trial court issued a temporary injunction against a farmer conducting a hog enterprise near a city—the purpose being to give him an opportunity to eliminate the smell. The case was appealed to the Supreme Court of Massachusetts where it was reversed,

---

[30] *E.g.*, ILL. REV. STAT. ch. 54, §§ 31-35 (1979).

[31] *E.g.*, ILL. REV. STAT. ch. 100 1/2, § 26(8)(1979).

the court holding that it is not possible to eliminate the smell of pigs and that the most the court could do was give the farmer a period of grace within which to move his establishment. In this case the complaint was based on several factors including odor, the presence of rodents and insects, noise, air pollution, and dust. In a Missouri case the court held that a pigsty from 14 to 18 feet away from a residential property was a nuisance per se.[32]

Examples of other activities which have amounted to nuisance are: setting a threshing machine so smoke, dust, and chaff flew into the complainant's house (*Winters v. Winters*, 78 Ill. App. 417, 1898), main-taining stables so they were offensive to adjoining owners (*Oehler v. Levy*, 234 Ill. 595, 85 N.E. 271, 1908), depositing offal and permitting it to remain (*Seacord v. People*, 121 Ill. 623, 13 N.E. 194, 1887), and piling manure near the plaintiff's well during the rainy season (*Van Brocklin v. Gudema*, 50 Ill. App. 2d 20, 199 N.E.2d 457, 1964). But in *Ward v. Illiopolis Food Lockers* (9 Ill. App. 2d 129, 132 N.E.2d 591, 1956), the court held that maintaining a slaughterhouse, food locker, and meat market was not a public nuisance or a nuisance per se. The cases which follow give some indication of how the courts feel about farm-created nuisances.

NUISANCE—VILLAGE ORDINANCE

VILLAGE OF PLYMOUTH v. McWHERTER
Illinois Appellate Court, 1909
152 Ill. App. 114

The question involved in this appeal is the validity of section one of an ordinance of the Village of Plymouth entitled, "An ordinance regulating the letting of stallions, asses and bulls to the opposite sex and the handling and keeping of the same" which section, omitting the formal part, is as follows:

That no person or persons shall stand any stallion, ass or bull within the corporate limits of the Village of Plymouth, Illinois, without the consent in writing of all the property owners and persons living within one block each way from the barn or stable where it is proposed to stand such stallion, ass or bull, and any person or persons violating the provisions of this section shall be fined not less than ten dollars, nor more than one hundred dollars for each offense.

Upon the trial of the case in the Circuit Court, without a jury, upon an agreed statement of facts, there was a finding for the defendant and judgment against the plaintiff, Village of Plymouth, for costs.

The due passage and publication of the ordinance is admitted, and it further appears from the agreed statement of facts that on and prior to April 8, 1908, the defendant was conducting and maintaining a breeding

---

[32] *See*, Annot., 2 A.L.R. 3d 931–55 (1965).

barn facing one of the main streets of the village, within one block of the public square of said village, and in a residence portion thereof, in which barn defendant kept four stallions for breeding purposes and stood them in said barn within the corporate limits of said village for more than ten days prior to the commencement of this suit; that during said time at least five mares were bred to said stallions on at least five different days; that said barn is situated in a residence block, and that one widow living on the lot adjacent to said barn had refused to give her consent verbally or in writing to the keeping of said barn at said place; that several other residences are located within one block of said barn and the consent of the owners in writing had not been obtained.

It is an inflexible rule that an ordinance adopted by a municipal corporation within the delegated and limited powers conferred upon it by the legislature is presumed to be reasonable and valid, and the burden is upon one attacking such ordinance to clearly establish its unreasonableness and invalidity.

In *Laugel v. City of Bushnell*, 197 Ill. 20, it was said:

Nuisances may be thus classified: First, those which in their nature are nuisances per se or are so denounced by the common law or by statute; second, those which in their nature are not nuisances but may become so by reason of their locality, surroundings, or the manner in which they may be conducted, managed, etc.; third, those which in their nature may be nuisances but as to which there may be honest differences of opinion in impartial minds.

The breeding of male animals to those of the opposite sex, when conducted in an enclosure out of public view and hearing does not constitute a nuisance per se but is in its nature a nuisance or may become so by reason of the locality or surroundings in which the same is conducted. Whether the ordinance here involved be held to be the conclusive declaration of a nuisance by the village authorities based upon the exercise by such authorities of their judgment and discretion, or whether the declaration of the thing prohibited, as a nuisance, is to be determined as a question of fact, we do not think the ordinance is unreasonable and void.

As bearing upon the question of the reasonableness of the ordinance, we fully concur in what was said by Mr. Justice Boggs in *Hoops v. Village of Ipava*, 55 Ill. App. 94, as follows:

The business of keeping a stallion for service, because of the inevitable indecent noises and other offensive accompaniments attendant upon the business, if permitted in the principal or thickly settled parts of a village, is in its nature offensive to the public sense of decency, detrimental to public morals and a source of annoyance and discomfort to others.

Unquestionably, it was within the power of the president and board of trustees of the Village of Plymouth to absolutely prohibit by ordinance the location of a breeding stable within the corporate limits of the village, and it cannot be said that because the consent of all of the property owners and persons residing within certain territory contiguous to where such stable is proposed to be kept, is required to permit the location of the same in a particular locality within the corporate limits, the ordinance is unreasonable and therefore void.

The judgment is reversed and the cause remanded.

NUISANCE—OPERATING A COMMERCIAL POULTRY ENTERPRISE

GRIFFITH v. NEWMAN
Supreme Court of Georgia, 1962
217 Ga. 533, 123 S.E. 2d 723

The plaintiffs, residents and neighbors in the City of Austell, Georgia, filed a suit on March 29, 1961, in the Cobb Superior Court against the defendants D.L. Griffith and his wife, Myrl, seeking to restrain and enjoin the construction and operation of a broiler house. Their petition alleged: that the defendants own land partially inside and partly outside the city limits of Austell, on which the defendants are constructing a broiler-house building, which will accommodate some 12,000 to 13,000 chickens; that the broiler house, which is located partly within and partly without the city in Cobb County, is to be constructed in a highly congested residential area comprised of homes ranging in value from $15,000 to $25,000; that the defendants do not have a permit from the City of Austell to construct such broiler house, and are also proceeding illegally contrary to the zoning laws of Cobb County; that, unless equity intervenes, the plaintiffs will suffer irreparable damages to their property by depreciation of value; and that the desirability of residing in the area will be so diminished by the nuisance created that the petitioners will be required to dispose of their property and remove from the vicinity; that the operation of the broiler house would create a sanitary hazard; that the stench and the attraction of insects and vermin would affect the health and welfare of the plaintiffs and their children; that there will be unnecessary noise and traffic as a result of the operation of such business.

It was further alleged: that the plaintiffs made timely request that the defendants refrain from the construction; and that the operation of a broiler house in a residential area constitutes a nuisance. The petition also showed that the dimensions of the broiler house were approximately 400 feet in length and 32 feet in width.

The witnesses for the defendant testified that a properly run broiler house would have very few insects or rodents; that dust and odor could be kept to a minimum; that with modern antibiotics disease was controlled, and that there was scant possibility of infectious diseases being spread.

The plaintiffs showed by the testimony of a witness who conducted extensive operations in the broiler business and by two doctors that the probability of disease, the concentration of vermin and swarms of insects, the foul, persistent, and far-reaching odors and dust particles, the noise and congestion of trucks hauling the waste products, feed, and broilers were all an inherent part of the poultry operation. The defendants did not attempt to prove that the most modern practices would entirely eliminate the objectionable features, but insist that through proper control and maintenance the most objectionable aspects would be relatively insignificant and would not constitute a nuisance.

There was no evidence presented as to the Cobb County zoning laws, but the plaintiffs' witnesses did testify that it was necessary to obtain a building permit in the City of Austell and that the defendants had attempted to comply with this requirement.

The defendants bring to this court their bill of exceptions complaining of the order overruling their general demurrers, and of the denial of their motion for new trial.

The sufficiency of the petition to set forth a cause for injunctive relief to restrain the defendant from erecting a large broiler house near the plaintiffs' homes in a densely populated residential area, and upon the completion of the building from using the same in raising a great number of chickens must be decided according to the principles pronounced by this court in factually similar cases. A principle applied in numerous cases is that a lawful business may, by reason of its location in a residential area, cause hurt, inconvenience, and damage to those residing nearby in the vicinity and become a nuisance per accidens (a nuisance by reason of circumstances and surroundings), against which an injunction will be granted. However, when the petition in a case of this kind undertakes to allege a cause to enjoin a business before it is begun, more than mere apprehension of injury to the plaintiffs or damage to their property must be made to appear.

A court of equity will only exercise the power to restrain the erection of a building and the maintenance therein after construction of a lawful business, on the ground that the operation of such business will constitute a nuisance, where it is made to appear with reasonable certainty that such operation necessarily constitutes a nuisance, the consequences of which will be irreparable damages.

This is accomplished where the petition, not by way of mere conclusions but averments of fact, shows with reasonable certainty that the business will actually work hurt, inconvenience and damage to the plaintiffs and will constitute a nuisance per accidens.

There was sufficient evidence to support the verdict, and the trial judge did not err in overruling the general grounds of the motion for new trial.

Judgment affirmed.

NUISANCE—TRADITIONAL APPROACH

PENDOLY v. FERREIRA
Supreme Judicial Court of Massachusets, 1963
345 Mass. 309, 187 N.E. 2d 142

Residents of Topsfield by this bill in equity seek to enjoin the defendants (the Ferreiras) from conducting nearby in Boxford a piggery which the plaintiffs contend constitute a nuisance. They also seek damages. The plaintiffs and the Ferreiras have appealed from the final decree which permanently enjoined the Ferreiras

from operating their piggery...in such an unreasonable manner as to cause a stench to emanate therefrom which materially interferes with the reasonable enjoyment of the property of a large number of people living in the vicinity, and from keeping four dogs which bark and yelp, at their piggery, unattended at night.

Nine of the plaintiffs were awarded damages in amounts between $200 and $415.88, and in an aggregate amount of $2,665.88.

The plaintiffs live in Topsfield near the Boxford line, in an area varying from 250 yards to about six tenths of a mile from the Ferreiras' piggery. Topsfield since 1950 has changed greatly with "the development of industry on route 128." That "rural community has become predominantly residential."

The Ferreiras started the piggery in 1949 on a farm of about 25 acres. They have worked hard on it. In 1950, they had 4 to 5 employees, 400 pigs, and 100 piglets; in 1960, 10 employees, 850 pigs, and 225 piglets. There "would be very little salvage value in the structures [probably about $5,000] if the piggery had to be moved. Most of the equipment would be used in a different location with little loss." A forced sale of the pigs would result in a loss of about $20,000. The Ferreiras "are good hog farmers. Their piggery is in the upper 5% to 10% of...[comparable] piggeries insofar as quality of operation is concerned."

The master's conclusion that a nuisance exists is consistent with common knowledge that the offensive odors of a piggery with a large number of pigs ordinarily cannot be confined to a small area, here twenty-five acres. These owners of residences within a distance to which substantial piggery odors carry are entitled to specific relief against the frequently recurrent smells which interfere substantially with the enjoyment of their property "to the discomfort and annoyance of a large number of residents." As the master pointed out, "Legally, a course of conduct that would have been without fault in...[a] rural area, has, with the change in the environs of the farm to a residential district, become unreasonable."

The master has found that the Ferreiras will suffer a large loss if operation of the piggery is enjoined entirely. Some part of this loss can probably be avoided if reasonable time is afforded for an orderly disposition or removal of the pigs now on the premises and for finding other premises. Some structures will have little salvage value. The extent of total loss may be somewhat less than the $75,000 estimated by the master, because of his failure to make allowance for depreciation. The dollar loss to the plaintiffs is much smaller than that of the Ferreiras, but the injury affects their residences and their reasonable enjoyment of them. It, of course, is appropriate, on usual equitable principles, to take into account the damage to the Ferreiras compared to the benefit to the plaintiffs in determining the type and scope of the relief to be granted. This consideration, however, is not necessarily conclusive.

In considering the form and extent of the injunction, we give substantial weight to the fact that the injury to the Ferreiras is economic, whereas the material interference with the rights of the plaintiffs is in the day to day use and comfort of the places where they live. This aspect of the case is of importance, for the plaintiffs obviously can avoid the serious unpleasantness of the piggery only by moving, an inconvenient and costly process which would deprive them of their lands and houses. Nevertheless, their interest in having their residences comfortable and free from "stench" is entitled to adequate injunctive protection.

Upon the facts appearing in the master's report, the Ferreiras cannot be expected to correct the offensiveness of the piggery. The Ferreiras' difficulty lies in the inherently offensive aspects of any piggery in a residential neighborhood and in the material discomfort which piggeries cause to others. Consequently, there is no reason to suppose that the piggery will become less detrimental to the general neighborhood or less of a nuisance. Indeed, on the facts before us, it may be inferred that it presents an unreasonable deterrent to the normal growth of the area.

Giving due weight to all factors, the injunction granted by the final decree seems to us too limited. In the first place, there might be difficulty in enforcing such a generally phrased injunction which may not constitute an adequately "clear and unequivocal command." Even apart from this question, we think that the plaintiffs are entitled to have the offensive operation terminated entirely within a reasonable time. Due consideration, however, must be given to the Ferreiras' economic interest in an orderly, rather than a hurried, liquidation of their pigs, and to affording them opportunity to find new premises. Accordingly, a permanent injunction against any operation of the piggery is to be granted, but the final decree is to provide (a) a reasonable opportunity for the Ferreiras to dispose of, or to move, the pigs, structures, and equipment, and (b) that the injunction is to take effect completely only at a specified future date, with provisions for the protection of the plaintiffs in the interim in some practicable manner. The period of delay should allow only the time essential for a reasonable liquidation or adjustment of the Ferreiras' affairs. The details of the decree are to be settled in the Superior Court after such further hearings before the master or a judge as may be deemed appropriate. It shall provide for the payment of the damages hitherto awarded with any upward adjustment necessary because of the delay in the effective date of the injunction.

The final decree is reversed. The case is remanded to the Superior Court for further proceedings consistent with this opinion.

NUISANCE—DEVELOPER TO PAY RELOCATION COSTS

SPUR INDUSTRIES, INC. v. DEL E. WEBB DEVELOPMENT CO.
Supreme Court of Arizona, 1972
108 Ariz. 178, 494 P. 2d 700

CAMERON, Vice Chief Justice.

From a judgment permanently enjoining the defendant, Spur Industries, Inc., from operating a cattle feedlot near the plaintiff Del E. Webb Development Company's Sun City, Spur appeals. Webb cross-appeals. Although numerous issues are raised, we feel that it is necessary to answer only two questions. They are:

1. Where the operation of a business, such as a cattle feedlot is lawful in the first instance, but becomes a nuisance by reason of a nearby residential area, may the feedlot operation be enjoined in an action brought by the developer of the residential area?
2. Assuming that the nuisance may be enjoined, may the developer of a completely new town or urban area in a previously agricultural area be required to indemnify the operator of the feedlot who must move or cease operation because of the presence of the residential area created by the developer?

The facts necessary for a determination of this matter on appeal are as follows. The area in question is located in Maricopa County, Arizona, some 14 to 15 miles west of the urban area of Phoenix, on the Phoenix-Wickenburg Highway, also known as Grand Avenue.

Farming started in this area about 1911. By 1950, the only urban areas in the vicinity were the agriculturally related communities of Peoria, El Mirage, and Surprise. The community of Youngtown was commenced in 1954. Youngtown is a retirement community appealing primarily to senior citizens.

In May of 1959, Del Webb began to plan the development of an urban area to be known as Sun City. For this purpose, the Marinette and the Santa Fe Ranches, some 20,000 acres of farmland, were purchased for $15,000,000, or $750.00 per acre. This price was considerably less than the price of land located near the urban area of Phoenix, and along with the success of Youngtown was a factor influencing the decision to purchase the property in question.

By September 1959, Del Webb had started construction of a golf course south of Grand Avenue and Spur's predecessors had started to level ground for more feedlot area. In 1960, Spur purchased the property in question and began a rebuilding and expansion program extending both to the north and south of the original facilities. By 1962, Spur's expansion program was completed and had expanded from approximately 35 acres to 114 acres.

Accompanied by an extensive advertising campaign, homes were first offered by Del Webb in January 1960 and the first unit to be completed was approximately 2 1/2 miles north of Spur. By 2 May 1960, there were 450 to 500 houses completed or under construction. At this time, Del Webb did not consider odors from the Spur feed pens a problem and Del Webb continued to develop in a southerly direction, until sales resistance became so great that the parcels were difficult if not impossible to sell.

By December 1967, Del Webb's property had extended south and was within 500 feet of Spur. Del Webb filed its original complaint alleging that in excess of 1,300 lots in the southwest portion were unfit for development for sale as residential lots because of the operation of the Spur feedlot.

Del Webb's suit complained that the Spur feeding operation was a public nuisance because of the flies and the odor which were drifting or being blown by the prevailing south to north wind over the southern portion of Sun City. At the time of the suit, Spur was feeding between 20,000 and 30,000 head of cattle, and the facts amply support the finding of the trial court that the feed pens had become a nuisance to the people who resided in the southern part of Del Webb's development. There is no doubt that some of the citizens of Sun City were unable to enjoy the outdoor living which Del Webb had advertised and that Del Webb was faced with sales resistance from prospective purchasers as well as strong and persistent complaints from the people who had purchased homes in that area.

It is noted, however, that neither the citizens of Sun City nor Youngtown are represented in this lawsuit and the suit is solely between Del E. Webb Development Company and Spur Industries, Inc.

MAY SPUR BE ENJOINED?

The difference between a private nuisance and a public nuisance is generally one of degree. A private nuisance is one affecting a single individual or a definite small number of persons in the enjoyment of private rights not common to the public, while a public nuisance is one affecting the rights enjoyed by citizens as a part of the public. To constitute a public nuisance, the nuisance must affect a considerable number of people or an entire community or neighborhood.

Where the injury is slight, the remedy for minor inconveniences lies in an action for damages rather than in one for an injunction. Moreover, some courts have held, in the "balancing of conveniences" cases, that damages may be the sole remedy.

Thus, it would appear from the admittedly incomplete record as developed in the trial court, that, at most, residents of Youngtown would be entitled to damages rather than injunctive relief.

We have no difficulty, however, in agreeing with the conclusion of the trial court that Spur's operation was an enjoinable public nuisance as far as the people in the southern portion of Del Webb's Sun City were concerned.

Arizona statutes include within the definition of a public nuisance any condition or place in populous areas which constitutes a breeding place for flies, rodents, mosquitoes and other insects which are capable of carrying and transmitting disease-causing organisms to any person or persons.

It is clear that as to the citizens of Sun City, the operation of Spur's feedlot was both a public and a private nuisance. They could have successfully maintained an action to abate the nuisance. Del Webb, having shown a special injury in the loss of sales, had a standing to bring suit to enjoin the nuisance. The judgment of the trial court permanently enjoining the operation of the feedlot is affirmed.

MUST DEL WEBB INDEMNIFY SPUR?

A suit to enjoin a nuisance sounds in equity and the courts have long recognized a special responsibility to the public when acting as a court of equity:

§ 104. Where public interest is involved.

Courts of equity may, and frequently do, go much further both to give and withhold relief in furtherance of the public interest than they are accustomed to go when only private interests are involved. Accordingly, the granting or withholding of relief may properly be dependent upon considerations of public interest....   [27 Am Jur. 2d, Equity, page 626.]

In addition to protecting the public interest, however, courts of equity are concerned with protecting the operator of a lawfully, albeit noxious, business from the result of a knowing and willful encroachment by others near his business.

In the so-called "coming to the nuisance" cases, the courts have sometimes held that the residential landowner may not have relief if he knowingly came into a neighborhood reserved for industrial or agricultural endeavors and has been damaged thereby.

People employed in a city who build their homes in suburban areas of the county beyond the limits of a city and zoning regulations do so for a reason. Some do so to avoid the high taxation rate imposed by cities, or to avoid special assessments for street, sewer and water projects. They usually build on improved or hard surface highways, which have been built either at state or county expense and thereby avoid special assessments for these improvements. It may be that they desire to get away from the congestion of traffic, smoke, noise, foul air and the many other annoyances of city life. But with all these advantages in going beyond the area which is zoned and restricted to protect them in their homes, they must be prepared to take the disadvantages.   [Dill v. Excel Packing Company, 183 Kan. 513, 525, 526, 331 P. 2d 539, 548, 549 (1958). See also East St. John's Shingle Co. v. City of Portland, 195 Or. 505, 246 P. 2d 554, 560–562 (1952).]

Were Webb the only party injured, we would feel justified in holding that the doctrine of "coming to the nuisance" would have been a bar to the relief asked by Webb, and, on the other hand, had Spur located the feedlot near the outskirts of a city and had the city grown toward the feedlot, Spur would have to suffer the cost of abating the nuisance as to those people locating within the growth pattern of the expanding city.

We agree, however, with the Massachusetts court that:

The law of nuisance affords no rigid rule to be applied in all instances. It is elastic. It undertakes to require only that which is fair and reasonable under all the circumstances. In a commonweath like this, which depends for its material prosperity so largely on the continued growth and enlargement of manufacturing of diverse varieties, extreme rights cannot be enforced.... [Stevens v. Rockport Granite Co., 216 Mass. 486, 488, 104 N.E. 371, 373 (1914).]

There was no indication in the instant case at the time Spur and its predecessors located in western Maricopa County that a new city would spring up, full-blown, alongside the feeding operation and that the developer of that city would ask the court to order Spur to move because of the new city. Spur is required to move not because of any wrongdoing on the part of Spur, but because of a proper and legitimate regard of the courts for the rights and interests of the public.

Del Webb, on the other hand, is entitled to the relief prayed for (a permanent injunction), not because Webb is blameless, but because of the damage to the people who have been encouraged to purchase homes in Sun City. It does not equitably or legally follow, however, that Webb, being entitled to the injunction, is then free of any liability to Spur if Webb has in fact been the cause of the damage Spur has sustained. It does not seem harsh to require a developer, who has taken advantage of the lesser land values in a rural area as well as the availability of large tracts of land on which to build and develop a new town or city in the area, to indemnify those who are forced to leave as a result.

Having brought people to the nuisance to the foreseeable detriment of Spur, Webb must indemnify Spur for a reasonable amount of the cost of moving or shutting down. It should be noted that this relief to Spur is limited to a case wherein a developer has, with foreseeability, brought into a previously agricultural or industrial area the population which makes necesary the granting of an injunction against a lawful business and for which the business has no adequate relief.

It is therefore the decision of this court that the matter be remanded to the trial court for a hearing upon the damages sustained by the defendant Spur as a reasonable and direct result of the granting of the permanent injunction. Since the result of the appeal may appear novel and both sides have obtained a measure of relief, it is ordered that each side will bear its own costs.

Affirmed in part, reversed in part, and remanded for further proceedings consistent with this opinion.

Weeds

Weeds are a nuisance to farmers and ranchers and to their neighbors. Many states have adopted specific legislation to help in the control of weeds. Such a control program is illustrated in the following Illinois provisions.[33]

Weeds, which experience has shown to be particularly difficult to control, are designated as noxious by a committee of three composed of the director of the Illinois Department of Agriculture, the dean of the College of Agriculture of the University of Illinois, and the director of the Agriculture Experiment Station at the University of Illinois. Formerly, the legislature classified by statute which weeds were noxious, but this was changed in 1971 to put flexibility of classification and control in the determination back in the hands of people in agriculture. Lists describing noxious weeds can be obtained from the Illinois Department of Agriculture. Also, lists must be published periodically in the newspapers.

All persons are required to control the spread of weeds and eradicate noxious weeds on land owned or controlled by them. This includes railroads and highway authorities.

Each county governing body is designated as the local weed control authority and may employ a weed control superintendent to detect and treat noxious weeds. When the owner or person in control of the land fails to eradicate noxious weeds on his or her land, the weed control authority will notify the person in writing of the duty to cut them and when and how the weeds are to be eradicated. If the owner or person in control of the land fails or neglects to eradicate the noxious weeds, the authority may come in and do so at the owner's expense. The weed control superintendent or other authorized personnel will not be liable for damages or trespass when they enter on private land to eradicate noxious weeds or take specimens. Persons dissatisfied with the costs levied against them for the eradication by the authority must file an appeal within 5 days after being advised of the amount to the state director of agriculture.

Funds for the eradication of noxious weeds can come from any appropriate general fund of the county board, or, if approved by the voters of the county, a weed control fund may be established and the county board can set the tax rate and levy a tax which cannot exceed 0.01 percent on the value of the taxable property in the county. From either of these sources of revenue, purchases of the necessary machinery and equipment are to be made

---

[33] ILL. REV. STAT. ch. 18, § 101–24 (1979).

plus the cost for operation of such equipment is to be paid. This equipment may also be used by the weed control authority on public lands to eradicate weeds that have not been declared noxious.

Most states also have laws regulating weed seeds in agricultural seed. A detailed discussion of these laws appears in Chapter 12, "Sale and Transportation of Agricultural Products and Machinery."

The principal duties of the county weed control superintendents are to determine if all the land under their authority is in compliance with the Noxious Weed Act, to compile data on infested areas and other information the director of agriculture might require, to consult and advise on the most practical methods of noxious weed control, to render assistance and direction in practical methods of control, and to aid in the investigation and prosecution of anyone violating this act. The superintendents are paid at a rate determined by the county board.

Since weed seeds can be transmitted from one area to another in machinery and equipment, the state committee may publish a list of machinery and equipment and the designated treatment that must be done before these machines or articles can be moved. The weed control authority can prevent the movement of these machines from one premise to another until the designated procedures are followed. The authority could also stop the movement of a machine and direct the operator in its movement if the designated treatment has not been followed.

Further, when it appears to the authority that a tract of land is infested with noxious weeds beyond the ability of the person in control or owner to eradicate,

the weed control authority may take the action necessary if the state director of the department of agriculture appoves of quarantine of the infested land. Written notice must be given prior to the entry on the land, and the expenses shall be split equally between the weed control authority and the owner of the land.

The state, county, and township lands are subject to control of the authority. Expenses for state lands are to come from state funds, and in counties where there is a noxious weed control fund, both the county and township land expenses are to come out of the fund. Otherwise the expenses are shared by each governmental unit, with each unit paying for the work it receives.

Any violation of the Noxious Weed Act is a misdemeanor, and the violator may be fined $100 for a first offense and $200 for each offense after that.

7.6 ZONING AND LAND USE CONTROLS

Generally

Police power is the exercise of the government's sovereign right to promote the safety, health, morals, and general welfare of society within constitutional limits. Under the police power, the private use of land is regulated for the advancements of some acknowledged public interest. Zoning is one type of governmental activity authorized under the police power of the state.

The power to zone was established in *Village of Euclid v. Ambler Realty Co.*[34] The court decided that the zoning ordinance

[34] Euclid v. Ambler Realty Co., 272 U.S. 365, 47 S. Ct. 114 (1926).

in question was a valid regulation under the police power and did not violate the appealing landowner's constitutional property rights. Zoning ordinances must, however, relate substantially to the public health, morals, safety, or welfare.[35]

From the economic and social standpoint of zoning and with regard to the benefits which a well-administered county zoning law may confer, it has been maintained that county zoning can do the following:

1. Control development in the outskirts of cities
2. Minimize unnecessary and speculative land subdivision
3. Prevent real estate values from depreciating and thus weakening the tax base
4. Prevent unsightly and dangerous roadside development
5. Assist in conserving water resources
6. Prevent lake and stream pollution
7. Set aside adequate space for parks and other recreational areas
8. Help plan for future highway and transportation facilities
9. Reduce the cost of installing public utilities
10. Stabilize and enhance real estate values
11. Protect the best agricultural lands for farming purposes
12. Provide suitable space and protection for business and industrial areas
13. Protect recreational areas from undesirable uses
14. Guide future development in accordance with a carefully considered master plan

Most planning and zoning has occurred at the municipal level. The legal justification for controlling the type and intensity of land use has been relatively clear at this level. There also has been general acceptance of regulations in "urban-rural fringe" areas. Controls beyond this point have not readily been approved by rural citizens and landowners. However, regulation of predominantly rural areas by various zoning techniques is increasing.

Zoning of unincorporated or rural areas is authorized in all fifty states and in more than three-fourths of the 3000 counties in the United States. The number and kinds of governmental units empowered to zone and the areas each governmental unit may zone vary somewhat from state to state.

A report by the U.S. Department of Agriculture summarizes what some states currently are doing.[36]

1. Zoning to protect agriculture is a state-level activity in Hawaii. Prime agricultural lands are placed in agricultural zoning districts, and forest and watershed lands in conservation districts ....
2. State agencies are empowered to zone floodplains in Iowa and Minnesota, coastal wetlands in Rhode Island, unorganized boroughs in Alaska, shorelands in Minnesota and Vermont, and floodplains and shorelands in Wisconsin. The state highway commission in Mississippi is empowered to establish and enforce setback regulations. Similar state agencies in Louisiana, Maryland, Minnesota, Montana, Oklahoma, and Wisconsin are authorized to zone certain roadsides. Selected roadsides are zoned by the legislature in South Dakota.

---

[35] Nectow v. City of Cambridge, 277 U.S. 183, 48 S. Ct. 447 (1928).
[36] ECONOMIC RESEARCH SERVICE, U.S. DEPARTMENT OF AGRICULTURE, RURAL ZONING IN THE UNITED STATES: ANALYSIS OF ENABLING LEGISLATION (Misc. Publication No. 1232 Washington, D.C., 1972).

3.   Any land not zoned by a local government can be zoned by the governor of Oregon. In Maine a land use control commission is empowered to provide planning, zoning, and subdivision regulations in unorganized townships for all areas located within 500 feet of the edge of public roads and within 500 feet of shorelines of certain classes of lakes and ponds.

4.   Open-space land, under one classification in a Washington State differential assessment and tax law, must be so designated in an adopted city or county land use plan and zoned accordingly.

5.   In many other states, selected cities and towns are empowered to zone adjacent areas outside their boundaries.

6.   A half dozen statutes authorize zoning regulations requiring that automobile graveyards and junkyards be screened from view. Other statutes permit creation of historic zoning districts to safeguard and promote educational and recreational aspects of historic areas.

7.   A few enabling statutes confer express authority to create exclusive-type agricultural zoning districts for farming and related uses only. Support for exclusive agricultural zoning is growing in some parts of the agricultural community. Livestock producers are increasingly aware of the threat of nuisance suits (usually because of odor) that might be filed by urban workers living in the rural areas. Even though constitutional questions still cloud the use of exclusive zoning, it is being tried. However, strict enforcement of this type of ordinance may bring legal objections.

Planning and zoning traditionally have been practiced at the lowest level of government. But "a major trend away from the municipal monopoly on the land use regulatory powers has emerged and there are strong tendencies toward the reorganization of governments at the state and local levels and the assignment of land use regulatory powers to higher echelons."[37]

The conflict between private property and the public interest in that property will probably intensify as more innovative regulatory plans are tried. The problem today is that complete control by the individual over property is not practical, while absolute control by the state is inconceivable. To find the proper balance between these two extremes is the challenge now confronting the law and those who develop and administer it.[38]

The Illinois Example.

The Illinois legislature provided for regional planning by counties many years ago. Such comprehensive planning is accomplished through the appointment by the county board of a planning commission. The commission may be involved in planning for a portion of a county, for a whole county, or for two or more counties. The plan which is eventually developed is advisory only, but if zoning is contemplated, it should have a material effect on the kind of ordinances adopted, depending on the thoroughness and breadth of the planning effort.

The county's authority to zone is similar to that granted municipalities. The first legal step consists in appointment of a zoning commission by the county board. It then becomes the duty of the commission to draft an ordinance and establish zones and permitted uses within zones.

---

[37] Heyman, *Legal Assaults on Municipal Land Use Regulation*, 5 THE URBAN LAWYER (1973).

[38] J. CRIBBET, PRINCIPLES OF THE LAW OF PROPERTY (1962).

This ordinance must be subjected to a series of hearings in the townships in the county, following which the commission makes a report and recommendation to the county board. During this process there may be changes or modifications in the proposed ordinance. Once adopted by the county board, the ordinance goes into effect and is administered by a zoning officer appointed by the board.

Another important entity required by the law is a zoning board of appeals, also appointed by the county board of supervisors. A zoning ordinance cannot be retroactive; hence, one using property for a particular purpose may continue to use it for such purpose though the area is zoned against it. This is known as a *nonconforming use* and may be continued as long as there is no cessation or material change. Property owners who feel they are injured by enforcement of the zoning ordinance may ask for a variation in its application. Property owners who wish to establish a business in an area zoned against it may ask for a special use permit. Within limits, these can be granted by the zoning officer or the zoning board of appeals. However, the granting of too many special use permits or variances tends to weaken the effect of the zoning ordinance. Also, a variance may be held invalid if the authorities exceeded

their permissible discretion in issuing the variance.

Control is exercised over the addition or modification of structures through a permit system. Generally, permits are required to establish any new use of property—to excavate or build; to erect, construct, reconstruct, enlarge, or move any building or structure; to change the use of any building, structure, or land from one classification to another; or to change a nonconforming use. Generally, a small fee is charged for permits.

Under the Illinois law, permits are not necessary for agricultural buildings and no fees may be charged. In some counties, permits are required to check on setback requirements and to ascertain that the proposed building will be for agricultural purposes. Property owners who feel that the zoning ordinance creates a hardship on them may get relief by going to the zoning officer. The next step would be an appeal to the board of zoning appeals. If the board of appeals doesn't grant their request, they may go into court and ask to have the ordinance declared invalid.

Most county ordinances establish industrial, business, residential, and agricultural zones as a minimum. Some of these zones may be further subdivided, and others such as forestry or recreation may be added.

ZONING

LAKELAND BLUFF, INC. v. COUNTY OF WILL
Illinois Appellate Court, 1969
114 Ill. App. 2d 267, 252 N.E. 2d 765

The owner of the property involved in the cause before us first sought to have the property in Will County rezoned. When this request was denied, plaintiff Lakeland Bluff, Inc., sought to have the Will County zoning ordinance, as it relates to the property of plaintiff, declared invalid. The trial court decreed that the Will County ordinance was invalid as it applied to the property of plaintiff and granted the injunctive relief requested. The County appealed from such judgment.

In 1962, Patrick D. Fahey of Joliet, Illinois, purchased 700 acres of land near Braidwood in Will County, Illinois. The land was a former strip mine that had been redeveloped and was not fit for farming. In 1966 Mr. Fahey conveyed the 160-acre tract, which is the subject of the present litigation, to Lakeland Bluff, Inc., a corporation, in which Mr. Fahey owned all the stock. The property in question was zoned "F" (Farm District). There was no specific provision which would allow mobile home developments in such "F" district, and, accordingly, plaintiff sought rezoning of the 160-acre tract to "B-5" district. After application to the Will County Zoning Board of Appeals, this request was denied, and the denial was approved by the Board of Supervisors of Will County in October of 1967. The present injunction action was then undertaken, after a showing that the plaintiff had exhausted its remedies in seeking rezoning relief.

The presumption of validity which arises from enactment of a zoning ordinance can be overcome by clear and convincing evidence that the ordinance, as applied to the subject land, was arbitrary and unreasonable and without real or substantial relation to the public health, safety, morals and welfare. The courts of this State have recognized that the validity of each zoning ordinance must be determined on its own facts and circumstances. The court in *LaSalle Nat. Bank v. County of Cook*, 12 Ill. 2d 40, 145 N.E. 2d 65 (1957) grouped the various factors for consideration under six general headings, stating:

Among the facts which may be taken into consideration in determining the validity of an ordinance are the following:

(1) The existing uses and zoning of nearby property....
(2) The extent to which property values are diminished by the particular zoning restrictions....
(3) The extent to which the destruction of property values of plaintiff promotes the health, safety, morals or general welfare of the public....
(4) The relative gain to the public as compared to the hardship imposed upon the individual property owner....
(5) The suitability of the subject property for the zoned purposes....
(6) The length of time the property has been vacant as zoned considered in the context of land development in the area in the vicinity of the subject property....

Apparently, one of the major reasons that Will County refused to rezone the property when first requested may have been the feeling that the development would possibly cause an increase in local government costs for schools, roads and other facilities. Such considerations, however, could not be a justifiable basis for rejecting an appropriate use of the property. It is obvious that if future developments were limited to commercial or industrial enterprises, there would be more tax money without the addition of any school children; that the fiscal position of the school board would be strengthened but only at the cost of circumventing the reason for having schools. We do not believe that such consideration should be a basis for rejection of a request for rezoning or usage which is consistent with the general objectives of the zoning ordinance.

While we do not predicate our conclusion upon the need for lower cost housing, we believe that this was an element which should be considered in determining the reasonableness of the restrictive zoning ordinance. The need must necessarily be balanced as against the question of its effect upon the neighboring property, etc. While many of the uses which are authorized by the "F" zoning classification would be more detrimental than the mobile home development, we believe that the court rightfully considered the mobile home development on the basis of its impact in the community, and not as a lesser evil.

In applying the six factors which were emphasized as basic considerations in the *LaSalle Nat. Bank v. County of Cook* case (12 Ill. 2d 40, 145 N.E. 2d 65), we believe that the trial court was correct in its findings and judgment. The trial court should have, and apparently did consider the factors referred to in making its determination.

The existing uses and zoning of the property adjacent and nearby to the property in question is a factor to be considered. Although the area around the 160-acre tract was zoned "F," it was shown that the tract in question could not be farmed or used for many of the uses which were permitted in the "F" zoning. The existing uses of nearby property were shown by the record to be compatible with the mobile home development, since the adjacent property was used for recreational areas which included campers and trailers.

The relative gain to the public as compared to the hardship imposed upon the individual property owner should also be considered. The hardship to the plaintiff in the case before us is apparent. His property has very little value as farmland and might well be worth $15,000 an acre if developed for moble homes. The circumstance that plaintiff purchased the tract knowing that it was zoned "F" does not preclude the plaintiff from objecting to such classification.

In view of the record and the precedents to which we have referred, we do not feel that this court would be justified in rejecting the determination of the trial court. The judgment of the Circuit Court of Will County will, therefore, be affirmed.

UNREASONABLE ZONING RESTRICTIONS

PETTEE v. THE COUNTY OF DE KALB
Illinois Court of Appeals, Second District, 1978
60 Ill. App. 3d 304, 376 N.E. 2d 720

Plaintiff, Gary Pettee, owner of the subject property, applied to the Zoning Board of Appeals of De Kalb County for a change in zoning from A-Agricultural District to E-2 Estate Residential District (single-family residences of not less than one acre) and a small area of B-3 Commercial, Wholesale and General Service District under the De Kalb County Zoning Ordinance. In addition, he requested a special use permit for an aircraft landing field, which can be allowed in an E-2 district under the ordinance. The Zoning Board of Appeals recommended to the Board of Supervisors of De Kalb County that plaintiff's application be denied. On October 17, 1973, the Board of Supervisors accepted that recommendation and refused to grant the requested changes in zoning or issue the special use permit. Plaintiff instituted this action against defendants, the County of De Kalb and the Zoning Board of Appeals of De Kalb County on March 12, 1974, requesting that the trial court hold the zoning ordinance, as applied to the subject property, arbitrary and unreasonable and bearing no substantial relation to the public health, safety or welfare and order that his proposed uses be allowed.

The trial court concluded that the De Kalb County Zoning Ordinance, as applied to the subject property, was not unreasonable and entered judgment in favor of defendants. In arriving at its conclusion the trial court found that plaintiff's proposed use would not decrease the value of the surrounding property and that the value of the subject property would increase from $1,600 per acre as presently zoned to between $2,000 to $2,500 per acre if rezoned as requested. Ths court also found, however, that the subject property would be prime farm land if properly tiled; that if this property had remained a part of a large farm, as it must have once been, the cost of tiling it would be relatively insignificant when amortized over many years; that plaintiff's residential subdivision would not be compatible with the surrounding agricultural uses; and that plaintiff's proposed use would create problems with respect to police and fire protection and sanitary waste and garbage disposal, although no evidence was introduced in this regard.

A determination as to whether the present agricultural zoning classification is reasonable as applied to plaintiff's property depends, as all zoning cases do, upon the particular facts involved.

Our supreme court has stated that among the factors which may be taken into consideration in determining the validity of zoning ordinances are the following: (1) the existing uses and zoning of nearby property; (2) the extent to which property values are diminished by the particular zoning restrictions; (3) the extent to which the destruction of property values of plaintiff promotes the health, safety, morals or general welfare of the public; (4) the relative gain to the public as compared to the hardship imposed upon the individual property owner; (5) the suitability of the subject property for the zoned purposes; and (6) the length of time the property has been vacant as zoned considered in the context of land development in the area in the vicinity of the subject property.

When we apply these factors to the instant case, as the parties urge, we conclude that prohibition of the proposed residential and aircraft landing uses on the subject property by the existing zoning restrictions is unreasonable, but that prohibition of the proposed commercial use, as was also determined by the trial court, is reasonable. The evidence fairly shows that the subject property is largely unsuitable for farming, or is at best marginal farmland, because approximately 25 acres suffer from a serious drainage problem. The present cost of properly tiling it to alleviate this condition was estimated at $30,000, a significant sum in our view. Both plaintiff and Wilton L. Battles, his planning and zoning consultant, testified there was a need for developments of the proposed type in the area. While Donald Taylor testified that there was no such need, it is noteworthy that he had recently developed a similar project nearby and had an obvious competitive interest at stake. If the proposed use were allowed it was estimated that the value of the subject property would rise from $1,600 per acre to between $2,000 and $2,500 per acre with no resultant decrease in the value of any neighboring property. Evidence was introduced that three of the bordering property owners, as well as other persons in the area, were in favor of the proposed use. Plaintiff's experts testified that the proposed use would be compatible with the surrounding farming uses and that it would have no adverse affect on them. Taylor corroborated this testimony by stating that his similar development had caused no adverse effects on its rural surroundings of which he was aware. Plaintiff's experts also stated that they were of the opinion that the highest and best use of the subject property would be the proposed use. The expert testimony of William H. Lawrence to the contrary, that the highest and best use was agricultural, deserves less weight. His view that the proposed use was incompatible with, and would have serious adverse affects on the surrounding farmland was based only on a general objective of the County of De Kalb to preserve a natural resource, farmland, and his bare assertion that this was a goal important to the general welfare of De Kalb County. We note that the combined residential and landing strip development proposed by plaintiff is contemplated by defendants' ordinance as a special use allowed in its E-2 Estate Residential District which permits single-family residences on not less than an acre of land. It would appear that such specialized developments must necessarily be carved out of rural, sparsely populated areas of the county and those would normally be currently applied to and zoned for agricultural purposes. It would be unrealistic to strike such areas from consideration for residential-landing-strip developments; these would appear to be far less compatible to a more densely populated suburban area. While farmland might well be characterized as an essential natural resource, as defendants suggest, the evidence fails to disclose why plaintiff's land specifically should be so preserved for the general benefit. The gain to the public from continuation of the existing restrictions on this 80 acres of marginal farmland, as suggested by Lawrence, finds little specific support in this record, whereas the hardship imposed upon plaintiff is real and substantial. Under such circumstances this court is fully justified in declaring the zoning restrictions before us to be unreasonable and void insofar as they prohibit a residential-landing-strip development on plaintiff's land.

Plaintiff met his burden of showing by clear and convincing evidence that the zoning restrictions as applied to him were unreasonable and the trial court's holding to the contrary is against the manifest weight of the evidence.

We do not believe, however, plaintiff has shown that application of the ordinance, insofar as it denies him the right to commercial use of his property, is unreasonable. Little evidence was presented in regard to this use and the need for it other than that it would include a large building from which plaintiff would operate his landscaping business and an aircraft maintenance garage. These uses would not generally be in keeping with a residential development and we cannot say the decision of the trial court in this regard was against the manifest weight of the evidence.

Therefore, the judgment of the trial court is affirmed insofar as it holds the zoning restrictions prohibiting the proposed commercial uses are reasonable. The judgment of the trial court is reversed insofar as it holds that the zoning restrictions prohibiting the proposed residential and aircraft landing uses are reasonable and the cause is remanded to the trial court with directions that the court hear further evidence as to the particular use and conformation of the aircraft landing field proposed by plaintiff together with any recommendations by defendants as to its regulation and enter an appropriate order permitting the residential and aircraft landing uses in accordance with the evidence presented.

7.7 LIMITATIONS ON FARM OWNERSHIP

Rules and regulations concerning who may own farmland in the various states have been the subject of much discussion in recent years. At the heart of this discussion has been the fear that purchases of farmland by large corporations and aliens constitute a threat to "family farms." In response to this fear, both the federal and state governments have enacted laws which, in one form or another, regulate farmland ownership.

Federal Regulation of Alien Ownership

The Agricultural Foreign Investment Disclosure Act of 1978 represented the first comprehensive effort of the federal government to obtain reliable data on foreign investments in agricultural land.[39] This act is a reporting law and imposes no restrictions on present holdings or future acquisitions of farmland by anyone.

[39] 7 U.S.C. §§ 3501–3508 (1978).

The federal law evolved from certain underlying facts. There had been numerous reports that the purchase of U.S. agricultural land by foreign interests was escalating. These reports were viewed as possible indicators of a trend.

Also, there was widespread concern, especially in the agricultural community and the rural sector, over the implications and impact of foreign investment in agricultural land. This concern was focused on the effects of such investment on the price of farmland, local taxes, economic vitality of rural communities, farm commodity prices, conservation practices, and entry of new farmers into agriculture, among other things. The conditions encouraging foreign investment in U.S. farmland were not diminishing. Such conditions included the decline in the value of the dollar relative to the value of other currencies, the stability of our government and social system compared with the growing instability in many others, and tax advantages available to foreign buyers but unavailable to U.S. farmers.

The lack of reliable data on foreign investment in U.S. agricultural land made it difficult, if not impossible, to determine if such investment did, in fact, pose a threat to the United States as a whole, or to the family farms and rural communities in this country. Clearly, such information was needed before a reasonable, responsible analysis of the situation could be made.

The act requires any foreign individual or organization that either acquires or transfers an interest in agricultural land to file a report with the U.S. Secretary of Agriculture. This report must identify the foreign owner and the land involved, reveal the purchase price, and disclose the use the owner intends to make of the land. Foreign individuals and organizations already owning agricultural land must file the same kind of report. If the foreign owner is not an individual or a government, the Secretary may require the organization also to report the names, addresses, and nationalities of all those holding an interest in the organization. A foreign owner that does not file this report or knowingly files an incomplete, false, or misleading report is subject to a civil penalty of up to 25 percent of the value of the land. Any report filed is open to public inspection, and the Secretary is to send a copy of each report to an appropriate agency of the state where the land is located. The Secretary is to determine the effects that foreign investment in agricultural land has on family farms and rural communities and is to periodically report the findings to the President and Congress.

State Regulation of Alien Ownership

Many states have enacted laws which either require reporting of farmland transactions involving aliens or place some constraints on aliens acquiring or holding farmland.[40] Some of the states inhibit or prohibit individual alien investors residing outside the United States from owning real estate in their names; some have laws that limit the total acreage that aliens can acquire or hold; some have laws that restrict aliens from owning land for more than a specified time; and some require aliens to dispose of all or part of their landholdings within specified times if they do not become U.S. citizens or residents of the

---

[40] Reynolds, *State Statutory Restrictions on Alien and Corporate Ownership of United States Agricultural Land*, 1 AGRICULTURAL L.J. 415 (1979).

state. Legislation to place additional constraints on foreign ownership of land or to require reporting of such holdings has been proposed in several states. In most of these states, restrictions of some type were already in effect. Some of these laws have been challenged on constitutional grounds.

CONSTITUTIONALITY OF LAWS REGULATING ALIEN OWNERSHIP

LEHNDORFF GENEVA, INC. v. WARREN
Supreme Court of Wisconsin, 1976
74 W. 3. 2d 369; 246 N.W. 2d 815

DAY, J.

The principal questions on this appeal are whether sec. 710.02, Wis. Stats. limiting nonresident alien ownership of land violates the equal protection clause of either the United States or Wisconsin constitutions. We conclude that the answer to these questions is no.

LGI is a Texas corporation duly qualified to do business in Wisconsin with its principal place of business, Chicago, Illinois. The entire stock of LGI is owned by nonresident aliens, citizens of West Germany. The limited partners are citizens of West Germany. Farms alleges in the complaint for declaratory judgment that it is owner of options to purchase certain real estate in Wisconsin in excess of 640 acres and that if it acquired such properties the attorney general would enforce the forfeiture provision of sec. 710.02, Stats.

The cases which called for a "heightened judicial solicitude" toward aliens dealt with statutes which obstructed the normal affairs of life even though the national government had determined that the aliens in question could live in this country. As residents, these aliens bore the burdens imposed by society but not the sought-after benefits. Nor could they participate in the political process, which is the normal avenue of redress for a citizen unhappy with a governmentally-imposed burden. In this type of situation, the court repeatedly held, "heightened judicial solicitude" is appropriate.

None of these considerations appears in the instant case, in which foreign nationals who reside outside our borders have voluntarily associated with each other simply to have an investment vehicle here. The duties and burdens shared by the resident alien in common with the citizen entitles him to most of the benefits enjoyed by citizens. But burden sharing, except for payment of taxes in connection with the ownership or development of the land, is lacking in the case of the nonresident aliens in the case before us.

[7]   We conclude the plaintiffs do not possess the characteristics which warrant heightened judicial solicitude and the state has acted in an area traditionally within its province. Therefore the proper test is found in *Simanco v. Dept. of Revenue* (1973), 57 Wis.2d 47, 54, 203 N.W.2d 648. Only if a challenger can show that the classification is arbitrary and has no

reasonable purpose or relationship to the facts or a justifiable and proper state policy will a legislative classification fall on the grounds of a denial of equal protection.

The state argues that absentee ownership of land can be potentially detrimental to the welfare of the community in which it is located and persons who are neither citizens nor residents are least likely to consider the welfare of the community in which the land is located.

[8]   The classification of nonresident aliens is sufficiently related to the state's asserted desire to limit possibly detrimental absentee land ownership to survive the test applied here. Limiting the benefits of land ownership to those who share in the responsibilities and interests of residency is not an unreasonable exercise of legislative choice.

We conclude that 710.02 Stats. does not violate the equal protection clause of the United States Constitution or Article I, Section 1 of the Wisconsin Constitution.

State Regulation of Corporate Ownership[41]

Many states also have adopted some form of restriction on corporate involvement in agricultural production. The statutes range from mere reporting requirements in some states, such as Nebraska, to outright prohibition from engaging in the business of farming in others, such as North Dakota. Most of the states with such prohibitions make exceptions for closely held farm corporations, as is seen in the following discussion of the Kansas restrictions.[42]

For more than four decades, limitations have been imposed on farm corporations in Kansas. At present, corporations in that state cannot, "directly or indirectly engage in the agricultural or horticultural business of producing, planting, raising, harvesting, or gathering of wheat, corn, grain sorghums, barley, oats, rye, or potatoes or the milking of cows for dairy purposes."

However, corporations may engage in even the prohibited activities if specified requirements are met. The corporation may have no more than 10 shareholders, all of whom must be individuals or trustees, executors, administrators, or conservators for individuals, and all incorporators must be Kansas residents. Also, the corporation is limited to 5,000 acres of land owned, controlled, managed, or supervised. And none of the shareholders may own stock in another corporation authorized to engage in the prohibited purpose.

Corporations engaged in other activities such as beef cattle raising are not similarly restricted. Corporations owning or leasing land "used or usable for farming or agricultural or horticultural purposes" are required to report information on land owned and

---

[41] Id.; see generally THE FARM CORPORATION, WHAT IT IS, HOW IT WORKS, HOW IT IS TAXED (North Central Regional Extension Publication No. 11, 1979).
[42] KAN. STAT. ANN. §§ 17-5901 et seq. The discussion of the Kansas provision is taken from THE FARM CORPORATION, WHAT IT IS, HOW IT WORKS, HOW IT IS TAXED at 4 (North Central Regional Extension Publication No. 11, 1979).

leased, number of shareholders and value, stated separately, of nonagricultural and agricultural assets.

STUDY QUESTIONS

1. What trends may affect rights and limitations in the use of farm property?

2. What are easements, and how are they created? What are covenants running with the land, and how are they created? Who can enforce them? What kinds of covenants cannot be enforced?

3. What rights does a landowner have to lateral and subjacent support?

4. What acts might constitute trespass? What is the difference between civil and criminal trespass? What remedies does a landowner have for trespass?

5. What duties are owed to trespassers, licensees, and invitees by occupiers of land? By absentee landowners?

6. What actions might one take to prevent trespass?

7. What is the meaning of "attractive nuisance"?

8. What special rules apply regarding liability to persons using property gratuitously for recreational purposes?

9. How are pesticides classified under federal law, and what is the effect of this classification?

10. What standards have been developed to protect employees who are working in fields treated with pesticides?

11. What kinds of state regulation might affect pesticide applicators?

12. What is the basis of liability for pesticide application? Who is potentially liable?

13. What is a nuisance? What factors are important in determining whether a nuisance is present?

14. What special regulations apply to weeds?

15. How is zoning related to the police power?

16. What kinds of zoning restrictions might be unreasonable?

17. What federal laws regulate alien ownership? What is the nature of the regulatory scheme?

18. Can corporations own farmland?

19. Frank Farmer took possession of a 320-acre newly purchased farm. The 320-acre farm was completely surrounded by other land owned by Initial Landlord, who had sold the 320-acre farm to Frank Farmer. The contract for purchase and the deed were silent as to access. What is the right of Frank Farmer to use a private road across Mr. Landlord's property to gain access to the 320-acre farm? Assume this road had been used by Initial Landlord in recent years to gain access to the 320-acre parcel. Discuss.

20. New Farmer began farming operations on a 320-acre newly purchased farm. After the crops were planted, New Farmer hired Cut-Rate-Aerial-Applicators to apply a herbicide. Cut-Rate-Aerial-Applicators negligently applied the chemical and caused extensive property damage and personal injury in a nearby town.

New Farmer also hired College Student to assist generally with farming operations. College Student was directed to apply a chemical to a pond located on the 320-acre farm. The chemical was to control mosquitoes. The chemical was labeled as being dangerous to humans. College Student applied the chemical to the pond. Later that day, College Student saw two persons swimming in the pond but did not warn them of the danger. These swimmers suffered injury from exposure to the chemical. One of the swimmers, Ima Freeloader, had been invited to swim at any time by New Farmer. The other swimmer, Loel Sneak, had not received any permission and had walked past a "no trespassing" sign on his way to the lake.

Discuss the potential liability of Cut-Rate-Aerial-Applicators and New Farmer for the spraying damage in the nearby town. Discuss the potential liability of College Student and that of New Farmer for the injuries to Ima Freeloader and Loel Sneak.

8
Water and Drainage

Water is of critical importance to agriculture. On the one hand, water can bring life to parched, dry earth as it falls from the heavens or trickles from an irrigation ditch. On the other hand, too much water can destroy newly planted crops in low-lying fields and can take buildings or even human life as it breaches protective levees.

At common law, five distinct classes of nonatmospheric water were recognized:

1. natural surface waters
2. diffused surface waters
3. underground streams
4. percolating groundwaters
5. springs

In addition, a sixth category of artificial waters, such as the water in artificial channels and ponds, was often recognized.

Separate common-law rules developed for the management of each type of water. These rules have survived in their original form in some states, but elaborate modifications have been made in others. The "humid" Eastern states have traditionally followed riparian water laws based on the common law. The Western states adopted systems more satisfactory for an arid region—based on the doctrine of prior appropriation—although some continue to recognize the riparian doctrine to some degree. In light of water shortages in some of the Eastern states, efforts have been made to modify traditional riparian water laws to take on characteristics of prior appropriation. Such formerly riparian states as Iowa, Florida, and Kentucky have adopted variations of administrative permitting systems; Mississippi had adopted a version of prior appropriation. Other states are currently studying their allocation systems in light of what is perceived to be an impending "water crisis" in some areas.

As will be apparent in the following discussion, the right of a farmer or rancher to use water often depends upon whether the source of that water is a surface or underground stream, groundwater, or diffused surface water and whether that person lives in the arid West or some other part of the country. Similarly, a person's right to be rid of excess surface water depends on the particular law recognized in the landowner's jurisdiction.

8.1 GROUNDWATER

Water found below the surface of the earth, except clearly defined underground watercourses, is classed as *percolating groundwater*. Because of the early courts' method of basing water rights upon the source of supply, the use of percolating groundwater is governed by rules of law that differ substantially from those that regulate the use of water in watercourses. Underground or subterranean watercourses which flow in well-defined channels are governed by the same rules as surface watercourses in jurisdictions following the common law. However, the channels of such streams must be defined and capable of being proved in court; otherwise they will be considered as percolating groundwater and will be governed by the rules applicable to percolating groundwater.

General Rules

The law of percolating groundwater use is not clearly defined. Until recent years, pumping systems could not draw large volumes of water from great depths. Most wells were shallow and were used only to supply domestic requirements. As a result, not enough groundwater was used to deplete the supply and cause conflict between competing users. Therefore, the courts were seldom called upon to decide water rights involving groundwater.

In addition, the movement of groundwater could not be seen or followed, and the early courts hesitated to lay down rules regulating the use of something whose "existence and progress cannot be known or regulated," something that "rises to great heights, and moves collaterally, by influences beyond our apprehension," as was noted by a Connecticut court. The courts felt that while a *riparian proprietor* (one who owns land adjacent to a stream) could not interfere materially with the flow of stream water without knowing that it would affect a lower riparian proprietor, a user of groundwater often did not know who, if anyone, would be affected by his or her use.

However, as the use of groundwater for consumptive purposes (by municipalities, industry, and agriculture) increased with the development of more efficient pumping methods, the courts and legislatures in some states have laid down rules defining the rights of different users and uses. Many areas of the law pertaining to groundwater uses are left unsettled or entirely untouched.

In states recognizing a distinction between underground streams and percolating waters, rights to use the latter rest upon one or some variation of three bases—prior appropriation, the English rule of absolute ownership, and the American rule of reasonable use. Some Western states have specifically imposed prior appropriation on percolating waters. Other states have included percolating waters within broad appropriation statutes. In some Western jurisdictions, percolating waters are subject to the basic common-law rules, rather than to statutory appropriation.[1]

Some states have developed permitting schemes for groundwater allocation—especially in critical groundwater areas. The restrictions imposed by these systems are insignificant compared with those in Western states that limit the use of groundwater to certain purposes and amounts. If the water supply should ever become seriously inadequate, even in a part of a state, such laws would probably multiply and the price of water would undoubtedly increase.

The English rule of absolute ownership holds that the owner of overlying lands is the absolute owner of all percolating waters thereunder. Under the rule of capture, owners generally may withdraw as much as they desire, regardless of the effect on other wells or of the reasonableness of their use. The American rule of reasonable use modifies the English rule by limiting landowners' water use to the amount necessary for some reasonable beneficial purpose in connection with their land. Waste of water or its export for distant use is not reasonable if other overlying landowners are thereby deprived of reasonable use of the water on their lands.

GROUNDWATER

SMITH-SOUTHWEST INDUSTRIES v. FRIENDSWOOD DEVELOPMENT CO.
Court of Civil Appeals of Texas, Houston (1st Dist.), 1977
546 S.W. 2d 890

This is an appeal from the granting of a summary judgment against the plaintiffs, Smith-Southwest Industries and other landowners similarly situated, who brought this class action against Friendswood Development Company and its corporate parent, Exxon Corporation, alleging that the severe subsidence of their lands was caused by the defendants' withdrawal of vast quantities of percolating underground water from wells located on defendants' land in the immediate vicinity of the plaintiffs' land.

The plaintiffs' petition alleged four theories of recovery: (1) nuisance, (2) negligence, (3) intentional interference with appellants' property by way of the diversion of water onto and across their property and (4) wrongful and unconstitutional taking of property without just compensation and conversion of such property for private use. Friendswood and Exxon each filed a general denial.

[1]   The trial court had before it depositions, interrogatories and answers, affidavits, and exhibits but concluded, as a matter of law, that the plaintiffs had failed to state a cause of action against the defendants.

---

[1] States that provide for the appropriation of both surface water and groundwater sources, without distinguishing between percolating waters, underground streams, or other groundwaters, include Alaska, Kansas, Nevada, North Dakota, and Oregon.

The appellants' petition recites that they are landowners in the area of Seabrook and Clear Lake. The appellees own property inland from that owned by appellants and pump massive amounts of subsurface fresh water from their property to sell to industrial purchasers.

The appellants contend this extensive withdrawal of fresh water has proximately caused the sinking and loss of elevation above mean sea level of their property and the property of others similarly situated along the shores of Galveston Bay and Clear Lake which has resulted in the destruction of the land and improvements by flooding. The appellants say that this is not a water rights case and that neither the trial court nor this court is called upon to decide any competing claims by property owners to any water rights. They contend that this case concerns damage to land and that their petition presents four individual causes of action upon which relief can and should be granted.

The appellees' position is that whether the damage results from the lowering of the water table, from destruction of wells, or from subsidence, the damage is damage to land resulting from the exercise of a neighboring owner's right to the unlimited withdrawal of water beneath his land. They say that in Texas there is no right to recover for damages resulting from withdrawal of underground water or to enjoin withdrawal, regardless of the fact that neighboring lands sustain damage.

[2,3]   The rules in the courts of the United States with respect to the right of a landowner to the abstraction and use of percolating water beneath his land are the "common law" or "English" rule and the "American" or "reasonable use" rule, which is also referred to as the doctrine of "correlative rights." 78 Am. Jur. 2d 607, Water § 158. The American or reasonable use rule is that

the rights of each owner being similar and their enjoyment dependent on the action of other landowners, their rights must be correlative and subject to the maxim that "one must so use his own as not to injure another," so that each landowner is restricted to a reasonable exercise of his own rights and a reasonable use of his own property, in view of the similar rights of others.   78 Am. Jur. 2d 607, Waters, § 158.

The English rule of absolute ownership stems from *Acton v. Blundell*, 12 Meeson & Welsby, 324, 152 English Reprint 1223 (1843), in which the court said:

That the person who owns the surface may dig therein, and apply all that is there found to his own purposes, at his free will and pleasure; and that if, in the exercise of such right, he intercepts or drains off the water collected from the underground springs in his neighbor's well, this inconvenience to his neighbor falls within the description of damna absque injuria, which cannot become the ground of action.

Among jurisdictions that apply the English rule we have found no subsidence cases holding, that a cause of action may be grounded on a neighbor's withdrawal of percolating waters from his own land, absent malice or waste.

The Texas Supreme Court in *City of Corpus Christi v. City of Pleasanton*, 154 Tex. 289, 276 S.W. 2d 798, 801–802 (1955), spelled out its adherence to the English rule:

> With both rules before it, this Court, in 1904, adopted, unequivocally, the "English" or "Common Law" rule. *Houston & T.C.R. Co. v. East*, 98 Tex. 146, 81 S.W. 279, 280.
>
> Having adopted the "English" rule it may be assumed that the Court adopted it with only such limitations as existed in the common law. What were these limitations? About the only limitations applied by those jurisdictions retaining the "English" rule are that the owner may not maliciously take water for the sole purpose of injuring his neighbor, 55 A.L.R. 1395–1398; 67 C.J., sec. 257, p. 840; or wantonly and willfully waste it. 56 Am. Jur., sec. 119, p. 602; *Stillwater Water Co. v. Farmer*, 89 Minn. 58 [93] N.W. 907, 60 L.R.A. 875. There certainly was no limitation that prohibited the use of the water off of the premises where it was captured. Neither was there any restriction of its use to a particular area. Under the so-called "common-law" or "English" rule, which prevails in some jurisdictions, the right to extract artesian water for use outside the basin or district in which it is found would seem to be unrestricted. 56 Am. Jur., Sec. 118, p. 601.[2]

[4]   Two basic principles of law appear to be applicable: the English rule of absolute ownership and the well-settled Texas principle of law that imposes upon all persons a duty to use due care in the use of their property or the conduct of their business to avoid injury to others.

[5]   Because of a landowner's absolute right to take all of the water which he can produce from his land, the fact that this taking causes the land of others to subside will not, standing alone, give them a cause of action. But if the landowner is negligent in the manner by which he produces the water, and the negligence is a proximate cause of the subsidence of another's land, the fact that he owns the water produced will not insulate him from the consequences of his negligent conduct.

[6]   We sustain the appellants' first four points of error. We cannot say that they failed to state a cause of action against the appellees based on the theories of negligence and of nuisance in fact.

We reverse and remand the trial court's order granting summary judgments on the pleadings in favor of the appellees.

---

[2] Illinois seems to follow the English rule. *See* Edwards v. Haeger, 180 Ill. 99 (1899).

In *State v. Michels Pipeline Construction Co., Inc.*, 63 Wis.2d 278, 217 N.W.2d 339 (1974), there was surface property damage caused by land subsidence, together with damage from the loss of water wells. The Wisconsin Supreme Court chose not to adopt the English rule, the reasonable use rule, or the correlative rights rule, but rather to adopt the rule set forth in Tentative Draft No. 17 of the Restatement of the Law of Torts, Second, as proposed on April 26, 1971, for adoption by the American Law Institute. [Tentative Draft No. 17 has been approved in principle by the Institute; see *State v. Deetz*, 66 Wis.2d 1, 224 N.W.2d 407 (Wis. 1974), note 5 at page 415.]

Proposed Section 858A reads:

NON-LIABILITY FOR USE OF GROUND WATER—EXCEPTIONS.

A possessor of land or his grantee who withdraws ground water from the land and uses it for a beneficial purpose is not subject to liability for interference with the use of water by another, unless
(a) The withdrawal of water causes unreasonable harm through lowering the water table or reducing artesian pressure,
(b) The ground water forms an underground stream, in which case the rules stated in sec. 850A to 857 are applicable, or
(c) The withdrawal of water had a direct and substantial effect upon the water of a watercourse or lake, in which case the rules stated in secs. 850A to 857 are applicable. [*State v. Michels Pipeline Construction Co., Inc.*, supra.]

The American Law Institute's section dealing with subsidence, Section 818, was amended in May 1969 to read:

"Withdrawing Subterranean Substances. One who is privileged to withdraw subterranean water, oil, minerals or other substances from under the land of another is not for that reason privileged to cause a subsidence of the other's land by such withdrawal."

Other Restrictions

No one is allowed to unlawfully pollute groundwater. Likewise, no one is allowed to deplete groundwater for the malicious purpose of drying up a neighbor's supply. In addition, state laws have been passed to regulate the construction and maintenance of water wells,[3] including provisions for minimum spacing requirements in some states, such as Texas.[4]

If a landowner desires, he or she may grant to another person the right to come upon the land and make exclusive use of percolating groundwater. Although the question has not been decided in all jurisdictions, it appears that a grant by a landowner of percolating groundwater to another, without a concurrent grant of an easement to come upon the land to remove the water, would include an implied ease-

---

[3] For example, Illinois law contains the following provisions: (1) A log of all drilled wells must be filed with the State Geological Survey. ILL. REV. STAT. ch. 104, § 34 (1979). (2) A permit must be obtained from the state department of mines and minerals before a well can be drilled. *Id.* § 63.1. (3) An abandoned water well must be plugged. It is a criminal offense to leave it unplugged. ILL. REV. STAT. ch. 100 1/2, § 28.1. (4) If water from a new well is to be used for human consumption, the well must conform to regulations published by the Department of Public Health as to location, construction, and modification. ILL. REV. STAT. ch. 111 1/2, §§ 116.111–116.118.

[4] Texas law empowers underground conservation districts to enact spacing requirements for water wells. TEX. WATER CODE ANN. tit. 4, § 52.117 (Vernon 1972).

ment to come upon the grantor's land for the purpose of utilizing the grant.

8.2 RIGHTS TO USE STREAM WATER

The Riparian Doctrine of the East, Southeast, and Midwest

Owners and occupants of land adjoining a watercourse have certain rights—riparian rights—to use the water. Riparian rights attach to both surface and subterranean watercourses and to other definite natural sources of water supply on the surface of the earth. As a general rule, riparian rights exist only in *natural* watercourses or other natural bodies of water such as lakes, and in waters naturally flowing therein.

Riparian rights do not ordinarily attach to artificial streams in artificial channels, such as an artificial drainage system. However, artificial watercourses may in time take on the characteristics of natural watercourses. Additionally, interests in artificial watercourses can arise by grant, contract, or prescription.

Two theories have evolved to measure riparian rights. Under the *natural flow theory*, each riparian proprietor was entitled to have the water of the stream maintained in its natural state, not sensibly diminished in quantity or impaired in quality. Under the *reasonable use theory*, the riparian proprietor had a right to be free from an unreasonable interference with use of the water. The natural flow theory was recognized in early cases. In most jurisdictions, it was discarded as impractical, especially in developing communities needing water for consumptive uses. As stated by the Oregon Supreme

Court in an early case, to hold that there could be no diminution whatever in the streamflow as a result of the proprietor's use of the water would be to deny any valuable use of it; hence, each landowner is allowed to make a reasonable consumptive use of the common supply.[5]

A distinction between so-called "natural" or "ordinary" uses of water and "artificial" or "extraordinary" uses was made in many American and English cases. *Natural uses* of water are those arising out of the necessities of life on the riparian land, such as use of water for household purposes, for drinking needs, and for the watering of domestic animals. For these purposes, the riparian owner often may be allowed to take the whole flow of the stream if necessary, leaving none to go down to lower riparian proprietors. *Artificial uses*, on the other hand, are all those that do not minister directly to the necessities of life upon the land. Such uses are primarily for the purpose of improvement, trade, or profit. For these business uses, the riparian owner may not take all the water to the exclusion of other riparian owners, but may take what is reasonable with due regard to the uses of others on the same stream.

Stock Watering. From the standpoint of riparian rights to use water for stock watering, two classifications are involved—domestic (natural) use and commercial (artificial) use.

The riparian right at common law entitled the landowner to water stock from the stream. As in the case of use for household purposes, the landowner generally could take as much of the water as needed for watering farmstead domestic animals, even to the extent of consuming, *if neces-*

---

[5] Weiss v. Oregon Iron & Steel Co., 13 Oreg. 498, 498–502, 11 Pac. 255 (1886).

sary, all the water of the stream for that purpose. The preference accorded to the use of water for watering domestic animals as one of the primary uses of water usually applied only to the number of domestic animals required for ordinary farm domestic uses.

While the watering of large or small herds of stock on a commercial scale is a proper riparian use, subject to the rule of reasonableness, it usually is not a preferred use of the water. Therefore, the riparian landowner who raises stock on a commercial scale is ordinarily neither entitled to exhaust the stream flow for watering stock, nor to claim preference, as against another riparian owner who uses the water for irrigation.

Irrigation. The use of water to irrigate cultivated and uncultivated land has generally been characterized as an artificial use. The irrigation right is usually subordinate and applies only to the surplus of water above the quantities required for domestic purposes and for the watering of farm livestock. Once these natural wants have been supplied and protected, the right of the riparian proprietor to reasonable use of the surplus water for irrigation purposes in common with others in like situation, has been acknowledged and recognized.

Hunting, Fishing, and Swimming.   Riparian owners also have the right to hunt, fish, swim, and use the water for other forms of recreation, although their rights are subject to reasonable regulation by the state. Such rights accompany ownership of the land under the water. If the adjoining landowner holds title to the bed of the stream or lake, the landowner may use the water for recreation and, in some states, exclude others from using the water for recreational purposes.

Rights of the Public.   Citizens, as members of the public, have the right to hunt, fish, swim, and make other recreational use of navigable streams and meandered or navigable lakes. Meandered lakes are those outlined on maps by the federal surveyors when they surveyed the Northwest Territory, placing title to the beds in the state. Thus members of the public may use such waters for recreation.

Navigable streams and lakes are subject to an easement of navigation, which gives the public the right of transportation over the water. To be considered navigable, the stream or lake must be naturally capable of transporting enough boats for commercial purposes for sufficient time during the year to be of some practical value. The government may also have the right to make improvements for navigation and to exercise other rights over navigable waters.[6]

---

[6] The Illinois Department of Transportation has certain jurisdiction and control over interference with the use of navigable waters and other public waters of Illinois. Lakes and streams that discharge into navigable waters may also be considered public waters. A permit must be obtained from the Department to erect or make any structure, fill, or deposit in any public waters. Other states have similar provisions. Similar jurisdiction over navigable waters of the United States is exercised by the Corps of Engineers, U.S. Army.

RIPARIAN DOCTRINE

HARRIS v. BROOKS
Supreme Court of Arkansas, 1955
225 Ark. 436, 283 S.W. 2d 129

The issues presented by this appeal relate to the relative rights of riparian landowners to the use of a privately owned non-navigable lake and the water therein.

Factual Background.   Horseshoe Lake, located about 3 miles south of Augusta, is approximately 3 miles long and 300 feet wide, and, as the name implies, resembles a horseshoe in shape. Appellees, John Brooks and John Brooks, Jr., are lessees of Ector Johnson who owns a large tract of land adjacent to the lake, including three-fourths of the lake bed.

For a number of years appellees have intermittently raised rice on Johnson's land and have each year, including 1954, irrigated the rice with water pumped from the lake. They pumped no more water in 1954 than they did in 1951 and 1952, no rice being raised in 1953. Approximately 190 acres were cultivated in rice in 1954.

The rest of the lake bed and the adjoining land is divided into four parts, each part owned by a different person or group of persons. One such part is owned by Ed Harris, Jesse Harris, Alice Lynch and Dora Balkin who are also appellants. In March 1954 Mashburn leased from the above named appellants a relatively small camp site on the bank of the lake and installed the business above mentioned at a cost of approximately $8,000, including boats, cabins, and fishing equipment. Mashburn began operating his business about the first of April, 1954, and fishing and boat rentals were satisfactory from that time until about July 1st or 4th when, he says, the fish quit biting and his income from that source and boat rentals was reduced to practically nothing.

Appellees began pumping water with an 8 inch intake on May 25, 1954 and continued pumping until this suit was filed on July 10, and then until about August 20th. They quit pumping at this time because it was discovered fish life was being endangered. The trial was had September 28. After a lengthy hearing, the chancellor denied injunctive relief, and this appeal is prosecuted to reverse the chancellor's decision.

Two Basic Theories.   Generally speaking two separate and distinct theories or doctrines regarding the right to use water are recognized. One is commonly called the "Appropriation Doctrine" and the other is the "Riparian Doctrine."

[2]   *Appropriation Doctrine.*   Since it is unnecessary to do so we make no attempt to discuss the varied implications of this doctrine. Generally speaking, under this doctrine, some governmental agency, acting under constitutional or legislative authority, apportions water to contesting claimants.

It has never been adopted in this state, but has been in about 17 western states. This doctrine is inconsistent with the common law relative to water rights in force in this and many other states. One principal distinction between this doctrine and the riparian doctrine is that under the former the use is not limited to riparian landowners.

[3] *Riparian Doctrine.* This doctrine long in force in this and many other states is based on the old common law which gave to the owners of land bordering on streams the right to use the water therefrom for certain purposes, and this right was considered an incident to the ownership of land. Originally it apparently accorded the landowner the right to have the water maintained at its normal level, subject to use for strictly domestic purposes. Later it became evident that this strict limitation placed on the use of water was unreasonable and unutilitarian. Consequently it was not long before the demand for a greater use of water caused a relaxation of the strict limitations placed on its use and this doctrine came to be divided into (a) the natural flow theory and (b) the reasonable use theory.

[4]   (a) *Natural Flow Theory.* Generally speaking again, under the natural flow theory, a riparian owner can take water for domestic purposes only, such as water for the family, livestock, and gardening, and he is entitled to have the water in the stream or lake upon which he borders kept at the normal level. There are some expressions in the opinions of this court indicating that we have recognized this theory, at least to a certain extent.

Reasonable Use Theory. This theory appears to be based on the necessity and desirability of deriving greater benefits from the use of our abundant supply of water. It recognizes that there is no sound reason for maintaining our lakes and streams at a normal level when the water can be beneficially used without causing unreasonable damage to other riparian owners. The progress of civilization, particularly in regard to manufacturing, irrigation, and recreation, has forced the realization that a strict adherence to the uninterrupted flow doctrine placed an unwarranted limitation on the use of water, and consequently the court developed what we now call the reasonable use theory. This theory is of course subject to different interpretations and limitations. In 56 Am. Jur., page 728, it is stated that

The rights of riparian proprietors on both navigable and unnavigable streams are to a great extent mutual, common, or correlative. The use of the stream or water by each proprietor is therefore limited to what is reasonable, having due regard for the rights of others above, below, or on the opposite shore. In general, the special rights of a riparian owner are such as are necessary for the use and enjoyment of his abutting property and the business lawfully conducted thereon, qualified only by the correlative rights of other riparian owners, and by certain rights of the public, and they are to be so exercised as not to injure others in the enjoyment of their rights.

It has been stated that each riparian owner has an equal right to make a reasonable use of waters subject to the equal rights of other owners to make the reasonable use, *United States v. Willow River Power Co.*, 324 U.S. 499, 65 S.Ct. 761, 89 L.Ed. 1101. The purpose of the law is to secure to each riparian owner equality in the use of water as near as may be by requiring each to exercise his right reasonably and with due regard to the rights of others similarly situated. *Meng v. Coffey*, 67 Neb. 500, 93 N.W. 713, 60 L.R.A. 910.

[5]   This court has to some extent recognized the reasonable use theory, *Thomas v. La Cotts*, 222 Ark. 171, 257 S.W. 2d 936; *Harrell v. City of Conway*, Ark., 271 S.W. 2d 924, but we have also said in the City of Conway case that the uniform flow theory and the reasonable use theory are inconsistent and, further that we had not yet made a choice between them. It is not clear that we made a choice in that case. The nucleus of this opinion is, therefore, a definite acceptance of the reasonable use theory. We do not understand that the two theories will necessarily clash in every case, but where there is an inconsistency, and where vested rights may not prevent it, it is our conclusion that the reasonable use theory should control.

In embracing the reasonable use theory we caution, however, that we are not necessarily adopting all the interpretations given it by the decisions of other states, and that our own interpretation will be developed in the future as occasions arise. Nor is it intended hereby that we will not in the future, under certain circumstances, possibly adhere to some phases of the uniform flow system. It is recognized that in some instances vested rights may have accrued to riparian landowners and we could not of course constitutionally negate those rights.

The result of our examination of the decisions of this court and other authorities relative to the use by riparian proprietors of water in non-navigable lakes and streams justifies the enunciation of the following general rules and principles:

[7-10]   (a) The right to use water for strictly domestic purposes—such as for household use—is superior to many other uses of water—such as for fishing, recreation and irrigation.

(b) Other than the use mentioned above, all other lawful uses of water are equal. Some of the lawful uses of water recognized by this state are: fishing, swimming, recreation, and irrigation.

(c) When one lawful use of water is destroyed by another lawful use the latter must yield, or it may be enjoined.

(d) When one lawful use of water interferes with or detracts from another lawful use, then a question arises as to whether, under all the facts and circumstances of that particular case, the interfering use shall be declared unreasonable and as such enjoined, or whether a reasonable and equitable adjustment should be made, having due regard to the reasonable rights of each.

[11]   We do not minimize the difficulties attendant upon an application of the reasonable use rule to any given set of facts and circumstances and particularly those present in this instance. It is obvious that there are no definite guide posts provided and that necessarily much must be left to judgment and discretion. The breadth and boundaries of this area of discretion are well stated in Restatement of the Law, Torts, § 852c in these words:

The determination in a particular case of the unreasonableness of a particular use is not and should not be an unreasoned, intuitive conclusion on the part of the court or jury. It is rather an evaluating of the conflicting interests of each of the contestants before the court in accordance with the standards of society, and a weighing of those, one against the other. The law accords equal protection to the interests of all the riparian proprietors in the use of water, and seeks to promote the greatest beneficial use of the water, and seeks to promote the greatest beneficial use by each with a minimum of harm to others. But when one riparian proprietor's use of the water harmfully invades another's interest in its use, there is an incompatibility of interest between the two parties to a greater or lesser extent depending on the extent of the invasion, and there is immediately a question whether such a use is legally permissible. It is axiomatic in the law that individuals in society must put up with a reasonable amount of annoyance and inconvenience resulting from the otherwise lawful activities of their neighbors in the use of their land. Hence it is only when one riparian proprietor's use of the water is unreasonable that another who is harmed by it can complain, even though the harm is intentional. Substantial intentional harm to another cannot be justified as reasonable unless the legal merit or utility of the activity which produces it outweighs the legal seriousness or gravity of the harm.

In all our consideration of the reasonable use theory as we have attempted to explain it we have accepted the view that the benefits accruing to society in general from a maximum utilization of our water resources should not be denied merely because of the difficulties that may arise in its application. In the absence of legislative directives, it appears that this rule or theory is the best that the courts can devise.

[12]   *Our Conclusion.*   After careful consideration, an application of the rules above announced to the complicated fact situation set forth in this record leads us to conclude that the Chancellor should have issued an order enjoining appellees from pumping water out of Horseshoe Lake when the water level reaches 189.67 feet above sea level for as long as the material facts and circumstances are substantially the same as they appear in this record. We make it clear that this conclusion is not based on the fact that 189.67 is the normal level and that appellees would have no right to reduce such level. Our conclusion is based on the fact that we think the evidence

shows this level happens to be the level below which appellants would be unreasonably interfered with.

We think the conclusion we have reached is not only logical but practical. Although appellees had quit using water from the lake when this case was tried yet they testified that they intended to use water therefrom in 1955. We might assume that they would want to also use water in subsequent years, so it would seem to be to the best interest of all parties concerned to have a definite level fixed at which pumping for irrigation must cease in order to avoid useless litigation.

[13]   Appellees make the point that the Chancellor should be sustained because they have acquired a prescriptive right to the unlimited use of the water in Horseshoe Lake, and, to the same effect, that appellants are estopped from asserting any rights to the contrary. We cannot sustain this contention. Although appellees, according to the record, have used this water for irrigation purposes on several occasions in previous years, dating back for more than seven years, yet it appears that appellants had not been disturbed in the exercise of their riparian rights previous to 1954. Prior to that year appellees had merely been exercising their lawful rights as riparian owners and their exercise of those rights was in no way adverse to the rights of any one. (56 Am. Jur. p. 730, § 343.)

Reversed with direction to the trial court to enter a decree in conformity with this opinion.

The Doctrine of Prior Appropriation in the West[7]

Generally. Two basic doctrines govern the use of water in Western watercourses. They are (1) the doctrine of prior appropriation, and (2) the riparian doctrine. The riparian doctrine, which had such broad application in the eastern United States, was not a satisfactory doctrine for an arid region. Such a philosophy of water rights law could not have been indigenous a century ago to the undeveloped West, where the water potential fell far short of meeting the needs of large areas of arable land. The history of Western agriculture and water law refutes such a possibility. As a practical matter, the riparian doctrine was found to be unsuited to water development in the more arid areas, and as a legal matter, it was repudiated in the predominantly arid jurisdictions. Had the riparian doctrine been recognized and applied in Utah, said the supreme court of that state, "it would still be a desert."[8]

Nevertheless, in ten of the Western states, the riparian doctrine is recognized in some

---

[7] *See generally* W. A. HUTCHINS, WATER RIGHTS LAWS IN THE NINETEEN WESTERN STATES, Vols. I-III (U.S.D.A. Misc. Publication No. 1206, 1971).

Substantial portions of the following material have been adapted from these volumes.

[8] Stowell v. Johnson, 7 Utah 215, 26 P. 290 (1891).

degree concurrently with the doctrine of appropriation, and in Hawaii, without such concurrence. This degree of riparian recognition varies widely from one jurisdiction to another: in some states, riparianism, both in law and in fact, is an important part of the state water jurisprudence; in others, very little vestige of the doctrine is left. Eight Western states have generally repudiated the riparian doctrine of water rights. Where the two doctrines exist simultaneously, they are often in conflict.[9]

The prior appropriation doctrine, in contrast, has been established in each of the seventeen contiguous Western states and Alaska. This doctrine contemplates the acquisition of water rights by diverting water and applying it to reasonable beneficial use for a beneficial purpose, in accordance with procedures and under limitations specified by constitutional and statutory law or acknowledged by the courts. The water may be used on or in connection with lands away from streams, as well as with lands contiguous to streams. A distinctive feature of the doctrine as it was developed in the West is the principle of "first in time, first in right"—the prior exclusive right of the earliest appropriator of water from a particular watercourse to the use of the water to the extent of the appropriation, without material diminution in quantity or deterioration in quality, whenever the water is available; each later appropriator has a like priority with respect to all those who are later in time. In the absence of constitutional or statutory modifications, the principle of "first in time, first in right" is still valid. However, certain states have authorized preferences and imposed restrictions upon appropriations made under prescribed statutory procedures, the effects of which under some circumstances vary from the right of the first applicant to be accorded the first priority. The appropriative right relates to a specific quantity of water and is good as long as the right continues to be properly exercised. The right may be acquired for any use of water that is beneficial and reasonable.

State Administrative Procedures.   Administrative procedure governing the acquisition, determination, and administration of water rights has become highly developed throughout the West. Present administrative procedures are based largely upon those which originated in Colorado and Wyoming. The states' supervision and control are usually exercised through the state engineer or other corresponding official, and through the courts. In some states a board or department of the state government exercises control.

In Wyoming, all these functions are vested primarily in state administrative officers. The exclusive procedure for initiating the acquisition of a water right in Wyoming is to apply to the state engineer for a permit to make the appropriation. Adjudications or determinations of existing rights are made by the Board of Control, composed of the state engineer and the water division superintendents, all of whom are constitutional officers. Appeals from the board's decision can be taken to the courts. The distribution of water according to priorities of right is under the control of the organization of division superintendents and district commissioners, headed by the state engineer.[10]

---

[9] *E.g.*, Valmont Plantations v. State of Texas, 163 Tex. 381, 355 S.W. 2d 502 (1962).

[10] WYO. STAT. ANN. §§ 41-3-503, 41-3-640, 41-3-909, 41-4-201, 41-4-301, 41-4-401 (1977).

The Colorado system provides for judicial or judicially supervised determinations of water rights and priorities. Responsibility for the administration, distribution, and regulation of waters, subject to such determinations, is placed upon the division engineers, under the general supervision of the state engineer. However, permits to appropriate water are not required. If an appropriator desires a determination of his or her water right and the amount and priority thereof, an application for such determination is filed with the water clerk. Jurisdiction to hear and adjudicate such questions is vested exclusively in the water judges and their designated referees.[11]

In most of the seventeen contiguous Western states, the statutory procedure to appropriate water is held or conceded to be the exclusive method by which an appropriative right may be acquired. The exceptions are Colorado and Montana which do not utilize an administrative procedure for supervising the acquisition of appropriative rights, and Idaho, which recognizes a constitutional method of appropriating water that supplements the statutorily created administrative procedure.

Whatever the method of determining water rights—which are a form of property—jurisdiction in the last analysis is necessarily vested in the courts. For example, although the powers of the Wyoming Board of Control are quasi-judicial, it is true that appeal from the board's determinations may be taken to the courts. In no event are individuals precluded from recourse to the courts for protection of their water rights.

8.3 FEDERAL INVOLVEMENT: THE INTERSTATE ALLOCATION OF WATER; ACREAGE AND RESIDENCY LIMITATIONS IN RECLAMATION LAW[12]

The Interstate Allocation of Water

In many instances, states have been able to reach agreement concerning the allocation of waters from interstate water sources. In fact, over twenty interstate compacts providing for the apportionment or allocation of water within the Western states have been consented to by Congress. Congress often has expressly given advance authorization to particular states to negotiate specified interstate compacts, and often a federal representative has participated in the negotiations. In consenting to a number of compacts—for example, the Yellowstone River Compact—Congress has expressly reserved the right to alter, amend, or repeal the compact.

When states have been unable to agree on how to divide waters, Congress has acted to allocate water. For example, the Boulder Canyon Project Act of 1928 resulted from the gravity of the Southwest's water problems and the failure of the states to agree on how to conserve and divide the waters of the Colorado River.[13]

In the case of *Arizona v. California*, the U.S. Supreme Court concluded that the Boulder Canyon Project Act specified each state's share of the mainstream lower-basin water, and the Court gave the Secretary of the Interior authority to accordingly

[11] COLO. REV. STAT. §§ 37-92-202 to 302.
[12] *See also* Simms, *National Water Policy in the Wake of United States v. New Mexico*, 20 NAT. RE-SOURCES J. 1 (1980).
[13] Pub. L. No. 70-642, 45 Stat. 1057 (codified at 43 U.S.C. § 617-617u (1979).

apportion the water by making contracts for delivery of water, thereby allocating the water among the states.[14] In doing so, the act was construed to give the Secretary discretionary authority to determine which users within each state would get that state's share of water from the mainstream, subject to limitations and directives in the act. The Court said such apportionment was not controlled by state laws, by the doctrine of equitable apportionment, or by the Colorado River Compact.

The Court said that in previous cases in which it had used the doctrine of equitable apportionment, "Congress had not made any statutory apportionment. In this case, we have decided the Congress has provided its own method for allocating among the Lower Basin States the mainstream water to which they are entitled under the compact."[15] The Court also concluded that while the compact pertained to a division of waters between the Upper and Lower Basin States, it did not import to make any division among the Lower Basin States, which was the principal issue in this case. In the event of a shortage of available water, the Secretary was required to follow cer-

tain provisions set out in the act, but otherwise the Secretary had discretion to choose among recognized methods of apportionment or to devise his or her own reasonable methods.

Acreage and Residency Limitations of Federal Reclamation Law

Early Legislation and Judicial Interpretations. Irrigation in lands of many of the Western states is possible primarily by federal reclamation projects. The Reclamation Act of 1902, the Reclamation Act of 1914, and the Omnibus Adjustment Act of 1926 constitute the basic federal reclamation law.[16] The federal legislation includes both a 160-acre limitation and a residence requirement for establishment of a right to use water on privately owned land. The validity of the limitation was upheld in 1958,[17] but the dispute over applicability, in light of the lack of enforcement, has continued. The following case addressed the acreage limitation as it applied to certain lands, but the residency issue and the acreage limitation issue as it applies to other lands were not resolved.[18]

[14] Arizona v. California, 373 U.S. 546 (1963), decree entered 376 U.S. 340 (1964). This important case has been discussed in a number of secondary sources, including Trelease, F.J., *Arizona v. California: Allocation of Water Resources to People, States, and Nation.* 1963 SUP. C. REV. 158; Meyers, *The Colorado River,* 19 STAN. L. REV. 1 (1966). *See also* Hanks, *Peace West of the 98th Meridian—a Solution to Federal-State Conflicht over Western Waters,* 23 RUTGERS L. REV. 33, 40–41 n. 32

(1968), citing other sources.
[15] 373 U.S. at 565.
[16] *See* 43 U.S.C. § 431, 43 U.S.C. § 418 and 43 U.S.C. § 423 respectively.
[17] Ivanhoe Irrigation District v. McCracken, 357 U.S. 275 (1958).
[18] *See also* National Land for People, Inc., v. The Bureau of Reclamation, 417 F. 449 (D.C. Col. 1976); 42 Fed. Reg. 43,044 *et seq.* (August 25, 1977).

THE 160–ACRE LIMITATION

IMPERIAL IRRIGATION DISTRICT v. YELLEN
Supreme Court of the United States, 1980
_____U.S. _____; 100 S.Ct. 2232

MR. JUSTICE WHITE delivered the opinion of the Court.

When the Boulder Canyon Project Act, 45 Stat. 1057. 43 U.S.C. § 617 *et seq.* (Project Act) became effective in 1929, a large area in Imperial Valley, Cal., was already being irrigated by Colorado River water brought to the Valley by a privately owned delivery and distribution system. Pursuant to the Project Act, the United States constructed and the Imperial Irrigation District (District) agreed to pay for a new diversion dam and a new canal connecting the dam with the District. The Project Act was supplemental to the reclamation laws, which as a general rule limited water deliveries from reclamation projects to 160 acres under single ownership. The Project Act, however, required that the Secretary of the Interior (Secretary) observe rights to Colorado River water that had been perfected under state law at the time the Act became effective. In the course of contracting with the District for the building of the new dam and canal and for the delivery of water to the District, the United States represented that the Project Act did not impose acreage limitations on lands that already had vested or present rights to Colorado River water. The United States officially adhered to that position until 1964 when it repudiated its prior construction of the Project Act and sued the District, claiming that the 160-acre limitation contained in the reclamation law applies to all privately owned lands in the District, whether or not they had been irrigated in 1929. The District Court found for the District and its landowners, 332 F. Supp. 11 (SD Cal. 1971), but the Court of Appeals reversed and sustained the Government's position, 559 F. 2d 509 (CA9 1977). We now reverse the Court of Appeals with respect to those lands that were irrigated in 1929 and with respect to which the District has been adjudicated to have a perfected water right as of that date, a water right which, until 1964, the United States Department of the Interior officially represented foreclosed the application of acreage limitations. The judgment is otherwise vacated.

I

Imperial Valley is an area located south of the Salton Sea in southeastern California. It lies below sea level, and is an arid desert in its natural state. In 1901, however, irrigation began in the Valley, using water diverted from the Colorado River, which in that area marks the border between California and Arizona. Until at least 1940, irrigation water was brought to the Valley by means of a canal and distribution system that were completely privately financed. On June 25, 1929, when the Project Act became effective, the

District was diverting, transporting, and delivering water to 424,145 acres of privately owned and very productive farmland in Imperial Valley. Under neither state law nor private irrigation arrangements in existence in Imperial Valley prior to 1929 was there any restriction on the number of acres that a single landholder could own and irrigate.

The Project Act was the culmination of the efforts of the seven States in the Colorado River Basin to control flooding, regulate water supplies on a predictable basis, allocate waters among the Upper and Lower Basin states and among the States in each Basin, and connect the River to the Imperial Valley by a canal that did not pass through Mexico. In 1922, the seven States executed the Colorado River Compact (Compact) allocating the waters of the River between the Upper and Lower Basins, and among other things providing in Art. VIII that "[p]resent perfected rights to the beneficial use of the waters of the Colorado River System are unimpaired by this compact." The Project Act, passed in 1928 and effective in 1929, implemented and ratified the Compact; contained its own formula for allocating Lower Basin water among California, Arizona and Nevada, *Arizona v. California*, 373 U.S. 546 (1963); and authorized the construction of the works required for the harnessing and more efficient utilization of the unruly River. The principal works of the Project, consisting of the Hoover Dam at Black Canyon and the storage facilities behind it, served to implement the division of the Compact. The dam was completed and storage began in 1935.

Section 6 of the Project Act, of critical importance in this case, mandated that the works authorized by § 1 were to be used: "First, for river regulation, improvement of navigation, and flood control; second, for irrigation and domestic uses and satisfaction of present perfected rights in pursuance of Article VIII of said Colorado River compact; and third, for power." Section 9 authorized the opening to entry of the public lands that would become irrigable by the Project but in tracts not greater than 160 acres in size in accordance with the provisions of the reclamation law.

Section 14 provided that the Project Act should be deemed supplemental to the reclamation law, "which said reclamation law shall govern the construction, operation, and management of the works herein authorized, except as otherwise herein provided." The "reclamation law" referred to was defined in § 12 as the Act of June 17, 1902 (Reclamation Act), 32 Stat. 388, and acts amendatory thereof and supplemental thereto. One of the statutes amendatory of or supplemental to the Reclamation Act was the Omnibus Adjustment Act of 1926 (1926 Act), § 46 of which, 44 Stat. 649, 43 U.S.C. § 423e, forbade delivery of reclamation project water to any irrigable land held in private ownership by one owner in excess of 160 acres, and required owners to execute recordable contracts for the sale of excess lands before such lands could receive project water.

III

We are unable, however, to agree with the Court of Appeals that Congress intended that the 160-acre limitation of the 1926 Act would apply to the lands under irrigation in Imperial Valley in 1929. Under § 14 of the Project Act, the construction, operation, and management of the project works were to be governed by the reclamation law, but only if not otherwise provided for in the Project Act. Section 46 of the 1926 Act is one of the reclamation laws; and its acreage limitation, which expressly applies to contracts for "constructing, operating, and maintaining" project works, would appear to govern the delivery of project water unless its applicability is foreclosed by some other provision of the Project Act. The Court of Appeals, erroneously we think, found no such preclusion in § 6 of the Act.

Concededly, nothing in § 14, in § 46, or in the reclamation law in general would excuse the Secretary from recognizing his obligation to satisfy present perfected rights in Imperial Valley that were provided for by Art. VIII of the Compact and § 6 of the Project Act and adjudicated by this Court in *Arizona v. California, supra*. The Court of Appeals nevertheless held that § 46 could be applied consistently with § 6 because the perfected rights in Imperial Valley were owned by and would be adjudicated to the District, not to individual landowners, who were merely members of a class for whose benefit the water rights had been acquired and held in trust. Individual farmers, the Court of Appeals said, had no right under the law to a particular proportion of the District's water. Applying § 46 and denying water to excess lands not sold would merely require reallocation of the water among those eligible to receive it and would not reduce the water to which the District was entitled to have delivered in accordance with its perfected rights.

We find this disposition of the § 6 defense to the application of the 1926 Act's acreage limitation to be unpersuasive. *Arizona v. California* recognized that "one of the most significant limitations" on the Secretary's power under the Project Act was the requirement that he satisfy present perfected rights, a matter of great significance to those who had reduced their water rights to beneficial use prior to 1929. Accordingly, in our initial decree, the perfected right protected by § 6 was defined with some care: a right that had been acquired in accordance with state law and that had been exercised by the actual diversion of a specific quantity of water and its application to a defined area of land. In our supplemental decree, entered prior to the opinion of the Court of Appeals denying rehearing and rehearing en banc, there was decreed to the District a presently perfected water right of 2.6 million acre feet of diversions from the mainstream or the quantity of water necessary to supply the consumptive use required to irrigate 424,145 acres and related uses, whichever was less, with a priority date of 1901. 439 U.S. at 529. We thus determined that as of 1929, the District had perfected its rights under state law to divert the specified amount of water and had actually diverted that water to irrigate the defined quantity and area of land. As we see it, the Court of Appeals failed to take adequate account of § 6 of the Project Act and its implementation in our opinion and decrees filed in the *Arizona v. California* litigation.

In the first place, it bears emphasizing that the § 6 perfected right is a water right originating under state law. In *Arizona v. California*, we held that the Project Act vested in the Secretary the power to contract for project water deliveries independent of the direction of § 8 of the Reclamation Act to proceed in accordance with state law and of the admonition of § 18 of the Project Act not to interfere with state law. 373 U.S., at 586–588. We nevertheless clearly recognized that § 6 of the Project Act, requiring satisfaction of presently perfected rights, was an unavoidable limitation on the Secretary's power and that in providing for these rights the Secretary must take account of state law. In this respect, state law was not displaced by the Project Act and must be consulted in determining the content and characteristics of the water right that was adjudicated to the District by our decree.

It may be true, as the Court of Appeals said, that no individual farm in the District has a permanent right to any specific proportion of the water held in trust by the District. But there is no doubt that prior to 1929 the District, in exercising its rights as trustee, delivered water to individual farmer beneficiaries without regard to the amount of land under single ownership. It has been doing so ever since. There is no suggestion, by the Court of Appeals or otherwise, that as a matter of state law and absent the interposition of some federal duty, the District did not have the right and privilege to exercise and use its water right in this manner. Nor has it been suggested that the District, absent some duty or disability imposed by federal law, could have rightfully denied water to individual farmers owning more than 160 acres. Indeed, as a matter of state law, not only did the District's water right entitle it to deliver water to the farms in the District regardless of size, but the right was equitably owned by the beneficiaries to whom the District was obligated to deliver water.

These were important characteristics of the District's water right as of the effective date of the Project Act, and the question is whether Congress intended to effect serious changes in the nature of the water right by doing away with the District's privilege and duty to service farms regardless of their size. We are quite sure that Congress did not so intend and that to hold otherwise is to misunderstand the Project Act and the substantive meaning of "present perfected rights" as defined by this Court's decree.

The Court of Appeals said it would not be a breach of trust by a water district to obey the dictates of § 46, relying on *Ivanhoe Irrig. Dist. v. All Parties and Persons*, 53 Cal. 2d 692, 712. 3 Cal. Rptr. 317, 329, 350 P. 2d 69, 81 (1960). But the issue here is whether § 46 applies to lands already being irrigated in 1929. In the *Ivanhoe* proceedings, the courts were not dealing with perfected rights to water that the project there involved would furnish, nor with a Project Act that specifically required present perfected rights to be satisfied. Here, we are dealing with perfected rights protected by the Project Act; and because its water rights are to be interpreted in the light of state law, the District should now be as free of land limitations with respect to the land it was irrigating in 1929 as it was prior to the passage of the Project Act. To apply § 46 would go far toward emasculating the substance, under state law, of the water right decreed to the District, as well as substantially limiting its duties to, and the rights of, the farmer-beneficiaries in the District.

It should be recalled that we defined a present perfected right as one that had not only been acquired pursuant to state law but as one that had been exercised by the diversion of water and its actual application to a specific area of land. We did not intend to decree a water right to the District under this definition, conditioned upon proof of actual diversion and use, but nevertheless to require the District to terminate service to the lands on the basis of which the right was decreed. The District has itself no power to require that excess lands be sold, and it is a contradiction in terms to say, as the Court of Appeals did, that the District has presently perfected rights but that § 46 requires it to terminate deliveries to all persons with excess lands who refuse to sell. We consequently hold that the perfected water right decreed to the District may be exercised by it without regard to the land limitation provisions of § 46 of the 1926 Act or to any similar provisions of the reclamation laws.

V

There remains a further consideration. The parties stipulated and the District Court found that at the outset of this litigation, the District was irrigating approximately 14,000 more acres than the 424,145 acres under irrigation in 1929. If, in light of our perfected rights holding, an Art. III case or controversy remains with respect to the applicability of acreage limitations to this additional 14,000 acres, there would remain to be disposed of those arguments of petitioners for reversing the Court of Appeals which we have not addressed and which, if sustained, would exempt from acreage limitations all privately owned lands in Imperial Valley, a result which the District Court seemingly embraced. The parties, however, have not separately addressed the status of this additional 14,000 acres; nor does the record invite us to deal further with this case without additional proceedings in the lower court. We do not know, for example, whether the District is still irrigating the additional 14,000 acres, whether any of the 14,000 acres consists of lands held in excess of 160 acres, or whether for some other reason of fact or law there is not now a controversy that requires further adjudication. Even if a live dispute remains, it would be helpful to have the Court of Appeals, or the District Court in the first instance if the Court of Appeals deems it advisable, adjudicate the status of the 14,000 acres, freed of any misapprehensions about the applicability of the 160-acre limitation to lands under irrigation in 1929.

Accordingly, the judgment of the Court of Appeals is reversed with respect to those lands that were irrigated on June 25, 1929 and with respect to which the District has been adjudicated to have a perfected water right as of that date. The judgment is otherwise vacated and the case is remanded to that Court for further proceedings consistent with this opinion.

The Recent Legislative Response. The *Imperial Valley* case effectively lifted the 160-acre limitation that was on those farmers in the valley whose lands had been under irrigation in 1929. But the general application of that limitation outside the Imperial Valley was untouched by the decision. Whether the 160-acre restriction should be more narrowly applied was to be a political issue of great magnitude.

Reportedly, a significant portion of the farmers in the seventeen contiguous Western states are in compliance with the 160-acre limitation set by the 1926 amendment to the federal Reclamation Act. But because this limit was not actively enforced, some farms using the water subsidies grew to immense size. Through 1976, some $5 billion in subsidies—providing water at a cheaper price than its delivery costs—were provided to irrigators by the reclamation program. These irrigators included railroads, oil companies, canning companies, and multinational corporations in addition to the more traditional "family farmers."

Pending legislation would substitute a 1280-acre limitation for the 160-acre limitation. The bill would also ban the leasing of additional acres and prohibit large corporate participation in the water subsidy program.[19]

8.4 BOUNDARIES—ACCRETIONS AND AVULSIONS

The landowner whose property is located next to a stream or lake is sometimes faced with questions concerning the property boundary—given the changing nature of many watercourses. The property owner's rights will vary depending on the navigability of the stream, the property description appearing in the deed to the land, and the type of physical changes that occur in the stream itself.

If a landowner owns property which is adjacent to a navigable stream or a navigable or meandered lake, in most states the landowner does not hold title to the bed of the stream or lake, but title is retained by the state.[20]

The exact boundary line will vary depending on state law. Many states follow common law and extend the property owner's line to the ordinary high-water mark, while others have made statutory modifications. In *Silver v. Dreger*, 183 Kan. 419, 327 P.2d 1031 (1958), the Kansas Supreme Court stated:

[Kansas statutes] 71–106 provides that the *bed and channel* of any river within this state and all islands and sand bars lying therein shall be considered to be the property of the state of Kansas unless this state or the United States has granted or conveyed an adverse interest therein. Since the early case of *Wood v. Fowler*, 26 Kan. 682, 40 Am.Rep. 330, it has been clear in Kansas that a riparian owner owns only to the bank and not to the center of a navigable stream.

Our cases appear to hold that the ordinary high-water mark is the boundary line

---

[19] S. 14, 96th Cong. 1st Sess. (1979). But in June 1980, the *House* Committee on Interior and Insular Affairs recommended H.R. 6520 which *inter alia* would allow the additional leasing of up to 2,400 more acres under certain conditions.

[20] Accordingly, legal title to islands in navigable waters is often held by the state. Missouri has some interesting legislation in this regard. Generally, Missouri has transferred title to land created by the recession of navigable waters or by the formation of an island in navigable waters to the county to be held for school purposes. MO. ANN. STAT. § 241.290 (Vernon 1952). But for all islands formed in the Missouri and Mississippi Rivers within the state after September 28, 1971, title is transferred to the conservation commission or state park board for wilderness or recreational purposes. MO. ANN. STAT. § 241.291 (Vernon Supp. 1980).

between the bed of the river and the land of the riparian owner.

In those situations where a landowner owns property on both sides of a nonnavigable stream, the streambed would be considered the exclusive property of the landowner.[21]

If a landowner owns land adjoining a nonnavigable stream on one side of the stream only, the usual rule is that ownership of the bed extends to the middle thread or course of the main current of the stream—sometimes called the *meander line*. This general rule could be varied if a land description was sufficiently precise to indicate that the bed of the stream was expressly reserved or excepted from the property conveyed in the deed.[22]

BOUNDARY ON NONNAVIGABLE STREAM

KNUTSON v. REICHEL
Court of Appeals of Washington, Division 2, 1973
10 Wash. App. 293, 518 P. 2d 233

This case involves a dispute over the ownership of certain lands lying between the bank and thread (center) of a non-navigable river. In summary, the facts are as follows:

Plaintiff Anna Knutson's mother died in 1944. Included in her estate was a large tract of land situated in Thurston County. This property was divided by the DesChutes river. As part of the settlement of the estate, a portion of the property was conveyed to the plaintiff by the remaining heirs (her brothers and sisters). This parcel was described as follows:

That part of the northeast quarter of the northwest quarter of Section 34, Township 16 North, Range 2 East, beginning at the southwest corner of said northeast quarter of the northwest quarter of said Section 34, running thence due North 20 rods, thence due east 48 rods, thence North to the county road, *thence following the south or west line of said county road to the Des-Chutes River; thence following along the North bank of the DesChutes River* to its intersection with the North and South line between the East half and the West half of the northwest quarter of said section; thence North along said line to the point of beginning, containing 18½ acres, more or less.

(Italics ours.)

---

[21] In a few states, nonnavigable streams are classified as either private or public, depending on whether the stream is floatable. In Missouri, for example, a stream may be nonnavigable but still subject to public access if it will float canoes, rowboats, and other small floating crafts. The bed of the stream, however, belongs to the individual property owners who adjoin such streams. *See* Elder v. Delcour, 269 S.W. 2d 17 (Mo. 1954).

[22] *See* Annot. Deeds: Description of Land Conveyed by Reference to River or Streams as Carrying to Thread or Center or Only to Bank Thereof—Modern Status, 78 A.L.R. 3d 604 (1977).

In connection with this distribution the plaintiff conveyed to the other heirs her interest in the balance of the property. In 1969, plaintiff filed an action to reform the deed and quiet title in her to the land lying between the north bank and the thread of the river, alleging that due to a mutual mistake the parties to the original deed inserted "thence...along the North bank of the DesChutes River" when they intended the thread of the river to constitute the boundary.

The trial court characterized the italicized portion of the deed as ambiguous and admitted testimony from two of the surviving heirs that the center of the stream had been intended as the boundary of the parcel. Based in part upon this testimony, the trial court reformed the portion of the deed in controversy to read:

thence following the south or west line of said county road to the DesChutes River; *then following along the thread of the DesChutes River* to its intersection with the North and South line.

[3,4]   Generally, a call in a deed to a non-navigable river means to the center (thread) of the stream. There exists, moreover, a presumption that when a private individual grants property belonging to him and bounds it generally upon a natural stream, he does not intend to reserve any land between the upland and the stream, and the grant will carry title to the grantee so far as the grantor owns unless the shoreland or bed of the stream be *expressly reserved* from the grant.

[5]   Furthermore, as to a deed which employs a call to a river, though the thread of the river is not specifically described as a boundary, it can be said in light of the above presumption that the shorelands and bed are appurtenant to the basic grant.

[6]   In our opinion, the cumulative effect of these principles is this: a deed which employs a river as one of the calls in its description will be construed against the grantor, and if he owns to the water he will be deemed not to have cut off the grantee from the water, absent an express reservation.

[7]   There is clearly no express reservation of the shorelands or bed of the river in the deed in this case. In applying this rule of construction we must accordingly conclude that the grant passes title to the thread of the stream.

While the trial court considered the problem as one of ambiguity warranting reformation of the deed, and we have viewed it as one of construction, the result is the same. Accordingly, the judgment and decree quieting title to the land between the north bank and thread of the DesChutes river is affirmed.

The boundary line along a stream may change with the continual changing of the stream itself. Along a navigable stream, the boundary line might shift as the high-water mark changes. Along a nonnavigable stream, the boundary would change as the middle thread or the main current shifts. The extent to which the boundary changes will vary depending on whether the change is by accretion or avulsion. *Accretion* is the slow, almost imperceptible addition caused by the washing action of the water. And land slowly added to the banks of the body of water by accretion ordinarily belongs to the adjoining landowner. *Avulsion* is the sudden and perceptible loss or addition of land by the actions of the water or a sudden change in the course of a stream. In such cases the boundary does not change but remains at the original place.[23]

ACCRETION AND AVULSION

VALDER v. WALLIS
Supreme Court of Nebraska, 1976
196 Neb. 222, 242 N.W. 2d 112

This is an action to quiet title to accretion lands formed by the Missouri River. At the time of the Iowa-Nebraska Boundary Compact of 1943 the land was in Nebraska. By virtue of a shift in the bed of the river, the land, although on the Nebraska side of the boundary line, is on the Iowa side of the river. The defendants own land in Iowa adjoining the property in dispute and claim ownership by adverse possession and accretion. The court decreed a division of the land in accordance with an existing river chute. Defendants appeal. We affirm the judgment of the District Court.

[1]   The following facts appear to be clearly established by the evidence. In the early 1940's the Missouri River abutted the land of defendants in the State of Iowa. In the ensuing years the river moved westward and crossed to the Nebraska side of the state line fixed by the Iowa-Nebraska Boundary Compact of 1943. See Appendix, Vol. 2A. R.R.S. 1943. In moving westward it left an island protected by dikes constructed by the United States Army Corps of Engineers on the original Nebraska bank. Accretion formed downstream from this original island and dike and a substantial chute was left on the Iowa side of the island. Additional accretion formed on the Iowa bank to the east of this chute. The land in dispute comprises a part of the large island which formed below the original dike and the small island. The chute carried a substantial volume of water sufficient for a 58-foot work boat to navigate it until dikes were constructed across it in the early months of 1961. Although defendants base their claim on adverse possession by reason of pasturing the

---

[23] Some states provide for state acquisition, by condemnation of the new bed of a navigable stream created by avulsion or flood. *See* KANS. STAT. ANN. § 82a-201 (Supp. 1979).

island prior to 1961 and so testified, the evidence clearly establishes that the island was unfenced and not pastured prior to that time. This action was commenced in July 1970. Defendants have not established their claim to the island by reason of adverse possession.

The land in dispute is in Burt County, Nebraska, although on the present Iowa side of the river. Plaintiff seeks also to claim the land lying between the chute and the original Iowa bank as accretion to the original small island formed by avulsion. It is therefore apparent that in addition to the defendants' claim of adverse possession, we have conflicting accretion claims as defendants also assert that the land is accretion to their Iowa property. The evidence clearly and without contradiction established that defendants did obtain title to the land east of the chute by adverse possession. Have they established title by accretion to the land west of the chute which formed as part of the island? This presents a question of law.

[2]   "'Avulsion' is a sudden and perceptible loss or addition to land by the action of water, or a sudden change in the bed or course of a stream." 78 Am. Jur. 2d, Waters, s. 406, p. 852.

[3,4]   In the present instance we have such a change. The river cut around the small island protected by the dikes above mentioned. This island remained a part of the property of the individual who owned it prior to the change in the riverbed. This is the general rule in cases of avulsion to which Nebraska subscribes. It was held, on rehearing, in *Kinkead v. Turgeon*, 74 Neb. 580, 109 N.W. 744:

Under the common law a riparian owner of lands on one side of a navigable river above the flow of the tide holds to the thread of the stream, subject to the public easement of navigation, and, if the river suddenly changes its channel and leaves its former bed, the boundary does not change, and he still holds to the same line. This is also the rule of the civil law....

[6]   Again, in *State v. Ecklund*, 147 Neb. 508, 23 N.W. 2d 782, it was held:

Where a river changes its main channel, not by slowly excavating and gradually passing over the intervening space to a new position, but changes it by flowing around intervening land, as by gradually, during many years, deepening a smaller channel which was on the other side of an island until it becomes the main channel, the boundary which was fixed as the original main channel remains, under such conditions, in that original channel.

The evidence here will not sustain a finding that plaintiff's predecessors in title still owned, after the change in the riverbed, to the thread of the original stream but clearly establishes retention of ownership of the original island. As to that portion of the land east of the island lying in the original streambed, defendants, as noted, have acquired title by adverse possession.

[7]   Accretion has formed on the Iowa bank and also on the island. These accretions were separated by the chute mentioned above. In such instances the law, pertaining to the rival claims, is well established in this state. We have held:

Title by prescription may be acquired to an island in a river or stream, which otherwise would belong to a riparian owner. Accretions to an island so held and occupied for more than the statutory period belong to the owner of the island, and not to the riparian owner to whom the island or a part of it would otherwise belong.

[8]   In *Durfee v. Keiffer*, 168 Neb. 272, 95 N.W. 2d 618, this court ruled:

Where the accretion commences with the shore of the island and afterward extends to the mainland, or any distance short thereof, all the accretion belongs to the owner of the island; but, where accretions to the island and to the mainland eventually meet, the owner of each owns the accretions to the line of contact.

See, also, *Burket v. Krimlofski*, 167 Neb. 45, 91 N.W. 2d 57; *Roll v. Martin*, 164 Neb. 133, 82 N.W. 2d 34.

[9]   Under Nebraska law, titles to riparian lands run to the thread of the contiguous stream.

[10]   In the present case the contiguous stream between the accretion lands on the Iowa bank and on the island is the chute which separates them. It is therefore apparent that the District Court was correct in designating the boundary line as the thread of the chute.

The judgment of the District Court is affirmed.

8.5 DIFFUSED SURFACE WATER AND DRAINAGE LAW: CIVIL LAW RULE, COMMON-LAW RULE, RULE OF REASONABLE USE

In general, *diffused surface waters* are waters which, in their natural state, occur on the surface of the earth in places other than natural watercourses, lakes, or ponds. Floodwaters that have escaped from streams are exceptions in some jurisdictions. Where such exceptions do not prevail, diffused surface waters may originate from any natural source. They may flow vagrantly over broad lateral areas or occasionally for brief periods in natural depressions, or they may stand in bogs or marshes. The essential characteristics of diffused surface waters are that they are short-lived and are spread over the ground and not yet concentrated in channel flows that constitute legal watercourses or not yet concentrated in natural bodies of water that conform to the definition of lakes or ponds.

The rights of landowners regarding diffused surface waters may be classified into two groups: (1) the right to avoid some waters, i.e., drainage, obstruction, and riddance of such waters, and (2) the right to use those waters that may be wanted. Regarding this latter right, the Eastern states generally recognize landowners' absolute right to capture and impound diffused surface water for their use while it is on their lands. In many of the Western states, this absolute right of a landowner to collect and use such waters is not as clear.

Issues concerning the right of a landowner to be rid of diffused surface waters have been before the courts on many occasions. The courts have followed various rules with respect to this aspect of diffused surface waters. The following classification portrays the sometimes complex judicial distinctions: (1) civil law or natural flow rule,[24] (2) common-enemy and/or common-law rules,[25] and (3) rule of reasonable use.

DRAINAGE RULES

BUTLER v. BRUNO
Supreme Court of Rhode Island, 1975
1475, 115 R.I. 264; 341 A. 2d 735

During the summer season, the litigants presently before us are next-door neighbors. The plaintiffs are husband and wife. They seek damages which result from the defendant's deflection of surface water from his property onto their premises. A nonjury trial was held before a justice of the Superior Court. At the conclusion of the presentation of all the testimony, the trial justice found for the defendant. The plaintiffs have appealed.

The trial justice found that before Bruno began building, the surface water had flowed from west to east and would gather on the Bruno lot. He

---

[24] See Peck v. Herrington, 109 Ill. 611 (1884) (right to improve drainage under civil rule); City of Peru v. City of LaSalle, 119 Ill. App. 2d 211, 255 N.E. 2d 502 (1970) (cities must follow the rule of Peck v. Herrington); Geis v. Rohrer, 12 Ill. 2d 133, 145 N.E. 2d 596 (1957) (lower owner's duty to take water). But see Templeton v. Huss, 57 Ill. 2d 134, 311 N.E. 2d 141 (1974) (Illinois Supreme Court seemed to drift toward the reasonable use rule. The court held that a new subdivision on the upper land may create an unreasonable rate of flow of water on the lower land. The court said: "A dominant, or higher, estate for drainage does not have an unlimited right to increase the rate or amount of surface-water runoff flowing onto a servient, or lower, estate, and, in determining whether the owner of the higher estate is liable for increasing the rate of such runoff, the question that must be confronted is whether the increased flow of surface waters, regardless of its cause, is beyond a range consistent with the policy of reasonableness of use."). See generally Annot., Modern Status of Rules Governing Interference with Drainage of Surface Water, 59 A.L.R. 2d 421 (1958).

[25] Missouri, Wisconsin, and Indiana have followed some form of the common-enemy rule. Kansas followed the common-enemy rule until 1911, when the legislature enacted the following provisions. "Owners of land may drain the same in the general course of natural drainage, by constructing open or covered drains, into any natural depression, draw, or ravine, on his own land, whereby the water will be carried by said depression, draw or ravine into some natural watercourse, or into any drain upon a public highway, for the purpose of securing proper drainage to such land; and he shall not be liable in damages therefor to any person or persons or corporation...." See Goering v. Shrag, 167 Kan. 499, 207 P. 2d 391 (1949).

also found that the additional 3 feet of fill and the construction of the retaining wall stopped the easterly flow of the surface water, causing it to flood the Butler property. The trial justice observed that if he were to rule that Bruno was liable to the Butlers, he would order the entry of a money judgment in their favor for $5,200. This sum was the figure used by a real estate expert in estimating the loss of value of the Butler property which was attributable to the flood.

At this juncture, the trial justice ruled that the Butlers' loss was *damzum absque injuria,* or in the vernacular, while the Butlers sustained damages, there could be no recovery because Bruno did not violate any recognized legal or equitable right. In making this observation, the trial justice commented on the paucity of precedent to guide him, and after examining the literature that has been written in this area of the law, accepted as the law of this state the so-called "common-enemy" doctrine as modified by the rule of "reasonable use." He thereupon held that although the Butlers had sustained damage, there would be no recovery since Bruno had used "reasonable care" in developing his property and he had not "unnecessarily injured" the Butlers.

We cannot fault the trial justice's attempt to decide what is or should be the surface water law of this jurisdiction. It is true that at the turn of the century this court, in deciding an issue different from the one now before us, assumed that the common-enemy doctrine was the law of Rhode Island. We will, however, opt for another rule which shall be discussed after we first define the term surface water and discuss the various views which have been expressed by courts which have considered the rights of neighboring landowners and the damages resulting from the diverting of surface water.

[1]   As used in this opinion, the term surface water means the water from rains, springs, or melting snows which lies or flows on the surface of the earth but does not form part of a well-defined body of water or a natural watercourse. It does not lose its character as surface water merely because some of it may be absorbed by or soaked into the marshy or boggy ground where it collects. *Enderson v. Kelehan,* 226, Minn. 163, 32 N.W. 2d 286 (1948).

There are three basic rules which have been used to resolve the surface water disputes that have arisen in the United States.

[2]   The first is the common-enemy doctrine. The common-enemy doctrine is so named because at one time surface water was regarded as a common enemy with which each landowner had an unlimited legal privilege to deal as he pleased without regard to the consequences that might be suffered by his neighbor. This rule received judicial approbation in a time when the law held in high regard one's freedom to do with his land as he wished. One of the earliest cases to espouse this view was *Gannon v. Hargadon,* 92 Mass. (10 Allen) 106 (1865). New Jersey was the first jurisdiction to describe the rule by employing the phrase "common enemy." *Town of Union v. Durkes,* 38 N.J.L. 21 (1875). Several courts in adopting this rule have said that it encourages the development and improvement of real estate and

clearly delineates the rights of all interested parties. Concededly, litigation is kept to a minimum because in its application no one's rights are invaded. However, the simplicity of the rule does create problems, for, as one commentator has expressed it: "landowners are encouraged to engage in contests of hydraulic engineering in which might makes right, and breach of the peace is often inevitable." Maloney & Plager, *Diffused Surface Water: Scourge or Bounty*, 8 Nat. Resources J. 73, 78 (1968).

The Butlers might have invoked the common-enemy rule. The engineer testified that they could have alleviated their drainage problems by raising the level of their land with fill. Such a step, the witness said, would cause the surface water to gather and accumulate on the land of the Butlers' westerly neighbor. Presumably, if the Butlers were to pursue this remedy, they, rather than Bruno, would be the defendants as the domino theory of litigation enveloped the Maple Avenue residents. One obvious drawback to the common-enemy approach is the risk that its adoption can encourage a proliferation of litigation and engender neighborhood ill will.

The second principle upon which some courts have relied in resolving surface water disputes is called the "civil-law" rule.

[3]   The civil-law rule was first adopted in this country by Louisiana in 1812. *Orleans Navigation Co. v. New Orleans*, 2 Martin (O.S.) 214 (1812). It is said to have its roots in Roman Law and the Napoleonic Code. Annot., 59 A.L.R. 2d 421, 429 § 5 (1958). The rule is usually expressed in terms of an easement of natural drainage so that the owner of the lower land must accept the surface water which naturally drains onto his land but the upper owner may do nothing to increase the flow. Expressed in a more precise manner, the rule is that "A person who interferes with the natural flow of surface water so as to cause an invasion of another's interests in the use and enjoyment of his land is subject to liability to the others." Kinyon & McClure, *Interferences with Surface Waters*, 24 Minn. L. Rev. 891 (1940). The civil-law rule has the virtue of predictability in that it tells a prospective purchaser or acquirer of a parcel of real estate just what is expected of him. If it is applied to the letter, the rule can impede the physical and economic development of a locality. Its application can cause an evidentiary problem as the courts seek to determine what was the exact course of the "natural flow" of the surface water before the bulldozers arrived on the scene.

Both the common-enemy and the civil-law rules are encrusted with the verbiage that is usually associated with the law of real property. When they are used, one hears such terms as easements, the dominant estate, the servitudes, and the classicist has the opportunity to try his hand at translating such ponderous Latin phrases as *cujus est solum, ejus est usque ad coelum et ad infernos*[26] or *aqua currit, et debet currere ut currere solebat.*[27]

---

[26] "To whomever the soil belongs, he owns also to the sky and to the depths."

[27] "Water runs, and ought to run as it is accustomed to run."

Because of the harsh and often inequitable consequences of a strict application of either rule, courts through the years have created numerous exceptions, distinctions, and permutations to alleviate otherwise unjust results. Sometimes these modifications have caused the two antithetical doctrines to produce the same results. Thus, although the basic common-enemy rule allows each owner a *carte blanche* to deal with unwanted surface water, courts have held that the owner may not discharge the unwanted water upon neighboring land by collecting it into a concentrated flow by artificial means and then discharging it, if by so doing he causes his neighbor injury. *E.g., Johnson v. White, supra.* And although the basic civil rule held that no one may change the natural drainage flow, some courts have recognized that the upper owner may change the natural flow by collecting the water at one point thereby not increasing the amount of overall flow but causing greater volume at one point rather than another, so long as the increased flow is in a natural water course and injury is not too great to the lower land. *Stouder v. Dashner*, 242 Iowa 1340, 49 N.W. 2d 859 (1951), and cases cited in Kinyon & McClure, *supra*, at 921 et seq.

This convergence of the two theories has been aptly described as creating a situation in which

the civil-law owner may *never* drain his land *except* by following the natural drainage, but the common-enemy owner may *always* drain his land except that he may not use artificial channels. The civil-law owner may *never* obstruct the natural flow of surface waters *unless* he acts reasonably, while the common-enemy owner may always obstruct the flow *if* he acts reasonably. Maloney & Plager, *supra*, at 79.

A common modification of both rules holds that the landowner may change the flow of surface waters by either increasing or damming up the flow so long as he does so "in good faith" or "non-negligently" or "in a reasonable manner."[28] This is the modification to which the trial justice alluded and which he tacked onto the common-enemy rule.

The effect of these modifications is to bring disputes over surface water interference into the realm of modern tort concepts, and to depart from the rigid formulations, of property law. Thus, civil-law jurisdictions are now more chary about awarding either equitable or monetary relief for a mere technical trespass upon plaintiff property owners' rights, requiring instead a finding of "unreasonably injury." *See, e.g., Schmitt v. Kirkpatrick*, 245 Iowa 971, 63 N.W. 2d 228 (1954): *Cowan v. Baker*, 227 Miss. 828, 87 So. 2d 74 (1956). Common-enemy jurisdictions now recognize that the absolute right

---

[28] *See, e.g.,* Chamberlain v. Ciaffoni, 373 Pa. 430, 96 A. 2d 140 (1953); Seventeen, Inc. v. Pilot Life Ins. Co., 215 Va. 74, 205 S.E. 2d 648 (1974), applying the modification to the common-enemy rule; and Ratcliffe v. Indian Hill Acres, Inc., 93 Ohio App. 231, 113 N.E. 2d 30 (Ct. App. 1952), applying the modification to the civil law rule.

to fend off surface waters can be limited by the requirement that it not cause another "unnecessary harm." *See, e.g., Stacy v. Walker*, 222 Ark. 819, 262 S.W. 2d 889 (1953).

It is interesting to note that the court in *Johnson v. White, supra*, while alluding to the owner's right to fend off the surface water on his land as he pleased, in almost the same breath qualified the common-enemy rule by remarking that the owner was not privileged to discharge by artificial means upon the adjoining property large quantities of surface water. This exception is said to be a judicial recognition of another Latin maxim, *sic utere tuo ut alienum non laedas*.[29] *Norfolk & Western R.R. v. Carter*, 91 Va. 587, 22 S.E. 517 (1895).

Other courts, perhaps in recognition of the problems that have arisen by the application of the above two rules with all their modifications, have chosen a third doctrine. Instead of using the tort concepts as an overlay to mitigate the harsh results of the property law doctrine, they have instead created the standards for behavior entirely out of tort law, and abandoned the notions of servitude or absolute ownership.

[4]   Thus we come to the third surface water doctrine, which is generally known as the "rule of reasonable use." Under this rule, the property owner's liability turns on a determination of the reasonableness of his actions. The issue of reasonableness is a question of fact to be determined in each case upon the consideration of all the relevant circumstances. This approach was first employed in *Swett v. Cutts*, 50 N.H. 439, 446 (1870).

The doctrine of reasonable use is not the same as the reasonable-use modification to the common-enemy rule referred to and adopted by the trial court below.[30] Although there has been some confusion due to the striking similarity in the names of the two standards, and both have strong roots in tort law, they do differ.

[5]   It will be remembered that the reasonableness modification rests on determinations of "negligence," "malice," and "good faith." Absent negligence, or an intentional injury, the common-enemy or the civil-law rule would be applied. The New Hampshire rule of reasonable use does not rest on negligence, nor does it focus solely on the character of the property owner's action. Instead, it focuses on the results of the action, the consequent interference with another's use and enjoyment of his land—much like the nuisance branch of tort law.[31]

---

[29] "So use your property as not to injure the rights of another."

[30] The trial justice at the time he spoke of the "reasonable use modification" was discussing an annotation entitled Liability as regards surface waters, for raising surface level of land. Annot., 12 A.L.R. 2d 1338 § 3 (1950). This section describes cases which carve out exceptions to the common-enemy rule. They in no way relate to the cases which embrace the rule of reasonable use.

[31] This court has given recognition to the fact that the invasion of one's property by surface waters can be a nuisance, no different from an invasion by noise, noxious vapors, or the like. Sweet v. Conley, 20 R.I. 381, 385, 39 A. 326, 328 (1898). "[t]o wrongfully and illegally cause the surface water of a street to collect and remain in front of one's premises, so as to materially injure and damage him in the use and enjoyment thereof, is a nuisance...."

The New Jersey Supreme Court in adopting the rule of reasonable use expressed it in this manner:

"each possessor is legally privileged to make a reasonable use of his land, even though the flow of surface waters is altered thereby and causes some harm to others, but incurs liability when his harmful interference with the flow of surface waters is unreasonable." *Armstrong v. Francis Corp.*, 20 N.J. 320, 327, 120 A. 2d 4, 8 (1956).

The jurisdictions which have adopted this principle have set forth varying formulations of the test for determining liability. We find the clearest and most appropriate to be that adopted by Minnesota and expressed in *Enderson v. Kelehan, supra,* where the court considered the following factors:

(a)   Is there a reasonable necessity for such drainage?
(b)   Has reasonable care been taken to avoid unnecessary injury to the land receiving the water?
(c)   Does the benefit accruing to the land drained reasonably outweigh the resulting harm?
(d)   When practicable, is the diversion accomplished by reasonably improving the normal and natural system of drainage, or if such a procedure is not practicable, has a reasonable and feasible artificial drainage system been installed?

[6,7]   At one time only two jurisdictions, New Hampshire and Minnesota, had adopted the reasonable-use rule. Since that time, however, at least nine other jurisdictions[32] have embraced this view. In determining one's legal responsibility for the use of the surface water flowing across his land, we shall adopt the rule of reasonable use. One known advantage of the rule is its flexibility. It can be applied in situations unthought of in the day when surface water was truly considered to be the common enemy. Unlike the civil-law rule, it will not hamper land development, and in contrast to the common-enemy rule, the standard which we embrace today will permit a more equitable allocation of the costs of such improvements, for the owner improving his land must take into consideration the true cost of such development to the community.

In embracing the principle of reasonable use, we are aware of those whose support of either of the two property-based rules is based on their conviction

---

[32] Weinberg v. Northern Alaska Dev. Corp., 384 P. 2d 450 (Alaska 1963); Keys v. Romley. 64 Cal. 2d 396, 412 P. 2d 529, 50 Cal. Rptr. 273 (1966); Rodriguez v. State, 52 Hawaii 156, 472 P. 2d 509 (1970); Klutey v, Commonwealth of Ky., Dep't of H'ways, 428 S.W. 2d 766 (Ky. 1968); Armstrong v. Francis Corp., 20 N.J. 320, 120 A. 2d 4 (1956); Jones v. Boeing Co., 153 N.W. 2d 807 (N.D. 1967); Houston v. Renault, Inc. 431 S.W. 2d 322 (Tex. 1968); Sanford v. University of Utah, 26 Utah 285, 488 P. 2d 741 (1971); State v. Deetz, 66 Wis. 2d 1, 224 N.W. 2d 407 (1974).

that adherence to either rule gives to a concerned landowner the advantage of predictability. However, such a belief overlooks the fact that today as we enter the last quarter of the 20th century, no jurisdiction follows the strict requirements of either the common-enemy or the civil-law rule. With the numerous judicial exceptions and modifications that have been appended through the years to the two original concepts, we fail to see how the modern versions of either afford more predictability than the rule of reasonable use. However, even if we were to assume that each did possess a higher predictability factor, a desire for certainty of liability should not and must not serve as a judicial pardon for the unreasonable conduct which has been manifested by any landowner in our modern society. *Keys v. Romley*, 64 Cal. 2d 396, 412 P. 2d 529, 50 Cal. Rptr. 273 (1966).

Since the trial justice rested his decision on a theory that is completely at odds with the ultimate holding of this appeal, we must reverse and remand for further proceedings so that a new judgment which conforms to this opinion may be entered.

The plaintiffs' appeal is sustained, the judgment appealed from is vacated, and the case is remanded to the Superior Court.

JOSLIN, Justice (dissenting).

The majority today hold that a landowner's liability for the diversion of surface water from his land to that of another hinges in each case upon a factual determination of whether in view of all the circumstances his conduct in the use and improvement of his property is reasonable or unreasonable, and they enunciate four guidelines to aid the factfinder in making that determination. Because I believe that the proposed factual test is no "rule" at all and that it fails to provide a landowner any reasonably certain standards governing the use of his land, I respectfully dissent.

It may well be that unless specific exceptions are made both the common-enemy doctrine as presently prevailing in this state and the civil-law rule lack the flexibility to lead to the fairest result in a particular case, and that the concept of "reasonable use" reflects better than either of those rules contemporary sentiment toward the use and development of real property in light of the interests of neighboring owners. But in my opinion neither the majority nor the decisions they cite have defined that concept as a principled standard of law, with sufficient certainty to enable counsel to advise a landowner-client how he may use his property without incurring liability for surface water diversion. The requirement that a landowner thus either proceed at his peril or resort to the courts is an excessive burden. For that reason, until adequate reasonable-use standards are formulated this court should adhere to its present rule, which sets forth its requirements with precision, clarity, and certainty, and which can from time to time, if the occasion demands, be fully reviewed and further refined.

The reasonable use rule was also applied in the agricultural drainage case of *Pell v. Nelson*, 294 Minn. 363, 201 N.W.2d 136 (1972), which concerned the mechanical discharge of drainage water onto the adjacent farmer's land. The Pells undertook an extensive drainage project, utilizing almost 40,000 feet of tile which connected to a 3500-gallon sump. The sump was drained by an automatic electric pump which could discharge 1200 gallons per minute through a 12-inch outlet, located within 70 feet of Nelson's property. The court found that after the system was installed, water from the Pell land inundated 38 acres of Nelson's pastureland and an area of cropland devoted to corn and beans. The gathering and disposing of surface water under these circumstances was deemed to be an unreasonable use of Pell's land that would be enjoined under the reasonable use rule.

8.6 OTHER WATER-RELATED LAWS

Special Districts

Many states have enacted legislation providing for the creation of special districts with functional powers relating to water. Levee and drainage districts and soil and water conservation districts are examples of such districts.

Legislation enabling drainage districts typically provides that on petition by a majority of the landowners in an area a drainage district may be created. Such districts generally have the power to acquire easements, often by condemnation, and to construct and maintain drainage systems. The costs of constructing, operating, and maintaining such drainage works are usually collected by assessments, whereby landowners contribute to the costs in proportion to their share of the total benefits conferred by the programs. Even landowners who do not want to contribute can be forced to pay their proportional share of costs.

Illinois has placed the following powers and duties in the hands of drainage district commissioners:

1. to go upon the land, employ necessary assistance, and adopt a plan or system of drainage

2. to obtain the necessary lands and right-of-way by agreement or, if necessary, by eminent domain proceedings

3. in the corporate name of the district, to enter into contracts, sue and be sued, plead and be impleaded, and do "all such acts and things as may be necessary for the accomplishment of the purposes of this act"

4. to compromise suits and controversies and employ necessary agents and attorneys

5. to carry out specific provisions of the law relative to making various types of assessments, employing a treasurer or other assistance, annexing lands, borrowing funds, enforcing payment of assessments, and consolidating and dissolving districts

6. to let contracts for the surveying, laying, constructing, repairing, altering, enlarging, cleaning, protecting, and maintaining of any drain, ditch, levee, or other work; to let contracts by bid if the work to be done is the construction of the principal work and the cost is more than $1000

7. to borrow money, without court authority, in the amount of up to 90 percent of assessments unpaid at the time for the payment of any authorized debts or construction

8. to widen, straighten, deepen, or enlarge any ditch or watercourse, and to

remove driftwood and rubbish whether the ditch is in, outside of, or below the district

9. to cause railroad companies to construct, rebuild, or enlarge bridges or culverts when necessary

10. to make annual or more frequent reports as required by the court, including an annual financial report

11. to conduct meetings in the county or counties in which the district is located

12. to use public highways for the purposes of work to be done

13. to keep the works of the district in operation and repair

14. to sell or lease any land owned by the district

15. to own and operate necessary machinery and equipment

16. to construct access roads and level spoil banks

17. to abandon works no longer useful to the district

18. to contract with other public agencies, including the federal government

Weather Modification

Attempts at controlling the weather have a long and colorful history. Certainly, the control of weather could have a tremendous impact upon agriculture. Some degree of control can be effected through current technology which involves cloud seeding with silver iodide or other chemicals to augment precipitation.

Cloud seeding has been attempted in numerous projects in recent years. For example, the Colorado River Basin Project involved attempts to increase snowfall in the mountains. Other projects involved seeding summer cumulus clouds in Kansas, South Dakota, and California; additional rainmaking projects in Minnesota, Iowa, Michigan, Wisconsin, and Illinois during the late 1970s; and attempts to suppress destructive hailstorms in the Soviet Union.

The success of weather modification efforts are difficult to determine. The snowpacks in Colorado were reportedly increased by 30 to 35 percent. Precipitation in Kansas, South Dakota, and California was thought by some to have been increased by 10 to 20 percent. The Soviets claim a 90 percent reduction in hail damage, but the effects of the Midwest projects remain uncertain.[33]

A number of issues and problems are raised by weather modification activities. These issues and problems include ensuring competency of weather modifiers, determining liability for damages, avoiding international disputes, and encouraging the development of new, improved technology. Additional problems include reconciling differences between private persons or groups who want weather modification and those who don't. For example, corn growers want rain when hay growers may want dry weather; farmers generally may want rain when the construction industry or resort owners want sunshine. A final issue involves regulation: should regulation exist, and if so, at what level of government?

The regulation of weather modification activities has not been extensive in recent years. Litigation has produced mixed re-

---

[33] The Soviet Union reportedly seeds potential hailstorm clouds with artillery and rockets to protect 6 million acres of farmland. The Soviets claim benefits-to-cost ratios as high as 17 to 1 from their hail suppression program. *We're Doing Something about the Weather*, 141 NAT'L. GEOGRAPHIC 519, at 553-4 (April 1972). Assuming the Soviet claims to be valid, the potential value of such a hail suppression program in the United States is suggested by the fact that hail now destroys approximately $700 million worth of crops yearly in this country, and damages buildings and machinery as well. *Whatever Happened to Efforts to Control Weather*, U. S. NEWS 80:61 (Jan. 5, 1976).

sults.[34] In some instances such activity has been enjoined or has resulted in awards for damages, while in other instances recovery has been denied. Congress, through legislation enacted in 1971 and 1976, has required that weather modification activities be reported to the Department of Commerce, and that the Department study the subject and recommend appropriate federal involvement.[35] Some states have enacted regulatory statutes. The Illinois Weather Modification Act, for example, requires the licensing of persons involved in such activities and the issuance of a permit before weather modification activities can be attempted.[36]

STUDY QUESTIONS

1. What is percolating groundwater? Explain the various rules that govern the use of such water. Which of these rules is the best?

2. What are the two theories that have evolved regarding the right to use stream water under the riparian doctrine? How do they differ, and which one predominates today?

3. What distinction is made in the riparian doctrine between "natural" and "ordinary" uses of water?

4. What are the rights of the public in navigable streams and meandered or navigable lakes?

5. How does the prior appropriation doctrine differ from the riparian doctrine? What state administrative procedures are likely to be present in states following the prior appropriation doctrine?

6. How are multistate sources of water allocated?

7. What is the status of acreage and residency limitations in federal reclamation law?

---

[34] Weather modifiers have been the targets of lawsuits initiated by individuals seeking redress for alleged negligent or wrongful conduct. To date, plaintiffs seeking damages due to flooding allegedly caused by cloud seeding have failed to establish the requisite causal relationship necessary to permit recovery. *See, e.g.,* Samples v. I.P. Krick, Inc., Civ. Nos. 6212, 6223, 6224 (W.D. Okla. 1954); Auvil Orchard Co. v. Weather Modification, Inc., Civ. No. 19268 (Super. Ct. Chelan County, Wash., 1956); Adams v. California. No. 10112 (Super. Ct. Sutter County, Cal. 1964). Landowners have been more successful in obtaining injunctions where they have sought to stop cloud seeding designed to suppress hail, claiming that the seeding deprived them of needed moisture. Cloud seedings to suppress hail were enjoined in the Texas case of Southwest Weather Research, Inc. v. Jones, 160 Tex. 104, 327 S.W. 2d 417 (1959), but were allowed to continue in the Pennsylvania case of Pennsylvania Natural Weather Association v. Blue Ridge Weather Modification Association, 44 Pa. D. & C. 2d 749 (C.P. Fulton County, Pa., 1968). It appears that some type of balancing approach will be used in the future, as exemplified by Slutsky v. City of New York, 97 N.Y.S. 2d 238 (Super. Ct., 1950).

In that case, resort owners sought to enjoin cloud seeding which New York City was conducting to break a drought, attempting to replenish the city's water supply. The court held for New York City, reasoning that the needs of the two conflicting parties must be balanced against one another letting the greater public need prevail. The balancing of private rights against private rights will require judicial resolution in the future.

[35] Pub. L. No. 92-205, 85 Stat. 735, enacted in 1971 requires all weather modification activities or attempts to be reported. It also provides for a penalty upon failure to comply. The National Weather Modification Policy Act of 1976, Pub. L. No. 94-490, 90 Stat. 2359-2361, provides for a study of the state of scientific knowledge concerning weather modification, the present state of weather modification technology, and other related matters in order to develop a comprehensive and coordinated national weather modification policy and a national program of weather modification research and development.

[36] Weather Modification Control Act of 1973, Pub. Act. No. 78-674 [codified at ILL. REV. STAT. ch. 111, §§ 7301-7344 (1979)].

8. What is an accretion? An avulsion? How do they affect boundaries?

9. Regarding drainage, compare and contrast the civil law (natural flow) rule, the common-law (common-enemy) rule, and the rule of reasonable use.

10. What role do special districts play in the management of water resources?

11. What issues and problems are raised by weather modification activities? How are these activities regulated?

12. Suppose that you are a farmer planning to invest in irrigation equipment. Indicate how secure you would feel in making such an investment if the source of your water were: (1) percolating groundwater; (2) a nonnavigable stream; (3) a navigable stream; (4) surface water you have impounded by damming a course of natural drainage on your property.

9

Protecting the Environment and the Productivity of Agricultural Land

Pollution is by no means a new problem in agriculture. For hundreds of years, farmers have been constructing barns and feedlots downwind from their houses and taking protective steps in areas of soil erosion and sedimentation. Nevertheless, increases in population with its resulting needs and the intensification of farming techniques have increased our concern with pollution. The effects of pollution are more than mere temporary discomfort, for they can result in serious adverse consequences to all forms of life. A greater awareness and concern with the environment has initiated action from all levels of government in an attempt to improve and preserve the quality of our land and of our environment as a whole.

While a large amount of pollution comes from obvious sources such as industry, automobiles, etc., very few activities are pollution-free. Agriculture is no exception. Some of the causes of pollution from agricultural activities are erosion, irrigation return flows, misused commercial fertilizers and pesticides, and livestock enterprises which generate animal wastes and odors. Legislation from state and federal governments is concerned with these causes, and this will be discussed under the separate headings of Water Pollution, Air Pollution, and Noise Pollution.

Farmers and ranchers should not view environmental regulations solely as restrictions that interfere with their agricultural activities, for environmental regulations can protect agriculture. For example, more rigorous soil and water conservation can help retain the productivity of agricultural property for generations to come, as well as help to reduce water pollution. Also, to the extent that farmers and ranchers are more aware of potential pollution problems associated with mining coal, drilling for oil, extracting other mineral resources, and transporting mineral resources and energy through utility rights-of-way, these agricultural producers will be in a better position to negotiate mineral leases or deeds or utility rights-of-way that better protect agricultural activities on the surface.

9.1 WATER POLLUTION

Water pollution is of greater concern to agriculture than any other pollution category. In discussing the regulatory mechanism for controlling water pollution, it will be helpful first to differentiate between point sources of water pollution and nonpoint sources of water pollution. *Point sources* of water pollution can be generally described as those for which an "end of pipe" technology can be used to control pollution from that source. For example, the discharge of untreated human waste into a lake or a stream is a point source of pollution. Such a pollution source can be controlled by building an adequate waste treatment facility to process the sewage before it is discharged into the lake or stream.

Similarly, a large livestock feeding operation which releases animal wastes into a stream or lake could be categorized as a point source of pollution. *Nonpoint sources* of pollution, on the other hand, can be generally described as causes of pollution when pollution is generated by diffused land use activities and conveyed to waterways through natural processes such as storm runoff or groundwater seepage. Nonpoint sources of pollution are not susceptible to end of pipe treatment, but generally can be controlled only by changes in land management practices.

Point Sources of Pollution

The Federal Water Pollution Control Act (FWPCA) Amendments of 1972 provided a total revamping of federal law in the area of water pollution control.[1] The FWPCA identified certain national goals of water quality, and established a joint federal and state system of attaining these goals. The most important goal is the total elimination of point source discharges of pollutants by 1985. An interim goal—the elimination of such discharges to the extent necessary to protect fish, shellfish, wildlife, and recreation in and on navigable waters—is to be attained by July 1, 1983. The FWPCA also expressed the policy that the federal government will delegate to the states the primary responsibility for dealing with water pollution.

To meet these goals, the FWPCA established water quality standards which set the maximum amounts of certain contaminants or pollutants, such as phosphorus and ammonia nitrogen, that are to be found in the water. These standards ensure that water can be used for certain purposes, e.g., human

---

[1] Federal Water Pollution Control Act amendments of 1972, Pub. L. No. 92-500, 86 Stat. 816 (amending 33 U.S.C. ch. 26, 1948).

consumption, recreation, etc. To attain these water quality standards, the FWPCA also imposes limitations (*effluent limitations*) on the amount and type of pollutants which may be discharged into receiving waters.

The mechanism for enforcing the water quality standards and effluent limitations of the FWPCA is the National Pollutant Discharge Elimination System (NPDES). Unless exempted, all persons discharging pollutants are required to obtain an NPDES permit, which is given only if it is shown that the discharge of pollutants will be within the adopted limitations. The administration of the NPDES system was originally assigned to the regional offices of the U.S. Environmental Protection Agency. However, this responsibility has now been delegated to most individual states.

Many agricultural activities are not presently affected by the provisions of the FWPCA, because these provisions directly regulate only point sources, e.g., pipes, ditches, wells, etc. Nevertheless, there is one area of agricultural activity specifically designated by the FWPCA as a point source of discharge—concentrated animal feeding operations. Some of the types of pollutants generally traceable to feedlots and related activities are:

1. Biochemical oxygen demand (BOD): a measure of oxygen required to decompose plant and animal wastes in water. A sufficient amount of dissolved oxygen in water is necessary to sustain aquatic animal life. A high amount of BOD will result in a depletion of the dissolved oxygen in water and a corresponding loss of aquatic animal life.

2. Bacterial contamination: bacteria which may include water-borne diseases are usually associated with fecal matter.

3. Ammonia nitrogen.

4. Phosphorus.

5. Odors.

Although not every livestock operation is subject to the NPDES requirements, the U.S. Environmental Protection Agency has established certain criteria in determining whether a facility is required to obtain a permit. These criteria and the exceptions thereto are set forth in Table 9.1.[2]

State Regulation of Water Pollution. To help achieve a safe, comfortable, and healthy environment and to carry out responsibilities delegated to the individual states by the FWPCA, many states have enacted environmental protection acts. For example, the Illinois Act[3] and subsequent amendments established three agencies to carry

[2] See *Natural Resources Defense Council, Inc. v. Costle*, 568 F. 2d 1369 (D.C. Cir. 1977), for some insights regarding controversies surrounding the definition of "concentrated animal feedlot." Irrigation return flows were also deemed to be point sources of pollution under this decision, but Section 33 of the Clean Water Act of 1977 provided that irrigation return flows were not to be considered point sources and should be dealt with in the 208 planning process discussed *infra*. 33 U.S.C.A. §§ 1288 (b) (2) (F), 1342, 1362 (14).

[3] P.A. 76-2429, ILL. REV. STAT. ch. 111 1/2, §§ 1001 *et seq.* (1979). Action under the Illinois Environmental Protection Act can be initiated by a private citizen. In *Buckles v. Pope & Osborn*, P.C.B. 73-210 (1973), Buckles filed a formal complaint with the Pollution Control Board alleging that Pope was discharging animal waste which drained across complainant's (Buckles's) land into Clear Creek. However, after hearing the evidence in this case, the board concluded that complainant had not proved the allegations. The complaint was dismissed.

If the Pollution Control Board decides not to hold a hearing or denies relief to a complaining party, the act provides that the party can file suit in a court of law against the violator, requesting that the violation stop. Such a suit is for injunctive relief. The suit cannot, however, be brought until 30 days after the board has denied relief. If a suit is filed, the party prevailing is awarded costs and reasonable attorneys' fees.

TABLE 9.1 Livestock Facilities Where NPDES Permits Are Required

A livestock feedlot or facility (1) where animals are confined and fed or maintained for a total of 45 days or more in any 12-month period and (2) where crops, vegetation, forage growth, or postharvest residues are not present in the lot or facility during the normal growing season is required (exceptions are noted below) to obtain a permit if any one of the following three criteria is present:

Criterion A: The facility confines more than:

1. 1000 slaughter and feeder cattle, or
2. 700 mature dairy cows (whether milked or dry cows), or
3. 2500 swine weighing over 55 pounds, or
4. 500 horses, or
5. 10,000 sheep or lambs, or
6. 55,000 turkeys, or
7. 100,000 laying hens or broilers (if the facility has continuous overflow watering), or
8. 30,000 laying hens or broilers (if the facility has a liquid manure harvesting system), or
9. 5000 ducks, or
10. 1000 animal units*

Criterion B: (This criterion is only applicable (1) where pollutants are discharged into navigable waters† through an artificial ditch, flushing system, or other similar artificial device; or (2) pollutants are discharged directly into navigable waters† which originate outside of and pass over, across, through, or otherwise come into direct contact with the animals confined in the operation.) When applicable, Criterion B requires a permit if the facility confines more than:

1. 300 slaughter or feeder cattle, or
2. 200 mature dairy cows (whether milked or dry cows), or
3. 750 swine weighing over 55 pounds, or
4. 150 horses, or
5. 3000 sheep, or
6. 16,500 turkeys, or
7. 30,000 laying hens or broilers (if the facility has continuous overflow watering), or
8. 9000 laying hens or broilers (if the facility has a liquid manure handling system), or
9. 1500 ducks, or
10. 300 animal units*

Criterion C: The operator of the livestock lot or facility is notified in writing by appropriate authorities that an NPDES permit is required. Such notification can only occur after an on-site inspection of the operation and a determination that the operation should be regulated under the permit program.

---

*The term "animal unit" is calculated by adding the following numbers: the number of slaughter and feeder cattle multiplied by 1, plus the number of mature dairy cattle multiplied by 1.4, plus the number of swine weighing over 55 pounds multiplied by 0.4, plus the number of sheep multiplied by 0.1, plus the number of horses multiplied by 2.

†The term "navigable waters" is given a very broad definition and includes: (1) all navigable waters of the United States; (2) tributaries of navigable waters of the United States; (3) interstate waters; (4) lakes, rivers, and streams which are utilized by interstate travelers for recreational or other purposes; (5) lakes, rivers, and streams from which fish or shellfish are taken and sold in interstate commerce; and (6) lakes, rivers, and streams which are utilized for industrial purposes by industries in interstate commerce.

TABLE 9.1   Livestock Facilities Where NPDES Permits Are Required (continued)

Exceptions:

1. The owners or operators of livestock feedlots or facilities are not required to apply for and obtain permits if there is no discharge of pollutants into navigable waters.† Thus, totally enclosed systems, such as many poultry operations, which do not discharge into navigable waters are not subject to the permit requirements regardless of their size. Also, no permits are required from owners or operators who recycle all pollutants to the land, absorb all animal wastes in filter strips, or otherwise prevent such wastes from reaching navigable waters. Thus, any feedlot operator who uses alternative management techniques and prevents all discharge from reaching navigable waters would not be required to obtain a permit.
2. No livestock feedlot or facility is required to obtain a permit if the facility discharges only in the event of a 25-year, 24-hour storm (highest rainfall likely to occur in a 24-hour period from a storm that comes only every 25 years.).

Source: 40 C.F.R. § 124, 82 (a) (2) (1978).

out the goals of environmental protection. These agencies are the Illinois Institute of Natural Resources, the Environmental Protection Agency (EPA), and the Pollution Control Board.

The Institute of Natural Resources is responsible for long-range research, planning, and policy-making regarding environmental quality and other natural resource issues. One of its duties is to work with existing state and federal agencies in finding answers to practical problems of environmental contamination, and to make recommendations to the agency, the board, and the legislature. The institute has an Agricultural Advisory Committee, composed largely of prominent members of the state's agricultural community, to advise on significant agricultural pollution issues.

The Environmental Protection Agency is the pollution investigation agency. Its staff investigates complaints, maintains monitoring devices throughout the state, and inspects alleged or potential sources of pollution. In short, this agency polices the quality of the Illinois environment. In order to carry out its responsibility, the agency is vested with the authority to enter any private or public property at any reasonable time and

to investigate and inspect in accord with constitutional limits. The agency also administers a permit program, and may recommend regulations relating to permits for adoption by the Pollution Control Board. The agency presents data and evidence in any hearing before the board, and serves as a receiving unit for federal units.

The Pollution Control Board is the rulemaker and adjudicator under the act. The board has five members appointed by the governor who are responsible for the adoption of standards and regulations under the act. The board must give notice to the public of proposed regulations and hold public hearings where appropriate. The board also hears: (1) complaints of violations of EPA regulations brought by the agency and others, (2) petitions for variances from EPA regulations in special instances, (3) petitions for review of the agency's denial of a permit, and (4) petitions to remove a seal placed by the agency in what it felt was an emergency situation.

The Illinois Environmental Protection Act provides for a maximum civil penalty of $10,000 per violation, but requires the board to take into consideration the circumstances surrounding a violation when the board assesses a penalty.[4] The act also provides that any party dissatisfied with the board's action may petition the appellate court for judicial review.

Many states have enacted similar provisions. These provisions emphasize the extent to which environmental matters can be handled by administrative agencies rather than by the courts.[5] The foregoing discussion illustrates many principles of administrative law, such as the right of the public to participate as regulations are developed, guarantees of due process afforded at administrative hearings, and the ultimate right of judicial review after an administrative determination has been made.[6]

The Problem of Livestock Wastes. Livestock feedlots and facilities can be designed to minimize or prevent water pollution. Design criteria that accomplish this goal have been established in various states. Such criteria may be considered good management practices and, in many cases, have been incorporated into state environmental regulations. Also, many states have developed regulations regarding the disposal of livestock waste. The following guidelines are rather typical.

Livestock facilities should not contain within their boundaries any stream or surface waters other than small accumulations resulting from precipitation. Furthermore, a facility should not be located in a floodplain unless it is protected from possible flooding. Waste treatment facilities should not be located on soils with a high degree of permeability, such as sand or gravel, unless leachate from the waste treatment structure can be prevented from reaching groundwater. To prevent an odor nuisance, a facility should not be located within close proximity to populated areas.

Facilities should be designed to divert excessive surface waters from flowing through a feedlot. This should be accomplished, for example, by using a diversion terrace. To prevent feedlot runoff from entering and polluting other surface waters, runoff should be directed to an area such as a holding pond, pending disposal by other more proper methods such as a dispersal field. Facilities should also have a holding pond to receive this runoff.

Wastes stored in excess of 6 months should be contained in a storage structure for manure that is impermeable. Temporary manure stacks should be constructed to prevent rainfall or surface water from entering the stacks and carrying materials to other surface or groundwaters. Likewise, manure stacks should not be within 100 feet of any

---

[4] The relevant considerations are: (1) the degrees of damage or injury caused by the violation; (2) the social and economic value of the pollution source; (3) the suitability of the pollution source to the area in which it is located; and (4) the technical practicability and economic reasonableness of reducing or eliminating the emissions.

[5] For example, the Illinois Environmental Protection Act does not impair any existing civil or criminal remedy for damages caused by acts which also violate the act. Accordingly, an action against the violator for money damages could be brought in a civil suit based on nuisance theory, even though the acts causing the nuisance also violate the Environmental Protection Act. For a discussion of the measure and elements of damage for pollution

of a stream see 49 A.L.R. 2d 253-314 (1956). Among the items discussed are damages to trees, crops, fish, and livestock and to swimming and boating activity and the deprivation of water uses.

[6] The reader may also want to examine environmental legislation in other states, such as the Michigan Environmental Protection Act, MICH. COMP. LAWS ANN. §§ 691.1201–.1207 (West Supp. 1977) and the Minnesota Environmental Rights Act, MINN. STAT. §§ 116B.01–13 (1978). The Minnesota act is especially interesting because it includes an exemption for "a family farm..." *Id.* § 116B.02(2). *See generally* Bryden, *Environmental Rights in Theory and Practice,* 62 MINN. L. REV. 163 (1978).

water well. Livestock handling facilities should be constructed to prevent wastes from escaping into surfaces or ground-waters.

Field application of livestock wastes should be carried out in a careful manner. Several factors are to be considered—the type of soil, its permeability, its condition (frozen or unfrozen), the slope of the land, cover mulch, and the area's proximity to surface waters, among other factors.

The extent to which the disposal of live-stock wastes or spoiled feed can be proble-matic and the kind of administrative dif-ficulties that a livestock producer can encounter are illustrated in the following cases that were heard before the Illinois Pollution Control Board.

POLLUTION PENALTY—MITIGATING CIRCUMSTANCES

ENVIRONMENTAL PROTECTION AGENCY v. LOVELESS
Illinois Pollution Control Board, 1976
Ill. PCB 75-56, 23 Opinions 199

This matter is before the Board on a Complaint filed by the Environment-al Protection Agency on February 6, 1975, alleging that Respondent Loveless' operation of a cattle feedlot in Macoupin County, Illinois caused violation of Sections 12(a) and 12(d) of the Environmental Protection Act.

An unnamed natural stream runs through Respondent's property, adjacent to the pit silos and certain of the individual cattle feeder lots. That unnamed natural stream discharges into Spanish Needle Creek, which also runs through Respondent's property, approximately 150 yards south of the feedlot facility.

The Complaint alleges that Respondent's operations have caused contam-inants to enter both the unnamed natural stream and Spanish Needle Creek, in violation of Section 12(a) of the Act. Those same discharges are alleged to have caused the presence of unnatural sludges and bottom deposits, unnatural color, turbidity and odors in both the unnamed natural stream and Spanish Needle Creek, in violation of Rule 203(a), as well as dissolved oxygen and ammonia nitrogen levels in violation of Rules 203(d) and 203(f). Finally, Respondent is alleged to have caused the deposition on land of contaminants (manure, silage, etc.), so as to cause a water pollution hazard with respect to both streams in violation of Section 12(d) of the Act.

Respondent argues that because the United States Environmental Protec-tion Agency issued an NPDES permit for Respondent's operation, which permit contained later compliance dates than some of the dates for which violation was alleged, and which contained exceptions for adverse weather conditions, that permit—in whose issuance the Illinois Environmental Protec-tion Agency was involved—provides an absolute defense. We find that the issuance of an NPDES permit is, prior to State assumption of NPDES author-ity, immaterial to the issues here.

Having found that the Agency has made its case and shown all the viola-tions alleged, we must now turn to consideration of those factors in Section 33(c) of the Act, and the various matters pleaded in mitigation by Respondent. First, considering the nature of the injury caused by Mr. Loveless' operations, we find that such injury was significant, and resulted in degradation of the quality of the unnamed natural stream and, more importantly, Spanish Needle Creek. Agency testimony concerning biological surveys of Spanish Needle Creek indicate that the degradation in the area immediately downstream of the confluence of the unnamed natural stream with Spanish Needle Creek was serious.

The Agency's brief does not question the social and economic value of Mr. Loveless' feedlot operations. Nor, by virtue of its rural setting, do we have any doubt regarding the suitability or unsuitability of Mr. Loveless' operation for the area in which it is located. While there may be some question regarding the location of the feedlots adjacent to a stream, in such a manner as to allow run-off to enter that stream, we find that proper controls can make such a location entirely suitable. It is evident, as will be discussed below, that Mr. Loveless has initiated such controls.

The technical practicability and economic reasonableness of eliminating Mr. Loveless' discharges has also been resolved. Testimony indicated that by approximately the same time that the Complaint in this matter was filed, Mr. Loveless' operation achieved compliance with the applicable regulation. As early as 1968 or 1969, Mr. Loveless constructed a small holding lagoon for run-off from the feedlots. Subsequently, in his efforts to achieve compliance, Mr. Loveless has closed approximately one-half of the individual feedlot areas on his property, constructed an additional larger lagoon to hold run-off, and built and later strengthened a berm separating a run-off interceptor ditch from the unnamed natural stream.

Although testimony indicates that during the period alleged in the Complaint there were breaches and overflow from the small lagoon and the run-off interceptor ditch, it now appears that this is no longer a problem. Mr. Loveless has constructed a piping system to remove run-off liquids from the smaller holding pond, and pumps those liquids to the larger holding pond, which is estimated to have two years holding capacity.

In addition, Mr. Loveless has closed two of his pit silos, which discharged leachate into the unnamed natural stream, and has installed equipment to pipe liquid discharges from the remaining pit silos into the larger of his two holding ponds. The sum of these actions apparently serves to—for at least the present—alleviate all problems from the Loveless feedlot operation.

All of the above actions were taken by Mr. Loveless during what seem to have been relatively constant, if disorganized and occasionally haphazard, good faith attempts to achieve compliance with the applicable rules and regulations. Mr. Loveless attended conferences with the Agency and, although he did not achieve compliance within the period envisioned by the Agency, he apparently did offer considerable cooperation to the Agency. These facts, coupled with the Agency's admission that it has allowed longer periods for other feedlot operators to achieve compliance, lead us to find that no penalty would be appropriate in this instance.

We shall, therefore, instead of imposing a penalty, order that Respondent Loveless cease and desist all violations. We shall also require that he submit to the Agency, within one year, a plan for permanent compliance with the Regulations which this Record indicates were violated. We leave to Mr. Loveless the substance of such a plan.

WATER POLLUTION—FISH KILL

ENVIRONMENTAL PROTECTION AGENCY v. WEIDE
Illinois Pollution Control Board, 1976
Ill. PCB 75-353, 23 Opinions 211

This matter comes before the Pollution Control Board (Board) upon the September 9, 1975 Complaint of the Environmental Protection Agency (Agency) charging that Mr. Edward H. Weide (Weide) violated Rule 203(a) of the Water Regulations (causing unnatural sludge or bottom deposits harmful to human, animal, plant or aquatic life) and Section 12(a) of the Environmental Protection Act (allowing the discharge of any contaminants into the environment so as to cause water pollution in Illinois) on or about August 9, 1974. Weide is accused of causing or allowing the discharge of corn silage wastes into an unnamed tributary of Big Sandy Creek resulting in unnatural sludge or bottom deposits, odor, unnatural color, and a fish kill. Respondent is also charged with violation of Water Rules 203(f) (causing said stream's ammonia nitrogen level to exceed acceptable levels) and 203(d) (causing said stream's dissolved oxygen to be less than 5.0 mg/l).

Mr. Michael Conlin testified that he was called to investigate a fish kill in August, 1974. Mr. Conlin traced the upper limit of the fish kill to the entrance of an unnamed tributary to Big Sandy Creek. The fish kill covered 2.6 miles, the water being cloudy, dirty, and milky, and having a putrid odor. Mr. Conlin followed the unnamed tributary by sight and smell to white, turbid water on Weide's pasture. He found the banks to be saturated with waste materials. Mr. Conlin spoke to Weide, who admitted placing corn silage at that spot two days before.

Mr. Conlin set up three sampling areas each consisting of 150 feet, in light, moderate and heavy kill areas respectively. Mr. Conlin then counted the fish in these areas and projected a fish kill of approximately 25,000 fish. Mr. Conlin testified that corn silage has a high BOD which could result in oxygen depletion thereby suffocating fish.

Mr. Weide testified that on August 9, 1974, he cleaned his silo putting the waste in a manure spreader. Using the manure spreader, Weide placed the silage in the ditch to help stop erosion; no water was seen in the ditch at that time. Mr. Weide neither cultivated under the silage nor seeded on top. A total of 6 to 8 cubic yards of silage was deposited, having a fairly high moisture content. The silage was placed on top of soil and concrete foundations which had been placed previously to control erosion.

Mr. William Tucker testified that high organic material, such as corn silage, will cause oxygen depletion and could cause an instantaneous fish kill. In addition, he testified that the stream could recover in as little as 1 1/2 days. He measured the dissolved oxygen (DO) to be 9.3 + 10.3 ppm upstream and downstream from the discharge. At the point of discharge the DO was 0.6 ppm.

It is the Order of the Pollution Control Board that:

1. Weide is found to have violated Rule 203(a), (d) and (f) of the Water Regulations and Section 12(a) of the Act.
2. Weide shall pay, as a reasonable value of the fish killed through said violations, $2600.00 by certified check or money order payable to the Game and Fish Fund, State of Illinois, 2200 Churchill Road, Springfield, Illinois 62706 within thirty-five days of the date of this Order.
3. Weide shall cease and desist from depositing corn silage wastes in such a way as to contaminate the unnamed tributary to Big Sandy Creek.

Nonpoint Sources of Pollution[7]

Nonpoint sources generally coincide with types of land use. Since they are sources that diffuse and discharge pollutants to water by way of widely dispersed pathways, they are generally significant sources of pollution only when they involve large land areas. Agricultural management techniques can significantly affect various categories of nonpoint source pollution. The following discussion will identify some of the categories of nonpoint source pollution that are important to agriculture. The discussion will also identify the planning process from which a regulatory control program for nonpoint sources of pollution is evolving, and will illustrate the agricultural nonpoint source pollution program that has recently evolved in one state. The purposes of the following discussion are to acquaint farmers and ranchers with the problems attributable to agricultural nonpoint source pollution; to identify the mechanism whereby control programs are being developed, so that agricultural producers can participate in that process and help create a control program that will be reasonable and effective; and to emphasize that a mandatory pollution control regulatory program with potentially harsh regulatory constraints is much less likely in the future if agricultural producers voluntarily adopt management practices that reduce nonpoint source pollution.

Nonpoint Source Pollutants. Categories of nonpoint source pollutants include sediments, nutrients, minerals, pesticides, oxygen-demanding wastes, and pathogens. Sediments carried by soil erosion represent by far the greatest volume of wastes entering surface waters. Although it is not possible to keep all waters crystal clear, excessive

---

[7]See U.S. Environmental Protection Agency, Institutional Bases for Control of Nonpoint Source Pollution (1979) for an excellent discussion of nonpoint source pollution. Much of the following discussion has been developed from this publication.

sediment loads raise water treatment costs for municipalities.[8] They cause aesthetic degradation, damage to domestic and industrial water supplies and water recreation, destruction of wildlife, and clogging of reservoirs and channels. In addition, sediment has frequently been identified as the principal transport mechanism for much of the plant nutrient waste load that accelerates lake eutrophication. Finally, sediment is an important transport mechanism for pesticides, organic and inorganic wastes, and pathogens.[9]

Cropland is one of the chief sources of sediment on a total mass basis, accounting for 50 percent or more of the sediment deposited in streams and lakes.[10] Well-managed forests, on the other hand, are exceptionally free of erosion and sediment pol-

lution; but harvested forests are subject to erosion, highly so if timber harvest is poorly managed.[11]

Nutrient elements, chiefly phosphorus and nitrogen, enter waters in municipal discharges, urban storm runoff, and combined storm and sanitary sewer overflows, as well as runoff, seepage, and percolation from lands managed for intensive production of livestock and crops.[12] Because of the contribution of phosphorus and nitrogen to lake eutrophication and the potential pollution of groundwater drinking supplies by nitrates, nutrients are sometimes considered a more serious pollution problem than sediments per se.[13] Runoff from agricultural lands has been identified as a major contributor to nutrient levels in the Southeast, Southern Plains, Midwest, and Central

---

[8] This is because flowing waters have fixed minimum carrying capacities. If control of discharges reduces suspended solids below these minimum levels, the flowing waters will attempt to restore these minimum levels by scouring the beds and banks of the watercourse.

[9] Staff report to the National Commission on Water Quality IV-22 (1976); MIDWEST RESEARCH INSTITUTE AND HITTMAN ASSOCIATES, INC., METHODS FOR IDENTIFYING AND EVALUATING THE NATURE AND EXTENT OF NONPOINT SOURCES OF POLLUTANTS 240 (EPS-43019-75-014, 1973). However some scientists have disputed that phosphorus absorbed in clay is an important cause of the eutrophication of all but very shallow lakes. They have asserted that eutrophication of deep lakes results mainly from dissolved phosphorus (which is released from municipal outfalls, septic tanks, and runoff-borne animal wastes and fertilizers) not incorporated in sediment. K. PORTER ET AL., NITROGEN AND PHOSPHORUS, FOOD PRODUCTION, WASTE, AND THE ENVIRONMENT 15-16, 82-84, 210-13 (N.Y. State College of Agriculture and Life Sciences 1975).

[10] MIDWEST RESEARCH INSTITUTE et al., supra note 9, at 1. The National Commission on Water Quality's staff report found that high concentrations of suspended solids were linked to cropland in the Great Plains, Midwest, Southwest, and Central Valley of California. In significant portions of

those regions, the polluting effect of agricultural activities is augmented by the natural high erodibility of the soil in the drainage basins. Staff Report, supra note 9, at IV-22, IV-30.

[11] Forestry practices which disturb the land surface have caused increased turbidity in streams of the Pacific Northwest and Appalachian regions. Staff Report, supra note 9, at IV-22, IV-30. See also U.S. DEPARTMENT OF AGRICULTURE PLANNING STAFF, NORTH COASTAL AREA OF CALIFORNIA AND PORTIONS OF SOUTHERN OREGON—MAIN REPORT ON SEDIMENT YIELD AND LAND TREATMENT 65-59 (1972).

[12] Phosphatic detergents have been identified by some scientists as the largest source of phosphates in municipal discharges. It should be noted that, in areas where such detergents have not been banned, they are released into groundwaters and surface waters by sources not included in the NPDES— septic tanks and fields—as well as municipal point sources.

[13] Nutrients received a great deal of attention in the early and mid-1970s because nutrient levels in many areas were continuing to rise, whereas the levels of oxygen-demanding wastes, coliform bacteria, metals, and chemicals (including pesticides) were declining. U.S. Environmental Protection Agency, National Water Quality Inventory 3 (1975); U.S. Council on Environmental Quality, Environmental Quality 1974, at 284-87 (1974).

Valley of California, although in some areas nitrate pollution of groundwater occurs naturally. A committee of the National Research Council has found that relative losses of nitrogen from cropland vary significantly as a result of such agricultural practices as timing and amounts of fertilizer application.[14]

Most nonpoint source pollution from minerals other than nitrates and phosphates results from mining activities, and, to a lesser extent, urban runoff. In agricultural production, the chief mineral pollutant from a nonpoint source is salinity in irrigation return flows. Both point source and nonpoint source salinity pollution from irrigated lands are exacerbated by natural saline conditions in the Colorado basin.[15]

Pesticides are widely used in agriculture and less extensively used in silviculture, construction, and urban land uses. They are transported from soil to water directly in runoff and sediment and indirectly by careless application and spray drift. The chief damage of pesticides to water quality has resulted from the persistence of some kinds of pesticides in the aquatic environment, where they are accumulated by fish and other food chain organisms, causing damage to wildlife high in the food chain. Because persistent pesticides are no longer in common use, this problem is decreasing.

Organic wastes that are transported by nonpoint sources to streams in sediment and runoff have essentially the same adverse effects as the much greater loadings of organic wastes from municipal and industrial point sources and feedlots. Crop debris, livestock wastes, waste petroleum products, forest litter, and numerous solid waste materials are included in this type of pollution.[16]

Health hazards in the form of infectious pathogens are generally assumed to be present when evidence of animal or human fecal matter, as measured by noninfectious, fecal coliform bacteria, is found in the water. While these pathogens can be effectively controlled in drinking-water supplies by suitable treatment processes, their presence in surface waters can make those waters unfit for contact recreation. Although some of the coliform bacteria emanate from range and cropland runoff, by far the greatest part of the bacteria comes from point sources.

Section 208 Planning. Section 208 of the Federal Water Pollution Control Act amendments of 1972 deals with areawide waste treatment management. This section was originally interpreted by the federal EPA as applying only to areas of particularly complex water pollution problems resulting from large urban populations and industrialization or other causes. However, in the 1977 case of *Natural Resource Defense Council v. Costle*, the D.C. Circuit Court of Appeals affirmed a U.S. district court ruling that planning of the type specified in Sec. 208 must be done in all areas, not just those designated by the governor, and that the state is responsible for conducting the planning.[17] This expanded 208 planning process requires public participation. The process has attempted to identify all agricultural sources of nonpoint source pollution and methods to control, to the extent possible, such sources of agricultural pollution.

The "Culver amendment" of the Clean Water Act of 1977 [Sec. 208(j) of the FWPCA] authorizes a program of assistance to landowners and operators for installing best management practices for nonpoint

---

[14] MIDWEST RESEARCH INSTITUTE *et al. supra* note 9, at VII; Staff Report, *supra* note 9, at IV-19, IV-38.
[15] Staff Report, *supra* note 9, at IV-19, IV-38.

[16] MIDWEST RESEARCH INSTITUTE *et al.*, *supra* note 9, at VIII.
[17] National Resources Defense Council, Inc. v. Costle, 564, F. 2d 573 (D.C. Cir. 1977).

source pollution control and authorizes appropriations through the Secretary of Agriculture for this program.[18] The Culver amendment authorizes the Secretary (acting through the Soil Conservation Service and such other agencies as the Secretary designates) to enter into 5- to 10-year contracts with landowners and operators to provide cost-sharing and technical assistance for carrying out best management practices identified in the agricultural portion of the 208 plan and incorporated in plans approved by the soil conservation district. Such contracts would only be entered into in areas where Sec. 208 plans had been certified by the governor and approved by EPA and where the designated management agency assured an adequate level of participation by owners and operators controlling rural land. Priority in providing assistance is to be given to those areas and sources that have the most significant effect on water quality. The principal incentive for a state to establish and implement a Sec. 208 plan is the availability of federal grants for states with approved Sec. 208 plans.

The *Train* case and EPA's water management planning regulations[19] have given the states "backstop" responsibility for establishing and implementing the land use control and land treatment aspects of the Federal Water Pollution Control Act. In so doing, they have put the responsibility at the level of government that is most capable of exercising it, on the basis of both legal powers and political acceptability. The U.S. Environmental Protection Agency has issued a final program guidance memorandum, which establishes implementation criteria for EPA approval of nonpoint source elements of water quality management plans.[20] This memorandum states that nonpoint source *regulatory* programs will be required whenever the 208 agency, in consultation with the EPA regional administrator, determines that a regulatory program is "the only practical method" to assure that nonpoint source controls are implemented.

The memorandum does not go so far as to say that all 208 plans for areas of significant nonpoint source problems must contain regulatory programs. The memorandum provides that regional administrators may grant approval of nonpoint source control programs that do not contain enforcement provisions only where the regional administrator is convinced that such nonregulatory programs will result in sufficient implementation of nonpoint source controls to achieve water quality goals. Nonregulatory programs that merely continue existing programs which have not been successful in the past, without substantial changes, are not to be approved. Moreover, approval of nonregulatory programs shall be withdrawn if progress reports do not show continuing and substantial improvement.[21]

Agricultural producers can expect that the initial 208 nonpoint source control program will utilize voluntary controls as much as possible. In Illinois, for example, the water quality management plan was initially approved without any major mandatory provisions in the soil erosion and sedimentation control portion. The Illinois plan and the plans of many other states initially will try to solve erosion and sedimentation problems as well as other

[18] Federal Water Pollution Control Act, 33 U.S.C. § 1288 (j) (1977).
[19] 40 C.F.R. § 130 *et seq.* (These sections were later removed. *See* p. 808 of 40 C.F.R.)

[20] ACTING DEPUTY ASSISTANT ADMINISTRATOR FOR WATER PLANNING AND STANDARDS, REGULATORY NONPOINT SOURCE CONTROL (SAM-31, 1977).
[21] *Id.* at 6–8.

agricultural nonpoint source pollution problems with educational efforts, tax incentives, and cost-sharing funds to encourage adoption of best management practices. Agricultural producers must be prepared, however, for a more stringent water quality management plan in the future if the agricultural sector does not vigorously respond to the voluntary approach.

9.2 SOIL AND WATER CONSERVATION

The preservation of our soil and water resources is one of the most important tasks facing agriculture. All of the fifty states, the Virgin Islands, and Puerto Rico have statutes enabling the creation of special-purpose local governments called "soil conservation districts," "soil and water conservation districts," or simply "conservation districts." All of the statutes resemble each other, for they were originally passed in the late 1930s or early 1940s in response to the serious wind and water erosion problems of that time. They were all based on a 1936 Standard State Soil Conservation District Law, which was developed and proposed to the states by the U.S. Department of Agriculture (USDA) to provide responsible state and local cooperation required by the Soil Conservation Service's new program of soil conservation and improvements on private land.[22] Some

of these laws were subsequently amended to emphasize other soil erosion–related concerns, such as flood prevention and land use planning.[23]

Although concern about the on-farm effects of erosion, such as reduced productivity, continues to be important, our society is also becoming more concerned about the off-farm effects, such as sedimentation of streams and reservoirs. Soil and water conservation districts, which were originally created to deal with the on-farm problems of erosion, are logical organizations to help control the off-farm problems as well.

In 1971, Iowa passed the first statewide sediment control statute regulating agriculture.[24] Many other states now have sediment control laws, most of which are based, at least in part, on the 1973 Model State Act for Soil Erosion and Sediment Control, prepared by representatives of the National Association of Conservation Districts, the U.S. Environmental Protection Agency, the USDA, and state governments. More recently, "alternative provisions" have been developed for the purpose of transforming the Model Act so that it could provide a more adequate legal basis for an agricultural nonpoint source pollution regulatory program. In the following paragraphs, traditional soil and water conservation district laws as well as the newly evolving regulatory provisions found in the 1973 Model Act are discussed.

---

[22] Act of Apr. 27, 1935, Pub. L. No. 74-46, 49 Stat. 163 (codified at 16 U.S.C.A. § 590 *et seq.*).
[23] A good example of this is the Wisconsin Soil and Water Conservation District Law, Wis. Stat. Ann. §§ 92.01–92.21 (West). Originally enacted in 1937, it was amended in 1955 to give the state soil conservation agency and to give the districts authority to sponsor SCS-assisted small watershed projects. It was amended in 1972 to require that

district conservation plans in counties included in regional planning commission jurisdictions be consistent with the plans of the planning commission.
[24] Iowa Code Ann. §§ 467A.42-467A.53, §§ 467D.1-467D.24 (West). The act amended the Iowa soil conservation districts law to require, *inter alia*, that all conservation districts set and implement soil loss limits.

The 1936 Standard Act

Virtually all state conservation district laws authorize districts to study the needs and problems regarding resources, develop conservation plans for soil resources of the district, educate land occupiers about the plans, and offer land occupiers technical advice and services, financial assistance, and other assistance (including machinery, equipment, fertilizers, and seeds) for the installation of conservation practices on private land.

State conservation district laws permit districts to require land occupiers (as a condition of receiving benefits and services from districts) to enter and perform agreements to carry out conservation practices or farm conservation plans. But state laws generally provide no penalties for failure of land operators to carry out such "cooperative agreements." Although it is possible that districts could obtain court orders for specific performance of such agreements as contracts, districts have not sought to do so because of their emphasis on the voluntary nature of their programs.

Procedurally, assistance is provided to districts by federal and state agencies, and district programs are coordinated with programs of other levels of government through "memoranda of understanding" and other similar documents. An umbrella memorandum of understanding is executed between each district and USDA, outlining the assistance to be provided and the conditions that must be met to receive it. Supplemental memoranda are developed between each district and each USDA agency cooperating with the district.

Virtually every district has a memorandum with the Soil Conservation Service, (SCS), the only USDA agency that receives appropriations earmarked for direct assistance to districts. Under these memoranda, the SCS generally agrees to furnish each district with the services of a professional conservationist specially assigned to the district, with other personnel qualified to carry out resource planning, conservation, and development activities, and with facilities for their use.

Most districts also have a memorandum with the county Agricultural Stabilization and Conservation (ASC) Committee. Under these memoranda, county committees generally agree to take district long-range objectives and annual work plans into consideration in developing county ASC programs, inform district cooperators of the availability of the Agricultural Conservation Program (ACP) cost-sharing for installing practices that may be included in their conservation plans, and give priority to providing cost-sharing for installing practices required for specified district priority programs. In addition, districts generally agree to participate in the development of county ACP programs. Memoranda of understanding between districts and county committees frequently specify that cost-sharing priority be given to land in resource and community development and water shed projects. There is no apparent reason why a similar arrangement could not be made, giving cost-sharing priority to lands found by areawide water quality managment studies to be causing nonpoint source pollution problems.[25]

---

[25] A new set of memoranda of understanding is likely to be drawn up as a result of the Culver amendment, which provides that the Secretary of Agriculture shall make arrangements with districts (where practicable) to administer long-term contracts to install and maintain agricultural best management practices included in approved 208 plans. The Secretary has promulgated regulations for a rural clean water program (RCWP) to carry out the Culver amendment, which delegates to SCS responsibility to make arrangements with districts to administer such contracts. SCS has

The Standard Act also gave districts the power to promulgate land use regulations in the form of enforceable conservation ordinances. This power is now included in about half of the state's enabling statutes (usually in restricted form) and has been very seldom used.[26] Some observers suggest that a major obstacle to enactment of land use regulations is the high percentage of supporting votes required by various state statutes. The range is from 50 percent plus 1 vote to 90 percent of those voting.[27]

The Standard Act and most state acts give the districts themselves no money-raising authority, because the Standard Act contemplated that all district operations would be funded from state appropriations for districts and federal contributions (chiefly through the Soil Conservation Service). The law passed by the Illinois Soil and Water Conservation Districts is an exception to this general rule, for it provides for the creation of subdistricts with the power to levy a tax.[28]

The 1973 Model Act for Soil Erosion and Sediment Control

The Model Act (followed by most of the state sediment control laws based on it) requires the state soil and water conservation commission to prepare a state program to control soil erosion and sediment damage from land-disturbing activities, including guidelines for development of regulatory programs by the districts.[29]

Land-disturbing activities are defined as any land changes which may result in movement of sediment into waters or onto land, including tilling, clearing, grading, excavating, transporting, and filling of land (other than federal land), except for minor activities such as home gardening, landscaping, repair, and maintenance.

The Model Act gives the state commission responsibility for developing a comprehensive sediment control program, in cooperation with the state water quality agency, other appropriate state and federal agencies, and an advisory board representing housing, financing, industry, agriculture, recreation, and local government agencies.

As a part of this program, the commission is required to adopt guidelines[30] for carrying out the program by a date specified in the individual state law. The commission is required after giving due notice (as defined in the state conservation district law) to conduct public hearings, before adopting or revising the guidelines.

---

published a Rural Clean Water Program procedural manual to provide specific guidance about the RCWP. Other types of arrangements with relevance to agricultural NPS control can be made between districts and Farmers' Home Administration (FmHA), state extension services, ESCS, and other federal and state agencies.

[26] *See, e.g.* ARK. STAT. ANN. § 9-910 (1976); COLO. REV. STAT. ANN. § 128-1-9 (1973); VA. CODE § 21-66 (1975).

[27] Alabama (80), Arkansas (75), Colorado (50+), Florida (50+), Georgia (50+), Illinois (75), Kentucky (90), Louisiana (66 2/3), Maryland (50+), Mississippi (66 2/3), Montana (50+), Nebraska (60), Nevada (50+), North Carolina (66 2/3), North Dakota (75), Oregon (66 2/3), South Carolina (66 2/3), Tennessee (66 2/3), Texas (90), Utah (50+), Vermont (50+), Virginia (66 2/3), West Virginia (60), Wisconsin (50+), Wyoming (75).

[28] ILL. REV. STAT. ch. 5, § 131b (1979). It is presumed that subdistricts have the same powers as soil and water conservation districts, in addition to the following special provisions: (1) to develop plans for flood prevention and flood control; (2) to levy a tax not in excess of .125 percent; (3) to cooperate with the federal government in carrying out the Watershed and Flood Prevention Act; (4) to make assessments for works of improvement, using the assessment procedure in the Local Improvement Law of the Illinois Municipal Code; (5) to pay subdistrict directors a maximum of $10 a day for services performed concerning subdistrict business.

[29] COUNCIL OF STATE GOVERNMENTS, SUGGESTED STATE LEGISLATION, 11–19 Vol. XXXII (1973) hereinafter cited as Model Act.

[30] The Model Act states that the guidelines must: (1) be based upon relevant physical and develop-

Every district in the state is required to develop and adopt its own sediment control program, consistent with the state program and guidelines, within a time period after adoption of the state guidelines to be specified in the individual state law. The district is to be assisted in developing its program by an advisory committee (representing the same interests represented on the state advisory board) and is entitled to assistance from the state commission, on request.

Upon adoption of its program, the district is required to submit the program to the commission for review and approval. If the district fails to submit the program within the statutory time period, the commission is required (after appropriate hearings or consultations with local interests) to develop and adopt an appropriate program (by implication, including standards) to be carried out by the district.

After the program has been approved by the commission, the district is given a time period (to be set by the state statute) in which to adopt conservation standards for various soil types and land uses.[31] These standards are required to include "criteria, guidelines, techniques, and methods for control of erosion and sediment resulting from land-disturbing activities" Before adopting any conservation standards or changes in existing standards, the district is required to give "due notice" and to conduct a public hearing on the proposed standards or changes. Although the Model Act requires district standards to be consistent with state guidelines concerning conservation standards, the act makes no provision for commission review and approval of district standards. Both program and standards must be made available for public inspection at the principal office of the district.

The Model Act provides different mechanisms for controlling prohibited land-disturbing activities of different classes of land users. Owners, occupiers, or operators of private agricultural land and forestland who have district-approved farm or ranch conservation plans for normal agricultural and forestry activities and are maintaining such plans, or whose normal agricultural and forestry activities comply with district conservation standards, are entitled to cost-sharing and technical assistance to help them avoid violating the act. Such persons are not deemed to be engaged in prohibited land-disturbing activities, unless at least 50 percent cost-sharing assistance or adequate technical assistance is made available for installation of the erosion and sediment control measures required for compliance with their approved farm or ranch conservation plans or district conservation standards.

The Model Act authorizes the district to make on its own initiative on-site inspections to determine whether the resident owner, operator, or occupier is com-

---

mental information concerning the watersheds and drainage basins of the state, including, but not limited to, data relating to land use, soils, hydrology, geology, size of land area being disturbed, proximate water bodies and their characteristics, transportation, and public facilities and services; (2) include such survey of lands and waters as may be deemed appropriate by the commission or required by any applicable law to identify areas, including multijurisdictional and watershed areas, with critical erosion and sediment problems; and (3) contain conservation standards for various types of soils and land uses, which standards shall include criteria, techniques, and methods for the control of erosion and sediment resulting from land-disturbing activities.

[31] The "program," which must first be approved by the State Commission, is understood to include goals, organization, time frame, manpower and other administrative details. The "standards" mean technical performance standards and may include, among other things, soil loss limits and best management practices.

plying with his or her approved farm conservation plan or conforming with district conservation standards. The district is required to give the resident owner, operator, or occupier notice that the inspection will be made and an opportunity to accompany the inspector. If the inspection reveals that the land occupier is not complying with the approved farm plan or the district's standards, the occupier must be notified by registered mail of the measures needed for compliance. The notice shall require commencement of such measures within 6 months from the date of the notice. If the land occupier fails to comply with the notice, the occupier will be deemed in violation of the act and subject to its penalties.

The decision of the district that a violation exists is subject to judicial review, provided an appeal is filed within 30 days. Judicial review is available on the same terms from all other decisions of the district and the commission.

Assuming no appeal is taken, violators of the act may be prosecuted for a misdemeanor and subject to a fine of up to $500 or up to 1 year imprisonment for each violation. Every day that the violation continues shall constitute a separate offense. It should be noted that not all states have

adopted these penalty provisions. The Illinois version, for example, authorizes the district to seek voluntary compliance. If voluntary compliance is not obtained, formal hearings are held to determine the reason for noncompliance. In lieu of a fine, the provision requires the findings to be published and made available.[32]

In addition, the district, the commission, or "any aggrieved person who suffers damage or is likely to suffer damage because of a violation" may apply to the court for injunctive relief. The county attorney shall take whatever legal action is needed to enforce the act, on request of the district; and the state attorney general, on request of the commission.

In early 1978, the National Association of Conservation Districts published a set of alternative provisions for use with the Model Act by states considering the adoption of sediment control laws or amendment of existing sediment control laws to meet the needs of the Sec. 208 planning effort. The main thrust of the alternative provisions is to put more emphasis on the pollution control aspects of erosion and sediment control and to extend the coverage of state and district programs under the Model Act to pollutants other than sediment.

CONSTITUTIONALITY OF MANDATORY SOIL LOSS LIMITS

WOODBURY COUNTY SOIL CONSERVATION DISTRICT v. ORTNER
Supreme Court of Iowa, 1979
279 N.W. 2d 276

This appeal involves a dispute concerning the obligation of landowners to comply with the provisions of ch. 467A, The Code, 1975, commonly referred to as the Soil Conservation Districts Law. The trial court found § 467A.44 of the act, and the section fixing the rules and regulations under

---

[32] ILL. REV. STAT. ch. 5, § 138.8 (1979).

which the soil conservation district operates, unconstitutional. We reverse the trial court and remand the case for further proceedings.

The defendants Ortner and Schrank each own farm land in Woodbury County. In 1975, an adjacent landowner, John C. Matt, filed a complaint with the soil conservation district alleging that his farm was suffering damage from water and soil erosion from defendants' land. An investigation made under § 467A.47 resulted in a finding that the soil loss on the Ortner and Schrank farms was in excess of the established statutory limits. The district issued an administrative order finding defendants in violation of the district soil erosion control regulations and requiring them to remedy the situation within six months.

The order offered defendants two alternatives to bring the soil within acceptable limits. They were directed to either seed the land to permanent pasture or hay or to terrace it. Defendants failed to do either within the time allowed by the commission's order and the district brought this action as authorized by § 467A.49, The Code.

Even with state grants which were available through the Department of Soil Conservation to defray part of the cost, terracing would cost the Ortners more than $12,000.00 and the Schranks approximately $1,500.00. There was also testimony that this process would render a number of acres of each farm untillable. The other alternative—pasture or hay seeding—would be less expensive but would also remove some of each farm from active production. The defendants introduced evidence that either alternative would decrease the value of their land, although there was considerable evidence to the contrary.

[1]   In considering the constitutionality of legislative enactments, we accord them every presumption of validity and find them unconstitutional only upon a showing that they clearly infringe on constitutional rights and only if every reasonable basis for support is negated.

[2]   Important to our decision here is a determination as to whether the restrictions and conditions imposed by ch. 467A, The Code, amount to a taking of property under eminent domain or simply a regulation under the police power of the state. The latter entitles the property owner to no compensation; the former requires that he be paid for the appropriation of his property for public use.

In *Van Zee* and *Hakes* we stated that the test is whether the "collective benefits [to the public] outweigh the specific restraints imposed [on the individual]." Factors of particular importance include the "economic impact of the regulation on the claimant and, particularly, the extent to which the regulation has interfered with distinct investment backed expectations." To be considered also is the "character of the governmental action." *See Penn Central*, 437 U.S. at 124, 98 S.Ct. at 2659, 57 L. Ed. 2d at 648. It is important therefore to consider the nature of the public interest involved and the impact of the restrictions placed on defendants' use of their land by ch. 467A, The Code.

It should take no extended discussion to demonstrate that agriculture is important to the welfare and prosperity of this state. It has been judicially recognized as our leading industry. *See Benschoter v. Hakes*, 232 Iowa at 1360, 8 N.W. 2d at 486.

The state has a vital interest in protecting its soil as the greatest of its natural resources, and it has a right to do so. *Iowa Natural Resources Council v. Van Zee*, 261 Iowa at 1297, 158 N.W. 2d at 118. This is the purpose of ch. 467A as is apparent from this declaration:

To conserve the fertility, general usefulness, and value of the soil and soil resources of this state, and to prevent the injurious effects of soil erosion, it is hereby made the duty of the owners of real property in this state to establish and maintain soil and water conservation practices or erosion control practices, as required by the regulations of the commissioners of the respective soil conservation districts.

Defendants' argument is two-fold. They assert first that the statute amounts to a taking of private property without just compensation. Next, they say the statute is an unreasonable and illegal exercise of the state's police power.

[4]   We hold defendants have failed to establish § 467A.44 is unconstitutional. Its provisions are reasonably related to carrying out the announced legislative purpose of soil control, admittedly a proper exercise of police power.

[5]   While this imposes an extra financial burden on defendants, it is one the state has a right to exact. The importance of soil conservation is best illustrated by the state's willingness to pay three-fourths of the cost. In Ortner's case, the state's share is $36,760.50 and in Schrank's it is $4,413.00. The remainder to be paid by defendants ($12,253.50 by Ortner and $1,471.00 by Schrank) is still substantial, but not unreasonably so. A law does not become unconstitutional because it works a hardship. The argument that one must make substantial expenditures to comply with regulatory statutes does not raise constitutional barriers.

[6]   What we have already said is relevant, too, on defendants' claim the regulations established by the soil conservation district amount to a taking of their property without compensation in violation of the federal and state constitutions.

As we have already pointed out, an exercise of police power may be so sweeping in its scope and so all inclusive in its operation that it becomes a taking rather than a regulation. However, this did not happen here. Defendants still have the use and enjoyment of their property, limited only by the necessity to prevent soil erosion beyond allowable standards.

[7]   Defendants raise one other objection. They say the statute is invalid because it is designed "solely as a means of furthering the purely private property interests of a very limited class of landowners" rather than for the

benefit of the public generally. This is based on § 467A.47 which, they allege, provides for action by the soil conservation district upon the complaint of one damaged by erosion, rather than upon the initiative of the district itself. We believe this argument ignores other sections of the act under which the soil conservation district is authorized to act. *See* § 467A.44(3), under which the commissioners may require owners to act, and § 467A.52, under which, in limited circumstances, they may take independent action. *See also Miller v. Schoene*, 276 U.S. 272, 281, 48 S.Ct. 246, 248, 72 L.Ed. 568, 572 (1928), where a similar provision was held unobjectionable. We find no merit to this complaint.

The judgment of the trial court is reversed and the case is remanded for such other proceedings as may be appropriate.

9.3 AIR POLLUTION

The regulation of air pollution is of concern to agriculture at two levels. To some extent, agricultural activities contribute to air pollution, although these agricultural sources are of much less significance than the air pollution problems created by large urban and industrial areas. Regulatory efforts directed at the agricultural sector will be the principal focus of this section. At a more philosophical level, however, agricultural producers should recognize that the growth in the amount and complexity of air pollution brought about by urbanization, industrial development, and the use of motor vehicles, has resulted in mounting dangers to the public health and welfare of our country, including injury to agricultural crops and livestock. Thus, the regulation of air pollution is a double-edged sword—a sword that not only regulated agricultural activity but also helps to protect agricultural activities from such environmental problems as acid rain.

Legislation concerning air pollution can be found at both the federal and state levels of government. At the federal level, the Clean Air Act establishes national air quality standards and gives the individual states primary responsibility in assuring these standards will be met, maintained, and enforced.[33] While the federal legislation and regulations promulgated thereunder set goals for the quality of air, state law is of primary concern, since it deals with the method of obtaining these goals. State regulatory programs vary somewhat, although the administrator of the U.S. Environmental Protection Agency has encouraged the enactment of uniform state and local laws relating to the prevention of control of air pollution.[34]

Odor Problems

Although odor problems in agriculture have been traditionally handled under nuisance concepts discussed in Section 7.5 some states provide additional regulation of

[33] Clean Air Act, Pub. L. No. 88-206, 77 Stat. 392 (1963) (codified with amendments in 42 U.S.C. § 7401 *et seq.*).
[34] *See* 42 U.S.C.A. § 7402(a).

odors through environmental legislation.[35] For example, the Illinois Environmental Protection Act prohibits anyone from discharging or emitting any contaminant into the environment which causes or tends to cause air pollution. Air pollution occurs when a sufficient quantity of one or more contaminants is present in the air so as to be injurious to human, plant, or animal health or to property, or to unreasonably interfere with the enjoyment of life or property.[36] The Illinois act also prohibits anything which causes or tends to cause a violation of any regulation or standard adopted by the Illinois Pollution Control Board. The Board is given authority in the act to adopt regulations more specifically controlling air pollution and has adopted such air pollution control regulations.[37]

CHICKENS—AIR POLLUTION

PROCESSING AND BOOKS, INC. v. POLLUTION CONTROL BOARD
Supreme Court of Illinois, 1976
64 Ill. 2d 68, 351 N.E. 2d 865

A complaint filed by the Illinois Environmental Protection Agency with the Illinois Pollution Control Board on April 7, 1972, charged that the respondents, Processing and Books, Inc., an Illinois corporation, and National Mellody Farm Fresh Egg Company, its wholly owned subsidiary, had caused air pollution consisting of odors from chicken manure and incinerators used to dispose of dead chickens, in violation of Section 9(a) of the Environmental Protection Act. The Board fined the respondents $3,000 and entered a cease and desist order.

The respondents appealed, raising issues concerning the propriety of the relief ordered. The appellate court reversed on the ground that the Board's order does not specifically indicate that it took into consideration four factors set out in the Act as bearing on the reasonableness of the pollution. We granted leave to appeal.

The offense charged is set out in Section 9(a) of the Environmental Protection Act: "No person shall: (a) Cause or threaten or allow the discharge or emission of any contaminant into the environment in any state so as to cause or tend to cause air pollution...."

"Air pollution" is defined in Section 3(b) as "the presence in the atmosphere of one or more contaminants in sufficient quantities and of such characteristics and duration as to be injurious to human, plant, or animal life, to health, or to property, or to unreasonably interfere with the enjoyment of life or property."

---

[35] Interestingly, the Minnesota Environmental Rights Act disallows suits based solely upon violation of odor regulations. See MINN. STAT. §116B.02 (5) (1978).

[36] ILL. REV. STAT. ch. 111 1/2 § 1003 (b) (1979).
[37] Ch. 2, ILLINOIS POLLUTION CONTROL BOARD RULES AND REGULATIONS.

Section 33 provides:

(c)   In making its orders and determinations, the Board shall take into consideration all the facts and circumstances bearing upon the reasonableness of the emissions, discharges or deposits involved including, but not limited to: (i) the character and degree of injury to, or interference with the protection of the health, general welfare and physical property of the people; (ii) the social and economic value of the pollution source; (iii) the suitability or unsuitability of the pollution source to the area in which it is located, including the question of priority of location in the area involved; and (iv) the technical practicability and economic reasonableness of reducing or eliminating the emissions, discharges or deposits resulting from such pollution source.

The property involved is a portion of the large Hawthorne-Mellody farm, which is leased to National Mellody Farm Fresh Egg Company, which conducts an egg-producing operation. This operation is located southeast of the village of Mundelein and south of the village of Libertyville in an area zoned for agricultural uses. In 1965, the cattle and dairy operations to which the farm had been primarily devoted were terminated, and since that time the poultry operation has been greatly expanded. The total chicken population ranges between 296,000 and 330,000, and the farm produces between 160,000 and 170,000 grade "AA" eggs per day, 95 percent of which are sold to the National Tea Company.

The Board found that

some of Respondent's neighbors had lived in the area for almost 20 years. Some of them had their own farm animals and therefore had to dispose of manure. Although they tolerated the past odors emanating from a much smaller operation they found they could no longer enjoy their homes and property because of the chicken manure odor and the even more permeating odor of burning chickens and feathers.

The Agency has not disputed that the operation has substantial social and economic value.

The Board's order summarizes the evidence that showed that the odors emanating from the egg farm had interfered with the public's enjoyment of life and property in an area extending more than a mile beyond the boundaries of the farm. Expert and lay testimony was presented as to the sources of the odors: chicken manure spread on the farm's fields; holding tanks in each of 16 chicken houses where the manure, which accumulates at the rate of 75,000 pounds per day, was allowed to remain for three or four weeks before being taken away; a dryer used to convert some of the manure into marketable fertilizer; and two incinerators used to burn about 175 chickens which die every day. There was extensive evidence that residents of the area were prevented from holding cook-outs and relaxing out of doors, became nauseated while driving past the farm, and occasionally were even awakened at night by what one witness termed "a foul odor."

Complaints had been brought to the respondents' attention by private citizens, the county health department and the sheriff's office, but the odors persisted. The evidence showed that the odors might be substantially diminished if the manure in the holding tanks was disposed of within a week of its expulsion from the chickens since it takes approximately that long for bacterial decay to produce hydrogen sulfide, sulfur dioxide and other obnoxious gases. There was also evidence that incinerators of multichamber design would produce less air pollution than the single-chamber incinerators used by the farm.

The problem of interpreting the Air Pollution Statute stems from the use of the word "unreasonably." Each of the four criteria mentioned in Section 33(c) bears upon the reasonableness of the conduct involved, and so it might be argued that, in order to establish the type of Section 3(b) offense that is here involved, the complainant bears the burden of proof with respect to each of those criteria. But this interpretation of the word "unreasonably" as used in Section 3(b) would appear to place upon the complainant a burden more stringent than he would bear in a common law nuisance action, and thus to frustrate the purpose of the Act "to establish a unified, state-wide program supplemented by private remedies, to restore, protect and enhance the quality of the environment, and to assure that adverse effects upon the environment are fully considered and borne by those who cause them."

There is little that any person can do which does not in some degree "interfere with the enjoyment of life or property" of other persons. The very act of breathing consumes oxygen. In our opinion the word "unreasonably" as used in Section 3(b) was intended to introduce into the statute something of the objective quality of the common law, and thereby exclude the trifling inconvenience, petty annoyance or minor discomfort. The word is used in a similar sense in the disorderly conduct statute. As used in this statute it removes the possibility that a defendant's conduct may be measured by its effect upon those who are inordinately timorous or belligerent. This is the meaning that was given to the word "unreasonably" in the *Incinerator* case when the appellate court referred to "a substantial interference with the enjoyment of life and property."

The penalty of $3,000 was imposed after hearings which revealed that the respondents seriously interfered with the enjoyment of life and property in ways that could reasonably have been prevented. The Board did not abuse its discretion in fixing that fine.

In our opinion the determination of the Board was correct, and the judgment of the appellate court is reversed.

Agricultural producers must recognize that large livestock enterprises and residential developments simply do not mix. Furthermore, when the two come in conflict, the livestock enterprise often loses. Perhaps the best protective action that livestock producers can take to prevent conflict over odors is to locate in areas that are remote from other residential developments and to encourage the development of land use controls that will preserve the agricultural character of that area. In addition, agricultural producers may find that the best defense against an air pollution complaint from persons already located in the vicinity is a "good-neighbor" policy.

Health Hazards

Not all air pollution problems in the agricultural sector are odor-related. In some cases, agricultural activities can produce air pollution that constitutes a health hazard. In particular, discharges of organic compounds and particulate matter can be troublesome. The following discussion describes how one state has regulated these kinds of discharges.

Stationary Sources—Particulate Matter. The Illinois air pollution control regulations set forth limitations on the amount and types of contaminants that may be emitted into the air from sources that are stationary and not self-propelled, e.g., a grain dryer. One type of contaminant specifically regulated is particulate matter, e.g., dust and grit. The regulations limit the number of pounds of particulate matter that may be emitted in any hour, depending upon the weight of material processed during that period. These regulations apply to grain handling and grain drying operations, unless an operator decides to comply with other regulations concerned specifically with such activities.

The regulations are concerned with grain handling and grain drying operations. However, there are two types of agricultural equipment totally exempt from all regulations—portable grain handling equipment and one-turn storage space. All nonexempt grain handling and grain drying operations, regardless of their size, must implement and follow certain "housekeeping practices," such as cleaning air pollution and dust control filters. In addition to this requirement, certain large operations are required to obtain an operating permit from the Illinois Environmental Protection Agency. This requirement applies only if the grain handling operation's annual throughput exceeds 300,000 bushels. A permit is required for grain dryers only when its manufacturer's rated capacity exceeds 750 bushels per hour at 5 percent moisture extraction. In effect, these two provisions exempt most farming operations.

Organic Matter. A second type of regulated contaminant is organic material, i.e., a chemical compound of carbon. It is unlawful to cause or allow the loading of volatile organic material, such as motor fuels, into any stationary tank with a storage capacity of over 205 gallons, unless the tank is equipped with a submerged loading pipe or equivalent device. These devices prevent the escape of vapors from the fuel that occurs in the natural evaporation process. This rule includes all organic materials and not necessarily just volatile ones, but unless an odor nuisance exists, the requirement applies only to the latter.

Other types of regulated contaminants also exist in Chapter 2 of the Illinois Pollution Control Board Rules and Regulations.

Mobile Sources. Another section of the air pollution regulations affecting agriculture involves emission standards for mobile sources such as tractors, trucks, and cars. It is unlawful to fail to maintain in good working order, to remove, or to cause to be inoperative any pollution control device on a motor vehicle. Also, all motor vehicles shall not have any visible emissions of smoke. However, a different rule covers diesel engines.

Open Burning.   Open burning is another area of the air pollution regulations affecting agriculture. In general, the regulations prohibit the open burning of matter, but certain exemptions are made, providing that the burning does not cause air pollution. Whether matter may be openly burned depends on the type of waste it is and other relevant factors. The types of wastes are classified into three groups—agriculture, landscape, and domicile waste.[38]

9.4 NOISE POLLUTION

At the turn of the century, Robert Koch, the Nobel laureate who worked to control contagious disease, wrote: "The day will come when men will have to fight noise as inexorably as cholera and plague." Robert Koch was, indeed, a man of foresight, for in recent years we have witnessed noise—unwanted sound—increasing at an alarming rate. The impact of noise goes well beyond mere unpleasantness, stress, and other psychic effects. It may cause serious physiological effects on the human body, ranging from deafness to enhanced risk of cardio-vascular disease or alteration of fetal nervous systems.

To help combat the problems of noise pollution, legislation has been enacted at both the state and federal levels of government. The federal Noise Control Act of 1972[39] required the administrator of the Environmental Protection Agency to establish noise emission standards for newly manufactured products such as vehicles, construction equipment, and other machinery. The act also required the administrator to promulgate noise criteria reflecting all the identifiable effects of different quantities and qualities of noise on public health or welfare. Individual states and local governments, however, retained the primary responsibility for setting and enforcing limits on environmental noise. The following discussion illustrates how one state has responded to the need for increased noise control.

Noise pollution in Illinois is primarily governed by the Pollution Control Board's regulations.[40] The noise control regulations classify land according to its various uses. Noise is regulated on the basis of the classification of land from which the noise is emitted, e.g., industrial, and the classification of the receiving land, e.g., residential. As a general rule, the maximum intensity of noise received by residential property is lower than the maximum intensity permitted on business or industrial property.

---

[38] Agriculture wastes include any refuse produced on a farm or ranch by crop and livestock production practices, such as seed bags, cartons, dry bedding, structural materials, and crop residues. It does not include garbage (refuse resulting from the handling, preparation, and consumption of food), dead animals, and landscape wastes. *Landscape wastes* are defined as any vegetable or plant refuse, except garbage and agriculture waste. Examples of landscape wastes are trees, tree trimmings, branches, stumps, brush, weeds, grass, shrubbery, and yard trimmings. *Domicile wastes* include any refuse generated on a single family residence as a result of domiciliary activities, except landscape waste, garbage, and trade waste. It should be noted that there is an exception to the general rule for the open burning of leaves. The open burning of leaves is permitted unless prohibited by local ordinance, or unless the Illinois Pollution Control Board has restricted or prohibited such burning in a specific geographic area.

[39] Pub. L. No. 92-574, 86 Stat. 1234 (codified in 42 U.S.C. §§ 4901–4918).

[40] Ch. 8, ILLINOIS POLLUTION CONTROL BOARD RULES AND REGULATIONS.

Similarly, lower levels are required at night-time than during the day.

The noise regulations do not directly affect agriculture and related activities, because a specific exception is provided in the regulations. That exemption states that the regulations controlling noise "shall not apply to sound emitted from lawn care maintenance equipment and agricultural field machinery used during daytime hours. For purposes of this sub-section, grain dryers operated off the farm shall not be considered agricultural field machinery."[41] It should be noted that to be excepted from the noise limitations, grain dryers must be operated on the farm. Furthermore, this exception covers only daytime operations.

COUNTRY ELEVATOR: NOISE POLLUTION

ENVIRONMENTAL PROTECTION AGENCY v. TABOR AND CO.
Illinois Pollution Control Board, 1976
PCB 75–89, 23 Opinions 85

Respondent has an elevator in Tallula, Illinois. Tallula is a village of approximately 650 people located in Menard County. The elevator has throughput of over a million bushels of grain per year. Tabor and Company leased the elevator in 1971 and purchased the elevator for $225,000 in 1972. The drying season when the noise problem arises is from October through December.

In the complaint the Agency alleges violation of Rule 202. Rule 202 deals with noise being emitted from a class "C" land use (industrial) to a class "A" land use (residential). The Regulations designate land activities by means of numerical codes. It is Respondent's contention that the code has no classification for country grain elevators and that the Tabor elevator is unclassified and without regulation. The Board finds this argument to be without merit. Class "C" generally denotes industrial use. All agriculture and agricultural related activities are classified as "C" land uses. Codes 811 through 829 are agriculture or agricultural related activities. Under the latter category are included ginning, milling, shelling, baling, threshing and all other agricultural processing services. Although grain elevators are not specifically listed they would be included in "other agricultural processing services."

Respondent further contends that the receiving property is not land of class "A" use. The chief complainant to the Agency in this case was Joseph Feagans. Mr. Feagans runs a two-way radio business in a separate building at the rear of his house. The noise caused him to move his service area to the front of the house. Respondent contends that because of Mr. Feagans' business his property is a class "B" land use and is not covered by Regulation 202. The Board rejects this contention. At the time of adoption of the Noise Regulations, the Board recognized in its adopting opinion that "land use is not necessarily co-extensive with land ownership." Included as an

---

[41] *Id.* at Rule 208 (c).

example was a high rise apartment building, "where the apartments themselves are class A uses while ground level businesses are class B uses. In the present situation Feagans' business is class B but his residence is class A. It should also be noted that the Feagans are surrounded on all sides but one, the northwest where the Tabor elevator is, by other residences or class A uses. Thus Feagans' property would come under the "C to A" classifications of Rule 202. The Agency did find that the noise emitted from Respondent's elevator constituted a violation of Rule 202. We agree.

In determining what if any penalty should be assessed the Board must consider the factors listed in Section 33(c) of the Act. First to be considered is the character and degree of the injury. That injury has and does occur from noise was acknowledged by the General Assembly in Section 23 of the Act. Noise can cause hearing losses, both temporary and permanent. Noise can interfere with speech, be annoying and affect the mental and motor performance of individuals. The Feagans testified concerning the interference with their lives mostly in terms of loss of sleep and annoyance as did several other citizens of Tallula. The irritation and annoyance to the personal well being of the citizens of Tallula living close to the elevator is quite high during the three months of the drying season.

During this time of annoyance is also when the grain elevator with the dryer is of the most value to the farming community within the five mile radius of Tabor and also to the citizens of Tallula who work at the elevator and provide services to the farmers of the area. Farmers need ready access to elevators to allow them to harvest in good weather conditions and to store their grain safely. The grain is harvested at various moistures and must be dried sufficiently to avoid growth of molds and fungi. During the harvesting season a dryer may have to run continually to allow farmers to store all they can while good weather prevails. It is apparent that this function is of extreme importance to a small rural village such as Tallula. The importance of Tabor to the community is further documented by the 268 signatures on a petition requesting the Board not to impair the functioning of Tabor elevator.

The Board does find Respondent in violation of Rules 102 and 202 of the Noise Regulations and Section 24 of the Act. In considering a penalty it is clear that there has been injury to the citizens of Tallula in dealing with the effects of the noise. However, it is also clear that the elevator is of great importance of the community. Respondent has investigated and gone ahead with measures to abate the problem.

The Board notes that Tabor sought aid in noise abatement from the Brunswick Corporation, Fansteel, the Aeroglide Company and the George A. Rolfes Company. Only the George A. Rolfes Company made an offer which was accepted with alacrity.

The elevator has spent, or contracted to expend, well over $130,000 in an effort to reduce noise and emissions from its elevator. Since these monies were apparently expended as soon as management was convinced such expenditures would offer relief, the Board does not find Respondent unduly dilatory.

The good faith shown by Respondent and the expenditures made to achieve compliance without increasing capacity or productivity, and the fact that environmental harm has been minimized, convinced the Board that a penalty would not, in this case, aid enforcement.

It is the Order of the Pollution Control Board that:

1.   Tabor and Company is found to have been in violation of Rules 102 and 202 of the Noise Regulations and Section 24 of the Act.
2.   Tabor and Company shall cease and desist from all future violations of the Regulations or Act.

9.5 MINERALS, TIMBER, AND OTHER RESOURCE USE PROBLEMS

Farmers and ranchers have genuine concern about other environmental issues such as mining, the exploration and extraction of oil and gas, the cutting of timber, and other activities pertaining to our natural resources. Farmers and ranchers are generally not the target of environmental regulations in these areas; however, agricultural producers are affected by these activities because of the potentially significant impacts of these activities upon agricultural lands. It will be helpful to note some of the legislation governing the exploitation of natural resources and also to identify ways in which agricultural producers can better protect the surface of their farming lands through private agreements. In particular, it will be useful to examine some of the legal issues concerning coal mining, oil and gas exploration and development,

the cutting of timber, and other resource problems.

Coal and the Agricultural Interest

The United States is witnessing a renewed interest in coal as a fuel. The depletion of domestic oil reserves and the uncertainty of supply from foreign sources coupled with the safety and environmental controversy surrounding nuclear power have caused this nation to take a second look at its abundant coal reserves. These reserves have been estimated to comprise at least a fifth to a sixth of the world's coal reserves. About an eighth of the United States has underlying coal, with the coal-bearing strata located in at least thirty-seven states.[42] Vast coal resources lie under much of the farmland and ranchland in America.

Farmers and ranchers have been selling or leasing their coal rights to coal companies for many years.[43] Many of these agreements have involved subsurface rights only. Con-

---

[42] J. A. SIMON AND M. E. HOPKINS, GEOLOGY OF COAL 20 (1973).

[43] At common law, a mineral estate could be severed from the fee, either by granting the general estate and reserving the mineral rights or by granting only the mineral estate. See, e.g., Jilek v. Chicago, Wilmington & Franklin Coal Company, 382 Ill. 241, 47 N.E. 2d 96 (1943); Uphoff v. Trustees of Tuffs College, 351 Ill. 146, 184 N.E. 213 (1932). See generally 54 AM. JUR. 2d Sec. 103, 108, 120 (1971).

sequently, some farmers were not too concerned about the price they received for such rights, tending to view any payment received as an added bonus, no matter what the price. Many of these same farmers have not been sufficiently aware of the consequences of the sale or lease, such as potential damage to the surface from the underground mining operations, and of the meaning of a clause waiving their rights to collect for surface damages.[44]

Other farmers have been deeply concerned about the impact of coal mining activities upon the surface—either because underground mining was contemplated and the farmers were aware of the potential subsidence problems or because surface mining was to take place with the obvious disturbance to the land surface.

Agriculture and Underground Mining. A landowner may be able to include a number of desirable provisions in the sale or lease of the mineral estate. The amount of compensation received is the most obvious one. Unfortunately, an individual landowner is in a very weak position to demand higher compensation than that being offered. If the landowner does not sell, the coal company may simply mine around the land. In such a case, the holdout coal probably never will be mined, because a new coal company

would not be likely to have the vast acreage needed to justify the expense of bringing in equipment and sinking a new shaft at a small site.

As a rule, a few initial acquisitions in a coal bed tend to give the first coal company in the development a virtual monopoly over the entire area, especially if the initially purchased tracts formed columns or rows through the area. Such initial acquisitions make it very difficult for a competing coal company to acquire a sufficient block of relatively contiguous acreage for development, unless the initial purchaser is willing to transfer its interest to the second company.

Perhaps as a result of the rather weak bargaining position of individual landowners, royalties received by individual landowners have been substantially less than those demanded by the federal government. Many individual landowners receive royalties approximating 3 percent of the value of the coal, whereas the federal government demands a royalty of at least 8 percent of the value of coal extracted from federal lands by underground mining.[45] In an effort to improve their bargaining position, landowners in some states have formed cooperative organizations to negotiate the sale or lease of coal.[46]

---

[44] Absent such a disclaimer, a mining company which damages the soil by removing its subjacent support is liable to the owner of the surface estate without regard to the degree of care with which the minerals were removed. *See* Jilek v. Chicago, Wilmington & Franklin Coal Co., 382 Ill. 241, 47 N.E. 2d 96 (1943); Ciuferi v. Bullock Mining Co., 332 Ill. App. 1, 73 N.E. 2d 855 (1947). However, the owner of the surface estate may, by deed conveying mineral rights or by separate contract, agree to waive and release all damages caused by loss of subjacent support; and the waiver or release of this nature is not against public policy and will be fully enforced if the agreement is otherwise binding. Mason v. Peabody Coal Co., 320 Ill. App. 350, 51 N.E. 2d 285 (1943); Wesley v. Chicago,

Wilmington & Franklin Coal Co., 221 Ill. App. 427 (1920). If such waivers are aptly worded, they can be binding on future surface owners. Therefore, the owner of the surface estate must be cognizant of any releases or reservations of this nature made by anyone in the chain of title.

[45] 43 C.F.R. § 3473.3-2 (a)(3); 44 Fed Reg. 42,584, 42,648 (July 17, 1979). The regulation provides: "A lease [for federally owned coal] shall require payment of royalty of not less than 8 percent of the value of the coal removed from an underground mine, except that the authorized officer may determine a lesser amount, but in no case less than 5 percent if conditions warrant."

[46] *See* Uchtmann, *Coal, Farmers, and Collective Sale of Mineral Rights*, 17 ILL. AGR. ECON. 1 (1977).

Other provisions which a landowner may desire to have included in the mineral deed or lease include limiting the sale or lease of rights to a specified mineral, such as "coal and the integral minerals of it," rather than transferring the rights to all minerals—coal, oil, gas, gravel, and so on. In fact, the description of the mineral estate may be limited to a particular seam of coal in order to prevent any misunderstanding.[47]

The scope of the coal company's rights in mining the coal can also be specified and limited where desirable. Where some surface will be needed for roads, reservoirs, cleaning plants, and the like, a farmer should get at least a fair rental for temporary use, or a fair market price where the surface use will be perpetual—for example, where rock refuse and gob material are deposited as an incident of the cleaning process. The rental or fair market value for perpetual use of the surface should be paid in addition to compensation for the actual sale or lease of the mineral. In many instances, farmers and ranchers prefer to specify that any use of the surface will be prohibited unless a separate agreement regarding surface use is consummated.

A clause providing for a waiver of damages in the mineral deed or lease would be undesirable to the farmer. For example, many "form" leases or deeds contain provisions whereby all rights to damages occasioned by the mining and removal of coal are waived. Although some damages are foreseeable and may not be great, other damages, such as damages from subsidence, are not as predictable and generally should not be waived.

Clearly, the sale or lease of coal is an event that should not be taken lightly. It is an event that generally happens only once in a landowner's lifetime. It is an event that can have substantial impact upon the surface of the land. Prudence demands that landowners seek out competent legal assistance before any agreements concerning the sale or lease of coal are consummated. Regrettably, far too few landowners have followed this very simple rule.

Surface Mining.   Historically, an outright sale of the fee simple estate has preceded surface mining activity, at least on privately owned lands. With the advent of stricter reclamation laws, however, has come an increasing interest in mineral leases. Landowners who enter into mineral leases providing for the surface mining of coal should consider a reclamation clause that contains a covenant providing how the surface will be cleaned up and restored, or that "the lessee shall comply with all applicable laws, rules and regulations of the State and United States governments relating to such mining operations." Failure to comply with state reclamation acts generally results in the forfeiture of a bond to the state, but state law generally does not provide for compensation to the surface owner. Thus, the landowner, also may want a separate bond or security to reinforce this duty of the lessee. Landowners should also consider other lease provisions required by the federal government on federally owned lands.[48]

Under the Surface Mining Control Reclamation Act of 1977,[49] the primary governmental responsibility for control-

---

[47] Coal seams are identified by a number that is sometimes preceded by a geographic point, e.g., Herrin (No. 6) coal. Seams with lower numbers are older; those with higher numbers are relatively younger and occur above the lower-numbered seams, as one observes a cross-section of the coal-bearing rock formations. The geographic point represents a location where the seam can be readily observed near Herrin, Illinois; however, that seam extends under much of the surface of the state.

[48] See 43 C.F.R. § 3473 et. seq.; 44 Fed. Reg. 42,584, 42,606. (July 17, 1979).

[49] Surface Mining Control and Reclamation Act, Pub. L. No. 95-87, 91 Stat. 448 (codified in 30 U.S.C.A. § 1201 et seq., 1977).

ling surface mining rests with the states which were authorized to assume exclusive jurisdiction by submitting a state program to the newly created Office of Surface Mining Reclamation. The act also established reclamation standards to be effective until final adoption of a state or federal program.

The act established minimum environmental protection performance standards which required operators to (1) restore land to the original contour and to support the same use or a higher use than the land use prior to mining; (2) stabilize areas to control erosion and pollution; (3) separate, preserve, and restore topsoil, and take special precautions with prime farmland to maintain a comparable and uniform root zone; (4) create water impoundments where necessary; (5) minimize disturbances to the prevailing hydrologic balance by keeping acids and other toxic materials out of drainage systems and restoring recharge capacity of mined areas; (6) seal auger holes to prevent drainage; (7) stabilize waste piles to assure a final contour compatible with the natural surroundings; (8) refrain from surface mining within 500 feet of an underground mine; (9) construct access roads to prevent erosion, pollution, and damage to water flow; (10) blast only if adequate notice is given to the local government and residents, if a log is kept of all blasting done for 3 years, and if a preblasting survey is conducted if requested; (11) establish a permanent vegetative cover and assume responsibility for revegetation for 5 years, after the last year in which revegetation is complete; (12) protect off-site areas from slides and other damage due to operations; (13) dispose spoil to prevent mass movement and spoil erosion.[50]

Oil and Gas Leasing— the Agricultural Interest

All parties to an oil and gas lease view development as the ultimate goal. To this end, a lease should permit the oil operator freedom to carry out an efficient exploration and drilling program. However, such freedom should be tempered by the interests of the landowner and, to some extent, of society in preserving the surface for agricultural production. Also, as a matter of equity, the landowner should be adequately protected from drainage by wells on neighbors' lands.

Selecting an operator to develop the oil and gas is an important decision. An owner who has desirable land for leasing should not lease prematurely, because the result may be speculation instead of legitimate development. The landowner is often injured by speculation because of an overriding interest for the speculator. If the override is large, it may cause the well to be abandoned before the oil is exhausted, because production will become uneconomical at an earlier date. Usually a landowner will receive the best return by leasing to a reputable operator who intends to drill promptly.

To assure the oil operator's good faith in drilling operations, the landowner should make regular inspections and inquiries at

---

[50] The act also provides that the Secretary of the Interior will promulgate rules and regulations to control the surface effects of underground coal mining. Minimum standards include requiring operators to (1) adopt measures to prevent subsidence and maintain value of surface lands; (2) seal all openings no longer needed; (3) stabilize waste piles to protect water quality and to assure that the final contour is compatible with natural surroundings; (4) stabilize and revegetate the site; (5) protect from offsite damage, fire hazards, hydrologic imbalance and disturbance; (6) use the best technology to minimize disturbances to fish, wildlife, and related environmental values.

the drilling site and should have access to all logs and other information concerning the well or be furnished with a copy of such records. Most operators are willing to furnish this information voluntarily, but it is advisable to insert a clause in the lease allowing these rights to the landowner.

Lease forms are usually preprinted, and most of them are called "Producers 88" leases. Many problems have arisen from the use of what appear to be standard lease forms. Although there is a considerable degree of uniformity in the provisions of these leases, substantial differences do appear. The landowner and oil operator should negotiate both because of the differences in fine print and because each leasing situation involves individual preferences.

These variations make it essential that a farmer consult an attorney when considering an oil and gas lease. Still, farmers should understand the document they are to sign, the effect it will have on their use of the surface, and their position if oil or gas is found. The following discussion briefly explains oil and gas interests and the usual lease clauses, primarily from the farmer's viewpoint.

The Three Interests. The owners of the *mineral estate* have the right to any oil and gas. Because most landowners do not have the capital or experience necessary to carry out a drilling operation, they frequently contract to an oil operator the right to explore for and extract oil and gas. The oil operator agrees to pay all expenses and to pay a share, usually one-eighth of the oil and gas produced, to the landowner free of cost.

The share paid to the landowner is a *royalty*. The oil operator's share—often seven-eighths—must pay all expenses of exploring and producing the oil and gas. The oil operator's share is called the *working interest*.

Mineral Estate. Oil and gas are legally treated as minerals like limestone, sand, gravel, and coal. The owner of minerals may separate them from the surface either by conveyance in a mineral deed or by reservation of the minerals when land is sold. If no reservation is made at the time land is sold, the law presumes that the grantor conveyed all of the mineral interest.[51] The mineral deed or reservation may be either in perpetuity or for a term of years.[52]

Royalty. A *royalty* is the landowner's share as provided in the oil and gas lease. All or part of the royalty may be sold and conveyed by the landowner. It is also possible to reserve a royalty interest when conveying land or minerals. In this case, the new owner of the land or minerals has the sole right to lease oil and gas rights, while the old owner has a share of any minerals that may be produced in the future. In this way, the power to lease can be kept in one person, while the right to the oil and gas produced can be shared.[53]

Working Interest. The working interest bears the entire cost of drilling and producing. It may be carved up by the grant or reservation of overriding royalties. The landowner who is in a strong bargaining position

[51] There is always the possibility that some prior owner may have reserved or sold a portion of the minerals.
[52] A common method is to reserve the minerals for a term of years and for so long thereafter as oil or gas is produced from the land. This method allows the person selling or reserving the minerals

to keep an interest and also assures that the minerals will eventually go to the person owning the surface when the term expires or production ceases.
[53] The person with the power to lease has the right to any lease bonus, but does not have the power to pool or unitize the royalty owner's interest.

is often able to demand an overriding royalty in addition to the standard one-eighth royalty. Usually the overriding royalty is some fraction, such as 1/32 of the 7/8 working interest, although it may be 1/32 of the total production of oil and gas. Where the mineral owner owns only a fraction of the minerals, the overriding royalty may be on the same fraction of the well as the owner's interest or on the entire well. An overriding royalty is also created when the person or company leasing land does not wish to develop the oil and gas and instead sells or "farms out" the lease, reserving an overriding interest. Overriding royalty does not share any of the costs of exploring and producing and differs from a royalty interest in that overriding royalty is carved out of the working interest, whereas a royalty interest is carved out of the mineral estate.

Power to Lease.   If the mineral estate has been divided, each owner usually becomes a tenant in common of an undivided interest in the minerals. All must sign a lease, but each is free to bargain for as large a cash bonus or overriding royalty as can be obtained.[54]   There is no compulsion for all to lease to the same oil operator, although it is generally advantageous to do so.

When the mineral estate is owned by several persons, there may be difficulty in getting them all to execute a lease; for example, if one of them has disappeared, is a minor, or refuses to execute, he or she cannot execute the lease. Some states have passed a law to protect the majority owners of the oil and gas from wells on adjoining land by permitting the owners of one-half or more of the oil and gas, or the owners of

leases covering one-half or more of the oil and gas under a tract, to petition the court for an order allowing them develop the oil and gas. All the owners, both known and unknown, are made parties to the action. If the petition is approved by the court, all nonsigning owners become participants in the lease.

Leasing becomes more complicated when land is subject to a life estate or is held by a trustee or guardian. Generally, a guardian or trustee needs a court order to be able to execute an oil and gas lease. Life tenants and remaindermen must usually join in executing an oil and gas lease. They may agree to apportion the proceeds in the lease or in a separate agreement.[55]

A farm tenant has a right to possess the surface. Although the law is not clear, a landlord might be held liable for damages to the crops of the tenant and for interference with the tenant's use of the surface by the oil and gas operator. If the agricultural lease has not reserved to the landlord the right to lease for oil and gas, the landlord should have the oil and gas lease made subordinate to the agricultural lease, or should insert a clause covering reimbursement to the tenant for any damage the tenant may sustain. The oil operator may then make an agreement with the farm tenant to enter upon the land to begin oil operations.

Leasing Separate Tracts.   When the mineral owners of several tracts join in a single oil and gas lease for a specified term and as long thereafter as oil or gas is produced, production from any part of the leased land will extend the term of the lease on the entire acreage. This rule probably ap-

---

[54] If the surface estate has been separated from the mineral estate, it is not necessary that the surface owner sign the lease.

[55] In the absence of agreement, the law provides a formula for computing the share of each one.

plies even if the tracts are located several miles apart.[56]

As a general rule, using separate leases for each tract of land is preferable to leasing separate tracts on the same lease form.

Other Problems of Leasing. A problem often arises when one small producing well that has been kept in operation ties up a large body of land for years, because the landowners have not been able to prove that wells drilled in other locations would be commercial producers. This problem can be avoided by including provisions for a drilling program in the lease or by splitting the large tract into smaller tracts.[57]

There are three powers granted to the oil operator in the standard lease form that can easily be abused: (1) the right of operating conjointly with neighboring lands; (2) the right of pooling or unitization; and (3) the right of subsurface injection of brine, water, or gas for secondary recovery. All of these powers are often necessary, but the landowner may wish to restrict their use to protect his or her own interest. In order to get full protection the landlord could strike the right of conjoint operation and the right of pooling or unitization from the lease and provide that these powers and the power of secondary recovery be granted by separate agreement when and if they will be in the best interests of both parties.

Usual Lease Clauses of Special Interest. The *granting clause* describes the land leased and the purposes for which the premises may be used. The law implies that the lessee has the right to do whatever a reasonably prudent oil operator would do in the circumstances. A provision that the lessee may operate the land "alone or conjointly with neighboring lands" means that the lessee may build across the lessor's land roads and pipelines which may be used to operate the oil wells on an adjoining farm.[58] Other provisions may be inserted to include any small adjoining parcels which the lessor owns, or to permit the oil operator to drive the oil or gas to wells on adjoining land, without requiring counter-drainage.

The royalty, typically one-eighth of gross proceeds, will be stated in the *royalty clause*.[59]. A landowner in a strong bargaining position can increase this share by increasing the royalty or by taking an overriding interest.

The purpose of a *dry hole clause* is to relieve the operator of paying delay rental for a year after a dry hole is drilled. Generally, whenever a lease does not provide for delay rental, the dry hole clause should be stricken. A dry hole clause may be coupled with a clause providing for payment of rental to extend the life of the lease.

---

[56] This rule also applies to a mineral deed. For example, if the separate (or same) owners of two farms convey one-half of the oil and gas under both farms in one deed for 10 years and as long thereafter as oil and gas are produced, a producing well on the farm will extend the term on the other farm.

[57] For example, it could be required that, in the event of commercial production, a well be drilled every 6 months or that a minimum number be drilled during the basic lease term. Or a person desiring to lease 160 acres could give the oil operator four separate 40-acre leases. If separate leases were used and there was only production on one 40-acre plot, the other leases would lapse at the end of the lease period unless tested.

[58] In the absence of this clause, the oil operator does not have the right to use any land to operate an adjoining oil well. A clause providing for compensation for the use of the surface should be inserted in the lease.

[59] The royalty could be increased to a larger fraction, such as 5/32 or 3/16. (In situations where only one tenant in common is to receive a larger share, a separate document granting an overriding royalty might be preferable.)

When the lessor owns less than the entire estate being leased, a *lessee interest clause* is used to limit the royalty to the same proportion as that of the minerals the lessor owns. The lessor may request, pursuant to the *use of surface clause*, that the operator bury pipelines (below plow depth) and locate the structures necessary for operations so that they interfere minimally with the lessor's use and enjoyment of the property.[60]

To compensate for damage to the surface, a crop-damage clause has been used. Under common law, the oil operator is not liable for damages to the surface unless the operator is guilty of negligence or unless the operator uses more of the surface than is reasonably necessary.

A clause is often inserted which says that *commencing a well or commencing operations within the primary term extends the lease.* This clause requires only that the operations be commenced within the primary term. Actual drilling could be delayed if the delay was in good faith.

Timber and Other Natural Resources

Farmers, ranchers, and other private citizens own approximately 3 out of every 5 acres of America's commercial forestland, and they supply more than half of the wood used by industry. A variety of planning and managing assistance is available to these private woodland owners through programs funded by the state and federal governments. Farmers and ranchers should be aware of these assistance programs and of important provisions that may appear in cutting contracts between landowners and timber cutters. Some of the laws and regulations providing assistance to, and protec-

tion for, woodlot owners are noted below, in addition to information regarding cutting contracts.

State and Federal Assistance to Private Woodlot Owners. The Cooperative Forestry Assistance Act of 1978 consolidated and clarified several previously existing cooperative forestry assistance programs.[61] Under these cooperative state-federal programs, state foresters can provide private landowners with technical advice and assistance in the management of their forestland. This assistance includes advising landowners on multiple-use management plans, on the selection of trees for cutting, and on steps for improving the remaining stand and for reestablishing a stand of trees through planting or natural regeneration. Foresters also can assist landowners and loggers in the harvesting, processing utilization, and marketing of forest products.

Landowners are also provided with incentives to plant trees, perform timber stand improvement work, and perform other forest resource management activities. The incentives are generally in the form of cost-sharing programs for small forestland owners—including farmers, ranchers, recreation-home owners, and others.

Licensing and Bonding of Timber Buyers. Many states regulate timber buyers so as to provide additional protection to landowners who sell timber. The Illinois Timber Buyers Licensing Act, for example, provides that any person engaged in the business of buying timber shall obtain a license from the Department of Conservation.[62] Such persons are required to file a surety bond with the department. In the event the timber buyer fails to pay the timber grower for purchased timber or for legally determined

---

[60] Landowners must place a restrictive clause in the lease if they wish to control the proximity of wells to their house or barn.

[61] Pub. L. No. 95-313, 92 Stat. 365 (codified at 16 U.S.C. § 2101 *et seq.*).

[62] ILL. REV. STAT. ch. 111, § 701 *et seq.* (1979).

damages for timber wrongfully cut by the buyer, the bond is forfeited. The proceeds are first applied to any sums owed to the timber grower.

Timber Cutting Contracts. Timber cutting contracts provide an excellent opportunity for the landowner to avoid numerous problems. The contract should clearly identify the tract where cutting is to occur, the method of designating the particular trees to be cut, and the payment agreement. The contract may also specify a number of conditions such as access provisions; a final date for cutting and removing trees; protection for unmarked and young timber, including a method of determining damages if such trees are destroyed; risk of loss, if the trees are destroyed during the term of the agreement; and a way of handling disputes that might arise during the course of the cutting process. It is advisable that both the seller and the purchaser employ legal counsel to review the cutting contract prior to its endorsement.

9.6 UTILITY RIGHTS-OF-WAY[63]

The production of energy is an important concern of our nation. In addition to finding less expensive and more efficient energy supplies, the nation's energy industries are involved in planning efficient and inexpensive methods for transporting and distributing energy and energy resources. Currently, thousands of miles of pipelines and power lines crisscross the country for the distribution of oil, natural gas, petroleum products, and electricity. In order to acquire the land needed for pipelines and power lines, public utility companies purchase rights-of-way across private property. The public utility right-of-way is essentially an easement for the purposes of constructing and maintaining a utility line.

Landowners should have a basic understanding of the likely impacts of utility line construction and maintenance upon agriculture. Utility line installation usually will affect farming operations, such as the herding of livestock and the rotation of crops.[64] Land features and soil conditions may also be disturbed. Pipeline installation, and the installation of some electric poles, generally requires the cutting of drainage tiles. In addition, after a pipeline is installed, rocks usually move to the surface and disturb farming operations. Trees around power lines must be trimmed when necessary, and pipeline right-of-way must be kept clear of large foliage, such as trees, to protect the integrity of the pipeline and to make aerial inspection possible. The utility company may wish to defoliate the right-of-way by the aerial spraying of herbicides.

An understanding of the long-term effects of pipelines and power lines is also important. The long-term effects of pipelines include some interference with farming operations because of the test leads, markers, or other structures. Also, pipeline accidents are possible, even though properly maintained pipelines generally present very little risk. The long-term effects of electrical transmission lines include interference with field-work because of utility structures or the line itself, noise and interference with radio and television reception, and the potentially

---

[63] For an excellent discussion of general legal considerations surrounding utility rights of way acquisitions, *see* Uchtmann and Schreck *Representing the Farm Owner in Utility Right of Way Acquisitions*, 1978 So. ILL. U. LAW J. 365.

[64] Prior to the installation of the utility line, the utility company will survey the right-of-way and may plant survey stakes in the ground. The utility company may have to remove fences to gain access to the right-of-way, and if roads are unavailable, the utility company may have to cross cropland and pastureland.

harmful effects of electromagnetic induction in extra high voltage lines.[65] Scientists disagree as to the degree and significance of these effects, but some risk is clearly present.

Negotiating the Right-of-Way Contract

Landowners have an opportunity to assert their rights and protect their interest when the utility company first offers to negotiate a contract for the purchase of the right-of-way. The right-of-way contract provides landowners with the means of controlling the effects of the utility line on their property and of establishing the responsibilities of the utility company to protect the land and pay for damages. The utility company will usually provide the landowners with a standard form easement contract that describes the rights and responsibilities of both parties. In addition, the landowner can request that special clauses be added to the contract to take care of specific conditions, such as location, access, types of structures, land restoration, and payment of damages.

The typical easement contract provides the utility company with the right to construct, operate, maintain, repair, remove, and relocate the utility line. The utility company also has the right of access to the right-of-way for utility line purposes and the right to remove obstructions. The landowner has the right to use the right-of-way for all purposes that will not interfere with the utility line. The standard easement contract also provides that the utility company will compensate the landowner for damages caused by the utility line and the operations of the utility company.

The standard easement generally reflects the rights of both parties as dominant and servient owners. In addition, the utility company might include a clause that specifically limits certain activities of the landowner in the right-of-way strip, such as drilling a well or constructing a building. The utility company may also include provisions for constructing additional facilities or for obtaining additional space during construction.

Utilizing Other Forums

Generally, public utilities are regulated by special commissions within the various states. For example, public utilities in Illinois are regulated by the Illinois Commerce Commission. If a utility company wishes to construct a new pipeline or additional power lines in a new area, it generally must obtain permission from the commission. If the farm or ranch owner cannot reach a private agreement with the utility or if the owner believes that the utility line is unnecessary or the route is unreasonable, then the landowner can generally contest the utility company's petitions before the appropriate state commission. With the support and assistance of other landowners, and by proposing more reasonable routes, the landowner may be able to present a concerted and effective challenge in the commission proceedings.

Alternatively, the landowner may challenge the utility line in a condemnation suit. Although the utility company benefits from landowners' fear of condemnation, the costs, delays, and resulting community ill-

---

[65] See Davis, *Health and High Voltage*, SIERRA, 23–25 (July/Aug. 1978); Young, *Danger: High Voltage*, ENVIRONMENT, 16–20, 37–38 (May 1978); Miller & Kaufman *High Voltage Overhead*, ENVIRONMENT, at 6–15, 32–36 (Jan/Feb. 1978). For a comprehensive review of research and literature in this area, see A.R. SHEPPARD AND M. EISENBUD, BIOLOGICAL EFFECTS OF ELECTRIC AND MAGNETIC FIELDS OF EXTREMELY LOW FREQUENCY (1977). For a study of the impact of a 765 K V transmission line in rural Ohio, L. YOUNG, POWER OVER PEOPLE (paperback ed. 1974).

will make condemnation unattractive to the utility company as well as the farmer. However, the landowner should not be afraid of condemnation if it is necessary. The condemnation proceedings provide an additional opportunity to determine issues such as the reasonableness and the necessity of the proposed utility line. The proceedings defer the issue of fair compensation to a jury of one's peers, which will arrive at a lump-sum condemnation award. The landowner may sue in tort for damages later caused by the utility company's negligence.

STUDY QUESTIONS

1. What is the difference between "point" and "nonpoint" sources of pollution? What kinds of agricultural pollution fit into each category?
2. What are the national goals of water quality that were identified in the Water Pollution Control Act amendments of 1972?
3. What is the National Pollutant Discharge Elimination System, and how does it function? What kinds of agricultural enterprises require NPDES permits?
4. How are individual states involved in the regulation of water pollution?
5. What pollution problems are created by erosion?
6. Describe the goals and mechanics of "208 planning."
7. What are the origins and missions of soil and water conservation districts? How has the mission changed in recent years?

8. Compare and contrast the 1936 Standard State Soil Conservation District Law and the 1973 Model State Act for Soil Erosion and Sediment Control.
9. What legislation concerning air pollution has been promulgated by the federal government? The state governments?
10. Air pollution problems associated with agriculture involve both odors and health hazards. Discuss.
11. What generalizations can be made regarding the respective roles of federal and state governments in the control of water, air, and noise pollution?
12. What kind of lease provisions in an underground coal lease could help protect the agricultural interest?
13. What special agriculturally related problems are generated by surface mining? What is the nature of federal legislation designed to minimize these problems?
14. Regarding oil leases, what is the nature of the mineral estate, royalty, and working interest?
15. What typical oil lease clauses are of special interest to agriculture?
16. What kind of governmental assistance is available to private woodlot owners?
17. What kinds of protection may be available to woodlot owners in their dealings with timber buyers?
18. Describe the initial and long-term effects of power lines and pipelines on agricultural lands.
19. What opportunities are available to a landowner to help protect agricultural lands from the adverse effects of utility lines?
20. Is environmental regulation a help or a hindrance to agricultural producers?

10

Farm and Ranch Animals

Owing to certain characteristics of farm animals, a large body of "livestock law" has developed concerning trespass, fences, grazing, branding, marketing, diseases, injuries to persons, and many other problems. Many of these issues are discussed below. However, discussion of laws pertaining to the marketing or sale of livestock is contained in Chapter 12, and discussion of odor and livestock waste problems is contained in Chapters 7 and 9.

Ancient laws, particularly those of Babylonia, Greece, and Rome, contained many provisions on domestic animals. For example, the Code of Hammurabi, formulated about 2000 B.C., provided that cow doctors should receive compensation for their services only if an animal recovered, but should give the owner the value of the animal if it died; and the Code of Moses prescribed the death penalty for one whose bull kills a person, provided the owner is aware that this bull is "wont to push with its horns."

Livestock laws differ from state to state, owing largely to variations in the predominance of different kinds of livestock and to the manner in which they are handled. In the Western range country, laws on grazing and brands are important, whereas in the Corn Belt, laws on fences and animal trespass become more important.

10.1 RIGHTS IN ANIMALS AS PROPERTY

Generally

According to the common law, dogs and cats were never considered as property. Therefore, the usual rights in the case of theft and injury by others did not exist in owners of cats and dogs. This rule has now been changed, allowing a value to attach to such animals.

Captured wild animals are subject to property rights only so long as they are retained in confinement or are pursued and kept within the possibility of recapture. There is a theory that if a wild animal shows a will to return, or an *animus revertendi*, it can be retaken as the property of the owner.

Killing or mortally wounding, along with taming, confining, and domesticating, have generally been held sufficient acts to create a property interest in wild animals. One famous old case held that a fox hunter, who, with his hounds, had practically overtaken a fox, had no right against an interloper who happened along, shot the fox, and carried it away. The court said the hunter had never had the fox under control; consequently, it had never been his property.

All the useful domesticated farm animals are regarded as property and can be recovered wherever found, subject to laws on strays and animals at large.

In cases where domestic animals are made pregnant either by trespassing male animals or by trespassing of the dam, the offspring belongs to the owner of the dam—the expression of the rule being, "as her owner is the loser by her pregnancy, he ought to be the gainer by her brood."

Under rules developed at common law, bees were regarded as wild animals, and once they escaped from one person, were any other person's property. Because of the growth of the bee industry, a different rule now obtains, at least in those states where bees are economically important. So long as the bees can be found and identified, the right of the original owner will not be lost, regardless of where or when they swarm or on whose property they finally settle. Beekeepers are seldom liable for injury caused by their bees, because people are presumed to understand the nature of bees and are expected to conduct themselves accordingly. In the case of employees who are severely stung, liability would still not attach, unless the employer were negligent or subject to a state employer's liability law. In most cases, the employer would not be subject to the latter, since beekeeping qualifies as an agricultural pursuit under the agricultural exemption in such laws.

LARCENY

THE PEOPLE v. HERMENS
Supreme Court of Illinois, 1955
5 Ill. 2d 277, 125 N.E. 2d 500

Mr. Justice Maxwell delivered the opinion of the court:

Sam Hermens, plaintiff in error, Hal Griffith and Clarence Davis were, on March 5, 1954, indicted for the larceny of nine hogs from a farm in

Greene County. They were arraigned on March 19, 1954. Griffith pleaded guilty and was sentenced to the penitentiary for a term of three to five years. Davis pleaded guilty and applied for probation. A hearing on this application was held and the decision was pending at the time of plaintiff in error's trial. Plaintiff in error, hereinafter designated as defendant, pleaded not guilty, was tried by jury, convicted and sentenced to the penitentiary for a term of three to five years. He brings the cause here by writ of error.

On the night of February 17, 1954, nine hogs were taken from the uninhabited farm of one Ernie Ballard, were loaded into the car belonging to codefendant Davis, taken to Woodson, near Jacksonville, where they were sold by codefendant Griffith for the sum of $100. The defendant Hermens contends the evidence heard by the jury is not sufficient to show beyond a reasonable doubt that he participated in this larceny, and if he did, he was too intoxicated at the time to form the specific intent which is a necessary element of that crime.

This case involves three very bibulous miscreants and nine little pigs that illegally went to market. Alcohol, one of our best clients, attendance-wise, played the leading role, supported by the defendants, its puppets. The defendant Hermens testified that he and Mrs. Hermens spent the day of February 16 at their home drinking whiskey, wine and beer; that on the morning of the 17th they resumed this fascinating sport, after he had gone to town to replenish their fast shrinking supply, and on that day he consumed a quart of whiskey, a quart of wine and 18 bottles of beer. In the early afternoon Griffith and Davis arrived, apparently unheralded and without preconceived plan, bringing with them, at least in the unconsumed state, only a small contribution to the refreshment supply, insufficient to offset the increase in consumption engendered by the jolly fellowship of the occasion. So the four of them, in Davis's car, motored to town to replenish their spirits and brighten the spirits of the supplier.

While gay camaraderie and perfect harmony ruled the day on February 17, the dull and sober atmosphere of the court room, at Hermen's trial, completely destroyed the beautiful friendship and loyal devotion theretofore existing between the parties. As a consequence, we have difficulty in accurately narrating the subsequent events. According to the testimony of the Hermenses and their still-devoted friend, Griffith, they returned directly to the Hermens home, where Hermens, completely overcome by the affluent events of the day, passed out. But according to Davis, whose friendship was as brief as his acquaintance, they did not return directly to the Hermens home, but Hermens directed them to drive past the Ballard farm, not just because of his sentimental attachment for the place where he had lived as a child, but to view some readily marketable shoats residing there in a temptingly unprotected environment. Mrs. Hermens did not consciously participate in this inspection expedition, as she slept peacefully in the rear seat of the Davis car. At this point, to be fair with Mrs. Hermens, we should point out that she was enjoying the comforts of the back seat before and not after the shoats. Unfortunately, as subsequent developments proved, the parties failed to perceive that one of the nominated quarry had some very distinctive marking, as described by the owner "his ears were red and there was a little red back of his tail and the rest of him was all white." We are unable to locate the "the red back of his tail," and still remain on the same pig, but for our purpose here the red ears will suffice. But to get back to the Davis version of our story, having completed their preliminary survey for the contemplated project, they returned to the Hermens home for a refreshing interlude, awaiting nightfall. Then under cover of darkness, Davis, Griffith and Hermens stealthily returned for a more intimate association with the shoats. Having previously reconnoitered the physical surroundings and selected their choice of pigs, according to ease of handling and suitability for their transportation facilities, they parked their car close to the fence at a corner of the pig lot. They then herded the desired number of their unsuspecting quarry into this corner and completed their capture by seizing them, one at a time, by the extremities which the housewife would best recognize as being the shanks of the hams, passed them over the fence to the one who gently, or otherwise, deposited them through the back window in the back part of or on the back seat of the automobile, in such manner that those previously placed there did not escape. On the ride to the town where the prospective new owner resided, the three culprits occupied the front seat of the car with their load of pay dirt in the rear. The record, at least, is silent during this ride. The Davis version of the story then leaves him and Hermens sitting, unoffendingly, in a tavern until Griffith returns, sans shoats, but with a $100 check. Then, being one or two o'clock in the morning, with a bright and flush tomorrow to look forward to, the three of them procured a room from a not-too-discriminating hotel clerk, who "wouldn't have rented them a room if they had been drunk" but was willing to overlook that they smelled like whiskey but "no more than usual" and the fact that their clothes weren't "very clean," and retired, registered as "Hal Griffith and guests." Arousing about 8:00 a.m. on the morning of the eighteenth, their first stop was a tavern in the vicinity of the hotel for a liquid breakfast. There they found a trusting bartender willing to exchange some custom and cash for the check. En route to Hermens' home, says Davis, Griffith divided the spoils, giving him $25 and laying some currency of an unknown amount on Hermens' knee. Davis couldn't say that Hermens took it but he didn't find it in the car. After stopping at a garage to get the high gear of their car back in operation, having tired of traveling in second gear, they proceeded to Hermen's home where Sam got it over with as Mrs. Hermens "gave Sam cain for being out all night." Sam's reaction or explanation is not in the record although there was some questioning by counsel bearing the implication that Mrs. Hermens brandished the domestic butcher knife. The principals did not regard this as serious, nor shall we. Sometime during the morning, between drinks, Griffith suggested to Davis that his car was "a sight." Davis said he drove it across the road from Hermens' home, parked it near a schoolhouse and attempted to wash it out. Apparently giving up in despair, he abandoned it there and hitched a ride to the county seat. Arriving there about noon, still "loaded," both financially and otherwise, he spent the rest of the day touring the taverns of the town, he didn't know how many but he guessed all of them. About 11:00 p.m., with his guilty conscience becoming more than the finer traits of his character could bear, he sought sanctuary at the county jail where the sheriff put him up for the night. This new association and law-abiding influence resulted in full repentance for his sins and conscience-relieving confession signed and delivered into the hands of the sheriff on February 20. The day he testified in court was the forty-fourth day he was enjoying as the sheriff's guest.

There was other evidence offered by the state, including the stark, mute testimony of the pigs. Since these famous creatures are going to become a part of the permanent archives of this court by reason of the six beautiful photographs attached to the record of this case, and will remain here as a precedent for the guidance of all the courts and counsel in all future pig cases in this state, we should relate their further thrilling experiences after the midnight ride in the back seat of the Davis car. Their new owner, temporarily at least, was a local stock dealer and auctioneer residing in Jacksonville who apparently had no qualms about making a profitable deal late at night, so he willingly exchanged his $100 check for the nine little shoats. By coincidence he had an auction sale over at Mt. Sterling in Brown County the following day, so he took the shoats along and found a new owner who unknowingly gave him a $62 profit on the deal. But the stock dealer hadn't permanently parted company with the little pigs that had gone to market. About a week later, their first owner and the sheriff, on the trail of the lost animals, called upon him to take him to the farm of the purchaser. And when the first owner saw that little shoat with the red ears, and when he spoke to them and they came running to him, he knew his lost prodigals had been found. Upon their return home they were photographed, in six different poses, both with and without a group of their brothers and sisters. While these photographs are not in color, to show the identifying red ears, they are not without color, dramatically. In addition to the aesthetic and artistic value which they add to the record, their evidentiary value, cursorily inconsequential, is subtly inferential. A lingering concentration, such as true art deserves, reveals that these pigs appear just as well fed and contented as their stay-at-home kin; nor is there anything in their forms, figures or faces indicating that they possess more daring or adventurous spirits. Consequently, any possible inference that they voluntarily ran away from home, either because of mis-treatment or a spirit of wanderlust, is effectively dispelled.

The confusion resulting from the various terms used by the witnesses was satisfactorily cleared away when the state introduced the testimony of an experienced pig grower who stated that "swine," "hogs," "pigs" and "shoats" were all appropriate designations for these little creatures, thus legally estab-lishing, at long last, the oft-heard profundity that "pigs is pigs."

The owner of the pigs, the sheriff, the stock dealer, the hotel clerk, and the state police officer who got wind of the Davis car and its tell-tale con-tents, all testified as to the parts they played and the State's Attorney rested.

Hermens testified in detail as to what he didn't know about any pig larceny; that he went to sleep at home about 5:00 p.m. in the afternoon of the seventeenth and awakened in a hotel room in Jacksonville on the morning of the eighteenth. Anything in between was impenetrable blackness. He denied the preliminary reconnoitering expedition, denied that he ever had any intent to commit larceny, and asserted, somewhat convincingly, that he was mentally incapable of having any intent to do anything. Mrs. Hermens denied the afternoon ride past the pig farm, never heard anyone talk about any pigs, and didn't even think her husband had spent the night in Jacksonville since he was in bed at home at 7:00 a.m. on the morning of the eighteenth. A tavern owner found Hermens too drunk about 3:00 p.m. on the seventeenth to buy a drink at his tavern, and a barmaid had him falling off a stool in a tavern where she worked in Roodhouse about 9:00 or 10:00 p.m. on the same day. Hal Griffith, testifying as a court witness at the request of defendant, claimed all the credit for locating the pigs, their asportation and conversion. Davis aided and abetted the asportation, but Hermens was at home asleep so far as he knew until he and Davis went for him after the pigs had been put to bed, and took him along to Jacksonville to do a little drinking.

The defendant tells us a great wrong has been done him by the court and jury, who should never have believed Davis's testimony. Davis, says defendant, is a tramp, a confessed thief, a traitorous liar against his drinking pal to get leniency for himself, and, worst of all, he's a drunkard. Davis admitted on cross-examination that he had just come to Illinois on February 14 to visit his brother-in-law; that he had two dollars in his pocket when he came but was broke on the seventeenth; that he had been drunk for three weeks prior to the seventeenth; and he admitted that he had pleaded guilty to this crime, had applied for probation, that this application was pending at the time and that he was "really hoping" that he would get a break from the state for his testimony against Hermens. He did—six months in the penal farm, for what offense the record doesn't show, as contrasted with the three to five years in the penitentiary meted out to his two trusting pals. Defendant further complains that he was not given sufficient time to prepare for trial, the court erred in instructing the jury as to the defense of drunkenness and the court erred in permitting the State's Attorney to cross-examine the character witnesses as to other dishonest acts.

As we view this evidence, there was no reliable corroboration of Davis's testimony that Hermens participated in this larceny other than the inferences which might be drawn from the relative knowledge of the parties involved. The testimony of the hotel clerk is not impressive. He said the three men's clothing was dirty, and that Davis and Hermens were dirtier than Griffith, who admittedly handled the hogs twice, in loading and unloading them. The clerk further qualified his statement by saying Davis and Hermens were dirtier because they were dressed in coveralls while Griffith was not. Hermens explained the clerk's testimony that they were dirty, saying "Well maybe he thinks clothes like I wear is dirty around a hotel." The mere statement that their clothes were dirty, with no description of the degree or nature of the dirt, and no testimony of mud or odor does not corroborate testimony that Hermens had handled these hogs.

At common law the uncorroborated testimony of an alleged accomplice was sufficient to warrant a conviction if it satisfied the jury beyond a reasonable doubt. This rule has always been followed and has frequently been pronounced in Illinois. It is, however, universally recognized that such testimony has inherent weaknesses, being testimony of a confessed criminal and fraught with dangers of motives such as malice toward the accused, fear, threats, promises or hopes of leniency, or benefits from the prosecution, which must always be taken into consideration.

Under the circumstances of this case, where the jury had the difficult question of choosing between the testimony of Davis and that of Griffith and defendant, we think that eliciting from the character witnesses such statements as "I heard he done some dishonest acts" and "He's been in trouble before but I don't know what for" were highly prejudicial and may have influenced the jury in reaching their verdict of guilty.

Because the testimony of the accomplice Davis lacks material corroboration, is denied by the defendant and another accomplice whose testimony is not such as to be unworthy of belief, and because of the prejudicial statements about other offenses, we are not satisfied that defendant's guilt has been established beyond a reasonable doubt. The judgment is reversed and the cause is remanded for a new trial.

Dogs and Cats

A's Doberman one morning took a long walk during which the following events transpired: He trampled and completely ruined a petunia bed under B's window; he killed C's cat; he growled at D, an elderly lady, causing her to step off the sidewalk and sprain her ankle; he chased E's sheep into a corner of the pasture, where one lamb was trampled and killed. While the dog was crossing F's property, F shot him and broke the dog's left front paw, after which the Doberman hobbled home.

Two days after this eventful morning, E saw the dog lying just outside A's yard by the roadside and shot and killed him.

What causes of action exist—by whom, against whom, and for what? Here is how these questions might be answered, unless affected by state law or local ordinances.

B can recover damages for the loss of her petunia bed. Dogs and cats are not by common law denied the right to roam, but if they damage anyone's property during their excursions, the owner may be held liable for the damage caused; and if a dog or cat engaged in a series of damaging visitations to one's property, he or she could get a restraining order compelling the owner to keep it off the property. The owner of a dog or cat with a communicable disease can likewise be held liable for spreading the disease to the animals of others—or to human beings—if the owner knew or had reason to know the dog or cat had such a disease and still did not confine it.

C can recover for the loss of his cat if it was killed on C's premises. Otherwise it would be difficult to make a case, because dogs and cats are presumed to act the way nature ordained while in each other's presence; and if death or damage results, an owner could be held liable only if the owner were personally negligent—or had arranged the fight! The same principles are also held for dog versus dog. Of course, there are always seeming exceptions. The owner of a known vicious dog might very well be held responsible for the dog's damage to other people's dogs and cats—but this would imply negligence on the part of the owner of the vicious dog, so the rule still holds.

D could probably recover—providing the dog's growling was the proximate cause of her injury. Detailed facts would need to be adduced about the circumstances surrounding the incident—the intensity of the growl, the dog's distance from the woman, the sudden appearance of the dog, and similar data. Were these facts such as to produce this effect on persons of this age? It is a harder question than the petunia bed. There are more variables. Certainly, if a dog or a cat attacks a person going peaceably about his or her business, the odds are in favor of recovery despite the common-law theory that it takes a first bite to inform the owner that the dog will bite. Some states have by statute changed the common-law "one-bite" theory to liability for the first bite when the injured party is not a trespasser and has not been negligent (teasing the dog, for example).

E can recover for his lamb. Also, had he been present, he could under the law of many states have pursued and killed the dog. Killing the dog 2 days later while the dog is lying peacefully on his owner's property is not permissible. The court would say E's remedy was against the owner for damages and not against the dog this long after the fact!

F had no right to shoot the dog. Only if the dog were injuring or killing his live-stock, threatening persons, or had the appearance of being rabid, could F resort to this expedient. None of these requirements were present in the above example. Cats no doubt enjoy this same immunity even more, since their ability to threaten or disturb and the likelihood of their being rabid are not so great. By this same token, we could assume also that the size and age of a dog would be material facts in cases where a claim is based on chasing livestock or threatening persons.

What is one's liability when a dog joins up with a pack of dogs and the pack inflicts damage? There is good authority that the liability is joint and several, and that if one is so unfortunate as to be the only identifiable owner of a member of the pack, that person can be sued for the whole damage.

In summary, unless this is changed by state law or local ordinance, a dog or cat owner is: (1) not bound to confine pets; (2) not liable simply because pets set foot on or cross the property of another; (3) liable for actual damages caused to others or their property. In the case of disease transmission, however, liability would depend on knowledge; (4) entitled to recover damages from anyone who, without good cause, detains, injures, or kills the owner's dog or cat; (5) not liable for damage caused when pets escape from a competent custodian—a small animal hospital or boarding kennel, for example. But the custodian may be liable to anyone injured and also to the owner if there is negligence.

10.2 ANIMAL CONTROL LAWS

Although common-law principles are still important in the animal control area, much of the law is statutory and regulatory. Many states have passed animal control legislation. These acts generally contain provisions pertaining to the control of stray animals, prevention of rabies, and reimbursement for domestic animals wounded or killed by dogs. Some states statutorily define the liability of a person owning a dog which attacks or injures a person,[1] while other states rely on the common law.

Destroying Stray Dogs

It is generally recognized that, in the absence of statute, a landowner has no right to kill a dog merely because it is trespassing on the premises. However, the common law does give a landowner the right to use whatever force is necessary against a trespassing dog in defense of family, person, or property, even to the extent of killing the dog.[2]

In several states, statutes have been enacted authorizing the killing of dogs under certain circumstances. It has been held by all of the courts which have considered the question that these statutes do not abridge the common-law right to defend property generally. It has also been held that, in many instances, these legislative enactments have enlarged the common-law right by frequently conferring the right to pursue and kill the dog after the act of depredation has been committed.[3]

It is hard to develop a general rule as to whether a landowner is justified in killing a trespassing dog not actually engaging in harmful or destructive acts. Cases interpreting the common law seem to be about equally divided on the question. However, statutes which define the right to kill dogs that are worrying, wounding, or killing sheep or other livestock, offer a more uniform rule—the majority of courts holding that under the particular statute the dog need not necessarily be caught in the act for the killing to be justified.[4]

RIGHT TO KILL DOGS

BUNN v. SHAW
Supreme Court of New Jersey, 1949
3 N.J. 195, 69 A. 2d 576

An action was instituted in the Morris County District Court for the value of plaintiff's fox hound which had been shot and killed by defendant's son, on her orders, while the dog was on her property. The case was tried by the court without a jury and resulted in a judgment being rendered in favor of the plaintiff in the sum of $500.

---

[1] *E.g.,* ILL. REV. STAT. ch. 8, § 366 (1979).

[2] 15 A.L.R. 2d 580, 581 (1949).

[3] *E.g.,* Anderson v. Smith, 7 Ill. App. 354 (1880). It was held that a statute authorizing the owner of sheep to kill a dog under certain circumstances did not take away the natural right of a person to defend his or her other domestic animals upon the person's own premises from the attacks of dogs. The court further said that such a statute enlarged the common-law right to kill a dog that is engaged in the act of depredation by conferring upon the landowner the right to pursue and kill the dog after the killing of the sheep by the dog had been accomplished.

[4] *E.g.,* ILL. REV. STAT. ch. 8, § 368 (1979); KAN. STAT. ANN. § 47-646 (authorized killing if "found injuring or attempting to injure"); VA. CODE § 29-197 (1973) (may be killed if found "in the act of killing or injuring"). *See generally* Annot. 15 A.L.R. 2d 584 (1949).

On September 26, 1946, defendant's thirty-three bred ewes and a ram were grazing on her farm which had been posted against hunting and trespassing. The sheep were within two weeks of lambing. Plaintiff released his two fox hounds within a few hundred feet of defendant's lands. They picked up a cold fox scent and followed the trail into the pasture where the sheep were grazing. The dogs were barking and were heard by defendant's seventeen year old son. He notified his mother of their presence whereupon defendant told him to get his twenty-two caliber rifle and frighten the dogs away. Six shots were fired but the dogs continued to bark and run in the direction the sheep were going and were, in fact, within ten, twenty or thirty feet of some of them when defendant instructed her son to shoot them. One of the dogs was shot and killed, the other ran away. The evidence tended to show that the dog killed was deer and stock proof, but there is nothing to indicate the defendant or her son had knowledge of that fact.

The findings in the District Court were that the dog in question "was not in the act of chasing or worrying the defendant's sheep but that Cracker (the dog's name) was actually following the scent and track of a fox through the property of the defendant without regard for the presence of sheep or other animals," and that "Cracker had no intention to chase, worry or harm the defendant's sheep." The court found that the sheep were running away from the dogs, not that the dogs were chasing them.

The defendant, in the District Court, relied upon the common law rule that one may kill a dog in defense of his property where circumstances justify a reasonable belief that such action is necessary to protect his property. This defense was rejected by the trial court. The trial court based its verdict on the non-applicability of the New Jersey statute which provided "a person may humanely destroy a dog in self defense, or which is found chasing, worrying, wounding or destroying any sheep, lambs, poultry or domestic animal," and on his factual finding that the dog in question was not actually in the act of chasing or worrying the sheep, but was actually in the act of following the scent and track of a fox.

"Worry" as used in statutes providing that one may destroy a dog worrying sheep means "to run after; to chase; to bark at." Such is the meaning given to the word by courts of cattle raising states such as Colorado and Wisconsin.

The common law justified the act of defendant's son if there was reasonable belief that such a measure was necessary to protect defendant's sheep from injury. The statute merely broadens the common law; its enactment was intended not to restrict the common law rule but to enlarge it. It permits the shooting of a dog if it is found "chasing, worrying...sheep"; it does not limit the right to kill given by the common law but enlarges and expands the right. It could have been found, as was done by the District Court, from the following evidence that there was neither ground for a reasonable belief on the part of the defendant that harm was about to come to her sheep nor that the dog was chasing and worrying them. Her son testified he thought the dog might have been on a fox track and nothing the dogs had done up to the time of the shooting led him to believe they were going to harm the sheep. The defendant made an admission the dog was shot because it was trespassing. To a witness she stated she did not see the dog "attack or in any way bother the sheep" and "he had no right on the property, we don't allow dogs on the property."

Dogs do much damage to domestic farm stock and cause large monetary losses to farmers. On the other hand dogs of some breeds are valuable aids in the protection of cattle, sheep and poultry. The counties pay out considerable sums in bounties for the killing of foxes and other animals which are a greater menace to stock than are dogs. There is continual friction between dog lovers and owners and stock farmers. Opinions may well differ as to the equities of a particular case and we may sympathize with the views of the respective parties, but they are not our concern. Courts are bound to give effect to the law deemed applicable to the ascertained facts of each case.

We hold the statute to mean that a landowner has no right to kill a dog under circumstances giving rise to a reasonable belief that the dog is chasing, worrying, wounding or destroying stock or domestic animals, his person, his property, or that of other persons. Applying that law to the facts as found by the trial court the judgment must be affirmed.

Statutory Reimbursement and Predatory Animal Control

The owner of injured animals in seeking recovery against a known dog owner may file suit for damages. Often, however, the owner of the dog cannot be determined. Many states have enacted a statutory reimbursement plan for such circumstances. The state of Illinois, for example, has a statutory scheme whereby owners of injured animals may receive compensation out of an animal control fund.[5] Dog registration fees provide the major source of funding. Recovery from the fund does not bar a suit against the dog owner for damages, but if the lawsuit is successful, the amount paid from the animal control fund is replaced and the balance goes to the owner of the injured animal.

Some states have adopted legislation to control and eradicate predatory animals. The state of Colorado, for example, has set up a predatory animal fund which is funded through a tax on goats and sheep and through the sale of furs, skins, and specimens taken by hunters whose salaries are

---

[5] ILL. REV. STAT. ch. 8, § 369 (1979). Persons whose animals are killed or injured are entitled to make a claim by notifying the administrator within 24 hours after the injury or killing.

No claim will be honored unless the claimant is a resident of Illinois. The claimant must file an affidavit stating the numbers of animals killed or injured, the amount of damages, and the owner of the dog, if known. The damage must be proved by not less than two witnesses who are landowners in the county.

The maximum amounts recoverable per head

from the Fund are: $150—cattle, $100—horses and mules, $25—swine, $15—goats and sheep, $5—turkeys, and $1—other poultry. There is a 50 percent increase in the maximum amount for purebred animals.

If there is not enough money in the fund to cover all of the claims when they are paid each March, recovery is based upon a pro rata share of available funds. One-third of the registration fees must be retained for paying such claims. The remaining two-thirds can be used for carrying out other provisions of the act.

paid out of the fund.[6] A bounty is set for each wolf and coyote killed within the state. Annual permits for the poisoning of predators are available for issuance. Control programs for the protection of sheep and cattle may be set up by the board of county commissioners of any county upon the recommendation of sheep and cattle raisers associations. License fees may be imposed on both cattle and sheep to provide funds for the program.

Dog Bite

The owner's liability for injury caused by the vicious actions of a dog will depend on whether the state establishes statutory requirements for liability or on whether the state follows common-law rules. Generally, the past actions of the dog and the knowledge of the owner concerning the dog's past actions are crucial factors.

Cases against dog owners for dog bites may be based on one or more of five legal principles: (1) common-law liability for injury by a dog of known and vicious propensities, (2) liability under a statute, (3) violation by the dog owner of leashing or other restraining requirements, (4) negligence in restraining a dog, (5) deliberate inducement of a dog to attack or bite another.

DOG BITE—COMMON-LAW RULES

BLAIR v. JACKSON
Court of Appeals of Tennessee, Western Section, 1973
526 S.W. 2d 120

Plaintiff below, Eulyse E. Blair, has appealed and assigned error to the action of the lower Court in directing a verdict in favor of the defendants at the conclusion of all the proof. The plaintiff brought suit for personal injuries sustained on June 11, 1970, when a white German Shepherd dog named Casper kept in the defendants' back yard jumped to the top of a four-foot chain link fence and bit or tore a major portion of the plaintiff's left ear from his head. The plaintiff was not in the back yard with the dog but was in the front yard of the defendants' home looking over the fence for plaintiff's ten-year-old son. Plaintiff was standing near the chain link fence when the dog suddenly jumped and bit him as above set out. Plaintiff did not see the dog until after he had been bitten. The defendants contended that the plaintiff Blair actually leaned over the fence and was bitten but the plaintiff testified affirmatively that he was not leaning over the fence. Whether he was or was not leaning over the fence became a question for the jury.

The plaintiff, Eulyse Blair, resided on University Street about 200 feet south of Mr. and Mrs. Jackson. On the afternoon in question, Mr. Blair had gone up to the home of Mr. and Mrs. Havens looking for his ten-year-old son being of the impression that the son was playing in the Havens' back yard. Plaintiff walked from University Street up the driveway of the Havens' home and then walked between the Havens' home and the Jacksons' home on a

---

[6]COL. REV. STAT. § 35-40-101 *et seq.* (1973).

well-worn path used, without objection on the part of Mr. and Mrs. Jackson, by people using the gate to enter the Havens' back yard. Neighborhood children often played in the Havens' back yard. Mr. Blair reached the gate entering the back yard of the Havens' property. He did not enter the Havens' back yard but stepped to his left and across the property line a couple of feet over on the property of Mr. and Mrs. Jackson for the twofold purpose of getting a better look into the back yard of the Havens' property for his son and also to avoid a small dog owned by the Havens.

Plaintiff testified that he did not see the dog before he was bitten but only heard a growl at or about the time he was struck from the left rear. There were no signs on the Jackson property to beware of the dog and no signs to keep off the property of the Jacksons, either front or back yard. In 1969, the dog, Casper, had tried to bite the garbage collector, Mr. Bowman, while he was picking up the garbage at the Jacksons' home and often times the dog would lunge at the fence when Mr. Bowman was picking up garbage at the house next door. On at least one occasion, Mr. Bowman discussed with Mrs. Jackson the fact that the dog would bite; that he was afraid of him. Mrs. Jackson insisted to Mr. Bowman that the dog would not bite. On one occasion prior to the time Casper bit the plaintiff, young Eddie Havens was bitten or scratched by the dog, Casper. Mr. Jackson learned about it and discussed the matter with Eddie Havens' parents and was assured that Eddie was not harmed by the incident.

At the conclusion of all the proof His Honor the Trial Judge held that the plaintiff was an inadvertent trespasser and under the authority of *Bramble v. Thompson*, 264 Md. 518, 287 A.2d 265, and *Missio v. Williams*, 129 Tenn. 504, 167 S.W. 473, the defendants' motion for a directed verdict should be granted.

In *Hood v. Waldrum*, 58 Tenn. App. 512, 434 S.W.2d 94, Judge Todd reviewed in detail many of the cases in Tennessee relating to dog bites. He announced that the following principles do apply to the common law of liability of dog owners in Tennessee:

(1) A dog owner who has no reason whatever to expect any mischief from his dog ordinarily is not negligent and not liable for the first mischief which occurs.

(2) The occurrence of mischief, of any other pertinent circumstance, creates a duty upon the owner to exercise ordinary care in keeping with the events or circumstances which have occurred. His failure to exercise ordinary care in this situation is ordinary negligence, for which he may be held liable, unless

(3) The injured party failed to exercise ordinary care under the circumstances, in which event the injured party is guilty of ordinary negligence and cannot recover for ordinary negligence of the dog owner, but

(4) If the dog has exhibited such a fixed or customary or characteristic disposition as to be classified as a dangerous or ferocious dog, then the owner may be guilty of gross or wilful negligence by the mere act of harboring such

a dangerous animal upon his premises without adequate safeguards. In such event the owner could be held liable for injury notwithstanding the ordinary negligence of the injured party, however,

(5) Ordinary negligence of the injured party will mitigate damages for the owner's gross negligence, and

(6) If the injured party's negligence was gross or wilful, such as voluntary assumption of a known risk, then the dog owner may not be liable even for gross negligence.

If the jury believed the testimony of the garbage collector, Mr. Bowman, and the neighbor, the jury could reasonably find that the dog, Casper, was, in fact, a vicious dog and accustomed to biting people and that Mr. and Mrs. Jackson had some knowledge of his vicious propensities.

On the authority of *Sherfey v. Bartley*, 36 Tenn. 58, we hold that in the present case the jury might reasonably have found in favor of the plaintiff Blair even though he was a trespasser if the jury should find from a preponderance of the evidence that the dog, Casper, was in fact a vicious dog accustomed to bite or attack people and that the defendants, Jackson and/or wife, had knowledge of such viciousness.

It was for the jury to determine whether plaintiff had carried the burden of proof in proving that defendants had knowledge of the vicious propensities of the dog, Casper; whether defendants were negligent in failing to give warning to plaintiff and others that they had a vicious dog in their back yard; and whether defendants were negligent in failing to erect a higher fence to keep said dog and whether plaintiff was guilty of proximate or remote contributory negligence. His Honor the Trial Judge was in error in directing a verdict and assignment of error No. I is sustained. The judgment for defendants will be set aside and plaintiff granted a new trial.

STATUTORY LIABILITY FOR DOG BITE

NELSON v. LEWIS
Appellate Court of Illinois, 5th Dist., 1976
36 Ill. App. 3d 130, 344 N.E. 2d 268

Plaintiff, by her father and next friend, brought an action under the Illinois "dog-bite" statute (Ill. Rev. Stat., ch. 8 par. 366) for injuries inflicted upon her by defendant's dog. From judgment entered on a jury verdict for the defendant, she appeals.

On the date of her injury, plaintiff Jo Ann Nelson, a 2½-year-old, was playing "crack-the-whip" in defendant's backyard with his daughter and other children. Jo Ann was on the end of the "whip." The testimony shows that after she had been thrown off the whip, Jo Ann fell or stepped on the dog's tail while the dog was chewing a bone. The dog a large Dalmatian, reacted by scratching the plaintiff in her left eye. There was no evidence that plaintiff or anyone else had teased or aggravated the dog before the incident, nor was there evidence that the dog had ever scratched, bitten, or attacked anyone else. According to its owner, the dog had not appeared agitated either before or after the incident. As a result of her injuries, Jo Ann incurred permanent damage to a tear duct in her left eye. It was established that Jo Ann's left eye will overflow with tears more frequently but that her vision in the eye was not affected.

Our statute pertaining to liability of an owner of a dog attacking or injuring persons provides:

If a dog or other animal, without provocation, attacks or injures any person who is peacefully conducting himself in any place where he may lawfully be, the owner of such dog or other animal is liable in damages to such person for the full amount of the injury sustained.   [Ill. Rev. Stat., ch. 8, par. 366.]

Under this statute there are four elements that must be proved: injury caused by a dog owned or harbored by the defendant, lack of provocation; peaceable conduct of the person injured; and the presence of the person injured in a place where he has a legal right to be. There is no dispute but that the dog caused the plaintiff's injury; the defendant owned the dog; the plaintiff's conduct was peaceable; and she was injured in a place where she had a legal right to be. The issue presented is whether plaintiff's unintentional act constitutes "provocation" within the meaning of the statute.

At common law in Illinois, one injured by a dog could recover from the owner only if he could prove that the dog had manifested a disposition "to bite mankind" and that the dog's keeper or owner had notice of this disposition. He could not recover for an injury resulting from his own contributory negligence either by knowingly exposing himself to the dangerous dog or by provoking the dog. A dog owner's liability rested upon negligence, and he could be liable only if he harbored a "vicious" dog. Thus, one injured by a dog bore a substantial burden of proof.

The instant statute, and its immediate predecessor, substantially eased this burden imposed by the common law. It eliminates the requisite proof that the dog was vicious towards humans and that the owner knew of this disposition, and made irrelevant questions of the injured person's contributory negligence (other than provocation). *Beckert v. Risberg*, 33 Ill. 2d 44, 210 N.E. 2d 207 (1965).) We do not believe, however, that it was meant to impose strict liability on dog owners for all injuries caused by dogs, except those intentionally provoked. Instead this act was apparently drawn to eliminate as much as possible any inquiry into subjective considerations. A determination of provocation does not require consideration of the degree of willfulness which motivates the provoking cause. Had the legislature intended only intentional provocation to be a bar to recovery we think it would have so specified. Its conclusion apparently was that an owner or keeper of a dog who would attack or injure someone without provocation should be liable. This implies that the intent of the plaintiff is immaterial. Nor do we think that the plaintiff's status as a child of tender years should relieve her of all responsibility for a provoking act. Our Supreme Court in *Beckert v. Risberg*, 33 Ill. 2d 44, 210 N.E. 2d 207 (1965), sanctioned a jury instruction in the language of the statute where the plaintiff was a 3-year-old boy. Although the court did not specifically address the issue, it appears by implication that a young child is not exempted from responsibility for his or her acts which provoke a dog under this statute.

Although we believe that the instant statute does not impose liability upon a dog owner whose animal merely reacts to an unintentionally provocative act, the present appeal does not involve a vicious attack which was out of all proportion to the unintentional acts involved. The Dalmatian here apparently only struck and scratched plaintiff with a forepaw in response to the plaintiff's stepping or falling on its tail while it was gnawing on a bone, an act which scarcely can be described as vicious. Therefore we hold that "provocation" within the meaning of the instant statute means either intentional or unintentional provocation; that the defendant's dog was provoked by the plaintiff's unintentional acts and did not viciously react to these acts; and that no reversible error was committed in the trial court.

For the foregoing reasons, the judgment of the Circuit Court of St. Clair County is affirmed.

DOG BITE—INJURY TO CHILD—TRESPASS

FULLERTON v. CONAN
District Court of Appeals of California, 2d Dist., 1948
87 Cal. App. 2d 354, 197 P. 2d 59

Action by Penelope Joan Fullerton, an infant, by her guardian ad litem, Dorothy Fullerton, against R.G. Conan and wife, for personal injuries sustained as the result of being bitten by the defendants' dog. Judgment for defendants, and plaintiff appeals.

The complaint alleges that while plaintiff, a child of the age of five years, "was lawfully upon the premises consisting of defendants' yard," defendants' dog bit plaintiff "on and about the mouth, inflicting severe pain, lacerations and wounds to said plaintiff's face and flesh." The trial court found for defendants.

It is contended by plaintiff on appeal that the "judgment for respondent based on the finding that appellant was a trespasser, is without support in the evidence and should be reversed." In that connection appellant argues, "It is our contention that appellant having shown that the minor came upon respondent's property under the invitation extended to her mother the burden was cast upon respondent to show that although lawfully arriving upon the premises she subsequently did something which changed her status."

The findings recite:

The Court finds that the plaintiff had been instructed not to go into that portion of the said premises where the dog was maintained, namely, in the back yard of said premises; that notwithstanding said warning and instruction not to go in said portion of said premises, plaintiff did go therein without the permission or consent of the defendant and was a trespasser therein, and that defendant was not guilty of any negligent, wilful or wanton act or conduct toward plaintiff.

Chap. 503, Statutes 1931, p. 1095, Gen. Laws, Act 384a, provides that:

The owner of any dog which shall bite any person while such person is... lawfully on or in a private place, including the property of the owner of such dog, shall be liable for such damages.... A person is lawfully upon the private property of such owner within the meaning of this act...when he is on such property upon the invitation, express or implied, of the owner thereof.

Appellant bases the within action on the foregoing provision and in that connection argues;

In plain language, the statute provides that, if appellant came upon respondent's premises lawfully and was bitten by his dog, respondent is liable. Because the statute is clear and unambiguous, there is no room for judicial construction.

The court's duty is to apply the statute. The definition, that one is lawfully upon the owner's property if there pursuant to express or implied invitation, leaves no room to discuss the nice distinctions between invitee, business invitee, social guest, or trespasser. Every person, other than a trespasser, comes upon premises by invitation. Any invitation is sufficient to satisfy the requirement of the statute.

It should be noted at the outset that gates and doors have been the generally accepted means of indicating privacy for centuries; their use for such a purpose is traditional and is still sanctioned by universal custom. A gate is a barrier just as a door to a home; both in effect are notifications that what is beyond them is private. And it must be assumed that when gates and doors are a part of the property involved they represent such a purpose. Nor is an invitation without limitation. It would be presumptuous indeed to assume that a social invitation includes authorization or permission to ignore the customary formalities and establish by judicial decision that such an invitation includes the right, as a matter of law, to enter without observing the customary formalities.

As the testimony of the mother recited above indicates, the child was left in the yard unattended. Although there is no direct evidence as to just what happened, the inference is warranted that the child opened the gate and entered the back yard. Manifestly, the host was not responsible for such conduct on the part of the child. And, in that connection, it should be emphasized that the responsibility of the mother for the welfare of her child does not shift to the host upon a visit by the mother and child to the latter's residence.

In the circumstances here presented, "The owner of any dog which shall bite any person" is liable only when such person is, "lawfully upon the private property of such owner." The conclusion reached by the trial court that the child was a "trespasser" simply means that the child was not lawfully upon the property of the dog owner at the point where the biting occurred. And the findings in this regard are supported by the evidence. Whether the child or the mother were lawfully upon the property at other points is beside the issue. The owner of a dog is not an insurer.

For the foregoing reasons, the judgment is affirmed.

Rabies

The legislation from state to state is very similar with regard to rabies. Statutory provisions generally require dogs to be innoculated against rabies. Dogs which have not been innoculated may be impounded and disposed of. Dogs which exhibit signs of rabies are to be confined, and proper authorities are to be notified. If a dog bites a person, the dog must be confined for a period of observation. If there is imminent danger that rabies may spread, the local health department or health officer has broad authority to require owners of animals to take preventative measures to ward off the spread of the disease.

10.3 FENCE LAWS

Early in the history of agriculture, conflicts arose between grain farmers and livestock farmers over the right of the latter to permit unrestrained grazing. In localities where grain farming predominates, landowners have been successful in securing legislation prohibiting unrestrained grazing and requiring the owners of livestock to keep the stock fenced in. In some of the Western states, where grazing is more important than grain farming, the opposite rule exists, whereby the owner of livestock is not required to fence in animals. This latter rule existed in some of the Corn Belt states for a time during the middle of the nineteenth century and was contrary to the earlier common law. Many statutes requiring fencing are simply reversions to the old common-law rule.

Unless negligent in some way, the owner of a fence is not liable for injuries caused by a fence. If a person constructs a barbed-wire fence across a path used by the public, liability might be imposed on this person for injury to a person using the path. If an owner maintains a division fence in poor repair and if, because of that fact, the neighbor's cow becomes entangled in it and is severely injured, the fence owner can be held responsible. A landowner has no duty, however, to provide safe fencing for trespassing persons or livestock and cannot be liable for injuries suffered by them. Nor is there a duty to fence dangerous premises (an old well or a gravel pit) to save trespassing animals from injury. However, a landowner may find it advisable to do so for the protection of his or her own animals lawfully on the farm. Also, there may be a state law, even a criminal statute, requiring the safe covering of abandoned wells or the fencing of deep pits or holes.

Some states have laws or regulations concerning the use of barbed wire. Horses are especially prone to injuring themselves on this type of fence.

Division Fences

Many farmers who keep no livestock feel that any fencing between their own and adjoining property should be maintained by the owner of the adjoining land. Their view is supported by the common law, which states that a landowner is under no obligation to build or maintain or contribute toward a partition fence absent prescription, agreement, or statute.[7] Texas still follows this common-law doctrine, although most states have by statute abrogated the common-law position and require each adjacent owner to contribute to the construction and maintenance of the partition fence. Each state, however, defines the extent of the contribution in slightly different terms. California considers coterminous owners mutually bound to maintain the partition fence.[8] Illinois requires each of the owners of adjoining land to maintain a "just portion" of a division fence.[9] Kansas requires the owners to maintain a partition fence in "equal shares" so long as both parties continue to occupy or improve such lands.[10] New York requires each owner to maintain a just and equitable portion, whereas Montana requires coterminous owners to be "mutually bound equally" to maintain fences.[11] The precise language of the statutes varies from state to state, although the substantive provisions are quite similar. Consequently, an in-depth analysis of a statute in a state such as Illinois will best serve to illustrate the substantive rights and obligations of adjoining owners.

An Illustration. When a landowner desires to enclose land with a division fence, an adjoining landowner is required to pay for the building and maintenance of a just proportion of the fence. The landowner can escape this duty by electing to let land lie open, uncultivated, and unpastured. This provision does not apply in counties with a population that is greater than 1 million, inside municipalities, or to fences on lands held by public bodies for roadway purposes.

There are some justifications for this statute. Since property ownerships are usually divided by some kind of fence, the owner who wishes to escape responsibility for the fence should have the burden of showing why the responsibility ought not to be shared. Permitting an owner merely to remove connecting fences and say "my land is now lying open" tends to create one of the very situations that the law regarding division fences sought to avoid—the uncertainty caused by frequent shifting of responsibility, which is always to the detriment of the owner who maintains fences.

The courts have held, therefore, that an owner's obligation starts at the time the fence becomes a division fence. If, for example, an owner sells a part of the farm, the owner and the purchaser must share responsibility for the division fence from the date of sale. It should be understood, however, that owners whose properties

---

[7] 36A C.J.S. *Fences* § 5 (1961).
[8] Cal. Civ. Code § 841 (West 1954).
[9] Ill. Rev. Stat. ch. 54, § 3 (1979).
[10] Kan. Stat. Ann. § 29-301 (1973).
[11] Mont. Rev. Code Ann. § 67-802 (1970).

adjoin are not compelled by law to build a particular kind of division fence, or any fence at all, if they can agree.

School districts in Illinois bear the full responsibility for all division fences between school grounds and adjoining lands, and are required to keep such fences and maintain them in good repair. Although the kind of fence that must be maintained is not prescribed, it can be assumed that

the fence should be a legal one as described in the fence law—one capable of turning hogs, sheep, cattle, and horses.

Illinois law provides that, "If the property adjoining any State Park is used for farming purposes, fences shall be maintained between the park and such adjoining land in accordance with the division fence law."[12]

Highway officials are not required to fence the road right-of-way.

DIVISION FENCES—ESCAPING LIVESTOCK

D'ARCY v. MILLER
Supreme Court of Illinois, 1877
86 Ill. 102, 29 A.R. 11

This was an action brought to recover damages for certain crops destroyed, in the years 1873 and 1874, by the hogs of defendant. The parties occupy adjoining farms, divided by a line fence. Defendant's hogs passed through this fence and did the damage complained of.

Now, if it be true, as the testimony tends to show, that defendant and Swalm, the former owner, agreed upon a division of the fence, and built and kept in repair in accordance with the agreement, and that after plaintiff's father purchased he recognized and acquiesced in the division so made, and planitiff, since he acquired an interest in the land from his father, continued to recognize the division, we are aware of no reason why the fence may not be regarded as a division fence between the parties. A division fence may be established by agreement, or it may be established under the statute regulating partition fences. By the common law, every man was bound to keep his cattle on his own land, or respond in damages for their trespasses. And it was one of its rules that no man is bound to fence his close against an adjoining field, but every man is bound to keep his cattle in his own field at his peril. But this legal obligation might be changed by prescription and by covenant. And in this state it can be done under the statute regulating partition fences. If parties desire to avoid the common law duty in cases of adjoining fields, they may do so under our statute by compelling contribution for the erection and maintenance of such fence.

Plaintiff seems to have tried his case on the theory that at common law each adjoining owner was required to keep his stock on his own land, at his peril. In this he would have been correct had no partition fence been established, but when it was proven that a partition fence had been agreed

---

[12] ILL. REV. STAT. ch. 105, § 468b1 (1979).

upon and erected, it developed upon plaintiff to show that the damages he sought to recover arose from stock passing through the portion of the fence defendant was bound to keep in repair. As he failed in this, the judgment will be reversed, and the cause remanded for another trial consistent with the views here expressed.

Judgment reversed.

The Right to Discontinue Maintenance. The Illinois law prescribes the conditions under which an owner may legally stop maintaining a part of a division fence. Stated briefly, the owner must give the adjoining owner 1 year's written notice of such intention and must let adjacent lands lie uncultivated and unpastured. Even under these conditions, however, the adjoining owner may prevent the owner's *removal* of a portion of the fence by refusing to give permission for the removal. Where such permission is refused, the owner is entitled to the value of that portion as determined by fence viewers.

If an owner removes a fence without giving the adjoining owner written notice or obtaining the adjoining owner's permission, the person who removes the fence can be held for all damages that may result. Should an unlawful removal be made, the adjoining owner may rebuild the fence at the expense of the person who made the unlawful removal. A further provision in regard to fence removal states that a landlord is bound by the acts of a tenant.

If an owner has mistakenly built a division fence on the adjoining owner's land, it may be moved to the true line, provided the owner pays for any fence materials that may have been taken from the adjoining land and does not remove the fence at a time when the crops of the adjoining owner would be exposed to livestock. The removal must be made within 6 months after the true line has been run. If, within that 6-month period, moving the fence would expose crops of either party to livestock, removal must be made within a reasonable time after the crops are harvested. This statute does not alter the general rule in Illinois that a fence mislocated for 20 years or more cannot be moved unless both parties consent.

Which Portion of a Fence Must One Maintain? Owners having adjoining lands are required to maintain a just, as well as a distinct, proportion of the division fence, but the law does not mention which portion or how much of the fence each owner must maintain. Owners ordinarily assume responsibility for a designated one-half of the fence, usually the half on their right as, standing on their own property, they face the division line. This is not a part of the law, however; it is simply a custom. Evidence can always be admitted to show that the fence should be maintained another way.

When owners cannot agree on the proportion of the fence that each should maintain, the law provides that the township fence viewers can specify the proportion to be maintained by each. This provision applies also to the building of division fences. In making their determination, the fence viewers may question previous owners and tenants and hired hands who worked on the farm to see which end of the fence was maintained by former owners. One decision that fence viewers cannot make, however, is that each owner should maintain his or her own side of a hedge fence.

Inclosing on Another's Fence. The Illinois fence law provides for the case of a person who incloses land upon the inclosure of another. That person must, while taking such action, either pay the owner of the adjoining land a just proportion of the value of the division fence that the adjoining owner may have built, or build a share of the fence immediately.

If the parties cannot agree on the value of the fence or the share that each should assume, either they may call in the fence viewers or the aggrieved party may bring an action in court. If an owner removes a fence and later connects to the new fence built by the adjoining owner, one-half the cost of that fence must be paid. The adjoining owner cannot prevent the neighbor from connecting to the division fence, but can insist on reimbursement. Also, in the future each is responsible for a share of the fence.

What Kind of a Fence Must One Construct? One adjoining owner can make the other build a fence that meets the standard defined in the law—a fence 4½ feet high that will turn hogs, as well as other stock.[13] The only purpose of this definition is to avoid disputes about division fences. This definition does not apply to other fences on the farm, or even to a division fence if the adjoining owners can agree on what they want. If the parties are in agreement, a barbwire fence or an electric fence will suffice on the division line, or, if they like, they need have no fence at all.

An adjoining owner cannot force the other to use certain kinds of material in the construction of a division fence. The statute states that any fence

in good repair, consisting of rails, timber boards, stone, hedges, barbwire, woven wire, or whatever the fence viewers of the town or precinct...shall consider equivalent thereto, suitable and sufficient to

prevent cattle, horses, sheep, hogs, and other stock from getting on the adjoining lands of another, shall be deemed legal and sufficient.

An owner therefore cannot be forced to build an expensive fence or one that will turn animals other than those specified in the law. Neither can an owner be held liable for animals injured on the fence, unless the injury results from negligence in maintaining the fence.

Construction and Repair. Illinois law provides that if an owner neglects to repair or rebuild a share of a division fence, the adjoining owner may have two fence viewers of the town or precinct examine the fence. If the fence viewers find that the fence is insufficient, they are required to direct the negligent owner to repair or rebuild a share of the division fence within such time as they think is reasonable.

This procedure seems to be an alternative to a provision by which an owner may give 60 days' written notice to an adjoining owner that a fence be built or 10 days' written notice that a fence be repaired and by which the owner may build or repair the fence alone, should the adjoining owner fail to comply with such notice. Under this provision, too, the owner may hold the adjoining owner liable for any damage resulting from neglect of the fence, and recover the expense of building or repairing the fence, along with costs of suit, before a court of competent jurisdiction. However, use of the fence viewers is recommended, particularly if court action is likely to arise.

This part of the law also provides that when fire, flood, or other casualty damages or destroys a division fence, the person responsible for that fence has to rebuild or repair his or her portion of it within 10

---

[13] Electors at an annual town meeting, however, may determine what shall constitute a legal fence in their town, and the county board in counties not under township organization may regulate the height of fences.

days after receiving written notice from an interested party to do so. If, however, a flood destroys a floodgate or a part of the fence that crosses a stream or natural watercourse, the person responsible has to rebuild or repair within 2 days after being notified by an interested person. Should an owner, under these circumstances, fail to repair or construct the fence within the time specified by law, the injured party may do the work and recover expenses, as well as costs of suit if legal action is necessary.

Ordinarily, a floodgate or water gap is maintained by the owner in whose end of the fence it happens to be. However, since the law states that each owner shall maintain a "just proportion" of the fence, there is no reason why an owner who maintains a floodgate or water gap should not be compensated by having a smaller proportion of the fence to take care of.

Fences—Viewers, Hedge Removal

Fence Viewers.   In connection with laws on division fences, the Illinois Legislature has created a local body known as "fence viewers," whose duties are:

1.   To determine the value of a division fence when adjoining owners cannot agree on the amount that one owner should contribute to another for building the fence, or when the owner intends to let land lie open and the adjoining owner wishes to buy a portion of the fence
2.   To fix, when disputes arise, the proportion of a division fence to be maintained by each owner
3.   To examine the fence on the complaint of one owner that an adjoining owner has failed to make necessary repairs, and, if they find the fence in need of such repairs, to order the delinquent party to

make them within a reasonable, specified time

In counties under township organization, town boards of auditors are ex officio fence viewers. In counties not under township organization, the county board appoints, for a term of 1 year, three viewers for each precinct.

Each party may choose one of the viewers, and the viewers, if they disagree between themselves, may choose the third to act with them. Should an owner neglect to choose a viewer, the other owner may choose both, provided that this owner gives the other party 8 days' written notice.

In addition to their other powers and duties, fence viewers may determine what the equivalent of a legal fence is for their town or precinct. They may also compel testimony when considering a fence dispute. Their decisions must be recorded and filed with the town clerk or, in counties not under township organization, with the county clerk.

Trimming Hedge Division Fences.   By Illinois law, an owner of a hedge division fence is required to trim his or her fence to a height of 4 feet or less the year after the hedge becomes 7 years old, and to 5 feet every 2 years after that time. This law further specifies that trimming is to be done on or before June 15. If an owner fails to cut his or her hedge as required by law, an adjoining owner who is injured may give 10 days' written notice and, after that time, cut the hedge alone and recover the cost from the owner of the hedge.

However, 60 rods of hedge may be left untrimmed in a division fence to protect wildlife, orchards, and buildings, to serve as windbreaks, or to protect against soil erosion. The hedge must actually be serving as protection if this exception is to be made. The mere prospect of such use is not considered a sufficient reason for failure to trim the hedge.

In trimming a hedge fence, even one neglected by an adjoining owner, a person is entitled only to his or her share of the posts that might be taken out of the trimmings.

Trimming Hedges along Highways.   An Illinois law gives highway authorities the right to protect roads from adjoining and over-hanging hedge trees. This law provides that the owner of a hedge fence lining a public highway must trim his or her fence to a height of 5 feet or less the year after the hedge becomes 7 years old, and to 5 feet at least once every year after that time, so that it will not obstruct the public highway, impair its usefulness, or endanger the pub-lic. Osage orange hedge is subject to the same regulations, except that annual trim-ming need not start until the second year after it is first trimmed and trimming must be to a height of 4 feet. However, as much as one-fourth of the length of a hedge fence along a highway may, with the consent of the highway commissioner, be left un-trimmed for windbreak purposes. Owners failing to trim their hedges by October 1 are liable annually to a fine of $10 to $50, which the highway commissioner may recover by a suit.

Planting willow hedge fences on the margin of highways has been made illegal in Illinois. Where such hedge fences already exist, the appropriate highway authority may contract with the owner for their destruction prior to tiling.

10.4 LIABILITY FOR TRESPASS— RIGHTS OF INJURED PARTY

Owners may be held liable in damages for injuries caused to the property of others. Except for some of the Western states where livestock are handled under range conditions, it is the legal duty of an owner of livestock to keep them off the property of others. If the livestock owner fails and the cattle get in the neighbor's corn, damages may be imposed. Also, the courts hold that the owner of animals that are wrongfully on the land of another may be held responsible for all damage that can reasonably be attributed to such trespass. So, if trespassing hogs have cholera and transmit it to other hogs, recovery may be had for cholera losses; or if cows are bred by a trespassing bull, damages may be recovered by the owner of the cows. The amount of damages in such a case would be based on the difference in value to the owner between the actual progeny and the progeny intended. Damages may be sub-stantial when the cows are purebred and the culprit is a scrub.

It is obvious that the probability of being held responsible for damages caused by trespassing animals is quite high. The best policy, therefore, is to do whatever is necessary to prevent trespass. This will vary depending upon the kinds, natures, and habits of animals. Also, the promptness with which the owner of a trespassing animal goes after it will influence the extent of liability.

General Rules

The condition of fences on an owner's land, and also on the land subject to animal trespass, has an important bearing on lia-bility for damage done by trespassing animals. The predominant views of state courts on various factual situations in-volving livestock, fences, and disgruntled owners may be expressed as follows:

1.   An owner of livestock who maintains good fences (legal fences, if state law

defines these), who is not aware that the animals are in the habit of breaking out, who does no negligent act causing them to break out, and who makes an immediate attempt to retake them when they do break out is not liable for damage caused by them.

However, the courts of some states follow the common-law rule and hold the owner strictly liable even under these circumstances.[14] As a result, the owner is under an absolute duty to keep the animals restrained on his or her own property and effectively becomes an "insurer" for damage caused by them. Many states have statutes which modify the common-law liability and predicate liability on negligence. In these states, the owner of trespassing animals is not an "insurer," but must be negligent to be held liable. Other statutes reject, adopt, or restore the common-law liability either in whole or in part.[15] Under many state fencing laws, the owner of trespassing animals is liable only to those who enclose their lands with a legally sufficient fence.[16]

2. When animals break through an adjoining owner's part of a division fence and such fence is not in good repair or is not legally sufficient, the owner of the animals cannot be held liable for their trespass.

3. An owner of trespassing animals may be held liable:

   a. when the animals are in the habit of breaking out, regardless of the condition of the owner's fences

   b. when the fences are defective or insufficient

   c. when negligence causes the trespass (e.g., frightening the animals until they break out or leaving a gate open)

State laws generally provide that the owner of land on which animals are trespassing may do anything reasonably necessary to terminate the trespass. The animals may be driven back to their own fields. The owner may be asked to remove the animals. Necessary force may be used to drive the animals, and if injury results from the application of such an amount of force, the owner of the animal cannot complain. However, the law does not tolerate greater force than is needed.

An additional right accorded by most states is that permitting the confinement, watering, feeding, and taking care of trespassing animals until the owner comes and takes them, making good any damage suffered.[17] Generally, a landowner is not privileged to do this unless free from fault or negligence. The "taker-up" must notify the owner immediately and give the owner an opportunity to come after the animals. The cost of feed and care during confinement must be paid by the owner.

An *estray* is a domestic animal of unknown ownership running at large. It does not refer to dogs, cats, or poultry. Estrays differ from animals that are simply trespassing in that the latter have known owners. The laws of most states provide that landowners may confine estrays and care for them. A reasonable attempt must then be made to locate the owner. Some laws require public posting and the giving of notice in local papers. If the owner comes for the animals, the claims of the taker-up for feed, housing, care, and any other costs involved must be satisfied. If the owner does not claim the animals, they become the property of the taker-up. Some state laws provide for sale of the

[14] 3A C.J.S. *Animals* § 241 (1973). *See generally* 7 N. HARL, AGRICULTURAL LAW §§ 3.01 *et seq.* (1980).

[15] 3A C.J.S. *Animals* § 242 (1973).
[16] *Id.* § 243.
[17] *E.g.*, ILL. REV. STAT. ch. 54, § 21 (1979).

animals, reimbursement of the taker-up, and transfer of the balance to county funds.

Estrays may be impounded by local (generally township) authorities when state law so provides. In this case, the animals are sold at public auction on failure of the owner to appear and claim them.

CROP DAMAGE BY CATTLE—MEASURE OF DAMAGE

JOHNSON v. SLEAFORD
Appellate Court of Illinois, 2d Dist., 1963
39 Ill. App. 2d 228, 188 N.E. 2d 230

This is an action by the plaintiffs against the defendants based upon Ch. 8 Ill. Rev. Stats. 1959, par. 1, which reads as follows, so far as applicable:

Hereafter, it shall be unlawful for any animal of the species of...cattle... to run at large in the State of Illinois: Provided, that no owner or keeper of such animals shall be liable for damages in any civil suit for injury to the person or property of another caused by the running at large thereof, without the knowledge of such owner or keeper, when such owner or keeper can establish that he used reasonable care in restraining such animals from so running at large.

The defendants were charged with not making adequate provision for keeping and retaining certain cattle on their premises, which roamed at large from July 24, 1960, the day of their escape, to January 1, 1961, when the last thereof were recovered, and which allegedly damaged certain crops of the plaintiffs. The jury rendered a verdict for the plaintiffs, separately assessing their respective damages, upon which the court entered a judgment for $788.50, $794.50, and $1206.00 for the respective plaintiffs, from which this appeal is taken by the defendants. It appears from the evidence that the defendants James Thompson and Frank Sleaford operated a farm and cattle enterprise in Bureau County, Illinois, jointly with the defendant Leonard Crossell, and that on Saturday, July 23, 1960, Thompson and Sleaford went to Carbon Cliff, Illinois where they inspected and purchased thirty-five head of Black Angus cattle. They drove the cattle from one pen to another while making their examination and inspection. At this time, the cattle apparently were tame, did not seem unruly, were normal, and appeared no different than any other cattle. They had an average weight of 480 pounds. On Sunday, July 24, 1960, the cattle purchased were transported to the farm where the defendants conducted their cattle operation and were unloaded, about 9-10 a.m., into a corral about 200 square feet in size. During the loading process they did not seem unruly. During the unloading nothing out of the ordinary occurred.

The corral had been holding other feeder cattle which had been removed in order to put the newly acquired cattle in. It was a cement corral lot. The fence around the corral was constructed of one inch by twelve inch boards with wood posts of six inch creosote, four and one-half feet high with the boards vertical—there were solid boards all the way around. The gate was about fifteen feet wide and was secured with double strands of barbed wire at all four corners. It was not hinged. It was constructed of one inch by six inch boards. When last seen at 11:30 a.m. that Sunday morning the cattle were standing normally in the corral.

On the same day, however, July 24th, the cattle broke down the gate, sometime before 12:30 p.m., broke through a four stranded barbed wire fence by jumping into it, and then broke through a third enclosure, a three stranded barbed wire fence. The top wires that secured the gate at the corral had been snapped and the cattle had pushed the gate down so it was lying flat.

Thompson discovered the cattle when they had broken through one enclosure and tried unsuccessfully to head them back. They scattered and went in different directions and upon various properties. He, together with Sleaford and other persons who were hired and who volunteered to assist, made efforts that day and subsequently to recapture the animals with horses, trucks, jeeps, and an airplane. They made efforts to comb the neighboring corn fields, driving the roads, and going through timber trying to locate the cattle and drive them to a place where they could be corraled. Some of the cattle stayed in the growing corn until after picking time because there was no place to corral them. The sight of the searchers scared the cattle and they ran farther away. Nine persons were involved in the search. Seven head were recaptured during the first week, and in the first two weeks about twelve head were recaptured. Some were recaptured by a veterinarian shooting them with a rifle containing tranquilizer drugs. The search covered about 22 square miles. Three weeks from the day of the escape twenty-two head were still at large, and one-half of these were on the fields of the plaintiffs. The last of the cattle were not returned to the defendants until the first of January, 1961, more than 5 months after they had escaped. The plaintiffs sought damages for the loss, damage, and destruction of and to their growing oats, soybeans, and corn by these cattle.

It is admitted by the defendants that the cattle were actually running at large and that the plaintiffs had thereby established a prima facie case, but the defendants argue that the plaintiffs offered no competent evidence to show that the defendants did not use reasonable care in restraining the cattle.

The plaintiffs' theory is that the verdict is amply supported by the evidence, and is according to law. They say the defendants failed to provide reasonable care to restrain the cattle and permitted them to run at large after having knowledge of their escape.

The general rule is that where an accident occurs as a proximate result of the violation of the statute making it unlawful for stock to run at large, there is a presumption of negligence on the part of the owner and keeper of the stock, which is, normally, sufficient to carry the case to the jury so far as that issue is concerned. The defendants owners are not liable "when such owner or keeper can establish that he used reasonable care in restraining such animals from so running at large." If the defendants cannot so establish that they so used reasonable care they are liable. The defendants claim the benefit of the proviso in the statute; the proof to be established under the proviso was within the knowledge of the defendants and not the plaintiffs; and the burden of evidence, after the plaintiffs rested their case in chief, was on the defendants. It was a question of fact for the jury to determine whether the evidence introduced by the defendants was sufficient to overcome the prima facie case made by the plaintiffs; the credibility of the witness and the weight to be given their testimony were questions to be determined by the jury; the inferences to be drawn from the evidence were matters for the jury; it was their peculiar province to determine the preponderance of the evidence. The motions for directed verdict and for judgment notwithstanding the verdict presented the single question whether there is any evidence which, standing alone and taken with all its intendments most favorable to the plaintiffs, tends to prove the material elements of the plaintiffs' case. We think there is, and that there is no complete absence of probative facts to support the inference drawn by the jury here. Hence, the Court properly denied the defendants' motions for directed verdict and for judgment notwithstanding the verdict.

On the issue of damages, the plaintiffs' witnesses testified generally as to the number of acres or percentages of crops or number of bushels of grain lost or damaged by eating, trampling, etc., the kind of crops lost or damaged, the average probable yield per acre of the respective crops of oats, soybeans, or corn, the market prices at the time of maturity, and in some instances the number of bushels actually harvested from a damaged tract. Each plaintiff produced testimony as to the loss or damage that he suffered, all of which was in the area of the money damages claimed and allowed. They say this is the only type of evidence of damages that could have been submitted under the circumstances. The defendants urge that all of such evidence was improper and incompetent and the Trial Court should have sustained their objections to such, that in an action for damages to unmatured crops it is improper to allow evidence of market value of matured crops, and unmatured crops have no value on the market.

The plaintiffs were entitled to plant, cultivate, mature, and harvest their crops—to secure the full benefit to arise from the annual harvest according to the season; evidence tending to show how much the land would yield, and as to the usual market value of the product at the usual market, at the harvesting season, was admissible; out of this it was proper to deduct the expense of tillage, harvesting, and marketing; the remainder is the legitimate fruit of the land, labor, and expense; the measure of damages is the worth of the growing crops at the time they were destroyed, not for immediate use in the condition they then were, but with a view to the use of the ground until maturity, with the right to cultivate and harvest the crops; this is ascertained by the probable amount of grain the crop would produce, and the probable value of the same in the market at the market season, deducting therefrom the necessary cost of cultivating, harvesting, and taking the same to market; the amount and value are necessarily hypothetical and an opinion thereon can only be formed by considering the average yield at the place and under like circumstances and the average value of the products in the market at the place and time of market. That value was necessarily a matter of estimate on conclusion of the mind of the witnesses to be arrived at from all the material facts which would affect it, including the quality of the land on which the crops were growing, its fertility, and productivity—and including the probability or improbability that a particular crop would mature on a particular tract.

Accordingly, considering the continuing, day to day, nature of trespass and damage by these cattle, considering the character of the products, growing crops, to which damage was done, and considering all the relevant facts in evidence, we believe the Court did not err in overruling the objections which the defendants made to the evidence as to damages and properly denied the motion for new trial.

The judgment will, therefore, be affirmed.

Animals on the Highway

Farm animals frequently get out on highways. If a user of the highway collides with a loose animal and is injured or has a vehicle damaged, the owner of the animal may be turned to for compensation. Although it is not possible to predict with accuracy what damages, if any, may be recovered in particular instances, there are certain general rules which apply:

1.   If a farmer is negligent in maintaining fences and allows animals to get on the road, liability may be imposed for damage to persons using the highway.
2.   If a farmer maintains fences in good repair but has one or more animals which are in the habit of breaking out, the owner may be held liable for damages caused by such animals if their habits are known.
3.   If adequate fences are maintained in good repair and animals which are not in the habit of breaking out get through the fence and onto a highway, the owner of

the animal may be held liable for damages if he or she knew the animal was out and made no reasonable effort to confine the animal.
4.   When animals are being driven across or along a highway, particularly a paved highway, the owner should use the degree of care necessary to keep them under control. Naturally, if animals are being driven at night or when visibility is poor, more care is necessary in order that motorists will be properly warned and the animals kept under control. Also, the amount and nature of the traffic will affect the amount of care which is necessary. When a road is jammed with traffic, it might be negligent to try to drive a herd of cattle across the road, no matter how much caution was exercised When animals are being driven along or on a highway, the basis of a farmer's liability is negligence.

Stock-crossing signs do not excuse a farmer from using due care in driving animals on the highway—such signs simply increase to some degree the care which motorists must exercise.

ANIMALS ON HIGHWAY

O'GARA v. KANE
Appellate Court of Illinois, 5th Dist., 1976
38 Ill. App. 3d 641, 348 N.E. 2d 503

Plaintiff, Patrick O'Gara, brought suit to recover for personal injuries received when an automobile in which he was a passenger collided with a horse owned by Dr. C.C. Kane, defendant, on Route 40, St. Clair County, Illinois, on November 2, 1971. At the close of all the evidence the defendant moved for and was granted a directed verdict from which plaintiff appeals.

The issue presented is whether the court erred in directing a verdict for the defendant.

The complaint was in two counts. The first alleged negligence in allowing the horse to run at large and the second alleged a violation of chapter 8, section 1, of the Illinois Revised Statutes which reads in pertinent part:

[I]t shall be unlawful for any...horse...to run at large in the State of Illinois: Provided, that no owner or keeper of such animals shall be liable for damages in any civil suit for injury to the person or property of another caused by the running at large thereof, without the knowledge of such owner or keeper, when such owner or keeper can establish that he used reasonable care in restraining such animals from so running at large.

Dr. Kane testified that nine colts were kept in a fenced pasture on his farm and that all nine escaped from the enclosure on the evening of the accident. The fence around the pasture had been renewed just a few weeks before the incident. Those repairs consisted of a new corner post, a creosoted railroad tie, other posts of 6" by 6" creosoted wood, all buried 3 or 4 feet deep and sticking up 5 to 5¼ feet and placed 8 feet apart. The cross bars were two 2" by 6" boards, nailed approximately 16 inches apart.

We believe the verdict was properly directed for the defendant. The only evidence presented which went to the allegation of negligence on the part of defendant was that of Robert Shrodes to the effect that he might have seen the defendant's horses out once or twice before the accident. However, this testimony is so unclear on this point that it cannot be relied upon standing alone as it does. Such a conclusion does not constitute an evaluation by this court of his credibility. He was, by his own admission, unsure of what he saw. Even if it were possible to deduce that he meant the defendant's horses were out and running loose at some point before the accident there is no indication if such occurred before or after the repairs to the fence or what condition caused or permitted their escape.

As to the second count alleging a statutory violation, the plaintiff argues that animals encompassed by the statute are running at large unlawfully if on the public highway unattended, unrestrained and uncontrolled, relying on the case of *Fugett v. Murray*, 311 Ill. App. 323, 35 N.E. 2d 946. The language from *Fugett* upon which plaintiff relied is, however, meant to describe the rule of law established by the early cases prior to the amendment of the law in 1931. Such rule is inapplicable here. The statute was amended by the addition of the proviso that an owner would not be held liable if able to prove that he used reasonable care in restraining his animals and if he was without knowledge that they were running at large. As stated in *Fugett* the proviso was intended by the legislature to relieve the owner of livestock of the harshness of the law as established in the early cases.

The testimony of Dr. Kane was that he had no knowledge that the horses were out until notified after the accident and that testimony was uncontradicted. The only remaining element required to be established under the statute is that the defendant used reasonable care in restraining the animals from running at large. The question then becomes whether the fence described by Dr. Kane and Fred Williams constituted the use of reasonable care in restraining the horses.

Defendant adduced proof of the construction of the fence which established that a reasonable effort had been made to restrain the colts in the absence of any proof from plaintiff as to what would have constituted a reasonably secure fence, if the one described was not. Plaintiff offered no evidence bearing on the reasonableness of the construction of the fence.

The judgment is affirmed.

BULL ON HIGHWAY—LIABILITY OF BAILEE

MORENO v.BECKWITH
Appellate Court of Illinois, 2d Dist., 1967
77 Ill. App. 2d 443, 222 N.E. 2d 918

This is an appeal from the Circuit Court of McHenry County. The suit was for personal injuries sustained by plaintiff, Joseph Adolph Moreno, when an automobile he was driving struck a Black Angus bull on Route 14. The jury returned a verdict against both defendants and assessed plaintiff's damages at $10,000. The Trial Court granted defendant Beckwith's post-trial motion to set aside the verdict.

Defendant Krohn, a dealer in cattle, rented the bull to defendant, George E. Beckwith for $35. Beckwith was to use the bull for two months to breed his cattle. On September 6, 1961, the date of the accident, Krohn asked Beckwith if he could use the bull for a few hours to breed a cow belonging to Edgar Pierce. Beckwith agreed. Beckwith then helped Krohn load the bull on a truck. Krohn, as he left, told Beckwith he would be back with the bull in a couple of hours. Krohn took the bull to the Pierce farm. Beckwith did not share in the fee paid by Pierce to Krohn.

At about 7:30 p.m., Krohn returned to the Beckwith farm with the bull. Neither Beckwith nor his wife were at home at the time. While Krohn, unaided, was attempting to unload the bull from his truck, the bull escaped and started off down Route 14. Krohn spent about 30 minutes trying to capture the bull but lost it in the darkness. Believing the bull had gone to a nearby farm, Krohn returned to the Beckwith farm and asked the nurse employed by Mrs. Beckwith to tell Beckwith "that the bull is out there,...[at a nearby farm], and that he would be out in the morning to pick him up and bring him home."

Upon being told what happened, he said he took a lantern and went to try to find the bull. Beckwith testified he looked for the bull for about 45 minutes before going into his house to retire for the night.

Plaintiff, Joseph Moreno, testified he did not see the bull on the highway until he was about 10 feet from it. He struck the bull at about 10:30 p.m. on September 6. The point of impact was on the highway alongside the Beckwith farm.

We turn our consideration to an analysis of the evidence and all of its aspects most favorable to the plaintiff. From the time on the evening of September 6 when Krohn picked up the bull, Beckwith had neither possession nor control of the bull. The animal was never returned to his custody or control. It escaped from the custody and control of Krohn, an experienced dealer in cattle. Krohn's message for Beckwith was that the bull was at a nearby farm and that he would return it to Beckwith in the morning.

At the time the bull escaped and was at large, it was the object of a bailment. Beckwith was the bailor and Krohn was the bailee. The Bailee is liable for injuries resulting to a third party from animals which are the subject of the bailment. A bailor cannot be held responsible to a third party for injuries resulting from his bailee's negligent use of bailed property.

Judgment affirmed. Beckwith not liable.

10.5 ANIMAL DISEASE LAWS

General Principles

Both the federal government and the states have enacted a large number of laws and carry on an extensive regulatory program with regard to animal disease. Although most specific laws have been provided by state legislatures, the federal government has, through its authority under the interstate commerce clause and through grants-in-aid and other devices, come to play a major role in animal disease eradication. The Secretary of Agriculture is authorized to issue federal regulations regarding animal diseases. The Animal and Plant Health Inspection Service, a division of the U.S. Department of Agriculture, performs this function. Usually, the state department of agriculture is the administrative agency empowered to promulgate regulations implementing the state legislation. Such regulations have the force of law and must be complied with by individual producers.

The U.S. Department of Agriculture must operate within the limits of legislative delegation. Consequently, the Department has the power to make rules and regulations for the suppression, prevention, and eradication of infectious and contagious animal diseases, but is not empowered to determine which diseases are dangerous and contagious. Among the regulated diseases at the federal level are tuberculosis, brucellosis, dourine, foot-and-mouth disease, pleuropneumonia, rinderpest, scrapie, anaplasmosis, hog cholera, Texas (splenetic) fever, scabies, exotic Newcastle disease, and psittacoses.[18] This listing is not all-inclusive and is subject to change by legislative action. The states regulate some of these same diseases as well as others that are not regulated at the federal level.

The federal government cooperates with the states in disease eradication programs. For example, major programs to control bovine tuberculosis and brucellosis and to stamp out hog cholera have been carried on by the federal government in cooperation with the states.

State legislatures have generally authorized their departments of agriculture to investigate all cases of contagious and infectious diseases among animals within the state, and, if necessary, quarantine and destroy all animals infected or suspected of being infected with contagious or infectious diseases. Such animals are a public nuisance and come under the exercise of the police power. Buildings and premises may also be quarantined and destroyed if they cannot be properly disinfected. Both the federal government and the states provide indemnification for animals destroyed owing to their status as diseased, suspect, or exposed animals or as reactors. Such indemnification is not a constitutional right, but rather a matter of legislative discretion. If necessary, the state department of agriculture may quarantine geographical districts in the state when there is a disease outbreak.

LIVESTOCK DISEASES—POWER OF STATE

DURAND v. DYSON
Supreme Court of Illinois, 1916
271 Ill. 382, 111 N.E. 143

The averments in the bill are, substantially, that appellees R.W. Patterson, B.J. Shanley and L.F. Brown, individually and collectively as members of the Board of Livestock Commissioners of the State of Illinois, and Oliver E. Dyson, individually and as State veterinarian of Illinois, and various agents, employees and assistants of appellees, threaten and are about to kill sixty-one head of pure-bred and registered Guernsey cattle belonging to the appellants and located on their farm in the township of Shields, in said county, which are of the value of not less than $35,000; and also insist that appellants' said cattle are afflicted with such a malady (known as the hoof and mouth disease), and that said statute authorized them to kill all of said herd, and requires appellants to consent thereto and to accept therefor the sum of $13,500, the valuation at which they have been appraised, and upon failure of appellants to so consent, that then appellees are authorized by the statute to take and kill said animals without any compensation whatever to appellants.

---

[18] 9 C.F.R. 50-56, 82 (1979). For an excellent treatment of liability for spread of contagious animal diseases, *see* 2 N. HARL, AGRICULTURAL LAW §§ 9.01 *et seq.* (1980).

When the said board...determines that any animal is affected with, or has been exposed to, any dangerously contagious or infectious disease, the board or any members, thereof,...may agree with the owner upon the value of such animal or of any property that it may be found necessary to destroy, and in case such an agreement cannot be made, said animals or property shall be appraised by three competent and disinterested appraisers.

Upon such appraisement being made, it shall become the duty of the owner to immediately destroy such animals and to dispose of the carcasses thereof, and to disinfect the premises occupied by such animals, in accordance with the rules prescribed by said board governing such destruction and disinfection. And upon his failure so to do, said board...shall cause such animal or animals or property to be destroyed and disposed of, and thereupon such owner shall forfeit all right to receive any compensation for the destruction of said animal or animals or property.

All Claims against the state arising from the slaughter of animals as herein provided for, shall be made to the Board of Livestock Commissioners,...and it shall be the duty of said board to determine the amount which shall be paid in each case on account of the animals so slaughtered and fix the fair cash value thereof.

In speaking of the extent and limits of what is known as the police power, the Supreme Court of the United States said in *Lawton v. Steele*, 152 U.S. 133:

It is universally conceded to include everything essential to the public safety, health and morals, and to justify the destruction or abatement, by summary proceedings, of whatever may be regarded as a public nuisance. Under this power it has been held that the state may order the destruction of a house falling to decay or otherwise endangering the lives of passersby; the demolition of such as are in the path of a conflagration; the slaughter of diseased cattle; the destruction of decayed or unwholesome food; the prohibition of wooden buildings in cities;...the restriction of objectionable trades to certain localities; the compulsory vaccination of children; the confinement of the insane or those afflicted with contagious diseases;...the prohibition of gambling houses and places where intoxicating liquors are sold. Beyond this, however, the state may interfere wherever the public interests demand it, and in this particular a large discretion is necessarily vested in the legislature to determine not only what the interests of the public require but what measures are necessary for the protection of such interests.

The court then lays down the further rule that to justify the state in thus interposing its authority it must appear, first, that the public generally, as distinguished from those of a particular class, require such interference; and, second, that the means are reasonably necessary for the accomplishment of the purpose and not unduly oppressive upon individuals. While it is true that such legislation is subject to the supervision of the courts, it is only in such cases where the state arbitrarily and unnecessarily interferes with private business or imposes unusual and unnecessary restrictions upon lawful occupations that such legislation will be declared as in contravention of the fourteenth amendment.

Cattle afflicted with a dangerous and contagious disease are public nuisances as defined by the common law, and under the common law such a nuisance could not be legalized because it invaded the peace and safety of the people. Prevention of the spreading of dangerous diseases among cattle is now universally recognized in this country as within the domain of the police power, as it is so essential to the public safety and health. It is also now generally recognized that where the disease among cattle is so very dangerous and of so contagious or infectious a character as to be communicable to human beings through the consumption of the flesh or milk of such animals as have the disease, as the foot and mouth disease is generally considered to be, legislatures may, and should, confer upon boards of commissions the power to destroy animals afflicted with such a disease when thought to be necessary to public safety.

The decree is affirmed in favor of the State Board of Livestock Commissioners.

The federal government extensively regulates the interstate movement of diseased animals and the importation of animals into the United States. Some states have tried, with limited success, to restrict the importation of animals from diseased areas in other states. Many states have enacted statutes providing for the confinement of animals which are being transported into the state and unloaded while in transit.[19]

Penalties are set forth in the statutes for persons who violate statutory transportation and quarantine measures. In addition, there may be civil liability for damages caused by the communication of a disease if a person is aware that his or her animals are diseased and allows them to run at large.[20]

HOG CHOLERA—POTENTIAL LIABILITY

UNITED STATES v. STARKEY
United States District Court, E.D. Ill., 1943
52 F. Supp. 1

Defendant is charged with violation of the statute and the regulation promulgated in pursuance thereof, forbidding shipping in interstate commerce hogs afflicted with cholera or other contagious, infectious or communicable diseases.

---

[19] *E.g.*, ILL. REV. STAT. ch. 8, § 182 (1979).

[20] ILL. REV. STAT. ch. 8, § 191.1 (1979); Herrick v. Gary, 83 Ill. 85 (1876).

The seller of the pigs, a farmer, having employed a veterinarian to examine the animals, weighing about 110 pounds each, being advised that they had fever, and having learned, from a post-mortem examination of one of them by the veterinarian, that they were not well and might have cholera or some other disease, took 16 of his 19 pigs to market, retaining two, which afterwards died. Defendant purchased the pigs. Defendant examined them before the deal was completed. He was advised that they had fever. He saw that the hogs were not in good, marketable condition as they were young, unfattened and thin, and knew that the price paid for them was much below the normal market prices of market-ready hogs. The pigs were immediately taken by truck to Indianapolis and upon examination the next morning, most of them were found to be afflicted with cholera.

The circumstances, it seems to me, point irresistably to the conclusion that if defendant, dealing in hogs and knowing of the prohibition of shipping cholera hogs, had exercised the reasonable care of a reasonably prudent dealer, as he was bound to do, he would have discovered the cholera and would not have shipped the pigs. He closed his eyes to obvious sources of information, ignoring results of inquiries readily accessible with regard to immature pigs not fattened for market which he was advised were afflicted in some way. I conclude, therefore, that his willful failure to pursue inquiries, his actual knowledge and what he could have discovered, point irrefutably to the ultimate fact that he is guilty of knowingly shipping in interstate commerce hogs afflicted with cholera.

Individual producers in need of information concerning animal disease laws and regulations should contact their local veterinarian. Local veterinarians have a good working knowledge of such laws and are also in touch with state and federal health officials. Federal regulations can be found in the Code of Federal Regulations printed by the U.S. Government Printing Office. Most states have developed informational programs and provide copies of all the regulations and also provide separate pamphlets on animal disease laws upon request. Much of this material is detailed and contains numbers, facts, and figures which change with new discoveries and evolving needs.

Perhaps the best way to understand general principles of animal disease laws is to select a particular disease and see what happens to livestock owners whose animals contract that disease. The following case study of an actual disease outbreak serves this purpose well.

Brucellosis: A Case Study

On May 2, 1979, Mr. X, a southern Illinois farmer, took two cows which had aborted to a local livestock auction market.[21] The purchaser wanted to use the cows for breeding purposes, and, therefore, they had to be tested for brucellosis. Both of the cows tested positive and had

---

[21] He had attributed the abortions as well as several other abortions during the winter to leptospirosis contracted from deer in the area and had consulted with his veterinarian about the problem although no tests had been made.

to be slaughtered. Mr. X did, however, receive the market value of the cows.[22]

On May 21, Mr. X received an official notice of quarantine from the Illinois Department of Agriculture Division of Meat, Poultry and Livestock Inspection.[23] Under the quarantine, sales could be made for slaughter only and the animals would have to be branded "S" on the left jaw before leaving the farm.[24]

Mr. X wanted to get his herd tested immediately to determine how many reactors were present, to send them to slaughter, and to eventually have the rest of his herd released from quarantine. The tests performed shortly thereafter revealed twenty reactors.[25] On May 22, the reactors were branded with a "B" by state veterinarians and shipped to slaughter.[26] Mr. X then had to decide whether to conduct a retest or depopulate.[27] Due to the serious

infection of his herd, he chose to depopulate. Federal and state approval to depopulate was obtained on June 28 and was to be performed any time after July 1.[28] The remainder of the herd was branded "B" and sent to slaughter on July 16.

Mr. X received the market price of the animals sold for slaughter as well as indemnification from both the state and federal governments.[29] Each provided $50 per head to total $100 per head in indemnification proceeds.[30] The indemnity is designed to put less of a burden on the individual farmer by compensating the farmer for the governmental action taken. Producers are compensated for the fact that they are required to sell their animals whether or not the animals meet optimal market weight and condition criteria.

The Division of Meat, Poultry and Livestock Inspection traced the source

---

[22] The purchaser had to sell the cows for slaughter and may have suffered a slight loss if he paid a premium to take the cows back out to the country for breeding. He was not entitled to indemnification proceeds.

[23] Unofficially, he was already under quarantine as of the date the reactor cows were retested.

[24] Branding had to be done by a hot iron and the animals had to be identified by an approved ear tag.

[25] The test was at state expense, as are all the retests of suspects and retests to qualify a herd for release from quarantine, as long as funds are available for this purpose.

[26] All reactor cattle are branded with a "B" brand as opposed to an "S" brand. The "S" brand is used for suspects and exposed animals which are sold for slaughter. The animals had to be shipped within 15 days after tagging and branding to qualify for state and federal indemnification. The animals were shipped to National Stockyards, Illinois.

[27] If he had chosen to retest, he would have been required to retest every 6 months until he had one "clean" test in which all of the animals tested negative.

[28] The option to depopulate was available since

more than 10 percent of his herd were disclosed as reactors on a single herd test.

[29] There is a slight discount for cattle branded "B" as fewer plants are equipped to handle them. The kill floor must be cleaned both prior to and after the cattle are killed, the workers must change their clothing, and the carcasses must be hung in separate coolers. Once the meat passes inspection, it is safe for consumption purposes. The main concern is the health hazard to workers in packinghouses who may contract undulant fever. There are several packers who have had a large number of employees infected with brucellosis at one time. This has been costly and troublesome to them in terms of hiring and training substitute employees, downtime, and additional expenditures. *See, e.g.,* Donald C. Utterback, L.C.I. Annual Meeting Report, 1973. In addition, Mr. X intimated a valid concern that packer buyers may not bid competitively on "banger" cattle and may collusively take advantage of the owner's predicament. Consequently, it can be argued that the statutorily fixed indemnification proceeds are not enough to make the producer "whole."

[30] Registered animals are entitled to additional indemnity by statute.

of the infection to a purchase by Mr. X of thirty-two heifer calves at an Interstate Producers Livestock Association (IPLA) sale on January 5, 1978. The heifer calves had originated from Indiana. The proper Indiana authorities were then notified to help in the job of tracing.[31] In addition, all of the sales made by Mr. X after January 5, 1978, were traced. The Missouri Department of Agriculture was notified in the event that they desired to do a follow-up on two groups of heifers purchased by Missouri residents.

Mr. X was required to clean and disinfect with an approved disinfectant all of his barns and lots.[32] He also signed an agreement not to restock for a period of 30 days following depopulation. A list of recommendations was then made available to Mr. X to help him avoid any future problems with brucellosis, and on August 28 his farm was released from quarantine.[33] He did reenter the cattle business within 5 months and has had no further problems with brucellosis.

10.6 OTHER LAWS

Brands

In the range country, it is necessary to provide a means of determining the ownership of animals. Consequently, the legislatures of all the states in which open grazing is practiced have enacted comprehensive laws regarding the recording and inspection of brands and the transfer of branded animals.[34] These laws generally contain the following provisions:

1. A requirement that each owner of certain kinds of livestock (generally cattle, horses, and mules) adopt a brand and have it recorded. The brand must differ from any already recorded. When approved, it must be applied to the owner's livestock.
2. When animals are sold, a bill of sale or other written evidence of the transfer must be signed by the seller and given to the purchaser. There are exceptions to this requirement in the laws of some states, but

[31] The heifer calves were less than 6 months of age when they crossed the state line and thus were not required to be tested for brucellosis. In Illinois, feeding or grazing cattle consisting of heifers over 6 months and under 18 months of age may only enter the state when accompanied by an official interstate health certificate and a permit from the division. They are placed under quarantine at destination and may be held under quarantine for a period of feeding not to exceed 12 months. One sale or transfer of feeding or grazing cattle under quarantine is permitted. The quarantine is released when the owner reports the shipment of the quarantined animals to a public stockyard or a livestock auction market, the sale of the quarantined cattle for immediate slaughter, or the slaughter of the cattle for the owner's own use. Quarantine is also released if the animals die or if a negative brucellosis blood test is obtained. Generally, all female cattle 18 months of age and over for feeding or grazing purposes only and all dairy or breeding cattle over 6 months must test negative within 30 days prior to entry or be under 24

months of age and officially calfhood vaccinated against brucellosis. If dairy or breeding cattle are from a certified brucellosis-free herd they need not be tested as long as the animals are properly identified and accurate records are maintained.
[32] The Division of Meat, Poultry and Livestock Inspection had a list of approved disinfectants from which Mr. X could select. He indicated that the availability of the disinfectants at local farm supply stores and elevators was less than desirable in light of the fact that the premises had to be disinfected within 15 days.
[33] It was recommended that he avoid assembling a herd from random unknown sources, isolate all newly purchased additions, avoid the addition of any bred heifers or cows with calves from a feedlot to an established breeding herd without a negative brucellosis test, avoid sharing common pastures and co-mingling with other herds, and annually test for brucellosis.
[34] See, e.g., COLO. REV. STAT. §§ 35-43-101 et seq. (1973); WYO. STAT. ANN. §§ 11-20-101 et seq. (1977).

it is quite general. The purpose of the bill of sale is to overcome presumptions of wrongful possession by someone who has animals with different brands.

3.   Local brand inspectors, usually working under authority of the state department or commissioner of agriculture, must inspect all animals leaving their district to determine if any are being sold by a person other than the owner.

4.   An inspection of hides at slaughterhouses is frequently required as a further means of disclosing theft and wrongful sale.

5.   Usually, there is a provision that animals shall not be skinned in remote locations which make difficult the detection of theft.

6.   Penalties of a substantial nature are provided for violation of these laws, especially for attempted defacing or changing of brands.

Cruelty to Animals

Some think of cruelty to animals in terms of external violence, and picture the members of societies for the prevention of cruelty to animals as the only persons seriously concerned about maltreatment. As a matter of fact, the law on the subject is extensive. Many people, including authorities in the field of animal husbandry, have pointed to the failure of some farmers to afford adequate feed, shelter, and footing for farm livestock, especially during bad weather, as a cause of economic loss and, in the worst cases, as a species of cruelty to animals.

Some state legislatures have given counties the power to take necessary measures and to institute proceedings to enforce laws for the prevention of cruelty to animals. Other states place enforcement responsibilities with a state agency, such as the state department of agriculture. Enforcement often utilizes a complaint system, followed by a formal investigation and the imposition of sanctions, varying from injunctions to potential jail sentences and fines.

The usual forms of cruelty designated by statute are the following: overloading, overdriving, overworking, cruelly beating, torturing, tormenting, mutilating, and cruelly killing animals; cruelly working any old, maimed, infirm, sick, or disabled animal; unnecessarily failing to provide any animal with proper feed, drink, and shelter; abandoning any old, maimed, infirm, sick, or disabled animal; carrying or driving an animal in an unnecessarily cruel manner.[35]

Although such laws were aimed primarily at abuses of horses in the pre-automobile and pre-tractor days, they are sufficiently comprehensive to cover cruelty to other animals.

Legislatures have also made it unlawful for railroads or common carriers to allow animals to be confined for more than a specified number of hours without being fed and watered, unless the carriers are delayed by storm or accident.

The keeping of pigeons to be killed for sport, the mutilation of horses' tails, and the maintenance of a place for, or the paying of admission to see, the fighting of bulls, bears, dogs, cocks, or other creatures are prohibited in many states.

---

[35] *See, e.g.,* ILL. REV. STAT. ch. 8, §§ 701 *et seq.* (1979).

CRUELTY TO ANIMALS—COCKFIGHTING

STATE OF NEW MEXICO v. BUFORD
Supreme Court of New Mexico, 1958
65 N.M. 51, 331 P. 2d 1110

The Assistant District Attorney of Lea County filed an information charging the defendant (appellee) with violation of the New Mexico Cruelty to Animals Statute, in that, on or about the 21st day of February, 1958, the defendant

did promote, procure, counsel, and aid a cockfight in which two roosters, or cocks, were permitted and encouraged to engage in combat, armed with artificial spurs, and in which said cocks were permitted and encouraged to inflict dangerous wounds one upon the other at a public exhibition and before a crowd of spectators in Lea County, New Mexico.

The State now prosecutes this appeal from the action of the trial court in sustaining defendant's motion to quash the information on the ground that the term "any animal," as used in the statute, includes gamecocks, but that as a matter of law the language of the statute does not contemplate the fighting of gamecocks in the manner described in the information above.

The sole issue presented is whether or not cockfighting, as above described, comes within the terms of New Mexico's Cruelty to Animals Statutes 40-4-3, N.M.S.A. 1953, which reads in part as follows:

If any person torture, torment, deprive of necessary sustenance, cruelly beat, mutilate, cruelly kill or overdrive *any animal,* or unnecessarily fail to provide the same with proper food or drink, or cruelly drive or work the same when unfit for labor, he shall be punished by a fine...." [Emphasis supplied.]

We are concerned primarily with the emphasized portion. The State contends that the fighting of gamecocks, as above described, is torture and torment to animals within the meaning of this statute, whereas the defendant asserts that gamecocks are not animals as that term is used, and that if they are, cockfighting is not prescribed by the statute.

Nowhere in the statutes are the terms "animal," "torture" or "torment" defined. Several sister states have, however, provisions specifically defining these terms as used in their cruelty to animal statutes.

"Animal" has been defined to include "every living creature except men," or "the human race," or "human beings;" "every living dumb creature;" "the whole brute creation," or "any domestic animal."

In view of these definitions and the finding of the trial court that "any animal" includes gamecocks, from which no cross-appeal or cross-error was taken, we assume for purposes of this opinion that the finding is correct.

The words "torture" and "torment" are commonly defined to include every act, omission, or neglect whereby unjustifiied physical pain and suffering or death is *caused or permitted.*

(After citing statutes and cases from several jurisdictions the court said:)

There is authority that cruelty to animals is strictly a statutory offense and if prohibited it must come within the terms of the statute.

Certainly from early times, cockfighting has been considered a lawful and honorable sport in New Mexico. In 1875 the Territorial Legislature passed Sunday Laws which contained a specific prohibition of cockfighting on Sunday. It should be noted that a statute which had the effect of amending this statute was passed on February 17, 1887, five days after the original cruelty to animals statute was approved. Thus, the legislature again recognized that cockfighting was legal on weekdays, this time after passage of the cruelty to animals provision.

While it is true that in the minds of some men, there is nothing more violent, wanton, and cruel, necessarily producing pain and suffering to an animal, than placing a cock in a ring with another cock, both equipped with artificial spurs, to fight to the death, solely for man's amusement and sport, others consider it an honorable sport mellowed in the crucible of time so as to become an established tradition not unlike calf-roping, steer riding, bull-dogging, and bronco busting. As stated in the case of Mikell v. Henderson, supra 63 S. 2d 509:

Everyone familiar with roosters and particularly game roosters, knows that they need no encouragement to fight. It is not necessary that their tail feathers be pulled, or that any other inducement be offered, or stimulant applied, in order to produce a fight.

Admittedly the words "torture" and "torment," under the prevailing definitions which include pain and suffering "permitted" would seem to embrace fighting cocks equipped with artificial spurs or gaffs capable of cutting deep wounds and sharp gashes in the cocks, but when looking at the statute as a whole we are not convinced the legislature so intended it to be construed.

Penal statutes are to be strictly construed since every man should be able to know with certainty when he is committing a crime. Such a statute should define the act necessary to constitute the offense with such certainty that the person violating it must know that his act is criminal when he does it.

The language of the statute, however, seems to apply only to brute creatures and work animals and the history shows that it was passed in relation to other laws governing livestock. No specific definition of the meaning of the controversial terms was set forth nor does the statute itself contain words making it unlawful for a person to allow two animals to do what they by nature would do in the absence of such person under similar circumstances.

The appellee has favored us with an appendix to his brief showing the states having a specific provision prohibiting cockfighting and those having only a general cruelty law. After a careful examination of those provisions we note the following: Forty-one states, Hawaii, the District of Columbia, and Alaska, have specific prohibitions against fighting game cocks. Seven states have only general cruelty to animal laws, but no case has been found dealing with cockfights under these general laws, other than the Florida case noted above. Of those states having specific provisions against cockfighting, none were found to be without a general cruelty statute similar to, but more comprehensive than the New Mexico statute. Notwithstanding the fact that many states specifically defined the controversial terms, they still had a specific prohibition, some including it within the general cruelty law.

Thus we reach the conclusion that the type of cruelty to animal statute we are construing was not passed with the intention of prohibiting such sports as cockfighting. We further believe that, to so construe the statute, would open up many other activities to prosecution, though they are not within its spirit. For example, using live minnows to bait hooks.

We deem any prohibition of cockfighting must come from the legislature and hold the judgment should be affirmed.

Disposal of Dead Animals

Most states have laws which are concerned with the proper disposal of refuse, including dead animals. For example, one Illinois statute directs that animals, poultry, or fish which have died are not to lie about the premises, but must be disposed of within 24 hours as prescribed by regulations of the Department of Agriculture. These regulations concerning on-the-farm disposal prohibit all open burning. Disposal by burning is permitted only in an incinerator approved by the Illinois Environmental Protection Agency.

Disposal by burying is the normal procedure. Illinois Department of Agriculture regulations require the carcass to be buried deep enough to allow at least a 6-inch soil cover and to prevent any disturbance by animal or mechanical means. The burial site should be located to prevent contamination of water supplies. The regulations further provide that the abdominal cavity of large carcasses should be punctured to allow the escape of gases. Finally, lime and other chemicals should not be used to prevent decomposition.

Game and Fish

The common-law theory is that all game and fish belong to the state and can be legally reduced to possession by individuals only in accordance with such laws, rules, and regulations as the state prescribes. Under its police power, the state has the right to prescribe hunting or fishing seasons, species which may be taken, number which may be taken daily or possessed at any one time, method of taking, and conditions essential to procuring a license.

Under the common-law theory, an animal wild by nature is nevertheless the subject of property once it is domesticated and has the will to return to its owner's premises. However, most states prescribe the conditions under which wild animals can be taken and kept. Presumably, if these conditions are not met and a permit is not obtained, the common-law rule would not protect the taker.

With respect to licenses for hunting, fishing, and trapping, it is a general policy in most states to excuse the occupants of farmland from having to procure licenses as long as the activity takes place on the premises occupied by them and as long as game, fish, and trapping laws are adhered to. Persons under 16 years of age often are not required to procure a license for fishing with hook and line. Other exceptions may be made, such as on behalf of persons in the armed forces, persons over 65 years of age, or other classes of people for whom the courts would regard as reasonable to extend such special privileges.

Migratory waterfowl are subject to federal regulation, and on federal lands, hunting, fishing, and trapping are subject to federal law.

Hunting, Fishing, and Trespass.   Farm owners are under no duty to admit hunters and fishers to their property, and, unless permission is given, entry for this purpose constitutes trespass. Under certain circumstances, the trespass not only gives rise to a civil action on the part of the landowner but also constitutes a criminal offense. The same is true if the premises are posted at the main entrance, but hunters or fishers enter nevertheless without permission. Entering to fish is a trespass, even if the entry is by boat on a stream, unless the stream is designated as a public one by applicable state law.

In any case, one who enters the property of another, whether with or without permission, is responsible for damage to property, including that which may be caused to animals, fences, or crops. If the land is rented, the farm tenant is ordinarily the person who has the right to extend or refuse permission. In the absence of proof to the contrary, it would be presumed that when hunters or fishers ask permission and it is given, the permission applies only to the particular day on which they come. If the owner said "come back any time you want to," this might amount to a license for the current season. An early law providing that if one hunts on land by invitation of the owner, the person needs no license was held invalid. Also, in a 1904 Illinois decision, *Cummings v. People*, 211 Ill. 392, 71 N.E. 103, it was held that neither stockholders in a corporation owning land for a hunting lodge in Illinois nor members of the hunting club are privileged to hunt without a license on land belonging to the club.

Wildlife Habitat Management Areas and Controlled Shooting Areas.   In most states, landowners who want to aid in the conservation of wildlife may cooperate with the appropriate state agency by leasing land for wildlife habitat management areas. The state may cooperate with the landowners in improving wildlife cover. Generally some portion of the area must be open for public hunting during the regular season. No hunting is permitted on the remaining land. These laws usually provide rules for hunting, removing surplus game, protecting the farm premises from hunters, and supervising the project. The state may reimburse the farmer at an agreed price for hay or any other crops the farmer leaves standing for the benefit of game. The law permits and regulates hunting clubs.[36]

---

[36] ILL. REV. STAT. ch. 61, § 3.27 (1979). Among the Department of Conservation's licensing requirements for upland game shooting are the following: (1) The shooting area must be not less than 320 acres nor more than 1280 acres of contiguous land, and the land must be controlled for 5 years or more. (2) Every controlled shooting area must release 250 Bobwhite quail, Chukar partridges, or pheasants each season. (3) All game must be banded with special bands provided by the Department of Conservation. (4) The hunting club must not kill more than 80 percent of the game released, except that a club may kill 100 percent of the Chukar partridges and certain other birds which are native.

The Right to Kill Game Damaging Crops or Property.[37] Many states provide that the owners and tenants of lands may destroy certain wild birds or mammals when such wild bird or wild animal is destroying property on his or her land, by obtaining written permission from an appropriate state agency.[38] Following such a request, the agency will make a determination and, if it agrees that the game should be destroyed to prevent damage, will instruct the farmer about the measures to be taken and the disposition to make of any game so killed. It is quite likely that where severe damage is suffered and time is important, the farmer would by common law be excused if the destruction of game was undertaken prior to receiving a permit. To some extent, this view is supported by court decisions holding that the state is not liable for damage done by protected wild animals. One could argue that if this is true and if it is not possible to procure a permit before the damage is done, then the farmer would have a constitutional right to protect property.

GAME—RIGHT OF FARMER TO KILL DESTRUCTIVE ANIMALS

CROSS v. STATE
Supreme Court of Wyoming, 1962
370 P. 2d 371, 93 A.L.R. 2d 1357

This case involved the question as to whether or not a man may protect his property against depredation by protected game animals.

By stipulation filed in said district court on March 6, 1961, the defendant Albert "Ab" Cross admitted the killing of the moose in question, admitted they were killed out of season and at a time when the defendant did not possess a proper license or permit, and admitted to all facts set forth in the complaint of the state, upon which the defendant was tried on appeal. Defendant, however, asserted and presently asserts that he is not guilty of any of the crimes charged against him despite such admission of fact by reason of the fact that such killing was done by him in defense of property. The State of Wyoming therein admits that the moose in question were causing damage at the time of killing, that the damage being caused by said moose was sufficient under the law to justify the defendant's killing of said moose in the defense of his property, if the defense of justification is a proper and legal defense under the laws of this state and the facts agreed upon in the case.

---

[37] For a discussion of N.Y. court cases involving liability of the state for damage done by protected wild animals, see an article under this title by Judge Bartlett Rummel in the September 1965 issue of *American Rifleman*, pages 45 to 47. Also, there is a good discussion of the right of farmers to kill game animals damaging their crops or livestock in Annot. 93 A.L.R. 2d 1367 (1962). This discussion follows the report of Cross v. State, 370 P. 2d 371, 93 A.L.R. 2d 1357 (Wyo. 1962), in which the court held that the facts showed justification on the part of a farmer for killing two moose.

[38] ILL. REV. STAT. ch. 61, § 2.37 (1979).

The defendant, Albert Cross, and his father before him, have owned about 7,200 acres of land on the Dunoir River in Fremont County. George Cross, father of defendant, moved there in 1907. Wild game was non-existent there in 1907, but game animals started to appear in that area in 1915, avoiding the meadowlands. The big increase in game population and resultant trespass on meadowland became noticeable from 1937 onward.

There has been a large and increasing herd of wild game having its fall and winter range within and along the Dunoir and upper Wind River regions in Fremont County, near the town of Dubois, Wyoming, and adjacent to the Game and Fish Dennison Refuge. During the summer and fall months, these animals range and forage on the Shoshone National Forest, near the Refuge, staying well back in the mountains and away from the private lands of the defendant and his neighbors. As winter sets in, the annual migrations of wild animals begin, leading them to follow various natural courses, through the Forest Reserve, down creek bottoms, and along ridges, many of which natural trails converge and enter upon the "H—" Ranch, belonging to defendant.

These animals each year have done serious and substantial damage to the defendant's ranch, the extent of these damages ranging annually from fifteen hundred dollars to four thousand dollars; the principal items of damage are the consumption of pasture and other forage reserved for defendant's livestock, injury to the turf, curtailing the production of hay and other natural grasses growing on the ranch lands, serious and costly destruction of fences caused by the attempts of the moose, elk and other wild animals to jump over the fences, and either becoming entangled in the wires or breaking through them; the interference of the wild game, especially moose, with the normal ranching operations, due to the necessity for patrolling the areas which are constantly threatened by the moose in the destruction of the necessary reserves of winter and spring feed for the domestic animals, and the necessity for driving them away; the damage to fences requiring interruption of ranching operations; and finally, the disturbance caused by the moose themselves in driving them off the ranch, exciting domestic livestock thereon; and the refusal of domestic livestock to graze on, forage or eat hay or other edible substances after the same has been trampled, urinated upon and defecated upon by the moose; and the stench of moose offal, especially the urine, is so offensive to both domestic animals and humans, that it constitutes a serious menace.

It is virtually impossible to keep the moose and elk off the defendant's ranch property by fencing, for the reason that fences do not offer a serious enough obstacle to prevent entry by wild game.

The defendant has, over the years, done everything in his power to get assistance from the State Game and Fish Department to help solve his plight; he has hired and paid for riders to get the wild animals driven away; he has expended considerable sums of money hiring airplanes to "spook" the moose and elk away from his premises; he has been forced into long drawn out and expensive litigation with the Game and Fish Department to enforce sufficient control to protect the residents in this area; this defendant and various of his neighbors have been forced to support and maintain this ever-increasing herd of wild game species and have been helpless to prevent the wild game from virtually "taking over" the ranching operations by belligerently driving cattle from feed grounds, by chasing horses, by chasing hired help and their families indoors, by usurping and defending their usurpation of sheds, barns hay corrals, etc.; children are permitted to carry firearms from ranches to school as a protection against the quarrelsome moose; and defendant has experienced perennial frustration in attempting to control the wild game herds and protect his property with insufficient help from the Game and Fish Department.

Both parties further agreed in the district court that by reason of the foregoing Stipulation of Fact there remained no factual issue for determination by the jury, and that none of the facts which constitute grounds for prosecution by the state nor none of the facts which constitute grounds for the defense of justification by the defendant were in conflict or dispute and that there remained, therefore, only the single issue of law to be determined by that Honorable Court, namely;

"Under the laws of the State of Wyoming and the facts agreed upon in the case, is the defense of justification available to the defendant in avoidance of the criminal charges made against the defendant."

The parties further stipulated therein that in the event such defense be available to the defendant, the complaint against him and all counts therein contained ought to be dismissed, but that in the event that such defense be not available to defendant in the district or supreme court, that he be guilty as charged.

A lengthy argument as to the police power of the legislature has been made in the brief of counsel for the state. The rights of individuals are subject to certain reasonable regulations by the legislature under the police power, but the police power too has its limitations and cannot come in direct conflict with constitutional provisions. So we shall proceed to consider whether or not the legislature can, pursuant to police power, prohibit a man from protecting his property from the depredations of wild animals. The authorities are practically unanimous on that point. (The Court cited numerous authorities and then concluded:)

Counsel for the state claim that these cases are not in point. They say that they have been decided under a constitutional provision which directly gives the right to protect property. For instance, the Constitution of Pennsylvania, as also the constitutions of a number of other states, provides:

All men are born equally free and independent, and have certain inherent and indefeasible rights, among which are those of enjoying and defending life and liberty, of acquiring, possessing and protecting property and reputation, and of pursuing their own happiness.   [Art. 1, Sec. 1, Const. Pa., P.S.]

Our Constitution does not have the exact wording of the Constitution of Pennsylvania and so counsel claim that the right to protect property is not a constitutional right. We think that the brief of counsel for the state does a grave injustice to the intelligence and statesmanship of the able framers of our Constitution, the memory of some of whom like that of the late Chief Justice Potter has not yet faded into the distant past. It is unbelievable that the inherent and inalienable right to protect property, as well as life and liberty, recognized long before the Declaration of Independence, was ignored or omitted from our Constitution or is nullified thereby.

Section 23-117, W.S. 1957, provides that a person whose property is damaged by wild animals may file a claim with the Game and Fish Commission for the amount of damages sustained. It is argued by the state that this gives such landowner an adequate remedy. We hardly think that a landowner should be compelled to waive his constitutional rights by filing a claim for damages, perhaps every month, every two months, every year, or at other intervals, and recover damages perhaps after protracted litigation. The argument of the state carried to its logical conclusion would mean that a person must, before killing a wild animal, permit his property, even his own home, to be invaded and destroyed. It would mean a relinquishment of his constitutional rights for money which may be recovered by a claim filed with the commission.

In conclusion, though we may be guilty of tautology, we think that before a defendant can resort to force in protecting his property from wild animals protected by law he should use every remedy available to him before killing such animals. He should use only such force as may be reasonably necessary and suitable to protect his property and must use only such force and means as a reasonably prudent man would use under the circumstances.

However, in view of the stipulation between the parties herein, judgment herein is reversed and the complaint against the defendant should be dismissed.

Reversed with direction.

Pet Shop Operators, Dog Dealers, Bull Lessors

Many states have enacted legislation in other areas affecting animals. Among others, pet shop operators, dog dealers, and bull lessors are subject to regulation. Licensed pet shop operators and dog dealers are often required by statute to maintain sanitary conditions, ensure proper ventilation, provide adequate nutrition and humane care and treatment, and take reasonable care to release for sale, trade, or adoption only those animals which are free of disease, injuries, or abnormalities.[39] Bull lessors are frequently subject to licensing requirements and may be required to maintain proper identification and records of all bulls loaned or leased for breeding purposes. Breeding bulls may also be required by statute to have brucellosis tests made within a certain period of time prior to the loan or lease of the breeding bull.[40]

---

[39] ILL. REV. STAT. ch. 8, § 301-322 (1979).

[40] ILL. REV. STAT. ch. 8, § 251-267 (1979).

STUDY QUESTIONS

1. At common law, what property rights were afforded persons in possession of dogs and cats? Wild animals? The offspring of trespassing male animals? Bees?

2. What rules now generally govern dogs and cats?

3. What is the right of a livestock owner to destroy stray dogs that might be a hazard to livestock? What typical changes in the common law have been made by statute?

4. If a livestock owner loses livestock to an unidentified dog, does the livestock owner have any recourse in most states?

5. What is a dog owner's liability for injury caused by vicious actions of the dog?

6. Describe the common regulatory scheme to control rabies.

7. Who has responsibility to build and maintain a division fence? How can this rule be justified? What part of the fence should an adjacent landowner maintain?

8. Under what conditions is the owner of trespassing livestock likely to be held liable for resulting damage?

9. Your livestock escapes onto a nearby road where some are hit by a passing car. The livestock, the driver, and the car are damaged or injured. Who is liable? What would be your potential liability if the livestock had escaped from a stockyard to which they had been consigned?

10. What animal diseases are regulated by the U.S. government? What is the nature of the federal regulation? Do states also get involved?

11. How are brands protected?

12. How are animals protected from cruelty?

13. At common law, who owns all game and fish? What are the rights of landowners to hunt and fish? What are their rights to destroy animals damaging crops or other property?

11

Agricultural Credit and Finance – A Legal Perspective†

The credit devices which apply to other businesses also apply to the farmer. The farmer writes checks and maintains bank accounts, executes promissory notes, pays interest on borrowed money, purchases stocks and bonds for investment, makes financial statements, becomes familiar with drafts, bills of lading, and warehouse re-

---

†The authors are indebted to Professor Thomas L. Frey, Dept. of Agricultural Economics, University of Illinois for his helpful suggestions regarding the content of this chapter.

ceipts, and in many other ways engages in commercial transactions. Because of the nature of the farming enterprise and of farm property and, also, because of the kinds of transactions in which a farmer sometimes engages, there are often special rules which apply in the use of some of these devices and instruments.[1]

The sections which follow present an overview of credit sources and the mechanics of borrowing as a general foundation for the more detailed discussion in later sections. The loan agreement and some particularly troublesome clauses—acceleration and confession of judgment clauses, for example—are also discussed. Since farmers and ranchers, as a class, are constantly buying and selling real estate, a special discussion of mortgages and installment land contracts is included, noting some of the protections afforded debtors and creditors by the law and some additional protections that could be negotiated and included in the formal instrument. A similar discussion of security interests in personal property as governed by Art. 9 of the Uniform Commercial Code follows. Finally, bankruptcy is discussed. Debtors of farmers and ranchers can and do go bankrupt, and even agricultural producers can go bankrupt because of the ever-present cost-price squeeze in agriculture.

11.1 SOURCES OF CREDIT

The sources of credit available to farmers range widely, but may generally be classified as either institutional or noninstitu-tional. In selecting the appropriate source of credit, the borrower must first understand the type of credit needed. There are three basic types, the first being *short-term* credit. Working-capital loans for seasonal production best illustrate this type of credit. *Intermediate-term* credit is used most frequently to finance the acquisition of farm equipment and machinery and the making of farm improvements. The third type of credit is *long-term* credit, which is used primarily to finance the acquisition of land or the building of a home.

Once the borrower has determined which sources of credit offer the particular type of credit needed, the decision of which source to utilize will be based upon both the willingness of each source to lend and the relative advantages of the financing offered by each source. The borrower should be alert to the legal and practical factors which distinguish one loan from another.

Institutional Lenders
Commercial Banks. Banks offer short- and intermediate-term and some long-term credit. Banks commonly provide services, such as financial advisement, to their clients. If a producer has checking and savings accounts at a local bank, it would be not only convenient to borrow there, but advantageous in that the farmer might already have established a personal relationship with the bankers.

There are some disadvantages to borrowing from commercial banks. Banks often make intermediate-term loans for periods

[1] For greater detail on the matter of agricultural finance, the reader is referred to the following sources: P. J. BARRY, J.A. HOPKIN, & C. B. BAKER, FINANCIAL MANAGEMENT IN AGRICULTURE (1979); W.G. HOAG, THE FARM CREDIT SYSTEM: A HISTORY OF FINANCIAL SELF-HELP (1976); A.G. NELSON, W.F. LEE, & W.G. MURRAY, AGRICULTURAL FINANCE (6th ed. 1973); J.B. PENSON & D.A. LINS, AGRICULTURAL FINANCE—AN INTRODUCTION TO MICRO AND MACRO CONCEPTS (1980).

of 3 to 5 years. Farmers often want to extend the term of the loan to from 7 to 10 years to reflect the depreciable, or useful, life of the asset. Some commercial bankers may be reluctant to do this, and even if they do extend the term of the loan, there may be refinancing charges. Also, banks which accept deposits are required by law to maintain a certain amount of reserves. Banks also have limits as to the size of the loan they may make to each customer.

Insurance Companies.   These lenders are important sources of long-term mortgage credit.[2] They accept only first lien mortgages on real estate and concentrate their farm lending in major agricultural regions. Insurance companies often maintain minimum loan limits.

Farm Credit System: Federal Land Banks, Federal Intermediate Credit Banks, and Banks for Cooperatives.   The Farm Credit System began in 1916 when the Federal Land Banks were established.[3] Some government capital was originally used, but the cooperative system was designed to become farmer-owned and -controlled and to leave the farmer self-supporting. Government capital was totally repaid many years ago and fully replaced by private capital. The system is supervised and examined by the Federal Credit Administration, an independent government agency whose expenses are paid for by the banks and associations of the system. Three kinds of banks now exist within the system—Federal Land Banks, Federal Intermediate Credit Banks, and Banks for Cooperatives. At the local level, there are Federal Land Bank Associations and Production Credit Associations.

There are 12 district Federal Land Banks and more than 500 local Federal Land Bank Associations. The farmer-owned local associations own the land bank in their district. A farmer owning or purchasing agricultural land may obtain a first mortgage on the farm for any agricultural purpose and for other requirements of the farm family.[4] The loans are made for long terms ranging from 40 to 50 years. A farmer borrowing from a Federal Land Bank must buy stock in the local association in an amount equal to between 5 and 10 percent of the face value of the loan, which stock is redeemed for its full value when the loan is paid off.[5]

There are hundreds of local farmer-owned Production Credit Associations (PCA), which provide financing for seasonal operating purposes, living expenses, and capital expenditures for periods up to 7 years. The average size of PCA loans is larger than the average size of loans made by the commercial banks with which the PCAs compete. In order to tailor a seasonal loan to the borrower's budget, a PCA might use a line of credit arrangement.[6] A borrower from a PCA must buy stock in the amount of between 5 and 10 percent of the loan. Production Credit Associations

---

[2] A *mortgage* is a security interest in land (and the things permanently attached to it) given by a mortgagor (borrower) to the mortgagee (lender). Mortgages will be discussed more fully in Section 11.4.

[3] *See* H.R. REP. NO. 92-593, 92d Cong., 1st Sess. *reprinted in* [1971] U.S. CODE CONG. & AD. NEWS 2091, 2096.

[4] Other landowners, partnerships, corporations, trusts, estates, or other entities legally vested with authority to conduct business may obtain first mortgage loans used primarily for agricultural purposes. Also, loans may be made to nonfarm rural homeowners.

[5] Some districts pay dividends on this stock.

[6] Under a line of credit, a maximum loan amount is determined. The borrower may then draw upon that line of credit as the borrower's needs demand, so long as he or she does not exceed the maximum amount. Interest rates are minimized by such an arrangement, since the borrower only pays interest on each dollar for the number of days it was outstanding.

can make unsecured loans, as they claim to be "more interested in the farmer and his ability to repay than the collateral."[7]

There is one Federal Intermediate Credit Bank in each of the twelve districts. These banks serve three main purposes. Most important is their role in providing credit to local Production Credit Associations. Finally, these banks may discount agricultural paper held by commercial banks, finance corporations, and other institutional lenders.

There are thirteen Banks for Cooperatives, whose function is to make loans to farmer cooperatives.[8] They may provide commodity and working-capital loans on a seasonal basis for terms less than 1 year. They also provide working-capital and facility loans on a term basis for terms greater than one year.

Direct Lending through the Department of Agriculture. The U.S. Department of Agriculture makes direct loans through the Farmer's Home Administration, the Commodity Credit Corporation, and the Rural Electrification Administration. The Farmer's Home Administration (FmHA) is a federal lending agency operating within the U.S. Department of Agriculture. The FmHA performs two main functions. First, it provides supervised credit to farmers unable to obtain adequate credit from commercial lenders at reasonable rates and terms. This is primarily accomplished through three farmer-oriented credit programs—farm operating loans, farm ownership loans, and emergency loan programs. The second function is to improve rural communities and enhance rural development. This function is achieved through

rural housing loans, community development loans, and business and industrial development loans. The FmHA has rapidly expanded its guaranteed loan program, in addition to making direct loans.

The Commodity Credit Corporation makes price-supporting loans on certain stored farm products. It also handles the storage and disposal of accumulated products.

The Rural Electrification Administration (REA) finances the extension of electrical and telephone service to rural areas. Loans made by the REA may be for terms up to 35 years and up to 100 percent of the cost.

Noninstitutional Lenders

Individuals are a leading source of financing for the acquisition of real property. The two most common arrangements are mortgages and installment land contracts.[9]

Dealers are also involved in the financing of agriculture. For example, machinery might be leased from dealers. Far more common is an arrangement where the dealer takes a security interest in the item of personal property sold and receives a promissory note from the buyer, which the dealer may sell at a discount.

11.2 THE MECHANICS OF BORROWING

During the process of selecting the proper source of credit, it may be helpful to find out what type of credit is available from a particular lender and what collateral requirements each lender has. The next

[7] Generally, collateral can be real estate or a chattel. A *chattel* is an item of personal or movable property, as distinguished from real property. "Chattel" comes from the feudal word for cattle. A chattel mortgage is a security interest given in personalty. This matter will be discussed in Section

11.6.
[8] 12 district banks and a central bank in Denver, Colo.
[9] These two arrangements will be explored in Sections 11.4 and 11.5

step is to discuss with a lender the particular needs of the business.

Once the "threshold" (type of credit sought and collateral required) has been determined, the representative will ask the potential borrowers to produce a financial statement and to complete a loan application.[10] The financial statement basically shows what is owned and what is owed. The loan application will involve a statement of the purposes of the loan and a budget showing expected income and expenses. A loan application should be thoughtfully made, since it is technically an offer to enter into a binding contract. The lender could accept it as is, at which point it would be too late to modify the offer. If land is to be involved in the transaction, the borrower will eventually be required to produce an abstract of title or a title insurance policy. These are usually produced at the borrower's expense.

If the borrower and lender agree to enter into the loan, the legal documents will be prepared for signing. A wise borrower will not sign, at least initially, until after consulting a lawyer. Once the terms of the legal obligations are agreed upon, the completed documents will be executed (signed).

11.3 THE LOAN AGREEMENT[11]

A borrower is likely to encounter four legal instruments: promissory notes, mortgages, security agreements, and financing statements. The latter three instruments will be discussed in the sections dealing with mortgages and with the Uniform Commercial Code. In addition, state usury laws and federal truth in lending laws may be applicable.

Promissory Note

The note is the borrower's written promise to repay. There are several types of notes. A *demand note* states that the lender may demand repayment at any time. An *installment note* provides for debt reduction in a given number of periodic installments until the full amount is repaid. An *open-ended note* is used when a line of credit is arranged. A *collateral note* is used if personal property is pledged to the lender as security.[12]

The *promissory note* must state the amount of the loan. In addition, the interest rate is usually specified. Interest rates may be either fixed or variable (floating). Variable rates for farm loans have become very common in recent years, although their use varies from region to region. Even though a fixed interest rate may be stated, the borrower should be alert to other charges which effectively raise the cost of the loan. Closing fees, loan service fees, and costs to examine title to real property and to appraise personal property often fall upon the borrower.

The promissory note should clearly set forth the repayment plan adopted by the parties. This includes the amount of each payment, when it is to be made, and where it is to be made. It is important to be

---

[10] Additional information may be requested. For example, the Federal Land Bank in the Sixth District requires the production of federal income tax returns from the previous 3 to 5 years.

[11] Many aspects of this section were drawn from DOANE AGRICULTURAL SERVICE, INC., DO IT RIGHT THE FIRST TIME (1978).

[12] A *pledge* is when the borrower transfers some item of property to the lender as security. The lender has possession of the item until the debt is repaid.

aware of these terms, since a minor deviation may be deemed a technical default. In connection with default, there are a number of clauses which can have drastic consequences on defaulting borrowers. Borrowers should be especially alert to the significance of these terms.

Some notes contain clauses which state that "in the event of borrower's default, the borrower agrees to pay collection costs and reasonable attorney's fees." Some notes contain provisions for penalty interest which state that "after maturity, this note shall bear interest at the highest legal rate." These clauses can result in unexpected, additional costs in case of default.

Another such clause is an *acceleration clause*. A typical one reads,

If any installment is not paid when due, or if the holder deems himself otherwise insecure, the entire unpaid indebtedness shall thereupon, at the option of the holder, become immediately due and payable without notice to the maker.

The holder of the note is either the lender or someone to whom the lender has assigned or sold the note. The borrower is better protected if he or she receives notice of default, and perhaps a "grace period" of a few days to work out problems. Courts generally will not permit a holder to abuse the right to accelerate when the holder "deems himself insecure." Nevertheless, it might be possible for the borrower and lender to agree that only certain specified events would be grounds for acceleration.

Another potentially troublesome clause is a *confession of judgment*, or a *cognovit*, clause. If a borrower agrees to such a clause, any attorney may appear in court as the borrower's agent after payment is due and confess that the lender should have a judgment against the borrower in the amount of whatever payment is due. Such a procedure is carried out without notice to the borrower. To protect against this, the borrower should demand personal notification of default at least a week before any court action may be taken.[13]

Promissory notes should state whether the borrower may prepay all or part of the loan. Some lenders do not allow prepayments unless state law requires such an option; others may charge a penalty fee if prepayment is allowed. In contrast, Federal Land Banks usually allow partial or total prepayment without the assessment of penalty fees.

The lender may require someone in addition to the buyer to sign the promissory note as additional security. If the second person signs as co-maker, that person becomes primarily liable along with the borrower. On the other hand, a guarantor agrees to pay if the lender does not.

Interest Rate Ceilings

Both federal and state legislation protect consumers (borrowers) from excessive interest rates. The main tools for the accomplishment of this goal are state usury laws and the Federal Truth in Lending Act.

[13] Confession of judgment clauses have been challenged as unconstitutional. Due process requires that a party have notice and an opportunity to be heard before any judgment may be entered against the party. Confession of judgment clauses have been upheld by courts, however, when there has been a knowing and voluntary waiver of the due process requirement.

State Usury Laws.   Many states have enacted usury laws which limit the rate of interest a lender may charge. Parties to a contract may not avoid the statutorily imposed limits by merely stipulating a higher interest rate in their contract.

States frequently exempt certain transactions from the operation of the usury laws. For example, business or agricultural loans or loans in excess of a certain dollar amount may be unprotected.[14] The law of the state which governs the loan agreement should be consulted to find the applicable usury restrictions.

The remedies for an unlawful rate of interest also vary from state to state. As a general rule, a borrower may raise usury as a defense in an action by the lender to collect interest. Some states allow the borrower to sue to recover interest already paid.[15]

The Depositary Institutions Deregulation and Monetary Control Act of 1980[16] provides in part that state usury laws affecting business and agricultural loans of $25,000 or more have been preempted by the federal law for a period extending to April 1, 1983. However, the states may override this federal law by adopting a law or by certifying that the voters of a state have voted in favor of a provision that federal preemption is not wanted in that state.

Truth in Lending.   In 1968 the Federal Truth in Lending Act[17] was enacted in order to assure a meaningful disclosure of credit terms and to protect the consumer against inaccurate and unfair credit billing and credit card practices. The act imposes detailed reporting requirements on lenders. However, agricultural transactions are fully excluded from its application.[18]

11.4 MORTGAGES

A *real estate mortgage* is a conveyance of an interest in real property by the mortgagor (borrower) to the mortgagee (lender) on the condition that the transfer is void once the debt is repaid. The mortgage thus gives the lender an interest in the land and in permanent improvements on the land to secure the payment of the debt. The nature of the interest held by the lender varies from state to state. In some states, mortgagees are deemed to have title to the mortgaged property. In other states, such as Illinois, the lender has a lien on the real estate, but title remains in the debtor subject to the lender's mortgage.[19] In Illinois and many other states, the borrower is free to sell the property subject to the mortgage unless the mortgage instrument expressly prohibits such a

---

[14] For example, Illinois law provides that any rate of interest is lawful on a loan made to a corporation, on a business loan to a business association or copartnership, or on a business loan to a person owning and operating a business as sole proprietor or with another as joint tenants or tenants in common. The term "business" means in this context "a commercial, agricultural or industrial enterprise which is carried on for the purpose of investment or profit." ILL. REV. STAT. ch. 74, § 4 (1979).

[15] Illinois allows the borrower to recover twice the total of all interest paid, plus reasonable attorney's fees and court costs. ILL. REV. STAT. ch. 74, § 6 (1979).

[16] Pub. L. No. 96-221, 94 Stat. 132 (1980).

[17] 15 U.S.C. §§ 1601 *et seq.* (1976).

[18] Truth in Lending Simplification and Reform Act of 1980, Pub. L. No. 96-221, 94 Stat. 132. This act is effective as of April 1, 1982.

[19] This legal distinction becomes important in certain circumstances. For example, in Illinois, grant of title could sever a joint tenancy (and destroy the right of survivorship), but grant of a lien would not.

transfer. The lender's priority is not affected by such a sale.

The value of a mortgage to a lender lies in the priority which the lender acquires with regard to other creditors of the borrower. If the lender records the mortgage in the county where the land is located, and if this is the first mortgage on the land, then the lender has a prior claim against the whole of the mortgaged property for the full amount of the loan.[20] A "second," or "junior," mortgage exists when a loan is made on property already covered by a first mortgage, and the second lender accepts a mortgage of the property as security. In case foreclosure and sale become necessary, the second lender is entitled to the proceeds only after the full amount of the first mortgage claim has been settled.

The Mortgage Instrument

Illinois statutory law (Ill. Rev. Stat. ch. 30, § 10) provides that a mortgage of land may be in substantially the following form, which is fairly typical:

The mortgagor (here insert name or names), mortgages and warrants to (here insert name or names of mortgagee/s), to secure the payment of (here recite the nature and amount of indebtedness, showing when due and the rate of interest, and whether secured by note or otherwise), the following described real estate (here insert description thereof), situated in the county of ⸻, in the state of Illinois. Dated this ⸻ day of ⸻, A.D. 19⸻.

(signature/s)

The statute further provides that every such mortgage, when otherwise properly executed, shall be deemed and held a good and sufficient mortgage in fee to secure the payment of the moneys therein specified. If the mortgage contains the words "and warrants," the mortgage shall be construed the same as if full covenants of ownership, good right to convey against encumbrances of quiet enjoyment, and general warranty were fully written into the mortgage. If the words "and warrants" are omitted, no such covenants shall be implied. When the grantor in any such mortgage of any real estate desires to release or waive his or her homestead rights therein,[21] it is only necessary to insert in the mortgage after the words "state of Illinois" in substance the following words, "hereby releasing and waiving all rights under and by virtue of the homestead exemption laws of this state."

The mortgage instrument is likely to contain provisions detailing the rights and duties of the borrower and lender. The borrower should read the entire mortgage instrument in order to be aware of the terms of the agreement. There are numerous duties which may be imposed on the borrower, and if the borrower defaults on any one, an acceleration clause may take effect. For example, the borrower

---

[20] There are certain rights which can arise after the mortgage has been recorded, but which nevertheless become prior to the mortgage. For example, mechanic's liens and bankruptcy are prior to a first mortgage.

[21] *Homestead* may be generally defined as an exemption from debts for the head of a household. The concept was created by state laws or constitutions and represents a policy to protect the family to some extent. Originally, the exemption was probably large enough to preserve the family home, but the legislation has not kept pace with inflation in most states. In Illinois, for example, the homestead exemption is $10,000. ILL. REV. STAT. ch. 52, § 1 (1979).

may be expected to defend the land against all claimants. The borrower is usually expected to pay all taxes, liens and assessments and to insure the improvements against fire and hazard. (If the borrower defaults on these promises, usually the lender can pay the charges and then add the cost to the loan principal.) There also may be a requirement that if the property is condemned or taken under the power of eminent domain, the proceeds of the award will be applied to the underlying debt. The borrower may be expected to pay the reasonable costs of foreclosure.

Deed of Trust

In some states, it is customary for the owner of the property to convey title to a third party, in trust, to hold the property as security for the repayment of the loans made on the property. This conveyance is accomplished by a *deed of trust*. Deeds of trust are used in place of mortgages. The two instruments are similar in legal effect. A deed of trust must meet the same requirements as to signature, consideration, description of property, and other legal essentials as a mortgage. When the indebtedness secured by a deed of trust has been paid, the debtor is entitled to a release of record.

Foreclosure

Since a mortgage is security for a debt, the lender must be able to do something with the property when the debt remains unpaid after its due date. The legal method is through a suit to foreclose the mortgage or deed of trust. The ordinary foreclosure suit is nothing more than a request for sale of the property and application of the proceeds of sale to the debt. After proceedings have been properly brought, the date of the sale is advertised, the property is auctioned to the highest bidder, and the proceeds are used to pay taxes, assessments, costs, and unpaid debts. Any balance is returned to the mortgagor.

Redemption

A right of redemption is inherent in and essential to every mortgage. This right permits the mortgagor to buy back the land—even after foreclosure. To redeem the land, the mortgagor makes a payment or performs some other condition (as provided by statute). Anyone having an interest in the mortgaged premises has a right of redemption. For example, a junior, or second, mortgagee may exercise the right of redemption.

The right to redeem is a valuable property right and can be sold or transferred. The length of the period during which a redemption can be made is regulated by state law. Generally, it is between 1 and 2 years after the foreclosure sale of the property.

Since it is true that the mortgagee is entitled to the security benefits of any permanent additions to, or improvements of, the real estate, so is it true that the purchaser at a foreclosure sale will be entitled to the same improvements. Of particular interest are the rights which a purchaser at foreclosure obtains with respect to farmland and its incidents. If a tenant under an unexpired lease is on the premises, the purchaser will be entitled to the rent accruing after the redemption period. The purchaser is generally entitled to growing crops, growing fruit, nursery stock, and logs. During the period of redemption, the mortgagor is still entitled to rents and profits, and only loses such right when no redemption is made and a deed is finally executed to the purchaser. It is always possible for the mortgagor to assign his or her right of redemption.

FARM MORTGAGES—FORECLOSURE AND REDEMPTION

PHOENIX MUTUAL LIFE INS. CO. v. LEGRIS
Illinois Court of Appeals, Third District, 1975
30 Ill. App. 3d 678, 344 N.E. 2d 399

This appeal is from an order of the Circuit Court of Kankakee County which vacated part of a mortgage foreclosure decree and also vacated orders confirming the sale ordering distribution of the proceeds, and appointing a receiver for the premises.

On September 13, 1972, Phoenix Mutual Life Insurance Company (hereafter called "Phoenix") filed a complaint to foreclose its first mortgage (a lien for $125,000) which had been executed by Louis Legris, mortgagor, on May 17, 1963. The mortgaged premises consisted of a 350-acre farm, legal title to which was vested in First Trust & Savings Bank of Kankakee as trustee. In addition to Legris and First Trust, defendants to the foreclosure action included trustees under second- and third-mortgage trust deeds and owners of the debts secured by the second and third mortgages.

The decree of foreclosure and sale was entered December 1, 1972.

The sixth paragraph stated "It is therefore decreed" that the land shall be sold at a public sale on January 19, 1973. Paragraphs 7–12 contained the usual provisions for conduct of the sale and issuance of a certificate of sale by the sheriff with a reservation of jurisdiction to order distribution of the proceeds and, if necessary, to enter a deficiency decree and appoint a receiver to collect rents, issues and profits to apply to any deficiency. Paragraph 13 provided that the sale should be subject to rights of redemption but that the premises should be sold free and clear of all liens. The disputed Paragraph 14 stated:

The Court further finds that the date of service of summons upon the last Defendant to be served herein was October 3, 1972 when service was obtained by the Sheriff of Cook County upon the Defendant, Kraftco, Inc. That, according to law, the last date for redemption from said sale shall be October 3, 1973 or within six (6) months from the date of the foreclosure sale, whichever is later.

The final paragraph of the decree provided:

It is therefore ordered, adjudged and decreed that the foregoing Decree for Foreclosure be entered and that a sale of the property foreclosed be conducted as provided herein and a report thereof made as provided herein.

As a result of the sale, the premises were purchased by appellant Felesena, who was not a party to the foreclosure suit, for $295,000, and on February 5, 1973, an order confirming the sale was entered. Thereafter an order of distribution was entered which also included a deficiency decree against

Legris for $14,300 in favor of two of the junior lienholders, and on the same date a receiver was appointed.

On September 21, 1973, Legris filed a petition to vacate that part of the December 1, 1972, decree of foreclosure pertaining to its execution and all proceedings thereunder, including the sale, certificate of purchase issued to Felesena, report of sale, order approving the report of sale, order for distribution, deficiency judgment, and appointment of receiver. The petition alleged that the disputed portions of the order of foreclosure and sale were void and of no effect because the court failed to adjudicate the beginning of the period for redemption as required by statute. The petition asked that possession of the premises be returned to Legris and that the receiver account to Legris for all moneys received and paid out. The petition to vacate was granted by the circuit court on March 15, 1974, and Legris was given the relief requested.

The circuit court held the foreclosure decree void for want of judicial authority to enter a decree which failed to comply exactly with section 18e of the judgments act. That section provided, in part, as follows:

In any suit to foreclose the lien of a mortgage...the court shall order, adjudge and decree in the decree foreclosing the lien, that date when the owner of the equity of redemption, or if more than one, when the last of the owners thereof, have been served with summons or by publication as required by law, or have submitted to the jurisdiction of the court. Any defendant, his heirs, executors, administrators, assigns or any person interested in the premises, through or under the defendant, may,...within 12 months from the date so adjudicated in the decree, or within 6 months after the foreclosure sale, whichever is later, redeem the real estate so sold....The adjudication of such date in the decree of foreclosure has the effect of establishing the date for the commencement of the period of redemption under this Section and is binding on all persons and for all purposes. [Ill. Rev. Stat. 1971, ch. 77, sec. 18e.]

All parties agree that Paragraph 14 of the foreclosure order erroneously fixed the redemption period to begin on October 3, 1972, the date of service on the last defendant, Kraftco, Inc., a creditor, instead of September 18, 1972, which was the date of service on First Trust, the owner of the equity of redemption.

Legris contends that fixing an erroneous date, in contravention of the statute, had the legal effect of failing to adjudicate any date at all and consequently when the trial court ordered the foreclosure and sale, it exceeded its jurisdiction. Legris argues that the policy of the law favoring redemptions should be given effect here and directs our attention to cases holding that redemption statutes should be liberally construed.

In the case before us, we hold that the circuit court had jurisdiction of the parties and of the subject matter, and that the decree of foreclosure, although clearly an erroneous application of the statutory provisions governing redemptions, was nevertheless binding on all parties and not void. The decree of foreclosure adjudicated the date for the commencement of the period of redemption, and Legris was not prejudiced by the decree which allowed him the right to redeem until a later date than that permitted by statute. Since a direct appeal from the foreclosure decree was not taken within the time for appeal, that decree is final, and the motion to vacate should not have been granted.

Accordingly, the order of the circuit court vacating part of the decree of foreclosure and subsequent orders is reversed, and this cause is remanded with directions to reinstate the foreclosure decree, the order confirming the sale, and other orders erroneously vacated, and for such other proceedings as are consistent with this opinion.

Reversed and remanded with directions.

11.5 INSTALLMENT SALES OF FARMLAND

The usual methods of paying for farmland are straight cash sales, mortgage agreement with the seller or some third party, and installment land contracts. With a *straight cash sale*, the buyer pays the entire purchase price to the seller in exchange for an absolute deed. Where a *mortgage agreement with the seller* is used, the buyer pays a substantial portion of the purchase price to the seller as a down payment. The seller then gives the buyer a deed, receiving in return a mortgage to secure the balance. When a *mortgage agreement with a third-party lender* is used, the buyer borrows part of the money from a third party, pays the seller in full, receives a deed, and executes a mortgage of the land to the third party.

The *installment land contract* is also called a "contract for deed" or a "bond for deed." It is used when the seller wants certain income tax reporting advantages

and retention of title during the repayment period, even though the buyer will be in possession.[22] The buyer becomes the beneficial owner and takes possession of the land following the down payment. The seller retains legal title to the land as security for performance. Once the buyer has accumulated substantial equity in the land (by making installment payments over time), the arrangement may be converted to standard mortgage financing. Often with installment sale contracts, the deed and contract are deposited with an escrow agent until the conditions for delivery of the deed have been met.

Upon the formation of a valid contract for the sale of an interest in land, the buyer acquires what is known as "equitable ownership" of the land. This "divided ownership" caused some courts to rule that the buyer, although not entitled to a deed, is the true owner. These rulings are based on the equitable doctrine that "that will be regarded as done which ought to be done," thus anticipating the time when the buyer

---

[22] Installment land contracts provide advantages to both buyer and seller. The buyer puts up a down payment and gains immediate control of the farm. The seller can realize certain income tax benefits from an installment sale. The income tax advantages will be discussed in Chapter 17.

will assume full and exclusive ownership. However, the law varies from state to state on this point.

General Rules

Disposition of Property on Seller's Death. If the seller dies before all payments have been received, leaving no will, the right to receive the remaining installments passes to the estate as personal property in most jurisdictions. If the seller dies leaving a will which does not specifically bequeath the proceeds of the contract or the property subject to the contract, the contract interest passes to those beneficiaries entitled to take personal property. If the seller dies leaving a will which specifically bequeaths the property subject to the contract (e.g., "I give my farm to...."), the property usually passes to the legatee subject to the contract, regardless of whether the will was made before or after the contract.[23]

When the seller and spouse own land as joint tenants at the time the contract is made, the joint tenancy is controlling, and the survivor acquires the right to receive the remainder of the installments due under the contract.

Disposition of the Property on Buyer's Death. If the buyer and spouse acquire their interests as joint tenants, the interest of the buyer passes to the surviving spouse automatically upon death, even if there are contrary provisions in the will. If the property was not being acquired in joint tenancy, the property is treated as real estate and is distributed accordingly.

Buyer's Duty to Prevent Waste. Once the farm is in the buyer's possession, the buyer makes all decisions regarding the management and operation of the farm, unless the contract provides otherwise. There is, however, one qualification to the buyer's complete control. The seller has the right to prevent the buyer from committing acts which substantially impair the seller's security interest in the farm. The law refers to such acts as *waste*. For example, the seller would have a right to obtain a court decree demanding that the buyer refrain from cutting valuable trees, removing buildings or improvements or allowing them to fall into serious disrepair, or following improper crop practices that substantially reduce the productivity of the soil. Since these duties are not specifically defined in the law, a clause should be included in the contract covering the buyer's obligations.

As a general rule, the purchaser (once in possession) is liable to third parties who are injured because of defects on the premises. However, the seller may be liable to both the buyer and to third parties if the seller is aware of hidden defects on the premises that can cause injury and fails to warn the buyer of these defects.

Buyer's Duty to Pay Taxes. The payment of taxes and assessments levied on the farm during the term of the contract is another duty that passes to the buyer in possession. In the year of transfer, the party who receives the profits from the farming operation may bear the entire property tax burden, regardless of when the buyer went into actual possession of the farm, or the agreement may call for a pro rata sharing of taxes. For income tax purposes, the property tax deduction should be apportioned between the seller and buyer according to the time of year the sale was made, regardless of whether the parties actually apportioned the tax.

It is common practice to insert a provision in the contract that if the buyer fails to pay property taxes, the seller may

---

[23] *See, e.g.,* ILL. REV. STAT. ch. 110 1/2, §§ 4–8 (1979).

do so. Any amounts expended by the seller are then added, along with interest, to the amount due from the buyer under the contract.

Risk of Loss and Insurance. Another aspect of the buyer's "beneficial ownership" is that the risk of loss caused by fire, wind, and floods is usually borne by the purchaser. However, the seller is interested in seeing that there is adequate insurance coverage on improvements, since they serve, along with the land, as security for the purchase price. Therefore, unless the down payment exceeds the value of the improvements, the contract should place a duty on the buyer to maintain insurance on buildings.

The typical insurance clause requires coverage with a reputable insurance company, payable to both parties. The seller often agrees to assign existing insurance to the buyer, who agrees to pay the seller for a proportional share of the premium for the unexpired term.

There should be a provision in the contract that in the event of loss the insurance proceeds will be applied either to the replacement or repair of the structure destroyed or damaged, or to the unpaid balance due the seller under the contract. To minimize the risk of a misunderstanding or failure to maintain insurance, the contract should require the policies to be deposited with the escrow agent. As in the case of taxes, it is also common to provide that if the purchaser fails to pay the insurance premium, the seller may do so, with the amounts expended to be added to the balance due with interest.

Oil, Gas, and Mineral Rights. In the absence of a provision in the contract, neither the buyer alone nor the seller alone has the right to remove oil, gas, or mineral deposits from the realty, or the right to lease the mineral estate to third parties during the contract term. For this reason, especially in areas of oil and gas development,

the parties should agree on rights to minerals and incorporate this agreement into the contract.

Rights of Creditors. When one person obtains a judgment against another in court and files it in the proper county office, the judgment becomes a lien on the debtor's legal and equitable interests in any real estate in that county. Thus, the buyer's beneficial ownership in the property would be subject to liens imposed by those holding judgments against the buyer. In most states, the contract interest of the seller can also be reached by creditors. The buyer should prohibit the seller from any further encumbrance of title from and after the date of the contract so long as the buyer is not in default. The buyer should record the contract in the county where the land is located. In this way, the buyer can establish rights in the property and can obtain priority over subsequent lienors.

Right to Assign and Mortgage. Unless the contract provides otherwise, either party may sell or assign his or her interest, and the assignee acquires the same interest in the land as that held by the original party. When the seller assigns an interest, the assignee acquires the right to receive the purchase price from the buyer. Similarly, an assignee of the buyer acquires the right to receive the deed from the seller as provided in the contract.

It does not follow, however, that because the buyer has assigned the interest, there is no longer an obligation to the seller. Unless the seller has agreed to release the buyer, the original buyer may still be held responsible for payment of the purchase price.

Sellers frequently want to include a provision that prohibits assignment by the buyer without the prior consent of the seller. The same result can be obtained by inserting an option clause under which the seller is to be given the first opportunity to purchase the farm if the buyer decides to sell during the contract term.

A provision that the contract shall be obligatory upon the heirs and assigns of the parties is standard in installment land contracts. This provision is simply a statement of what the law would be in the absence of such a provision. It does, however, direct the attention of the parties to this aspect of their obligation.

What has been said with respect to assignment is equally applicable to a mortgage. In the absence of a contract provision to the contrary, either party has the power to mortgage an interest in the farm. The mortgagee, of course, acquires no greater interest than the mortgagor has under the contract.

Default on the Contract

Usually, the installment land contract provides that if the buyer defaults in the performance of the contract, the seller shall have the right to declare a forfeiture of the buyer's interest. In come cases, such a provision will be enforced by the courts. Thus, the seller can declare that the buyer's interest is at an end, retake possession of the land along with the buyer's improvements, and keep the amounts paid by the buyer as damages.

To recover possession, the seller usually gives written notice demanding possession and stating the nature of the buyer's default. If the buyer does not leave, the seller uses the legal remedy of *forcible entry and detainer*. Three considerations are taken into account by courts:

1. The nature of the buyer's default.
2. The extent of the seller's loss.
3. Whether the seller has fully complied with the terms of the contract in declaring the forfeiture.

Most contracts contain a "time is of the essence" clause, meaning that everything must be performed exactly at the time called for in the contract. These clauses, usually inserted for the seller's benefit, have been narrowly applied by the courts. For example, courts often find that such clauses are "waived" by the seller when late payments are repeatedly accepted. The seller may be able to change this situation by giving notice to the buyer that late payments will no longer be accepted.

The buyer's departure from the terms of the contract must be substantial; a forfeiture is not justified in the case of minor noncompliance. If the seller declares a forfeiture when it is not justified, the court may decide that the seller has rescinded the contract and force the seller to return to the buyer the payments on the purchase price as well as the value of the improvements made by the buyer.

Even if it is found that the buyer has made a substantial default, the courts usually will not enforce the forfeiture clause if it is found that a penalty would be imposed in doing so.

Assume, for example, that the seller has contracted to sell a farm to the buyer for $40,000, and that the agreement calls for a down payment of $10,000 and 10 annual installments of $3000 each. The fair rental value of the farm is $1500 per year. The contract has been in existence for 5 years, during which time the buyer has made improvements on the farm worth $10,000. Assume also that the seller has incurred $5000 of recoverable damages as a result of the buyer's default, which occurred at the end of the fifth year. In this situation, if the forfeiture were enforced according to its terms, the buyer would lose the following amounts:

Down payment	$10,000
Five annual $3,000 installments	$15,000
Improvements made	$10,000
Total	$35,000

The seller would have lost the following:

Rental income on farm for five years	$ 7,500
Recoverable damages	$ 5,000
Total	$12,500
Amount of penalty to buyer	$22,500

In this example, the courts would not enforce the penalty clause, and it would be necessary for the seller to foreclose and have the property sold.

If the buyer defaults and a forfeiture occurs, it is doubtful whether the buyer can be reimbursed for the value of any improvements that the buyer may have placed on the land. However, the parties may provide in the contract for payment for improvements if the buyer defaults.

The buyer may also secure some degree of protection if the contract calls for delivery of a deed to the buyer and a mortgage to the seller upon completion of a certain portion of the payments. Upon default, the buyer has all the rights of a mortgagor to have a sale through foreclosure.

If the seller refuses to deliver the title to the buyer at the time called for in the contract, the latter can obtain assistance from the courts in forcing delivery of the title.

If it is discovered that the seller's title is defective and that the seller has nothing worth conveying, the buyer's only remedy is an action for damages for breach of the contract. Before signing the contract, the buyer should always check to see that the seller has good title to the property.

COURTS DISFAVOR FORFEITURES

FISEL v. YODER
Court of Appeals of Indiana, Third District, 1974
162 Ind. App. 565, 320 N.E. 2d 783

The plaintiffs (Yoders) were buyers in a contract for the sale of farmland in Elkhart County. Fire destroyed a barn located on the premises. The Yoders received an insurance check made payable to themselves and to the seller, Fisel. The plaintiffs sent the check to Fisel for his endorsement, and received from him a notice that they had breached two of their obligations under the contract, namely to carry adequate insurance and to refrain from making major improvements without the written consent of the seller. Fisel gave them 10 days to cure the breach or else suffer forfeiture. Plaintiffs immediately tendered payment in full and demanded evidence of good title. Plaintiffs brought this action for specific performance; defendant counter-claimed for forfeiture and possession. The trial court found for plaintiffs and denied defendant's claims.

The trial court made findings of fact: the defendant had failed to object to the insurance policy when plaintiffs showed it to him, plaintiffs had re-modeled the bathroom, cleaned and re-sided the chicken house, and had generally improved the premises. These findings of fact stand, as they are not clearly erroneous.

Even if there had been a violation of these provisions of the contract, forfeiture would be improper. The Supreme Court of Indiana has said "in all but a few instances, forfeitures of land sales contracts are improper and such contracts should be considered to be in the nature of secured transactions with foreclosure as the seller's remedy rather than forfeiture."

Forfeiture might be appropriate in the case of an abandoning, absconding buyer, or in a case where the buyer has paid a minimal amount of the contract at the time of default and seeks to retain possession while the seller is paying taxes, insurance, and other upkeep to preserve the premises.

The Yoders had paid a substantial portion of the $42,000 contract price (approximately 37%). The ruling of the trial court is affirmed.

Important Contract Clauses

Prepayment Privilege. It appears to be the general rule that without a prepayment clause in the contract, any attempt by the buyer to make payments of principal to the seller before they are due may be rightfully refused by the seller—even if the full amount of interest is also tendered.

In years when farm income is high, the buyer may desire to pay ahead as a hedge against years when income may be low. If the seller agrees to this privilege, a special provision in the contract should give the buyer the right to prepay installments of principal that the buyer may apply against future installments. However, the usual agreement limits the number of future installments that may be paid at any one time and requires that these payments be in multiples of the regular payment. The provision should also state whether the installment is to be paid with interest, and if so, the amount of interest.

In earlier times, restrictions on prepayments in the first year were typically included in the contract because of income tax requirements. More recent amendments to the Internal Revenue Code concerning the installment reporting of income have deleted the requirement that no more than 30 percent of the total purchase price could be received in the first year of sale. Accordingly, such restrictions are no longer essential.

Grace Period. The usual period of grace in which to make overdue payments is 30 to 60 days. It is suggested that this period might be increased as the purchaser's equity increases. For example, a 60-day grace period might be allowed the buyer until 20 percent of the total purchase price has been paid, a 90-day grace period until between 20 and 40 percent has been paid, 120 days until between 40 and 60 percent has been paid, and so on.

Mortgage Provision. Many contracts provide that upon payment of a certain portion of the purchase price, the buyer is entitled to receive a deed if a mortgage is made to the seller. This provision entitles the buyer to fuller protection upon default. Such clauses often state that upon payment of 50 percent of the total price, a deed and mortgage shall be executed.

Arbitration Clause. An agreement to arbitrate future disputes is unenforceable generally if one party declines to use arbitration. Nevertheless, an arbitration clause is valuable because both parties are usually anxious to avoid the costs and consumption of time incident to litigation.

Once a dispute has arisen, and both parties agree to arbitrate, the decision of the arbitrators is binding under the law of some states.

11.6 SECURITY INTERESTS IN PERSONAL PROPERTY—ARTICLE 9 OF THE UNIFORM COMMERCIAL CODE[24]

Because a party who extends credit to another is often reluctant to rely only on the promise of the borrower to repay, the lender frequently requires the borrower to put up some collateral. Lenders may accept real property or personal property, or both, as collateral. The preceding sections have discussed the use of real property (land) as security for a loan. This section, deals exclusively, as does the Uniform Commercial Code, with the use of personal property (e.g., livestock, furniture, tractors) and fixtures (goods which become attached to real estate and become a part of it, e.g., a furnace, bricks, or cement). The collateral serves as security for the loan. If the proper steps are taken, the lender will have a security interest in the collateral. A *security interest* is a legal right in the collateral. Among other things, it gives the secured party (lender) a certain degree of protection against claims which other creditors may have against the borrower.[25]

Farmers and ranchers, knowingly or unknowingly, have frequent dealings that involve security interests. They borrow money, extend credit, and buy or sell everything from consumer goods to feed and seed. In all of these matters, the Uniform Commercial Code is important. It defines the conditions in which farmers or ranchers can or cannot lose property already paid for and those in which they can repossess items sold on credit or provide safe security for a loan. Persons working in agricultural finance and marketing also benefit from a basic understanding of Art. 9. The following discussion will emphasize some general concepts and identify some potential trouble areas that concern agricultural producers, lenders, suppliers, and purchasers.

As will be apparent in the paragraphs which follow, farmers, ranchers, and agricultural products receive much special treatment in Art. 9. This special treatment has probably evolved from the historical premise that agricultural producers are more like consumers than merchants. However, a trend toward treating agriculture producers just like other business persons seems to be evolving and is probably justified in light of the contemporary structure of agriculture.

General Concepts

Creation of the Security Interest. One creates a security interest by the use of a *security agreement*. The only formalities necessary

---

[24] *See generally* Clark, *The Agricultural Transaction and Equipment and Crop Financing*, 1 AG. LAW J. 172 (1979). Also, the authors are indebted to Barkley Clark and Keith Meyer, professors of law, University of Kansas Law School, for their stimulating lectures at the American Bar Association, National Institute on Agricultural Law, Kansas City, Missouri, May 9–10, 1980. Their presentations and reference materials were invaluable in focusing and documenting much of this section.

[25] The U.C.C. has greatly simplified this aspect of financing. Prior to its enactment, there were various ways to give security. For example, there were chattel mortgages and conditional sales contracts. These old instruments may still be used, but their effect will be to create a security interest under the U.C.C. (so long as its requirements are met).

for a valid security agreement are that it be in writing, that it be signed by the debtor, and that it contain a description of the collateral. If the collateral is in the lender's possession, no written security agreement is required. As between the borrower and the lender, the security interest is valid and enforceable once three things have happened: there has been a security agreement (or the collateral is in the lender's possession), the lender has given something valuable in exchange for the security interest, and the borrower has property rights in the collateral.

Perfection of the Security Interest. If the security interest is to be valid against third parties (for example, another party with a claim against the borrower), further steps must be taken to notify third parties of the secured party's claim. However, when the collateral is in the possession of the secured party, no additional steps need to be taken. Actual possession of the collateral is the most effective security. The process of giving public notice of a security interest is called *perfection*. The usual method of perfecting is by filing a financing statement in the proper place.[26] The *financing statement* is a very brief document. It must describe the collateral, give the names and addresses of both the debtor (borrower) and the secured party (lender), and be signed by the debtor.[27] The proper place for filing the financing statement varies with the type of collateral, and varies from state to state.[28] The filed financing statement (or security agreement) need not be refiled for 5 years. A statement properly filed usually continues to be effective within the state, even when the debtor moves or the location of the collateral is changed.

Priority. Where two or more lenders file a statement covering the same collateral, the general rule under the UCC is that the first to file prevails, regardless of who actually lends money first.[29] It makes no difference whether the party who filed first knew, when the money was advanced, that another had already made a loan on the same collateral.

Rights of the Parties on Default. Under the UCC, a secured party must take possession of the collateral within 60 days after the maturity of the loan. The right to possession must be exercised without breaching the peace. This does not mean that the secured party needs the debtor's consent, but only that force cannot be used to take possession. If it is not possible to take possession peacefully, the secured party must resort to the courts.

If the security agreement so provides, the secured party may require the debtor to bring together the collateral (which may be located in different places) and make it available at a place designated by the secured party and one that is mutually convenient.

---

[26] A financing statement filed in good faith but in the wrong place is still good against anyone who knows the contents of the statement.

[27] The security agreement may be filed in place of a financing statement so long as the agreement contains the additional information necessary in a financing statement.

[28] To find out which scheme a particular state follows, *see* § 9-401(1) of the state's Uniform Commercial Code.

[29] There is an exception to this rule when a purchase money security interest is involved. A *purchase money security interest* is one retained by the seller of the collateral to secure its purchase price. In this case, the secured party gets a 10-day grace period to file. For example, Dealer sells a tractor to Farmer on Day 1, taking a purchase money security interest in the tractor. On Day 5, Bank gets a judgment against Farmer and obtains a lien on Farmer's tractor. On Day 9, Dealer files a financing statement. Dealer's claim to the tractor is prior to Bank's since Dealer filed within the 10-day grace period. *See* U.C.C. § 9-301(2) (1972 version).

After possession is obtained, the UCC allows the secured party to sell, lease, or otherwise dispose of the collateral. He or she may sell it at a public or private sale with a right to claim a deficiency and a duty to account for surplus. The UCC encourages private sales through commercial channels. It is thought that this practice will result in a higher sale price for the collateral, which will be beneficial for all parties.

Classification of Collateral. The UCC classifies collateral as consumer goods, farm products, inventory, or equipment. Different rules and rights of parties are present, depending on which type of collateral is involved. The UCC's emphasis on the purpose and use of collateral in determining the classification of all goods except farm products demonstrates that the focus is not on the form of the agreement, but on what the parties intend to accomplish through financing.

Transactions Involving Consumer Goods

Consumer goods are those bought primarily for personal, family, or household purposes. Like everyone else, a farmer is a consumer and buys consumer goods such as refrigerators, radios, and television sets.[30] A buyer of consumer goods takes the goods free of all previous security interests in those goods so long as the purchase is made in the ordinary course of business. A purchase in good faith from a dealer or a person in the business of selling goods of that kind is a purchase made in the ordinary course of business. For example, if a farmer buys a refrigerator from an appliance store that regularly stocks refrigerators, the farmer buys free of any security interest in that refrigerator which was created by the seller. However, if a farmer buys a refrigerator from a dealer who does not ordinarily sell such items (for example, a refrigerator from a lumber dealer), the farmer buys at the risk of being subordinated to other security interests in the refrigerator. This would not be a purchase in the ordinary course of business.[31]

If a farmer buys consumer goods from another consumer, the farmer will take the goods free of any unfiled security interest so long as the farmer had no knowledge of the previous security interest and paid for the goods. This fact explains why dealers may be eager to file financing statements, though the act of filing might not be necessary to perfect their security interest.[32]

If a default occurs, repossessed consumer goods must be offered for sale within 90 days of repossession in cases where the farmer has paid either 60 percent of the purchase price or 60 percent of the loan to buy the goods. This sale may be public or private. However, after default has occurred, the debtor (farmer) may release the secured party from this obligation by signing a statement of renunciation.

---

[30] Automobiles are also consumer goods. They are covered by numerous special rules and will not be discussed here.

[31] When making a purchase out of the ordinary course of business, a farmer should check the records to see whether there is a financing statement covering the goods in question. For example, if a farmer purchases a refrigerator from a lumber dealer, the farmer should check the records to see whether anyone has a security interest in the dealer's equipment. In most states, the farmer would check the records of the Secretary of State or other central filing location.

[32] For example, an appliance dealer often gets a purchase money security interest in the goods when the farmer does not pay the full purchase price outright. The dealer does not have to file a financing statement to perfect the dealer's security interest in consumer goods (unless those goods are to become fixtures).

Transactions Involving Farm Products

Farm products receive special treatment under the UCC. They are not inventory to a farmer as refrigerators are to an appliance dealer. *Farm products* are crops, livestock, or supplies used or produced in farming operations, and products of crops or livestock in their unmanufactured state (e.g., milk, eggs, wool clips, seed), provided they are in the possession of a debtor engaged in raising, fattening, grazing, or other farming operations.[33]

Using Farm Products as Security for Production Loans. Farmers frequently borrow to meet the present costs of future production and commonly offer their crops or livestock as collateral. The UCC provides flexibility in such arrangements. For example, livestock and other goods acquired by the farmer in the future may be included as collateral for the present loan under an *after-acquired property clause.*[34] Also, the UCC allows parties to agree that future advances of money may be given when needed without making a new agreement.

The security interest created by the UCC is a very durable lien. Collateral may change in form as the process of production unfolds. Fertilizer and seed become growing crops. Livestock are fattened and sold. Still, the lien follows the changing collateral and travels through the stages of production; in the end it may attach itself to the proceeds from the sale of the products and the whole process may begin again.

Crops are often used as collateral for production loans, but livestock is preferred collateral since depreciation proceeds at a slow pace and resale value often increases during the term of the loan. Use of an after-acquired property clause creates a valid security interest in offspring, whether or not they were conceived at the time of execution of the agreement.[35] The after-acquired property clause thus appears to sidestep questions regarding the exact date of conception. It also makes it easier for the farmer to sell and buy livestock and to cull diseased cattle or poor producers and substitute new stock. The lender's interest automatically attaches to the replacements.

Where both a farmer's crop and livestock are items of collateral, a lender does not usually object to the farmer's using the crop as feed. The lender's filed financing statement describing the crop and animals would give sufficient notice of the continuing lien and would preserve the interest in the feed. However, when one lender has a lien on crops that are fed and another has a lien on the animals, the UCC does not give a clear answer. The lender on crops may have some difficulty in enforcing the lien, particularly if the lender knew that the borrowing farmer was in the livestock

---

[33] UCC § 9-109(3) (1972 version). For example, feedlot cattle are farm products, but livestock in the possession of a cattle dealer are inventory.

[34] UCC § 9-204 (1972 version). However, the 1962 UCC generally prohibited a security interest in crops planted more than 1 year after the security agreement was created. Thus it was necessary for a lender to reexecute a security agreement each

year. Some states have not yet adopted the less restrictive 1972 version.

[35] For example, a description might read "all (type and brand description) and other livestock and all additions, natural increase, replacements, and substitutions thereto, and all products thereof located at (location) and all accounts arising therefrom."

business.[36] The best protection for the lender is to have both the crops and the animals as collateral.

Lender's Problem of Description. The Uniform Commercial Code § 9-110 (1972 Revision) provides that, for purposes of Art. 9, any description of personal property or real estate is sufficient if it reasonably identifies what is described, whether or not the description is specific. Regarding crops, UCC §§ 9-203 and 9-204 require a description of the real estate on which the crops are growing or to be grown. Although, as is apparent in the following case,[37] a full legal description is not necessary, lenders should take care to reasonably identify the land because other courts have been less forgiving.[38] The lender also must identify the particular crop with care. In one case, a court reviewed a combined financing statement and security agreement which described "all crops of every kind grown or to be planted....Said crops to consist of 1,200 acres of soybeans, 28 acres of cotton, and 30 acres of rice." The Arkansas court held that the financing statement and security agreement did not reach the milo grown by the debtor on the same real estate.[39]

FINANCING STATEMENT—ADEQUACY OF DESCRIPTION

UNITED STATES v. BIG Z WAREHOUSE
United States District Court, Southern District of Georgia, 1970
311 F. Supp. 283

Plaintiff moves for summary judgment in this action for conversion by defendant of the 1964 tobacco crop of Oscar B. Chancey which was pledged as security for loans made to him by Farmers Home Administration in 1962 and 1963. The indebtedness was secured by bills of sale to secure debt covering certain farm machinery, livestock and all crops growing or to be grown on the debtor's 90 acre farm located 1 mile from Offerman, Ga. After the Uniform Commercial Code went into effect a new security agreement was

---

[36] *See* First National Bank of Brush v. Bostron and Colorado High Plains Agricultural Credit Corp., 39 Colo. App. 107, 564 P. 2d 964 (1977). In this case, cattle in which the lender had no security interest consumed feed that was the lender's collateral. The court held that the security interest was destroyed, noting that "cattle consume food as motor vehicles do gasoline. Once eaten, the feed not only loses its identity but...ceases to exist...."
[37] *See* United States v. Smith, 22 U.C.C. Rep. 502 (N.D. Miss. 1977); Production Credit Corp. v. Columbus Mills, 22 U.C.C. Rep. 228 (Wis. Cir. Ct. 1977). *See also* First Security Bank of Utah v. Wright, 521 P. 2d 563 (Utah 1974) (lender A with

imperfect security interest saved because lender B was on actual notice of A's security interest).
[38] *See* Piggott State Bank v. Pollard Gin Co., 243 Ark. 159, 419 S.W. 2d 120 (1967) (reference to 1965 crops on particular owner's land, Clay County, Arkansas, found to be inadequate); First Security Bank and Trust Co. v. Voelker, 252 N.W. 2d 400 (Iowa 1977) (inadequate legal description in financing statement prevented perfection); First National Bank of Atoka v. Calvin Pickle Co. 516 P. 2d 265 (Okla. 1973) (complete omission of real estate description for peanuts was insufficient).
[39] People's Bank v. Pioneer Food Industries, 253 Ark. 277, 486 S.W. 2d 24 (1972).

executed describing the same indebtedness and collateral and a financing statement was filed.

During the selling season in 1964 the defendant acting as agent for Chancey auctioned 4,136 pounds of tobacco delivered to the warehouse by the debtor to be auctioned to the highest bidder. The total sales price was $2,602.30 and the proceeds less commissions were paid to Chancey by Big Z Warehouse. The Government realized nothing.

In opposing plaintiff's motion for summary judgment the defendant has raised several issues.

III

Defendant challenges the adequacy of the description of the crop and the land. The collateral consisted of "crops" growing or to be grown on:

Farm(s)	Approximate acreage	Direction and distance from a named town
Oscar R. Chancey	90	1 mi. north of Offerman, Ga.

All in the County of Pierce, State of Georgia

Notice filing contemplates that the financing statement shall indicate "merely that the secured party who has filed may have a security interest in the collateral described." Further inquiry by another party is necessary to disclose the complete state of affairs. See Official Code Comment, Section 9-110:2. "Any description of personal property or real estate is sufficient whether or not it is specific if it reasonably identifies what is described." § 109A-9-110. According to § 109A-9-402(3), the financing statement shall describe the real estate in which the "described crops are growing or are to be grown." Security agreements covering crops must contain "a description of the land concerned." § 109A-9-103(1) (b).

In *Piggott State Bank v. Pollard Gin Company*, 243 Ark. 159, 419 S.W. 2d 120, the Supreme Court of Arkansas found the following description in the Financing Statement and the Security Agreement legally wanting:

CROPS. All of the following crops to be planted or growing within one year from the date hereof on the lands hereinafter described: 7 acres of cotton and 53 acres of soybeans to be produced on the lands of...Mary Gilbee; 4½ acres of cotton and 11 acres of soybeans to be produced on the lands of George Nixon; all of the above crops to be produced in Clay County, Arkansas during the year 1965.

[5]   The description in the present case is much more explicit. It would have sufficed under the chattel mortgage law. In *Yancey Brothers Co. v.*

Dehco, Inc., 108 Ga. App. 875, 134 S.E. 2d 828 the Court of Appeals said that the description in the security instrument must "raise a warning flag, as it were, providing a key to the identity of the property." By way of a footnote dictum, Judge Eberhardt added that the Uniform Commercial Code "[does] not appear to work any change in this rule."

A crop does not have to be described as a tobacco crop when all crops grown on the land are collateral for the debt. The description reasonably identifies what is described. It is adequate.

V

[8,9]   Defendant's remaining contention is that it has not been shown that the tobacco was produced on the debtor's 90 acre farm. The only evidence bearing on this phase of the case is a statement in a deposition of an official of Big Z Warehouse that he "reasonably assumed that this was tobacco grown on his farm." It should be readily provable that Chancey did not grow the tobacco on any farm except the one described in the security agreement and that he did not have a tobacco allotment on any other. The burden is on the plaintiff to show the source of the crop claimed to have been converted.

Since there may be an issue of fact in this and perhaps another area I deny the motion for summary judgment. The case will be given a non-jury trial assignment and disposed of in accordance with my notions of the law.

Lender's Problem of Classification. Lenders are confronted with at least two problems relating to whether particular collateral fits into one class or another. One problem relates to *where the financing statement should be filed*. Generally, financing statements are filed centrally, for example with the Secretary of State.[40] However, when the collateral is equipment used in farming operations, farm products, proceeds from the sale of farm products, or consumer goods, many states have opted for local filing, such as with the recorder of deeds of the county where the debtor resides.[41] In order to avoid this problem, lenders can simply double-file—both centrally and locally. Also, if crops "growing or to be grown" are the collateral, the lender must file in the county where the crops are growing. So if the crops are growing in one county and the debtor lives in another, the debtor must file in both counties.

The other problem, illustrated in the following case, relates to *describing the collateral by classification*.

---

[40] *E.g.*, ILL. REV. STAT. ch. 26, § 9-401(c) (1979).   [41] *E.g.*, ILL. REV. STAT. ch. 26, § 9-401(a) (1979).

COLLATERAL CLASSIFICATION PROBLEMS

K.L. SMITH ENTERPRISES, LTD. v. UNITED BANK OF DENVER
United States Bankruptcy Court, D. Colo., 1980
Bankruptcy No. 79 K. 0187, 28 U.C.C. Rep. 534

GLEN E. KELLER, Jr., Bankruptcy Judge.

This matter came before the court upon the complaint of the Debtor to determine the nature, extent, and validity of a claimed lien by the United Bank of Denver in certain property and certain cash.

The facts are in large measure undisputed. The principal officer of the plaintiff over a number of years pioneered a method of housing laying hens and collecting eggs which is, by all accounts, unique in the industry. The chickens are housed in "egg production units," which are large, circular structures containing four concentric circles of caged hens, 10 tiers high. The circles revolve through the building, passing stations for feeding, watering, egg collection, and manure removal. The chickens pass a collection station, which consists of an elevator which the operator rides up and down among the tiers, hand collecting the eggs. After the eggs are collected, they are cooled and then processed by washing, spraying with a light oil to seal the shell, and "candling." The candling operation is nothing more than passing the eggs in a rotating fashion over a light to detect cracks or other defects which render the egg nonmarketable to the consumer trade. The eggs are then sized by weight and packaged in cartons. Where appropriate, the cartons of the customer, which have been preprinted, are used, and on other occasions, the eggs are packaged in 30-dozen cartons, where they are separated by layers of fiberboard. On some occasions, the Debtor does not put the eggs through the entire process of candling, washing, and oiling and sells the eggs as "nest run eggs," which puts the processing burden upon the purchaser.

The United Bank of Denver loaned the total principal sum of $2,400,000.00 to the Debtor on November 5, 1976. Four separate security agreements were executed in connection with this loan, two of which have specific application here. The first grants to the Bank a security interest in all inventory, accounts and contract rights of the Debtor, plus the proceeds therefrom. The second gives the Bank a security interest in all equipment and machinery of the Debtor. Appropriate financing statements were filed in the requisite offices to perfect the security interest in all of the described collateral.

The Bank became concerned about the Debtor's financial condition in the spring of 1979. Its concern became progressively more pronounced until, on September 21, 1979, the Bank forced the resignation of Kenneth L. Smith as the president and executive officer of the Debtor. The petition herein was filed November 23, 1979, and Mr. Smith thereupon resumed active operation of the Debtor's business.

The Debtor's primary customer for a number of years had been Safeway Stores, Inc. Safeway and the Debtor had a written contract, pursuant to which all of the Debtor's egg production meeting minimum standards was sold to Safeway. On September 24, 1979, Safeway Stores gave notice of its cancellation of the contract effective 30 days later in accordance with the termination clause in the contract. Safeway did continue to buy eggs, however, by sending inspectors to the egg facility and selecting eggs which would be purchased from time to time. On November 19, 1979, Safeway took delivery of an egg shipment which was not invoiced until November 24, 1979, pursuant to the routine billing practices of the Debtor. In addition to the receivable for the eggs shipped on November 19th, the Debtor had at the close of business on November 22nd other accounts receivable, which totaled, together with the Safeway account, a stipulated $40,192.50.

On November 24, 1979, an occasional customer of the Debtor, Mr. Gonzales, picked up a shipment of "nest run eggs" for resale in Mexico and paid the sum of $11,205.00 cash for such eggs.

After the filing of the petition herein, the Debtor delivered several shipments of eggs to Safeway, the last of which occurred on December 1, 1979. In December, as well, three flocks of chickens, totaling some 120,000 birds, were sold to the Campbell Soup Company. These hens had passed the age of prime laying capacity and no longer had utility in the production of eggs.

The Bank contends that the eggs are inventory within the meaning of its security instruments and that the chickens may be inventory or may in fact be equipment. It asserts that it, therefore, had a valid security interest in chickens and eggs. Notwithstanding the status of the chickens and eggs, it asserts a security interest in all of the sales to Safeway, which it claims to have been pursuant to contract; the sale to Mr. Gonzales, likewise asserted to have been pursuant to contract; and the sale of the chickens to Campbell Soup Company, which the Bank suggests may have been pursuant to contract as well. The Bank further claims a security interest in the accounts receivable as of the date of the filing of the petition, thus concluding that all of the cash in the Debtor's possession is "cash collateral," to which the Bank's security interest extends.

The Debtor asserts that the chickens and eggs are "farm products" as that term is used in the Colorado version of the Uniform Commercial Code. 1973 CRS § 4-9-109. That section describes farm products as:

crops or livestock or supplies used or produced in farming operations or if they are products of crops or livestock in their unmanufactured states (such as ginned cotton, wool-clip, maple syrup, milk, and eggs), and if they are in the possession of a debtor engaged in raising, fattening, grazing, or other farming operations. If goods are farm products they are neither equipment nor inventory.

It would thus seem that if eggs are products of "livestock," the hens themselves must be "livestock" within the meaning of that section. There does at least seem to be a biological connection. Official Comment to UCC

§ 9-109; *United States v. Pete Brown Enterprises, Inc.*, 328 F Supp 600 [9 UCC Rep 734] (ND Miss 1971).

The Bank has not disavowed the biological connection but asserts that in an operation such as this, where the sole business is the production of eggs, the eggs lose their characteristic as farm products and instead become inventory in the operation of a business. Great emphasis is placed by the Bank on the fact that there are no residents on the property of the Debtor and that while certain wheat was grown on adjacent land owned by the Debtor, it was not harvested.

The Official Comment of UCC § 9-109 states:

Products of crops or livestock, even though they remain in the possession of a person engaged in farming operations, lose their status as farm products if they are subjected to a manufacturing process. What is and what is not a manufacturing operation is not determined by this Article. At one end of the scale some processes are so closely connected with farming—such as pasteurizing milk or boiling sap to produce maple syrup or maple sugar—that they would not rank as manufacturing. On the other hand an extensive canning operation would be manufacturing. The line is one for the courts to draw. After farm products have been subjected to a manufacturing operation, they become inventory if held for sale.

The pasteurization of milk or the boiling of sap seem to the court to be even more significant treatment of raw product than does the washing, candling, and spraying with oil of eggs. At the very least, they are in the same category, and the internal structure of the egg is not changed. The packaging of eggs in cartons does not seem to this court to be analogous to the "extensive canning operations" characterized by the Official Comment. Nearly all farm products must be packaged in some way for delivery to the farmer's customer. The facts that the packaging is done in the customer's package to eliminate a step in handling or that the operation is highly mechanized, do not seem to this court to disqualify the operation from the normal farm category. The language of the Code seems reasonably specific in its determination of what are farm products and does not appear to distinguish between the methods of producing the same product. The Bank's refreshing view that only conventional farming techniques which are unmechanized, unsophisticated, and labor intensive can produce farm products is unpersuasive. It is somewhat interesting to note that the loan at the Bank was made through its agricultural loan department.

The cases have uniformly found cattle feeding operations to be "farms" for the purposes of UCC § 9-109, although they are not farms in the traditional sense. See, for example, *In re Charolais Breeding Ranches, Inc.*, 20 UCC Rep 193 (ED Wis 1976), where the court held that a tax shelter cattle feeding operation produced farm products, saying: "Although the bankrupt was not a farmer in the conventional sense, its business consisted of raising, breeding, and maintaining cattle." See also, *Swift & Co. v. Jamestown National Bank*, 426 F 2d 1099 [7 UCC Rep 788] (8th Cir 1970). There are, of course, cases in which the courts should exercise judgment as to what constitutes a farm for purposes of a statutory construction. See, for example, *Weed v. Monfort Feed Lots, Inc.*, 156 Colo 577, 402 P 2d 177 (1965), where it was determined that a feed lot was not a farming operation under the state highway tax statute, which exempted farmers and ranches from certain taxes. Similarly, in *Mountain Credit v. Michiana Lumber & Supply*, 31 Colo App 112, 498 P 2d 967 [10 UCC Rep 1347] (1972), the court determined that a logging operation was not a "farming operation" within the meaning of 1973 CRS § 4-9-401 (1) (a). It was noted that trees could be farmed in a nursery setting, however. The construction of this statute, however, compels the conclusion that chickens are livestock and eggs are products of livestock. The statutory language is simply too clear. More importantly, the purposes of the Code could be badly abused. The Code was designed to provide a simple public explanation of claimed security interests so that the public might know under what conditions they were dealing with a debtor. To strain the statutory construction as sought by the Bank would seriously impair the public notice features which are the hallmark of the Uniform Commercial Code.

The court must conclude that the Bank has no security interest in the proceeds of either chickens or eggs, except to the extent such proceeds generated a prepetition "account" as defined in 1973 CRS § 4-9-106 (1978 Supp). The amount of prepetition accounts in which the Bank has a valid security interest is $40,192.50.

Buying and Selling Farm Products. Anyone buying farm products from a person engaged in farming operations takes the products subject to any prior security interest in them.[42] The "farm products" rule is an exception to the general rule that buyers in the ordinary course of business take free of security interests created by the seller. A farmer who has given a security interest in a crop is free to market the crop in a way that will bring the highest profit so long as the action is not inconsistent with the terms of the security agreement.

The lender is secure because the lien continues from seed to crop to proceeds of sale. If the farmer sells the collateral without authority from the lender, the lender also can sue the person to whom the farmer sold the farm products, either to repossess the goods or to get conversion damages. Conversion is a common-law tort action for wrongful interference with property rights. The usual measure of damages is the fair market value of the goods on the date of conversion (that is, the day on which the farmer made the unauthorized sale, plus

---

[42] UCC § 9-307(1) (1972 version).

interest from that date to the date of the judgment).[43]

In *Vermilion County Production Credit Assn. v. Izzard.*, 111 Ill. App.2d 190, 249 N.E.2d 352 (1969), a farmer gave the PCA a security interest in his crops and the proceeds of the crops. The PCA perfected its security interest by filing. The farmer sold the crops to the local elevator and kept the proceeds. The PCA sued the elevator for proceeds from the crops, claiming they had a perfected security interest since the elevator had purchased farm products from a farmer. The elevator defended by saying that the PCA had waived its security interest by allowing the farmer to sell the crops.[44] The court found that the PCA had made no express waiver of the security interest in the security agreement, nor could any waiver be implied. The court

held that the PCA could recover the proceeds from the elevator.

Whether the sale is authorized or unauthorized depends upon the facts of each case. This issue is often litigated.[45] Courts look at the course of dealing between parties, the trade customs, and the written security agreement to determine whether or not the lender has authorized the sale. To avoid potential problems it is important that the farmer and the lender discuss the matter of future sales of collateral in detail. In addition, the farmer should keep the lender informed throughout the relationship of any actions taken with respect to the collateral. It may be prudent for the lender to require that checks from the sale of farm products be payable jointly to the producer and lender. Producers should not be offended by such conditions in light

[43] In *First National Bank of Joliet v. Conness*, 33 Ill. App. 3d 765, 338 N.E. 2d 459 (1975), a cattle dealer purchased cattle from a farmer. The bank had loaned money to the farmer and had taken a security interest in the cattle. The bank had not consented to the sale and thus was able to sue the cattle dealer and win conversion damages. Similarly, in *Production Credit Assn. v. Columbus Mills*, 22 U.C.C. Rep. 228 (Wis. Cir. Ct. 1977), the farmer made an unauthorized sale of crops which were subject to PCA's security interest. The court found this to be clearly conversion, and said that the buyer of the crops had not only interfered with PCA's interest in the corn, but effectively eliminated its ability to exercise its right to repossess "the corn."

In addition to conversion damages and the right to repossess the collateral, two other legal effects may follow the unauthorized disposition of collateral. Some states impose criminal penalties on the farmer who sells property in which a security interest has been given if the proceeds of the sale are not paid to the lender. Finally, the original secured party may be entitled to recover the proceeds from the sale of the encumbered farm products.
[44] UCC § 9-306(2) (1972 version) says the security interest in collateral and proceeds continues at

their sale, unless the secured party gives up this right in the security agreement or loses it by waiver or estoppel.
[45] For cases holding that the sale was authorized and the buyer should prevail, *see* United States v. Central Livestock Association, Inc., 349 F. Supp. 1033 (D.N.D. 1972) (FmHA gave implied consent to livestock sale); Hedrick Savings Bank v. Myers, 229 N.W. 2d 252 (Iowa 1975) (bank gave implied consent); North Central Kansas PCA v. Washington Sales Company, 223 Kan. 689, 577 P. 2d 35 (1978) (court stated acceptance of proceeds from unauthorized sale was not implied consent, but court found express consent in a livestock sale); Clovis National Bank v. Thomas, 77 N.M. 726, 425 P. 2d 726 (1967) (court found implied consent in a livestock sale).

For cases holding that the sale was unauthorized and the lender should prevail, *see* Baker Production Credit Assoc. v. Long Creek Meat Company, 266 Or. 643, 513 P. 2d 1129 (1973) (court found the consent was upon condition that drafts received would be honored and paid); Southwestern Washington Production Credit Assoc. v. Seattle First National Bank, 92 Wash. 2d 30, 593 P. 2d 167 (Wash. 1979) (court found consent was conditional upon receipt of the proceeds).

of the lenders' potential problems in this area.[46]

Note that a farmer who buys seed or feed grain from a neighbor is also a buyer of farm products from a person engaging in farming operations and takes the goods subject to prior security interests in that grain.

SECURED CREDITORS AND THE PURCHASER OF FARM PRODUCTS

GARDEN CITY PRODUCTION CREDIT ASSOC. v. LANNAN
Supreme Court of Nebraska, 1971
186 Neb. 668, 186 N.W. 2d 99

A protected Kansas lender seeks in replevin to recover 161 head of cattle in the possession of an innocent Nebraska purchaser. The basic issue is whether, under the Uniform Commercial Code, the lender has waived his otherwise protected security interest. The judgment of the district court was against the lender. We reverse the judgment of the district court.

Section 9-306(2), U.C.C., provides:

Except where this article otherwise provides, a security interest continues in collateral notwithstanding sale, exchange or other disposition thereof by the debtor unless his action was authorized by the secured party in the security agreement or otherwise, and also continues in any identifiable proceeds including collections received by the debtor.

The cattle in question were from the ranch of Murlin and Doris Carter in Syracuse, Hamilton County, Kansas. The plaintiff, Garden City Production Credit Association, hereinafter referred to as P.C.A., extended the Carters a loan in 1965 to finance their farming and ranching operations. A signed financing statement, covering the cattle in question and executed and perfected pursuant to the Uniform Commercial Code of the State of Kansas, was filed with the Hamilton County register of deeds in Syracuse, Kansas, on May 2, 1966. Several subsequent security agreements were filed by P.C.A. pursuant to the Kansas Uniform Commercial Code covering farm machinery, crops, and branded livestock. On March 9, 1967, the Carters executed a security agreement which included the 161 head of cattle here involved. This agreement prohibited Carter from encumbering, removing, selling, or otherwise disposing of the cattle without the *written consent* of P.C.A., and provided the right to repossess in the event of default.

On several occasions, Carter sold cattle and endorsed the drafts over to Garden City, to be applied upon Carter's indebtedness. Later Carter arranged

---

[46] *See* Wabasso State Bank v. Coldwell Packing Co., 308 Minn. 349, 251 N.W. 2d 321 (1976) (court hints that buyer should have made proceeds payable jointly to lender and producer).

a large cattle sale. The purchaser, Western, gave Carter a small draft in part payment. Carter endorsed it over to Garden City. The draft included a notation that it was given as part payment for 165 head of cattle. Garden City therefore had knowledge of the intended sale. The second sight draft, for the major portion of the purchase price, was dishonored, and was returned for insufficient funds. Western, meanwhile, sold the cattle to defendant Lannan. Garden City P.C.A. then brought action against Lannan to enforce its security agreement.

There is no evidence in the record to support the defendant's allegation in his amended answer that P.C.A. had orally or in writing waived its security interest under the terms of the financing agreement. In essence, then, the defense to this action, in violation of the express terms of the security financing agreement, is based on the doctrine of implied consent or authorization (s. 9-306(2), U.C.C.) flowing from P.C.A.'s acknowledgment of the sale, and its failure to rebuke or object and require compliance with the express terms of the agreement when it accepted and applied the proceeds of the sale on the loan.

The evidence reveals a typical farm-ranch operation contemplating a course of dealing in the sale of farm products, and the necessity of securing credit financing for such an operation. The Uniform Commercial Code, whatever else its objects may be, was designed to close the gap in the classic conflict between the lender and the innocent purchaser and furnish acceptable, certain, and suitable standards which would promote the necessity of and the fluidity of farm credit financing in the modern context, and at the same time facilitate the sale and exchange of collateral by furnishing a definable and ascertainable standard which purchasers could rely on.

It is uncontested in the present case that there was strict compliance with the filing and notice provisions of the code. Lannan, the purchaser, was bound by the provisions of the code and must ordinarily take the risk of a failure to make the appropriate investigation contemplated by its provisions.

[3]   In this case we have a coupling of a provision prohibiting disposition of the collateral without written consent, together with a reservation of a security interest in the proceeds of any sale. These provisions cannot be construed otherwise than a further protection for the security holder under the terms of the code, and cannot be construed as provisions which open up the door to an expanded permissiveness or consent to the borrower, or a purchaser bound by the filing and notice provisions of the code.

The code does provide for certain situations where a security interest in collateral is defeated, even in the absence of authorization by the security agreement or by the secured party. These provisions need no detailed examination for the purpose of this case. They relate to purchasers in the ordinary course of trade and if applicable leave the secured party with only an interest in the proceeds from the sale. It is true that Western's purchase of the cattle from Carter was in good faith and without knowledge of the course of dealing between P.C.A. and Carter. It appears that the seller, Carter, was a person engaged in selling goods of the kind purchased and that Western was a buyer in the ordinary course of business. S. 1-201(19), U.C.C. *Such a buyer does not, however, take goods free of a security interest his seller created when he buys farm products from a person engaged in farming operations.* S. 9-307(1), U.C.C.

The cattle herein are by definition "farm products," and they were bought from Carter, a seller engaged in *"raising,* fattening, grazing, or other farming operations." (Emphasis supplied.) Section 9-109(3), U.C.C. This being the case, Western did not take the cattle free of the security interest created by the seller, Carter, under these applicable provisions of the code. It therefore appears that since Western received the cattle subject to P.C.A.'s security interest, no person who thereafter purchased the cattle from the seller was free of the security interest of P.C.A. P.C.A. had a continuously perfected security interest by virtue of its filing a financing statement in Nebraska within 4 months of the collateral's removal to this state. See ss. 9-103(3) and 9-401(4), U.C.C.

The conclusion we come to herein is in harmony with the express provisions of section 1-205(4), U.C.C., which states:

The express terms of an agreement and an applicable course of dealing or usage of the trade shall be construed whenever reasonable as consistent with each other; but when such construction is unreasonable *express terms control both course of dealing and usage of trade and course of dealing controls usage of trade.* (Emphasis supplied.)

We observe further that the record reveals that the secured agreements here between P.C.A. and Carter were periodically re-executed and contained a prohibition against resale without written authorization. The record shows that P.C.A. was engaged in a business involving the extension of loans on collateral involving some $60,000,000 or $70,000,000. We feel it cannot seriously be contended that P.C.A., by the methods by which it carried out its business and dealt with its debtors during the continuing contemplated process of sales of collateral farm products, intended to waive its security interest in the collateral against third party purchasers.

For the reasons given the judgment of the district court holding that there was a valid waiver of the perfected security interest of P.C.A. is reversed and the cause remanded.

Reversed and remanded.

NEWTON, Justice (dissenting).

Plaintiff relies on the provisions of section 9-307(1) of the Uniform Commercial Code. The unwarranted discrimination against purchasers of farm products contained in this section has been severely criticized, has been restricted in some jurisdictions by statute, and its demise is not contemplated. See, 26 The Business Lawyer, p. 314 (No. 2, Nov., 1970); Bender's Uniform Commercial Code Service, s. 9-307, p. 1-751. All other buyers in the "ordinary course of business" take free of a security interest created by the seller. One who extends credit necessarily does so on a basis of trust in the honesty and reliability of the borrower. A buyer in the ordinary course of business does not ordinarily rely on the trustworthiness of the seller. As between such a buyer and the holder of a security interest, the latter has the better opportunity to protect itself as the security holder knows with whom it is dealing whereas the buyer is often unaware of the origin of the products purchased and unable to trace them back to the original owner who created the security interest. The farm-product exception tends to restrict the free movement of such goods in commerce. It places an unwarranted responsibility on all commission firms, sale barns, auctioneers, and purchasers at public markets. In the case of fed cattle, it enables the security holder to follow through to the steak or meat on the consumer's table. Notwithstanding this situation, I am obliged to agree with the majority opinion which holds that under the existing Nebraska statute, the lien followed the cattle into defendant's hands, unless there was a waiver of the lien.

I disagree with the result arrived at by the majority of the members of this court. It is held that since the security agreement provides that consent to sale must be in writing, no other type of consent or waiver of this provision is valid.

We have held that a security agreement which covers proceeds may not be deemed to authorize sale by implication. See *Overland Nat. Bank v. Aurora Co-op. Elevator Co.*, 184 Neb. 843, 172 N.W. 2d 786. It is nevertheless a factor to be considered in determining whether an implied consent to sale has been given.

In *Clovis National Bank v. Thomas*, 77 N.M. 554, 425 P. 2d 726, cattle subject to a security agreement containing a similar provision forbidding sale without prior written consent was dealt with. The court stated:

> The plaintiff, if not expressly consenting to the questioned sales, certainly impliedly acquiesced in and consented thereto. It not only permitted Mr. Bunch, but permitted all its other debtors who granted security interests in cattle, to retain possession of the cattle and to sell the same from time to time as the debtor chose, and it relied upon the honesty of each debtor to bring in the proceeds from his sales to be applied on his indebtedness.
>
> Plaintiff was fully aware of its right to require its written authority to sell or otherwise dispose of the collateral, but it elected to waive this right. Waiver is the intentional abandonment or relinquishment of a known right.

There has been some criticism of the Clovis National Bank case due to the fact that in that case the security holder did not have actual knowledge of the particular sale at issue prior to delivery of the cattle. That is not true here. Plaintiff accepted and credited upon the debtor's note the downpayment made on the cattle. It likewise accepted and credited the final draft. It had frequently acquiesced in previous sales by the debtor and on the strength of this particular sale had made an additional loan to the debtor. Notwithstanding full knowledge of the sale before its final consummation and delivery of the cattle to the purchaser, it failed to object until the final draft was dishonored. By that time defendant had purchased the cattle in good faith and received possession. The conduct of plaintiff evidences an intentional relinquishment of its contract-right to stop the sale and a deliberate waiver of that right. "The essential elements of a waiver,...are the existence, at the time of the alleged waiver, of a right, advantage, or benefit, the knowledge, actual or constructive, of the existence thereof, and an intention to relinquish such right, advantage, or benefit." 56 Am. Jur., Waiver, s. 12, p. 113. All of the elements are present in this instance and, in addition, plaintiff accepted money on its contract with the debtor although it knew he had sold the cattle contrary to the strict terms of the security agreement.

There are also elements of estoppel present. By failing to question its debtor's sale of the cattle plaintiff made it possible for defendant to suffer from the acts of its debtor

Where one of two innocent persons must suffer by the acts of a third, the one whose conduct, act, or omission enabled such third person to occasion the loss must sustain it if the other party acted in good faith without knowledge of the facts, and altered his position to his detriment.   [Jordan v. Butler, 182 Neb. 626, 156 N.W. 2d 778.]

I respectfully submit that the judgment of the district court should be affirmed.

McCown, J., joins in this dissent.

Boslaugh, Justice (dissenting).

I concur in the opinion of Newton, J., that the circumstances in this case established both an authorization of the sale by the plaintiff, which waived its security interest in the cattle sold, and a ratification of the sale by the acceptance of the proceeds. These long-standing principles of law and equity have not been displaced by any provision of the code. See S. 1-103, U.C.C.

McCown, J., joins in this dissent.

Transactions Involving Inventory

Farm products may be converted into inventory and thus bought free of prior security interests. This change can come about in two ways: First, the farmer may pass the products along to a manufacturer or to a marketing agency, where they ultimately become inventory for sale; second, they may be subjected to a manufacturing process by the farmer. Pasteurizing milk or boiling sap to produce maple sugar would not be manufacturing, since these processes are too closely connected with farming. But a canning operation would be manufacturing, and the finished product would be inventory if held for sale. The buyer of manufactured products obtains a superior right, and the secured creditor of the farmer (seller) has an interest in the proceeds of sale but not in the items sold.[47]

Transactions Involving Farm Equipment

Goods are *farm* equipment if they are used or bought for use primarily in the farming business. Farm equipment typically requires local filing, while commercial equipment usually requires central filing.[48] Double filing by a lender may be the safest approach to this problem.

Using Farm Equipment as Collateral. There are two situations where a security interest in farm equipment is likely to be given. First, a dealer of farm equipment might retain a purchase money security interest in the equipment since it is unlikely that a farmer will be able to pay cash for equipment.[49] The second situation in which farm equipment might be used as collateral is in connection with a production loan. Equipment normally will be used as security in addition to, rather than instead of, crops and livestock. Farm equipment is probably the least favorable collateral for the lender.

For example, it may be subject to an outstanding purchase money security interest.

In order to create a security interest in farm equipment, the equipment must be described in the security agreement and financing statement. As with other types of collateral, the description only needs to "reasonably identify" the equipment. The UCC is generally liberal on this requirement.[50]

After-acquired property clauses are often used in conjunction with security interests in equipment. Equipment must be replaced from time to time, so an after-acquired property clause which includes replacements avoids the need to make a new agreement.

After default, a secured party has the right to render farm equipment unusable (without removing it from the premises).

Buying and Selling Farm Equipment. The purchase of farm equipment is similar to the purchase of consumer goods. If a farmer buys farm equipment from someone other than a person in the business of selling such goods, the farmer takes the tractor subject to prior security interests. If the farmer buys in the ordinary course of business, the farmer usually will take free and clear of any security interest created by the seller, but not always.

---

[47] *See* United States v. Hext, 444 F. 2d 804 (5th Cir. 1971) (cotton producer also owned ginning company; buyers of cotton took free of FmHA's security interest); First National Bank of Elkhart County v. Smoker, 153 Ind. App. 71, 286 N.E. 2d 203 (1972) (bank with security interest in meat packer's inventory prevails over farmer with unperfected security interest).

[48] *E.g., compare* ILL. REV. STAT. ch. 26, § 9-401 (1) (a) *with* § 9-401(1) (c) (1979).

[49] If a bank lends the farmer money to buy a piece of equipment, the bank will have a purchase money security interest.

[50] *But see* Mammoth Cave Production Credit Association v. York, 429 S.W. 2d 26 (Ky. App. 1968) (court found description in PCA's after-acquired property clause "vague and indefinite").

PURCHASING FREE OF DEALER'S CREDITORS: AN EXCEPTION

EXCHANGE BANK OF OSCEOLA v. JARRETT
Supreme Court of Montana, 1979
588 P. 2d 1006

The material facts are not in dispute. On September 8, 1976, Daniel F. Holland purchased a Michigan tractor-scraper through the Exchange Bank of Osceola (bank), located in Kissimmee, Florida. The bank retained a security interest in the tractor to insure full payment of the $13,000.00 purchase price. The bank took the necessary steps to perfect its security interest under Florida's Commercial Code.

On February 1, 1977, Daniel F. Holland, without plaintiff's permission and in violation of the security agreement, sold the tractor-scraper to C.B. and O. Equipment Co. of Council Bluffs, Iowa. C.B. and O., an Iowa merchant dealing in farm implements, transported the tractor-scraper from Florida to Council Bluffs, Iowa. The record shows that the tractor arrived in Iowa on February 7, 1977.

On February 21, 1977, defendant purchased the tractor-scraper from C.B. and O. for a good and valuable consideration. Defendant took possession of the tractor-scraper on or about February 21, 1977 and returned to Montana. The record indicates the tractor-scraper arrived in Miles City, Montana on March 9, 1977.

On April 4, 1977 (within four months from the date the tractor arrived in Iowa) the bank filed a financing statement in Iowa, pursuant to Iowa Code. Thereafter, plaintiff filed the same financing statement with the Montana Secretary of State.

When the original purchaser, Daniel F. Holland, defaulted on his obligation to the Florida bank, the bank instituted this action in the District Court, Custer County, to foreclose its security interest in the tractor possessed by Jarrett.

The sole issue for our determination is whether Spencer Jarrett purchased the tractor-scraper "free of" or "subject to" the bank's security interest when he purchased the tractor from the Iowa dealer.

Defendant contends that Iowa Code (UCC § 3-307) allowed him to purchase the tractor-scraper "free of" plaintiff's security interest. That section provides;

Protection of buyers of goods. 1. A buyer in ordinary course of business (subsection 9 of section 554.1201) other than a person buying farm products from a person engaged in farming operations takes free of a security interest *created by his seller* even though the security interest is perfected and even though the buyer knows of its existence. (Emphasis supplied.)

In the present case, defendant Jarrett purchased in good faith and without knowledge that the sale to him was in violation of the bank's security interest. Defendant also purchased the tractor in the ordinary course from a person in the business of selling tractors; therefore, he was "a buyer in the ordinary course of business" [UCC § 1-201-(9)]. However, § 9-307 contains the further limitation that the security interest must be "created by his [defendant's] seller." The Iowa implement dealer *did not* create plaintiff's security interest; therefore, defendant does not take the tractor "free of" plaintiff's security interest under the Iowa Code, *provided* plaintiff's perfected security interest has not lapsed.

It is agreed that the Florida bank perfected its security interest in the tractor-scraper by filing the financing statement required by UCC 9-302. The Uniform Commercial Code contemplates the continued perfection of a security interest if there has been no intervening period when it was unperfected. (UCC § 9-303.) A perfected security interest is generally not destroyed by the sale, exchange, or other disposition of the collateral, unless the action was authorized by the secured party in the security agreement or otherwise. Since Daniel Holland sold the tractor without plaintiff's permission and in violation of the security agreement, it is clear that C.B. and O purchased the tractor-scraper "subject to" the bank's security interest.

When C.B. and O. transported the tractor from Florida to Iowa, the continued existence of the bank's security interest was contingent on the provisions of Iowa's Commercial Code. The courts uniformly hold that UCC § 9-103 gives such a secured party a 4-month grace period during which the party's security interest is protected without any further action on that party's part:

The four-month period under the Uniform Commercial Code is different from the ten-day grace allowed under the former Conditional Sales Law for the original filing of a conditional sales contract. The four-month period provided in subsection 3, above, is an absolute period of protection of the vendor's security interest, designed to give him adequate time to make an investigation and locate the property. If the vendor fails to file within the four-month period, the protection of his security interest ceases upon the expiration thereof, and his unperfected security interest is thereafter subject to be defeated in the same way in which any unperfected security interest may be defeated under the code. A subsequent purchaser for value, without notice of the unprotected security interest, would take a superior title...But, a prior purchaser who purchased during the four-month period of statutory protection is not retroactively given a superior title.   [*First National Bank of Bay Shore v. Stamper* (1966), 93 N.J. Super. 150, 225 A. 2d 162, 3 UCC Rep. 949 (1966).]

When the provisions of the Iowa Code are applied to our fact pattern, it is obvious that the bank's security interest was viable at the time defendant purchased the tractor-scraper from C.B. and O. Equipment Company. The bank fully complied with UCC § 9-103 by filing their financing statement in Iowa on April 4, 1977, well within the 4-month period. Therefore, plaintiff's security interest continued and defendant purchased the tractor-scraper subject to the Florida bank's security interest.

Other Security Arrangements: Cannery and Marketing Contracts

Canning Contracts.   Many canning companies deliver seed to farmers under contract by which the farmer agrees to plant the seed and deliver the resulting crop. Under many of these contracts, the cannery retains ownership of the seed and the crops grown from it. The interest retained by the cannery is not a security interest and is not covered by the Uniform Commercial Code. The contract is not on public record; thus lenders on crops must be sure that the farmer whom they finance owns any seed planted. In a decision between the canning company and a creditor who loaned money on the collateral of growing crops, the canning company would probably win. A valid security agreement in the crop could not have been created because the debtor had no rights in the collateral.

Farmer's Contract with Cooperative Marketing Associations.   It is possible for the farmer to both borrow money on the crop and honor a cooperative contract. However, a problem may arise in the event of default. The lender may want to take possession and sell the crops, rather than wait for the cooperative marketing process. The co-op, on the other hand, is entitled to enforce its contract. Some states have statutes which provide that the interest of a cooperative association is subordinate to recorded liens. In those states, it would seem that the lender would prevail and could sell the crop immediately if the security interest was filed before the cooperative contract. If the contract came first, there might be a question of whether the lender had received notice, since such contracts need not be recorded or filed.

Other Special Problems

Landlord's Lien.   What happens if a tenant is not able to pay off either the production loan or the landlord's rent, both of which are secured by the crop? If the lease is a crop share lease or if the landlord is relying on a statutory landlord's lien, the priority of conflict would be settled outside of Art. 9, probably in favor of the landlord. In other instances, the priority rules of Art. 9 would be involved.[51]

Fixtures.   If the property used as security is to be affixed to real estate (hammer mill or feed processing center, for example), a conflict may arise with persons having or obtaining rights in the real estate. With timely filing of the security agreement or financing statement, the seller, according to the general rule, may remove a fixture even when the realty is mortgaged before or after the fixture attached. However, the seller of the fixture must restore or pay for any damage to the realty which is caused by removal of the collateral.

---

[51] *See* Clark, *The Agricultural Transaction: Equipment and Crop Financing* 1 AG. LAW J. 172, 191 (1979). *See also* Peterson v. Ziegler, 39 Ill. App. 3d 379, 350 N.E. 2d 356 (1976).

11.7 BANKRUPTCY

Certainly, farmers and ranchers are not completely immune from insolvency. The ratio of farm debt to non-real estate assets has increased dramatically in recent years. This increased reliance on borrowing rather than internal financing raises the specter of bankruptcy for some farmers and ranchers—particularly if fluctuating agricultural prices result in abnormally low income years. Additional reasons for having some understanding of bankruptcy law exist. Sometimes persons or businesses which owe money to farmers and ranchers go bankrupt—packers or commodity brokers, for example.

Our society has provided a mechanism whereby an honest debtor can pay into court most of the wealth that he or she may have, and the debtor can be discharged of all unpaid debts and start financial life all over again.[52] This mechanism is governed by bankruptcy laws at the federal level and insolvency laws at the state level. State insolvency laws have only a limited application today because the federal bankruptcy laws have superseded them to a large degree.[53]

There are two classifications of bankrupts. A *voluntary bankrupt* is one who subjects oneself to the bankruptcy law. A person and most corporations or associations may become voluntary bankrupts by filing a petition in the office of a bankruptcy judge. An *involuntary bankrupt*, on the other hand, is one who has been subjected to the bankruptcy law upon the petition of that person's creditors. Most natural persons, partnerships, and corporations owing debts exceeding $5000 can be forced into involuntary bankruptcy if such debtors are generally unable to pay a major portion of their debts as the debts become due. Interestingly, wage earners and farmers, among others, are exempt from the involuntary bankruptcy provisions and cannot be forced into bankruptcy by their creditors.[54] The filing of either a voluntary or involuntary petition for bankruptcy automatically delays the enforcement of any lien against the debtor's property or the recovery of any claim owed by the debtor. This automatic delay is one of the

---

[52] Certain debts are exempt from discharge under bankruptcy laws. Unpaid debts that survive the bankruptcy proceeding include some taxes, debts for obtaining property or services by false pretenses, debts arising from the debtor's willful and malicious conversion of property or from injury to other persons, debts for alimony or child support, debts for student loans until such loans have been due and owing for 5 years, and certain debts that the debtor owed before a previous bankruptcy case. All other debts, whether paid during the bankruptcy administration or not, are discharged at the end of the bankruptcy proceeding. The discharge acts as a total prohibition on debt collection efforts. 11 U.S.C.A. § 523.

[53] Bankruptcy law is codified in 11 U.S.C.A. § 101 *et seq.* Title 11 of the United States Code is divided into seven chapters: 1, 3, 5, 7, 9, 11, and 13. Chapters 1, 3 and 5 apply generally to all cases under Chap. 7 (Liquidation), Chap. 11 (Re-

organization), and Chap. 13 (Adjustment of Debts of an Individual with Regular Income). Bankruptcy cases are filed in only one of the four operative chapters—7, 9, 11, or 13. Chapter 9 deals with the adjustment of debts of a municipality. Chapter 11, Reorganization, is primarily designed for businesses, although individuals are eligible for relief under the chapter. Chapter 13 applies exclusively to individuals, but permits sole proprietorships to use the chapter. As a result of 1978 amendments to the 1978 Bankruptcy Act, the farmer-debtor is now granted access to Chap. 13 and may wish to pursue this alternative of debtor rehabilitation rather than liquidation.

[54] For purposes of this exception, a *farmer* is defined as a person who, during the previous taxable year, received more than 80 percent of his or her gross income from a farming operation which was owned or operated by this person. 11 U.S.C. § 101 (17). Individuals, partnerships, or corporations

fundamental debtor protections provided by the bankruptcy laws. It gives the debtor a breathing spell from the debtor's creditors. It permits the debtor to attempt a repayment or a reorganization plan, or simply to be relieved of the financial pressures that drove the debtor into bankruptcy.

Either the debtor or the bankruptcy court will appoint a trustee to represent the estate of the bankrupt. For all practical purposes, the trustee becomes the owner of the property with the power to use, sell, or lease the property while the creditors are filing and proving their claims against the debtor. Interestingly, bankruptcy operates as an acceleration of the principal amount of all claims against the debtor, but interest stops accruing at the date of the filing of the petition for bankruptcy.[55]

Bankruptcy law specifies the kinds of claims that are entitled to priority distribution. Generally, bankruptcy administration expenses and fees receive first priority. Priority is also given to employees of the bankrupt for up to $2000 of unpaid compensation, to consumer creditors for up to $600 for money deposited in connection with the purchase or lease of property or the purchase of services for their personal use, and to tax collectors.[56] To assist in bankruptcy administration and the identification of creditors, the debtor has the obligation to provide the court with a list of creditors, a schedule of assets and liabilities, and a statement of the debtor's financial affairs, and to cooperate with the trustee as necessary to enable the trustee to perform the trustee's duties.

In a liquidation proceeding, the assets of the bankrupt are first used to pay priority claims noted above. The remaining assets are used to pay off the creditors, with secured creditors being paid before unsecured creditors. However, under certain circumstances, the transfer of title or a security interest in property to a third party prior to the filing of a petition for bankruptcy may be rendered void. The trustee in bankruptcy may avoid fraudulent transfers if they were made with the actual intent to hinder or defraud a past or future creditor. Transfers made for less than a reasonably equivalent consideration are also vulnerable if the debtor becomes insolvent or if the debtor was engaged in business with an unreasonably small capital or intended to incur debts that would be beyond the debtor's ability to repay.[57] Also, under the voidable preference provisions of § 547, a creditor with a security interest in a floating mass, such as accounts receivable or crops or livestock, is subject to preference attack to the extent the creditor improves his or her position during the 90-day period before bankruptcy.[58]

Special provisions are made for the bankruptcy of commodity futures brokers. Several fundamental principles deserve particular attention. First, customer claims are granted the highest priority against the bankrupt's estate. Second, the commodity

---

can qualify as farmers for this purpose and thereby be exempt from involuntary petition. 11 U.S.C.A. § 101 (30). The exemption for farmers is based on the cyclical and unpredictable nature of the farming business. As was stated in the House report, one drought year or 1 year of low prices, as a result of which a farmer is temporarily unable to pay the creditors, should not subject the farmer to involuntary bankruptcy.

[55] 11 U.S.C.A. § 502 (b).
[56] 11 U.S.C.A. § 507.
[57] 11 U.S.C.A. § 548.
[58] *See* Clark *Preferences under the Old and New Bankruptcy Acts*, 12 UCC L.J. 154 (1979), for a discussion of the application of this provision to a typical agricultural financing transaction.

broker provisions strongly encourage the immediate transfer of customer accounts from the bankrupt to a solvent commodity broker, so as to minimize the possibility of default on margin payments and delivery.[59]

STUDY QUESTIONS

1. What is the role of commercial banks and insurance companies in supplying agricultural credit?

2. Describe the Farm Credit System.

3. What agricultural credit is available through the Department of Agriculture?

4. What is a promissory note? What provisions are usually contained in a promissory note? What clauses may be particularly troublesome and why?

5. What is the impact of interest rate ceilings on agricultural credit?

6. What is a mortgage? A deed of trust? Where are they used? How are they foreclosed?

7. What is redemption? Who does it protect? Why?

8. What duties does a buyer typically have under an installment land contract?

9. What may happen if a buyer defaults on an installment land contract?

10. Describe some of the important contract clauses that should be considered in an installment land contract.

11. Regarding Art. 9 of the Uniform Commercial Code, what is creation of a security interest? Perfection of a security interest? A financing statement?

12. How does Art. 9 classify collateral? Why are these classifications important?

13. How are farm products defined? What special treatment is afforded farm products under the Code?

14. What is the meaning and significance of an after-acquired property clause?

15. How important is the proper description and classification of collateral in a security agreement and financing statement?

16. What risks are present when a farmer buys "farm products"? What actions may be taken to reduce this risk?

17. What risks are present when a farmer buys farm equipment?

18. How are security interests through canning contracts, contracts with cooperative marketing associations, and the landlord's lien affected by Art. 9?

19. Is the special treatment of agricultural producers in Art. 9 of the UCC warranted?

20. What special treatment is afforded farmers and ranchers under bankruptcy laws? Is this special treatment warranted?

---

[59] *See generally* 11 U.S.C.A. § 761 *et seq.*

12

Sale and Transportation of Agricultural Products and Machinery

Many common-law and statutory provisions apply to the handling of agricultural products and to the products purchased by farmers and ranchers. Of prime importance are certain rules of contract, special laws protecting farmers or exempting them from the application of regulatory laws, statutes and common-law principles relating to pro-

duct liability, legal principles involved in sales and storage, the rights of farmers when they consign animals or other products to common carriers for transportation, and exemptions which apply when farmers provide their own transportation.

Before the government took an active part in the sale of farm produce, the only assurance of getting the type and quality of product bargained for was provided by the theory of implied warranty. Today, statutes and regulations, both state and federal, have removed much of the uncertainty from the buying of farm products. Those who sell farm products are strictly regulated and must truly represent the product they sell. State and federal inspectors keep watch over the processing, packing, and sale of farm products. Fines are provided for the misrepresentation of any product, and imprisonment may be imposed for the willful failure of a seller or inspector to abide by the statutory provisions.

In addition to state and federal regulations, local units of government often regulate the sale of perishable farm products. Many cities have their own ordinances and officials for the inspection and regulation of the sale of milk and fresh fruits and vegetables. Several of the more important laws and regulations and a few principles of law on the power to regulate are covered in the following sections.

12.1 SALES CONTRACTS GENERALLY

A sale is really a contract between the parties whereby title and possession of property are transferred in exchange for a consideration of value—either payment or a promise of payment. In a final sale, both title and possession are transferred to the buyer, and even in an executory sale (one not yet carried into full effect) title may pass to the buyer even though the seller may still have possession.

In conditional sales, title remains with the seller until the performance of a condition—often the payment of the price—even though the buyer may have possession and use. A conditional sale is made effective through a "contract for sale" made prior to the actual completion of the transaction.

Determining when title passes is often difficult. As a general rule, title cannot pass until there has been a definite agreement as to the property the buyer is to have. For example, a sale of ten calves out of a herd of forty would not be complete until the particular ten calves had been selected. On the other hand, a sale of ten bushels of wheat out of a bin containing a thousand bushels is complete without actual separation of the wheat since wheat is all alike. By law, such property is referred to as "fungible" goods.

Grain Sales

There are several important questions which should always be settled in a contract for the sale of grain. Is the sale by weight or by measure? In the absence of agreement, sale by weight is implied. Weight is always used when grain is sold to elevators or shipped to central markets. In purchasing corn from the neighbors for feed, bin measure is frequently used. However, it is good business to buy corn not only by weight but also according to its moisture content. Its value may vary several cents a bushel from the price paid when weight and moisture are considered.

What quality or grade is specified? When selling to an elevator, this is always determined and the price adjusted accordingly. In the absence of evidence as to what the grade should be, the most common grade for the community and season would be implied.

Who will be responsible for delivery and who will pay for delivery to the buyer's premises? In the absence of agreement, the buyer must take the grain from the seller's premises to the buyer's own premises and must bear the expense. There may be a question as to whether the grain is purchased in the field or harvested. In the absence of agreement, harvested grain available on the seller's farm would be implied. If the contract is for hay, there would be an implication that the hay be harvested, cured, and properly stored pending delivery. Local buying custom may alter this general rule, however. If everyone in the community bales his or her hay, then baled hay might be implied.

When will delivery be made, and will the seller charge for storage if the grain is not taken by a specified date? In the absence of agreement, the buyer would be expected to get the grain within a "reasonable" length of time. If the grain is not removed within a reasonable time or within the time agreed upon, the seller may be justified in charging for storage.

What is the price and when will payment be made? In the absence of agreement, the local market price payable at the time of delivery is implied.

Livestock Sales

The following questions are among the most important arising in the sale of farm animals.

Is the sale by the head or by weight? Sale by weight is preferable and is implied, unless there is an agreement to the contrary or unless circumstances or the type of animal indicate that weight was not intended. Breeding animals (ponies, dairy cows, horses, and dogs) are not likely to be sold by weight; farm animals (hogs, steers, lambs, and poultry) are. In the absence of agreement, there is an implication that animals sold by weight will be weighed on accurate scales and that weight will not be estimated. Unless agreed otherwise, weight at the time of delivery is used. If animals are running at large, the buyer may agree to take the whole herd, the statement in the contract reading: "(estimated number) more or less, to be weighed at . . . . when delivered."

What kind or grade of animals must the seller furnish? If the contract does not specify the kind or grade of animal, then the understanding between the parties becomes important. The parties must, and in practically all cases will, indicate the kind of animal wanted. If the buyer thought the contract was for feeder steers and the seller delivered dairy cows, there would be no contract. Failure to reach an understanding as to the grade of animal will not usually impair the contract, however, because in most cases the buyer will have seen the animals. Even if the buyer did not see them, it will be implied that animals fit for the purpose of the buyer will be delivered. For example, a farmer who contracts with a butcher to deliver six fat hogs for slaughter cannot fulfill the contract by delivering six hogs averaging only 100 pounds.

What warranties exist in favor of the buyer? A seller may make express warranties to the buyer. Even in the absence of an express agreement by the seller, there is a presumption that cattle sold for feeding purposes are fit for such an enterprise and are free from disease; that females sold for breeding purposes are not sterile; that a work animal sold as "sound" is free, at the time of delivery, of any disease, defect, or habits which would render it unfit for the intended use; and that an animal represented to be of "superior quality" is above average. The subject of warranties will be given special treatment in a later section of this chapter.

Auction Sales

Millions of dollars worth of farm property—particularly livestock—is sold annually at auction sales. Some of these sales are conducted regularly at the same location, and certain customs develop in the handling of the sale—particularly in regard to methods of making and receiving bids, settling for purchases, and taking possession of purchased property. These customs are generally binding on sellers and purchasers; but regardless of established practices there are certain rules of law contained in the Uniform Commercial Code which apply to all such sales. These are the most important ones:

§ 2-328. Sale by Auction

(1) In a sale by auction if goods are put up in lots each lot is the subject of a separate sale.

(2) A sale by auction is complete when the auctioneer so announces by the fall of the hammer or in other customary manner. Where a bid is made while the hammer is falling in acceptance of a prior bid the auctioneer may in his discretion reopen the bidding or declare the goods sold under the bid on which the hammer was falling.

(3) Such a sale is with reserve unless the goods are in explicit terms put up without reserve. In an auction with reserve the auctioneer may withdraw the goods at any time until he announces completion of the sale. In an auction without reserve, after the auctioneer calls for bids on an article or lot, that article or lot cannot be withdrawn unless no bid is made within a reasonable time. In either case a bidder may retract his bid until the auctioneer's announcement of completion of the sale, but a bidder retraction does not revive any previous bid.

(4) If the auctioneer knowingly receives a bid on the seller's behalf or procures such a bid, and notice has not been given that liberty for such bidding is reserved, the buyer may at his option avoid the sale or take the goods at the price of the last good faith bid prior to the completion of the sale. This subsection shall not apply to any bid at a forced sale.

An Illinois appellate court in interpreting these rules held that in a sale of sheep, announced to be without reserve, the seller could not resell the sheep merely because the seller didn't like the manner in which the auctioneer sold them.

Another appellate court case holds that in an auction sale possession of the property remains in the seller until the purchase price is paid or a mode of payment is agreed upon as required by the terms of sale. If the animal is sold as a purebred, there is an implied warranty that the seller will complete and transmit the necessary registry forms.

The person or organization in charge of a sale owes a duty to everyone attending the sale to conduct it in a safe manner and to see that the premises are safe. If anyone or anyone's property is injured through the negligence of the management, the injured party would have a right to damages regardless of any statement to the contrary in a sales catalog.

Buyers do not have to accept diseased animals or animals with material defects which they had no opportunity to discover. At community sales, it is unlawful to offer for sale animals known to be diseased, except that under regulations of the state department of agriculture, brucellosis reactors may be sold for immediate slaughter.

The auction sale is recognized, also, as a fair and impartial way to dispose of property which must by law be sold. When necessary, it can be used to sell the assets of an estate, pledged or mortgaged property which is unredeemed, property held to satisfy a lien, unclaimed property, public lands, tax-delinquent land, and school lands.

12.2 GROWER-PRODUCER AND DIRECT MARKETING ISSUES

Grower-Producer and Other Integration Contracts

It can be said that integration in American agriculture has been going on for more than

300 years. More and more things formerly done on the farm are done elsewhere. However, the term *grower-producer* has come to be used primarily to describe contracts between farmers and businesses which want a particular farm product. The business supplies the farmer with many of the elements of production, primarily credit, materials, and a certain amount of supervision. Contracts with canning companies for vegetable production, contracts for broiler production, and contracts for growing and processing of sugar are examples. Similar arrangements have been tried in pullet, hog, and egg production, and beef cattle feeding. The production of calves under cow-leasing contracts affords still another example. The following digest of important points to look for in grower-producer and other integration contracts contains useful suggestions on the legal implications of such contracts. Before such a contract is signed, it should be read carefully. The complete agreement should be in writing. Verbal agreements or incomplete contracts often lead to lawsuits.

Period of Contract. The period covered by the contract should be certain. Both starting and termination dates should be included.

Renewal Provisions. Some contracts call for automatic renewal in the absence of advance written notice of cancellation. The farmer should have the same rights as the company with regard to notice and renewal.

Cancellation Provisions. Many contracts have a wide range of cancellation provisions for the integrator. Few contain provisions for cancellation by the farmer. Without mutual protection, the farmer or the farmer's heirs must continue the contract to the end of the term. But the company may be able to step out of its commitment for any of the reasons stated in the contract.

Assignment of Interest. Some contracts prevent either party from assigning his or her duties to another party without written consent. An understanding of assignment provisions is especially important to a farmer who may wish to retire during the contract period and turn the operation over to another party.

Legal Relationship of Parties. The legal relationship of the parties should be stated in the contract. Is the farmer an employee or a partner of the integrator, or is the farmer an independent contractor? If the farmer is an employee, the integrator may be liable for actions of the farmer that cause injuries or losses to a third party. Or the integrator may find that social security contributions must be made for the farmer employee. These and other legal considerations would not hold if the farmer were deemed an independent contractor.

Supplies Furnished by Each Party. The production items (including hired labor) to be furnished by each party should be listed. The contract should also be explicit regarding what is furnished. For example, some egg production contracts state only that the integrator will supply a certain number of "birds." They do not state whether the birds are baby chicks or 24-week-old pullets, or whether they are all pullets or part pullets and part cockerels.

Ownership and Possession. Controversies may arise over the ownership and right to possession of animals or crops produced under these agreements. The contract should be carefully worded and specific in this regard.

Insurance.   The contract should clearly state who pays for insurance on the animals, buildings, equipment, and feed supplies.

Management Decisions.   The farmer should understand the extent to which the integrator can make management decisions. If the integrator controls these decisions, the farmer should become acquainted with the integrator's management program.

Producer Payments.   Some contracts guarantee the farmer a price so much above or below a certain market quotation at the time of marketing. A specific quotation on a specific market should be given. If prices are reported for several grades or weight classes, the specific grade on which the price is to based should be stated. Some price reports present a range of prices instead of a single price. In such cases, the top, bottom, or midpoint of the reported price range should be used as the basing price. If the contract calls for bonus or incentive payments to the producer, the basis and method of computing amounts should be written out in a clear and understandable formula or table.

Arbitration Provisions.   If the contract is well written and each party understands the rights and duties, disputes will not arise. In case disputes should arise, the contract should contain provisions for settlement without long and costly court procedures. These arbitration provisions should be explained in detail in the contract.

Controversies may arise over the ownership and right to possession of animals or crops produced under these agreements. The contract should be carefully worded and specific in this regard.

These are only some of the more important points to look for in integration contracts. They illustrate the need to read each contract carefully before signing. If questions arise regarding any points in the contract and the integrator cannot explain them satisfactorily, a lawyer should be consulted.

Direct Marketing of Agricultural Products

The direct marketing of fruits, vegetables, and other goods by producers has been increasing in recent years. For example, an estimated 750,000 to 1 million consumers do business at direct markets in Illinois each year. Producers who market their products directly to consumers face a variety of new and practical legal problems. For example, direct marketing activities may create additional sales, social security, and unemployment compensation tax liability. Also, hiring labor for direct marketing activities creates an entirely new set of legal issues involving the employment relationship. Additional legal responsibilities toward the consumers of goods are also created, and a variety of state and local regulations dealing with signs, zoning, and business registration may become applicable.

Sales Tax.   Most states have enacted some form of sales tax which applies generally to all retail sales. In general, farmers and ranchers are not required to collect and remit a sales tax, since their sales on grain or livestock are generally not to persons who actually consume such items. However, farmers and ranchers who engage in direct marketing activities to consumers would not be exempt from the state or municipal sales tax provisions.[1]

---

[1] For example, in Illinois the Retailers' Occupation Tax (sometimes referred to as the "sales tax law") exempts isolated or occasional sales at retail by persons who do not hold themselves out as engaging in the business of selling goods at retail. This exemption is not broad enough to include all

Federal and State Unemployment Compensation Tax. Payment of federal or state unemployment tax is typically avoided by farmers and ranchers since agricultural labor is exempt from coverage in most small- to medium-sized farming operations.[2] However, those farmers and ranchers who undertake sales of commodities directly to consumers will be required to remit unemployment compensation tax on wages paid to employees involved in retail activities.[3] Agricultural labor includes work of various types before actual retail sales, but work performed at a roadside stand or other sales facility would be retail labor subject to the tax.

Withholding Income Taxes. Agricultural producers generally can avoid withholding income taxes owed by employees so long as the employees are engaged in agricultural tasks and do not specifically request that

income tax be withheld. Agricultural producers who undertake retail sales of goods, however, cannot avoid withholding income tax from wages paid to employees working at roadside stands or other nonagricultural capacities.

Workers' Compensation Laws. In many states, agricultural producers are exempt from workers' compensation laws unless they employ exceptionally large amounts of agricultural labor. Unlike typical agricultural producers, operators who employ labor in the direct marketing phase of their operations may be unable to utilize available agricultural exemptions and may be subject to the mandatory coverage under the appropriate state workers' compensation law.[4]

Child Labor Laws. Generally, the child labor provisions of the Fair Labor Standards Act apply to agricultural producers only to a

---

farmers selling eggs or other produce on their own farms. To qualify their sales as isolated or occasional, farmers must not hold themselves as retailers of the property involved. Persons are not exempt from the tax merely because the quantity they sell is small. Also, the fact that the farmer selling the product is the producer is immaterial.

Sales made by farmers at roadside stands are subject to the tax. Sales by farmers using highway advertising signs would seem to be in the same category.

The Department of Revenue has ruled that, where persons engage primarily in the business of selling goods other than at retail (for example, at wholesale), the mere fact that a small fraction of their total sales are retail sales for use and consumption does not make the retail sale isolated or occasional within the meaning of the exemption. Thus, if farmers are considered to be primarily in the business of selling goods, including eggs, at wholesale, any sale of those goods at retail would be subject to the tax.

If a farmer is subject to the tax, a certificate of registration must be obtained from the Department of Revenue. The farmer is then required to make monthly reports and remittances of tax. Also, the farmer must keep the prescribed records.

See ILL. REV. STAT. ch. 120, § 440 *et seq.* (1979).

The Illinois sale tax law formerly contained a provision exempting "farm products or farm produce sold (at retail) by the producer." This was held unconstitutional in *Winter v. Barrett*, 352 Ill. 441, 186 N.E. 113 (1933).

[2] Generally, an employer must pay wages of $1500 during any calendar quarter of the current or preceding year, or employ one person for some portion of 20 days in separate weeks in any such quarter in order to be subject to the tax. Currently, the excise tax imposed is 3.2 percent of wages paid, and it must be paid together with social security taxes and contributions paid by employees.

As of 1979, employers who paid cash wages of $20,000 or more to *agricultural workers* in any calendar quarter in the current or preceding year or who employed ten or more agricultural workers for at least 1 day in 20 different weeks in the current or preceding year were subject to unemployment coverage. 26 U.S.C.A. § 3306.

[3] *Latimer v. United States*, 52 F. Supp. 228 (S.D. Cal. 1943).

[4] For example, in Illinois the act applied to all employers and farmers who employed persons in broadly defined extrahazardous activities. However, if a farmer employed less than 500 worker-days

limited extent.[5] For example, a child under 16 years of age who is employed in agriculture cannot engage in extrahazardous activities as defined by the U.S. Secretary of Labor. Agricultural producer-retailers who employ child labor will be subject to the full range of child labor regulations contained in the Fair Labor Standards Act. A similar disparity may exist in the applicable state child labor laws.

Minimum Wage, Maximum Hour, and Overtime Pay Regulation. Farmers and ranchers typically are exempt from federal minimum wage, maximum hour, and overtime pay regulations so long as their farming operations are relatively small and only agricultural laborers are employed. In addition, agricultural employers are exempt from maximum hour and overtime pay regulations regardless of the number of agricultural workers employed. However, whether agricultural producers who also engage in retail activities will be exempt from minimum wage as well as maximum hour and overtime pay regulations is a more difficult question. This rather complicated set of rules arises from an array of agricultural exemptions which may not benefit farmer-retailers with respect to employees engaged in retail sales activities, such as sales at roadside stands.

Handling Theft. Because producer-retailers have much more contact with the public, they face additional challenges in attempting to minimize theft. Such persons should be aware of at least one rule. The law does not favor a party exercising private control in the investigation and apprehension of suspected criminals. A strong emphasis must be placed on trained enforcement officers so that useless injuries to innocent citizens can be avoided. The prudent producer-retailer who suspects criminal activity of any sort by an employee or third party should immediately contact proper local law enforcement officials.

When a person has reasonable grounds to believe that a theft or other criminal offense has been or is being committed, either by an employee or a customer, two provisions exist to protect this person from civil liability in attempting to restrain the criminal action. Generally, persons who reasonably suspect retail theft may detain a suspect for a reasonable length of time to request and verify identification, to inquire whether the suspect possesses unpurchased goods, and to inform officers. Typically, one can only detain a suspect off the premises if one is in "hot pursuit" of the suspected criminal. A producer-retailer also may make arrests when there are reasonable grounds to believe that an offense is being committed. Certainly, witnessing a theft and verifying the theft by reasonable inquiry would constitute reasonable grounds

---

of agricultural labor per quarter during the preceding calendar year (excluding hours worked by the immediate family), coverage would not be mandatory. ILL. REV. STAT. ch. 48, § 138.3(19) (1979). Also, a farmer who undertakes retail sales may avoid mandatory coverage if the annual payroll for retail employees during the preceding year was less than $1,000, and other employees are exempt under the general agricultural exclusion. Obviously, most farmers who engage in a retail operation of any size may be subject to mandatory coverage under the act.

[5] Agricultural tasks exempt as of 1979 were specified for several age groups. (1) If the employee worked outside school hours in agricultural tasks, was less than 12 years old, and was employed by his or her parent on the parent's farm or with consent of the parents, the activity was not subject to child labor provisions. (2) So long as an employee was 14 years of age or older and worked in agricultural tasks outside school hours, the act was not applicable. (3) If the employee was 12 or 13 years old and employed with the consent of his or her parents, the act was not applicable. 29 U.S.C.A. § 213 (c) (1).

for arrest. If in doubt, one should be reluctant to exercise arrest powers because of potential civil liability and should seek the assistance of police officers instead. One must also be careful in restraining a suspect because physical conflict could result. Generally, use of force against a suspect will be justified only when the retailer reasonably believes force is necessary for self-defense or to defend another from imminent attack by the suspect. Deadly force is only authorized when persons believe such force is necessary to prevent death or great bodily harm to themselves or others. Use of force to protect property may be justified only if the use is necessary to prevent trespass or other criminal interference with property and if the force is not excessive.

Other Regulations. Persons involved in direct marketing activity may also be subject to a myriad of state and local regulations, such as those dealing with signs, zoning, state inspection of meat sold at retail, pasteurization laws, and many others. The potential liability for sale of unwholesome products is also of great importance; this issue will be discussed later in this chapter.

Some states have enacted "Farmers' Protection Statutes," which attempt to guarantee producers the right to sell their products.[6] Generally, such statutes do not exempt producers from reasonable health and safety regulations.[7]

12.3 FARMERS AND RANCHERS: THE MERCHANT'S EXCEPTION OF THE UNIFORM COMMERCIAL CODE

Questions often arise concerning whether contracts for the sale of agricultural products made between an agricultural producer and a merchant such as a grain elevator need to be in writing to be enforceable. Section 201 of the Uniform Commercial Code has now been adopted in virtually all of the states in the United States. This section reads as follows:

§ 2–201. Formal Requirements; Statute of Frauds
(1) Except as otherwise provided in this Section a contract for the sale of goods for the price of $500 or more is not enforceable by way of action or defense unless there is some writing sufficient to indicate that a contract for sale has been made between the parties and signed by the party against whom enforcement is sought or by his authorized agent or broker. A writing is not insufficient because it omits or incorrectly states a term agreed upon but the contract is not enforceable under this paragraph beyond the quantity of goods shown in such writing.
(2) Between merchants if within a reasonable time a writing in confirmation of the contract and sufficient against the sender

---

[6] *See, e.g.,* ILL. REV. STAT. ch. 5, § 91 (1979) which reads: "Every farmer, fruit and vine grower, and gardener, shall have an undisputed right to sell the produce of his farm, orchard, vineyard and garden in any place or market where such articles are usually sold, and in any quantity he may think proper without paying any state, county or city tax, or license, for doing so, any law, city or town ordinance to the contrary notwithstanding: Provided, that the corporate authorities of any such city, town or village may prohibit the obstruction of its streets, alleys and public places for any such purpose: And, provided further, that nothing in this Act shall be so construed as to authorize the sale of spirituous, vinous or malt liquors, contrary to the laws which now are or hereafter may be in force prohibiting the sale thereof."
[7] *See* City of Quincy v. Burgdorf, 235 Ill. App. 560 (1924). *But see* Youngquist v. City of Chicago, 405 Ill. 21, 90 N.E. 2d 205 (1950), where a license tax was held to be unreasonable as applied to a grower-wholesaler florist.

is received and the party receiving it has reason to know its contents, it satisfies the requirements of subsection (1) against such party unless written notice of objection to its contents is given within 10 days after it is received.

(3) A contract which does not satisfy the requirements of subsection (1) but which is valid in other respects in enforceable

(a) if the goods are to be specially manufactured for the buyer and are not suitable for sale to others in the ordinary course of the seller's business and the seller, before notice of repudiation is received and under circumstances which reasonably indicate that the goods are for the buyer, has made either a substantial beginning of their manufacture or commitments for their procurement; or

(b) if the party against whom enforcement is sought admits in his pleading, testimony or otherwise in court that a contract for sale was made, but the contract is not enforceable under this provision beyond the quantity of goods admitted; or

(c) with respect to goods for which payment has been made and accepted or which have been received and accepted (Section 2-606).

§ 2-104. Definitions. "Merchant"; "Between Merchants"; "Financing Agency"

(1) "Merchant" means a person who deals in goods of the kind or otherwise by his occupation holds himself out as having knowledge or skill peculiar to the practices or goods involved in the transaction or to

whom such knowledge or skill may be attributed by his employment of an agent or broker or other intermediary who by his occupation holds himself out as having such knowledge or skill.

. . .

(3) "Between merchants" means in any transaction with respect to which both parties are chargeable with the knowledge or skill of merchants.

It should remembered, however, that an oral contract normally required to be in writing, such as an agreement for the sale of grain, may also be enforceable independently of the merchant's exception. The concepts of *partial performance* or *estoppel* discussed in Sec. 2.2 of Chap. 2 may apply.

§ 1-204. Time; Reasonable Time; "Seasonably"

(1) Whenever this Act requires any action to be taken within a reasonable time, any time which is not manifestly unreasonable may be fixed by agreement.

(2) What is a reasonable time for taking any action depends on the nature, purpose and circumstances of such action.

As is apparent in the above section, if a farmer or rancher is deemed to be a merchant and enters into an oral agreement with another merchant, that contract is enforceable provided one of the merchants sends a written letter of confirmation that complies with the requirements of the Uniform Commercial Code. The question, of course, is whether farmers and ranchers have been held to be merchants within the meaning of the Uniform Commercial Code in a given state. Not all states have reached the same conclusion on this question.

THE FARMER AND THE MERCHANT'S EXCEPTION

KIMBALL COUNTY GRAIN COOPERATIVE v. YUNG
Supreme Court of Nebraska, 1978
200 Neb. 233 263 N.W. 2d 818

On July 26, 1973, the defendant telephoned the plaintiff and orally agreed to sell it 15,000 bushels of wheat at the price of $3.10 per bushel for delivery in January 1974. In accordance with its practice, the plaintiff drafted a written contract and held it for defendant's signature, but the defendant did not go to the plaintiff's elevator and sign that contract. Although the plaintiff attempted, unsuccessfully, to telephone the defendant several times between September 1973, and January 1974, and remind him of the contract, the plaintiff made no attempt to deliver the written contract or any other writing to the defendant during that period of time. On January 30, 1974, plaintiff's general manager did deliver the written contract to the defendant. The defendant neither signed it, nor did he object to its contents in writing within 10 days after he received it. The defendant ignored plaintiff's subsequent requests to deliver the wheat, and never did deliver any amount of wheat to the plaintiff under the oral agreement of July 26, 1973.

The District Court found that the parties had entered into an oral contract as alleged by the plaintiff, but concluded that it was not enforceable under the statute of frauds applicable to sales of goods, under section 2-201, U.C.C. The findings of the trial court in support of this conclusion were that (1) the defendant had not signed any writing sufficient to indicate that a contract for sale had been made between the parties; (2) the defendant was not a "merchant" as defined in section 2-104, U.C.C., and therefore the "merchant exception" to the statute of frauds, subsection (2) of section 2-201, U.C.C., did not apply; and (3) even if defendant was a "merchant," the oral contract was not enforceable under subsection (2) of section 2-201, U.C.C., because the defendant had not received a written confirmation of the oral contract "within a reasonable time." The District Court dismissed plaintiff's petition. Plaintiff has appealed, contending that the trial court erred in holding that the oral contract was not enforceable under the statute of frauds. We affirm the judgment of the District Court.

Subsection (2) of section 2-201, U.C.C., requires that a writing in confirmation of an oral contract be received "within a reasonable time." In the present case the oral contract was made on July 26, 1973. The defendant received no writing in confirmation thereof until January 30, 1974, more than 6 months after the oral contract was made, and only 1 day before the last possible delivery date under the oral contract.

AFFIRMED.

BRODKEY, Justice concurring.

Although authoring the majority opinion in this case, I do not believe it goes far enough, and I believe that this court should squarely face and resolve the question of whether the defendant was a "merchant" as defined in section 2-104, U.C.C. An important question of law has been left undecided, despite the fact that the question was properly raised, decided by the trial court, and thoroughly briefed on appeal. In view of the controversy over this issue in other jurisdictions, this court should resolve the issue so that farmers and grain elevators know what is required with respect to contracts for the sale of grain in this state.

In eight cases, with facts similar to those in the present case, courts from other jurisdictions have held that a farmer is a merchant. *See, Nelson v. Union Equity Co-op. Exchange*, 548 S.W. 2d 352 (Tex., 1977); *Sierens v. Clausen*, 60 Ill. 2d 585, 328 N.E. 2d 559 (1975); *Rush Johnson Farms, Inc. v. Missouri Farmers Assn., Inc.*, 555 S.W. 2d 61 (Mo. App., 1977); *Currituck Grain Inc. v. Powell*, 28 N.C. App. 563, 222 S.E. 2d 1 (1976); *Ohio Grain Co. v. Swisshelm*, 40 Ohio App. 2d 203, 318 N.E. 2d 428 (1973); *Continental Grain Co. v. Brown*, 19 U.C.C. Rept. Serv. 52 (W.D. Wis., 1976), *Continental Grain Co. v. Martin* 536 F. 2d 592 (5th Cir., 1976); *Continental Grain Co. v. Harbach*, 400 F. Supp. 695 (N.D. Ill., 1975).

Courts holding farmers to be merchants have rejected the view that a farmer is a simple tiller of the soil unaccustomed to the affairs of business and the market place. They have noted that the practices involved in the marketing of crops are well known to, and widely followed by, farmers, and that the marketing of a crop is as important to the farmer as the raising of it. *See, Sierens v. Clausen, supra; Rush Johnson Farms, Inc. v. Missouri Farmers Assn., Inc., supra; Currituck Grain Inc. v. Powell, supra; Ohio Grain Co. v. Swisshelm, supra.* Viewing the farmer as an agribusinessman, these courts have concluded that a farmer is not a casual or inexperienced seller, but that he is a professional with respect to the sale of his crop.

Courts holding a farmer to be a merchant have also relied on the language in the Comment, part 2, to section 2-104 of the code. In that comment it is stated that four provisions applicable to merchants in Article 2 dealing with the statute of frauds, firm offers, confirmatory memoranda, and modification "rest on normal business practices which are or ought to be typical of and familiar to any person in business. For purposes of these sections almost every person in business would, therefore, be deemed to be a 'merchant' under the language 'who...by his occupation holds himself out as having knowledge or skill peculiar to the practices...involved in the transaction...' since the practices involved in the transaction are non-specialized business practices such as answering mail." Courts relying on this language have stated that holding the farmer to be a merchant, insofar as the statute of frauds is concerned, places no greater burden on him or her than to answer mail and object to a written confirmation of an oral contract.

The purpose of the merchant exception to the statute of frauds was to put professional buyers and sellers on an equal footing by changing former law under which a party who received a written confirmation of an oral agreement of sale, but who himself had not signed anything, could hold the other party to the contract without himself being bound. Holding established grain producers to be merchants is consistent with this purpose.

This is not to say that farmers, as a class, are merchants as a matter of law. The inquiry in each case must be whether the farmer in question is in fact engaged in the business of raising and selling crops for a profit, as evidenced by his individual experience and prior activities.

In the present case, the relevant facts are not in dispute. The defendant has been a wheat farmer for more than 30 years, and presently cultivates approximately 1,000 acres of land each year. He makes it his business to be conscious of wheat prices and changes in the market. He has sold his wheat to grain elevators many times, and sold more than 74,000 bushels of wheat to the plaintiff alone between 1967 and 1973. On these facts, I believe that the trial court erred in concluding that the defendant was not a merchant. Defendant's primary occupation was clearly raising and selling wheat for a profit, and therefore he was a person who, by his occupation, held himself out as having knowledge peculiar to the practices involved in the transaction of selling grain.

Although I conclude that the defendant was acting as a merchant when he entered into the oral contract, I agree that the contract is unenforceable because the defendant did not receive a confirmation in writing of the oral contract within a reasonable time.

SPENCER, Justice, concurring.

I fully concur with the opinion herein. I do disagree, however, with the concurring opinion of Brodkey, J., suggestiong that the defendant was acting as a "merchant," as defined in the code, when he entered into the oral contract.

I am in full agreement with the five cases cited by the concurring opinion that a farmer who only sells his crop annually is not a professional with respect to such sales but is merely a casual seller within the meaning of the Uniform Commercial Code. [See *Sand Seed Service, Inc. v. Poeckes*, 249 N.W. 2d 663 (Iowa, 1977); *Decatur Cooperative Assn. v. Urban*, 219 Kan. 171, 547 P.2d 323 (1976); *Lish v. Compton*, 547 P.2d 223 (Utah, 1976); *Loeb & Co. Inc. v. Schreiner*, 294 Ala. 722, 321 So. 199 (1975); *Cook Grains, Inc. v. Fallis*, 239 Ark. 962, 395 S.W. 2d 555 (1965)]. I do not believe we should extend the Uniform Commercial Code by construction to cover an area which was not specifically considered by its drafters. I am certain it was not considered by our legislators when the Uniform Commercial Code was adopted in Nebraska.

The question as to whether or not a farmer in a particular instance is a merchant is a question of fact. If the farmer bought products only for his own use and sold only the products he raised himself, regardless of how much knowledge he might have in those two activities, I would not consider him a merchant. It would be in the instance where he was dealing with farm products raised by others that I would so consider him.

MERCHANT'S EXCEPTION—RECEIPT OF CONFIRMATION

PILLSBURY CO. v. BUCHANAN
Appellate Court of Illinois, Fourth District, 1976
37 Ill. App. 3d 876, 346 N.E. 2d 386

The plaintiff, Pillsbury Company, sued the defendant Buchanan for damages for a breach of contract. A bench trial was held. The trial court found for the plaintiff, Pillsbury Company, and the defendant Buchanan brings this appeal.

There is no dispute that an agent of the Pillsbury Company and the defendant, Buchanan, entered into an oral agreement on January 17, 1973, by which Buchanan agreed to sell and deliver to The Pillsbury Company a quantity of Number 1 grade yellow soybeans at a price of $4.55 per bushel and that Buchanan delivered about 2,057 bushels of such soybeans to The Pillsbury Company in March of 1973. The present controversy arose because the plaintiff Pillsbury Company claims that the parties had agreed that the defendant Buchanan would sell 3,150 bushels of soybeans although the defendant Buchanan contends that he had agreed to sell only 2,100 bushels.

The plaintiff, Pillsbury Company, sued for breach of contract for the alleged failure of the defendant, Buchanan, to sell the remaining 1,093 bushels of soybeans. Buchanan pleaded the Statute of Frauds as an affirmative defense. Pillsbury Company answered that defense by arguing that it had mailed a letter of confirmation of the oral contract in satisfaction of Section 2-201 of the Uniform Commercial Code. The parties stipulated that they are "merchants" within the meaning of the Statute of Frauds provision of the Uniform Commercial Code.

At trial, Pillsbury Company presented evidence that its agent had entered into an oral agreement on January 17, 1973, to the effect that the defendant Buchanan would sell 3,150 bushels of soybeans and that its agents had prepared and mailed a written letter of confirmation on the same day addressed to the defendant Buchanan at Toledo, Illinois. However, the defendant, Buchanan, testified that the parties had agreed that he would sell only 2,100 bushels of soybeans. Furthermore, Buchanan testified that his address was not Toledo, Illinois, but has been R.R. 1, Greenup, Illinois, for the past 19 years and that he had not received the written confirmation. Buchanan conceded that he is known around the Toledo area. Pillsbury's agent admitted that the wrong address had been placed on the confirmation but pointed out that the letter to the defendant, Buchanan, had not been returned although the return address of Pillsbury Company appeared on the envelope.

The trial court held in favor of the plaintiff, Pillsbury Company, and entered judgment against the defendant, Buchanan, for damages in the amount of $2,819.94. The trial court made a finding that the written confirmation had been received by the defendant, Buchanan. That finding is the narrow point challenged by Buchanan on this appeal.

In order for the plaintiff, Pillsbury Company, to have overcome the Statute of Frauds defense asserted by the defendant, Buchanan, the evidence must have established that Buchanan received the confirmation.

In the present case, there can be no presumption of receipt of the letter of confirmation. Although the mailing of a properly stamped and addressed letter raises a presumption of its receipt, Pillsbury Company admits that it had incorrectly addressed the letter. Where, as in this case, the receipt of a written confirmation is denied, the question of receipt is a question of fact.

The trial court in determining the credibility of the witnesses and the weight to be given the evidence could have believed the version of the facts offered by Pillsbury Company. That is, the court could have believed that Pillsbury Company's agents prepared and mailed a written confirmation to the defendant, Buchanan, at Toledo, although Buchanan lived in Greenup and that the letter was not returned to Pillsbury Company, although the company's return address was present on the envelope. The court could have taken judicial notice that Toledo and Greenup are small communities within Cumberland County only about five miles apart. The court could have accepted the admission of the defendant, Buchanan, that he is known in the Toledo area but could have rejected Buchanan's testimony that he had not received the letter of confirmation. From such a state of the evidence, the trial court's conclusion that Buchanan had received the confirmation was not against the manifest weight of the evidence.

Accordingly, the judgment of the trial court is affirmed.

12.4 DAMAGES FOR BREACH OF GRAIN CONTRACTS

FARMER'S BREACH OF GRAIN CONTRACT—DAMAGES

OLSEN v. SCHOLL
Appellate Court of Illinois, Second District, 1976
38 Ill. App. 3d 340, 347 N.E. 2d 195

Edward Olsen, the operator of the grain elevator in Polo, Illinois, brought this action against Thomas and Loren Scholl, who are farmers, alleging breach of a series of written contracts by failure to deliver 8,800 bushels of soybeans. The trial court entered judgment on a jury verdict in favor of the plaintiff assessing damages in the amount of $25,924.80. The defendants appeal contending that the damages awarded were excessive.

The contracts between the plaintiff and the defendants, who live near Polo, Illinois, were entered into during the latter part of November, 1972 and called for delivery of the soybeans to Illinois Grain Elevator in Hennepin, Illinois, during January, 1973. They provided, "Should elevator be full or incapacitated in any way, when grain is tendered, grain shall be delivered as soon thereafter as elevator can receive same." The contracts also provided, "Any extension of time to be at buyer's option." The parties understood that the sellers would be responsible for transporting the beans to Hennepin.

Late in December arrangements were made for delivery of some of the beans to Hennepin on January 2, 1973. On that day, after two loads of beans had been loaded, it was learned that the elevator at Hennepin was unable to take soybeans. In an effort to accommodate the sellers, Olsen made arrangements for the trucks already loaded to deliver the beans to Calumet Harbor. However, the beans were not taken to Calumet Harbor. On January 5, 1973, the sellers went to the buyer's place of business seeking to make arrangements for the immediate delivery of some beans on the contracts. They also sought partial payment in advance and stated they were in urgent need of money. The buyer was unable to arrange for immediate delivery and refused to make any advance payment. At that time the buyer had learned that the beans were described in a recorded security agreement between the sellers and a third party. During the rest of January and the early part of February, the buyer contacted the sellers several times to determine when the beans would be delivered. Between January 5 and 15 he informed the sellers that the elevator at Hennepin was taking delivery. On February 16, the buyer filed suit against the sellers seeking, *inter alia*, an injunction to restrain the sellers from disposing of the beans. On February 27, 1973, Olsen covered his obligation to his buyer by payment of the market price on that date, which was $6.63 a bushel. The contract prices of the beans ranged from $3.67 to $3.80 per bushel. The market price of soybeans during the first week of January was between $4.04 and $4.12 a bushel. The jury's verdict represented the difference between the contract prices and the market prices of $6.63 per bushel on February 27, 1973. Defendant appeals the measure and amount of damages.

In Illinois, when the time for delivery of goods on a contract is extended to an indefinite time, the measure of damages is the difference between the contract price and the market price at a reasonable time after performance is demanded. A demand may be made by the filing of suit and damages should be measured as of a reasonable time thereafter, as determined by the jury. On this record the jury could have found that the plaintiff exercised his option to extend the time for delivery and informed the sellers of his election to do so. Considering the time normally consumed for service of process, the jury could have determined that the buyer did not exceed the bounds of reasonableness when he waited 11 days before deciding that the sellers were not going to perform their part of the contract even under threat of suit. Therefore, we conclude that the award of damages based on the difference between the contract prices and the market prices on February 27, 1973, was not excessive.

GRAIN CONTRACTS—ELEVATOR SURCHARGE
FOR SHORT DELIVERY

HEEREN v. SONNEBORN BROS.
Appellate Court of Illinois, Fourth District, 1976
38 Ill. App. 3d 726, 348 N.E. 2d 495

This action was brought by the Heerens to recover $925.64 which was withheld by the defendants, purchasers on two contracts for the sale of soybeans. Defendants argued at trial that the first contract was for 2,200 bushels at $4.31½ per bushel and that the second was for 1,500 bushels at $5.05 per bushel. Plaintiffs insisted that the quantity terms were couched in "more or less" language because they were really selling by estimates of bin content. Both contracts were oral at the outset, but defendants confirmed the second with a written memorandum which specified 1,500 bushels.

Whe defendants took delivery, plaintiffs tendered 1,896.21 and 1,375.67 bushels on the respective contracts. Defendants took the difference between these quantities and those they felt they had contracted for, multiplied it times the difference between the contract price and the market price at the time of delivery, and deducted that amount, $925.64, from their payment to the Heerens. The Heerens, on the other hand, expected $4.31½ per bushel for 1,896.21 bushels and $5.05 per bushel for 1,375.67 bushels and no deductions.

The jury returned a verdict for plaintiffs granting a recovery of $813.74 on both contracts. However, the trial court then granted defendants a new trial as to the first contract and judgment *n.o.v.*, or, in the alternative, a new trial, on the second contract. Hence, we will rule on the issues relevant to the second contract in this opinion. These issues go to the appropriateness of the judgment *n.o.v.*

The trial court should enter a judgment *n.o.v.* only in those cases in which all of the evidence, when viewed in its aspect most favorable to the opponent, so overwhelmingly favors the movant that no contrary verdict based on that evidence could ever stand. Here, the plaintiffs, opponents of the motion, introduced a sufficient amount of evidence showing the contract to be for 1,500 bushels "more or less" to justify a jury verdict in their favor. Plaintiffs themselves testified that the quantity term was 1,600 bushels "more or less" and that they could not know exactly how many bushels of beans they had in their bins because they never took them into town for weighing. Plaintiffs also submitted testimony of another party that if he delivered less than the quantities mentioned in the contract he was not surcharged. Furthermore, Mrs. Sonneborn testified that defendant began sending out confirmation slips at some point in time between the two contracts with the Heerens because "we was having problems." From the testimony of these witnesses the jury could infer that quantity terms are often left uncertain and that the custom of the trade is not, as defendants would have it, to surcharge on short deliveries. Contradictory evidence at trial did not so overwhelmingly favor defendants that no verdict against them could ever stand. Therefore,

the trial court improvidently granted judgment *n.o.v.*
Reversed and remanded for a new trial.

12.5 REGULATION OF GRAIN AND LIVESTOCK DEALERS

Grain and livestock dealers of one kind or another are the focal point through which the entire incomes of millions of farmers and ranchers are funneled. The honesty and solvency of persons who store, buy, or sell grain or livestock is of the utmost importance to agricultural producers. A rather comprehensive regulatory scheme has been developed at both the federal and state levels of government to help protect agricultural producers from potentially disasterous financial loss when dealing with grain and livestock merchants and dealers.

Federal Grain Warehouse Regulation

Agricultural producers often store grain at country elevators or other commercial facilities. Among the biggest problems surrounding grain warehouse operation is protection of the grain producer from negligence or misappropriation by the warehouse operator. The U.S. Warehouse Act[8] addresses these problems, first, by requiring a bond of every applicant for a federal warehouse license. The bond is to secure obligations stated in the act and federal regulations promulgated thereunder, as well as obligations assumed by the warehouses under contract with agricultural producers. Second, the federal law tries to prevent injury to the grain producer by requiring that the products of one producer be kept separate from those of another, except in the case of fungible products such as grain

of the same kind and grade. Additionally, the law gives the Secretary of Agriculture, who is charged with the administration of the act, discretion to require fire or other insurance as a prerequisite to a warehouse license.

As orginally enacted,[9] the act made federal regulation of grain warehouses subservient to state regulation. But in 1931 Congress amended the act and substituted an exclusive system of federal regulation of warehouses that are licensed under the federal act. In the leading case of *Rice v. Santa Fe Elevator Corp.*, 331 U.S. 218 (1946), the U.S. Supreme Court held that Congress had formulated a policy on numerous phases of the warehouse business. The policy on rates was not to fix them but to exercise control through issuance, supervision, or revocation of licenses. Dual or conflicting positions of warehouses such as those that might arise where a warehouse operator is also a grain dealer, were regulated by disclosure, by general prohibitions against discrimination between customers, and by control over the license. Producers were protected from unsafe and inadequate warehouses by the power of the Secretary of Agriculture to determine whether the warehouses of applicants were suitable. Mixing of grain was authorized under specified conditions and prohibited under others. The court held that in areas such as those described above, individual states could not regulate federally licensed warehouses.

---

[8] 7 U.S.C.A. § 241 *et seq.*

[9] 39 Stat. 486 (1916).

BOND FORFEITURE—RIGHTS OF SCALE TICKET HOLDERS

FARMERS ELEVATOR MUTUAL INSURANCE COMPANY v. JEWETT
United States Court of Appeals, Tenth Circuit, 1968
394 F. 2d 896

Appellant, Farmers Elevator Mutual Insurance Company, issued a warehousemen's bond under the United States Warehouse Act, 7 U.S.C. §§ 241–273, to Sam Croft doing business as Sam Croft Grain Company in Kansas. The district court gave summary judgment for appellee Jewett and 40 others. Farmers has appealed on the ground that the Jewett group held only scale tickets rather than warehouse receipts and, hence, are entitled to no recovery on the bond.

As a licensed warehouseman under the United States Warehouse Act, Croft gave the required bond with Farmers as surety. Pertinent provisions of the bond secure the faithful performance by Croft, as a licensed warehousemen, of his obligations under the Act and regulations of the Secretary of Agriculture promulgated thereunder. The Jewett group delivered wheat to Croft and received only scale tickets which show the amount of wheat, the date of delivery, and the name of the owner. This wheat was commingled with wheat for which warehouse receipts were issued. Croft did not make delivery of wheat to various depositors including the Jewett group. Farmers satisfied the claims of those holding warehouse receipts but denied liability to those holding only scale tickets.

The form and printing of warehouse receipts are covered in the regulations of the Secretary. See 7 C.F.R. §§ 102.18 and 102.22. The scale tickets held by the Jewett group admittedly do not comply with these regulations. Section 102.30, 7 C.F.R., provides that receipts must be issued for all grain stored in a warehouse.

Warehouses licensed under the Act are required to issue receipts for grain stored therein but not for "nonstorage grain." See 7 U.S.C. § 259 and 7 C.F.R. § 102.30. Those delivering grain to such warehouses are charged with knowledge of the provisions of the statutes and the regulations. The licensed warehouseman is charged also with such knowledge. No claim is made that the wheat with which we are concerned was "nonstorage grain." The stipulation of the parties recites that the warehouseman received the wheat "for deposit"; that he commingled it with wheat covered by warehouse receipts; that he issued the scale tickets; that he did not pay for the wheat; and that he cannot satisfy the claims for wheat. The receipt of the quantities claimed appears on the scale tickets. Nothing on those tickets indicates any reason for delivery except storage. They are not, and do not purport to be, sales slips.

One of the conditions of the bond is that the warehouseman shall faithfully perform "all obligations of a licensed warehouseman under the terms of the Act." The Act, § 247, requires a bond to secure performance of obligations under the Act and of "such additional obligations as a warehouse-man as may be assumed by him under contracts with the respective deposit-ors of agricultural products in such warehouse." The Jewett group deposited wheat. The warehouseman received it. He did not give the depositors the receipts which the Act requires. He violated his duty under the Act. By re-ceiving the wheat for storage he was under an obligation to redeliver upon demand and payment of his charges. This was an obligation which he assumed with the depositors and, in our opinion, is an obligation within the intent of § 247 and consistent therewith.

To permit the surety to take advantage of the failure of the warehouse-man to do what the law compels him to do would permit a surety to profit by its principal's wrong. We see nothing in the Act which requires such a result.

It must be remembered that in the case at bar the total claims of the ware-house receipt holders and of the scale ticket holders do not exceed the penal sum of the bond. We are not called upon to decide—and do not decide—whether warehouse receipt holders should recover first and in full if total claims exceeded the penal sum of the bond.

Affirmed.

State Regulation of Grain Warehouses and Dealers

Warehouses. Most state warehouse laws mirror several of the federal requirements. For example, most states which have ware-house laws require filing of a bond with an application for a state license.[10] The bon-ding requirements are typically based on storage capacity, with maximum and mini-mum bonds somewhere between $5000 and $500,000.[11] The warehouse bond is available to grain producers whose stored grain has been misappropriated. Generally, if the amount of the bond is insufficient to compensate all producers holding warehouse receipts, the bond is divided among the producers on a pro rata basis.

Great divergence in state warehouse laws often occurs in the insurance provisions. Montana, for example, leaves the amount of the required insurance up to the discre-tion of the director of agriculture.[12] Kansas and Georgia require insurance up to the fair market value of the stored grain.[13] Texas and Kansas have elaborate provisions for the settlement of insurance claims, including a provision for certain deductions by the warehouse operator.[14]

Grain Dealers. Elevators typically deal in the purchase and sale of grain as well as providing storage. Accordingly, they are subject to either federal or state regulation of their warehouse activities and also state regulation of their grain dealer activities. There is no greater threat to farmers who store or sell grain at an elevator than an un-regulated run of bad luck where the dealer buys high and sells low. Elevator bankrupt-cies that result from speculation or bad management can be particularly trouble-

[10] See, e.g., ILL. REV. STAT. ch. 114, § 214.8 (1979); GA. CODE ANN. § 111-506 (Cum. Supp. 1978).
[11] ILL. REV. STAT. ch. 114, § 214.8 (1979).
[12] MONT. REV. CODES ANN. § 3-228.6 (Cum. Supp. 1980).
[13] GA. CODE ANN. § 111-506 (Cum. Supp. 1979); KAN. STAT. ANN. § 34-236.
[14] KAN. STAT. ANN. § 34-236; TEX. STAT. ANN. § 5577b-9b (Vernon) (Cum. Supp. 1980).

some to producers who have sold grain on *delayed pricing contracts*. Under such contracts, title to the grain passes to the elevator, but the farmer does not receive an immediate cash payment. Rather, the amount of payment and the actual transfer of cash will occur in the future based upon a future price. On the other hand, grain producers who store grain at an elevator retain title to that grain and are entitled to a warehouse receipt. The warehouse receipt is a security interest in grain inventory that the elevator may have on hand.

State regulation of grain dealer operations provides some protection for grain producers when elevators become insolvent. Typically, state grain dealer acts require that all grain dealers conducting operations within a state be licensed. The licensing procedure provides an opportunity for the state regulatory agency (typically the state department of agriculture) to periodically review the financial condition of grain dealers and to require an appropriate bond to help protect farmers. Grain dealer acts also may provide for a periodic audit of grain dealers and may authorize the regulatory agency to close an elevator and take custody of all grain where the elevator is found to be insolvent. The grain inventory, grain dealer's bond, and warehouse bond are available

to compensate producers who otherwise might not be paid at all.

Some states, such as Illinois, include provisions that closely supervise the use of price-later purchase agreements and provide additional protections to farmers where such agreements are in use. The Illinois provision, for example, requires grain dealers purchasing on price-later contracts to have grain, rights in grain, or proceeds from the sale of grain totaling 90 percent of the obligations on price-later contracts. Also, a grain dealer would be in violation of Illinois's act if the dealer is in a speculative position in excess of normal merchandising practices. The Illinois Department of Agriculture has set specific bushel amounts for each commodity as the limit for a long or short position in the grain market. These limits are based upon the net worth of the entity.

Generally, the various state regulatory schemes attempt to regulate management activities so that grain dealers do not become insolvent. In addition, the acts generally require bonding that may provide some relief to grain producers if a licensed elevator should go bankrupt.[15] In order to share in the bond, producers who are not paid for grain may be required to notify the state department of agriculture in writing within a specified time period.

ELEVATOR BANKRUPTCY: A CASE STUDY[16]

IN RE RICHARD ALLEN SWARRINGIM d/b/a ALSEY ELEVATOR
United States Bankruptcy Court, Central District of Illinois
No. S–BK–76–1409

On October 13, 1976 petitioner filed for bankruptcy under Chapter XI of the Bankruptcy Act. Schedule A (Debts) and Schedule B (Property of

---

[15] *See, e.g.,* ILL. REV. STAT. ch. 111, §§ 301 *et seq.* (1979).
[16] The authors are indebted to representatives of the Illinois Department of Agriculture, Division of

Agricultural Industry Regulation, and, particularly, to Michael Crews, an accountant with the division, for assistance in developing this actual case study.

Bankrupt) of the petition can be summarized as follows:

Schedule A (Debts)

A-1 (Priority claims): Federal, state, and local taxes . . . .$ Unknown
A-2 (Secured creditors): Banks and other commercial
    lenders, a scale company, and a furniture store 631,924.70
A-3 (Claims without priority):
    Grain dealer accounts payable (85 claims, the
       largest of which was for $83,614.90) 669,798.76
    Grain warehouse accounts payable (78 claims,
       the largest of which was for $73,485.29) 376,569.98
    Other accounts payable (110 claims, the
       largest of which was from a bank with a
       $78,860 unsecured note). 227,867.60
Total Debts $1,906,161.00

Schedule B (Property)

    Total property. $457,297.00
    Less homestead exemption . . . .(10,000.00)
    Less personal property exemption. . . . . .(1,000.00)
                                           $ 446,297.00
Approximate Deficiency . . . .($1,459,914.00)

The insolvency at Alsey Elevator had previously been brought to the attention of the Illinois Department of Agriculture by a telephone call from a terminal elevator which disclosed that some of the producers who had sold grain to Alsey Elevator had received Nonsufficient Funds checks. The department dispatched examiners to the facility to ascertain its solvency. When it was apparent that the company was unable to pay producers for grain, the license was suspended and operations were halted in September 1976. Department personnel were assigned to the location to make a determination of producer liability and to control the assets. Because there was not enough grain on hand to cover the outstanding warehouse receipts, the grain inventory was liquidated. Bids were solicited from local terminals and the grain was sold to the highest bidder. Personnel of the Illinois Department of Agriculture monitored the shipment of grain to ensure physical control of the commodities, proper allocation to sales contracts, and control of receipts from terminals. The Department also assisted producers who had contracts for delivery to Alsey Elevator.

Advertisements, which were placed in three area newspapers for three consecutive weeks, announced the cessation of business at Alsey Elevator and that claims should be filed with the Department of Agriculture. The names of the producers who submitted claims to the Department were checked against the grain creditors discovered in the audit by Department personnel. Anyone who had not filed a claim, but was thought by the Department to have a valid claim was required to sign a waiver of claim.

A notice was sent to each claimant informing the claimant of the time and place of the hearings held to adjudicate the claims and each claimant was assigned a specific time to present the claim. The owners of the insolvent elevator and the bonding companies who wrote the surety bonds were also given official notice of the hearing. The hearings for the Alsey Elevator claimants were held on October 16 and 25, 1976, June 23, July 12, 13, and 14, 1977 and February 7, 8, 9, and 10 and March 16, 1978.[17]

To determine the validity, type, amount and bond coverage of the claims, all of the documentary evidence relating to the grain transactions included in the claim was examined. This included scale tickets, settlement sheets, contracts, warehouse receipts, NSF checks, delayed pricing contracts, and the date of closing. The testimony and documentary evidence was utilized to determine if the claim was for grain produced in Illinois, if the grain was stored or sold, the date of sale, price, number of bushels, discounts and dockages, amount of any advances, and the existence of any accounts due to the elevator. The value of the claims disallowed in the course of the hearing was $279,934.79. The amounts due the elevator from the producers were used as set-offs in arriving at a net claim amount for the remaining valid claims.

The amounts of the claims, amount of monies available for distribution, and percent of approved net claim received are represented in the following table:

		Warehouse		*Grain Dealer*
Net Valid Claims:		$327,862.69		$304,384.22
$ Available for Distribution:[18]	Bond:	19,558.30	Bond:	100,875.66
	Grain:	18,558.65		
Percent Payout:		11.63%		33.14%

[17] The proceedings are of a formal, evidentiary type. An official transcript is made of the testimony. Each claimant is given the opportunity to explain the nature of the claim under oath. The department's attorney and members of the staff of the Bureau of Warehouses question each claimant in such a manner that the type, validity, and amount of a claim can be determined and, what, if any, bond coverage is applicable can be determined as well. In some cases, testimony is needed from the manager or owner to ascertain the required information. Representatives of the bonding companies or any other party to the proceedings are allowed to cross-examine the claimants. Documentary evidence is marked as exhibits and becomes a part of the record. At the conclusion of each claimant's testimony, the hearing officer rules as to the validity, type, amount, and bond applicability of the claim. Within 30 days after the conclusion of the hearing, a hearing order is prepared and sent to each claimant. The order constitutes formal notification of the decision rendered orally in the hearing. The bonding companies are also issued an order which includes a demand for that portion of their bond needed to make the valid claimants whole. Any affected party can petition the director of the department for reconsideration of the hearing officer's decision within 30 days from the date of the hearing order. Petitions received by the director must be ruled upon within 30 days of the day they are received. The next and last recourse for an affected party is the filing of a complaint in a circuit court for administrative review of the hearing order. This filing must be made within 35 days from the date that the decision being reviewed was served upon the affected party.

[18] All funds include accrued interest earned from date of receipt by department of agriculture to date of distribution. Grain sale proceeds reflect

The Department of Agriculture worked independently of the bankruptcy proceedings. At the conclusion of the Department's action, the Department provided to the Trustee in Bankruptcy a schedule showing the amount and classification of each person's claim, the pro rata share of funds applicable to the claim, and the amount received by the claimant from the Department.

The administration of the bankruptcy estate continued in the bankruptcy court. The Order Approving Final Report and for Distribution was entered January 31, 1980. That order and its contents can be summarized as follows.

1. The Final Report of the Trustee was filed August 9, 1979.
2. An Order consolidating the case of Betty Estella Swarringim (wife) and Richard Allen Swarringim was entered August 29, 1979.
3. The Final Report came up for a hearing at the Final Meeting of Creditors held September 19, 1979 after notice of the filing of the Final Report and Final Meeting of Creditors had been given to all interested parties.
4. The fee for the Referee's Salary—Expense Fund and the Trustee's Fee should be based on the sum of $294,626.76.
5. Total Fees should be paid as follows:

Attorney for Trustee	$9,592.00	plus $233 expenses
Attorney for Bankrupts	$1,500.00	plus $300 expenses
Trustee	$3,361.27	plus $200 expenses

6. The claims of two employees for prior wages should be paid in full (less federal and state payroll taxes).
7. Taxes payable to the U.S. Director of Internal Revenue and the Illinois Department of Revenue should be paid in full.
8. The $104,625.20 remaining in the Trustee's hands should be paid as a first and final dividend to the general, unsecured creditors whose claims were filed and allowed.

On February 13, 1980 an Order was entered which required the sum of $104,625.20 to be paid to individually listed creditors as an 11.6415% dividend on specifically listed claims that had been allowed. These allowed claims totaled $898,726, the largest single approved claim being from a bank in the amount of $87,410.97. A seed company, equipment company, agricultural service and scores of farmers who had done business at the elevator were included in the list of those with approved claims.

The claim of one producer in the preceding case has been followed through both the Department of Agriculture and the bankruptcy action. A *grain dealer* claim was submitted to the department for corn (1883 bushels) valued at the contract price of

---

the amount remaining after payment of shipping expenses. All distributions are made on a pro rata basis. If there is more than one fund, a separate distribution is made for each fund using the valid claims entitled to participate in that fund. All of these distributions for any one claimant are totaled so that only one check is issued to each claimant. The department, of course, has no control over the manner in which the bankruptcy action uses the department's distribution of funds as an offset against the claim filed with them. The department is of the opinion, however, that the bonds are penalty bonds and as such should not be used as an offset against the bankruptcy claim.

$3 per bushel. An advance of $17,000 had been received by the producer prior to the elevator closing. Alsey Elevator issued a check for the remaining balance, $18,651, which was returned to the producer because of insufficient funds. The elevator settlement sheet showed that all deliveries of grain were made within the bond protection time limits of the grain dealers bond. It also showed the price per bushel, the advance payment received, and the check number. Based upon this evidence, a valid grain dealer claim under the bond was allowed in the amount of $18,651, which yielded a 33.14 percent payout of $6181.

Grain warehouse claims were submitted to the Department by this same producer for both wheat and soybeans. The claim for wheat (1032 bushels at $2.26 per bushel) totaled $2334, and claims for soybeans (2876 bushels at $5.66 per bushel) totaled $16,279. The total warehouse claims of $18,614 were allowed and yielded an 11.63 percent payout of $2164.

In the *bankruptcy proceeding*, this claimant filed only the grain dealer portion of the claim. This claim for $18,651.25 was allowed and received an 11.64 percent payout of $2171.29. Thus, this particular individual experienced actual total "out of pocket" losses of $26,750—the difference between the producer's valid claims and the combined amount recieved from the Department of Agriculture and the Trustee in Bankruptcy.

Federal Packers and Stockyards Act

In recent decades, the American livestock industry has witnessed dramatic changes in the structure of livestock markets. When the Packers and Stockyards Act of 1921 was originally enacted, well over 80 percent of all livestock was sold through large terminal markets. Today, the Department of Agriculture estimates that well over 80 percent of all slaughter livestock is purchased by packers directly from producers and custom feedlots. As originally enacted, the act provided for close supervision by the Secretary of Agriculture of transactions involving the purchase and sale of livestock at terminal markets. The more recent experience of livestock producers indicated a clear need for expanded regulation of transactions involving direct purchases.

Between 1958 and 1975, over 150 packers failed, leaving livestock producers unpaid for over $43 million of livestock. By far the largest of the failures was that of the American Beef Packers (ABP), which went bankrupt in 1975, leaving producers in thirteen states unpaid for a total of over $20 million in livestock sales. Under the applicable law at that time, ABP's principal source of financing, General Electric Acceptance Corporation, stood ahead of the livestock producers by virtue of its duly perfected security interest in ABP's inventory, i.e., livestock and derivative products which the producers had sold on a cash basis and for which they had not been paid. In 1976 the federal Packers and Stockyards Act was amended to provide greater protection to livestock producers. Some of the more important provisions of the amended act are discussed below.

Bonding. The Secretary of Agriculture is authorized to require reasonable bonds from marketing agencies, dealers, and packers.[19] The proceeds of the bond are available to help compensate livestock producers who are not paid for the livestock that they have sold. However, only packers whose average annual purchases exceed $500,000 are required to be bonded under the federal law.

---

[19] 7 U.S.C.A. § 204.

Prompt Payment. The Packers and Stock-yards Act also provides that packers, market agencies, and dealers purchasing livestock must issue a check for the full amount of the purchase price before the close of the next business day following the purchase of livestock. However, this requirement can be waived by an express prior written agreement between the buyer and the seller.[20]

Statutory Trust. The federal act also requires that all livestock purchased by a packer in cash sales as well as inventories and proceeds from the sale of meat or livestock products be held in trust for the benefit of all unpaid cash sellers of livestock until full payment has been received by such sellers. Importantly, an unpaid seller loses the benefit of the trust unless the seller gives written notice to the packer and to the Secretary of Agriculture shortly after the final payment becomes delinquent or after the payment check has "bounced." This statutory trust applies only to packers whose average annual purchases exceed $500,000.[21]

State Regulation of Livestock Dealers

State laws and regulations also may govern the livestock industry to the extent that such laws and regulations are not inconsistent with the federal regulatory scheme. For example, Illinois law provides for the regulation of commission merchants,[22] feeder swine dealers,[23] livestock dealers,[24] and buyers of livestock for slaughter.[25] Generally, such laws require the dealer to be licensed by the state department of agriculture and to post a bond to ensure the faithful performance of the dealer's obligations. Most of these laws

exempt dealers who have been licensed and have posted a bond in accordance with federal law.

12.6 STANDARDS AND GRADES— LABELING AND INSPECTION

Farmers and ranchers are frequently involved in the purchase or sale of grain, livestock, seed, feed, and fertilizer. In all of these transactions agricultural producers are indirectly touched by an extensive federal and state regulatory system. This system involves the creation of uniform standards and grades for many agricultural products, accurate labeling of many products, and frequent inspections to ensure that grading and labeling comply with appropriate standards. Information concerning this broad regulatory scheme is of interest to agricultural producers because they rely on this system to facilitate the marketing of their products and because this regulatory system offers protection to agricultural producers when they purchase many agricultural inputs.

Grain and Livestock Inspection, Standards, and Grades

Grain. We had no federal or state standards or inspection and grading systems when commercial marketing of grain began in the early 1800s. Early sales were entirely local, and grain traders generally evolved their own set of rough standards to denote differences in quality and condition of grain.

As railroad and barge transportation capacity increased, the need for more uniform grades and standards became apparent. To fill this need, some states began in-

---

[20] 7 U.S.C.A. § 228b.
[21] 7 U.S.C.A. § 196.
[22] ILL. REV. STAT. ch. 111, §§ 101 *et seq.* (1979).
[23] ILL. REV. STAT. ch. 111, §§ 201 *et seq.* (1979).
[24] ILL. REV. STAT. ch. 111, §§ 401 *et seq.* (1979).
[25] ILL. REV. STAT. ch. 111, §§ 501 *et seq.* (1979).

spection and grading systems in the late 1800s. At the federal level, Congress enacted the U.S. Grain Standards Act in 1916. The act provided mandatory *national* grade standards[26] and a "two-level" national inspection and grading system. The first level was operated by inspection employees belonging to state, trade, and privately owned agencies and licensed by the U.S. Department of Agriculture. A second level of supervisory and appeal inspectors was employed by the Department.

The grain industry operated under the 1916 act until 1968. During that period, the industry expanded from a largely domestic operation into a multi-billion dollar domestic and export operation. In general, the revised act of 1968 retained the two-level national inspection system; removed most of the inspection requirements for grain shipped by grade in interstate commerce; provided flexibility and safeguards in the inspection and grading procedure to meet ongoing changes in grain production, harvesting, merchandising, and transportation; and added safeguards for grain exports.

Serious problems existed in the system as amended by the 1968 act. Generally, the Department of Agriculture's role as overall supervisor had certain inherent limitations. Weaknesses in the national inspection system led to extensive criminal abuses, such as the intentional misgrading of grain, short weighing, and using improperly inspected carriers. Disclosures of these matters in the world press and in congressional hear-

ings led to the enactment of the U.S. Grain Standards Act of 1976.

The principal provisions of the 1976 act required (1) that all grain inspections at export elevators and major inland terminal elevators be made by employees of the Federal Grain Inspection Service; (2) that all grain transferred into or out of export elevators be officially weighed by Federal employees; (3) that grain may be officially weighed at major inland terminal elevators, either by federal employees or by state employees under federal supervision; (4) that large companies engaged in merchandising grain be registered with the administrator of the Federal Grain Inspection Service. Also, the act enhanced the civil and criminal penalties available in order to enforce honest and accurate grain inspection and weighing.[27] The act increased the harshness of these penalties and also increased the scope of conduct subject to these penalties.

Section 24 of the 1976 act also addressed the question of whether existing grain standards were appropriate. The administrator of the Federal Grain Inspection Service was required to conduct an investigation regarding the adequacy of previously established federal grain standards. Could standards be developed that would reduce grading errors? Should grain be subclassed according to color or other factors not affecting quality of grain? Should the protein factor be included in the standards? Should broken grain be grouped together with other foreign material?[28]

---

[26] The concept of national standards remains intact even today. 7 U.S.C.A. § 76 provides for the establishment of standards for corn, wheat, rye, oats, barley, flaxseed, sorghum, soybeans, and other grains. The applicable national standards have been promulgated in 7 C.F.R. §§ 26.1 *et seq.*

[27] 7 U.S.C.A. §§ 71 *et seq.*

[28] A report of this investigation was submitted to Congress by the administrator. *Report of the Adequacy of the Existing Official Standards for Grain* (submitted by the Federal Grain Inspection Service to the Committee on Agriculture, Nutrition, and Forestry, U.S. Senate, and to the Committee on Agriculture, House of Representatives; November 1978, U.S. Government Printing Office 1979 0-280-931/FGIS-74).

Livestock. The adoption and implementation of uniform standards and grades has proceeded more slowly for livestock than for grain. *Live animal* grades are not officially applied in the marketing of livestock, but the USDA Market News Service publishes price quotations by grade. In direct selling by *carcass* grade and weight, the USDA standards may be used in grading the carcasses. Some packers insist on using their own grading system, while others use USDA grades. In the marketing of livestock, buyers rely more heavily on direct inspection of animals to be purchased than on a uniform grading system, such as the one used for grain.[29]

Other Federal and State Provisions. Additional federal standards have been developed for many other agricultural products, but a number of state laws also may be applicable insofar as they do not interfere with federal authority. For example, Illinois has special legislation dealing with the handling, inspection, labeling, processing, sale, and transportation of eggs[30] and has general legislation authorizing the director of the Illinois Department of Agriculture to promulgate official standards for grading and classifying agricultural products grown or produced in the state and to promulgate official standards for containers of agricultural products.[31]

The definitions of basic units of weight and measure, the tables of weight and measure, and weight and measure equivalents are published by the National Bureau of Standards. Weights and measures in conformity with these standards have been supplied to the various states by the federal government for the states' use and safekeeping. State law usually provides for the inspection and testing of all commercial weights and measures.[32]

Seed, Feed, and Fertilizer

Seed. The federal seed laws apply to seed which moves in interstate commerce. The following material describes the labeling requirements of the federal seed law, which has served as the model for many state seed laws.

All seeds traveling in interstate commerce must bear a label with the following information:

1. Name of the kind or kind and variety of each agricultural seed component in excess of 5 percent of the whole and the percentage by weight of each.
2. Lot number or other identification.
3. Origin of each agricultural seed. If origin is unknown, that should be stated.
4. Percentage by weight of weed seeds, including noxious weed seeds.
5. Kinds of noxious weed seeds and rates of occurrence of each.
6. Percentage by weight of inert matter.
7. Percentage by weight of agricultural seeds other than those under "1" above.
8. For each agricultural seed in excess of 5 percent and each kind or variety of type of agricultural seed shown in the labeling to be present in the proportion of 5 percent or less of the whole (a) percentage of germination inclusive of hard seed; (b) percentage of hard seed, if present; (c) calendar month and year when test was completed.
9. Name and address of the person who transports or delivers said seed in interstate commerce or person to whom the seed is

---

[29] *See generally* J. McCoy, Livestock and Meat Marketing 282-331 (2d ed. 1979).
[30] Ill. Rev. Stat. ch. 56 1/2, §§ 55-1 *et seq.*

(1979).
[31] Ill. Rev. Stat. ch. 5, §§ 92 *et seq.* (1979).
[32] *See, e.g.,* Ill. Rev. Stat. ch. 147, § 110 (1979).

shipped for resale, together with a code designation indicating such person.

10.   The year and month beyond which an innoculant is no longer claimed to be effective.[33]

The federal seed law also contains special requirements for the labeling of *treated* seeds, including (1) a statement that the seeds have been treated, (2) the name of chemicals used, (3) a warning of any harmfulness to humans, and (4) a description of the treatment process. The law prohibits defacement or alteration of labels in such a way as to defeat the labeling provisions; makes it unlawful to sell any agricultural seed bearing a false label, or to label a seed certified unless the seed has been certified by an authorized agency and issued a label by such agency; and requires that the label indicate percentage by weight of weed seeds, including noxious weed seeds and occurrence rates of weed seeds.[34] The only other federal law regulating weed seeds requires persons moving noxious weed seeds in interstate commerce to have a permit.[35]

Generally, state seed laws are quite similar and appear to be based on the federal law. For example, most state statutes have labeling requirements for agricultural seeds, treated seeds, and germinated seeds, and also require an indication on the label of the incidence of noxious weed seeds in excess of certain occurrence rates. In addition, most states have provisions forbidding false labeling and the alteration or defacement of labels in such a way as to undermine the seed laws.[36] The state laws also have broader application than the federal law in that state laws usually apply even though the seed is not transported in interstate commerce.

Many state laws also provide for seed certification programs. In Illinois, for example, the certification of seed is a voluntary program. Its purpose is to ensure high-quality seed and allow the grower a premium for producing it. To be acceptable in interstate sales, the certification must be accomplished by an official agency of the state. In Illinois, the University of Illinois Agricultural Experiment Station has been designated as the official certifying agency for the state of Illinois.[37] Under its authority to appoint an appropriate agency to actually carry out the certification program, the Experiment Station has designated the Illinois Crop Improvement Association, a not-for-profit corporation.[38]

Feed.   Although federal law does not contain any statutes regulating the labeling of commercial feed, the state laws are fairly uniform. They typically require commercial feeds to be labeled with weight, name, guaranteed analysis, name of each ingredient, and the name and principal address

---

[33] 7 U.S.C.A. § 1571 (1976).
[34] *Id.*
[35] 7 U.S.C.A. § 2803(a).
[36] *See, e.g.*, ILL. REV. STAT. ch 5., § 405.1(1) (1979).
[37] ILL. REV. STAT. ch. 5, § 409 (1979).
[38] In *Albin v. Ill. Crop Improvement Association*, 30 Ill. App. 2d 283, 174 N.E. 2d 697 (1961), the court considered the question—"Does the certifying agency owe a duty to those who purchase in reliance upon its tags, even though no privity exists between the certifier and purchaser?" In answering that there was no duty, the court said that actions on an express warranty cannot be maintained unless there is privity of contract. It also said that without privity, actions cannot be maintained on an implied warranty unless: (1) the product is inherently dangerous, (2) there have been fraudulent or deceitful statements or misrepresentations, (3) it is an implied warranty of fitness for human consumption.

The court held that this case did not fit into any of these exceptions. It should be noted that this is not a "sales" case brought under the Uniform Commercial Code. Presumably, the buyer would have some recourse against the seed seller for breach of warranty.

426 Sale and Transportation of Agricultural Products and Machinery

of the person responsible for distributing the commercial feed. Additional requirements may be present regarding customer formula feeds, which are a mixture of commercial feeds mixed according to the instructions of the final purchaser or contract feeder.

Illinois, Georgia, and Montana have virtually identical laws requiring commercial feeds to be labeled with the following:

1. net weight
2. name or brand
3. guaranteed analysis
4. common or usual name of each ingredient used in the manufacture of the commercial feed
5. name and principal address of person responsible for distributing the commercial feed

Customer formula feed must be labeled on the invoice with the following:

1. name and address of mixer
2. name and address of purchaser
3. date of sale
4. brand name and number of pounds of each registered commercial feed used in the mixture.

New York adds to these provisions a requirement that all feeds containing drugs or requiring special handling be labeled with adequate directions and warnings. Texas gives the director discretion to require the presence on the label of a number of materials. The customer formula feed requires listing of the names of any ingredients added by the purchaser. Kansas and California add to the basic provisions some special requirements for labeling mineral feedstuffs, including minimum percentages of protein, fat, and fiber. Customer feed labels are the same as those of the other states, with the addition of percentage or quantity of protein, mineral, vitamin, or other nutritive components. Kansas also requires listing of nonnutritive components used in the treating of disease. California further requires that the labels of commercial feed list salt content, a guarantee of any special quality, and a quality index for any animal protein concentrate.[39]

Generally, every brand of commercial feed sold in a state must be registered with the state department of agriculture. The label to be attached to the feed must usually be submitted to the department, which may be authorized to sample feeds and analyze their content. Any company guilty of mislabeling, adulterating, or operating without a license may be subject to a penalty.

Fertilizer. Many states have commercial fertilizer laws that typically require manufacturers, dealers, and blenders who sell fertilizers in the state to have their products analyzed and tagged and to pay an annual registration and license fee. Such laws regulate the sale of commercial fertilizers to assure the customer of a product identical to the analysis shown on the tag or invoice. Typically, such laws do not regulate limestone, manure, or burnt or hydrated lime or sewage sludge, nor do they regulate

---

[39] *See* ILL. REV. STAT. ch. 56 1/2, § 66.5 (1979); GA. CODE ANN. § 3-2028 (Cumm. Supp. 1977); MONT. REV. CODES ANN. § 3-2028 (Cumm. Supp. 1977); N.Y. AGRIC. MKTS. LAW § 130 (McKinney); TEX. CIV. CODE ANN. § 3881 (Vernon); KAN. STAT. ANN. § 2-1002(E)(6); CAL. FOOD & AGRIC. CODE § 14962 (Deering).

the spreading or application of commercial fertilizers.[40]

12.7 PRODUCTS LIABILITY— BREACH OF WARRANTY THEORIES[41]

Several theories are available to plaintiffs in products liability cases. Some of these theories are in the nature of contract actions, while others have their origins in tort law. Some of these theories focus primarily upon the product and its characteristics, while others focus upon the conduct of the seller or manufacturer. All are important to farmers, ranchers, and persons in agribusinesses who have an interest in products liability as consumers or as sellers.

Express Warranties

Two important kinds of warranties—express and implied—accompany the sale of personal property. An express warranty results from plain statements the seller makes about the goods. The express warranty may be oral or written, as in the case of statements printed on fertilizer, feed, and seed tags. Often a seller or a seller's agent, in trying to sell a product, will make representations which while not true are not stated expressly enough to constitute a warranty. Such language is referred to as "puffing" and does not become a part of the contract of sale. Many cases which have arisen because of a claimed breach of warranty depend on the jury's or the court's opinion of the language used.

There is a good discussion of oral warranties and the questions of law and fact involved in Annot., 67 A.L.R. 2d 619 (1959). Of interest to those in agriculture are cases noted in this article covering warranties of alfalfa seed; the age, birth date, breeding capacity, temperament, soundness, species, and workability of animals; apples, blood meal, bulls, feed, corn, seed, corn pickers, fertilizers, fruit trees, grain elevator capacity, hay, hay loaders, hay stackers,

---

[40] The Illinois law, for example, provides that a statement of the commercial feed contents must be filed with the Illinois Department of Agriculture before any commercial fertilizer is sold. If approved, the same information must appear on a tag attached to each bag or package, and in case of bulk shipment, to the invoice. The following information is required: (1) Weight; (2) Brand and grade; (3) Guaranteed analysis (in percent): (a) Nitrogen (b) Available phosphoric acid (c) Potash soluble in water; (4) Name and address of the person responsible for the statement and the guaranty.

Any fertilizer with two or more of these elements (nitrogen, phosphoric acid, and potash) must contain a combined percentage of at least 20 percent. The department is required to make one or more analyses each year of all registered fertilizers.

When a customer formula is prepared, the blender is required to register the various grades which the blender prepares on order from the farmer; also, the blender is required to give the purchaser an invoice showing the weight of each ingredient and the guaranteed analysis of each ingredient. These ingredients are to be thoroughly mixed before they are sold as a blend. Banking on a truck would not qualify as a blend. ILL. REV. STAT. ch. 5, § § 55.1 *et seq.* (1979).

A Florida case, *Shaw v. Armour and Company*, 175 F. Supp. 213 (1959), considered the issue of whether a statutory formula for damages where fertilizer fails to meet guaranteed analysis would preclude an action for common-law damages. The court held that the common-law remedy remains. For a discussion of the constitutionality, construction, and application of statutes relating to testing or sampling of agricultural fertilizers, *see* Annot., 105 A.L.R. 348–359 (1936).

[41] *See* 2 N. HARL, AGRICULTURAL LAW § 7.04 (1980) for an excellent discussion of these theories.

insect sprays, lily bulbs, manure, mascara, oats, peas, pork, potatoes, rape, rhubarb, and rye. Harking back to the day of the stationary threshing machine is *J. I. Case Threshing Machine Co. v. Stein*, 133 Ill. App. 169 (1907), in which the purchaser refused to accept delivery of a steam threshing machine engine, claiming that it was an old engine and that he had purchased a new one. So the company tendered another. The purchaser again refused, claiming they had simply painted the old one. The court held for the purchaser.

Several other Illinois cases are also interesting. In *Matthew v. Croene*, 2 Ill. App. 2d 529, 119 N.E.2d 830 (1954), the buyer visited the seller's farm in response to an advertisement of bred cattle. The seller expressly warranted that they had been bred. Based on this warranty, the buyer paid a price far above the unbred value. Some of the animals were not in fact bred. It was held that the purchaser could recover for the difference between what he paid and the market price as unbred animals.

In *Kenner v. Harding*, 85 Ill. 264 (1977), an inexperienced buyer examined a mule in a dark stall. The seller assured him that the mule was sound. The mule was in fact not sound. The court held that there was a warranty of soundness; in this case, it extended even to visible defects. This case illustrates that the rule of caveat emptor has always had its limitations—despite the fact that in the sale and trading of horses, outwitting the other person and getting the other person to buy an unsound horse was considered by many to be a fair game. In *Dayton v. Kidder*, 105 Ill. App. 107 (1902), when asked by a purchaser why cattle were so thin, the auctioneer said it was because they had been on short pasture. The owner overheard the auctioneer's answer and said nothing. The purchaser relied on this statement. The cattle were in fact diseased. The court held that under the circumstances, the owner was guilty of fraud and the purchaser was entitled to rescind the contract and recover damages.

HOG CHOLERA—EXPRESS WARRANTY

KELLER v. FLYNN
Appellate Court of Illinois, Second District, 1952
346 Ill. App. 499, 105 N.E. 2d 532

Defendants-appellants Ed Flynn and Samuel Lazarus, co-partners d/b/a Sterling Sales Company, appeal from a judgment for $956.50 damages, in favor of plaintiff-appellee, W.E. Keller, entered by the Circuit of Whiteside County on a jury verdict.

Some of the facts are undisputed. Appellee purchased sixty-six hogs at appellants' sales barn on July 27, 1950. They were purchased by appellee in three groups. A group of seventeen hogs consigned to the sales barn by an Illinois farmer are not in dispute. The dispute arises over two groups of hogs, one thirteen in number and the other thirty-six in number that had been shipped to appellants' sales barn from Missouri. Appellee purchased the hogs from the sales ring, and on the same day paid for the hogs at the sales office and received a printed sheet which provided in part "not responsible for stock after leaving the premises. Title to livestock does not change from Sterling Sales, Inc., until buyer's check has cleared." He also received two vaccination certificates. Appellee had the hogs delivered to his farm and they were mixed with other hogs owned by him. A number of the hogs died. The cause was submitted to the jury on a complaint consisting of two counts. Count I was based upon an express warranty theory. Motions for directed verdicts, for judgment notwithstanding the verdict, and for a new trial were denied.

The final issues involved whether or not the necessary elements exist which raise an express warranty. Appellee testified that Appellant Flynn stated, "Buy them, Doc, they are safe. They are long time treated." "Doc, they are long time treated, you better buy them." "If you need any hogs, Doc, there are some nice ones. They are long time treated and they are safe."

Considered alone, these statements are positive averments of fact in regard to the hogs made at the time of the sale for the purpose of assuring the appellee of the truth of the facts stated, and inducing him to buy the hogs. Taking the testimony of appellee that, "I would not have purchased the hogs if Mr. Flynn had not said they were long time treated and safe," there is substantial evidence in the record that appellee relied on the statement made by the appellant.

In the instant case there is evidence to be fairly inferred from all the testimony in the record that the defendants did warrant the hogs to have been long time treated for cholera and safe, and that the hogs died of cholera. The representations were made by the defendant, and the plaintiff relied upon them and there is evidence in the record establishing these facts. These were questions of fact for the jury to determine, and we cannot say that the finding of the jury that the warranty was made and breached, thus causing damages to the plaintiff, is manifestly against the weight of the evidence. We find no reversible error in this record; accordingly the judgment of the trial court is affirmed.

Implied Warranties and Caveat Emptor

Important in contract, particularly with reference to warranties, is the doctrine of *caveat emptor*, meaning "let the buyer beware." This rule is simply a way of saying that when a person buys something and fails to see defects which the average person would detect, the buyer is nevertheless bound by the contract. The extent to which this rule is effective depends, of course, upon the kind of contract, the nature of the property involved, and whether or not the purchaser had an opportunity to see the property or a representative sample of it. The rule could not possibly apply to some things a farmer purchases such as food, feed, livestock remedies, and chemical products.

Caveat emptor is applied much less literally today than it was a century ago. The various states have adopted provisions of the Uniform Commercial Code that clarify warranties implied when a product is purchased. Sections 2-314 and 2-315 of the UCC are set out below.

§ 2-314.   Implied Warranty: Merchantability; Usage of Trade

(1)   Unless excluded or modified (Section 2-316), a warranty that the goods shall be merchantable is implied in a contract for their sale if the seller is a merchant with respect to goods of that kind. Under this Section the serving for value of food or drink to be consumed either on the premises or elsewhere is a sale.

(2)   Goods to be merchantable must be at least such as
   (a) pass without objection in the trade under the contract description; and
   (b) in the case of fungible goods, are of fair average quality within the description; and
   (c) are fit for the ordinary purposes for which such goods are used; and
   (d) run, within the variations permitted by the agreement, of even kind, quality and quantity within each unit and among all units involved; and
   (e) are adequately contained, packaged, and labeled as the agreement may require; and
   (f) conform to the promises or affirmations of fact made on the container or label if any.

(3)   Unless excluded or modified (Section 2-316) other implied warranties may arise from course of dealing or usage of trade.

§ 2-315. Implied Warranty: Fitness for Particular Purpose

Where the seller at the time of contracting has reason to know any particular purpose for which the goods are required and that the buyer is relying on the seller's skill or judgment to select or furnish suitable goods, there is unless excluded or modified under the next section an implied warranty that the goods shall be fit for such purpose.

No statement of any kind is necessary to create an implied warranty. The obvious purpose of the product, with nothing having been said or done to make the seller believe that the purchaser intends to use it for some different purpose, is sufficient. Important to the farmer are the following implied warranties: that livestock feed is fit for consumption by farm animals, that seed will grow if planted under normal conditions, that various types of farm implements will perform in a satisfactory manner the operations for which they are designed, and that serums and viruses are effective for the use for which they are manufactured.

The Uniform Commercial Code provides that unless the seller states otherwise, a warranty that goods are merchantable is implied in a contract for their sale if the seller is a *merchant* for those goods. Thus, a farmer purchasing grain from an elevator may assume that the grain is of average quality within the description and fit for ordinary purposes unless the elevator operator tells the farmer to the contrary. However, purchasing an item the elevator doesn't normally carry, like lumber, would not give rise to the implied warranty. It would have to be purchased at a lumberyard for the implied warranty. The one exception to this is when the seller knows the buyer is relying on the seller's knowledge and what the buyer will use the goods for. In that instance, the seller warrants that the goods are fit for the purpose that the buyer intends to use them for.

WARRANTY OF FEED—IMPLIED WARRANTY OF FITNESS FOR PARTICULAR PURPOSE

TEXSUN FEED YARDS, INC. v. RALSTON PURINA COMPANY
United States Court of Appeals, Fifth Circuit, 1971
447 F. 2d 660

Texsun Feed Yards, Incorporated, (Texsun), a Texas corporation, a feed lot operator of Hereford, Texas, brought this suit against the Ralston Purina Company (Ralston), a Missouri corporation doing business in Texas, in the district court seeking damages for negligence, breach of warranty, and strict products liability in connection with Ralston's sales of feed supplement to Texsun during the spring of 1967. The jury awarded Texsun $27,000 as compensation for refunds, rebates, and adjustments which Texsun made to its customers and $10,000 as compensation for Texsun's loss of profits and diminished business reputation.

In March 1967, Texsun began to purchase a different ration supplement from Ralston. Ralston's assigned nutrition consultant, Dr. Mel Karr, advised Texsun to feed the new ration supplement to the cattle in Texsun's yard at the rate of 1.5 pounds per head per day. Texsun followed Dr. Karr's instructions, with disappointing results. It was subsequently determined that Dr. Karr should have told Texsun to supply the ration supplement to the cattle at the rate of 2 pounds per head per day.

Soon after Texsun began feeding the new ration supplement at the rate of 1.5 pounds per head per day, the rate of weight gain of the cattle in the yard decreased. To compensate for this diminished rate of gain Texsun kept many of its customers' animals in the yard longer than usual to attain the desired gain in weight. This additional time in Texsun's yard resulted in higher costs per pound of gain. Some of Texsun's customers removed their cattle from Texsun's yards because they were dissatisfied with the rate of gain. Texsun's customers demanded that Texsun extend cash refunds and account adjustments to compensate them for the additional feeding periods required to bring the cattle up to the desired marketing weight. In the spring of 1967 Texsun made cash refunds, rebates, and adjustments to its customers in an aggregate of $35,858.22.

Texsun alleged in its complaint that the ration supplement supplied by Ralston was defective and that the defect in the supplement proximately caused Texsun to suffer economic losses. In addition to feeding an insufficient amount under Ralston's recommendations, the defect in the supplement claimed by Texsun was characterized in two ways: (1) there was some deficiency in the ration supplement of a nature known only to Ralston, or (2) the manner in which the ration supplement interacted with the other feed that Texsun was using led to a weight gain rate below acceptable levels. As the case developed, the latter theory emerged as the mainstay of Texsun's case.

Where the seller at the time of contracting has reason to know any particular purpose for which the goods are required and that the buyer is relying on the seller's skill or judgment to select or furnish suitable goods, there is an implied warranty that the goods shall be fit for such purpose.

Ralston, in an effort to avoid liability for breach of implied warranty fitness for a particular purpose, characterizes its dealings with Texsun in the following manner.

Appellant submits that in essence here, the Defendant furnished a professional service to the Plaintiff and in connection therewith also manufactured and sold a specially formulated product consisting of the ration supplement in question. That the evidence viewed as a whole establishes that the product sold was not defective, there being no evidence whatsoever to indicate this fact, but that the professional advice of Dr. Karr to feed the supplement at the rate of 1½ pounds per day was incorrect, which conduct the jury likewise found to constitute negligence. The Trial Court perceived after the trial had progressed to a certain point that what was involved was a question of erroneous professional advice or instructions rather than defective product....

Ralston was in the business of selling ration supplement to feed lot operators. Its assignment of nutrition consultants such as Dr. Karr was designed to promote increased sales and to cultivate the good will of potential and existing customers. It is commercially unrealistic to treat separately the sale of the ration supplement and the rendering of professional advice and assistance. If Texsun was given inaccurate instructions by Ralston's nutrition consultant and if Texsun relied on those instructions to its economic detriment, we can perceive no reason for preventing Texsun's recovery under a breach of warranty theory.

Possible Defenses

Disclaimer of Warranties.[42]   A seller will often include language in the contract for sale, such as "as is" or "with all faults," which attempts to limit or modify the implied warranty of merchantability or fitness for a particular purpose. Generally, such disclaimers must be conspicuous to be effective, but even then the disclaimer will not be given effect where the limitation is un-

---

[42] UCC § 2-316 (1972 version) provides in part: "(2) Subject to subsection (3), to exclude or modify the implied warranty of merchantability or any part of it the language must mention merchantability and in case of a writing must be conspicuous, and to exclude or modify any implied warranty of fitness the exclusion must be by a writing and conspicuous. Language to exclude all implied warranties of fitness is sufficient if it states, for example, that 'There are no warranties which extend beyond the description of the face hereof.'

"(3) Notwithstanding subsection (2)

"(a) unless the circumstances indicate otherwise, all implied warranties are excluded by expressions like 'as is,' 'with all faults' or other language which

conscionable. In the case of consumer goods, a disclaimer of liability for personal injury is "prima facia unconscionable."

Obvious Defects. The UCC § 2-316(3)(b) (1972 version) specifically provides that if the purchaser has examined the product or refused to inspect it after the seller makes a demand for inspection, no implied warranty is created regarding defects that would have been discovered by such examination.

Privity of Contract. Historically, the fact that a person injured by a product did not have a contractual relationship with the manufacturer or seller (privity of contract) would bar recovery. This rule was a significant barrier to recovery by consumers against manufacturers with whom a consumer does not directly deal and third parties such as bystanders who deal with neither the manufacturer nor the seller. The UCC § 2-318 (1972 version) has greatly restricted the applicability of the privity defense to liability under breach of warranty.[43] Illinois, for example, has adopted Alternative A;[44] Kansas has adopted Alternative B;[45] and Virginia has adopted a modified version of Alternative C.[46] Most states have adopted one of these alternatives.

Alternative A

A seller's warranty whether express or implied extends to any natural person who is in the family or household of the buyer or who is a guest in the buyer's home if it is reasonable to expect that such person may use, consume or be affected by the goods and who is injured in person by breach of the warranty. A seller may not exclude or limit the operation of this section.

Alternative B

A seller's warranty whether express or implied extends to any natural person who may reasonably be expected to use, consume or be affected by the goods and who is injured in person by breach of the warranty. A seller may not exclude or limit the operation of this section.

Alternative C

A seller's warranty whether express or implied extends to any person who may reasonably be expected to use, consume or be affected by the goods and who is injured by breach of the warranty. A seller may not exclude or limit the operation of this section with respect to injury to the person of an individual to whom the warranty extends.

Subsequent Adulteration or Damage. The implied warranty theory is often used in cases dealing with food. In *Tiffin v. The Great Atlantic and Pacific Tea Company*, 18 Ill. 2d 48, 162 N.E.2d 406 (1959), the court noted that when food is furnished to the

in common understanding calls the buyer's attention to the exclusion of warranties and makes plain that there is no implied warranty; and

"(b) when the buyer before entering into the contract has examined the goods or the sample or model as fully as he desired or has refused to examine the goods there is no implied warranty with regard to defects which an examination ought in the circumstances to have revealed to him; and

"(c) an implied warranty can also be excluded or modified by course of dealing or course of performance or usage of trade.

"(4) Remedies for breach of warranty can be limited in accordance with the provision of this Article on liquidation or limitation of damages and on contractual modification of remedy (Sections 2-718 and 2-719)."

UCC § 2-719(3) (1972 version) provides, in part: "Consequential damages may be limited or excluded unless the limitation or exclusion is unconscionable."

[43] *See* 2 N. HARL, AGRICULTURAL LAW §7.05 (1980).
[44] ILL. REV. STAT. ch. 26, § 2-418 (1979).
[45] KAN. STAT. ANN. § 84-2-318 (1967).
[46] VA. CODE § 8.2-318 (1964).

general public, the manufacturer and retailer both impliedly warrant that the product is fit for human consumption at the
time it leaves their respective control, and
where the food proves to be deleterious,
either or both may be required to respond
in damages to the injured consumer. However, since a manufacturer's product may
pass through many hands before it reaches
the ultimate user, public policy does not
require the manufacturer to warrant that
no one will tamper with or adulterate the
food after it leaves the manufacturer's control and before it is received by the consumer; and where a party elects to hold the
remote seller liable the seller must, in the
absence of direct evidence of contamination by the manufacturer, prove that there
was no opportunity for subsequent adulteration.

Nonuniform Provisions Regarding Implied Warranties in Livestock Sales

Recently, a number of states have enacted special sections in their commercial
codes concerning implied warranties in
livestock sales. The South Dakota provision, for example, provides as follows:
"Notwithstanding [the above general provisions dealing with implied warranties, a
seller creates] . . . no implied warranty . . .
that such cattle, hogs or sheep are free
from disease."[47]

Iowa also has recently amended its commercial code.[48] The Iowa version appears
to exempt the sellers of livestock from *all*
implied warranties provided certain requirements are met, including *inter alia*
that an express statement be made that the

livestock has been properly inspected and
appears to be free of communicable disease.

The influx of similar nonuniform provisions in various states has some advantages
and disadvantages. Sellers of livestock may
benefit because they are less likely to be
held liable for breach of implied warranties.
Indirectly, livestock marketing associations
may benefit because such provisions effectively remove the seller's agent from the
controversy between seller and buyer.

On the other hand, buyers of livestock
have fewer protections where such nonuniform provisions have been enacted. Also,
aside from destroying much of the uniformity in state commercial codes, such provisions appear to be inconsistent with public
policy. As between a purchaser and seller
of livestock, who should be liable for disease? Shouldn't it be the person who was in
the best position to prevent the disease in
the first place?

12.8 PRODUCTS LIABILITY— NEGLIGENCE AND STRICT LIABILITY IN TORT

Negligence[49]

Products liability based on negligence is
really no different from general tort liability based on negligence. At an earlier
time, this theory of recovery was limited
by court decisions that had limited the class
of persons to whom a duty of reasonable
care was owed to those in privity of contract with the defendant. The modern
trend is to define the class of persons to
whom a manufacturer owes a duty to in-

---

[47] S.D. CODIFIED LAWS ANN. § 57-4-35.1 (1980 Interim Supp.).
[48] Iowa House File 2546 (enacted into law, Summer
1980).

[49] *See* 2 N. HARL, AGRICULTURAL LAW § 7.06
(1980).

clude all those who might reasonably be expected to come in contact with the product.[50] Thus, manufacturers have a duty to exercise reasonable care in the manufacture or design of a product and to warn of its foreseeable dangers. Persons who might reasonably be expected to come in contact with products may recover for breach of this duty.

UNWHOLESOME FOOD—NEGLIGENCE

GRAY v. PET MILK CO.
Circuit Court of Appeals, Seventh Circuit, 1940
108 F. 2d 974

There was substantial evidence to support the following facts: Appellee, a woman in her early thirties, kept house for her father, an unemployed coal miner. On the morning of November 16, 1936, she sent him to a grocery store to purchase a can of Pet Milk, which she opened in order to prepare cocoa for lunch on that day. Her method of opening the can was by punching two small holes in the top from which she then poured enough milk to make the cocoa, setting the can containing the balance of the milk in the refrigerator. For the meal she served only the cocoa and some cookies which her father had also purchased from the same store when he bought the milk. She drank part of one cup of cocoa, but did not eat anything. He drank two cups. About an hour after the meal, the father became violently ill. He went to bed, and about an hour later, went to see a physician, Dr. Pearce. While he was gone, appellee also became ill, suffering from a severe headache and vomiting. Appellee testified that prior to this time the health of both herself and her father had been good. When her father returned from the doctor's office he brought a friend with him, and appellee got up and prepared the evening meal, eating nothing herself. When she attempted to pour some of the milk from the can for coffee for the friend, she found that it would not pour freely, whereupon she took the can opener and made the opening larger, cutting the lid halfway off. She then found that the obstruction was caused by the body of a mouse, and set the can aside in a place where it was in sight of all of them. After the meal, her father and his friend both investigated, and they also saw the mouse. Another friend came in and they showed it to him, and then her father took the can over to show it to Dr. Pearce, who had attended him that afternoon. He also showed it to the manager of the store from which he had purchased it. The following morning, at the request of this manager, he left the can at the store in order that the latter might show it to the supervisor. The can was subsequently thrown into the fire

---

[50] *See* MacPherson v. Buick Motor Co., 217 N.Y. 382, 111 N.E. 1050 (1916). Many courts have adopted the foreseeability test first articulated by J. Cordozo in *MacPherson*.

because its smell was offensive, although the father had requested that it be kept for him.

Appellee continued to be very ill, and after five days went to a hospital operated by Dr. Pearce, where she remained ten or twelve days. After her return to her home she continued to have severe headaches and stomach cramps, and she lost a great deal of weight. In March, 1937, she returned to the hospital for two weeks, during which an operation was performed upon her. In April she returned for another two weeks at the hospital, suffering from the same headaches and cramps and severe weakness. She also, at this time, broke out in a rash, suffering from sores which came all over her body, and from which she testifies she was still suffering at the time of the trial. She was in the hospital for two more periods, one of two weeks and the last from some time in January, 1938, to March or April of that year.

On cross-examination Dr. Pearce admitted that he had never before treated a severe case of food poisoning; that he did not know what kind of poison a dead mouse could create, and could name no bacteria which could not be killed by a 200 degree temperature; that he had never seen a rash like the one on appellee's body and from an examination of it would not be able to say what caused it.

To prove the absence of negligence on its part, appellant produced as a witness the manager of the can-making department at the plant where the can here involved was made and filled. He described the method used, including sterilization of the filled can under steam pressure at a temperature of 240 degrees for thirty minutes. The description tended to prove the impossibility that a mouse could get into the can during the process. However, by cross-examination, and by a rebuttal witness, it appeared that, while ordinarily the cans moved continuously along a moving belt conveyor without stops from the time the flat strips of tin to be formed into cans were put on the conveyor until the cans were completed with covers, ready for filling, at times stoppages occurred in the line by jamming of the machinery. At such times the operation might be held up as long as five minutes, during which time the cans remained motionless on the conveyor, in a horizontal position, with open ends, protected by a guard rail only half as wide as the cans. It also appeared that there were a few places in the plant where it might be possible for a mouse to drop onto the conveyor or to jump up onto it, and that such places were not protected by any kind of cover. We think the evidence as to this point was sufficient to go to the jury on the question of negligence, when coupled with the fact of the uncontradicted evidence of three witnesses who saw the can opened and had it in view from that time until each actually saw the body of the mouse.

Judgment affirmed for plaintiff for $6,000.

Strict Liability[51]

A majority of American jurisdictions have adopted the *Restatement (Second) of Torts* Sec. 402A. This section provides that one who sells any product in a defective condition unreasonably dangerous to the person or property of the consumer is subject to liability for physical harm caused by the defective product.

PRODUCT LIABILITY—DEFECT IN DESIGN OF CORN PICKER

WRIGHT v. MASSEY-HARRIS INC.
Appellate Court of Illinois, Fifth District, 1966
68 Ill. App. 2d 70, 215 N.E. 2d 465

The plaintiff, Harold Wright, a farm employee, brought an action against the defendant, Massey-Ferguson, Incorporated, to recover for personal injuries sustained while operating a self-propelled corn picker. The defendant's motion to dismiss the complaint was allowed. The plaintiff appeals from that judgment.

Defendant claims that the complaint does not state a cause of action because (1) there are no facts alleged sufficient to show that the machine in question was inherently dangerous when put to the use for which it was intended, and (2) the complaint fails to allege facts sufficient to demonstrate that there was any hidden or latent defect in them, but on the contrary, the complaint shows that the danger would be obvious to anyone placing his hands in the corn husking rollers while the machine was in operation and the complaint therefore shows on its face that there is no liability to the plaintiff for the occurrence alleged.

While this cause was pending in this court, the Supreme Court of Illinois rendered a landmark decision in the case of *Suvada v. White Motor Co.*, et al., 32 Ill. 2d 612, 210 NE 2d 182, in which it not only shattered the privity defense in Illinois in actions against manufacturers, sellers, contractors, those who hold themselves out to be manufacturers, assemblers of parts, suppliers and manufacturers of component parts, but also held these same parties to strict privity-free liability for any injury or damage caused by any unreasonably dangerous products which one or all of them might place into the stream of commerce.

The Court based its holding solely on the same public policy which had heretofore motivated the Illinois Courts to impose strict liability on the sellers and manufacturers of food, saying at page 619:

---

[51] *See* 2 N. HARL, AGRICULTURAL LAW § 7.03 (1980).

Without extended discussion, it seems obvious that public interest in human life and health, the invitations and solicitations to purchase the product and the justice of imposing the loss on the one creating the risk and reaping the profit are present and as compelling in cases involving motor vehicles and other products, where the defective condition makes them unreasonably dangerous to the user, as they are in food cases.

The Supreme Court traced the history of products liability law in Illinois and the various extensions of that law leading up to its decision. It recognized that public policy was the primary factor for imposing strict liability on the seller and manufacturer of food in favor of the injured consumer, and that implicit in the reasoning of the cases imposing strict liability is that "liability is imposed by law and the refusal to permit the manufacturer to define the scope of its own responsibilities for defective products."

Specifically, the Suvada case held: ...

2   That lack of privity is no longer a defense in a tort action against the manufacturer, seller, contractor, supplier, one who holds himself out to be a manufacturer, the assembler of parts and manufacturer of component parts.

3   That henceforth strict tort liability is imposed against the above parties in cases involving products where the defective condition makes them unreasonably dangerous to the user.

4   The liability of the above-named parties is imposed by operation of law as a matter of public policy for the protection of the public for the following reasons:

a The public interest in human life and health demands all the protection the law can give against the sale of unreasonably dangerous products;

b The manufacturer solicits and invites the user of his product by advertising or otherwise representing to the public that it is safe for use. Having thus induced the use of the product, the law will impose liability for the damage it causes;

c The losses caused by unreasonably dangerous products should be borne by those who have created the risk and reaped the profit by placing these products in the stream of commerce.

6   That the views expressed in Suvada by the cases cited therein and also by Professor Noel, Professor James and Dean Prosser in various articles they have written on the subject of strict liability coincide with the language of Sec. 402A, Restatement of the Law, Second, Torts, which is as follows:

(1)   One who sells any product in a defective condition unreasonably dangerous to the user or consumer or to his property is subject to liability for physical harm thereby caused to the ultimate user or consumer or to his property, if

(a) the seller is engaged in the business of selling such a product, and

(b) it is expected to reach the user or consumer in the condition in which it is sold.

(2)   The rule stated in subsection (1) applies although

(a) the seller had exercised all possible care in the preparation and sale of his product, and

(b) the user or consumer has not bought the product from or entered into any contractual relation with the seller.

7   The plaintiff must prove that his injury or damage resulted from a condition of the product, that the condition was an unreasonably dangerous one and that the condition existed at the time it left the manufacturer's control.''

The present case involved a claimed defect in design rather than a defect in manufacture and we interpret Suvada to mean that the strict liability imposed upon a manufacturer includes injuries which arise from defects in design as well as defects in manufacture. Whether the design defect in the present case is of a nature upon which liability can be imposed involves the factual question of whether it creates an unreasonably dangerous condition, or, in other words, whether the product in question has lived up to the required standard of safety.

We believe that the complaint in the present case states a good cause of action in negligence and also a good cause of action in strict liability if we treat all of the allegations in excess of those required by Suvada as surplusage. For the foregoing reasons the judgment of the trial court in favor of the defendants is reversed. We remand the case for further proceedings not inconsistent with this opinion.

Although a manufacturer has a duty to make its product reasonably fit for intended use, the liability of a manufacturer to others encompasses only those individuals to whom injury from a defective product may reasonably be foreseen and the manufacturer is only liable in those situations where the product is being used for the purpose for which it was intended or for which it is reasonably foreseeable that it may be used. A foreseeability test for a manufacturer's liability under the concepts of strict tort liability is not intended to bring within the scope of the manufacturer's liability every injury that might possibily occur, for foreseeability means that which it is objectively reasonable to expect, not merely that which might conceivably occur. Courts have had some difficulty deciding what kind of injury is reasonably foreseeable and what kind of product is unreasonably dangerous, as illustrated by the following case.

DANGEROUS AUGER—STRICT LIABILITY

RICHELMAN v. KEWANEE MACHINERY AND CONVEYOR COMPANY
Appellate Court of Illinois, Fifth District, 1978
59 Ill. App. 3d 578, 375 N.E. 2d 885

Defendant appeals from a judgment in the amount of $75,000 entered by the circuit court of St. Clair County after a jury found the issues in favor of the plaintiff.

On November 17, 1972, Mark Richelmen, then 2 years 9 months of age, suffered a traumatic amputation of his right leg when he became entangled in a grain auger located in his grandfather's farm yard. The minor plaintiff's grandfather, Arthur Richelman, purchased the Kewanee Model 260 Grain Auger in 1967 from an implement dealer located in Steeleville, Illinois.

In 1972 plaintiff's parents, Donald and Elaine Richelmen, were living with their minor son in a mobile home located approximately 30 feet west of the farmhouse where plaintiff's grandparents resided. As the children were unable to sleep, Mrs. Richelman dressed them and took them to their grandmother's house nearby.

Less than five minutes later both parents heard Mark's screams and rushed to the grain elevator in time to pull their son from the hopper. The minor plaintiff's right leg had been amputated by the grain auger. However, no one had witnessed precisely how the young child had become entangled in the machinery.

There was a great deal of evidence adduced at trial concerning the methodology employed in testing the various guard designs. James Suhr, who had been instrumental as a design engineer in the employ of Kewanee during the 1965 tests was called as a witness for the plaintiff. He testified that in designing the guards he considered only the safety of the implement operator; the safety of a bystander was not even a factor. He explained that he anticipated that anyone, male or female, of high school age could be an operator of the auger. Nevertheless, in determining the width of the gap between the guard bars, Suhr measured only the width of his own size 12-B shoe and accordingly spaced the bars 4 5/8″ apart. Finally, he stated that although the engineers were fully cognizant that augers are generally located in a farmhouse complex where small children often play, their safety was not a consideration in designing the auger guard. In short, the guard was designed for the safety of "the majority of users." The study concluded that the parallel type guard which was replaced in 1967 was safer than the vertical type guard used in the 1967 design involved in this accident.

The only issue for review is whether Mark Richelman's injury was foreseeable as a matter of law under the rationale of *Winnett v. Winnett*, 57 Ill. 2d 7, 310 N.E. 2d 1, which involved an injury to a four-year-old child who was, in the court's own language, "permitted to approach an operating farm forage wagon or...permitted to place her fingers in or on the holes in its moving screen." In rejecting the usual categorization of plaintiffs, the court adopted the following test of liability:

In our judgment the liability of a manufacturer properly encompasses only those individuals to whom injury from a defective product may reasonably be foreseen and only those situations where the product is being used for the purpose for which it was intended or for which it is reasonably foreseeable that it may be used.

The court continued:

Whether the plaintiff here is an individual who is entitled to the protections afforded by the concepts of strict tort liability depends upon whether it can be fairly said that her conduct in placing her fingers in the moving screen or belt of the forage wagon was reasonably foreseeable. A foreseeability test, however, is not intended to bring within the scope of the defendant's liability every injury that might possibly occur. 'In a sense, in retrospect almost nothing is entirely unforeseeable.' Foreseeability means that which it is *objectively reasonable* to expect, not merely what might conceivably occur.

A detailed recitation of the evidence regarding foreseeability would serve no purpose here. We need only repeat that questions of foreseeability as well as questions whether a product is defective or unreasonably dangerous are ordinarily for the jury to resolve. While the supreme court in *Winnett* felt that the facts there in issue were such that nonliability could be found as a matter of law, we regard the evidence in this case as presenting factual questions upon which reasonable men might differ and thus believe that it was properly submitted to the jury. (*Ney v. Yellow Cab Co.*, 2 Ill. 2d 74, 117 N.E. 2d 74.) We cannot say as a matter of law that injury to the plaintiff in this case was not objectively reasonable to expect. For reasons stated earlier in this opinion, we do not find the *Winnett* case and its progeny controlling on this issue.

For the foregoing reasons the judgment of the circuit court of St. Clair County is affimed.

Mr. JUSTICE JONES, dissenting:

The majority recognizes the validity of the "foreseeability" rule for products liability cases as expressed in *Winnett v. Winnett*, but yet it refuses to follow it upon a set of facts strikingly similar to those of the *Winnett* case. It also concludes that the machine involved in the injury in this case was an unreasonably dangerous one. I disagree with the majority upon both facets of their conclusion, believing that upon the facts present in this case the trial court should have entered judgment for defendant notwithstanding the verdict. I accordingly respectfully dissent.

Here, as in *Winnett*, there is but one inference to be drawn from the evidence and the court should therefore have directed a verdict for defendant at the close of all the evidence, holding as a matter of law that it was not foreseeable by defendant that plaintiff would be injured in the manner in which the injury in fact occurred.

With regard to the character of the auger as an unreasonably dangerous machine it should be noted that the dangerousness did not result from a flaw in its manufacture, nor in its failure to conform to the intended design, nor from an inadvertent design error. It was a dangerous machine because of a conscious choice in design. The auger was being used in the manner for which it was designed and was functioning in its intended manner. A safety barrier or grid that would prevent any injury to any persons, including wandering minor children, would be manifestly less efficient as a device to auger grain into a bin. The dangerousness of the auger in use here may well be attributable to its usefulness. Its dangerousness is generic to its function. It in fact appears in the record here that another auger equipped for greater protection potential was available to plaintiff's grandfather. For reasons not apparent the particular machine in question was purchased instead.

The risk of harm from the auger is readily apparent and the design aspect of the machine that makes it dangerous may in fact play a role in the user's decision to purchase it. This factor is important since it bears heavily upon the question whether the auger is "unreasonably" dangerous, for liability is imposed only if the product is "unreasonably dangerous."(*Suvada v. White Motor Co.*, 32 Ill. 2d 612, 210 N.E. 2d 182.) Illinois courts have not adopted a rule imposing absolute liability upon manufacturers for injuries occasioned by their products. This is particularly true in instances where the dangerousness of the machine or instrumentality is readily apparent.

The trial court should have found, as a matter of law, that the auger, its dangerousness readily apparent and generic to its function, was not an unreasonably dangerous machine and that it was not objectively reasonable for defendant to expect that an injury would be incurred by the minor plaintiff, a nonuser bystander. Having so found the court should have directed a verdict for defendant at the close of all the evidence or entered judgment for defendant notwithstanding the verdict.

12.9 TRANSPORTATION OF AGRICULTURAL PRODUCTS

The transportation industry is heavily regulated by federal and state law. Much of this regulation is of importance to agriculture generally because it affects transportation costs and dependability. A few aspects of this regulatory scheme are also of practical importance to agricultural producers. One such consideration is the high duty of care that commercial carriers must exercise when transporting products.

TRANSPORTATION OF DAIRY CATTLE BY RAILROAD

PRINCE v. RAILWAY EXPRESS AGENCY, INC.
Appellate Court of Illinois, First District, 1950
341 Ill. App. 236, 93 N.E. 2d 102

The defendant express company appeals from a judgment, entered on a trial before the court without a jury, for $2,238.58, damages to a carload of dairy cows shipped by express from Milwaukee (West Allis), Wisconsin to New Bedford, Massachusetts.

There is no substantial dispute in the evidence. The cars were loaded at point of origin November 1, 1944 at 10:30 a.m., moved to Chicago and attached to New York Central train No. 10 until the train reached Cleveland, Ohio, where according to the practice of the railroad company at that time express cars were removed from the train and attached to the second train No. 10, which left Cleveland 36 minutes after the first train. The car arrived in Boston too late for connection with the night train for New Bedford, Massachusetts. Mr. White of the office of the general manager of defendant at Boston notified plaintiff by telephone that the cows would have to be unloaded. Plaintiff arrived at the Brighton stockyards as the cows were being taken from the express car to the barn. He told the representative of the stockyards to see that the cows were milked and watered. This request was not complied with. The cows were moved to destination the next morning. Ten cows suffered damage to their udders because of failure to milk them enroute. They were no longer useful as dairy cows. They were sold on the market at a loss to the plaintiff of the amount fixed by the judgment. An agent of the defendant, called by plaintiff under section 60 of the Practice Act testified that the car was in the possession of the carriers from the time it was loaded until it was delivered at New Bedford, Massachusetts, 44 hours and 10 minutes; that the usual and customary time required to transport the car would be about 45 hours, based on the 10:30 a.m. loading time.

Plaintiff contends that it was the duty of the express company to unload and milk the cows if their transportation was not concluded within 36 hours. Defendant's position is that it was under no obligation to do anything other than take the cows from the car and water and feed them, unless the shipper gave directions in writing for milking or other care of the cows. Defendant's contention is based upon the following provision of its tariff. "Instructions of shippers as to the feeding and care of animals in transit, when given in writing or plainly marked upon the container, must be complied with, and no charge will be made for feeding animals when the food accompanies the shipment." It contends that in the absence of written instructions it is not permitted under the law to render special service to a shipper by milking the cows enroute. No authorities directly in point are cited. It is our opinion that this provision is not a limitation on the right or duty of the carrier to care for animals entrusted to it. In an earlier case, plaintiffs brought suit to recover damages to a shipment of apples caused by freezing. The evidence on behalf of defendant merely shows that there was no delay in the shipment or any mishap during the transit. In affirming a judgment against the carrier the court said: "The law is well settled that a common carrier must anticipate and guard against all natural consequences that may occur during transportation." In 13 Corpus Juris Secundum 63 (a) it is said: "The fact that the carrier cannot make a charge for a service, unless such charge is provided for in the published tariffs and classification,...does not affect the existence of the duty to render such service as is necessary to the proper care of livestock in transit." In a Colorado case, a house-broke dog died enroute from a broken bladder, sustained by failure of the carrier to exercise the dog daily. The court said:

"No statute nor regulation has been pointed out which relieves the defendant, as a common carrier, of the usual responsibility of caring for animals, delivered to it for transportaiton, while the same are in transit. The fact that the carrier could not make a charge for a service, unless such charge is provided for in the published tariffs and classifications, does not affect the existence of the duty to render such service as is necessary to the proper care of live stock in transit."

Here plaintiff orally requested that the cows be milked. Payment for such service was neither requested nor refused. It appears without controversy that failure to milk dairy cows within 36 hours will cause the injuries suffered in this case. The waybill required the unloading of the cows within 36 hours. They arrived at Boston within 30 hours. It was the duty of the defendant to milk the cows when they were unloaded at the Brighton stockyards, especially in view of the request of plaintiff. Judgment affirmed.

Another feature of transportation regulation of practical importance to agriculture producers is the broad exemption available to such producers. For example, in the regulations applying to vehicles used for hire, there are exemptions for agricultural producers carrying their own products and for producers who incidentally pick up a neighbor's product or livestock for market.

STUDY QUESTIONS

1.   What are several important questions which should be settled in a contract for the sale of grain? Of livestock? What terms are generally assumed if these questions are not expressly addressed?

2.   Discuss some of the important points that should be included in grower-producer contracts.

3.   Is there a trend toward increased direct marketing by agricultural producers? What legal implications result from direct marketing activities?

4.   What is the UCC merchant's exception to the statute of frauds? Does the exception affect agricultural producers? Should it apply to agricultural producers?

5.   What levels of government regulate grain warehouses? Grain dealers? What is the purpose of this regulation? What regulatory provisions are typical?

6.   What can agricultural producers do to help assure that they will be paid for grain delivered to a warehouse or grain dealer? What special risks are present with delayed pricing contracts?

7.   Describe some of the significant changes that have occurred in the structure of the American livestock industry.

8.   How has the federal Packers and Stockyards Act been changed to better protect producers?

9.   What is the nature of the state regulation of livestock dealers?

10.   What significant changes have occurred in the grain marketing industry? What problems were created by these changes?

11.   Are there federal grain standards? Federal livestock standards?

12.   What labeling requirements apply to seed, feed, or fertilizer?

13.   What is an express warranty? Under what conditions does it arise?

14.   What is implied warranty of merchantability? Must the seller be a "merchant" for the warranty to arise?

15.   What is the implied warranty of fitness for a particular purpose? When does it arise?

16.   Can implied warranties be disclaimed?

17.   What legislation recently has been passed by several states regarding implied warranties in livestock sales? Are such laws good or bad?

18.   What is strict liability? Under what circumstances is it likely to be a basis of products liability?

19.   What standard of care is generally imposed upon common carriers such as railroads or truckers?

20.   Are broad exemptions from transportation regulations available to agricultural producers?

13
Farm Tenancy

Leases play an important role in farming. In fact, many farmers could not stay in business without operating through lease arrangements. Table 13.1 describes the frequency with which farmers rent all or part of their farmland. Many farm landlords and tenants know little about the legal aspects of the landlord-tenant relationship. Yet, when misunderstandings arise, the parties must depend upon legal principles for settlement of their differences. A better knowledge of the nature and effectiveness of agreements made by the landlord and tenant and of their rights and duties would prevent many misunderstandings that otherwise occur.

The lease agreement between the parties is crucial in determining what rights and duties exist between landlords and tenants. A lease is a contract and will be interpreted in the light of contract law. It is for this reason that it is important that the parties understand the details of their lease (contract) and the language used in defining the terms of the agreement. In addition, state law rather than federal law is the controlling force in determining the rights and duties of the parties.

Most states have enacted a series of statutes dealing with the landlord-tenant relationship. These statutes, many of which will be discussed in more detail in the sec-

Table 13.1   Tenure Status of Operators by Crop Reporting Region, 1964–1974

Region	% Full Owners		% Part Owners		% Tenants	
	1964	1974	1964	1974	1964	1974
Illinois	41	50	28	30	31	20
Northwest	45	53	17	24	38	23
Northeast	39	45	21	25	40	30
West	60	53	18	29	22	18
Central	29	40	28	32	43	28
East	24	35	29	35	47	30
West-Southwest	44	52	28	30	28	18
East-Southeast	42	51	40	38	18	11
Southwest	52	57	30	30	18	13
Southeast	54	61	37	32	9	7

Source: Bowling and Van Es, *Changes over a Decade in Illinois Agriculture*, ILLINOIS RESEARCH, Spring 1977.

tions that follow, typically deal with the following subjects:

1.   Statutes defining tenancy, sharecropping, and other terms relating to the tenure status

2.   The statute of frauds limiting the validity of oral leases

3.   Statutory provisions on the termination of farm leases, which are designed to force landlords and tenants to notify the other party of an intention to terminate the lease at some reasonable period prior to the expiration date of the lease

4.   Statutory recognition of the "tenancy from year to year," which is designed to continue farm tenancies where no written lease exists and where statutory notice has not been given

5.   Statutes providing that notice as required by law may be abrogated by special agreement

6.   General statutes on the committing of waste, which are designed to protect the landlord's property

7.   Statutes prohibiting, in certain specified instances, assignment of the lease without the consent of the landlord

8.   Statutes prohibiting tenants from violating the provisions of written leases and giving landlords a right to reenter when such a violation occurs

9.   Statutes on subleasing which are designed to protect the landlord's reliance on the personal characteristics of the tenant

10.   General remedies for the collection of rent, which are usually not designed specifically for farm tenancies

11.   Lien statutes of varying effectiveness and inclusiveness designed to protect the landlord's right against the tenant for rent and specifying conditions and procedures for enforcement

12.   Statutes limiting the landlord's lien

13.   Statutes exempting debtors' goods from execution, the purpose being to leave the farmer certain basic equipment necessary for farming

14.   Statutes giving the landlord a right to enter the premises, to mature and harvest crops, and to retain the rent in cases where the tenant abandons the farm

15.   Statutes providing penalties for holding over, which are designed to aid landlords

in recovering possession at the expiration of the lease

16.   Statutes of a general nature, providing that compensation shall be paid for improvements made prior to notice of an adverse title in case of dispossession by one having a better title

17.   Statutes allowing the tenant to remove certain fixtures erected during the term and not "attached" to the realty

The above list is undoubtedly incomplete, but it does indicate the general tenor of state law. No one state has laws on all the subjects listed, and some states have but a few. Some states even have constitutional provisions relating to leases.

13.1 NATURE OF THE LANDLORD-TENANT RELATIONSHIP

Requirements of a Legal Lease

The relation of landlord and tenant may be defined in general terms as that which arises from a contract under which one occupies the property of the other with permission for a payment known as *rent*. The following elements are essential to creation of the landlord-tenant relationship.[1] (1) A valid contract—this may be oral, providing it is taken out of the statute of frauds by partial performance or by actual occupancy; (2) provisions for a payment for use of the land—normally known as rent; (3) the transfer of substantial rights to the tenant so that it may be said an "estate" has passed—otherwise, the agreement may be only a license; (4) possession and control in the tenant; (5) a reversionary interest in the landlord; (6) real estate or some interest in real estate must be involved—otherwise, the agreement may be a bailment.

For the duration of the lease, except for rights which may have been retained by the landlord in a written lease and for certain customs which may exist, the tenant is much like an owner.

The relation between the landowner and the farm operator may be classified as a landlord-tenant relationship, an employee contract, or a partnership. How the relationship is classified depends on the provisions of the agreement.

Employee or Tenant

At first, the difference between a tenant and an employee is easy to see. An employee is paid a wage to produce a crop. The wages an employee receives may be a share of the crop or a share of the proceeds of the sale of the crop. The employee has no legal interest in the farm and usually no legal interest in the crops until they are set aside at harvest as part of the wages. In many states, the employee's sole remedy, if the employer fails to pay the wages, is to sue for damages for breach of contract.

A tenant, on the other hand, is entitled to exclusive use and possession of the real estate. The tenant may sue other parties, including the landlord, unless stated otherwise in the lease, for trespass on the premises. The crops, until divided, belong to the tenant exclusively, even if the landlord is to receive a part of the crops as rent. As the operator of the real estate, the tenant is potentially liable in negligence cases for the injury of invitees or licensees who come onto the property if injuries result from the poor upkeep of the premises.

---

[1] For a general discussion of farm leases and a checklist of items for landlords and tenants to consider, *see* MODERN LEGAL FORMS ch. 32, § 4001 *et seq.*

The problem arises when a contract contains elements of both an employer-employee contract and a landlord-tenant lease. For example, a contract may use words such as "rentals" or "landlord-tenant," but if the lease provides for control of the operation by the owner, with the owner supplying the seed, fertilizer, and machinery, a court may say the relation is employer-employee instead of landlord-tenant. The rules that regulate the agreement may then turn out to be much different than the original intent of the parties.

Partnership or
Landlord-Tenant Relationship

Legal problems can arise when the intent of the parties is not clearly expressed, because a court may interpret the relationship to be a partnership when the parties intended the relationship to be a landlord-tenant arrangement.[2] The importance lies in the fact that when a partnership exists, all partners are individually liable for all debts and obligations *of the partnership.* Generally, a landlord does not wish to assume the obligations of the tenant that arise from operation of the farming business. Therefore, it is important that a landlord-tenant relationship *not* be considered a partnership.

13.2 LEGAL CLASSIFICATION OF AGRICULTURAL TENANCIES

Leases can be classified according to the term of the lease. This classification is pos-

sible regardless of whether the lease is a cash lease, a crop-share lease, a livestock-share lease, or some combination of these. The classification is particularly important in determining the application of statutory provisions relating to the termination of farm leases and of notice requirements.

General Classifications

The usual classifications of agricultural leases are tenancies from year to year, tenancies for years or for a term, tenancies at will, and tenancies at sufferance.

Tenancies from Year to Year. The *tenancy from year to year* is a periodic tenancy that is common in the United States. The important characteristic of this tenancy is that it can last indefinitely; i.e., it is deemed to automatically renew itself unless adequate notice to terminate is given.

Typically, year to year tenancies are created by oral agreement. But a year to year tenancy can be and frequently is embodied in a written lease. Such leases are terminated by one party giving the other notice of termination which conforms to statutory requirements or notice requirements as stipulated in the written agreement.

Tenancies for Years or for a Term. The most important characteristic of this tenancy is that it is a tenancy measured by time. A *tenancy for years or for a term* lasts for a specified time agreed upon in the lease. The tenant's right of possession automatically terminates at the end of this period. It is not necessary to send notice in order to effect a termination. Tenancies for years or for a term are usually created by a written

---

[2] *Compare* In Re Estate of Drennan, 9 Ill. App. 2d 324, 132 N.E. 2d 599 (3d Dist. 1956) (court found a livestock-share lease to constitute a partnership) *with* United States v. Farrington, 244 F. 2d 111 (7th Cir. 1957) (court, applying Indiana law, held that a livestock-share lease did not create a partnership). Indiana, like Illinois, stresses intent in determining whether a partnership exists. For a discussion of partnership aspects of the livestock-share lease, *see* Note, 1957 U. ILL. L.F. 532.

lease, but sometimes they are oral if they are to terminate within a year after the lease is agreed upon.

Tenancies at Will. The *tenancy at will* can be terminated at any time by either party. Such tenancies may be created by express actions of the parties or by implication. For example, such a tenancy might be clearly established by terms of a lease which reserves a right of termination to either party. Courts tend to disfavor the tenancy at will because of its tenuous nature and, accordingly, tend to require a specific understanding as to the nature of the tenancy before such a tenancy will be found to exist.

Tenancies at Sufferance. The tenancy at sufferance defines the relationship between a landlord and a *holdover tenant*—a tenant whose lease has expired and who has not yet vacated the premises. The *tenancy at sufferance* is a condition which can exist only for a short time, after which the tenant must be physically dispossessed or be considered a tenant from year to year entitled to possession for another year.

Tenancies from Year to Year

Most states have enacted the essential elements of the old English act against frauds and perjuries (statute of frauds) providing, among other things, that under certain circumstances, parties cannot be held responsible for agreements that are not in writing. As discussed in Section 2.2, a writing is generally required for agreements concerning the sale of land and agreements that cannot be performed within 1 year of the date of the agreement.

Some courts have held that a lease is a "chattel real" and does not constitute a sale of property.[3] If leases are excluded, on the theory that they are "chattels real," from the operation of the section of the statute of frauds governing the sale of land, they may then fall under other provisions concerning agreements that cannot be performed within a year. This provision renders unenforceable oral leases which cannot be performed within 1 year from the date of making. In other words, an agreement to lease for a year, arrived at before the tenant is in possession, is generally unenforceable since more than 1 year must elapse before it is fulfilled.

To come under the statute of frauds, a lease must be wholly oral. The writing required under this section does not have to be a detailed contract. A memorandum or note is sufficient if it is, in fact, signed by a party or for that party. Various written communications, such as notes on separate pieces of paper, letters, telegrams, and other types of writings which serve as memoranda of the agreement,[4] have been found to comply with the statute. The absence of any writing at all in a large number of cases has emphasized the need for written leases; it has also led to the legal recognition of so-called "tenancies from year to year." In order to provide some measure of protection to both landlords and tenants under circumstances where inadequate oral agreements are used, the law of many states now recognizes these tenancies.

The rule is well established that an oral contract, even though it is unenforceable because of the statute of frauds, may be enforced if one party relies on the contract and makes substantial performance. Tenancies from year to year arise from the same principle. The legislatures and courts say, in effect, "if no notice is given by either party within a certain period a lease for another year exists." In many farm states,

---

[3] *E.g.*, People v. City of Chicago, 335 Ill. 450, 167 N.E. 79 (1929).

[4] *E.g.*, Gaines v. McAdam, 79 Ill. App. 201 (1st. Dist. 1898).

agricultural tenancies commence on March 1, so the usual effect of a statute on tenancies from year to year is to require that notice be given a set period of time prior to March 1. If the tenancy actually commenced on some other date, the statutory notice would have to be given the specified time prior to the anniversary date of the original tenancy. The provisions of such leases continue the same as in the original agreement. When written leases are not renewed and the tenant remains on the farm, a tenancy from year to year also exists. The statutory notice period applies only when there is no written lease covering the current lease year.

ORAL LEASE—TENANCY FROM YEAR TO YEAR

TREDICK v. BIRRER
Supreme Court of Kansas, 1921
109 Kan. 488, 200 P. 272

These are consolidated actions for the right of possession of two tracts of farming land in Gove county. In one of these, S.S. Reynolds as owner, leased forty-two acres to the defendant under a written contract for the crop year from September 1, 1918, to August 31, 1919. In the other case, Reynolds as agent of Charles E. Tredick, the owner, leased 160 acres to the defendant for the crop year from September 1, 1919, to August 31, 1920. No written contract for the Tredick land was executed. The defendant remained in possession of the Reynolds land the second year without a written contract. In June, 1920, according to the jury's findings, defendant had an oral conversation with Reynolds in which the latter assured him that he might have the land for another year; but on August 26, 1920, Reynolds served written notices on defendant of termination of tenancy and demand for possession on the ensuing date of August 31. Defendant refused to vacate. Hence these lawsuits.

The trial court gave judgment against defendant as to both tracts of land, and he appeals.

While the cases were tried as one lawsuit, it seems necessary to consider their respective phases separately. Of course, under well considered precedents, the contract founded on the oral promise of Reynolds made in June to rent these lands to defendant for another year which was to commence, not at that time but at a future date, September 1, was void under section 6 of the statute of frauds.

But as to the Reynolds land, the defendant had leased that land for a year under a written contract. The contract was for the year beginning September 1, 1918, and ending August 31, 1919. When that year expired, defendant was permitted by Reynolds to hold over without a new or a different contract. Another contract in writing was prepared, but it was not executed, and therefore entitled to no significance. In such a situation defendant became a tenant from year to year under the Kansas statute; and, as such, he was entitled to thirty days' notice prior to August 31, 1920 (the statutory notice period then required under Kansas law). He only received *five* days' notice, which was altogether insufficient to terminate his tenancy.

The judgment touching the right of possession of the Reynolds' land was incorrect.

Touching the defendant's tenancy of the Tredick land, he went into possession for one year only, for a term definitely fixed, September 1, 1919, to August 31, 1920; and therefore, no thirty days' notice nor any other notice to quit was necessary. It follows that the judgment entered for the plaintiff Tredick was correct.

The judgment for the possession of the Reynolds land is reversed, and the judgment for the possession of the Tredick land is affirmed.

Notice Requirements. The notice required to terminate a tenancy from year to year varies considerably from state to state. By Virginia law, such lease may be terminated by either party giving notice in writing 3 months prior to the end of the lease year.[5] In Illinois, the statute calls for notice not less than 4 months prior to the termination of the tenancy.[6] Since in Illinois most tenancies commence on March 1, the usual effect of the statute is to require that notice be given before November. In Kansas, the state legislature has attempted to distinguish leases for land with fall-seeded crops from leases for other types of land. The usual termination date for farm leases in Kansas is March 1, with a 30-day notice requirement.[7] For fall-seeded crops, however, if the crop has been planted, the notice is still required 30 days prior to March 1, but the lease does not terminate until August 1 or the last of harvest.[8]

Many oral leases of farm property will fit the classification of a tenancy from year to year because the parties contemplate a right in the tenant for at least a year's period. If, in fact, the parties do not contemplate that the lease will run for a period of a year, then it may be considered a "tenancy from month to month," in which a written notice prior to the end of the month is necessary to terminate the tenancy. The notice requirement for such leases is a short period of time—frequently 30 days in advance of the date when the rent is paid.

The statutory provisions with respect to the notice necessary to terminate a tenancy from year to year have been rigidly adhered to in court interpretations. The statutes typically require that the notice be in writing[9]

---

[5] VA. CODE ANN. § 55-222 (Repl. 1974).

[6] ILL. REV. STAT. ch. 80, § 5.1 (1975). This provision applies to agricultural leases only. A 60-day notice period is provided for nonagricultural year to year tenancies.

[7] KAN. STAT. ANN. § 58-2506 (Supp. 1979).

[8] KAN. STAT. ANN. § 58-2506 (b) and (c) (Supp. 1979).

[9] *E.g.*, ILL. REV. STAT. ch. 80, § 10 (1975), provides as follows: "§ 10. Service of demand or notice: Any demand may be made or notice served by delivering a written or printed, or partly writ-

and that it be given by the time provided by state law. In most states, the right to notice has been considered to be reciprocal.[10]

Naturally, the various tenancy and notice requirements do not apply if the agreement itself is in writing and provides that the tenancy will end at a certain time, or if it specifies that no notice is to be given. At the same time, the agreement between the parties could establish other notice require-ments, and these will be enforceable if they are a part of a written agreement.

Prior Lease Terms Carried over into the New Tenancy. A tenancy from year to year usually exists when written leases are not renewed but the tenant remains on the farm. However, the written lease no longer applies, except as the courts are willing to say that its provisions carry over.

TENANCY FROM YEAR TO YEAR

WANOUS v. BALACO
Supreme Court of Illinois, 1952
412 Ill. 545, 107 N.E. 2d 791

Plaintiff, Lawrence J. Wanous, brought an action in the Circuit Court of Madison County to obtain specific performance of a contract for the sale of land, or in the alternative for money damages. Defendants filed a motion for summary judgment or decree which was granted and plaintiff appeals to this court, a freehold being involved.

From the pleadings it appears that in 1945 plaintiff leased certain property from the defendant, Sam Balaco. A written lease was executed, the term of which was from June 1, 1945, to March 1, 1950. This lease contained no covenant or option for renewal or extension, but did contain the following provision, which plaintiff now relies upon to sustain his right to specific performance: "Lessors agree to give to Lessee the right to purchase the premises mentioned in this Lease, during any part of the term of said Lease for the sum of Thirteen Thousand Five Hundred Dollars ($13,500.00) cash."

Notwithstanding the expiration of the lease, plaintiff remained in possession and paid rent until March 29, 1951, when Balaco served notice on plaintiff that his tenancy would terminate May 1, 1951. It was apparently at that

---

ten and printed, copy thereof to the tenant, or by leaving the same with some person above the age of ten years, residing on or in possession of the premises; or by sending a copy of said notice to the tenant by certified or registered mail, with a returned receipt from the addressee; and in case no one is in the actual possession of said premises, then by posting the same on the premises."

In interpreting this provision, Illinois courts have held that a written notice is essential; that such notice must be signed by one having authority; and that it must accurately describe the property in question. Kansas follows similar rules as set out in KAN. STAT. ANN. § 58-2510 (1976).

[10] Kansas is an exception to this rule. The notice requirement in KAN. STAT. ANN. § 58-2506 applies to the tenant. No provision is made for notice to the landlord. *See* Nelson v. Ware, 57 Kan. 670, 47 P. 540 (1897).

time that plaintiff attempted to take advantage of the purchase option, for this action was commenced April 2, 1951.

On the record, it is uncontroverted that there was no agreement for the renewal or extension of the lease and option.

However, this does not dispose of the case, for plaintiff argues that, even in the absence of an agreement, the mere holding over after the term had expired made him a tenant from year to year upon the same terms as the original lease, including the option. We agree that the holding over and payment of rent made plaintiff a tenant from year to year. Therefore, at the time he attempted to exercise the option he was such a tenant, commencing his second year to year tenancy. The sole question which we must decide is whether the option to purchase became one of the terms of the year to year tenancy.

The continued possession coupled with the payment of rent did not renew the old lease, but created a new tenancy from year to year upon the same terms as the old lease, only so far as they are applicable to the new condition of things.

We believe, however, that even though a purchase option is held to be an integral part of a lease and, therefore, renewed when the lease is renewed, it is not such a provision as will be incorporated in a year to year tenancy created by operation of law. Not every provision in a written lease is made a part of a holdover tenancy—only those terms applicable to the new condition of things are so treated.[11] We believe that the option to purchase for a certain sum "during the term of this lease" is not such a provision as is applicable to the new tenancy and the new condition of things.

We, therefore, hold that the option was not a part of the holdover tenancy. The action of the trial court allowing defendants' motion for summary judgment and decree was correct and is affirmed.

Tenancies for Years or for a Term

Sometimes a landlord and tenant enter into an agreement which contemplates that the tenant will be in possession for only 1 year or some other specific term. If such an agreement is entered into before the lease year begins, a statute of frauds problem is present. Furthermore, the recognized tenancy from year to year does not necessarily apply because the tenant is not a holdover tenant who has been allowed to remain on the premises, nor is the tenant in possession indefinitely. Accordingly, such leases should be in writing as a general rule. Nevertheless, the law does offer some protection to a tenant who has relied upon an oral lease for a term by starting to perform responsibilities under that lease.

---

[11] In interpreting the term "the new condition of things," the court in Butz v. Butz, 13 Ill. App. 3d 341, 347, 299 N.E. 2d 782, 786 (1973), said: "We interpret this to mean that the former lease is no longer effective as a contract but that its terms may be consulted in determining rent, costs, and essential duties of both landlord and tenant under the tenancy from year to year. Special provisions created by the lease agreement, such as an option to purchase, a promise to make some improvement or to give the tenant a bonus for high yields, having lapsed with the lease which was not renewed or extended, and not being essential to the determination of usual farm landlord-tenant rights and duties, would not be a part of the tenancy from year to year."

ORAL LEASE—PART PERFORMANCE

ANDERSON v. COLLINSON
Appellate Court of Illinois, 1939
300 Ill. App. 22, 20 N.E. 2d 980

On March 9, 1937, the defendant, E.T. Collinson, who is the owner of the farm involved in this suit, obtained a judgment in justice of peace court in Knox County, in forcible entry and detainer against Edwin W. Anderson, for possession of said farm. Anderson appealed from the said judgment to the Circuit Court of Knox County, Illinois, where said question is now pending on said appeal.

On the 19th day of August, 1937, Edwin W. Anderson filed his original complaint in the Circuit Court of Knox County, and on the 22nd of November, by leave of court, filed an amended complaint, which charges in substance that on March 1, 1934, the appellee entered into a certain written lease for the premises involved, being the 220-acre farm, for a term of one year, from March 1, 1934, to March 1, 1935; that he entered into possession of said premises on March 1, 1934; that in the fall of 1934, the parties entered into an oral agreement extending the lease from March 1, 1935, to March 1, 1936; that in the fall of 1935, the lease was again extended from March 1, 1936, to March 1, 1937; that on the farm in question, the plaintiff has engaged in the breeding of purebred Poland China and Duroc hogs, and the farm in question was peculiarly well fitted for this purpose; that in the fall of 1936, the parties again entered into an oral agreement, by which the terms of the written lease were extended from March 1, 1937, to March 1, 1938; that it was the custom in the neighborhood where the said farm was located to rent the farms in the fall for the year following, and on account of said custom he could not rent any other farm after December, 1936; that in the fall of 1936, he plowed about 20 acres of land and plowed and sowed 15 acres of rye, which could not mature until the month of July, 1937, and that he spent much time and care in the improvement of the farm for his purebred hog business and in preparing the said farm for the year from March 1, 1937, to March 1, 1938.

The defendant filed his answer, in which he admitted the written lease from March 1, 1934, and the oral agreements extending the lease year to March 1, 1937. He denied that the plaintiff, Edwin W. Anderson, was in the purebred hog business, as alleged in the amended complaint, but avers that the business was conducted as a partnership, known as "Anderson Brothers." The defendant denies that the plowing and spreading of manure was done for the purpose and benefit of the farming season of 1937, but that it was done under the extension of the former lease. The defendant denies that he had any knowledge that the plaintiff had sown any rye on the premises, and says if it was sown it was done without his knowledge or permission. He denies there was any verbal lease entered into between the plaintiff and himself for the year from March 1, 1937 to March 1, 1938.

The court sustained the exceptions to the master's report, and entered a decree on July 15, 1937, of specific performance of the oral agreement to lease the farm from the first day of March, 1937, to the first day of March, 1938, on the same terms and conditions as the former written lease, and a writ of injunction was entered, restraining E.T. Collinson from prosecuting the proceeding in the forcible entry and detainer suit. It is from this decree that the appeal is prosecuted.

There is a sharp conflict in the evidence as to whether there was an oral lease of the premises for the year from March, 1937, to March 1, 1938. The plaintiff swears positively that there was such an agreement. The defendant, in his testimony, admits that there was some talk of an extension of the lease for the crop year of 1937, but says that he told the plaintiff that if he rented an adjoining farm, that he would not rent him his farm. The evidence shows that the plaintiff did not rent an adjoining farm. One or the other party is necessarily mistaken as to the conversations had at these different meetings. The trial court has found the issues in favor of the plaintiff, and unless this court, on reviewing the evidence, can say that his finding is against the manifest weight of the evidence, we would not be justified in reversing the case, because the chancellor erred in his finding of facts.

It is conceded that an oral lease, such as claimed in this suit, is within the statute of frauds, and unless the appellee relying upon such oral agreement, performed labor or services in contemplation of a renewal of the lease, then it is unenforceable and is void.

A verbal agreement to extend the terms of a lease for a period of one year, such year to commence at some future time, is within the statute of frauds, and as such it is unenforceable unless there is a part performance by the lessee in preparation of the land for a crop during the extended term in reliance upon the agreement. Plowing and sowing small grain was enough to justify the conclusion reached by the court that the part performance was sufficient to avoid and bar the statutes.

In this case, it is undisputed that the plaintiff in the fall of 1937 purchased rye for seeding and sowed 15 acres on the leased premises, and that he plowed 20 acres. These facts tend to support his contention there was verbal agreement to lease the farm for the ensuing year, and this work was done as part performance of the contract. The trial court so held, and on the record, as presented, we are not inclined to reverse the finding.

The decree of the trial court will be affirmed.

13.3 GENERAL RIGHTS AND DUTIES OF LANDLORD AND TENANT

Among the principles that the courts have laid down as a part of the tenant's duty are the following: (1) only a reasonable use of the property for the purpose for which it is obtained is permissible; (2) no waste should be committed; (3) the farming should be done in a husbandlike manner; (4) the soil should not be unnecessarily exhausted by negligent or improper tillage; and (5) repairs should be made. Unless a lease provides or implies otherwise, it is presumed that a tenant will conduct the farm business according to well-established customs or usages of the region in which the tenant lives. These and other rights and duties are discussed more fully below.

Tenant's Right to Determine Cropping System

Although the tenant must not farm in such a way as to injure the land, the tenant is not required to yield the land in the same condition it was in when the tenant's management began. On the other hand, the tenant cannot set up a claim for farming the land in a more beneficial manner than required. In the absence of specific agreement, the tenant has the right to determine the cropping system.

SELECTING THE CROPPING SYSTEM

BERT v. RHODES
St. Louis Court of Appeals, 1924
258 S.W. 40

On August 1, 1916, Edward J. Rhodes, being the owner of a farm in Perry County, Mo., leased the same to the plaintiff herein, Edward Bert, for a term of five years. The lease, which is informally drawn, provided for payment by the lessee of $750 per year as rent, $500 to be paid on or before August 1, or each year during the term, beginning August 1, 1917, and $250 on or before the 1st of the following March of each succeeding year.

Early in 1921, while plaintiff was in possession of the farm as such tenant, he instituted this action against Edward J. Rhodes as defendant. The second count of the petition charges, in substance, that on February 25, 1921, defendant (landowner) wrongfully entered upon the land and over plaintiff's (tenant's) protests, sowed clover seed in 30 acres of land upon which plaintiff then had growing wheat and 15 acres in which plaintiff had sowed oats, thereby interfering with plaintiff's ability to harvest the wheat and oats to plaintiff's damage in the sum of $500.

The answer to the second count likewise contains a general denial, and alleges that when plaintiff went into possession of the farm, 7 acres were in alfalfa, and that plaintiff, without the consent of the landowner, plowed up the alfalfa in 1920, contrary to good husbandry and with damage to the inheritance (the value of the land to the landlord when the lease terminates); that in compromise of this matter it was agreed between the parties that the whole farm should be sowed in clover in 1920 and 1921; and that on February 25, defendant sowed clover in plaintiff's growing wheat and oats as alleged in the petition; it being necessary to do so "to keep up the fertility of the soil." This is followed by a counterclaim wherein it is alleged that plaintiff plowed up the grass and clover on said land, planted the land in corn, and, in the autumn of 1920 and spring of 1921, sowed all the land in wheat and oats, thereby destroying the permanent grasses, destroying the rotation of crops, and impairing the fertility of the land, to defendant's (landowner's) damage in the sum of $1,000.

As to the second count, the testimony for plaintiff goes to show that when, in February, 1921, defendant Edward J. Rhodes with some employees of defendants began sowing clover on the lands which plaintiff had in wheat and on that which he had sowed oats, plaintiff appeared upon the scene and vigorously protested against the sowing of the clover seed, but that defendant Edward J. Rhodes insisted that plaintiff had given defendant permission to do so. Plaintiff denied that he had given such permission.

The trial court, over plaintiff's objection, permitted the defendant to offer much testimony tending to show the custom of farmers in the community in cultivating their farms, with reference to the rotation of crops and the sowing of clover to preserve the fertility of the soil, etc.

No right of action could accrue to defendant by reason of plaintiff's failure to sow clover or the manner in which he rotated the crops upon the land. The lease is entirely silent as to these matters, placing no restrictions upon plaintiff's cultivation of the land, and it is too clear for extended discussion that plaintiff was not required to sow clover, nor was he in any way restricted as to character of the crops which he might grow upon the land during the term of his tenancy. Consequently the evidence relating to the custom in the vicinity touching these matters adduced by defendants over plaintiff's objections, and which constitutes a very considerable part of the record before us, should have been kept out of the case altogether.

Under the facts in evidence, if there was any permission given by plaintiff to defendants to sow clover seed upon the land it was at most a mere oral license, revocable at will. The evidence conclusively shows that if such license ever existed plaintiff revoked it; and consequently it could not be invoked to excuse the act of defendants in persisting in sowing clover seed in plaintiff's wheat and oats lands over his protests, constituting an interference with his right to the exclusive possession, management, and control of the premises. It follows that plaintiff was entitled, as a matter of law, to at least nominal damages on this count.

The judgment should accordingly be reversed and the cause remanded. It is so ordered.

Duty Not to Commit Waste[12]

Another potential conflict is that arising over the duty of the tenant not to commit waste. In most states, the tenant is made liable for damages from waste committed while in possession of the property. Some

---

[12] See, e.g., KAN. STAT. ANN. § 58-2523 (1976) and VA. CODE ANN. § 55-211 et seq. (Repl. 1974), where waste is prohibited by statute.

state statutes set the damages at two times the value of the actual damages if the waste is wanton. An even higher duty is placed on the tenant during the pendency of any lawsuit, such as for possession of the property, because waste during that time may be considered contempt of court and additional damages may be assessed.[13]

Today, the term "waste" lacks definition. What practices are considered wasteful to the real estate? The most common requirement for proving waste is a finding of "permanent" or "substantial" injury to the real estate. With regard to poor soil practices, the problem of proving the decline in value of the land arises.

Courts draw a distinction between two types of waste. *Voluntary waste* is defined as waste resulting from a decisive action, such as removing topsoil, destroying buildings or fences, cutting or selling timber, or destroying shrubbery or other cover. *Permissive waste* is defined as waste resulting from a *failure* to do something, such as a failure to rotate crops or a failure to contour plow or plant a cover crop. Liability is greater for voluntary waste.

Although these terms are ill-defined, there have been some distinctions made between voluntary waste and permissive waste. Injunctions have been granted against injurious acts of tenants, such as pasturing cattle on wet ground, overtilling, and removing topsoil. But when permissive waste is involved, the ill effects are from what has *not* been done and, hence, there is nothing to enjoin. For example, courts have held in favor of tenants in cases where tenants have used poor conservation practices, such as permitting land formerly in cultivation to lie fallow or grow up in pine trees, or allowing land to grow up in weeds

and go uncultivated. In short, common law is not very effective in preventing permissive waste by tenants, and there is little legal recourse.

The definition of waste will be determined on a case-by-case basis. The statutes are designed to protect the property by prohibiting the tenant from taking action which would be permanently damaging to the real estate.

A distinction as to the amount of waste permitted has been drawn between a life tenant and a tenant for a term of years, giving a life tenant much more liberty to commit waste. The language of some wills and deeds creating life estates includes the statement "without impeachment for waste," which excuses the life tenant still further from making a reasonable use of the premises.

For the tenant's protection, specific provisions should be included in the rental agreement that detail what acts are permissible and what acts are expected as part of the normal course of husbandry.

Liability for Rent in Case of Fire or Other Disaster[14]

One question that sometimes arises in rental situations is the responsibility of the tenant to continue paying rent after the destruction of buildings by fire or other disasters. State law usually provides that if buildings are destroyed without any fault or negligence on the part of the tenant, then the tenant is not bound to continue to pay rent or to reerect the buildings. In fact, the tenant is entitled to a reduction in the rental for the value of the buildings until such time that they are again available for use. No duty is imposed on the landlord

[13] *See* VA. CODE ANN. § 55-216 (Repl. 1974).
[14] For a statutory provision relieving the tenant

from the obligation to pay rent in case of destruction, *see* VA. CODE ANN. § 55-256 (Repl. 1974).

to rebuild the structures. It is the landlord's option, unless some differing provisions are included in the agreement itself.

A related question arises concerning the disposition of insurance proceeds following a fire or other disaster. If the lease imposes a duty on the tenant to insure improvements, then any insurance proceeds paid to the tenant following the destruction of buildings should be used to rebuild. On the other hand, if the landlord is required to maintain insurance on improvements, no obligation is imposed on the landlord to rebuild unless the lease specifically includes such a provision. The tenant would be entitled to a rental reduction if the landlord did not rebuild, however.

vide various places for the crop to be divided, such as in the harvest field, in bins on the farm, or at elevators where the crop is sold. Although the rule that a growing crop belongs to the tenant is well established, insurance companies will insure landlord's interest in the crop, considering it simply another risk.

If a part of the farm is taken by condemnation, the tenant, and possibly the landlord, is entitled to damages to growing crops. If the award is for the value of a mature crop, the landlord should share in the award just as if the crop had been harvested. Tenants with long-term written leases should be able to collect damages for the overinvestment in labor and machinery resulting from the shrinkage in acreage.

Crop Ownership

The crop belongs to the tenant until it is harvested and divided.[15] A lease may pro-

TITLE TO CROPS

BABCOCK v. MISSISSIPPI RIVER POWER COMPANY
Court of Appeals, 7th Circuit, 1940
113 F. 2d 398

This was an action brought by Edward Babcock against the Mississippi River Power Company to recover damages growing out of the erection of a dam in 1913 across the Mississippi River at Keokuk, Iowa, by which the waters of the river were raised and held at the increased height.

The suit was commenced on September 25, 1930 and was tried by a jury on a declaration containing six counts, in which plaintiff sought to recover for damages because he had lost the avails and value of large quantities of

---

[15] As to the title to unharvested crops, see Sargent v. Courrier, 66 Ill. 245, (1972). Appellee landlord replevied the harvest from 190 rows of corn which had been raised under the arrangement that twofifths of the crop would constitute the rent when the crop was put in the cribs and measured. Appellant levied on the crop before it was cribbed and had it sold. Held, for appellant. "Although the rent was to be paid by a portion of the crop, the parties are not tenants in common of the crop, but the title to the whole is in the tenant until the stipulated rent is paid. Appellee had no ownership of it while standing in the field, neither had he a right of property or of possession at the time he sued out the writ of replevin."

farm products which would otherwise have been grown and harvested on the real estate in question for each of the years 1927 to 1930, inclusive.

At the trial of the case, the facts developed that the land in question had been rented during the years in question to tenants under written leases for cash as to pasture land and a share of the crops. Thereupon the parties stipulated that plaintiff did not seek to recover for any permanent injury or damage to the land, but sought only to recover for recurring and intermittent damages.

The question we are called upon to decide is: In whom, under the circumstances, is the right of action? In other words, can the plaintiff recover when his land is leased and in possession of a tenant who pays as rental part cash and a portion of the crop raised, the crop to be divided by the tenant and the landlord's part delivered to him in the bin.

An injury to annual crops is, as a general rule, an injury to the possession, and the right of action, therefore, is in the tenant alone, and where the relation of landlord and tenant exists and the rent to be paid is a portion of the crop, the title to the whole crop is in the tenant until the stipulated rent is paid.

Plaintiff's counsel also makes the point that this is a suit for damages to his reversionary interest against defendant for rendering plaintiff's land wet, miry and marshy. There can be no question that the owner of real estate may maintain an action where the injury is of a permanent nature, even though the real estate is in the possession of a tenant. Unfortunately, however, in our case the plaintiff has expressly stated that he does not seek to recover for any permanent injury or damage to the land in question.

Judgment for defendant affirmed.

Right to Sue for Injury to Farm Property

The right to sue for injury to the farm or property on it depends upon legal rights in the property damaged. Since growing crops belong to the tenant, the courts have held that the right to sue for damage to such crops belongs exclusively to the tenant, even though the landlord's rent is payable out of the crop. On the other hand, injury to the farmland, buildings, fences, trees, or drainage system gives the landlord a cause of actions.

DAMAGE TO FARM AND CROPS

LIBBRA v. MT. OLIVE AND STAUNTON COAL COMPANY
Appellate Court of Illinois, 1961
29 Ill. App. 2d 396, 172 N.E. 2d 813

Defendant, Mr. Olive and Staunton Coal Company, appeals from judgments entered against it on verdicts rendered by a jury in favor of plaintiff, Stella

Libbra, as owner of a 150-acre tract of land in Madison County and plaintiff, Mack Libbra, as tenant of the same premises. They had joined in a suit against the coal company alleging damages to the farm and its crops caused by slack, coal dust and other debris being deposited by the defendant in a stream of water which flowed through the premises. It was contended that by reason of the overflow of the natural watercourse on many occasions over several years time, the slack, dust and debris had been deposited in various quantities at different places on the land involved. Plaintiff, Stella Libbra, as owner, alleged that "the fair cash market value of the land as above-described had been greatly and permanently diminished and depreciated." The plaintiff, Mack Libbra, as tenant, asked for crop damages for the years 1953, 1954 and 1955 based on flooding of the premises in those years with the consequent deposit of the coal mining debris. He was the year to year tenant on the premises for some time, having farmed the place for the past 12 years prior to the time that this suit was filed.

The jury returned verdicts in the sum of $7,300 for plaintiff Stella Libbra and $1,700 in favor of the plaintiff Mack Libbra. The coal company filed a post-trial motion to set aside the judgments and to enter judgments notwithstanding, or, in the alternative, to grant a new trial. This motion was denied.

On appeal, the coal company seeks a reversal. The basis of the coal company's argument is that evidence of the wrong measure of damages, as to plaintiffs, was permitted to go to the jury.

Because damages are measured differently for the tenant than for his landlord, we must review the action separately.

Insofar as the landlord is concerned, her evidence at the trial, pertaining to her damages, was limited solely to showing diminution of market value of her farm after the contamination. Defendant contends that this is a proper measure of damages only when the injury to the land is permanent. Defendant then argues that there was a total failure of any evidence from which permanent injury to the land could be concluded, and that, therefore, defendant was entitled to a directed verdict.

There was testimony that corn would not grow in the areas affected due to its acidity and that, in order for crops ever to grow again, the contamination would have to be removed and the soil neutralized. It appeared that lime might be used as a neutralizer, but there would have to be laboratory tests taken to determine whether this would be feasible. It was suggested that nature itself might, in time, restore the fertility of the soil. Various witnesses testified as to the value before and the value after the contamination caused by the deposit of coal debris. The verdict for Mrs. Libbra was within the range of this testimony, as the witnesses' appraisal of the damage varied from $1,300 to $12,090.

What is the proper rule of damages insofar as the plaintiff, Stella Libbra, is concerned?

15 Am. Jur., Damages, Section 106, states on page 514:

There is no fixed rule for determining the measure of damages for injuries to, or destruction of, property in every case. The amount to be awarded depends upon the character of the property and the nature and extent of the injury, and the mode and amount of proof must be adapted to the facts of each case. In ascertaining the damages to be allowed, the jury may consider all the circumstances connected with the injury.

The question here presented is whether or not a fair determination of the damage to the owner of the farm could be arrived at by testimony of the value of the premises after the land was contaminated.

In our present case, the evidence showed damage to the owner's farm by the deposit of debris resulting from the operation of the coal mine; that the land was too acid to grow a crop; that the debris measured in various depths from 1/2 inch to 18 inches, and that it was deposited at irregular intervals, making it difficult to farm portions of the premises upon which there was no debris. Although it might be argued from the evidence that there was a possibility that the land might be reclaimed or restored by nature or some artificial neutralizing agent, it is well to note that "laboratory tests would have to be conducted to determine if it were feasible." In other words, we cannot say from the record before us that it is reasonable to believe that the premises could be completely restored by any certain process, natural or otherwise. Consequently, we think that to permit a showing of value before contamination and value after contamination was a reasonable approach to the measurement of the damages sustained. Presumably, the fact that the land might eventually be restored to fertility was taken into consideration by the witnesses in arriving at the values after contamination.

If the coal company felt that a different measure of damages would have lessened the amount, it should have introduced evidence to support its theory.

With regard to the tenant, who sued for his crop loss during the years 1953, 1954 and 1955, the defendant argues that the measure of damages was not the ultimate market value of the crop, but its value when lost. Defendant further argues that a tenant cannot claim damages for a crop loss after he knows that the ground's fertility has been impaired. Based on these two contentions, defendant claims it was entitled to a directed verdict against the tenant, and, as in the case of the landlord, seeks only a reversal in this court.

Testifying to his own damages, the son gave the number of bushels per acre of yield of the contaminated land compared with the number of bushels per acre of yield in the portion not damaged by the coal debris. The average was 85 bushels in the good land and 30 bushels where the debris was. He testified what the crop brought and also what the price of corn was for the 3 years.

The crop damages evidence consisted of the showing of a reduced crop and the market value of what the crop would have brought had it been a good crop. Based on the plaintiff's testimony for the years 1953, 1954 and 1955, the total loss came to $2,047.20. His verdict was $1,700.

Based on the record before us, we are in no position to say that the coal company is entitled to a directed verdict in the tenant's case. But, should the tenant be allowed more than one year's loss?

There are cases which permit a tenant to recover damages for each succeeding year notwithstanding the fact that he has knowledge of the condition. The damages complained of in such cases are referred to as continuing damages, and suit is permitted for such damages as long as the original obstruction remains.

The crop damages in this case are not exactly like the crop damages in any case cited. Here there was a repetition of flooding during the three years involved. True, there was a residue of debris from previous years but each year brought a new flooding and a new deposit of coal dust over debris. Thus, it appears to us that this case is more like the negligence case which could be prevented and we believe it reasonable to have permitted the tenant to recover for the three years inasmuch as the nuisance was renewed each year. It is not the same as though there was one flooding and one complete damage at one time. This case was one of a repetition of flooding and a repetition of damage to the crops.

However, we do not see how there could have been a verdict for the tenant in excess of $1,364.80. The evidence supported a maximum loss of $2,047.20 and the jury's verdict for him was $1,700. But the tenant under his leasing agreement would have to account to the landlord for one-third of any crops raised. A tenant in possession of the land on a year to year lease has the right to sue for all the damage to the crops and an injury to annual crops is an injury to the possession and the right of action for such injury lies in the tenant. Nevertheless to allow a tenant to recover the full amount of the crop damages, where the landlord is also recovering for his injury to the land, would be unconscionable for it would permit a double recovery for the landlord. Here, the landlord was awarded a verdict by the jury based on the difference between the value before and the value after the contamination. In making proof of damages in this manner, the landlord is compensated for all damages including her share of any crop loss.

We therefore feel that the extent of the tenant's damages would be two-thirds of the sum of $2,047.20, which amounts to $1,364.80.

Accordingly, we affirm the judgment of the plaintiff Stella Libbra, and we set aside the judgment in favor of the plaintiff, Mack Libbra, and enter judgment here in favor of the plaintiff, Mack Libbra, in the sum of $1,364.80.

Liability for Injuries on the Premises

As a general rule, the landlord is not liable to the tenant or to third parties for injuries resulting from conditions on the premises. The tenant has sole and exclusive possession and control of the premises and therefore has the basic responsibility to see that the premises are kept in safe condition. An exception to this general rule is when injury occurs to either the tenant or to third parties lawfully on the premises, resulting from concealed or hidden defects (for example a defective well platform or barn floor). Liability is imposed on the landlord if the landlord knew about the defect at the time the lease was entered into and if the landlord failed to warn the tenant of the defect.

If the tenant knows or should know of defects on the premises, invitees and licensees (but probably not trespassers) may hold the tenant liable for injuries resulting from the tenant's failure to correct the defect, even if the landlord has agreed to make all necessary repairs. The landlord is ordinarily not liable to third parties for injuries resulting from negligent acts of the tenant. The tenant is neither an employee nor an agent of the landlord. There may be some circumstances in which the landlord and the tenant can be held jointly liable for injuries to third parties, although the usual liability would be that of the party in control of the premises. For example, if a defective condition known to the landlord exists at the time the lease is entered and the tenant, with knowledge of the defective condition, admits members of the public, the parties may be jointly liable for injuries sustained by such persons who are injured by reason of the condition.

DETERMINING LIABILITY

BORDERS v. ROSEBERRY
Supreme Court of Kansas, 1975
216 Kan. 486, 533 P. 2d 1366

This case involves the liability of a landlord for personal injuries suffered by the social guest of the tenant as the result of a slip and fall on the leased premises. The facts in this case are undisputed and are as follows: The defendant-appellee, Agnes Roseberry, is the owner of a single-family, one-story residence located in Osawatomie, Kansas. Several months prior to January 9, 1971, the defendant leased the property on a month to month basis to a tenant, Rienecker. Just prior to the time the tenant took occupancy of the house the defendant-landlord had work performed on the house. The remodeling of the house included a new roof. In repairing the house the repairmen removed the roof guttering from the front of the house but failed to reinstall it. The landlord knew the guttering had been removed by the workmen, intended to have it reinstalled, and knew that it had not been reinstalled. The roof line on the house was such that without the guttering the rain drained off the entire north side of the house onto the front porch steps. In freezing weather water from the roof would accumulate and freeze on the steps. The landlord, as well as the tenant, knew that the guttering had not been reinstalled and knew that without the guttering, water from the roof would drain onto the front porch steps and in freezing weather would accumulate and freeze. The tenant had complained to the landlord about the absence of guttering and the resulting icy steps.

On January 9, 1971, there was ice and snow on the street and ice on the front steps. During the afternoon the tenant worked on the front steps, removing the ice accumulation with a hammer. The plaintiff-appellant, Gary D. Borders, arrived on the premises at approximately 4:00 p.m. in response to an invitation of the tenant for dinner. It is agreed that plaintiff's status was that of a social guest of the tenant. There was ice on the street and snow on the front steps when plaintiff arrived. At 9:00 p.m. as plaintiff Borders was leaving the house he slipped and fell on an accumulation of ice on the steps and received personal injuries. There is no contention that the plaintiff Borders was negligent in a way which contributed to cause his injuries. After a pretrial conference the case was tried by the court without a jury. Following submission of the case the trial court entered judgment for the defendant, making findings of fact which are essentially those set forth above. The trial court based its judgment upon a conclusion of law which stated that a landlord of a single-family house is under no obligation or duty to a social guest of his tenant to repair or remedy a known condition whereby water dripped from the roof onto the front steps of a house fronting north, froze and caused the social guest to slip and fall.

At the outset it should be emphasized that we do not have involved here an action brought by a social guest to recover damages for personal injuries from his host, a possessor of real property. The issue raised involves the liability of a lessor who has leased his property to a tenant for a period of time. Furthermore, it should be pointed out that the plaintiff, a social guest of the tenant, has based his claim of liability against the landlord upon the existence of a defective condition which existed on the leased property at the time the tenant took possession.

Traditionally the law in this country has placed upon the lessee as the person in possession of the land the burden of maintaining the premises in a reasonably safe condition to protect persons who come upon the land. It is the tenant as possessor who, at least initially, has the burden of maintaining the premises in good repair. The relationship of landlord and tenant is not in itself sufficient to make the landlord liable for the tortious acts of the tenant. When land is leased to a tenant, the law of property regards the lease as equivalent to a sale of the premises for the term. The lessee acquires an estate in the land, and becomes for the time being the owner and occupier, subject to all of the responsibilities of one in possession, both to those who enter onto the land and to those outside of its boundaries. Professor William L. Prosser in his Law of Torts, 4th Ed. 63, points out that in the absence of agreement to the contrary, the lessor surrenders both possession and control of the land to the lessee, retaining only a reversionary interest; and he has no right even to enter without the permission of the lessee. There is therefore, as general rule, no liability upon the landlord, either to the tenant or to others entering the land, for defective conditions existing at the time of the lease.

The general rule of non-liability has been modified, however, by a number of exceptions which have been created as a matter of social policy. Modern case law on the subject today usually limits the liability of a landlord for injuries arising from a defective condition existing at the time of the lease to six recognized exceptions. These exceptions are as follows:

1.   Undisclosed dangerous conditions known to lessor and unknown to the lessee.[16]

It should be pointed out that this exception applies only to latent conditions and not to conditions which are patent or reasonably discernible to the tenant.

2.   Conditions dangerous to persons outside of the premises.[17]

The theory of liability under such circumstances is that where a nuisance dangerous to persons outside the leased premises (such as the traveling public or persons on adjoining property) exists on the premises at the time of the lease, the lessor should not be permitted to escape liability by leasing the premises to another. The liability of the landlord for structural defects on leased property which causes injuries to persons outside of the premises has been recognized and made the basis of a judgment against the landlord.

3.   Premises leased for admission of the public.

The third exception arises where land is leased for a purpose involving the admission of the public. The cases usually agree that in that situation the lessor is under an affirmative duty to exercise reasonable care to inspect and repair the premises before possession is transferred, to prevent any unreasonable risk or harm to the public who may enter.[18]

---

[16] This exception is stated in RESTATEMENT, SECOND, TORTS 358 as follows: "358. Undisclosed Dangerous Conditions Known to Lessor: (1) A lessor of land who conceals or fails to disclose to his lessee any condition, whether natural or artificial, which involves unreasonable risk or physical harm to persons on the land, is subject to liability to the lessee and others upon the land with the consent of the lessee or his sublessee for physical harm caused by the condition after the lessee has taken possession, if (a) the lessee does not know or have reason to know of the condition or the risk involved, and (b) the lessor knows or has reason to know of the condition, and realizes or should realize the risk involved, and has reason to expect that the lessee will not discover the condition or realize the risk. (2) If the lessee actively conceals the condition, the liability stated Subsection (1) continues until the lessee discovers it and has reasonable opportunity to take effective precautions against it. Otherwise the liability continues only until the vendee has had reasonable opportunity to discover the condition and to take such precautions.

[17] This exception is stated in RESTATEMENT, SECOND, TORTS 379, as follows: "379. Dangerous Conditions Existing When Lessor Transfers Possession: A lessor of land who transfers its possession in a condition which he realizes or should realize will involve unreasonable risk of physical harm to others outside of the land, is subject to the same liability for physical harm subsequently caused to them by the condition as though he had remained in possession."

[18] This exception is stated in 359 of RESTATEMENT, SECOND, TORTS, as follows: "359. Land Leased for Purpose Involving Admission of Public: A lessor who leases land for a purpose which involves the admission of the public is subject to liability for physical harm caused to persons who enter the land for that purpose by a condition of the land existing when the lessee takes possession, if the lessor (a) knows or by the exercise of reasonable care could discover that the condition involves an unreasonable risk of harm to such persons, and (b) has reason to expect that the lessee will admit them before the land is put in safe condition for their reception, and (c) fails to exercise reasonable care to discover or to remedy the condition, or otherwise to protect such persons against it." *See* Mathes v. Robinson, 205 Kan. 402, 469 P. 2d 259 (1970) and the cases cited in Annot., 17 A.L.R. 3d 873 (1968).

4. Parts of land retained in lessor's control which lessee is entitled to use.

When different parts of a building, such as an office building or an apartment house, are leased to several tenants, the approaches and common passageways normally do not pass to the tenant, but remain in the possession and control of the landlord. Hence the lessor is under an affirmative obligation to exercise reasonable care to inspect and repair those parts of the premises for the protection of the lessee, members of his family, his employees, invitees, guests, and others on the land in the right of the tenant.[19]

5. Where lessor contracts to repair.

At one time the law in most jurisdictions, and in Kansas, was that if a landlord breached his contract to keep the premises in good repair, the only remedy of the tenant was an action in contract in which damages were limited to the cost of repair or loss of rental value of the property. Neither the tenant nor members of his family nor his guests were permitted to recover for personal injuries suffered as a result of the breach of the agreement. In most jurisdictions this rule has been modified and a cause of action given in tort to the injured person to enable him recovery for his personal injuries.[20]

6. Negligence by lessor in making repairs.

When the lessor does in fact attempt to make repairs, whether he is bound by a covenant to do so or not, and fails to exercise reasonable care, he is held liable for injuries to the tenant or others on the premises in his right, if the tenant neither knows nor should know that the repairs have been negligently made.[21]

---

[19] This exception is covered in RESTATEMENT, SECOND, TORTS 360 and 361, which provide as follows: "360. Parts of Land Retained in Lessor's Control Which Lessee is Entitled to Use: A possessor of land who leases a part thereof and retains in his own control any other part which the lessee is entitled to use as appurtenant to the part leased to him, is subject to liability to his lessee and others lawfully upon the land with the consent of the lessee or a sublessee for physical harm caused by a dangerous condition upon that part of the land retained in the lessor's control, if the lessor by the exercise of reasonable care could have discovered the conditions and the unreasonable risk involved therein and could have made the condition safe."

"361. Parts of Land Retained in Lessor's Control but Necessary to Safe Use of Part Leased: A possessor of land who leases a part thereof and retains in his own control any other part which is necessary to the safe use of the leased part, is subject to liability to his lessee and others lawfully upon the land with the consent of the lessee or a sublessee for physical harm caused by a dangerous condition upon that part of the land retained in the lessor's control, if the lessor by the exercise of reasonable care could have discovered the condition and the unreasonable risk involved there-

in and could have made the condition safe."

[20] This exception is found in RESTATEMENT, SECOND, TORTS 357, which states as follows: "357. Where Lessor Contracts to Repair: A lessor of land is subject to liability for physical harm caused to his lessee and others upon the land with the consent of the lessee or his sublessee by a condition of disrepair existing before or arising after the lessee has taken possession if (a) the lessor, as such, has contracted by a covenant in the lease or otherwise to keep the land in repair, and (b) the disrepair creates an unreasonable risk to persons upon the land which the performance of the lessor's agreement would have prevented, and (c) the lessor fails to exercise reasonable care to perform his contract."

[21] This exception is stated in RESTATEMENT, SECOND, TORTS 362, as follows: "362. Negligent Repairs by Lessor: A lessor of land who, by purporting to make repairs on the land while it is in the possession of his lessee, or by the negligent manner in which he makes such repairs has, as the lessee neither knows nor should know, made the land more dangerous for use or given it a deceptive appearance of safety, is subject to liability for physical harm caused by the condition to the lessee or to others upon the land with the consent of the lessee or sublessee."

Section 362(d) of the Restatement, Second, Torts declares that the lessor is subject to liability if, but only if, the lessee neither knows nor should know that the purported repairs have not been made or have been negligently made and so, relying upon the deceptive appearance of safety, subjects himself to the dangers or invites or permits his licensees to encounter them. Conversely it would follow that if the lessee knows or should know that the purported repairs have not been made or have been negligently made, then the lessor is not liable under this exception.

With the general rule and its exceptions (all of which have been recognized in Kansas) in mind we shall now examine the undisputed facts in this case to determine whether or not the landlord can be held liable to the plaintiff here. It is clear that the exceptions pertaining to undisclosed dangerous conditions known to the lessor (exception 1), conditions dangerous to persons outside of the premises (exception 2), premises leased for admission of the public (exception 3), and parts of land retained in the lessor's control (exception 4) have no application in this case. Nor do we believe that exception 5, which comes into play when the lessor has contracted to repair, has been established by the court's findings of fact. It does not appear that the plaintiff takes the position that the lessor contracted to keep the premises in repair; nor has any consideration for such an agreement been shown. As to exception 6, although it is obvious that the repairs to the roof were not completed by installation of the guttering and although the landlord expressed his intention to replace the guttering, we do not believe that the factual circumstances bring the plaintiff within the application of exception where the lessor has been negligent in making repairs. As pointed out above, that exception comes into play only when the lessee lacks knowledge that the purported repairs have not been made or have been negligently made. Here it is undisputed that the tenant had full knowledge of the icy condition on the steps created by the absence of guttering. It seems to us that the landlord could reasonably assume that the tenant would inform his guest about the icy condition on the front steps. We have concluded that the factual circumstances do not establish liability on the landlord on the basis of negligent repairs made by him.

In his brief counsel for the plaintiff vigorously argues that the law should be changed to make the landlord liable for injuries resulting from a defective condition on the leased premises where the landlord has knowledge of that condition. He has not cited any authority in support of his position, nor does he state with particularity how the existing law pertaining to a landlord's liability should be modified. We do not believe that the facts and circumstances of this case justify a departure from the established rules of law discussed above.

The judgment of the district court is affirmed.

Other Rights and Duties[22]

Right to Maintain Trespass Action. The right to maintain trespass belongs to the tenant once in possession, and may be enforced even against the landlord unless the landlord has reserved the right of entry in the lease or has entered for certain recognized purposes. If the landlord is on the property to collect rent, to prevent waste, to make improvements, to deliver a notice, or to perform duties imposed by state statute, liability for trespass may not be imposed in many jurisdictions.[23] The landlord may reserve additional rights of entry in a written lease.

Right of Tenant in Case of Sale. State law usually includes provisions to protect the tenant in case the property is sold by the landlord. Generally, after a sale or after a partition between co-owners, a person who is holding as a lessee will continue to have the same rights on the same terms as before. This should be construed in light of the requirement of a written agreement in certain situations because innocent purchasers without notice of the lease or rental agreement may not be bound thereby unless the lease is in writing. For complete protection, the tenant will not only wish to have a written agreement, but may wish to record the agreement. Most state statutes provide for the recording of leases if they are in the proper form.

Right to Assign or Sublet. In most states, a tenant may not assign the lease or sublet the farm or any part of it unless permitted to do so by the terms of a written lease. Some specific state statutes prohibit such transfers. Kansas, for example, prohibits the assignment or transfer of leases if they are for less than 2-year terms.[24] If a valid assignment is made, the new tenant has the same rights against the landlord as the original tenant had. A minority of jurisdictions allow a farm tenant to assign or sublease in the absence of an express restriction.[25]

13.4 SECURING THE PAYMENT OF RENT/RETAKING THE PREMISES

Generally, a written contract should detail the rights of either party in case of a breach of the contractual arrangement. Normally, leases include provisions for the right of the landlord to retake possession upon the failure of the tenant to pay rent as due. In those cases where these rights are not detailed by agreement, the law makes specific provisions for the collection of rent. Although these provisions do not always include specific items relating to the tenant's rights, it should be kept in mind that these provisions were written to provide the landlord with alternate ways of collecting rent and retaking possession of the premises.

Under the law of most states, the landlord is specifically authorized to retake the premises at any time the tenant abandons the premises. If the tenant leaves before harvest without having made any arrangements to take care of the growing crops, the landlord has the right to cultivate, harvest, and sell the crops. In most states, the landlord can retain the proceeds absolutely;[26] in others, the landlord can retain rent, labor, and expenses out of the crop

---

[22] See MODERN LEGAL FORMS, *supra* note 1.

[23] See 51C C.J.S. Landlord and Tenant § 318.

[24] KAN. STAT. ANN. § 58-2511 (1976).

[25] See, *e.g.*, Glanz v. Halperin, 251 Ill. App. 572 (1st Dist. 1929). For an example of the general rule see, Crump v. Tolbert, 210 Ark. 920, 198 S.W. 2d 518 (1946).

[26] This result is obvious in the case of a crop-share lease. In the cash lease, the landlord would have this option. See SPIES, LAW OF FARM TENANCIES IN VIRGINIA (Pub. No. 29 of the Southeast Land Tenure Committee (1958), at 21-22.

sales, plus damages for nonperformance of agreements of the lease.[27] The purpose of such provisions is to protect the landlord's security for rent.

In a more typical situation the tenant is still in possession and is in default for non-payment of rent. In such circumstances the landlord has a number of options available. Naturally, the landlord may bring an action in court against the tenant in order to attempt to collect the rent. In some states, such actions are referred to as debt and assumpsit. These are legal actions by which owners, executors, or administrators can sue for and recover rent or a fair and reasonable satisfaction for the use of lands. *Debt* is an action to recover a sum of money due from another. *Assumpsit* is an action to recover damages caused by failure to perform a simple contract.

Attachment of property and garnishment of wages or other income are remedies offered to any creditor as a means of asserting possession over the debtor's property and intangible assets (stocks, bonds, mortgages, etc.). When a landlord has established a right against the tenant for rent due, these actions may be used.

Distress for Rent

State law often allows a substitute procedure for collection of rent commonly called *distress for rent*. Basically, this procedure allows the landlord to obtain a distress warrant from a judge or court clerk upon affidavit of the landlord that rent is due.[28] The warrant authorizes the sheriff to levy upon any goods of the tenant found on the leased premises to the extent necessary to satisfy the rent due. The sheriff, in effect, attaches the tenant's property and holds it

until such time as proper orders of a court are entered regarding the disposal of the property and the payment of the rent.

Under the distress proceeding, the landlord is allowed to take possession of the leased property upon court order. Such an order will not be entered lightly. For example, the tenant will normally be given notice and an opportunity for a hearing, and the tenant has a right to post a bond and retain possession of the property until after the hearing. Such orders will not be entered in the first place unless the landlord has clearly established that the claim is valid and that there are no defenses likely to be raised by the tenant. A hearing may not be necessary if a written waiver of the right to hearing is signed by the tenant prior to the taking of possession. Therefore, some leases include such a waiver in order to expedite the process should rent be due and unpaid and should the landlord wish to retake possession.

The distress proceeding has limitations. First, the right may not extend beyond a specified period from the end of the lease term or termination of the tenancy. Second, the law exempts certain articles of the tenant's personal property from being distrained by the landlord. At the time the distress warrant is served, the tenant should be notified of these rights and given an opportunity to select exempt property.

In written leases today, it is common for tenants to waive these exemptions. However, these waivers have been held invalid as against heads of families on the ground that the exemption is as much for the families as for the debtors themselves. To be binding against the head of a family, the waiver must be made in advance by means of a chattel mortgage or security agreement.

Landlord's Lien on Crops

State law frequently gives a landlord a lien for rent upon crops grown or growing that attaches as soon as the crops begin to grow. It is often enforced by using the distress proceeding described earlier, or a legal action may be instituted to enforce the lien.

The landlord lien statutes vary considerably from state to state, but an examination of these statutes reveals a number of typical provisions:

1. The landlord's lien does not apply to any property of the tenant other than crops, and then only to crops grown on land for which the landlord is entitled to rent. It is good only for the rent for the year in which the crops are in the ground. However, fall-seeded crops, such as winter wheat, which grow in 2 different years are subject to the rent for both of those years.

2. The landlord's lien is superior to chattel mortgages or other claims against the crops, and can be lost only by waiver or failure to enforce within a specified period after the expiration of the lease term. A lien does not give the landlord a right to immediate possession of the crops. Before the landlord can recover a share, the crop must be harvested and the landlord's share designated. Until this is done, the crop belongs entirely to the tenant.

3. The landlord's lien is against the crop, not against the tenant. However, to enforce the lien against third parties, it is necessary to show that the purchaser knew that the crop was grown on rented land. If a purchaser, such as an elevator, has no knowledge of the tenancy and the origin of the grain, the purchaser is not subject to the landlord's lien. As a matter of protection, many landlords furnish a list of their tenants to all elevator operators in the community.

LANDLORD'S LIEN

KNAPP v. HIPES
Supreme Court of Kansas, 1952
159 Kan. 94, 152 P. 2d 805

This was an action on two promissary notes which had been assigned to the plaintiff by the payee after their maturity.

The defense was that the maker had been relieved of their payment by a compromise settlement with the payee which he had performed.

Briefly the pertinent facts were these: Defendant Hipes was a tenant farmer in Brown county. He was burdened with debts. The Morrill State Bank held two of his notes, one for $400 and another for $1,312.61. These bore a high rate of interest and both were past due on March 26, 1941, at which time the bank and Hipes made a written agreement of settlement. Its terms were that he was to pay the bank $150 in cash, and he was to sell fourteen shoats, five hogs, eight cows and four calves and deliver their proceeds to the bank, and he was to deliver his share of a wheat crop (estimated at fifty acres) at an elevator in Hiawatha to the account of the bank, but that the harvesting and threshing expense should be deducted from the sale price. The bank's part of this agreement was that it would surrender the notes to Hipes on his performance of the terms outlined above. Hipes paid the agreed $150, and sold his livstock for $382.86 and delivered the proceeds thereof to the bank. These payments were credited on Hipes' notes. Later, after harvest, Hipes delivered the wheat at the elevator to the account of the bank; but at that point Hipes' landlord claimed his statutory lien on the wheat for the nonpayment of the cash rent due for the pasture land on the farm occupied by Hipes. Of course that statutory lien took precedence of any claim the bank had on the wheat.

The satisfaction of the landlord's lien consumed the entire proceeds of the tenant's share of the wheat, and left an aggregate unpaid balance of $1,139.76 on its notes against Hipes.

On the assumption that by the interposition of the landlord's lien which deprived the bank of the proceeds of the wheat the compromise and settlement between Hipes and the bank was ineffective, the bank assigned the Hipes notes to plaintiff and she brought suit thereon. On the issues joined no material dispute of fact arose. The controversy below, as here on appeal, was whether the failure of the bank to get the beneficial proceeds of the wheat constituted a breach of the compromise and settlement between Hipes and the bank.

The trial court held that the compromise agreement had been fully performed, and gave judgment for defendant.

The plaintiff appeals, contending that the compromise agreement with the bank as plaintiff's assignor was vitiated through the fault of Hipes in not paying his cash rent, which failure alone prevented the bank from receiving the proceeds of the wheat. She also urges that the attaching of the landlord's statutory lien for the unpaid rent was not within the contemplation of the bank and Hipes when they made their compromise agreement.

Plaintiff stresses the elementary point that to make an accord effectual there must be satisfaction, and that there could be no satisfaction since the bank was deprived of the wheat delivered at the elevator to its account, that in effect Hipes did not keep his part of the agreement when by his own fault he failed to pay his cash rent, which failure caused the landlord's lien to attach.

There is a specious plausibility to this argument, but we think it is basically untenable. The landlord's lien is a long-standing rule of elementary Kansas law. Almost everybody is aware of it, certainly every country banker. No business man of any prudence will contract for any part of a crop grown by a tenant farmer, without taking the precaution to assure himself that the landlord's claim for rent (like the thresherman's claim for his labor) has either been paid or that satisfactory provision has been made for its payment, so that the crop he contracts for will not be subjected to one of these statutory liens.

Moreover, at the time of the compromise and settlement the bank knew of Hipes' financial difficulties. It knew he had other indebtednesses than those evidenced by his promissory notes which the bank held and which he could not pay according to their tenor. Under such circumstances it is quite just to say that the bank had notice of circumstances sufficient to put it on inquiry whether the pasture rent might be a lienable claim on the tenant's wheat.

It must be held that the compromise agreement should be construed in the light of the statute, and that it was only the net proceeds of Hipes' share of the wheat which the bank was to get. The parties estimated that there was fifty acres of wheat. In fact there was about seventy acres of it, and if the crop had been bountiful and the price had been good, perhaps there would have been sufficient money out of its sale not only to satisfy the landlord's lien, but to pay the bank also. That the crop and its proceeds did not do so, and left nothing for the bank after the landlord's lien was satisfied did not vitiate the agreement.

The judgment is affirmed.

Landlord's Lien for Advances

In some states, when an owner contracts with a tenant to raise livestock or crops and advances money, supplies, or other things to the tenant for the production of the crops or livestock, and as a part of the rent agrees to accept a share of such livestock or crops, the landlord then has a lien to the extent of all such advances.[29] This lien typically extends to any crops seeded, raised, or grown on the premises or to any livestock fed or raised on the land during the year that the advances are made. This lien usually may be enforced by the same procedure as for recovery of rent.

Eviction

Basic legal remedies are available to landlords for the purpose of removing tenants from the premises. When a tenant refuses to leave after the expiration of the lease and after proper notice, the landowner may file an action in court for "forcible entry and detainer" or "unlawful detainer."

In such cases, after a summons is issued to the tenant, a hearing may be held and a determination made as to whether or not the detention of possession was unlawful and as to which party is entitled to possession.

A second remedy available to a landlord to recover possession of property from a tenant after expiration or breach of lease is referred to as *ejectment*. Such cases are more involved than the unlawful detainer action, but the landlord may recover any rent due and any damages caused by the tenant while in possession.

13.5 TENANT'S FIXTURES AND IMPROVEMENTS

The question of whether a tenant has a right to remove certain kinds of improvements erected at the tenant's own expense frequently arises. Often, neither has given any thought to the question until the tenant proposes to take the improvements and discovers that the landlord claims they are part of the real estate and cannot be removed from the premises.

---

[29] *See* VA. STAT. ANN. § 43-29 (1974).

The recent trend, in both case law and in statutes, has been to allow considerable flexibility to the tenant so that improvements are encouraged.[30] The general rule is that the tenant may remove from the premises items (frequently called *removable fixtures*) that were erected by the tenant provided they are not so physically annexed to the land or buildings that severance would be impracticable and provided that severance would not cause material injury to the remaining real estate. Obviously, the difficulty is to distinguish between removeable fixtures and items that have become permanently affixed to the realty. This question is often one of intent of the tenant who erects the improvement. For example, individual hog houses, brooder houses, grain bins, or other similar structures which are not permanently fastened to another building or in a concrete foundation would most likely be considered removable fixtures. Such items should be distinguished from improvements to the farm—such as painting, fertilization, road building, etc.—for which the tenant has no right to reimbursement unless specifically stated in the lease.

If a lease is for a term of years, the tenant should remove any fixtures prior to the end of the lease term. If the lease is for an uncertain term, a reasonable time is usually permitted for removal following the termination of the lease.

Because of the frequent questions that arise concerning the tenant's rights relating to fixtures and improvements, these rights should be addressed in the written lease. If no written lease exists or if it does not address these issues, before construction or adding improvements the tenant should obtain a written statement from the landlord covering the right to remove the improvements or providing for reimbursement to the tenant for the unexhausted value of the item upon termination of the lease.

FIXTURES—REMOVAL

GOMEZ v. DYKES
Supreme Court of Arizona, 1961
89 Ariz. 171, 359 P. 2d 760

This appeal involves the incidents arising out of contracts for the sale of real and personal property wherein appellants Vidal Gomez and Jessie Gomez, husband and wife (hereinafter called plaintiffs), are the buyers, and appellees D.A. Dykes and Florence E. Dykes, husband and wife (hereinafter called defendants), are the sellers.

Prior to October 7 through 10, 1952, the parties hereto negotiated for the sale and purchase of a ranch located in south Phoenix, Arizona, composed of real and personal property owned by defendants. On or about October 10 the parties concluded their negotiations by signing and executing a contract and an agreement of sale which specifically described certain real and personal property to be transferred to plaintiffs for an agreed consideration.

---

[30] *See* Spies, *supra* note 26, at 33-34. The U.S. Supreme Court established an early policy in favor of severability of agricultural fixtures in Van Ness v. Pacard, 27 U.S. (2 Pet.) 137 (1829).

Dispute arose whereby plaintiffs claimed they were entitled to a trailer house which had been on the premises.

As relates to the trailer house the question arises, was the trailer house a fixture and therefore realty to pass under the realty agreement or, was it not a fixture so that it retained its character of personalty? The rule is set forth in *Fish v. Valley National Bank of Phoenix*, 64 Ariz. 164, 170, 167 P. 2d 197, 111:

> The mere affixing of personal property to real estate may or may not cause it to lose its personal characteristics. It may retain its identity as a chattel personal and not become a chattel real. The rule is that for a chattel to become a fixture and be considered as real estate, three requisites must unite: there must be an annexation to the realty or something appurtenant thereto; the chattel must have adaptability or application as affixed to the use for which the real estate is appropriated; and there must be an intention of the party to make the chattel a permanent accession to the freehold.

Based on this law we find that the evidence supports the trial court's findings and conclusions. The trailer house belonged not to defendants but an employee named Vale who brought it to defendants' premises when he came to work there. It was parked near the permanent employee house, temporarily attached thereto merely by a piece of tin held in place by temporary placement of cement blocks. With no evidence of electrical, water or gas connections of any kind having been made to the trailer house, the evidence discloses that there was no permanent annexation to the realty.

The second requisite to the rule could have been met. However, there is no evidence of the third requisite, intent, which as above mentioned, is the most important element of proof. Defendant Dykes could have no such intent. The trailer house did not belong to him but to his employee. Further, the rule provides that all three elements must unite. Since this did not happen the trailer house retains its character of personality. As such, it did not pass to plaintiffs under the personality agreement because it was not listed therein. The judgment of the trial court is affirmed.

13.6 EMBLEMENTS AND AWAY-GOING CROPS

When a tenant's lease expires through no fault of his or her own, the tenant may ordinarily return and harvest a crop, providing the crop was seeded before notice that the tenancy would be terminated was received. This is known as the *right to emblements* and such a crop is referred to as an *away-going crop*. It is an exception to the common-law rule that growing crops follow the title to real estate.

This principle also applies when the farm is rented from a life tenant. If the life tenant dies before the crops are matured and harvested, the lessee would be entitled to harvest under the right of emblements.

DOCTRINE OF EMBLEMENTS

FINLEY v. McCLURE
Supreme Court of Kansas, 1977
222 Kan. 637, 567 P. 2d 851

This is an action brought by a remainderman against the administratrix of a life tenant to recover the proceeds from the sale of wheat which were payable as crop rent on certain farmland. The plaintiff-appellant is Laurence Finley. The defendant-appellee is Ethel McClure, administratrix of the estate of D. Jessie F. Riley, deceased.

The case was submitted to the district court on an agreed statement of facts which essentially is as follows: Prior to her death on September 24, 1973, Jessie Riley was the owner of a life estate in certain farmland located in Wichita county, Kansas. The plaintiff Laurence Finley owned the remainder interest in this farmland. In 1973 the life tenant Riley leased the farmland for agricultural purposes to Wayne Marcy and Arthur McCowan, who were required to pay to Jessie Riley as rent one-third of the grain harvested by the lessees. Two weeks before Riley's death the lessees planted wheat on the property. After the death of Riley the crop was harvested by the tenants and deposited in an elevator under the names of Marcy and McCowan and the plaintiff Finley. Later by order of the probate court and without notice to the remainderman Finley, the wheat was sold and the proceeds of one-third of the wheat were paid to the defendant McClure as administratrix of the estate of the life tenant Jessie Riley.

Finley objected to the final settlement of the Riley estate, claiming that he was entitled to the proceeds from the sale of the wheat then in the hands of the administratrix. By agreement the controversy was certified to the district court. There the issue to be determined was stated to be as follows: whether the rent share of the wheat was owned by the life tenant Jessie Riley and now by her estate, or is owned by the remainderman, Laurence C. Finley, or should be apportioned between the life tenant's estate and the remainderman. The district court awarded the entire proceeds from the rent share of the wheat to Ethel McClure, as administratrix of the estate of the life tenant Riley. The remainderman Finley filed a timely appeal to this court.

We have considered the points raised by the defendant-appellee challenging the jurisdiction of the court and find them to be without merit. Hence we will proceed directly to the basic issue presented on appeal: "Did the trial court err in granting to the life tenant's estate the entire proceeds from the sale of the one-third rent share of the wheat and in failing to apportion the proceeds between the estate of the life tenant and the remainderman?" The controversy must be determined on the basis of the doctrine of emblements which comes into play when a life tenant of farmland dies before certain annual crops have been harvested. "Emblements" are corn, wheat, rye, potatoes, garden vegetables, and other crops which are produced annually, not spontaneously, but by labor and industry. The doctrine of emblements is of common law origin and was developed in reference to the ownership of such crops in the event of termination of the estate or tenancy of the person who planted them. Under the common law, if the life tenant sows a crop and dies before its maturity, the crop goes to his personal representative under the doctrine of emblements. The doctrine or right of emblements entitles one who holds land for a period subject to termination at a time which he cannot ascertain beforehand to remove from the land, after the termination of his tenancy, the annual crops or emblements which he has planted thereon prior to termination, provided termination is brought about without any fault on his part or without any act of his intention to bring about such a result. The basis of the doctrine is the justice of assuring to the tenant compensation for his labor, and the desirability of encouraging husbandry as a matter of public policy.

The doctrine is applied in controversies between the estate of a life tenant and remainderman. If the life tenant himself sows the crop and dies before it is mature, it goes to his personal representative under the doctrine of emblements. If the life tenant sells the crop during his lifetime and the life tenant dies before the crop is harvested, the grantee is entitled to the crop under the doctrine of emblements. The lessee of a life tenant is also protected by the doctrine and is entitled to the crops or his share thereof in the event his estate is terminated by the death of the life tenant during the term of the lease. If the life tenant dies between seedtime and harvest after having procured a "cropper" to operate the farm for a share of the crop, the life tenant is regarded as having had possession of the land and as having owned the growing crop or having an interest therein, and the crop passes to his estate, perhaps in conjunction with the cropper, the remainderman taking nothing. In each of the above instances the estate of the life tenant is entitled to his share of the matured crop on the theory that the life tenant at the time of his death was the owner, or at least part owner, of the growing crop.

A difference of opinion arises in the area where the life tenant leases land, with the rent payable with a share of the crop to be raised on the land by the lessees, and the life tenant dies before the crop is harvested. In this situation there is a decided split of authority among the various jurisdictions as to whether the estate of the life tenant or the remainderman is entitled to the crop share rent. Some courts take the view that the life tenant's estate is not entitled to the crop share rent but that it belongs to the remainderman, principally on the grounds that title to crops growing on leased land is in the lessee, not in the life tenant, that share rent is not due until the crop is harvested, and that the rent belongs to the owner of the fee at the time it becomes due. Other courts take the position that the life tenant, with respect to the landlord's share of the growing crop, was the owner of an undivided interest in the crop growing on the land at the time of his death and that such interest was personal property, title to which passes to his estate and not the remainderman, and similarly, that the life tenant's estate is entitled to the share rent, since such interest in the crop attaches after the crop commences to grow and is an inchoate interest which the life tenant may sell before maturity of the crop and which ripens into full ownership with such maturity. In a number of states the legislature by statute has settled the issue by providing for the apportionment of the crop rent or by creating in the life tenant a property right in the immature crop which entitles his estate to the crop rent share.

Like a number of other jurisdictions this court has struggled with the problem and encountered difficulty. The rule in Kansas has not been made clear, because it developed through a series of four cases, three of which disapproved of or overruled preceding cases in the series.

Finally, in *Sprick v. Beach*, 188 Kan. 296, 362 P. 2d24, this court in deciding the right to crops in a dispute between the grantee of a life tenant and a remainderman held that the grantee was entitled to a crop which he had previously planted on the land before the death of the life tenant. The court refused to apportion the proceeds from the sale of the crop rent, stating that a more definite rule than a theory of apportionment should be established for deciding these cases. The court did, however, state that the cases defendant cites are different because they involved leases and not outright sales. In the case now before us the district court, on the basis of Sprick, held that the entire proceeds from the one-third crop share rent were the property of the estate of the life tenant and that the remainderman had no interest therein.

We have concluded that the correct rule to be applied where a life tenant leases land for a share of the crop and dies before the crop is harvested is that the life tenant's estate is entitled to the entire crop share rent since under existing Kansas law his ownership in the landlord's share of the crop attaches after the crop is planted and his inchoate interest is one which he may sell before maturity of the crop and which ripens into full ownership with such maturity. In reaching this conclusion we have noted two Kansas statutes which recognize that a growing crop is to be considered on the death of the life tenant as personal property, not a part of the real estate, and that a landlord who leases his land for rent payable in a share of the crop is deemed to be the owner of such share and thus has an existing property interest therein.

The rule of *Sprick v. Beach*, supra, is to be applied in cases involving leases with rent based on crop shares as well as in cases involving outright sales.

The judgment of the district court is affirmed.

13.7 TAXATION, SOCIAL SECURITY, AND ESTATE PLANNING[31]

Generally, most farmers report net farm profit as "self-employment income" for tax purposes. Self-employment income normally would not include rental income from farm real estate or from personal property which is leased along with the farm real estate. Under some circumstances, the landlord participates in the operation. In such circumstances, the landowner may be subject to tax as a self-employed individual. The key in these cases is the "material participation" test applied to the landowner. Material participation may come about in a variety of ways. An agreement specifying participation by the landlord will serve as evidence that the income is self-employment income. In cases where there is no agreement for the landlord to participate, but the landlord does, in fact, materially participate in the production of agricultural products, the income received may be considered self-employment income. This actual participation may be in the form of physical labor or by a management contribution. The factors that are involved in determining whether or not a landlord materially participates in the operation include the following: the actual amount of work done; the participation in management decisions; the tools, equipment, and livestock furnished; and production expenses advanced, among others.[32]

In those situations where self-employment income is involved, it is subject to tax, and at the same time it generates social security benefits. Therefore, there may be circumstances under which an owner will desire to show material participation in order to qualify for social security benefits later.

In other situations, the individual may wish to avoid participation in order not to reduce current social security benefits.[33] Often, a direct lease agreement will provide that the decision making in the operation is left to the tenant. However, if the landowner continues to be involved and renders substantial services to the farming operation, any income may be considered as self-employment income and may serve to reduce current social security benefits. Up to age 72 (age 70 in 1982 and thereafter), any farmer who draws above a statutory maximum of earned income will incur the possibility of reduced social security benefits. The test in this case is "substantial services rendered in self-employment." This test is slightly different than the "material participation" test used to determine whether or not the income is subject to self-employment tax. The test is similar in that substantial services arise only from the actual participation by the landlord and cannot occur through the acts of an agent. Basically, the Social Security Administration will look at the nature of the services rendered and the time devoted to the entire operation. They will also compare the amount of work the individual landowner is contributing to the amount contributed prior to retirement in order to determine whether or not there has been a substantial change. These problems emphasize the benefit of having a carefully drawn and effective agreement which limits the activities of the landowner. In cases where it is effectively done, the landowner may be able

---

[31] For a review of the tax problems associated with the landlord-tenant relationship, see O'BYRNE, FARM INCOME TAX MANUAL § 1008 *et seq.* (1977).

[32] *Id. See also* Rev. Rul. 57-58, 1957-1 CB 270.
[33] *See* O'Byrne, *supra* note 31, at § 1023, for a review of how earnings after retirement reduce benefits.

to avoid taxation under self-employment and at the same time receive full social security benefits.

Whether a landowner materially participates in management also may affect several desirable estate planning options. For example, in order to qualify an estate for Internal Revenue Code § 2032A use valuation, the decedent or a member of decedent's family must have materially participated in management for 5 of the 8 years preceding the landowner's death. In order to qualify for Internal Revenue Code § 6166 or § 6166A installment payment of estate tax attributable to a closely held business, it may be necessary for the decedent to have materially participated in management, as a minimum.[34]

13.8 SOME ADDITIONAL ITEMS THAT SHOULD BE INCLUDED IN THE WRITTEN AGREEMENT

There are a number of additional items that should be specifically discussed between the parties and then included as part of the agreement. For example, a determination should be made as to who has the right to choose which crops will be planted on the farm. As a matter of law, it is the tenant who has the right to select crops to be grown so long as this selection does not constitute bad husbandry. It is irrelevant what the custom in the community is, unless custom tends to show the existence of an implied agreement. Such problems can be avoided by agreement as to what crops will be harvested and what cropping methods should be used.

The fundamental plans for crop rotation, soil management, and livestock management should be worked out and made a part of the lease. This should not be so rigid that changing conditions cannot be taken into account, nor should it be so general that the best use of land and improvements is not assured.

An understanding should be reached regarding the investment of each party, the expenses to be borne by each, the share of income which each shall take, and the manner of taking (cash, share of crop, share of livestock, or a combination of these). Many items need to be considered in arriving at an agreement on these points, including machinery, labor, power, fertilizers, taxes, and land value.

The lease agreement should include specific details as to the tenant's duty in regard to keeping up the premises and the tenant's duty to repair. The duties of the lessee should be so stated that there will be no doubt about the lessee's responsibility with respect to destroying weeds, hauling manure, pasturing the land, burning straw or other plant materials, cutting trees, and executing numerous other phases of the work in a husbandlike manner.

A provision should be made for remunerating the tenant for improvements made. A general statement about the kind of improvements the tenant may remove and the time within which they may be removed should be included.

Provisions should be made for the use of legume crops, homegrown lumber and wood, and other items of a special nature.

It is important that a determination be made as to who pays the insurance and taxes during the tenancy. This is particu-

---

[34] In Rev. Rul. 366, 1975-2 Cum. Bull. 472, a crop-share lease was construed as "an interest in a closely held business" for purposes of installment payment of federal estate tax where the landlord had participated in the business to a significant degree.

larly true with regard to improvements on the premises.

Details as to the rights of the tenant to assign or sublet the lease should be included, as should details regarding the survival of the lease upon the death of either party. An important portion of the lease should be devoted to determination of how the lease is to be renewed. An adequate period of notice with an automatic renewal clause in case of no notification is often desirable.

A minor detail that is often overlooked is a determination of the landlord's right to visit the farm. Quite often, the tenant will feel imposed upon if the landlord appears unexpectedly. It is more desirable to have these rights spelled out as part of the agreement.

The legal requirements of a farm lease have been discussed in this chapter. The essence of the lease, however, is the actual contractual arrangements between the parties. For this reason it is important that both parties understand the details of their lease agreement and the language used in defining the terms of the lease.

STUDY QUESTIONS

1. What are the essential elements for the creation of a legal lease?

2. What is the crucial difference between a landlord-tenant relationship and a partnership? An employer-employee relationship?

3. What is a tenancy from year to year, and what major problem is created when such a tenancy exists?

4. Who has the right to select the crops to be grown during the term of a lease?

5. What conduct is considered to be waste by the tenant? What acts are permissible?

6. Who has title to unharvested crops on rented land?

7. When is the landlord liable for injuries occurring on the leased property?

8. What rights does the tenant have if the leased property is sold to a new owner during the term of the lease?

9. What remedies are available to the landlord for the collection of rent? When may the property be retaken?

10. What is the effect of the "doctrine of emblements"?

11. Under what circumstances may a retired landlord's social security benefits be reduced owing to involvement in a landlord-tenant situation?

14
Farm Partnerships

Family partnerships offer flexibility so that the farmer can achieve lifetime income and retirement objectives. The partnership can be used to assure a smooth transition in the farm business and an equitable distribution to the next generation. The opportunity to acquire an ownership interest in the farm is often attractive to young farmers. By using a family partnership to accomplish this transfer of farm assets, a child may be encouraged to remain on the farm.

The partnership agreement may provide for periodic gifts of an interest in the farm. This may result in lower estate taxes. An installment purchase is often included in the partnership agreement or exists in a separate agreement. This has all the advantages of an installment sale. The parents receive greater income with a lesser tax burden as they grow less able to take part in the labor of farming. The child acquires more ownership as an ability to handle tasks of management is developed. At the father's death, further installments may be used to support the mother and to equalize the shares of other children.

The family partnership may have income tax advantages. It is not taxed as a separate business. Partners each report their share of profits on individual returns. Since children will generally be in lower income tax brackets, sharing profits with them as partners may reduce the overall tax of the family. Children may be treated as partners so long as they have a share of the business by contributions to capital or labor and so long as they participate to some degree in management.

Certain disadvantages also result from operating a business as a partnership. The major one results from the application of an important rule of partnership law—each partner is individually liable for all debts and obligations of the partnership. Since some partners may hold substantial personal assets which are not related to the partnership, they, in a sense, bear a greater share of the risk of business failure or risk of loss from other obligations that may be incurred in the business.

Another potential disadvantage for parents is that loss of some control of management and operational decision making may result since all partners have an equal voice in management. The partnership agreement can include provisions relating to authority of partners regarding certain decisions so that some of this disadvantage can be alleviated. The potential for conflict over rights and obligations does exist.

A major problem in partnership organization and operation is potential conflicts involving property of the partners and property of the partnership. Often, records are maintained that are inadequate to clearly distinguish property ownership, and conflicts can result when property is sold or when the partnership is dissolved.

14.1 PARTNERSHIP DEFINED; CHARACTERISTICS

A *partnership* is an association of two or more persons to carry on, as co-owners, a business for profit.[1] Partnerships are governed by a set of rules called the Uniform Partnership Act.[2] Additional rules may be adopted in the individual partnership agreement.

Elements
This definition from the Uniform Partnership Act includes several elements:

1. the association element
2. two or more persons having legal capacity
3. the business element
4. the profit element
5. the co-ownership element (including profit-sharing and joint control)

Association. The first element in the Uniform Partnership Act definition of a partnership is "association." This implies two or more persons acting voluntarily. This seems to imply that the intent of the parties is determinative of whether or not a partnership exists. But, even though the partners do not intend to form a partnership, if the elements of a partnership are present, the relationship may be established. The fact that the association element implies agreement does not necessarily mean

---

[1] The Internal Revenue Code definition is broader, *see* INT. REV. CODE § 761 (a).
[2] The Uniform Partnership Act (U.P.A.) is in effect, with certain modifications, in all states except Georgia, Louisiana, Maine, Mississippi, and New Hampshire. Sections of the U.P.A. cited herein are from VA. CODE ANN. § 50-6 *et seq.* (Repl. 1974).

that the relationship has to be established by written contract. The contract may be inferred, along with the intent, from the actions of the individuals.

Two or More Persons.   The second element of the definition indicates that two or more persons are to be involved. "Persons" in this sense can include individuals, other partnerships, corporations, or other associations. A person must have legal capacity to enter the relationship. Minors, incompetents, and other specific classes of individuals, may not qualify as capable parties. For example, a minor's contract is voidable. This would apply to a contract of partnership as well as contracts in general. Therefore, although a minor may be a partner, the minor may be able to repudiate the relationship and not be liable for a share of partnership obligations.

Business.   The third element of the definition of a partnership is the "business" element. Since the partnership is to carry on a business, it is necessary that the relationship be one which is more than co-ownership of property. While co-ownership of the business is essential, the mere ownership of property as co-owners does not establish a partnership, since the property may not be owned for the purpose of carrying on a business.

Profit.   An additional element of the relationship is the "profit" element. The carrying on of the business seems to indicate a profit objective. But there are nonprofit organizations. This part of the definition eliminates them as partnerships.

Co-ownership.   One of the important elements of the partnership relationship is the "co-ownership" element. This consists of the profit-sharing and the joint control components, both crucial for the partnership relationship to be established. The sharing of profits is prima facie evidence of a partnership. The sharing of control is also strong evidence, unless there is some intent or agreement to indicate otherwise.

Other Elements.   All of the above elements of a partnership give some substance to the definition. The crucial elements are sharing of profits and joint control. However, there are a number of other items that are considered in determining whether or not a partnership, in fact, exists.

The question of the existence of a partnership usually arises when a third party alleges that individuals have established a partnership arrangement. If the evidence clearly indicates a partnership, then all individuals involved can be held responsible for partnership debts.

Other important elements are (1) whether or not each person involved participates in management decisions; (2) whether assets are owned individually or jointly; (3) whether the individuals involved operate under a single name; (4) whether they have a single bank account used for business transactions; and (5) whether they keep a single set of business records.

The partnership agreement, if it exists, may also be indicative of a relationship. No single factor is determinative, and in a particular case, all of these questions may arise and be considered in determining whether in sum it is a partnership.

Joint Ventures, Landlord-Tenant Relationships, and Employment Contracts Distinguished

Joint Ventures.   Another type of business organization very similar to the partnership is the *joint venture.* The only real difference between a joint venture and a regular partnership is that the joint venture has a more limited scope. It is commonly a single undertaking, not requiring the entire attention of the individuals involved, and usually of fairly short duration. In most important respects, it is treated as a partnership.

Landlord-Tenant Relationships. The Uniform Partnership Act states that no inference of a partnership can be drawn in a situation where profits were received in payment of rent to a landlord. However, it is also sometimes difficult to distinguish the partnership from the landlord-tenant relationship. This is particularly true if the business operation is a family enterprise. The strongest determining factors in distinguishing a landlord-tenant relationship from a partnership are the intent of the parties and the amount of control of the business that is involved. It is for this reason that clauses are normally included in the lease excluding the possibility of a partnership. These are not entirely effective, but at least they serve as an expression of the intent of the parties. If the landlord retains joint possession with a tenant, the possibility of joint control is more likely and, therefore, the existence of the partnership may be inferred. Another aspect that is used to distinguish the two relationships is that a partnership agreement normally includes an express agreement to share losses. This is usually not true in a landlord-tenant situation. But, even in situations where a landlord-tenant arrangement includes a loss-sharing agreement, a partnership is not necessarily implied if other circumstances point to the existence of the landlord-tenant relationship rather than a partnership.

Employer-Employee Relationships. It is sometimes hard to distinguish between the partnership and the employer-employee relationship. Again, the Uniform Partnership Act indicates that no presumption of partnership arises from profit-sharing "as wages of an employee." Profit-sharing with employees is a fairly common practice. Again, the distinguishing characteristic is the intent of the parties and the amount of control. If the agreement clearly indicates the intent of the parties to establish an employer-employee relationship, then it is difficult to prove the existence of a partnership. In addition, if the situation is one in which the alleged employer is clearly in control of the business operation, this is strong evidence that an employer-employee relationship rather than a partnership exists.

There is a temptation to define a partnership by stating what it is not rather than what it is. The Uniform Partnership Act attempts to alleviate this temptation. However, the Uniform Partnership Act itself is subject to interpretation by courts. It is necessary to analyze the facts of a particular case in determining whether or not sufficient evidence exists to infer the existence of a partnership. The burden of proving the partnership is on the person who asserts the existence of the partnership. This burden is affected by interpretations of previous courts and by definitions that appear in the Uniform Partnership Act in those states which have enacted this set of rules.

EVIDENCE OF PARTNERSHIP

SHAWNEETOWN FEED AND SEED COMPANY v. FORD
St. Louis Court of Appeals, 1971
468 S.W. 2d 54

This is an action brought on an account due for seed corn against R.N. Ford who operated a combination grocery, feed and grain store. His wife, Clara Marie Ford, was joined as a party defendant on the theory that she was a partner in the business. At the close of plaintiff's case the court sustained a motion to dismiss as to Mrs. Ford. Defendants rested their case without putting on any evidence and a judgment of $1,000, with interest, was entered against R.N. Ford. The plaintiff corporation appealed, contending that the judgment should have been entered against both defendants.

There is no question before us relating to the amount owing to the plaintiff for the grain purchased. The points raised by the plaintiff all relate to the court dismissing as to Clara Marie Ford. It is contended here as it was below that the plaintiff made a *prima facie* showing that Ford and his wife were partners in the operation of the store and that the judgment should have been entered against both of them and not against R.N. Ford alone.

The testimony given by the officers of plaintiff corporation was that they had an account under the name of Ford Grocery and that payment was made to them by check. Printed at the top of the checks was R.N. Ford Grocery and Feed and Grain. They did not know whether Mrs. Ford signed the set of checks they received, but she did sign some. Neither did they know anything about the account that they were serving except that they carried it as Ford Grocery Company. No one testified that the defendants were partners in the operation of the store.

There was evidence that the Fords had a bank account at the Bollinger County Bank and another account at the Bank of Marble Hill, Missouri. Either party was authorized to sign checks on the accounts. A deposition of Mrs. Ford was offered in evidence by the plaintiff against interest. She stated in the deposition that both she and her husband had worked in the store together and that he kept the books. She did, however, occasionally write checks in payment of items delivered to the store. They both owned the store building and lived back of it until recent times when they moved to another house owned by both of them. She received no salary for her work but just worked "to help out." She drew upon the joint bank account for family expenses. The store had been closed prior to the time of trial but for about a year before it closed Mr. Ford had been working as a truck driver and Mrs. Ford was in the store most of the time.

It is next asserted that the evidence presented by plaintiff made *prima facie* proof of a partnership. This assertion is predicated in part upon 358.070 (4), RSMo 1959, V.A.M.S., which states: "The receipt by a person of a share of the profits of a business is prima facie evidence that he is a partner in the business, but no such inference shall be drawn if such profits were received in payment:..." This section is without application of the facts here considered. There is no evidence Mrs. Ford shared in the profits of the store. She drew from the checking accounts for family expenses but this was not for herself and was nothing more than the use of her husband's funds, with his consent, to carry out his obligation as a husband and father to support his family. Nor is there any proof that the Ford Grocery showed any profit.

Partnership must be proven by clear and convincing evidence. As in cases seeking to hold a husband and wife as joint venturers, the joint maintenance of a home by a husband and wife does not create a partnership, nor does the ownership of property by husband and wife as tenants by the entirety. A partnership does not arise necessarily by reason of a wife working in her husband's place of business, particularly when she works simply to "help out." In husband and wife cases the very nature of the relationship of parties tends to submerge adversity of individual interests. For the reasons stated, the plaintiff's evidence failed to establish the existence of a partnership between Ford and his wife.

THE NATURE OF A PARTNERSHIP

RIZZO v. RIZZO
Supreme Court of Illinois, 1954
3 Ill. 2d 291, 120 N.E. 2d 546

Defendants have appealed directly from a decree of the circuit court of Cook County, entered substantially in accordance with the master's findings and recommendations, and ordering defendants Michael, Joseph and John Rizzo, as surviving partners of Rocco Rizzo Sons and Company, to render an accounting to Catherine Miglore Rizzo, (herein called plaintiff,) administratrix of the estate of Rocco Rizzo, Jr., a deceased partner.

The essential issue in this cause is whether the evidence establishes that a partnership existed at the date of the death of Rocco Rizzo, Jr., between him and his brothers, defendants Michael, John and Joseph Rizzo.

From the evidence adduced before the master, it appears that in 1910, Rocco Rizzo, Sr., an Italian immigrant, who could neither read nor write English, operated a waste paper business under the name of Rocco Rizzo and Company.

Michael, the oldest son, went to work for his father in 1910. Joseph went to work in 1913, Rocco, Jr., in 1916, and John in 1920. Each son performed definite duties for the business; Michael, the most experienced, was the general manager; Joseph was the receiving clerk; and John and Rocco, Jr., were truck drivers. None of them received wages, but were given room and board, and all the profits, if any, were divided equally. However, in 1915, Rocco, Sr., retired from active participation. Michael, then age 21, urged his father to stay at home since their mother was dead.

On October 29, 1929, the father deeded the business property to Michael, who paid no consideration for either the business or the building, but merely handed the deed to his father to sign with his mark. Additional property adjoining these premises was subsequently acquired, and title was taken in the name of Frank Rosinia. There is evidence that the property was paid for with funds furnished by Michael, his brothers, and by the business which was the only source of income of the brothers.

Rocco Rizzo. Jr., died intestate June 27, 1931, leaving surviving his widow and two minor sons. Plaintiff testified that after her husband's funeral, Michael assured her that she would get her husband's share out of the business as she always had.

On the basis of the evidence the master found that Michael, Joseph, John, and Rocco, Jr., operated the business as a partnership from 1920 to June 27, 1931, the date of the death of Rocco, Jr.: that his estate was entitled to a one-fourth interest in the partnership as of the date of his death, and, at the option of the representative, either to interest at the legal rate on said one-fourth share or to the profits attributable to the use of his interest in the partnership from the date of his death to the date of the decree; and that plaintiff is entitled to an accounting from defendants Michael, Joseph, and John Rizzo of all partnership dealings from the time of the commencement to the date of the decree.

In the instant case the decree of the court in plaintiff's favor is predicated upon the existence of a partnership relation between plaintiff's deceased husband and his brothers. The requisites of a partnership are that parties must have joined together to carry on a trade or venture for their common benefit, each contributing property or services, and having a community of interest in the profits. It has been held that, as between the parties, the existence of a partnership relation is a question of intention to be gathered from all the facts and circumstances. Written articles of agreement are not necessary, for a partnership may exist under a verbal agreement, and circumstances may be sufficient to establish such an agreement. Such factors as the mode in which the parties have dealt with each other; the mode in which each has, with the knowledge of the others, dealt with other people, and the use of a firm name, have been deemed material in determining the existence of a partnership. The essential test, however, is the sharing of the profits, but it is not necessary that there be a sharing of the losses in order to constitute a partnership. Mere participation in the profits, however, does not of itself create a partnership.

Defendants contend that the evidence establishes that Michael Rizzo was the sole proprietor of the business on the date of the death of plaintiff's decedent. In support thereof, defendants point out that the business was turned over to Michael in 1915 when his father retired, that the profits were merely the measure of compensation for the brothers, that Michael was regarded as the boss by persons dealing with the firm, and that a formal partnership contract had to be drawn up at the request of the bank in order to negotiate a loan in 1937, indicating that there was no partnership prior thereto.

The fact that Michael, as the oldest son, had more authority in the management than the other brothers does not of itself preclude the existence of a partnership, particularly in view of the custom in such closely-knit immigrant families. In fact, Michael stated that the business was turned over to him because he was the oldest son. Furthermore, it is an accepted partnership practice that one partner may be charged with greater managerial responsibilities.

The fact that the brothers admitted that they all worked in the business, sharing equally in the profits and going without pay if there were none, tends to comply with the essential requirement for a partnership. That interpretation is enhanced by the admission of Michael on cross-examination that he was carrying on the business for all the brothers; by the testimony of the sister Rose Cambliglio, that Rocco, Jr., was a partner; and by the statement of an employee of 30 years that all the brothers were regarded as the owners.

Under the circumstances in the case at bar, therefore, there is ample evidence that the brothers, Michael, Joseph, John, and Rocco, Jr., were carrying on the business for their common benefit, each contributing his services and having an equal interest in the profits; hence, the finding of the master, as approved by the court, that the brothers were partners as of the date of the death of Rocco, Jr., could in no way be deemed to be manifestly against the weight of the evidence.

In the light of our analysis of this cause, the findings of the court are amply supported by the evidence, and the decree entered pursuant thereto is in accordance with the law and should properly be affirmed.

14.2 PARTNERSHIP AGREEMENTS[3]

A partnership is created by an oral or written agreement. In some cases, a partnership may be implied without an agreement if the business is being carried on like a partnership. A carefully drafted written agreement, however, is the best insurance against later misunderstanding between the partners.

A partnership agreement is the basis for the operation and management of the business, and it should be detailed and complete. Although the content and arrangement may differ, the agreement will usually contain the following:

1. A short introduction containing the date, the names of the parties, and the place where the agreement is made. There should be a statement that it is a partnership agreement.

2. The name, place, terms, and purpose of the partnership business. The term may be made continuous by stating a definite term with an automatic yearly renewal of the agreement unless notice of termination is given by one or more of the parties.

---

[3] *See* Bock, *Formalizing the Farm Partnership*, 54 NEB. L. REV. 558 (1975).

3. Capital contributions, provision for capital accounts of the partners and for withdrawal of money by partners, and a procedure for loaning money to the partnership by a partner.

Initial capital contributions by each partner should be listed in detail. There may be divided into cash, real and personal property, special assets, and service (labor and management) contributions. A stipulation to leave part of the profits in the business as contributions to capital may be included.

Provision should be made for keeping individual capital accounts, as well as complete books and records of the partnership that are available to all partners. This responsibility should be expressly given to one or more partners.

The amount of withdrawals from capital should be defined. For example, there could be a provision for withdrawals of cash by unanimous consent. Reductions in capital and distributions of capital to the partners could be allowed by a majority of the partners.

If it is contemplated that a partner may loan money to the partnership at some future time, a provision setting out the terms of such a loan is desirable.

4. Management by the partners, the time they devote to the business, and payment of salaries.

Unless there is a special provision to the contrary, a decision by a majority of the partners controls. However, there can be a requirement of unanimous decision in important questions such as incurring extraordinary expenses. It may also be provided that a decision by a majority of the partners in interest, rather than a majority in number, controls.

It is assumed that a general partner will devote substantially all of his or her time to the business, but it is advisable to include an express statement to this effect. If a partner is to devote only a portion of his or her time to the business, this should also be stated. In addition, provisions should be made for vacation and leave time for partners so that misunderstandings do not arise relating to time away from the business.

No salary payments are authorized without express agreement. Salary provisions should set out the amount and period of payment of any salary.

5. Sharing of profits and losses. Profits and losses are usually shared equally by the partners or shared on the basis of their capital contributions. However, the law permits a division in any way the partners desire.

A clause authorizing a maximum monthly withdrawal for living expenses is sometimes included.

6. A general statement of the partner's rights and obligations in connection with operating and partnership business.

Generally included is a partnership checking account, naming the bank and stating the limitations on the partners in drawing on it. It is desirable to definitely state who has power to sign checks and who, if anyone, must countersign.

7. Termination and dissolution of the partnership.

There should be a provision for voluntary dissolution. This may be done as follows:

a. By giving any partner the right to dissolve the partnership upon the providing of advance written notice. It may be agreed that a partner causing dissolution is personally liable for any loss incurred by the partnership as a result of dissolution.

b. By requiring the written agreement of a majority or all of the partners before there can be a voluntary dissolution.

The agreement may state that when a partner dies, the partnership is automatically dissolved. However, it is usually desirable to provide for continuation of the business after the death of a partner. This may be accomplished by binding the deceased partner's estate for a period of time to give the surviving partners an option to buy out the decedent's interest. Special buy-and-sell agreements with life insurance provisions may be used for this purpose.

A provision may be inserted to allow for the retirement of a partner. The agreement may also include provision for the expulsion of a partner for misconduct or for incapacitation for a stated period of time due to illness or injury.

8.   Miscellaneous provisions.

There may be an arbitration clause to be used when the partners cannot agree. A clause may also be included requiring that all notices or additions to the agreement be in writing.

14.3 PARTNERSHIP OBLIGATIONS

Since the partnership business is managed by the partners, they have the power to act for the partnership so long as they act within the scope of the business.

Every partner is an agent of the partnership. A partner who carries on the business of the partnership in its usual way binds the partnership even though expressly prohibited from carrying on such business by the partnership agreement. This is true unless the person with whom the partner is dealing knows that the partner is acting without proper authority.[4]

A notice given to any partner relating to partnership affairs is considered notice to the partnership, except in the case of notice of a fraud to a partner who allows the fraud to be committed.[5]

A partnership is liable for loss or injury caused to any person (including employees) by the wrongful act or omission of a partner, providing the partner was acting in the ordinary course of the partnership business or with the consent of the other partners. The partnership must also make good any loss caused by a partner misapplying money or property of a person outside the partnership which was received by the partnership or by a partner under apparent authority for the partnership.[6]

Each of the partners is also individually liable for loss or injury in the above cases if the partnership is liable. However, if an injured person recovers damages from an innocent partner for the wrongful act of a

---

[4] VA. CODE ANN. § 50-9. "Partner as agent; limitation of authority. (1) Every partner is an agent of the partnership for the purpose of its business, and the act of every partner, including the execution in the partnership name of any instrument, for apparently carrying on in the usual way the business of the partnership of which he is a member binds the partnership, unless the partner so acting has in fact no authority to act for the partnership in the particular matter, and the person with whom he is dealing has knowledge of the fact that he has no such authority. (2) An act of a partner which is not apparently for the carrying on of the business of the partnership in the usual way does not bind the partnership unless authorized by the other partners."

[5] VA. CODE ANN. § 50-12. "Knowledge of or notice to partner. Notice to any partner of any matter relating to partnership affairs, and the knowledge of the partner acting in the particular matter, acquired while a partner or then present to his mind, and the knowledge of any other partner who reasonably could and should have communicated it to the acting partner, operate as notice to or knowledge of the partnership, except in the case of a fraud on the partnership committed by or with the consent of that partner."

[6] VA. CODE ANN. § 50-13. "Partnership bound by partner's wrongful act. Where, by any wrongful act or omission of any partner acting in the ordinary course of the business of the partnership, or with the authority of his copartners, loss or injury is caused to any person, not being a partner in the partnership, or any penalty is incurred, the partnership is liable therefor to the same extent as the partner so acting or omitting to act.

co-partner, the innocent partner may recover that amount from the guilty partner.

14.4 PARTNERSHIP PROPERTY AND INTERESTS IN THE PARTNERSHIP

Unless the partnership agreement states otherwise, a partner is entitled to three general property rights. They are (1) rights in specific partnership property, (2) interest in the partnership, and (3) right to participate in management. The latter right will be discussed in Section 14.5.

Rights in Partnership Property

A partner is, with the other partners, a co-owner of specific partnership property (land, livestock, equipment, etc.), holding it as a "tenant in partnership." A partner has an equal right with the other partners to possess the property for partnership purposes without the consent of the other partners. One partner cannot assign his or her right in partnership property unless all the other partners also assign their rights at the same time. Claims against a partner cannot attach to that partner's right in specific partnership property, but can attach only to the partnership interest. When a partner dies, the right in specific partnership property goes to the surviving partners and they may possess it for partnership purposes. The deceased partner's representative may require an accounting and payment in cash for the net amount of the deceased partner's share.[7]

The Partnership Interest

A partner's interest in the partnership, which is a share of the profits and surplus, is personal property and is subject to attach-

---

§ 50-14. "Partnership bound by partner's breach of trust. The partnership is bound to make good the loss: (a) Where one partner acting within the scope of his apparent authority receives money or property of a third person and misapplies it; and (b) Where the partnership in the course of its business receives money or property of a third person and the money or property so received is misapplied by any partner while it is in the custody of the partnership.

§ 50-15. "Nature of partner's liability. All partners are liable: (a) Jointly and severally for everything chargeable to the partnership under §§ 50-13 and 50-14; (b) Jointly for all other debts and obligations of the partnership; but any partner may enter into a separate obligation to perform a partnership contract."

[7] Va. Code Ann. § 50-25. "Nature of right in specific partnership property. (1) A partner is co-owner with his partners of specific partnership property holding as a tenant in partnership. (2) The incidents of his tenancy are such that: (a) A partner, subject to the provisions of this chapter and to any agreement between the partners, has an equal right with his partners to possess specific partnership property for partnership purposes; but he has no right to possess such property for any other purpose without the consent of his partners. (b) A partner's right in specific partnership property is not assignable except in connection with the assignment of the rights of all the partners in the same property. (c) A partner's right in specific partnership property is not subject to attachment or execution, except on a claim against the partnership. When partnership property is attached for a partnership debt the partners, or any of them, or the representatives of a deceased partner, cannot claim any right under the homestead or exemption laws. (d) On the death of a partner his right in specific partnership property vests in the surviving partner or partners, except where the deceased was the last surviving partner, when his right in such property vests in his legal representative. Such surviving partner or partners, or the legal representative of the last surviving partner, has no right to possess the partnership property for any but a partnership purpose. (e) A partner's right in specific partnership property is not subject to dower, curtesy, or allowances to widows, heirs or next of kin."

ment of execution for claims against the partner.[8] It may be assigned and, on the death of the partner, becomes part of that partner's estate.[9]

An assignment of a partner's interest in the partnership entitles the assignee only to the profits to which the assigning partner would be entitled, unless the partners agree that the assignee shall also participate in the management.

Any one or more of the partners may be given the authority to transfer real property belonging to the partnership.[10] It is imperative that the partners agree on this matter

---

[8] VA. CODE ANN. § 50-26. "Nature of partner's interest in partnership. A partner's interest in the partnership is his share of the profits and surplus, and the same is personal property.

§ 50-27. "Assignment of partner's interest. (1) A conveyance by a partner of his interest in the partnership does not of itself dissolve the partnership, nor, as against the other partners in the absence of agreement, entitle the assignee, during the continuance of the partnership, to interfere in the management or administration of the partnership business or affairs, or to require any information or account of partnership transactions, or to inspect the partnership books; but it merely entitles the assignee to receive in accordance with his contract the profits to which the assigning partner would otherwise be entitled. (2) In case of a dissolution of the partnership, the assignee is entitled to receive his assignor's interest and may require an account from the date only of the last account agreed to by all the partners.

§ 50-28. "Partner's interest subject to charging order. (1) On due application to a competent court by any judgment creditor of a partner, the court which entered the judgment, order or decree, or any other court, may charge the interest of the debtor partner with payment of the unsatisfied amount of such judgment debt with interest thereon; and such court may then or later appoint a receiver of his share of the profits, and of any other money due to fall due to him in respect of the partnership, and make all other orders, directions, accounts and inquiries which the debtor partner might have made, or which the circumstances of the case may require. (2) The interest charged may be redeemed at any time before foreclosure, or in case of a sale being directed by the court may be purchased without thereby causing a dissolution; (a) With separate property, by any one or more of the partners, or (b) With partnership property, by any one or more of the partners with the consent of all the partners whose interests are not so charged or sold. (3) Nothing in this chapter shall be held to deprive a partner of his right, if any, under the exemption laws, as regards his interest in the partnership."

[9] VA. CODE ANN. § 50-25, *supra* note 7.

[10] VA. CODE ANN. § 50-10. "Conveyance of real property of partnership. (1) Where title to real property is in the partnership name, any partner may convey title to such property by a conveyance executed in the partnership name; but the partnership may recover such property unless the partner's act binds the partnership under the provisions of paragraph (1) of § 50-9, or unless such property has been conveyed by the grantee or a person claiming through such grantee to a holder for value without knowledge that the partner, in making the conveyance, has exceeded his authority. (2) Where title to real property is in the name of the partnership, a conveyance executed by a partner, in his own name, passes the equitable interest of the partnership, provided the act is one within the authority of the partner under the provisions of paragraph (1) of § 50-9. (3) Where title to real property is in the name of one or more but not all the partners, and the record does not disclose the right of the partnership, the partners in whose name the title stands may convey title to such property, but the partnership may recover such property if the partners' act does not bind the partnership under the provisions of paragraph (1) of § 50-9, unless the purchaser or his assignee, is a holder for value, without knowledge. (4) Where the title to real property is in the name of one or more or all the partners, or in a third person in trust for the partnership, a conveyance executed by a partner in the partnership name, or in his own name, passes the equitable interest of the partnership, provided the act is one within the authority of the partner under the provisions of paragraph (1) of § 50-9. (5) Where the title to real property is in the names of all the partners a conveyance executed by all the partners passes all their rights in such property."

in advance, and if any special problems are anticipated, an effort should be made to inform innocent third parties as to the true situation should they be dealing with a partner or partners.

Another point that bears emphasis is that each partner may sell personal property in the regular course of the business. If the purpose of the partnership business does not include the selling of personal property, this rule would not apply.

One problem that sometimes arises is distinguishing partnership property from that owned by the individual partners. This occurs most often at the time of the dissolution of the partnership or at a time when items of property are to be sold.

DISTINGUISHING PARTNERSHIP ASSETS

WILSON v. RODGERS
Supreme Court of Arkansas, 1971
250 Ark. 335, 468 S.W. 2d 739

This is an appeal by J.B. Wilson from an adverse decree of the Arkansas County Chancery Court in a case wherein J.B. contended that he is the owner of a one-half undivided interest in certain real property in Arkansas County, the legal title of which was held in the name of his brother, George, who is now deceased.

Until George Wilson's death, he and J.B. were partners in livestock and farming operations on the land involved in this case. The litigation arose when the widow and heirs of George Wilson filed a petition in chancery for the appointment of a receiver and for an accounting of the partnership assets, consisting primarily of cattle and hogs. J.B. Wilson filed a general denial and alleged rightful possession and control of the partnership assets. He filed a cross-complaint against the widow, Mrs. Kathryn Wilson, as well as against Joan Rodgers, Nancy Tullow, and Kalynn Harris, the three married daughters and surviving heirs of George Wilson, in which he alleged that the lands were partnership assets; that the legal titles to such lands as were held in the name of George Wilson were held in trust for the partnership; that he, J.B. Wilson, owned a one-half undivided equitable interest in the lands and he prayed for a decree to that effect. The chancellor confirmed title to the lands in the estate of George Wilson subject to the rights of dower and to outstanding mortgages and deeds of trust.

The undisputed evidence is clear that George and J.B. Wilson were near the same age, had held themselves out as business partners all of their adult lives. After their father died intestate they continued to operate an oil business left to them by their father. When George married, he brought his wife to the family home and J.B. continued to live with George and his wife until he also married. After losing the oil business and their home, through mortgage foreclosure during the depression years, George and J.B. remained closely associated with each other and got into the business of farming and raising livestock under the partnership title "Wilson Brothers," and this relationship continued until George's death on July 1, 1967.

All of the deeds of conveyance to the lands here involved were made to George Wilson and to his heirs and assigns forever, and the record is completely void of any competent evidence as to why this was done. It would be next to impossible, and of little value, to analyze the separate testimony of the many witnesses who testified, but the record is clear that most everyone considered the Wilson brothers as a partnership; and most everyone assumed that the partnership included the joint ownership of the land. A number of witnessess called by J.B. testified that George always referred to "us," "our," "Jay and I," and "mine and Jay's" when discussing the farm and its operation. In the sale of some of the land with conveyance to George, the grantors testified that they made the deal with J.B. One of the grantors testified that he dealt with J.B. and sold the land to the Wilson Brothers. The deed, however, was made to George, his heirs and assigns, and there is no evidence as to why this was done. Several witnesses testified as to business they conducted with the Wilson Brothers. Those witnesses called by J.B. testified that they dealt directly with J.B. in such matters as clearing land, sinking a well, arranging to rent land, baling hay, purchasing and selling livestock and feed, and in doing dragline work on the farm. Some of these witnesses testified that when they attempted to do business with George, he would delay final decision until he could talk with J.B.

The witnesses who were called by Mrs. George Wilson and the heirs, testified that they transacted all their business with George and that George did business with them without having to consult with J.B. One or two of these witnesses testified that George referred to the land as belonging to him and had stated that he intended it should go to his wife and children at his death. The overall testimony of all the witnesses leaves the preponderance of the circumstantial evidence fairly even on both sides.

The evidence is clear that George Wilson assessed the real property taxes for a number of years in the name of Wilson Brothers. On the income tax returns the profits from the farm were divided equally between George and J.B. Loans from the Production Credit Association were made to George and J.B. jointly until some individual judgments were obtained against them and the procedure was changed, at the insistence of the association. The amounts of the judgments against George were less than those against J.B., so they borrowed money and paid off the judgments against George and the P.C.A. loans thereafter were made to Geroge or in his name. All of this evidence definitely established a partnership relation between George and J.B. in the operation of the farm as the Wilson Brothers farm or ranch.

In spite of the voluminous record in this case, the record is vague or silent as to the two most important aspects of the case. It is vague as to the bank accounts and it is silent as to why the deeds were made to George, his heirs and assigns. J.B. testified that the bank accounts were joint accounts or Wilson Brothers partnership accounts, and that both he and George collected money from the farm operations and deposited all they made into the partnership accounts. He testified that they each drew money from the accounts by check when and as they needed it. J.B.'s primary contention is that the lands were purchased by the Wilson Brothers and paid for out of their joint funds.

Numerous canceled checks were offered in evidence. A number of them dated in the 1950's were signed "Wilson Brothers by J.B." Some were signed "Wilson Brothers by George," some were signed "J.B. & George Wilson," some were signed "George and J.B. Wilson by George," and some were signed "George and J.B. Wilson by J.B." Some of the checks were signed "George Wilson by J.B.," but most of the checks introduced by the appellees were dated in the 1960's and were simply signed "George Wilson." None of the checks indicate how the accounts were actually carried at the banks and no bank officer testified as to how the accounts were actually carried or what arrangements were made between the banks and the Wilsons in connection with the accounts. From the documentary exhibits it is impossible to tell whether the bank accounts were joint, or partnership accounts or whether they were the individual or personal accounts of George or J.B. with checking authority granted to the other.

The appellant J.B. Wilson's witnesses testified that George had indicated all along that he and J.B. owned the land together as partners. J.B. testified that the land was bought and paid for with partnership funds. The appellees' witnesses testified that George had indicated all along that the land belonged to him individually. The solemn deeds of record sustain the appellee's contention and although there is ample evidence that J.B. was a full partner in the livestock and farming operations, we are left to surmise and conjecture as to why the legal title to the real property rested in George Wilson, his heirs and assigns. George Wilson was in bad health for a considerable period of time before his death, the real property was heavily mortgaged without assistance or objections by J.B. The record only contains circumstantial evidence that perhaps the deeds should have been made to George and J.B. as joint tenants when the property was purchased but this was not done. There is no evidence at all of why the deeds were made to George, his heirs and assigns when the property was purchased, and there is no clear and convincing evidence of why this court should do so now. We find no merit to the appellant's other assignment of errors, so the decree is affirmed.

Affirmed.

DISSENTING OPINION

I am as yet unable to understand how the majority can find evidence to overcome appellant's contention that the real estate involved was partnership property or how the trial court could find that J.B. Wilson and George Wilson constituted a farming partnership which stopped short of ownership of the real estate. The evidence that Wilson Bros. owned the land seems stronger to me than that relied upon to show a farming partnership. I think that a partial explanation lies in failure to apply law relating to partnerships rather than to constructive or resulting trusts. Appellant has never sought to impress either upon the conveyances. He has simply sought to establish a trust under partnership law.

The receipt by a person of a share of the profits of a business is prima facie evidence that he is a partner in the business. Clear and convincing evidence is not required to prove a partnership. Its existence need be proved only by a preponderance of the evidence.

We have held that provisions of the Uniform Partnership Act are applicable to partnerships entered into prior to its passage and which had acquired real estate prior to its adoption.

Pertinent provisions other than the one cited hereinabove include the following:

1. Unless the contrary intention appears, property acquired with partnership funds is partnership property.
2. Every partner is an agent of the partnership for the purpose of its business and his acts for apparently carrying on the business of the partnership bind it.
3. A partner's interest in partnership property is as a tenant in partnership.

Until adoption of the Uniform Partnership Act in 1941 in Arkansas, the title to real property could not be held in the name of the partnership. The act recognizes, however, that title to partnership real property may be held in the name of one of the partners, but that this partner may not effectively convey title to the property unless the grantee in the conveyance is a holder for value without knowledge or the conveyance is one for apparently carrying on the business of the partnership. When the legal title is vested in the name of one of the partners, he becomes, in equity, a trustee for the other partners to the extent of their interest.

Real estate purchased for partnership purposes, paid for with partnership funds and held and used for partnership purposes, is treated as partnership property regardless of how or by what agency it is bought or in whose name the title is held, and the holder of the legal title is a trustee for the partnership. When land is purchased for use in carrying on the partnership business with partnership funds and there is no agreement or design that it be held for the partners' separate use, it will be treated in equity as vested in them in their firm capacity, whether the title is in all, or less than all the partners.

Proceeding upon these well established principles, we should turn aside from attempts to measure the evidence by the clear and convincing yardstick and abandon efforts to decide whether there was a constructive or resulting trust to answer the following pertinent inquiries:

1. Did J.B. Wilson receive a share of the profits of the business of Wilson Bros., consisting of him and George Wilson?
2. Is there any evidence that he received these profits as compensation for services as distinguished from his share as a partner?

3.   Does the evidence that a partnership existed preponderate?

4.   Were the lands in question purchased with partnership funds?

5.   If so, is there a preponderance of the evidence to show an intention that the lands not be held as partnership property?

6.   Does the evidence show that the property was used for partnership purposes?

I humbly submit that question 1, 3, 4, and 6 must be answered in the affirmative and questions 2 and 5 in the negative. This being so, the decree should be reversed for a decree declaring that George Wilson held the lands trustee for the partnership of Wilson Bros.

OPINION ON REHEARING

Upon original submission, the court was sharply divided upon the question whether a preponderance of the evidence supported the chancellor's finding that J.B. Wilson had no interest in the lands involved. The chancellor properly found that all farming operations were by a partnership consisting of J.B. and George Wilson.

The majority then sustained the chancellor's finding but found these deficiencies in the evidence:

1.   Deeds to only three of the five tracts involved were ever introduced in evidence, all of which named George Wilson as grantee. The identity of the grantor in the other two deeds was never disclosed. In spite of the fact that there was some evidence that some payments on the purchase price of some of the lands and some evidence that the grantors were dealing, or thought that they were dealing with Wilson Brothers, or J.B. and George Wilson, the record was silent as to the reason the title to the land was taken in George Wilson.

2.   The overall testimony of all the witnesses left the circumstantial evidence as to the ownership so evenly balanced that it could not be said that a preponderance lay either way.

3.   The evidence as to the names in which the bank accounts were carried, the source of the funds deposited, the identity of those authorized to draw checks on the account, the arrangements between the depositor or depositors and the bank was vague. No explanation was made or offered as to the failure of either party to produce bank records or bank statements or the testimony of bank officers or employees, other than one whose testimony related to transactions which took place many years ago. It was not possible to determine, with any degree of certainty, whether the pertinent bank accounts were joint accounts, partnership accounts or individual accounts of one or the other of the brothers, with checking authority to the other.

The affirmance of the chancellor's decree as to the ownership of the lands was based upon the want of evidence as to the reason the deeds introduced were made to George Wilson. We have considered this case, both on original submission and on petition for rehearing over a longer period of time than we usually devote to a single case, and are still divided and uncertained as to the correct result, because of the deficiencies in the evidence pointed out.

Because of our uncertainty as to the preponderance of the evidence, as to the theory upon which the case was decided, as to the rights and equities of the parties under the evidence before us, which seems not to have been fully developed, and in the furtherance of justice, we feel that this case should be remanded to the chancery court. There the parties shall be permitted to offer further evidence to show:

1.   How the record title to the land was held, and the identity of the grantee in any unrecorded deeds conveying the property
2.   The reasons for taking the title in the names of the grantees of all conveyances of lands alleged to be partnership property, rather than in the names of the two alleged partners
3.   The names in which bank accounts were held, the source of funds deposited thereto, the person authorized to draw checks on each such account, the arrangements between the depositors and the banks, and the disposition of the funds deposited
4.   The source of the funds used to pay the purchase price of any of the lands in which the grantee in the deeds when purchased was George Wilson
5.   Any accountings between the partners and withdrawal of partnership funds by the individual partners for their own account

14.5 RIGHTS AND DUTIES OF PARTNERS

The rights and duties of the partners in a general partnership are clearly detailed in the Uniform Partnership Act. The following sections deal with these rights and duties.

General Rules Determining Rights and Duties of Partners

The rights and duties of the partners in relation to the partnership shall be determined, subject to any agreement between them, by the following rules:

1.   Each partner shall be repaid his or her contributions, whether by way of capital or by advances to the partnership property, and shall share equally in the profits and surplus remaining after all liabilities, including those to partners, are satisfied. Each partner must contribute toward the losses, whether of capital or otherwise, sustained by the partnership according to his or her share in the profits.
2.   The partnership must indemnify every partner in respect of payments made and personal liabilities reasonably incurred by him or her in the ordinary and proper conduct of the partnership's business or for the preservation of its business or property.
3.   A partner, who in aid of the partnership makes any payment or advance beyond the amount of capital which he or she agreed to contribute, shall be paid interest from the date of the payment or advance.
4.   A partner shall receive interest on the capital contributed by him or her only from the date when repayment should be made.
5.   All partners have equal rights in the management and conduct of the partnership business.

6. No partner is entitled to remuneration for acting in the partnership business, except that a surviving partner is entitled to reasonable compensation for his or her services in winding up the partnership affairs.

7. No person can become a member of a partnership without the consent of all the partners.

8. Any difference arising as to ordinary matters connected with the partnership business may be decided by a majority of the partners; but no act in contravention of any agreement between the partners may be done rightfully without the consent of all the partners.[11]

Additional Rules[12]

Partnership Books. The partnership books shall be kept, subject to any agreement between the partners, at the principal place of business of the partnership, and every partner shall at all times have access to and may inspect and copy any of them.

Duty of Partners to Render Information. Partners shall render on demand true and full information of all things affecting the partnership to any partner or to the legal representative of any deceased partner or partner under legal disability.

Partner Accountable as a Fiduciary. Every partner must account to the partnership for any benefit, and hold as trustee for it any profits, derived without the consent of the other partners from any transaction connected with the formation, conduct, or liquidation of the partnership or from any use of its property.

Right to Formal Account. Any partner shall have the right to a formal account as to partnership affairs if wrongfully excluded from the partnership business or possession of its property by co-partners, if the right exists under the terms of any agreement, or if other circumstances render this right just and reasonable.

Continuation of Partnership beyond Fixed Term. When a partnership for a fixed term of particular undertaking is continued after the termination of such term or particular undertaking without any express agreement, the rights and duties of the partners remain the same as they were at such termination, so far as is consistent with a partnership at will.

A continuation of the business by the partners or such of them as habitually acted therein during the term, without any settlement or liquidation of the partnership affairs, is prima facie evidence of a continuation of the partnership.

14.6 PLANNING PARTNERSHIP FORMATION

Partnerships typically evolve from either an employer-employee arrangement or a profit-sharing agreement. A number of items should be considered in determining whether a partnership is a feasible alternative for the family. For example, consideration must be given to the potential income to be derived from the business and to the availability of living arrangements for the families to be involved. Additional important areas of consideration are noted below.

First, major questions must be answered concerning the transfer of property to the partnership. Unless the agreement provides for younger family members to acquire an interest in appreciating assets—particularly land—estate planning objectives may be defeated. Thus, crucial decisions concerning property—both real and personal—must be made prior to formation of the partnership.

---

[11] *See* VA. CODE ANN. § 50-18 (Repl. 1974).
[12] *See* VA. CODE ANN. §§ 50-19 to 50-23 (Repl. 1974).

A second major area of concern is the determination of how payments for capital contributions, labor and management are to be divided.

The third major area of concern at the time of formation of the partnership relates to potential income tax problems. Generally, at the time the partnership is formed, one who contributes property to the partnership does not realize gain or loss on the transaction. Nor is gain or loss realized by the partnership itself or by the other partners.[13]

Once the partnership is formed, each partner has a basis in the interest in the partnership which is essentially the original basis or contribution to the partnership, adjusted by subsequent contributions, distribution of property or money, partnership losses, partnership liabilities, and other items.[14] The basis of the partner cannot fall below zero in any event. A record of basis is important if the partner later transfers an interest in the partnership or if the partnership is dissolved.

Generally, the partnership receives as its tax basis in items transferred to it at the time of formation the same tax basis the items had in the hands of the transferors.[15] If the contributed asset is later sold by the partnership, a pro rata share of any gain is allocated to each partner.

14.7 PARTNERSHIP DISSOLUTION

The three separate terms which are often used regarding a change in the relation of partners are dissolution, termination, and winding up. As used in the Uniform Partnership Act, *dissolution* designates a point in time when the partners cease to carry on the business together. *Termination* is a point in time when all partnership affairs are wound up. *Winding up* is a process of settling of partnership affairs after dissolution. Winding up is also sometimes referred to as *liquidation*.

Partnerships can be dissolved in a number of ways. Under most partnership agreements, dissolution can occur without a violation of the agreement: (1) at the end of the term specified in the agreement; (2) by the will of any partner if no term is stated; (3) by agreement of all partners; (4) by expulsion of a partner under terms specified in the agreement.[16]

Normally, the agreement will provide for dissolution upon the death, incapacity, or retirement of a partner. The common way is by a "buy-sell" agreement, which is essentially a contract between the partners for the purchase of the interest of the deceased, retiring, or incapacitated partner. These agreements may be very specific and can provide for purchase price, interest, installment payments, and other details.

Dissolution may also occur in contravention of the partnership agreement between the partners. For example, if nothing is specified in the agreement itself, the death or bankruptcy of a partner will result in dissolution. Dissolution may also be by decree of court on application for or by a partner. Such a dissolution may be ordered in case of incapacity of a partner where one partner's conduct is such as to prejudice the carrying on of the business of the partnership, where one partner's conduct is a willful or persistent breach of the partnership, when the business can be carried on only at a loss, or under other such circumstances.

When a partnership is dissolved for any of the above reasons, the liability of the existing partners does not change. Natu-

---

[13] INT. REV. CODE § 721.
[14] INT. REV. CODE § 722.
[15] INT. REV. CODE § 723.

[16] *See* VA. CODE ANN. §§ 50-31 to 50-43 (Repl. 1974) for U.P.A. provisions on dissolution.

rally, one partner may have agreed to assume an existing obligation, but third parties and creditors are not bound by any such agreement unless they expressly consent to be so bound. The individual property of the partner continues to be liable for all obligations of the partnership incurred during the operation.

At any time that a partnership is dissolved or terminated, the liabilities of the partnership in order of priority are as follows: (1) liabilities owed to creditors other than partners; (2) liabilities owed to partners other than for capital or profits; (3) liabilities owed to partners in respect of capital; (4) liabilities owed to partners in respect of profits.[17] Once these distributions have been made, if the total assets of the partnership are inadequate to satisfy liabilities, each partner must contribute any amount necessary to satisfy partnership liabilities.

At dissolution, a number of tax problems may occur. In the case of a complete liquidation of a partner's interest, the tax basis in any property received is the same as the basis for the interest in the partnership adjusted by any money received as part of the liquidation.[18] Capital gain or loss may be involved if the property is subsequently sold.

If at the death of a partner the interest is liquidated, the payments from the partnership for the partner's capital interest are treated as a distribution.[19] If the remaining partners purchase the deceased partner's interest, the tax effect is essentially the same as the sale of any partnership interest. A special problem is often involved where the partnership agreement does not contain a provision regarding sale of the partnership interest at death. If no such agreement exists or if the agreement provides that the estate is to continue as a partner, additional income tax problems may arise.

14.8 TRANSFERRING OWNERSHIP TO YOUNGER PARTNERS

The operational partnership typically includes no provision for the children to acquire an interest in the real estate. Because of inflation and appreciating land values, the younger partner may be facing a real stumbling block in the future.

Sales

Consideration should be given to allowing the younger partner to purchase some interest in the real estate if the operation is profitable enough to allow the child to pay for the land. If it is not, perhaps both families should reevaluate the feasibility of the venture. The sale to the child can be handled in a number of ways.

The sale could involve (1) all of the real estate with a continuing operating partnership; or (2) part of the real estate at partnership formation and the remainder later. This latter method of handling the sale allows the younger partner to begin paying for part and gives this partner more "borrowing power" at a later point, should the parents wish to sell or if he or she has an option to purchase at the death of the parents.

The sale to the younger partner may involve special tax considerations. For example, if a father wishes to sell machinery and other eligible property which qualified for investment credit to a son, recapture provisions may apply if sold prior to the end of a designated investment credit life.[20] In such cases, it may be more practical for the father to lease the property to the partnership (or to the son) until the investment credit life is over.

A second problem may involve capital gains to the father for items of both per-

[17] See Va. Code Ann. § 50-40 (Repl. 1974).
[18] See Int. Rev. Code § 732 (b).
[19] See Int. Rev. Code § 736.
[20] Int. Rev. Code § 47.

sonal and real property sold to the younger partner. This may be a major problem in the transfer of livestock which have little or no basis. Caution must be exercised in this area because the sale of some livestock may result in ordinary income. The sale of machinery and equipment ordinarily would not result in gain, since the sales price would probably be equal to the basis. For real estate, the amount of gain may be substantial. To lessen the impact, consideration should be given a long-term installment sale which would qualify for special tax treatment. In many cases, such an arrangement may be necessary because the younger partner may be unable to obtain commercial financing for the purchase.

In many transfers, the financing arrangement may involve the assumption of existing debt as part of the transfer agreement.

Gifts

Many families have combined the organization of the family partnership with an overall estate plan, which often includes the use of gifts to transfer property to a younger partner. Under current federal gift tax provisions, a substantial amount of property can be transferred free of the federal gift tax. By taking advantage of the available exclusions and the unified credit, a younger partner can acquire a fair amount of property from the parents with which to commence the partnership without gift tax liability. For example, the parents each have a unified credit of $47,000 which can be used to offset the taxes due on up to $175,625 worth of property transferred by lifetime gift or at death. Some families find it advantageous to use this credit against lifetime gifts rather than at death. In addition, each parent can transfer up to $3,000 each year to each child (or other donee) free of gift tax. This exclusion can be used

annually to transfer property. (More detail on gift taxes is included in Chapter 17). Such transfers not only increase the younger partner's percentage interest in the business and effectively reduce the parent's estate, but may also serve as an incentive to the younger partner to remain in the family business. The basis of the parents in any property transferred is likewise transferred to the younger partner, so no gain is involved until such time as the younger partner disposes of the property. Special problems are involved in attempts to transfer partnership interests to minors by gift or by sale because minors are not legally competent to manage property and may disaffirm contracts made during their minority.

Partnership Buy-Sell (Business Purchase) Agreement

A *buy-and-sell agreement* is a contract between the partners for the purchase of a deceased partner's interest by the surviving partners. Such an agreement permits the business to continue and reduces financial problems at the death of a partner. A buy-sell agreement need not include a life insurance provision, but proceeds from such insurance assure funds to purchase the partnership interest.

Buy-sell agreements may set the price and terms of the transfer, may contain a formula for determining price, or may provide for an appraisal. The agreement may be either optional or mandatory and, if mandatory, can assist in setting values of the estate of the parents.

14.9 PARTNERSHIP TAXATION

For income tax purposes, the term partnership includes "a syndicate, group, pool, joint venture or unincorporated organization."[21] This is a broader definition than the concept of partnership under common law or under the Uniform Partnership Act.

The partnership itself is not a tax paying entity. The partnership must file an informational tax return (Form 1065) which reports the business income, losses, and deductions. Each partner then claims a proportional share of each tax item on the individual return and pays any tax due.

The following items *must* be separately listed on the partnership return and reported by each individual partner.

1. net short-term capital gain or loss
2. net long-term capital gain or loss
3. net Section 1231 gain or loss
4. charitable contributions
5. dividends received that qualify for the exclusion
6. partially tax-exempt interest
7. recoveries of previously deducted items
8. soil and water conservation expenses
9. land cleaning expenses
10. recapture of farm losses and land deductions[22]

In addition to the treatment of these items, the partnership return requires a computation of the self-employment income of each partner.

In many partnerships, advance withdrawals are made by each partner, perhaps in the form of a monthly "salary." Such withdrawals are considered to be a part of the individual's distributive share of income from the partnership.

Partners may decide to divide profits and losses for tax purposes in some way other than by the percentage interests of the partners. The partnership agreement controls so long as the principal purpose is not tax evasion. If there is no agreement, then income or loss is shared according to the percentage interests in the business. One special rule exists for partnerships that must be observed. A partner cannot deduct a share of losses in excess of that partner's basis in the partnership interest.[23]

During the term of the partnership, special tax problems may arise if sales or exchanges occur in transactions between the partnership and the individual partners. In cases where the partner owns directly or indirectly more than a 50 percent interest in the partnership, losses are disallowed.[24]

If a partnership distributes property to a partner who continues in the partnership, the partner takes over the basis the property had in the hands of the partnership. Gain is realized when the partner disposes of the property.

PARTNERSHIP TAXATION

SCHMITZ v. COMMISSIONER
U.S. Tax Court, 1978
37 T.C. Memo 1323

Petitioners, Raymond W. and Jeannette Schmitz (hereafter Raymond and Jeannette), husband and wife, filed joint Federal income tax returns for the years 1972 and 1973.

---

[21] INT. REV. CODE § 761(a). For more detailed information on partnership taxation, *see* O'BYRNE, FARM INCOME TAX MANUAL (1977).

[22] *See* Form 1065 and accompanying instructions.
[23] INT. REV. CODE § 469.
[24] INT. REV. CODE § 707(b).

Petitioner, Stephen Schmitz (hereafter Stephen), filed Federal income tax returns for the years 1972 and 1973.

In the early 1900's Joseph and Anna Schmitz (hereafter Joseph and Anna), the father and mother of Raymond and Stephen, started a cattle ranch in Brockton, Montana. Although raising cattle was their primary business, corn, wheat and other farm goods were also grown on the ranch. During the 1930's both Stephen and Raymond became one-third partners in the ranch with Joseph. All three provided services and participated in the ranch's management. Anna provided some services unconnected with the cattle but otherwise related to the ranch, but by 1972 she was 82 years old and could do very little.

On June 6, 1957, all the land used by the partnership to conduct its ranching operations was sold by Anna and Joseph to Raymond and Stephen for $5,000.

Upon Joseph's death in 1958, Anna inherited his one-third interest in the cattle and equipment used in the cattle partnership and Raymond and Stephen continued working the ranch. For each of the years 1972 and 1973, the Federal partnership returns filed by the Schmitzes listed Stephen and Raymond as the only partners. However, prior to Joseph's death, Raymond and Stephen orally agreed with their father that they would continue to pay Anna for life one-fifth of the yearly gross steer sales after his death in order to provide her with a sufficient income. Additionally, Anna was not to bear any losses on steer sales, and if there were no sales in a year, Anna would receive nothing. Raymond and Stephen never considered their mother to be a partner in the cattle farm, but they did believe she was entitled to the 20 percent interest on the steer sales and continued to pay her this amount out of the proceeds from the sales.

In 1972, the partnership paid Anna $5,215.65. This amount was deducted as pasture rent on the 1972 partnership return; however, this amount actually reflected 20 percent of the gross sales of steers (before any deductions for expenses, etc.). Anna did not share in any of the profits from grain sales or agricultural program payments. In 1973, Anna received $7,001.14 from the partnership or 20 percent of the gross steer sales of $35,005.70. This amount was excluded from the partnership income entirely which showed $28,004.56 income from the sale of steers. The $7,001.14 was reported by Anna on her income tax return for 1973.

The question which we must answer is whether payments made in 1972 and 1973 pursuant to the oral agreement were made to Anna as her share of profits in the partnership. Respondent contends that the partnership was not obligated to make the payments to Anna and that the payments were in the nature of support.

We must first look to Montana law to ascertain the extent of Anna's rights (if any) in the partnership profits. Under Montana law, there was a technical dissolution of the partnership upon Joseph's death in 1958.[25] Respondent assumes that any payments made by the partnership to Anna must be either for profits or interest for use of Anna's capital in the partnership or for support payments. He then argues that because the amount of payments was unrelated to either the value of Anna's share of capital or to the net profits of the partnership, they cannot be interest payments or profits in lieu of interest and, therefore, must be payments made by the partnership without legal obligation. Petitioners maintain that they were legally obligated to make the payments.

We disagree with respondent's basic assumption. To properly analyze the payments' character, we must deal first with the effect to be given the oral agreement between Joseph, Raymond, and Stephen (which respondent ignores). Mont. Rev. Codes Ann. sec. 63-514 sets forth the rights of the deceased partner's estate when the business is continued unless otherwise agreed. Thus, the rules governing accountings between partners upon dissolution and the rights of surviving partners are subject to agreements entered into which may be contrary to the usual statutory rules established in the absence of such agreements.

Here, the agreement modified the distributive shares each partner was to receive in such a manner that Anna received less than she otherwise would have received had she retained a one-third interest in the profits and losses of the ranch. Anna retained Joseph's one-third ownership in the cattle and equipment, however, and upon liquidation of her 20 percent interest in the gross receipts of the steer sales, Anna received the full fair market value of her one-third interest in the cattle and equipment.

Under the Internal Revenue Code, the partnership agreement includes any modifications of the partnership agreement agreed to by all the partners. Income Tax Regulations, specifically provide that such modifications may be oral. All the parties to the partnership agreed to the modification, and there is no dispute as to its terms. Therefore, the oral agreement is a valid modification of the original partnership agreement pursuant to the regulations.

We also believe that the agreement is binding under Montana law. The fact that the agreement was to take effect upon Joseph's death does not result in

---

[25] MONT. REV. CODES ANN. § 63-514 (1947) provides the following: "Rights of retiring or estate of deceased partner when the business is continued. When any partner retires or dies, and the business is continued under [conditions met here], without any settlement of accounts as between him or his estate and the persons or partnership continuing the business, unless otherwise agreed, he or his legal representative as against such persons or partnership may have the value of his interest at the date of dissolution ascertained, and shall receive as an ordinary creditor an amount equal to the value of his interest in the dissolved partnership; provided that the creditors of the dissolved partnership as against the separate creditors, or the representative of the retired or deceased partner, shall have priority on any claim arising under this section, as provided by section 65-513(8)."

a testamentary dispositon. The general rule is that such agreements are binding, even if not in writing. Finally, we believe that the agreement was supported by adequate consideration. Anna neither participated in the management of the partnership nor provided services to it. One would expect, therefore, for Anna to take a lower profit share than Joseph. Thus Stephen and Raymond provided consideration by their agreement to provide Anna with 20 percent of gross receipts in the steers, while Joseph provided the surviving partners with use of his share of the partnership assets. In addition, the reciprocal promises of the partners to operate (or remain operating) as a partnership furnish the necessary consideration for this later agreement which by its terms became incorporated into the original agreement.

Thus, we conclude that Anna had a property right under Montana law to 20 percent of the gross receipts of the partnership steer sales. We believe that the fact that this amount was arrived at solely by the partners' estimate of how much Anna needed for her support does not change this result. Because this interest is taxable to Anna as her share of partnership profits, it is not taxable to the remaining partners.

Decisions entered for the petitioners.

14.10 LIMITED PARTNERSHIPS

One common criticism of the partnership is the characteristic of unlimited liability of the partners for partnership debts and obligations. Personal assets of the individual partners may be used to satisfy partnership debts and obligations if the partnership itself has insufficient assets to meet the obligations.

As between partners, the liability problem can be minimized by including specific provisions in the partnership agreement. Such provisions do not affect the liability to third parties who deal with the partnership.

Most states have enacted the Uniform Limited Partnership Act, which is designed to protect partners whose involvement in a business is investment capital.[26] Such arrangements have been used extensively in cattle feeding and certain other types of farming operations.

The limited partnership involves one or more general partners and one or more limited partners. The general partners continue to operate the business and are for all purposes subject to the same liability as partners in a regular partnership. The limited partners are protected and are responsible for partnership debts only to the extent of their investment.

The limited partner can have no voice in management and the limited partner's name cannot appear in the partnership name. In addition, a certificate must be filed containing information as to the limited partner's interest and rights to share in profits.

The certificate must contain the following information:

1. The name of the partnership
2. The character of the business
3. The location of the principal place of business

---

[26] *E.g.,* ILL. REV. STAT. ch. 106 1/2, § 44 *et seq.* (1979).

4. The name and place of residence of each member, general and limited partners being respectively designated

5. The term for which the partnership is to exist

6. The amount of cash and a description of and the agreed value of the other property contributed by each limited partner

7. The additional contributions, if any, agreed to be made by each limited partner and the times at which or events on the happening of which they shall be made

8. The time, if agreed upon, when the contribution of each limited partner is to be returned

9. The share of the profits or the other compensation by way of income which each limited partner shall receive by reason of his or her contribution

10. The right, if given, of a limited partner to substitute an assignee as contributor in his or her place, and the terms and conditions of the substitution

11. The right, if given, of the partners to admit additional limited partners

12. The right, if given, of one or more of the limited partners to priority over other limited partners, as to contributions or as to compensation by the way of income, and the nature of such priority

13. The right, if given, of the remaining general partner or partners to continue the business on the death, retirement, or insanity of a general partner

14. The right, if given, of a limited partner to demand and receive property other than cash in return for his or her contribution.[27]

The limited partnership arrangement is an alternative to the corporate form of holding property—particularly land. As an estate planning device, it may allow the continuation of a business as an economic unit even after interests have been divided among a number of individuals.[28] For example, if a family wishes to divide farm assets but the parents choose to retain control of the business, the limited partnership arrangement could be used as a vehicle to accomplish this. The parents could be general partners with off-farm heirs as limited partners, and the agreement could be drafted to protect the rights of all parties.

STUDY QUESTIONS

1. How is a partnership distinguished from a landlord-tenant relationship?

2. Barry Picker and his brother "Banjo" orally agreed to go into the farming business. Each agreed to contribute $20,000 for a down payment on a farm and equipment. They borrowed the remaining money needed from an insurance company and both signed a promissory note which included repayment terms. They bought the land and equipment in late 1980 and farmed it in the 1981 crop season. They made about $8000 after all cash expenses were paid, which will not be enough to pay the annual payment plus interest due on the note.

If the insurance company sues and tries to prove that Barry and Banjo are partners, what are *five* of the factors that will be used to determine whether or not a legal partnership exists?

3. Under what circumstances may a partner's acts be binding on the partnership?

---

[27] VA. CODE ANN. §§ 50-44 to 50-73 (Repl. 1974).
[28] *See* Abbin, *Using the Multi-class Partnership to Freeze Asset Values for Estate Planning Purposes,* J. TAX. 66 (Feb. 1980); Dahl and Burke, *The Use of Limited Partnerships in Upper Midwest Agriculture,* 1 AGRIC. L.J. 345 (1979).

4. What is the concept of unlimited liability, and how does it apply to partners?

5. To what extent may a creditor of an individual partner reach that partner's interest in a partnership?

6. Why does the Uniform Partnership Act prohibit assignment of a partner's interest in the partnership?

7. On what grounds may a partnership be dissolved?

8. Why is bankruptcy of an individual partner considered to be grounds for partnership dissolution?

9. Assume that in forming the A B partnership, A contributed 75 percent of the property used in the business and B contributed 25 percent. Their partnership agreement provided that profits and losses would be equally shared and that each would have equal management responsibilities. If the partnership earns $40,000 in ordinary income, on what amount will each partner be taxed?

10. Sam Slick owns a greenhouse and nursery business. He has incurred financial difficulties the past 2 years and needs additional capital to expand the business in order for it to be profitable. His sister, Sue, is a successful attorney in Philadelphia. Sue has indicated that she would be willing to invest in Sam's business, but she does not want to lose more than her investment. She has suggested to Sam that they form a *limited partnership*.

What is a limited partnership?

What information must be included in the limited partnership certificate which must be filed (other than the *name of the business*)?

What restrictions must be complied with in order for Sam and Sue to operate as limited partners?

15

Farm Corporations

Farmers should not hesitate to select the business organization best suited to their needs. In the past, they have leaned heavily on the *sole proprietorship* type of organization because capital, labor, and management are usually concentrated in one person. Also, no organizational expense is involved and no special formalities are imposed by law. An operator's own judgment prevails. It is not necessary to ask anyone to approve the reasons or actions taken.

However, a few facts disturb the tranquility of this arrangement. Death terminates a proprietorship, and many times "splintered" ownership results. Testamentary provisions of the will are often nonexistent or inadequate, and, at best, wills do not usually solve the split ownership problem. Transferability of partial interests during lifetime is complicated. As opera-

tions get larger, the investment, as well as the risk, becomes greater. Credit is limited to the individual resources of a sole proprietor. Income tax rates rise to 70 percent. And, there is unlimited liability for debts and obligations of the business which extends to personal assets.

As a result of these problems, some farmers have turned to other forms of business organization. One form receiving considerable use is the *corporation*. This form can be used by a farm family, by several families, or by individuals who wish to combine capital in one operation. The corporation provides limited liability to the shareholders. Corporations are not affected by the life span or whims of any one owner. Ownership is in personal property, represented by shares of stock, which are easily transferable. The corporate income tax disadvantage of past years has partly disappeared and, in fact, there now are possible income tax advantages.

The purpose of this chapter is to show when and how the farmer may use incorporation in the farm business and the type of corporate structures that are available. This chapter deals with the regular and Subchapter S business corporation. The following chapter discusses cooperatives and not-for-profit corporations.

15.1 CORPORATE STRUCTURE AND FORMATION[1]

A corporation is a legal entity authorized by state law. Any kind of legitimate business may be incorporated. The procedure for incorporating a business is outlined by state law and must be followed exactly. The corporation begins its legal existence when the state issues a certificate of incorporation.

Once organized, a corporation is treated as an individual in its dealings with others. The owners of the corporation (called *shareholders*) are issued certificates representing shares to show the interest each holds in the corporate assets.

The Advantages of Corporate Structure: An Overview

Farm corporations can attain many of the advantages of a partnership while avoiding some of its disadvantages. A corporation differs from a partnership in that it is considered a separate business entity, apart and distinct from its owners. Owners conduct and control the business through the shares of stock they hold. They are liable for business debts and obligations only to

the extent of the value of their shares. Management obligations as well as rights of the shareholders are controlled by the corporation's articles of incorporation and by-laws, together roughly equivalent to the partnership agreement. Since the corporation is regarded as a separate entity, a transfer of an ownership interest by sale or gift of stock or by distribution upon the death of a stockholder does not terminate the business.

Like the partnership, the corporation provides an excellent means by which ownership of the farm may be transferred to children:

1. Gradual sale of stock allows parents to develop an adequate retirement plan, while children are encouraged to build and improve the farm.

2. Upon the death of the parents, the farm continues to function as a going concern.

3. Shares may also be gifts, providing parents with a means of treating their children equally. Children can shuffle their shares, depending upon their financial abilities and interest in farming, and thus plan their futures in relation to the family farm before the parents' deaths.

4, Transfers of stock by gift will reduce the size of the estate subject to estate and inheritance taxes.

Prior to 1958, the corporate income tax was a serious obstacle to farm incorporation in some cases, since a tax was levied first upon the corporate profits and then upon dividends of the owner-shareholders. There was, in effect, double taxation of corporate farm income. In that year, Subchapter S was added to the income tax laws to provide for optional tax treatment of

---

[1] *See generally* CAVITCH, BUSINESS ORGANIZATIONS.

corporations that is substantially identical to that of partnerships, so long as stock ownership is closely held. Like the partnership, the corporate device enables the farmer to distribute business earnings among children in low tax brackets in the form of salaries and dividends, thus reducing taxation on all farming earnings.

In 1978, the corporate tax rates and the income brackets for a regular (Subchapter C) corporation were revised, so that corporate income is taxed at rates ranging from 17 to 46 percent. The rates payable on net income are 17 percent on the first $25,000 of taxable income, 20 percent on the second $25,000 of taxable income, 30 percent on the third $25,000 of taxable income, 40 percent on the next $25,000, and 46 percent on all taxable income above $100,000. With these tax rates and income brackets, income tax savings may be achieved in the regular corporation by careful planning. The fact that the family-owned corporation has the option of selecting between two different methods of taxation provides opportunities for tax planning not available to the sole owner or the partnership.

Added advantages may be secured through various forms of corporate fringe benefits. These include insurance payments by the corporation for employees (officers and employees), medical and hospital plans paid by the corporation, pension and profit-sharing plans, and other benefits related to the income tax. Payments by the corporation are generally a business expense, fully deductible on the income tax return. Unlike the sole owner or partner, a stockholder may be treated as an employee of the corporation and is eligible for these benefits.

Disadvantages of incorporation include the following:

1. Initial cost of incorporating—fees, taxes, and professional advice
2. Capital stock tax on intangibles in some states
3. Annual tax for the privilege of operating as a corporation in some states
4. Formality of organization and operation
5. Restricted market for shares in the closely held family corporation
6. Possible income tax pitfalls upon incorporation

Corporate Formation

These are the usual steps in forming a corporation:

1. The incorporators (a) file an application to reserve a corporate name, (b) make a preincorporation agreement, (c) draft, sign, verify, and file the Articles of Incorporation and pay initial fees.
2. Capital is turned over to the corporation and stock issued in return.
3. The shareholders meet to elect directors.
4. The directors meet, elect officers, adopt bylaws (unless the Articles of Incorporation give this power to the shareholders), and begin business in the name of the corporation.[2]

The Preincorporation (Shareholders) Agreement. This agreement is not legally necessary but highly desirable. It serves as a guide for the incorporators while the corporation is still in its formative stages and unable to act for itself. It may also be used to restrict the rights of shareholders in the purchase and transfer of shares, and to restrict the powers and duties of directors, officers, and shareholders in the operation of the business.

---

[2] The exact procedure may vary somewhat from state to state. State statutes control the formation.

E.g., KAN. STAT. ANN. § 17-6001 et seq. See also ABA MODEL BUS. CORP. ACT (1960).

A preincorporation agreement for a farm corporation will usually include the following:

Agreement to Incorporate. The incorporators agree that the corporation shall be organized, that it shall issue a given kind and number of shares, and that they agree to buy these shares in stated amounts.

Naming of Employees, Directors, Officers, and Their Salaries. The agreement may name the shareholders who will work for the corporation, their duties, and their salaries. Since in a farm corporation the shareholders themselves usually will act as directors and officers, the agreement should state which position each will occupy.

Decisions of directors and officers which the incorporators feel should require unanimous approval may be included in this agreement and later written into the Articles of Incorporation and bylaws. Regulation of shareholders' votes and quorum requirements must be made a part of the bylaws, but also may be included in this agreement for later adoption as bylaws.

Restriction on Stock Transfers. Restrictions may be used to keep corporate control and assets in the hands of the original owners or selected successors. They may provide that if any shareholder resigns from the employ of the corporation, attempts to sell, pledge, or otherwise encumber his or her stock, becomes ill or incapacitated for a certain period of time, or dies, the corporation or the other shareholders, in proportion to their holdings, shall have the right to purchase this shareholder's shares. If this option to buy is to be a permanent restriction, it should also be included in the Articles of Incorporation.

An agreement for life insurance on the lives of the individual shareholders may be used to supplement the option to buy the shares of a deceased shareholder. The surviving shareholders, the corporation, or an independent trustee may be made beneficiary of the policy. The proceeds provide funds with which to pay the heirs, executor, or administrator of the deceased shareholder for the value of such shares.

The Articles of Incorporation. The Articles of Incorporation are the nucleus of the powers and limitations of the corporation and its shareholders. They should provide for possible future changes in size and type of farming operation, since amendments must be filed and additional fees paid if the Articles prove to be insufficient.

Articles of Incorporation are fairly standard from state to state. Most require inclusion of the items listed below.[3]

1. *Introduction.* The complete names and addresses of the incorporators must be listed.

2. *Name of the corporation.*

3. *Registered office and agent.* The address of the initial registered office, including the county in which it is located and the name of the initial registered agent at that address, must be stated.

4. *Duration.* The duration of a farm corporation usually is "perpetual." This means that the corporation will continue as a legal entity until it is formally dissolved by operation of law.

5. *Purposes.* A corporation has only the power to carry out the general purposes provided by law plus those stated in this article. This section should be brief and comprehensive, making the purposes very broad so that they cover any possible sideline business the corporation may enter. The general purpose will be to engage in farming and related businesses.

6. *Shares of stock.* The class, number, and value of authorized shares of stock as

---

[3] *See e.g.,* KAN. STAT. ANN. § 17-6002.

well as any preferences or restrictions with respect to the classes must be included.

In most states, shares may be par or no-par value and common or preferred class. *Par shares* have a predetermined and stated face value. *No-par shares* have no value stated on their face. They represent a proportionate interest in the business and the board of directors (the incorporators until the corporation is formed) sets the value at which they are issued.

Shares classed as *common shares* can pay dividends only when the directors declare a dividend out of current or past earnings, as long as the corporation remains solvent. The dividend must be the same for each share.

Holders of *preferred shares*, on the other hand, are entitled to receive dividends (up to a fixed amount) according to the terms of the contract. Usually, such dividends must be paid before any dividends may be paid on common shares or before earnings may be accumulated in the corporation. No-par common shares are the class most frequently authorized in a farm corporation. They allow flexibility of value and a simple financial structure.

7. *Number of directors.* Since the shareholders will also be the directors in a typical farm corporation, the number of directors will usually be determined by the number of shareholders owning the business. State law sets a minimum number to be elected—frequently three.[4] In many states, if there are less than three shareholders, the minimum number of directors is reduced to the number of shareholders.[5]

8. *Minimum stated capital requirement.* Many jurisdictions require that the certificate of incorporation include a statement that the corporation will not commence business until a minimum amount of stated capital is paid in.[6] This minimum is set by statute.[7]

9. *Oath and acknowledgment.* When the Articles of Incorporation are completed, the incorporators declare by their signatures that the statements made therein are true. The acknowledgment of signatures is then notarized.

Completed copies of the Articles must be sent to an appropriate state official along with the incorporation fees. If they are in proper order, the state files one copy and returns the other to the incorporators along with a Certificate of Incorporation. Local filing is usually required as well. Some states require incorporators to file a copy of the Certificate of Incorporation and the Articles of Incorporation in the county in which the registered office of the corporation is located. In other states, a copy is sent to local officials for recording directly from the state office.[8]

15.2 OPERATIONAL REQUIREMENTS

When the proper state official issues a Certificate of Incorporation, the corporation becomes a legal entity and is in official existence. However, before actual operation of a business—as a corporation—commences, the rules of operation must be detailed in corporate bylaws.

---

[4] *E.g.,* ARK. STAT. ANN. § 64-302; ILL. REV. STAT. ch. 32, § 157.34; OKLA. STAT. tit. 18, § 1.35a.
[5] *E.g.,* VA. CODE ANN. § 13.1-36.
[6] *See* CAVITCH, *supra* note 1, § 62.06.
[7] *Id.* Kansas, for example, once required a corporation to have $1000 of capital as a minimum for commencing business, but that requirement has been eliminated.
[8] *E.g.,* N. Y. GEN. CORP. LAW § 8. *Compare* ALA. BUS. CORP. ACT §§ 6, 9, 13.

The Bylaws

After the Articles of Incorporation are drafted and filed, the bylaws are considered. The Articles are more permanent provisions than the bylaws, and they are placed on public file, thereby giving people outside the corporation notice of them. The bylaws are regulations of a less permanent nature and are not on file in a public office. However, shareholders are presumed to know their contents and are bound by them. Bylaws provide general guides under which the business will be conducted, supplemented by resolutions of the board of directors and daily management decisions of the officers.

State law usually provides that bylaws may contain any provision for the regulation and management of the affairs of the corporation not inconsistent with law or with the Articles of Incorporation.

The bylaws spell out the rights, duties, and responsibilities of the shareholders, directors, and officers of the corporation. In the family corporation, the shareholders usually act as directors, officers, and employees of the corporation. It is important that the separate functions of each group be kept in mind so that the actions that are taken can be in the proper capacity.

Management—Division of Authority

The farm corporation has the same operating decisions to make as does the farm partnership, the landlord and tenant, or the single owner-operator. A corporate management system, however, handles such problems in a slightly different way than they are handled in the other types of business organizations.

There are three different management groups in a corporation. They are the shareholders, the directors, and the officers. Each group has the power to authorize certain things and perform certain acts in the operation of the corporation. Since the shareholders are usually also the directors and the officers in a farm corporation, the same people will be performing the functions of all three groups. However, it is important to know the separate functions of each group so that each person will act in the proper capacity.

The three management groups, in the order of their ultimate controlling power, are illustrated in Figure 15.1

Although state laws regarding the rights, duties, and responsibilities of each group vary, the following general principles are applicable to most states.

Shareholders.[9]   *Rights and Duties.*   Shareholders have the right to vote on questions before them, casting one vote on each question for each share of stock which they own. They have the right to direct the affairs of the corporation through directors elected by them.

In the election of directors, each shareholder is entitled to a number of votes equal to the number of shares owned. If cumulative voting is permitted by state law, this number is multiplied by the number of directors to be elected, and a shareholder may cast all votes for one director or distribute them among any number of directors. Shareholders also have the sole power to remove directors by a notice and hearing if there is sufficient cause to do so.

Shareholders transact all of their business at annual and special meetings. However, any action which may be taken there also

---

[9] For a general discussion of the director's rights and duties, *see* 5A CAVITCH, *supra* note, § § 108 *et seq.*

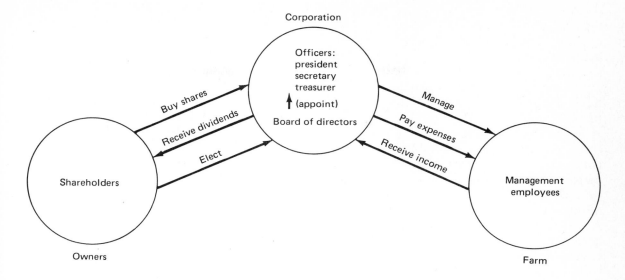

Corporation

Officers:
president
secretary
treasurer

↑ (appoint)

Board of directors

Buy shares

Receive dividends

Elect

Manage

Pay expenses

Receive income

Shareholders

Management
employees

Owners

Farm

Figure 15.1

may be taken without such meetings if all the shareholders give their written consent. Action by consent would be expected in a farm corporation where the shareholders are well acquainted and work closely in the business, or if one or more shareholders live a considerable distance from the farm business.

The power to make, alter, amend, or repeal the bylaws of the corporation may be given to the shareholders in the Articles of Incorporation. Otherwise, the directors have this power. Shareholders may amend the Articles of Incorporation if a resolution of amendment, adopted by the board of directors, is submitted to them and is passed by the required number of votes.

Meetings of shareholders must be in accordance with the bylaws. Unless state law, the Articles of Incorporation, or the bylaws require a greater vote to pass on a particular question, a majority vote of shareholders present is sufficient to approve any resolution which is properly before the shareholders.

A shareholder has the right to examine the books and records of the corporation for a "proper purpose." Almost any reasonable purpose is considered by law to be a proper purpose. The bylaws may state that the shareholders may examine the books at any time if it is in connection with the corporation business.

A shareholder has the right to sue in the name of the corporation to protect the corporation's interests. To do so, however, the shareholder must obtain from the board of directors a refusal to take legal action.

The shareholders of a corporation, by giving their unaminous written consent, may elect to voluntarily dissolve the corporation and wind up its affairs. When the president or vice president receives such written consent, the dissolution must be carried out according to law.

Liabilities. Since a corporation is a separate entity from its shareholders, the general rule is that a claim against the corporation is not a liability of the shareholders. If a shareholder has agreed with a creditor to personally be responsible for a corporate debt, however, that shareholder's personal assets are subject to the claim. Also, a person who has agreed to buy shares of the corporation for a certain price may be held liable for the unpaid balance of the purchase price.

A shareholder is not liable for injuries committed by agents or employees of the corporation unless that shareholder was personally responsible for or participated in the wrongful act.

Directors.[10] *Number, Term, Qualifications.* A director is considered an officer of the corporation and a "fiduciary" (one who occupies a position of trust and confidence), to the shareholders. A director is entrusted with the management of the business for the common benefit of each and every shareholder.

The number of directors to be elected at the first meeting of the shareholders is fixed by the Articles of Incorporation and remains the same at subsequent elections unless a different number is fixed by the bylaws. All directors are elected at each annual meeting of the shareholders and hold office for the following year.

If a vacancy occurs on the board of directors because of death, resignation, or other cause, a meeting of the shareholders may be held to fill the vacancy. Until the vacancy is filled, the remaining directors act as the full board. A director is free to resign at will, and a resignation is valid even if it is not accepted by the shareholders.

A director should not engage in business transactions which conflict with duties as a director of the corporation. If it is fair to the corporation, however, a director may enter into outside transactions, even to the extent of going into a business of the same nature as that of the corporation.

Powers and Duties—Meetings. The business and affairs of a corporation are managed by a board of directors. Courts have interpreted this to mean that an individual director has no authority as such, and that assent of a majority of the directors will not bind the corporation unless they act at a meeting as a "board."

A directors' meeting need not be formal or regularly called. If all directors are present, they may act as a board and bind the corporation. However, when advance notice of the meeting has been given in accordance with the bylaws, and a quorum is present at the meeting, a majority vote of the number present is sufficient to bind the corporation.

For example, the directors of a farm corporation having three directors may transact business at a meeting without giving notice of the meeting if all three are present. If all the directors are given proper notice, any two of them can act as a board, or if only the absent director had advance notice, the two directors present at the meeting can transact business. However, both directors would have to vote together on issues because one vote would constitute only one-half of the total vote present and not a majority.

The directors have a duty to meet often enough to know what the officers, agents, and fellow directors are doing and to keep the business in a sound condition. In a farm corporation, the directors will be working together as officers, agents, and employees in the business, and the frequency of meetings and the interest in the business should not present serious problems.

---

[10] For a general discussion of the director's rights and duties, *see* 6 CAVITCH, *supra* note 1, § § 126 *et seq.*

While the procedure that should be followed at meetings of directors is not defined by law, it is always best to take official minutes when the board is transacting business. Minutes provide a record of past decisions for the directors' use and give protection to persons dealing with the corporation. For example, if the board of directors decides that the president should purchase a tract of land or borrow money, a record of this in the official minutes will satisfy outside parties that the president has authority to do so. Except for keeping formal minutes of business decisions, the meetings may be conducted in an informal manner.

The directors are not entitled to a salary unless the bylaws so provide. There may be no real reason to provide compensation for the directors of a farm corporation since they are also the shareholders who gain from corporate profits and, in addition, may receive salaries as officers or other employees of the corporation.

The directors may elect to voluntarily dissolve the corporation, and if their resolution is adopted by a vote of the shareholders, the officers must carry out the dissolution.

Liabilities. In general, directors are not personally liable to the corporation to any greater extent than are the shareholders. However, they may be liable under special circumstances. A director may be held liable to the corporation for negligence in managing its affairs if the negligence causes loss to the corporation (for example, failure to perform a legal duty such as filing required reports with the state, or allowing another director to misappropriate corporate funds). A director is, of course, also liable to the corporation for intentional wrongs, such as fraud on the corporation. A director may also be liable if guilty of divided loyalty or of any other act in which the office is used as a means of personal gain at the expense of the corporation. Usually, a director is not liable for claims against the corporation unless personally bound by agreement.[11] If a director signs a promissory note on behalf of the corporation, the director will not be personally liable if authorized by a resolution of the board of directors to bind the corporation. However, if the director exceeds authority in executing the note in the corporate name, the director may be liable along with the corporation. Often a creditor will require that the directors bind themselves, as well as the corporation, before credit will be extended.

In summary, a director is personally liable for debts of the corporation:

1. When he or she agrees to become personally bound.
2. When he or she falsely leads the creditor to believe that the director intends to be personally liable.
3. When he or she attempts to bind the corporation in excess of authority.
4. When he or she misrepresents the financial condition of the corporation to persuade a third person to become its creditor.

---

[11] For example, in *Lowell Hoit and Company v. Detig*, 320 Ill. App. 179 (1943), plaintiff sought a recovery from the directors of a farmer's cooperative grain company, which operated an elevator, for conversion by the manager of grain stored in the company's elevator under a secret agreement with the manager.

The directors had no knowledge of the agreement or the conversion, and they could not have discovered these facts in the exercise of ordinary and reasonable supervision. The court held for the directors, noting that ordinarily directors are not personally liable for acts of omissions of officers or agents of a corporation, unless they took part in the wrong or failed to exercise ordinary care in preventing the act.

5. When he or she commits a wrongful act (or fails to act), causing physical or financial harm to an innocent person.

6. When he or she assents to a declaration of improper dividends.

ACTION BY DIRECTORS

BALDWIN v. CANFIELD
Supreme Court of Minnesota, 1879
26 Minn. 43

One King, the sole shareholder in the Minneapolis Agricultural and Mechanical Association, a corporation which had ceased active business, pledged part of his shares to a bank and part to Baldwin. He subsequently agreed in writing to sell the corporation's property to Canfield in consideration of $58,500 in market value of railroad bonds and notes of Canfield for $6500. King told Canfield that he owned all the shares in the corporation and he orally agreed to transfer these shares to Canfield. He then induced the directors, acting separately and without any meeting, to execute a deed which was signed as follows:

"The Minneapolis Agricultural and Mechanical
Association." [Seal.]

"By R.J. Mendenhall, Thomas Lowry, W.D. Washburn, C.G. Goodrich, G.F. Stevens, Wm. S. King, Levi Butler, W.W. Eastman, W.P. Westfall, Dorilus Morrison, Geo. A. Brackett, directors of said corporation."

Before delivering the deed King informed Canfield that the shares had been pledged but that the pledge would be redeemed with the bonds with which Canfield was to pay for the property. King subsequently delivered the deed, together with another deed executed in his own name but purporting to convey the corporate property, to Canfield, and the latter delivered the bonds and notes to King individually. The shares were never redeemed and Canfield forgot to demand them. Baldwin and the bank as pledgees of the shares sought to have the deeds cancelled as clouds on the corporation's title.

As conclusions of law, the court below finds as follows:

First. The purchase of all the stock of the Minneapolis Agricultural and Mechanical Association by King did not work a dissolution of the corporation.

Second. At the time of the conveyance by him to Canfield, King had not the legal title to the real estate purporting to be conveyed thereby, and he has never acquired the legal title thereto.

Third. At the time of the execution of the deed purporting to be executed by the association mentioned, the legal title to the real estate attempted to be thereby conveyed was in the Minneapolis Agricultural and Mechanical Association.

Fourth. Said deed was not the act and deed of said association, and did not convey to Canfield the legal title of the real estate purporting to be conveyed thereby.

This action was brought by Baldwin and the State National Bank of Minneapolis, as plaintiffs, against the Minneapolis Agricultural and Mechanical Association, and King and Canfield, as defendants. Canfield appeared and answered. Neither of the other defendants was served with process or appeared in the action.

The first, second and third of these conclusions of law are obviously right, and require no comment.

The fourth conclusion is called in question by the counsel for defendant Canfield, but we have no doubt of its correctness. As we have already seen, the court below finds that, by its articles of incorporation, the government of the Minneapolis Agricultural and Mechanical Association, and the management of its affairs, was vested in the board of directors. The legal effect of this was to invest the directors with such government and management *as a board*, and not otherwise. This is in accordance with the general rule that the governing body of a corporation, as such, are agents of the corporation only as a board, and not individually. Hence it follows that they have no authority to act, save when assembled at a board meeting. The separate action, individually, of the persons composing such governing body, is not the action of the constituted body of men clothed with corporate powers. In Vermont a somewhat different rule is allowed, as in the Bank of *Middlebury v. Rutland & Washington R. Co.*, 30 Vt. 159. In that case, and perhaps others in that state, it is held that directors may bind their corporation by acting separately, if this is their usual practice in transacting the corporate business. But we think that the general rule before mentioned is the more rational one, and it is supported by the great weight of authority. From the application of this rule to the facts of this case, it follows that the fourth conclusion of law, viz., that the deed purporting to be made by the association was not the act and deed of such association, and therefore did not convey the title to the premises in question to Canfield, is correct. The directors took no action as a board with reference to the sale of the premises or the execution of any deed thereof. So far as in any way binding the corporation is concerned their action in executing the deed was a nullity. They could not bind it by their separate and individual action. Hence it follows that the so-called deed is not only ineffectual as a conveyance of real property, but equally so as a contract to convey.

The finding that the two deeds, one purporting to run from the association to Canfield, the other from King to Canfield, are void and of no effect as against the plaintiffs calls for no remarks beyond what have been already made.

The finding that the two deeds mentioned are a cloud upon the title of the Minneapolis Agricultural and Mechanical Association to the real estate aforesaid is correct as respects the deed purporting to run from the association to Canfield. That deed purports on the face of it to be the deed of the association, and although, for reasons before assigned, it is not the deed of the association, that fact is not apparent upon its face. With regard to this deed, then, the court below properly adjudged it and its record to be void, as respected the plaintiffs.

With regard to the deed from King to Canfield, we see no ground upon which it can be said to cast a cloud upon the title of the association to the real estate mentioned. The title to the real estate was in the association.

[The court held that various additional points made in the defendant's brief were not well taken and that the judgment in favor of the plaintiffs should be modified with respect to the deed signed by King but affirmed as to the deed signed by the directors.]

Officers.[12]   *Qualifications, Election, Term.* Officers are elected annually by the board of directors or for a term stated in the bylaws. They may be removed by the board of directors if the board feels such action will serve the best interests of the corporation. Any special qualifications for an office should be in the bylaws. As pointed out earlier, officers in a farm corporation would usually be shareholders and directors.

In the operation of the business, the rules on conflicts of interest that apply to directors also apply to officers.

Powers and Duties.   The officers of a corporation are employed as its agents. The office itself confers no power to bind the corporation or to control its property. This power comes directly from the board of directors or is implied through custom and practice.

The president may sign contracts (including promissory notes) and perform other duties that are ordinarily part of the operation of the corporation's business. The president must have authority from the board of directors to enter into any unusual contracts, and the bylaws may require that approval of the board be obtained before certain other acts are done.

The vice president, unless the bylaws state otherwise, may act in any capacity where the president might act if the president is absent or when powers and duties have been delegated to the vice president.

The treasurer is in charge of receiving and paying out money in the operation of the business. The secretary is responsible for keeping minutes of meetings and for maintaining adequate records of business transactions. Both offices are frequently held by one person.

Liabilities.   Officers are generally no more liable to the corporation and to creditors for claims against the corporation than are directors and shareholders. They may, however, be liable both to the corporation and to creditors for fraud or other misconduct.

---

[12] For a general discussion of the officer's rights of duties, *see* 6 CAVITCH, *supra* note 1, §§ 128 *et seq.*

Table 15.1 Statutory Provisions in the Thirteen North Central States

	Illinois	Indiana	Iowa	Kansas	Kentucky	Michigan	Minnesota	Missouri	Nebraska	North Dakota*	Ohio	South Dakota	Wisconsin
Minimum number of incorporators	1	1	1	1	1	1	1	1	1	3	1	1	1
Minimum number of directors	1+	1+	1	1	1	1±	1+	1§	1+	3	1+	1	1
Must directors be residents of state?	No	No	No	No	No	No	No	No	No	No	No	One must be resident	No
Must directors be share holders?	No	No	No	No	No	No	No	No	No	No	No	No	No
Cumulative voting permitted?	Yes	Yes, if provided by articles	Yes, if provided by articles	Yes	Yes	Yes, provided by articles	Yes, unless denied by articles	Yes	Yes	Yes	Yes	Yes	Yes
Minimum paid in capital	$1000	$1000	None	None	None	None	$1000	None	None	$1000	$500	$1000	None
Perpetual life permitted?	Yes	Yes	Yes	Yes	Yes	Yes	Yes	Yes	Yes	Yes	Yes	Yes	Yes
Nonvoting stock permitted?	No	Yes	Yes	Yes	Yes	Yes	Yes	Yes	Yes	Yes	Yes	Yes	Yes

Source: "The Farm Corporation," North Central Regional Extension Publication No. 11.

*North Dakota law prohibits corporations from engaging in farming.

+If the corporation has only one shareholder.

±A provision in the articles of incorporation may provide that there shall be no board of directors if authority to manage is delegated to another group or individual.

§A corporation may have one or two directors if so stated in the articles of incorporation; otherwise it must have three or more.

15.3 LIABILITY CONSIDERATIONS

One of the general rules of corporate law is that the shareholders ordinarily are not personally liable for corporate obligations—neither contract nor tort. For example, if the corporation has debts in excess of its assets, the creditor could not look to the individual shareholders for payment of the corporate debts. An exception would be when they had individually obligated themselves to pay the debts of the corporation by co-signing notes or other debt instruments. This rule is in direct contrast to the partnership rule which makes the partners individually liable for all debts and obligations of the partnership. This rule has been suggested as one of the advantages of operating as a corporate entity and can be of advantage in some situations. However, lenders to family-owned corporations ordinarily require the shareholders to co-sign for corporate debts, thus defeating any claim of limited liability.

In the area of tort law, the fact that the corporate structure offers limited liability can make the structure attractive to families—particularly those with nonfamily corporate employees. In situations where an employee causes injury or property damage while working, the employer corporation might be held liable. This responsibility would not extend to the individual shareholders.

Often, the owners of family-owned corporations fail to observe the legal formalities of doing business in the corporate form. They may ignore the fact that the corporation is a separate legal entity and may fail to distinguish between personal activities and those of the corporation. In such cases, the shareholders run the risk of losing limited liability protection for corporate obligations. Courts have, in appropriate cases, disregarded the corporate form in order to prevent fraud or to achieve equity. This has been applied in cases where abuse of the corporate privilege is obvious, where the shareholders hold themselves out as being liable for corporate obligations, where the shareholders treat the corporate assets as their own and withdraw capital from the corporation at will, where the shareholders provide inadequate capitalization of the corporation, or in other situations where an obvious fraudulent or inequitable result would attain if the corporate form precluded personal liability.

PIERCING THE CORPORATE VEIL

DEWITT TRUCK BROKERS v. W. RAY FLEMMING FRUIT CO.
United States Court of Appeals, 4th Circuit, 1976
540 F.2d 681

Creditor brought action to impose individual liability on president of debtor corporation.

In this action on debt, the plaintiff seeks, by piercing the corporate veil under the law of South Carolina, to impose individual liability on the president of the indebted corporation. The District Court, making findings of fact which may be overturned only if clearly erroneous, pierced the corporate veil and imposed individual liability. The individual defendant appeals.

The corporation was, in practice at least, a close, one-man corporation from the very beginning. Its incorporators were the defendant Flemming, his wife and his attorney. It began in 1962 with a capitalization of 5,000 shares, issued for a consideration of one dollar each. In some manner which Flemming never made entirely clear, approximately 2,000 shares were retired. At the times involved here Flemming owned approximately 90% of the corporation's outstanding stock, according to his own testimony, though this was not verified by any stock records. Flemming was obscure on who the other stockholders were and how much stock these other stockholders owned, giving at different times conflicting statements as to who owned stock and how much. His testimony on who were the officers and directors was hardly more direct. He testified that the corporation did have one other director, Ed Bernstein, a resident of New York. It is significant, however, that, whether Bernstein was nominally a director or not, there were no corporate records of a real directors' meeting in all the years of the corporation's existence and Flemming conceded this to be true. Flemming countered this by testifying that Bernstein traveled a great deal and that his contacts with Bernstein were generally by telephone. The evidence indicates rather clearly that Bernstein was, "nothing more than [a] figurehead[s]," who had "attended no directors meeting," and even more crucial, never received any fee or reimbursement of expenses or salary of any kind from the corporation.

The District Court found, also, that the corporation never had a stockholders' meeting. This accorded with Flemming's own testimony when originally deposed. Later, it is true, he sought to disown this admission and produce minutes of five stockholders' meetings, which incidentally were identical in form. He would explain his earlier admission by saying he had misunderstood a simple question such as whether the corporation had ever had a stockholders meeting. The trial judge, who observed the witnesses and their demeanor on the stand, found the defendant's disavowal of his earlier testimony in this regard unconvincing and concluded that his earlier admission was correct. It is thus clear that corporate formalities, even rudimentary formalities, were not observed by the defendant.

Beyond the absence of any observance of corporate formalities is the purely personal matter in which the corporation was operated. No stockholder or officer of the corporation other than Flemming ever received any salary, dividend, or fee from the corporation, or, for that matter, apparently exercised any voice in its operation or decisions. In all the years of the corporation's existence, Flemming was the sole beneficiary of its operations and its continued existence was for his exclusive benefit. During these years he was receiving from $15,000 to $25,000 each year from a corporation, which, during most of the time, was showing no profit and apparently had no working capital. Moreover, the payments to Flemming were authorized under no resolution of the board of directors of the corporation, as recorded in any minutes of a board meeting. Actually, it would seem that Flemming's withdrawals varied with what could be taken out of the corporation at the moment: If this amount were $15,000, that was Flemming's withdrawal; if it were $25,000, that was his withdrawal.

To summarize: The District Court found, and there was evidence to sustain the findings that there was here a complete disregard of "corporate formalities" in the operation of the corporation, which functioned, not for the benefit of all stockholders, but only for the financial advantage of Flemming, who was the sole stockholder to receive one penny of profit from the corporation in the decade or more that it operated, and who made during that period all the corporate decisions and dominated the corporation's operations.

That the corporation was undercapitalized, if indeed it were not without any real capital, seems obvious. Its original stated "risk capital" had long since been reduced to approximately $3,000 by a reduction in the outstanding capital, or at least this would seem to be inferable from the record, and even this, it seems fair to conclude, had been seemingly exhausted by a long succession of years when the corporation operated at no profit. The inability of the corporation to pay a dividend is persuasive proof of this want of capital. In fact, the defendant Flemming makes no effort to refute the evidence of want of any capital reserves on the part of the corporation. It appears patent that the corporation was actually operating at all times involved here on someone else's capital. This conclusion follows from a consideration of the manner in which Flemming operated in the name of the corporation during the year when plaintiff's indebtedness was incurred.

The corporation was engaged in the business of a commission agent, selling fruit produce for the account of growers of farm products such as peaches and watermelons in the Edgefield, South Carolina, area. It never purported to own such products; to repeat, it (always acting through Flemming) sold the products as agent for the growers. Under the arrangement with the growers, it was to remit to the grower the full sale price, less any transportation costs incurred in transporting the products from the growers' farm or warehouse to the purchaser and its sales commission. An integral part of these collections was, as stated, represented by the plaintiff's transportation charges. Accordingly, during the period involved here, the corporation had as operating funds seemingly only its commissions and the amount of the plaintiff's transportation charges, for which the corporation had claimed credit in its settlement with its growers. At the time, however, Flemming was withdrawing funds from the corporation at the rate of at least $15,000 per year, and doing this, even though he must have known that the corporation could only do this by withholding payment of the transportation charges due the plaintiff, which in the accounting with the growers Flemming represented had been paid the plaintiff. And, it is of some interest that the amount due the plaintiff for transportation costs was approximately the same as the $15,000 minimum annual salary the defendant testified he was paid by the corporation. Were the opinion of the District Court herein to be reversed, Flemming would be permitted to retain substantial sums from the operations of the corporation without having any real capital in the undertaking, risking nothing of his own and using as operating capital what he had collected as due the plaintiff. Certainly, equity and fundamental justice support individual liability of Flemming for plaintiff's charges, payment for which he asserted in his accounting with the growers that he had paid and for which he took credit on such accounting. This case patently presents a blending of the very factors which courts have regarded as justifying a disregard of the corporate entity in furtherance of basic and fundamental fairness.

Finally, it should not be overlooked that at some point during the period when this indebtedness was being incurred—whether at the beginning or at a short time later is not clear in the record—the plaintiff became concerned about former delays in receipt of payment for its charges and, to allay that concern, Flemming stated to the plaintiff, according to the latter's testimony as credited by the District Court, that "he (i.e., Flemming) would take care of [the charges] personally, if the corporation failed to do so...." On this assurance, the plaintiff contended that it continued to haul for the defendant. The existence of this promise by Flemming is not disputed. Flemming simply would absolve himself of any obligation thereunder because the plaintiff has sued him individually instead of waiting patiently for the defendant to pay it at the latter's pleasure, if ever—a rather lame excuse since it was obvious that a legal action was the only recourse the plaintiff had to make Flemming abide by his promise. This assurance was given for the obvious purpose of promoting the individual advantage of Flemming. This follows because the only person who could profit from the continued operation of the corporation was Flemming. When one, who is the sole beneficiary of a corporation's operations and who dominates it, as did Flemming in this case, induces a creditor to extend credit to the corporation on such an assurance as given here, that fact has been considered by many authorities sufficient basis for piercing the corporate veil. The only argument against this view is bottomed on the statute of frauds. But reliance on such statute is often regarded as without merit in a case where the promise or assurance is given "at the time or before the debt is created," for in that case the promise is original and without the statute. A number of courts, including South Carolina, however, have gone further and have held that, where the promisor owns substantially all the stock of the corporation and seeks by his promise to serve his personal pecuniary advantage, the question whether such promise is "within the statute of frauds" is a fact question to be resolved by the trial court and this is true whether the promise was made before the debt was incurred or during the time it was being incurred.

For the reasons stated, we conclude that the findings of the District Court herein are not clearly erroneous and the judgment of the District Court is affirmed.

15.4 USE OF THE CORPORATION IN ESTATE PLANNING

Continued attention has been directed to the corporation as a device to assist in meeting family estate planning objectives. One major reason for the attraction of using the corporate form is to provide a vehicle for making gifts. By using the corporate form, one can convert real property and personal property into shares of stock which then can be gifted more conveniently. Gifts of corporate shares also allow the transfer of a large part of the estate while maintaining the economic unit intact. In fact, a large portion of the estate can be transferred while control is maintained by those with a majority interest in the corporation. One advantage of gifting minority interests is that they may be discounted in value because of the lack of marketability of such stock. Reference is made to the table on page 614 as a transfer plan for transfers of stock by gift over a period of time.

Single or Multiple Classes of Stock

The simple capital structure permits the transfer of assets to the corporation in exchange for stock—all of one type—with each shareholder entitled to share in corporate income based on the number of shares held.

This poses problems for some families because the income generated by the business may be barely adequate to pay expenses—including salaries to shareholder-employees. Thus, there may be little or no income left for distribution to the nonactive shareholders. For example, a retired widow who holds a substantial—but not a majority—interest in a business might find herself without income from the stock if the business does not generate sufficient income to pay all operating expenses and have any

left for dividends. One solution in such cases is to hold some property outside the corporation which could then be leased to the corporation, thus providing income to owners of such property. A second solution in such cases is to make sure retired individuals retain voting control of the business so that dividends can be declared if sufficient income is generated.

Another problem faced by some family corporations involves the matter of control. If gifts are made indiscriminantly to many family members—children, grandchildren, etc.- the situation may evolve where the business is owned by numerous individuals with no one group in control. The obvious method of avoiding this situation is to transfer shares in such a way that those active in the business gain eventual control. This naturally poses some problems for the off-farm heirs, who may find themselves holding shares of stock that generate no income but for which there is no market since they represent a minority interest in a family-owned business. Buy-sell agreements can alleviate some of these problems.

Another option that can alleviate some of the on-farm control and off-farm income problems is the use of debt securities as a part of the corporate capitalization. The usual debt security used in corporate capitalization is a debenture. A *debenture* is a debt instrument, which can be registered and which serves as evidence of an unsecured corporate obligation. At the time of corporate formation, some of those who transfer property to the corporation can receive debentures rather than shares of stock. The debenture provides for repayment at a set time with a set rate of interest. This can serve as a source of income to off-farm heirs or to retired owners, even if they hold minority interests. At the same time, control is assured to on-farm heirs because they hold voting stock. This technique can also provide a form of property—the debenture—which can be gifted easily and will not disrupt business operations. In addition, it serves as a "cap" on the estate of the holder. Assets in the corporation may increase in value—particularly if land is included in the corporation—whereas the fixed principal debt security is of a predetermined value which will not change at a later date. It is important that any such instruments be carefully drafted and carefully used so that they will be treated as loans rather than stock for income tax purposes.[13]

Another method, avaiable in most states, is to capitalize the corporation with two classes of stock—common and preferred. If these two classes are used in combination with both voting and nonvoting stock, considerable flexibility exists in providing control to some heirs and assuring income to others or to family members who retire. For example, common voting stock could be transferred to on-farm heirs. If the business generates dividends, the holders of preferred stock would be assured of receiving some income. Preferred stock usually carries not only a dividend preference but also liquidation preferences and may be subject to redemption at a fixed price. While considerable flexibility exists when multiple classes of stock are used, valuation questions and income tax problems may arise unless the capitalization is carefully planned and implemented.

Stock Transfer Restrictions/ Buy-Sell Agreements

Agreements between the shareholders or between the shareholders and the corporation may serve to assure that outsiders will not obtain corporate stock against the wishes of the other shareholders and that business continuity can be assured.

The Articles of Incorporation, the by-laws, or a separate agreement of the shareholders may contain restrictions on stock transfer. Such provisions usually restrict the transfer of stock to any outsiders unless first offered for sale to the remaining shareholders or perhaps to the corporation itself (stock redemption). They may provide for optional or mandatory purchase if the shareholder offers the stock for sale or upon the death of any shareholder.

Separate agreements are frequently used with an endorsement on stock certificates which indicates that the stock is subject to transfer restrictions. The separate agreement, often in the form of buy-sell agreements, can be cross-purchase agreements between the shareholders or stock redemption agreements with the corporation. In the *cross-purchase agreement* each shareholder agrees to offer stock to the other shareholders on a pro rata basis. In the *stock redemption agreement* the corporation, in effect, agrees to buy back any stock offered for sale or available upon the death of any stockholder.

Buy-sell agreements can serve as a vehicle for assuring business continuity by providing that upon the death of any shareholder, that person's interest in the corporation will be a liquid asset in the estate. Upon a shareholder's death, the remaining shareholders have either an optional right or a mandatory obligation to purchase the deceased shareholder's stock. The agreement can provide for set items including price, interest rate, payment period, etc., or can include a formula for determining price.

Similar agreements can be arranged for the retirement of any shareholder from active involvement in the business. The remaining shareholders may have the option (or have a mandatory obligation) of

---

[13] *See* INT. REV. CODE § 385; Scriptomatic Inc. v. United States, 397 F. Supp. 753 (E.D. Pa. 1975).

purchasing the retired owner's shares. This can provide a source of retirement income for the retired shareholder, but at the same time serve as a "cap" on estate value because the contract right has a set value as opposed to the fluctuating value of corporate stock.

The buy-sell agreement may actually provide a means of establishing estate values for federal estate tax purposes at death. Any stock bound by a restriction—such as mandatory transfer for a set price—may predetermine the stock value for estate tax purposes if the agreement is in strict compliance with Internal Revenue Service regulations.[14]

Funding for buy-sell agreements is frequently provided by the use of life insurance. In a cross-purchase plan, each shareholder owns a policy on the life of every other shareholder. If a stock redemption plan is used, the corporation itself owns policies on each shareholder. Upon death, the proceeds are available to carry out the provisions of the agreement. If life insurance is not available—for example, upon retirement or voluntary sale of shares—provisions for installment payments may be an attractive alternative. Naturally, if shareholders have outside sources of funds for use in carrying out buy-sell agreements, no special provisions are necessary.

15.5 EMPLOYEE BENEFITS, RETIREMENT PLANS, AND SOCIAL SECURITY

Employee Benefits

Various benefits may result from the fact that shareholders may become employees of the corporation rather than self-employed individuals or partners. Health and accident plans can be developed which can reimburse employees for medical expenses incurred. The reimbursement may serve as an income tax deduction to the corporation and may be excluded from income of the employee if properly designed.[15]

Group life insurance programs may also serve as a fringe benefit to all employees—including shareholder-employees. Premium payments may be deductible to the corporation and not taxable to employees, except for premiums on coverage in excess of $50,000.[16]

Most states require a minimum of ten employees in order to qualify for a group plan,[17] but "baby-group" plans are developed by some employers to achieve tax deductibility and other favored treatment. Internal Revenue Service requirements must be met to qualify for either type of group plan.[18]

A death benefit of up to $5000 may be paid to the surviving spouse or children of an employee which is not only free of income tax to the recipient but is deductible to the corporation.[19]

Retirement Plans

Various types of retirement programs may be developed for employees of a corporation which may result in more tax savings and better benefits than are found in programs available to self-employed individuals. Farm corporations may provide a defined benefit (pension) plan, which requires a fixed contribution each year, or a

---

[14] *See* Rev. Rul. 67-54, 1967-1 C.B. 269 and Rev. Rul. 59-60.

[15] *See* Nathan Epstein, T.C. Memo 1972-53; American Foundary v. Commissioner, 76-1 U.S.T.C. 9401 (9th Cir. 1976), Rev. Rul. 71-588, 1971-2 C.B. 91.

[16] INT. REV. CODE § 79; Treas. Reg. 1.61-2 (d) (2) (1957).

[17] *See* KANS. STAT. ANN. § 40-433 (1) (c) (Supp. 1975).

[18] Treas. Reg. 1.79-1 (b) (1972).

[19] INT. REV. CODE § 101 (b); Treas. Reg. 1.101-2.

defined contribution (profit-sharing) plan, which requires that a share of profit be set aside each year in the retirement fund. If these plans are properly designed, the corporation may claim as a current income tax deduction any payments to the plan on behalf of the employee. The employee is taxed on income after retirement.[20]

In addition to the usual retirement programs, farm corporations may establish employee stock ownership plans (ESOP) in which shares of stock are set aside for the employee. Also, salary continuation programs may be available for payments to the employee during disability or retirement or to survivors of the employee following the employee's death.[21]

Social Security

It is possible that an employee of a corporation could eventually receive higher social security benefits than from self employment assuming salary is at a higher level than self employment income. How-
ever, the cost of social security increases in the corporate form because both an employer's share and employee's share must be contributed to the social security system. The combined rate of the employer's plus employee's required contribution is higher than for a self-employed individual. The current rates for self-employment tax and the Federal Insurance Contributions Act (FICA) taxes are set by statute. The taxable wage base is subject to change based on changes in benefits which adjust with the Consumer Price Index. Actual rates are published annually.[22] Projected bases along with statutory rates are shown in Table 15.2.

15.6 TAXATION OF CORPORATIONS

The farm corporation is a separate taxpayer for most income tax purposes. When it is a family-owned corporation, it may have the option of selecting between two methods of taxation.

Table 15.2 Self-Employment and Social Security Tax—Projected Wage Base and Statutory Rates

Year	Projected Wage Base, $	Self-Employed Tax Rate, %	Combined Employer-Employee FICA Rate, %
1981	29,700	9.30	13.30
1982	32,100	9.35	13.40
1983	35,100	9.35	13.40
1984	37,800	9.35	13.40
1985	40,200	9.90	14.10
1986	42,300	10.00	14.30
1987	44,700	10.00	14.30
1988	44,700	10.10	14.30
1989	44,700	10.00	14.30
After 1989	44,700	10.75	15.30

[20] See Rev. Rul. 63-108, 196301 C.B. 87 and Rev. Rul. 72-4, 1972-1 C.B. 105.

[21] See Rev. Rul. 77-25, 1977-4 C.B. 10.
[22] See INT. REV. CODE §§1402 and 3101; Treas. Reg. § 31.3121 (a)(1) to 1 (a)(viii).

Subchapter C—Regular Corporation

The regular corporation is taxed under provisions of Subchapter C of the Internal Revenue Code. As a separate taxpayer, it reports income and claims deductions much the same as any other business taxpayer. The corporation reports its own gains and losses.

The federal income tax rates, payable on net taxable income, for 1979 and thereafter are 17 percent on the first $25,000 of taxable income, 20 percent on the second $25,000 of income, 30 percent on the third $25,000 of taxable income, 40 percent on the next $25,000 and 46 percent on all taxable income above $100,000. These tax rates have increased the interest in the farm corporation as a means of possible tax reduction.

The farm corporation may deduct the costs of doing business, such as salaries, lease payment, and interest payments, including reasonable payments to shareholders.[23]

Salaries must be reasonable and must be for work actually performed. If it is determined that distribution in the form of salaries is unreasonable or is for work not performed, the salaries will be classified as "constructive dividends" and taxed to the shareholder as dividends. The corporation, in turn, would lose the deduction.

One of the problems with corporate operation is the potential for double taxation when the corporation is successful. Income in excess of all deductions can be distributed as dividends to the shareholders. Dividends after tax distributions are nondeductible to the corporation. To the taxpayer, they are taxable income except for a limited exclusion. Thus, double taxation can result if distributions are made in the form of dividends or if salaries are classified as "constructive dividends."

Attempts are sometimes made to avoid the impact of double taxation by retaining profits in the corporation. Substantial accumulations of earnings and profits can be made annually. All corporations can accumulate up to $150,000 without penalty, but accumulations in excess of this amount may be subject to an accumulated earnings tax.[24] The purpose of the tax is to prevent the use of the corporation for tax avoidance on earnings and profits.

Even above the substantial allowable accumulation, additional amounts may be retained if amounts so retained can be justified by the reasonable needs of the business.[25]

Subchapter S—Tax Option Corporation

An additional option for corporate taxation is available for qualifying corporations if a proper election is filed indicating the consent of the shareholders to be so taxed. This option, under Subchapter S of the Internal Revenue Code, allows the corporation to be taxed substantially like a partnership.

The corporation pays salaries, interest, rent, and other costs of doing business as usual. The corporation then passes through to individual shareholders, in proportion to their shares, their pro rata share of undistributed taxable income. All shareholders report their share of such income on their individual tax returns.[26] If the corporation has long-term capital gains or operating losses, these too are passed through to the individual shareholders.[27]

In order to qualify for tax-option status, the corporation should have the following

---

[23] INT. REV. CODE §§ 162, 163.
[24] INT. REV. CODE §§ 531–537.

[25] Treas. Reg. 1.537-2 (b) (1959).
[26] INT. REV. CODE § 1373.
[27] INT. REV. CODE §§ 1374, 1375.

characteristics: (1) It must be a small business corporation with fifteen or fewer shareholders. For purposes of determining qualifications, husbands and wives who own shares jointly count as one shareholder. (2) All shareholders must be individuals (or estates of individuals). A corporation which has shares owned by another corporation, a partnership, or a trust does not qualify. (3) The corporation cannot have more than one class of stock outstanding. (4) The corporation's stock cannot be held by non-resident aliens. (5) At least 80 percent of the corporation's gross income must be from actual operation of the business. In other words, no more than 20 percent of the gross receipts of the corporation can come from rents, royalties, dividends, interest, annuities, and sales or exchanges of stock or securities.

To make the election, a corporation must submit an appropriate filing to the Internal Revenue Service reflecting the consent of all shareholders to the election. The election continues in force until terminated by the affirmative refusal of a shareholder to consent to the election. A corporation that has elected to be taxed under Subchapter C taxation can revoke the election in any year if the revocation is made at the beginning of the tax year. However, once the election is terminated a new election cannot be made for 5 years. Termination of the election can be involuntary if the corporation fails to meet the qualifications. [28]

TERMINATION OF TAX-OPTION STATUS

KENNEDY v. COMMISSIONER
U.S. Tax Court, 1974
1974 T.C. Memo 149

All the petitioners were shareholders of Freeport Development Company (hereinafter Freeport) during 1965 through 1968.

Freeport was incorporated on December 14, 1954, and commenced operations during 1955. On October 28, 1955, it acquired a 257–acre ranch near Sacramento, California. At the time of acquisition, the ranch was farmed by petitioner Joseph Borges (hereinafter Borges) under an existing sharecrop lease with its former owners.

Pursuant to an agreement between Borges, as lessee, and Freeport, Borges was to be given $5,000 worth of Freeport stock, when issued, for either canceling or orally promising to cancel the lease. In August 1960, Borges became a shareholder in Freeport.

In October 1960, Borges and Freeport entered into a new lease of the ranch for a period of seven years commencing January 1, 1961, and ending December 31, 1967. Under the terms of the lease, Borges, as lessee, continued to farm the land and pay Freeport specified percentages of various crops

[28] INT. REV. CODE §§ 1371, 1372.

as rental for the ranch. As lessee, he agreed to occupy, till, and cultivate the property in a good and farmer-like manner, and to keep and maintain the fences and buildings in as good condition as they were at the date of the lease, reasonable wear and tear and damage by the elements excepted.

In September 1963, at the suggestion of Freeport's accountants, a meeting of the shareholders was held to consider the advisability of liquidating the corporation and transferring its property to the shareholders or electing to do business "as a Sub-Chapter S 'tax option' Corporation."

On November 7, 1963, the attorney for the corporation met with Borges and discussed with him the cancellation of his lease on the ranch and the possibility of Freeport's electing to become a subchapter S corporation. On December 3, 1963, Borges was elected president of Freeport, and he held that position throughout the period in controversy.

Freeport timely elected to be treated as a small business corporation for its fiscal years 1965 through 1968. Borges continued to farm Freeport's property after the subchapter S election was made making percentage payments to Freeport substantially equivalent in amount to the payments that would be made under a sharecrop lease. He received no salary; his ownly remuneration was his share of the crop. Freeport paid none of the expenses of growing the crops, such as furnishing seed, fertilizer and labor. These expenses were borne solely by Borges. The Federal income tax returns filed on behalf of Freeport for its fiscal years 1965 through 1968 disclose no expenditures directly related to farming activities and show as income only its share of net crop proceeds.

During its fiscal years ending October 31, 1965, through October 31, 1968, Freeport had gross receipts, derived from farming activities as follows:

| 1965 | $5,370 | 1967 | 261 |
| 1966 | 6,061 | 1968 | 9,267 |

It had no other gross receipts during these years except the $14,508.20 received in its fiscal year ending October 31, 1965, from the sale of topsoil, which it reported as ordinary income.

In his statutory notices to petitioners, respondent determined that Freeport's passive investment income exceeded 20 percent of its gross income for its fiscal years ending October 31, 1965 through 1968, thereby terminating its election to be treated as a subchapter S corporation. Accordingly, the losses claimed by petitioners for these years from Freeport were disallowed.

Opinion

An election by a corporation to be treated as a subchapter S corporation terminates if, in any taxable year, more than 20 percent of its gross receipts constitutes passive investment income. The term "passive investment income" includes gross receipts derived from "rents" or "royalties."

Respondent maintains that Freeport's share of the crops grown on its land was rent and that its recipts from the topsoil sales were royalties. Since Freeport had no gross receipts of any other kind, respondent urges that Freeport's election of subchapter S status terminated in the taxable year ending October 31, 1965, and was, therefore, ineffective for all subsequent years in controversy. Petitioners deny that either the sharecrop income or the topsoil sales proceeds were passive investment income and maintain that the subchapter S election did not terminate.

We are compelled to hold for respondent.

The owner of farmland and the operator of the farm, are, of course, free to work out any kind of contract they choose for the management of the farm. In the instant case, the oral contract between Freeport and Borges called for a sharing of the proceeds of the crops grown on Freeport's land. Such a crop-sharing arrangement may create a landlord-tenant relationship, an employer-employee relationship, a partnership, or a joint venture. The kind of relationship which is created depends upon the terms of the contract between the parties and the manner in which it is carried out, and, within any one such type of relationship, the terms of the agreement may vary widely. In deciding what kind of relationship is created, the facts of the case, therefore, must be examined with great care.

As we interpret petitioners' position, they contend that beginning with Freeport's election to become a subchapter S corporation, the farm lease with Borges was cancelled and he became Freeport's employee in managing the farm's operation. Borges had farmed the land as a tenant for many years, and this relationship was allegedly a new one. While the record shows that the board of directors was informed that the corporation would be required to engage actively in the conduct of the farm in order to qualify for subchapter S status, we do not think the corporation actually did so.

An examination of Freeport's income tax returns for its taxable years ending October 31, 1965, 1966, 1967, and 1968 does not reflect that Freeport operated the 257-acre farm. The return for the fiscal year ended in 1965, for example, shows gross receipts of $5,370, evidently from crop shares, and other income of $14,508 from the sale of topsoil. The only deductions claimed were taxes of $12,335, depreciation of $1,628, and legal, auditing, insurance, and engineering fees totaling $2,037. The return reflects no expenditures by Freeport for labor, seed, fertilizer, planting, cultivation, insecticides, harvesting, or other items normally incurred by a farm growing the crops cultivated on the farm—corn, milo, safflower, barley, wheat, sugar beets, and tomatoes.

The record shows that it was Borges who paid all the expenses, bought the seed, hired the labor, supervised the cultivation, harvested the crops, and arranged to have a share of the crops' proceeds paid to Freeport. If Borges had been an employee operating the farm for the corporation, Freeport would have reported the total amount realized on the sale of the crops, not just its net share, and would have deducted the expenses. But Borges received all the crop income, paid Freeport its share, and paid the expenses as he did while he was concededly a tenant and Freeport his landlord.

Petitioners maintain that Borges was elected president of Freeport when the subchapter S election was made and that all his subsequent activities in managing the farm were performed on behalf of the corporation. It may not be possible to neatly segregate all of Borges' activities as share-crop-tenant from those activities which he carried on as a director and president of Freeport. However, he received no salary from Freeport. His only earnings from running the farm were his share of the crops. Since he paid all the expenses and received only a share of the crops, he bore virtually all the risk of loss in case of a crop failure. This risk-taking is characteristic of a tenant-entrepreneur rather than an employee. It is characteristic of a sharecrop arrangement rather than an employment arrangement (where the corpora-tion ordinarily would have borne all the expenses) or a joint venture (where the expenses would have been shared).

As we view the evidence, when the subchapter S election was made, the relationship between Freeport and Borges was not converted to that of an employer-employee. Freeport continued to be a landlord, and the crop shares which it received continued to represent rent. The minutes of the annual meetings of Freeport's board of directors reflect that a general report was made by the officers, including Borges, on the activities of the corpora-tion and the board ratified these acts. However, such formalities are not sufficient to show that a new relationship was created. Nor has petitioner shown that Freeport was actively engaged in the conduct of the farming business. There is no showing that the corporation participated to any material degree in the operation of the farm; it made on management deci-sions, furnished no supplies or services, and paid none of the farm expenses.

Petitioners next argue that a landlord-tenant relationship involves an interest in land and a contract effectuating such a relationship will not be implied "where the acts and conduct of the parties negate its existence." We do not question the correctness of this statement of the law. Nor do we intend to hold that a landlord-tenant relationship is implied from the facts in this case. Rather, we hold that the facts here show that such a relationship was created by the agreement and conduct of the parties—Freeport's fur-nishing nothing except the use of the land and receiving a crop share and Borges' furnishing all the management, labor supplies, etc., and receiving all the proceeds of the crops not turned over to Freeport, on substantially the same terms and in the same manner as during the period when a landlord-tenant relationship admittedly existed. A farm operator and a landowner cannot create a landlord-tenant relationship and then avoid the consequences of that relationship by calling it something else.

Having concluded that the income from the farm was rent, we need not make a decision as to whether the proceeds from the sale of topsoil consti-tuted royalties. The parties have agreed that if either the share-crop proceeds or the topsoil sale proceeds were passive investment income, the corporation is disqualified from subchapter S status.

To reflect the foregoing,

Decision will be entered for the respondent.

Tax Effect of Incorporation

Incorporation can normally be made as a "tax-free" exchange.[29] For a tax-free exchange to be successfully achieved, property must be transferred to the corporation solely in exchange for stock or securities of the corporation. In addition, those who transfer property to the corporation must be in control of the corporation immediately after the exchange. "Control" means that those who transfer property to the corporation must end up with at least 80 percent of the combined voting power and with at least 80 percent of the total number of shares of all other classes of stock.

Questions concerning the income tax basis of both the shareholders and the corporation sometimes arise at the time the shareholders wish to sell shares of stock or at the time the corporation wishes to sell property transferred to it in exchange for stock or securities.

The basis of stock in the hands of the shareholders is equal to the basis of the shareholders in any property transferred to the corporation if a tax-free exchange was successfully accomplished. The basis would be adjusted for any boot received in the exchange and for any gain recognized by the taxpayer in the exchange.[30]

The tax basis of the corporation in property received in exchange for stock or securities is the transferor's basis plus gain recognized, if any, to the transferor. The old basis is preserved for each asset transferred to the corporation.[31]

Tax Problems at Dissolution

Dissolution of a corporation can ordinarily occur by written consent of all shareholders or by approval of the board of directors plus a majority vote of shareholders. When a corporation is dissolved, the creditors have first priority on corporate assets and the shareholders then share in the distribution of remaining assets in proportion to each shareholder's interest in the corporation.

The actual procedure for dissolution is detailed in state statutes and varies from state to state.[32] Once dissolution is authorized, the appropriate state official is notified and the corporation ceases business operations. Liquidation of assets, after payment of creditors, may then follow.

The income tax consequences of dissolution vary, depending on the procedure chosen. Three options exist for handling of gains or losses. If properly planned, the dissolution may often be accomplished without a severe tax problem for the shareholders. This is particularly true if a complete liquidation and distribution of the assets is planned.[33] Generally, any cash and property received by the shareholders in excess of their tax basis results in taxable gain to the shareholders—usually at capital gain rates. Under available options, some assets may be received without the recognition of gain if undistributed earnings of the corporation are treated as ordinary income.[34]

---

[29] INT. REV. CODE § 351.
[30] INT. REV. CODE § 358.
[31] INT. REV. CODE § 362.

[32] See, e.g., KAN. STAT. ANN. §§ 17-6801 et seq.
[33] INT. REV. CODE §§ 331, 333, and 337.
[34] Id.

If improperly planned, a dissolution can result in unexpected tax problems for the shareholders. Each shareholder will likely have some gain to report if the value of corporate property exceeds the shareholder's income tax basis for the stock. If the corporation holds assets that have substantially appreciated in value—such as land—and the shareholders receive such assets upon dissolution, the gain may be substantial. A high tax liability could result, even though the shareholders are, in a sense, getting back their "own" property.

For example, assume a family incorporates an existing farm business and transfers substantially all assets—including land--to the corporation in exhange for stock. If after a number of years the corporation is dissolved and the shareholders receive the same land upon distribution of corporate assets, gain results if the corporate assets have appreciated in value. The shareholders may have a tax liability as a result of this distribution. Under some circumstances, distributions may even be treated as ordinary income. An additional pitfall for the corporation can result if assets are to be sold and the proceeds distributed to shareholders. Unless the proper method of dissolution is selected, the *corporation itself* may have a tax liability in addition to that of the shareholders.

Because of the possible tax pitfalls at dissolution, the choice of the option for handling gains or losses that best fits a particular corporation and its shareholders is crucial.

STUDY QUESTIONS

1. What are some of the potential advantages of use of the corporate structure in the farm business?

2. Assume X and Y own a business incorporated under state law. Suppose X causes injury to another person while acting in the ordinary course of business and on behalf of the corporation. Who can the injured person hold responsible for the injury?

3. If a corporation obtains a loan and the shareholders *do not* co-sign for the debt, who can be held responsible for the debt?

4. Distinguish between the functions of shareholders, directors, and officers in the corporation.

5. Under what circumstances may the shareholders of a corporation be held responsible for obligations incurred in the corporate name under the theory of "piercing the corporate veil"?

6. How is the corporation used as an estate planning tool?

7. Who is responsbile for payment of income taxes of a regular (Subchapter C) corporation?

8. If a regular (Subchapter C) corporation generates income in the amount of $40,000 above all business deductions, what is the amount of tax due under current corporate tax rates?

9. Barney Dore and his wife Housey have four children—Erpen, Cloise, Schlam, and Locket.

The Dores operated their farm as a partnership for a number of years, but incorporated the business in 1975 under the law of their state. The corporation was organized with 1000 shares of common stock. Barney and Housey each own 300 shares and each child owns 100 shares. All six are employees on the farm and have no other income. The farm income last year, after payment of all expenses, was $100,000. All of this was generated by operation of the various enterprises on the farm.

Will this corporation qualify for Subchapter S (tax-option) taxation? Why or why not?

How will the income tax on the $100,000 income be determined if the corporation elects Subchapter S taxation? (Assume it qualifies no matter what your answer is in the question above.)

10. Under what circumstances may a corporation be formed as a "tax-free" exchange?

16

Agricultural Cooperatives and Non-Profit Corporations

The American farmer has achieved much through organization. Many farm organizations, ranging from social and educational ones to those buying, selling, or performing other business services, are not formally organized and exist as unincorporated associations or societies. But, with growth and an enlargement of activities, such informal organizations find it to their advantage to incorporate. Generally, incorporation takes one of two forms—either that of a not-for-profit corporation or that of an agricultural cooperative. Associations organized to buy, sell, or render a service for remuneration are generally organized as cooperatives. For example, in the field of marketing, farmers have made extensive use of agricultural cooperatives. Such organizations afford farmers an opportunity to pool their efforts and deal with other individuals and corporations more effectively, at the same time keeping their private business interests separated from those of their organization. Associations to render an educational, social, or some other kind of service are generally organized as not-for-profit corporations. Examples of the latter are breed associations, local units of farm organizations, fair associations, and 4-H or other camps established as continuing enterprises.

16.1 AGRICULTURAL COOPERATIVES AND ANTITRUST LAWS

Two kinds of corporations predominate in agriculture—the nonprofit corporation, used generally for the organization of agricultural societies and bodies with educational objectives, and the agricultural cooperative association, organized to engage in selling, buying, and furnishing commercial services to farmers. Corporations of both kinds are subject to extensive legislative regulation. State laws outline the organizational procedure and functions of these two general types of agricultural corporations.

Cooperatives are essentially nonprofit enterprises operating on a cost basis, with benefits shared by all members as users of the cooperative. Control is democratic—often one person, one vote. Most are organized under state corporation laws designed specifically for agricultural cooperative operations.

Before the state and the federal government passed legislation expressly providing for and encouraging cooperative marketing organizations, these organizations were generally held to be in restraint of trade. They were attacked as monopolies, as violations of the Clayton Act,[1] as conspiracies under criminal statutes, and as violative of liberty and property rights.[2]

That the courts have caught the significance and importance of agricultural cooperative legislation is apparent from the language used in many cases. For example, in *Northern Wisconsin Cooperative Tobacco Pool v. Bekkedel*, the court said,

This legislation providing for the organization of cooperative associations, manifests a clear purpose on the part of the legislature, not only to authorize, but to

encourage cooperative effort. This legislation...being enacted subsequent to our general anti-trust statute, must be considered as modifying the scope of the former. The validity of cooperative marketing contracts, so far as they may constitute a restraint of trade is not to be tested by its provisions.[3]

In addition to state cooperative statutes, federal legislation also encouraged the formation of agricultural cooperatives. For example, Sec. 6 of the Clayton Act provided a limited exemption from antitrust laws for qualified agricultural cooperatives.[4] The Capper-Volstead Act of 1922 authorized associations of producers of agricultural products.[5] Associations operating on a one person–one vote principle for the mutual benefit of the members, can remain exempt if they do not deal in products of nonmembers in amounts greater in value than the same products handled for members.

Special Antitrust Problems[6]

The cooperative exemption from the antitrust laws is a limited one. Cooperatives which engage in coercive conduct such as boycotts or discriminatory pricing to maintain or enlarge their market share, or which use their power to deny their competitors access to a market will not receive

---

[1] The Clayton Act (15 U.S.C. § 15 *et seq.*) is reviewed in 5A CAVITCH, BUSINESS ORGANIZATIONS § 150B.01 *et seq.*

[2] Many such cases were decided prior to the enactment of cooperative statutes by the states involved. *See* citations in LEGAL PHASES OF FARMER COOPERATIVES PART 3, ANTITRUST LAWS, FCS Information 100 (May 1976).

[3] 182 Wis. 571, 197 N.W. 936 (1923).

[4] *Supra* note 1.

[5] 7 U.S.C. § 291.

[6] This section is excerpted from Berde, *An Overview of the Legal Problems Affecting Cooperatives*, 2 AGRIC. L. J. 40 (1980) at 53-55 (hereinafter cited as BERDE). Reprinted with permission of the author and from *The Agricultural Law Journal* published by Callaghan and Company, 3201 Old Glenview Road, Wilmette, Illinois 60091. Footnote numbering has been changed to correspond with those for this chapter, but footnotes 7 to 17 are taken directly from the original article.

much help from the Capper-Volstead Act.[7] Cooperatives which combine with nonco-op entities, by merger or otherwise, to restrain trade or monopolize markets are subject to the same antitrust penalties as nonco-op commercial enterprises.[8]

The difficult co-op antitrust exemption problems are those which arise when cooperatives, acting alone or with other cooperatives, achieve and exercise market power sufficient to enhance price, not by prohibited conduct, but by voluntary association of their constituent members so-called "no fault" exercise of monopoly power. A Federal appeals court has held, in two separate cases, that agreements between separate co-ops to fix price are permissible even though that is all they do.[9] It appears that the Justice Department and the FTC concur in that view.[10]

But those cases dealt with price-fixing, not monopoly. What happens if co-ops merge, federate or act through a common marketing agent to achieve and maintain monopoly power? For a number of years cooperatives have taken comfort from a jury instruction given by the court in the National Cranberry Association case that it is not unlawful for a cooperative "to try

to acquire even 100 percent of the market if it does it exclusively through marketing agreements approved under the Capper-Volstead Act..."[11] Up to now, the antitrust enforcement agencies appear to have applied the same rule to cooperative mergers. Although the three largest dairy cooperatives were formed by merger of 166 smaller cooperatives during 1968 and 1969, none were challenged as a violation of the antitrust laws.[12]

The issue still appears cloudy, however. One court has refused to dismiss a Sherman Act § 2 charge of monopolization and a § 7 Clayton Act complaint where a merger between three cooperatives was the sole basis for the action.[13] The court said that it needed to hear evidence to determine whether the mergers of the three co-ops "though for others monopolistic and in restraint of trade, are necessary to the achievement of the objective of the exemption legislation."[14]

It is difficult to reconcile that case with other cases which have approved the voluntary association of producers in organizations of sufficient size to constitute monopoly.[15] The court seems to have confused monopoly with "monopoliza-

---

[7] Pacific Coast Agricultural Export Ass'n v. Sunkist Growers, Inc., 526 F. 2d 1196 (CA 5th 1965) *cert. den.* 382 U.S. 977 (1966).

[8] Maryland & Virginia Milk Producers Ass'n v. United States, 362 U.S. 458 (1960); United States v. Borden, 308 U.S. 188 (1939).

[9] Northern California Supermarkets, Inc. v. Central California Lettuce Producers Cooperative, 413 F. Supp. 984 (ND Cal 1976); Treasure Valley Potato Bargaining Ass'n v. Ore-Ida Foods, Inc., 497 F. 2d 203 (CA 9th) *cert. den.* 419 U.S. 999 (1974).

[10] See MILK MARKETING, A REPORT OF THE UNITED STATES DEPARTMENT OF JUSTICE TASK GROUP ON ANTITRUST IMMUNITIES (January 1977), pp 207, 229; Central California Lettuce Producers Cooperative *et al.*, 90 FTC 18 (1977), 3 CCH Trade Reg Rep ¶ 21,337 (1977).

[11] Cape Cod Food Products, Inc. v. National Cranberry Ass'n, 119 F. Supp. 900, 907 (D Mass 1954); *see also*, Shoenberg Farms v. Denver Milk Producers, 231 F. Supp. 266 (D Colo 1964).

[12] FTC BUREAU OF COMPETITION STAFF REPORT ON AGRICULTURAL COOPERATIVES (Sept 1975) at 166.

[13] Muirbrook Farms, Inc. v. Western General Dairies, Civ C. 75-177 (D Utah, March, 1977) (unreported).

[14] *Id.*

[15] Sunkist Growers, Inc. v. Winckler & Smith Citrus Prod. Co., 370 U.S. 19 (1962); Case-Swayne Co. v. Sunkist Growers, 355 F. Supp (CD Cal 1971); United Egg Producers v. Bauer Int'l Corp., 312 F. Supp 319 (SDNY 1970); Cape Cod Food Prod. Inc., *supra* n. 11.

tion." The law does not prohibit monopoly per se.[16] Section 2 of the Sherman Act makes it unlawful to "monopolize, or attempt to monopolize...." any part of interstate commerce. To "monopolize" means to acquire monopoly power by anticompetitive conduct as distinguished from growth as a result of superior product, performance or authorized conduct.[17] Since the Capper-Volstead Act expressly authorizes producers to join together in associations and to have marketing agencies in common, it is difficult to understand how such authorized conduct could be condemned as unlawful "monopolization."

What Is a Cooperative?[18] The Capper-Volstead Act, that mighty charter of cooperative freedom, does not define or use the term "cooperative." It speaks, instead, of associations of "persons engaged in the production of agricultural products as farmers." In its simplest form, a cooperative may be any two or more persons who join together for their mutual benefit to promote a common purpose. To that simple definition may be added certain refinements such as ownership and democratic control by its members, service at cost, and distribution of gains on the basis of patronage. But as Mr. Justice Brandeis observed half a century ago "no one plan or organization is to be labeled as truly cooperative to the exclusion of others."[19]

The law draws distinctions between cooperatives and other forms of commercial activity for a number of purposes. State and federal regulatory provisions either exempt or provide special privileges to associations of farmers or other organizations "operated on a cooperative basis" with respect to access to credit, the antitrust laws, corporate income taxes, federal securities and state blue sky laws, public utility laws, and a variety of licensing and regulatory statutes.[20] An association's entitlement to the privileges or exemption provided by such regulatory statutes depends upon whether it has the organizational and operational characteristics set forth in the applicable statute; not upon what the organization thinks it is or claims to be. For example, Sunkist Growers[21] lost its Capper-Volstead antitrust exemption not because it was not a cooperative, but because there were included in its membership and represented on its board of directors, proprietary packing houses who were not producers. The Supreme Court said, in that case:

> [The Capper-Volstead Act] was designed to insure that qualifying associations be truly organized and controlled by and for producers...
>
> ...
>
> We think Congress did not intend to allow an organization with...non-pro-

---

[16] United States v. Grinnell Corp., 384 U.S. 563 (1966); Berkey Photo Inc. v. Eastman Kodak Co., 1979-1 CCH Trade Cas ¶ 62,718 (1979).
[17] *Id.*, 3 P. AREEDA AND D. TRUNER, ANTITRUST LAW § 613 (1978), p 34; "The monopoly attributable (solely?) to economies of scale, natural advantages, legal license, superior skill, or accident is apparently lawful."
[18] This section is also excerpted from BERDE at 42-45. Footnotes 19–34 are taken from the original article.
[19] Frost v. Corporation Commissioners, 278 U.S. 515, 564 (1929) (dissenting opinion).
[20] *See generally*, Packel, *The Organization and Operation of Cooperatives*, Joint Committee on Continuing Legal Education, American Law Institute, American Bar Association, (4th ed), at 32.
[21] Case-Swayne v. Sunkist Growers, Inc., 389 U.S. 384 (1976).

ducer interests to avail itself of the Capper-Volstead exemption.[22]

Courts do not hesitate to examine how a purported cooperative actually operates to determine whether it is entitled to a "patronage dividend" deduction from corporate income tax,[23] exemption from regulation under the Interstate Commerce Act,[24] exemption from the wages and hours provisions of the Fair Labor Standards Act,[25] or exemption from payment of minimum prices to producers under the milk order provisions of the Agricultural Marketing Agreement Act of 1937.[26] In a tax case cited, the court "lifted the cooperative veil and unmasked the economic realities of these transactions"[27] to find that the patronage rebates for which it claimed a tax deduction were nothing more than dividends paid to shareholders who "were no more than paper patrons."[28]

The cited cases teach that mere incorporation under the cooperative laws of some states is insufficient to confer on an organization the privileges and exemptions of cooperative status granted by various federal and state laws. Membership control plus actual operation in conformity with the requirements of the applicable regulatory statute is required to enjoy the privileges and exemptions accorded to cooperative status.

What Is a "Producer"? Section 1 of the Capper-Volstead Act authorizes "persons engaged in the production of agricultural products as *farmers* ... [to] act together in associations ... in collectively processing ... handling, and marketing" (emphasis supplied) their production. Section 521 of the Internal Revenue Code defines the cooperatives "exempt from taxation" as "farmers, fruit growers, or like associations organized and operated on a cooperative basis (A) for the purpose of marketing the product of members or other producers...." The Securities Act of 1933 exempts from regulation "[a]ny security issued ... by a farmer's cooperative organization exempt from tax under Section 524 of the Internal Revenue Code of 1954." The interrelationship of the three statutes plus the antitrust consequences to a cooperative of including a "nonproducer" as a member demonstrates the importance of the question: who, or what, is a "producer" within the meaning of the relevant statutes?

First of all, it is clear that the term "persons engaged in ... production ... as farmers" is not restricted to natural persons but may include partnerships or corporations, provided they are actually engaged in agricultural production and bear the risk of the farm enterprise.[29] Nor does it appear that the law imposes any size limitation

---

[22] *Id.* at 394, 396.

[23] Mississippi Valley Portland Cement Co. v. United States, 408 F. 2d 827 (CA 5th), *cert. den.*, 89 S. Ct 2015 (1969).

[24] Freight Consolidators Coop. Inc. v. United States, 230 F. Supp 692 (SDNY 1964).

[25] Fleming v. Palmer, 123 F. 2d 749 (CCA 1st, 1941), *cert. den.*, 316 U.S. 662 (1941).

[26] Elm Spring Farms v. United States, 127 F. 2d 920 (CCA 1st, 1942).

[27] 408 F. 2d at 833.

[28] 408 F. 2d at 834.

[29] Case-Swayne Co. v. Sunkist Growers, Inc., 369 F. 2d 449, 461 (CA 9th). *rev'd on other grounds,* 389 US 384 (1967); United States v. Maryland & Virginia Milk Producers Ass'n, 167 F. Supp 45 (DDC 1958).

[30] Central California Lettuce Producers Cooperative, 90 FTC 18 (1977), 3 CCH Trade Reg Rep ¶ 21,337 (1977); *see also,* National Broiler Marketing Ass'n v. United States, 436 U.S. 816 (1978).

on the persons or corporation who may qualify for membership in a cooperative so long as they are, in fact, engaged in production as farmers.[30] In the *Central California Lettuce Producers* case the FTC's challenge to the cooperative's antitrust exemption did not question the size of its members (which included United Brands, for example), but how the co-op operated. The concern in the *National Broiler Marketing Association* (NBMA) case was not with the fact that Ralston-Purina or Holly Farms were members, but whether they were engaged in production as farmers.

While the Capper-Volstead language: "persons engaged in agricultural production as farmers" seems clear, it was not clear enough for agreement among the judges who considered the NBMA case at the trial court level, in the appellate court and in the Supreme Court. After first observing that "the Act does not define the terms 'engaged in production' or 'farmers,'"[31] the trial judge held that the members of the NBMA were sufficiently involved in the production of broilers to be classified as "farmers" within the meaning of the Capper-Volstead Act. The appellate court reversed on the grounds that persons who "neither own nor operate farms"[32] are not within the class of persons Congress intended to protect under the Capper-Volstead Act.[33] The Supreme Court affirmed the appellate court, but on different grounds, with one separate concurring opinion and two Justices dissenting.[34]

PRODUCTION OF AGRICULTURAL PRODUCTS

NATIONAL BROILER MARKETING ASSOCIATION v. UNITED STATES
United States Supreme Court, 1978
98 S. Ct. 2122

The United States brought an antitrust suit against petitioner, a nonprofit cooperative association the members of which are integrated producers of broiler chickens. The complaint alleged that petitioner, which performs various marketing and purchasing functions for its members, had conspired with others, including its members, in violation of § 1 of the Sherman Act. Petitioner asserted that its activities with its members were sheltered from suit under § 1 of the Capper-Volstead Act, which permits "[p]ersons engaged in the production of agricultural products as farmers" to join in cooperative associations. The District Court concluded that the activities of petitioner's members justified their classification as farmers and that the Capper-Volstead protection claimed was therefore available. The Court of

---

[31] United States v. National Broiler Marketing Ass'n, 1975-2 CCH Trade Cas ¶ 60,059, p 67,220.
[32] United States v. National Broiler Marketing Ass'n 550 F. 2d 1380, 1381 (CA 5th, 1977).

[33] *Id*. at 1385-1386.
[34] National Broiler Marketing Ass'n v. United States, 436 U.S. 816 (1978).

Appeals reversed, holding that petitioner's members were not all "farmers" in the ordinary meaning of that word as it was used at the time the Capper-Volstead Act was passed.

Petitioner phrases the issue substantially as follows:

Is a producer of broiler chickens precluded from qualifying as a "farmer," within the meaning of the Capper-Volstead Act, when it employs an independent contractor to tend the chickens during the "grow-out" phase from chick to mature chicken?

NBMA is a nonprofit cooperative association organized under Georgia law. It performs various cooperative marketing and purchasing functions on behalf of its members. Its membership has varied somewhat during the course of this litigation, but apparently it has included as many as 75 separate entities.

These members are all involved in the production and marketing of broiler chickens. Production involves a number of distinct stages: the placement, raising, and breeding of breeder flocks to produce eggs to be hatched as broiler chicks; the hatching of the eggs and placement of those chicks; the production of feed for the chicks; the raising of the broiler chicks for a period, not to exceed, apparently, 10 weeks; the catching, cooping, and hauling of the "grown-out" broiler chickens to processing facilities; and the operation of facilities to process and prepare the broilers for market.

The broiler industry has become highly efficient and departmentalized in recent years, and stages of production that in the past might all have been performed by one enterprise may now be split and divided among several, each with a highly specialized function. No longer are eggs necessarily hatched where they are laid, and chicks are not necessarily raised where they are hatched. Conversely, some stages that in the past might have been performed by different persons or enterprises are now combined and controlled by a single entity. Also, the owner of a breeder flock may own a processing plant.

All the members of NBMA are "integrated," that is, they are involved in more than one of these stages of production. Many, if not all, directly or indirectly own and operate a processing plant where the broilers are slaughtered and dressed for market. All contract with independent growers for the raising or grow-out of at least part, and usually a substantial part, of their flocks. Often the chicks placed with an independent grower have been hatched in the member's hatchery from eggs produced by the member's breeder flocks. The member then places its chicks with the independent grower for the grow-out period, provides the grower with feed, veterinary service, and necessary supplies, and, with its own employees, usually collects the mature chickens from the grower. Generally, the member retains title to the birds while they are in the care of the independent grower.

It is established, however, that six NBMA members do not own or control any breeder flock whose offspring are raised as broilers, and do not own or control any hatchery where the broiler chicks are hatched. And it appears from the record that three members do not own a breeder flock or hatchery, and also do not maintain any grow-out facility. These members, who buy chicks already hatched and then place them with growers, enter the production line only at its later processing stages.

The Capper-Volstead Act removed from the proscription of the antitrust laws cooperatives formed by certain agricultural producers that otherwise would be directly competing with each other in efforts to bring their goods to market. But if the cooperative includes among its members those not so privileged under the statute to act collectively, it is not entitled to the protection of the Act. Thus, in order for NBMA to enjoy the limited exemption of the Capper-Volstead Act, and, as a consequence, to avoid liability under the antitrust laws for its collective activity, all its members must be qualified to act collectively. It is not enough that a typical member qualify, or even that most of NBMA's members qualify. We therefore must determine not that the typical integrated broiler producer is qualified under the Act, but whether all the integrated producers who are members of NBMA are entitled to the Act's protection.

The Act protects those who are "engaged in the production of agricultural products as *farmers, planters, ranchmen, dairymen, nut or fruit growers*" [emphasis added]. A common sense reading of this language clearly leads one to conclude that not all persons engaged in the production of agricultural products are entitled to join together and to obtain and enjoy the Act's benefits: the quoted phrase restricts and limits the broader preceding phrase "[p]ersons engaged in the production of agricultural products..."

The purposes of the Act, as revealed by the legislative history, confirm the conclusion that not all those involved in bringing agricultural products to market may join cooperatives exempt under the statute, and have the cooperatives retain that exemption. The Act was passed in 1922 to remove the threat of antitrust restrictions on certain kinds of collective activity including processing and handling, undertaken by certain persons engaged in agricultural production. Similar organizations of those engaged in farming, as well as organizations of laborers, were already entitled, since 1914, to special treatment under § 6 of the Clayton Act. This treatment however, had proved to be inadequate. Only nonstock organizations were exempt under the Clayton Act, but various agricultural groups had discovered that in order best to serve the needs of their members, accumulation of capital was required. With capital, cooperative associations could develop and provide the handling and processing services that were needed before their members' products could be sold. The Capper-Volstead Act was passed to make it clear that the formation of an agricultural organization, without antitrust consequences, could perform certain functions in preparing produce for market.

Farmers were perceived to be in a particularly harsh economic position. They were subject to the vagaries of market conditions that plague agriculture generally, and they had no means individually of responding to those conditions. Often the farmer had little choice about who his buyer would be and when he would sell. A large portion of an entire year's labor devoted to the production of a crop could be lost if the farmer were forced to bring his harvest to market at an unfavorable time. Few farmers, however, so long as they could act only individually, had sufficient economic power to wait out an unfavorable situation. Farmers were seen as being caught in the hands of processors and distributors who, because of their position in the market and their relative economic strength, were able to take from the farmer a good share of whatever profits might be available from agricultural production. By allowing farmers to join together in cooperatives, Congress hoped to bolster their market strength and to improve their ability to weather adverse economic periods and to deal with processors and distributors. NBMA argues that this history demonstrates that the Act was meant to protect all those that must bear the costs and risks of a fluctuating market, and that all its members, because they are exposed to those costs and risks and must make decisions affected thereby, are eligible to organize in exempt cooperative associations. The legislative history indicates, however, and does it clearly, that it is not simply exposure to those costs and risks, but the inability of the individual farmer to respond effectively, that led to the passage of the Act. The congressional debates demonstrate that the Act was meant to aid not the full spectrum of the agricultural sector, but, instead, to aid only those whose economic position rendered them comparatively helpless. It was very definitely special interest legislation. Indeed, several attempts were made to amend the Act to include certain processors who, according to preplanting contracts, paid growers amounts based on the market price of processed goods; these attempts were roundly rejected. Clearly, Congress did not intend to extend the benefits of the Act to the processors and packers to whom the farmers sold their goods, even when the relationship was such that the processor and packer bore a part of the risk.

We, therefore, conclude that any member of NBMA that owns neither a breeder flock nor a hatchery, and that maintains no grow-out facility at which the flock to which it holds title are raised, is not among those Congress intended to protect by the Capper-Volstead Act. The economic role of such a member in the production of broiler chickens is indistinguishable from that of the processor that enters into a preplanting contract with its supplier, or from that of a packer that assists its supplier in the financing of his crops. Their participation involves only the kind of investment that Congress clearly did not intend to protect. We hold that such members are not "farmers," as that term is used in the Act, and that a cooperative organization that includes them—or even one of them—as members is not entitled to the limited protection of the Capper-Volstead Act.

The judgment of the Court of Appeals is affirmed, and the case is remanded for further proceedings.

16.2 THE COOPERATIVE-MEMBER RELATIONSHIP

In addition to litigation regarding the antitrust status of cooperative organizations, a number of cases have dealt with issues concerning the agreements between members or between members and their associations. Cases have involved a wide range of issues including problems of earnings payouts, equity redemption, requests for accounting, and director's liability for wrongful actions. Also, in the case of associations organized for cooperative marketing purposes, the courts have taken active steps in enforcing members' contracts.

Agreements between Members and Their Cooperative

A question sometimes arises as to whether the delivery of products by the member to the association constitutes a sale or is an agency agreement. In all cases,

it is a question of fact and depends on the particular circumstances. Ordinarily, shipping associations are regarded as agents. Obviously, if they are only agents, they are not liable under members' contracts for nonnegligent injury to the products handled. Courts have generally required strict compliance with such agreements so that the objects of the association will be forwarded.

Whether or not a party can have a property right in a contract agreement may not be well settled, but it has been held that third parties can be enjoined from inducing a breach of a contract, and some states have laws forbidding such inducement.

A stipulation for liquidated damages carried in most cooperative marketing contracts has been upheld by the courts as reasonable and proper. A few courts have held that both liquidated damages and an injunction are proper for a single breach of a producer's contract with a cooperative when the producer agreed to market all produce through the cooperative.

LIABILITY TO COOPERATIVE

SANTO TOMAS PRODUCE ASSOCIATION v. SMITH
Supreme Court of New Mexico, 1961
68 N.M. 436, 362 P.2d 977

This case arose because of claimed liability of a member grower to a cooperative marketing association. The trial court found the issues in favor of the association and the defendant appeals.

The Santo Tomas Produce Association was incorporated in 1957 as a non-profit agricultural cooperative marketing association, and defendant Smith was one of the thirteen members who, by agreement, made the association the sole marketing agency for onions planted in the Fall of 1956. The original agreement was orally amended by the parties because of labor shortages, so that the association took care of gathering, harvesting and hauling of the onions to the sorting shed, at the expense of the individual members, including Smith. This was in addition to the written agreement, which contemplated the grading, processing, shipping and marketing of each member's crop. Unfortunately for Smith, who had seventeen acres of onions, the total cost of performing the above services was $14,328.65, whereas the onions were sold for only $6,371.24. The trial court credited Smith with the value of his stock in the association together with his portion of the savings made by the association, and rendered judgment against him for the difference of $6,738.04.

The defendant's first point relied upon for reversal is that the trial court erred in refusing to grant his motion for dismissal at the close of the plaintiff's evidence. This motion was grounded generally upon the fact that the marketing agreement provided that title to the product would be vested in the association upon delivery to the shed—thus, that a buyer and seller relationship existed, as distinguished from the association's contention that a principal and agent relationship was provided by the agreement. The defendant also, as a part of his motion, relied upon the fact that the agreement specified that the produce delivered "shall be pooled and marketed as fresh, processed, or other form, all in the sole discretion of the Association, and thereafter all net earnings shall be distributed to the grower members of the association ratably and proportionately according to individual deliveries so made."

Following the denial of defendant's motion, he proceeded to introduce evidence devoted principally to the claimed delay on the part of the association to promptly gather, harvest and haul his onions, together with some evidence as to the handling thereof after their shipment on the railway. The motion was not renewed at the close of the defendant's case, nor at any other time in the proceedings, and therefore, any error (if such it was) on the part of the trial court to grant the motion was waived.

However, even though this claim of error need not be considered, we have carefully examined the transcript together with the articles of incorporation, by-laws and the marketing agreement, and feel that, when they are considered together with the circumstances, the intention of the parties, and the provisions of the sections of the statute involved, it is obvious that the relationship created was that of principal and agent, or that the association is a bargaining agent, not an independent enterprise.

With respect to the pooling provision, it is plain that it was intended by the parties, as shown by all of the evidence, that it was purely for the purpose of convenience in the shipping of the product in order to make up carload lots, not pooling in its usual sense. There was no conflict among the witnesses as to such intent and even the defendant Smith testified that if there had been a profit from the sale of his onions, he would have been entitled to it. The processing and marketing charges, as determined by the board of directors and applicable to all of the members, were the association's only source of income. Separate accounts were maintained for the individual members as to costs and proceeds of sale. To accept defendant's premise would, in effect, be saying, "If I win, the profit is mine; if I lose, you must pay." Such strained construction of the agreement, considered with the articles of incorporation and by-laws, is not reasonable. We find no merit in defendant's first point.

The second point relied upon for reversal is claimed error in two of the findings of fact made by the court. The gist of this claim is that the charges for grading, processing, shipping and marketing were in the nature of advances from the association to the defendant and chargeable to the association.

Defendant, without the citation of any authority whatsoever, seems to contend that the association could not charge, or, in any event, recover for the processing and subsequent costs. Such contention is not in accordance with the general rules of law as we construe them.

Under this point, defendant apparently has no quarrel with the charge for the harvesting and hauling, and it is somewhat incongruous to draw the distinction which defendant attempts to make. Additionally, defendant's attack upon the two findings falls short of a proper attack under the rules, but, even so, there being no attack on the remaining findings made by the trial court, they amount to the facts before us and amply support the judgment.

The defendant's third and last point is based upon the court's refusal to find the association negligent in its handling of the produce, claiming that this was the proximate cause of the loss. However, here again the defendant has not attacked the trial court's findings, one of which was as follows:

16. That plaintiff's officers and directors acted in good faith and exercised reasonable discretion in the harvesting, hauling, processing and marketing of defendant's 1957 summer onion crop, and that no fraud or gross mistake on the part of plaintiff was shown or exists.

The authorities, almost without exception, hold that a cooperative marketing association is not liable for the loss due to delay in making sales, in the absence of unreasonable exercise of discretion. The tenor of all of the authorities is also that the judgment of the cooperative cannot be questioned, except for fraud or gross mistake.

Therefore, in view of the findings of the trial court, we find that defendant's point in this respect is without merit.

The judgment will be affirmed.

Suits against the Cooperative

As a corporate form of business, the cooperative is subject to most of the general rules relating to liability for the wrongful acts of officers and directors.[35] Generally, this means that cooperative officers and directors can be held liable for wrongful actions committed while serving in their

---

[35] See the discussion in Chapter 15, "Farm Corporations," on this point.

official capacity. This can include mismanagement, breach of fiduciary duty, negligence in the discharge of duties, or other acts of malfeasance. A member would ordinarily have a right to sue the directors or officers for these actions.

The degree of care required of directors in carrying out their duties and responsibilities is generally based on the "reasonable person" standard—the exercise of ordinary and reasonable care and diligence. The application of this standard means that a farmer-director cannot be indifferent as to the management of the cooperative, although this does not mean that the director is required to supervise the day-to-day operation of the business. A "business judgment" rule has traditionally been used in cases of director liability. This rule is that if a decision of a director is based on a valid business judgment and is not negligent, then liability will not be imposed for the director's conduct. On the other hand, a violation of the rule could result in liability being imposed.[36]

Redemption of Equity and Earnings Payout Problems

In the cooperative structure, each member-patron has a right to share in the "profits" of the cooperative, ordinarily through patronage dividends. These distributions are usually made on a pro rata basis in proportion to the amount or value of property bought from or sold to the cooperative or on the basis of other services of the cooperative utilized by the member-patron. The amount, time, and manner of the payment of patronage dividends are governed by both the bylaws of the cooperative and applicable state statutes. It is usually a matter within the discretion of the board of directors. Patronage dividends ordinarily do not have to be declared if the cooperative has no net earnings, and courts will not interfere with the directors' discretion as to when the financial state of the cooperative is such that payments are feasible. If, however, the directors' refusal is based upon an abuse of discretion, a breach of trust, fraud, or inequity, judicial relief may be possible.[37]

The same rules apply to directors' decisions regarding the redemption of member equities. In many cooperatives, a substantial portion of each year's net savings ("profits") is retained by the cooperative for capital use as "equity credits." This is a method of financing the business. The deferred patronage refunds are ordinarily payable at some future time at the discretion of the board of directors. The bylaws often provide for redemption of the "equity credits" of a member upon death or perhaps upon retirement or at a specified age.

---

[36] For an excellent discussion of this issue, *see,* Guenzel, *The Relationship Between Cooperatives and Their Members in Litigation,* 21 S. D. L. REV. 628 (1976).

[37] Lake Region Packing Ass'n. Inc., v. Furze, 327 So.2d 212 (Fla. 1976); Claassen v. Farmers Grain Cooperative, 208 Kan. 129, 496 P. 2d 376 (1971); Annot., *Cooperative Associations: Rights in Equity Credits or Patronage Dividends,* 50 A.L.R. 3d 435, § 21.

REPAYMENT RIGHTS

LAKE REGION PACKING ASSOCIATION, INC. v. FURZE
Supreme Court of Florida, 1976
327 So. 2d 212

As a tax exempt cooperative, appellee (petitioner herein), Lake Region markets the citrus produce of its patrons for a charge, remitting the proceeds from the fruit sales to the respective growers. Appellants (respondents herein), who are noncurrent, former members of the cooperative, brought this class action seeking sums concededly withheld from them by the cooperative in a reserve account.

While a cooperative form of organization provides advantages unavailable to the independent producer, it requires working capital and sufficient reserves to offset losses due to freezes or other contingencies. To establish such reserves a cooperative might either borrow money from outside sources (debt financing) or retain sums from members and patrons in order to accumulate working capital and reserves over a period of time (equity financing). In the case before us, since at least 1925 Lake Region has pursued the latter course and has charged its patrons such a fee, in addition to costs, in order to do so. Earnings withheld by the cooperative as contributions to its reserve account were recorded as noncash "allocations" to member and patron accounts. At the beginning of each fiscal year the board of directors set charges for the various services it was to perform for members and patrons during the coming year. At the end of that fiscal year net margins or net losses were determined by subtracting operating and other costs from the income received from charges. The difference was added to or subtracted from each member or patron's allocated reserve account in an amount proportionate to his transactions with the cooperative during that year. Although no definite schedule was followed, excessive reserves were used to redeem the earliest unrefunded allocations on approximately a ten to twelve year cycle. The directors on these occasions of redemption, pursuant to their duties as set forth in the bylaws, "declared" such excess. A 1962 amendment to the Internal Revenue Code, however, has caused considerable change in the cooperative's practice. As a consequence thereof, patrons' contributions to reserves since 1963 have designedly totaled less than the cooperative's net margins, and, with equal design, no contributions have been made since 1968. Moreover, no reserve allocations have been redeemed since 1963 and several letters by the president (now chairman of the board) clearly indicated that, until changed, the tax ramifications of the amendment would preclude repayment. Judicial review of a cooperative's refusal to redeem would be available if the directors' refusal to repay constituted an abuse of discretion, a breach of trust or was based upon fraud, illegality or inequity. However, in the absence of any such impropriety, the decisions to date indicate that repayment rights do not vest until dissolution unless applicable bylaws require earlier repayment. The District Court agreed with the trial court that no such abuse, impropriety or bylaw provision was demonstrated on the record in this case. In Florida, corporate directors generally have wide discretion in the performance of their duties and a court of equity will not attempt to pass upon questions of the mere exercise of business judgment, which is vested by law in the governing body of the corporation.

Were it necessary to characterize allocated retains as "debt" or "equity," we believe their characteristics more nearly resemble equity than debt. However, we do not deem it necessary to categorize retained reserves as either equity or debt since their treatment is defined by the bylaws of the cooperative in force at the time sums were retained from respondents. The agreement under which respondents undertook to participate in the cooperative effort of the association through incorporation of the bylaws by reference clearly spelled out the circumstances under which amounts would be retained for reserves and the method for distribution of such amounts. The fact that it had been the prior practice of the Association to revolve such retained reserves is not controlling in that the change in the tax law in 1962 provided a sufficient business judgment justification for the directors to discontinue the practice of revolving reserves as it had theretofore existed.

That does not mean that a forfeiture is worked upon the respondents or that recourse to the courts is foreclosed to them. Clearly, upon a dissolution of the Association, respondents will be entitled to their proportionate share of any then-existing reserves after payment of all other superior obligations of the Association. In addition, at any point in time at which respondents can demonstrate that the directors of the Association abuse their discretion or breach their trust by establishing charges to the producers at an inordinately low rate in relationship to the competitive market, by permitting the accumulation of excessive reserves, or by any other conduct, respondents have recourse to the courts under the principles expressed in the cases herein cited governing the conduct of directors.

We believe this result not only comports with the existing law on the subject, but also fulfills the intent and purposes of an agricultural cooperative as expressed in the Amended Articles of Incorporation. The plain purpose of agricultural cooperative associations is to advance the interests of active producers in the production and marketing of their crops. An agricultural cooperative is not in the nature of a business corporation in which the general public invests capital in the expectation of returns through appreciation in value or through dividends, nor is it an entity to which people lend funds in the form of bonds or debentures yielding a fixed sum by way of interest and return of the principal on a day certain.

That portion of the District Court's opinion affirming the judgment of the trial court is affirmed, but the balance thereof, including the remand to the trial court, is quashed.

16.3 TAXATION OF COOPERATIVES[38]

Tax treatment of cooperatives and their patrons is now covered in Subchapter T of the Internal Revenue Code, § §1381-1388. The sections apply to "any corporation operating on a cooperative basis" with certain statutory exceptions...

The essential character of cooperative tax treatment under Subchapter T is that net earnings on patronage business are excluded from taxation at the cooperative level if they are distributed or allocated to patrons on the basis of patronage in accordance with rules set forth in § §1382-1388. Under Subchapter T, "qualified" patronage refunds or capital retains, entitled to treatment as deductions from taxable income, must (1) be paid on the basis of volume or value of business done with or for such patrons, (2) be paid under a preexisting obligation, and (3) be determined by reference to net earnings of the cooperative from patronage business. Payments will not qualify for deduction as a patronage dividend if (1) paid out of earnings other than from patronage business or (2) out of earnings from other patrons to whom smaller amounts have been paid.

In order to qualify for deduction, a patronage refund or capital retain must either be paid in cash, as a qualified written notice of allocation, or in the form of other property. The written notice may be in the form of a simple book entry or other evidence of allocation provided that either (1) it is convertible into cash within 90 days at face value or (2) the patron has consented and agreed to include the entire allocation as part of his taxable income. In the case of a patronage fund allocation at least 20 percent must be paid in cash.

Qualification for "tax exempt" status under §521 of the Code has certain advantages not available to the "nonexempt" cooperative. An "exempt" cooperative may deduct: (1) amounts paid as dividends on capital stock or other forms of equity such as retain or revolving fund certificates; or (2) amounts paid on a patronage basis out of earnings derived from business done with or for the United States or from income from nonpatronage sources. Exempt status may be important to cooperatives obliged to pay dividends on capital stock or which realize substantial income from sources other than patronage.

Qualification for §521 "tax exempt" status is limited to marketing and supply cooperatives which: (1) "operate on a cooperative basis", (2) limit business with nonmembers, in the case of a marketing cooperative, to 50 percent of the co-op's total business, (3) limit nonmember, nonproducer business, in the case of supply co-ops, to 15 percent of the value of all purchases, (4) limit the dividend rate on capital stock to eight percent or the maximum legal rate in the state of incorporation, (5) treat members and nonmembers alike in pricing or allocation of earnings, (6) market only the products of members or other producers, subject to rigid and narrow exceptions for nonproducer purchases.

The problem with §521 status is the severe limitations placed on a co-op's activities by restrictive IRS rulings and interpretations of what the section permits. In most cases it would appear that the benefits of "nonexempt" status outweigh the dubious advantages of compliance with §521 under the restrictive interpretation of the section by the IRS.

---

[38] This section is excerpted from BERDE at 52-53. For a more detailed discussion see LEGAL PHASES OF FARMER COOPERATIVES, PART 2, FEDERAL INCOME TAXES, FCS Information 100 (May 1976).

COOPERATIVE TAXATION

CONWAY COUNTY FARMERS ASSOCIATION v. UNITED STATES
United States Court of Appeals, 8th Circuit, 1978
588 F. 2d 592

Conway County Farmers Association (CCFA) is an Arkansas agricultural cooperative association engaged primarily in the sale of agricultural supply products. It was organized in 1949 under the enabling legislation for agricultural cooperative associations with its principal place of business in Morrilton, Conway County, Arkansas. Though the stipulated facts describe CCFA as "an agricultural supply cooperative," its Amended Articles of Incorporation describe it as both a purchasing and marketing cooperative. Membership in CCFA may be obtained, on application, by any agricultural producer or person having farm income from crop rent. Members must (1) purchase a $10 common stock certificate, (2) refrain from competing with CCFA, and (3) trade with CCFA. Members must also agree that distributions with respect to patronage or volume of business conducted with CCFA shall be treated as required by applicable Internal Revenue Code provisions.

The authorized capital stock of CCFA consists of common stock, owned by the members, and two classes of preferred, noncumulative, nonvoting stock. Net income is first allocated to preferred stock in an amount not to exceed 6% of its par value. Income attributable to business with nonmembers is set aside as a tax-paid reserve. Remaining net income is allocated to member patrons in proportion to the volume of business each conducted with CCFA during the fiscal year.

For 1970 and 1971, CCFA filed corporation income tax returns (IRS Form 1120) claiming deductions for patronage dividends paid to members in the amount of $14,520 and $5,465, respectively. Upon audit, the Internal Revenue Service (IRS) ruled that CCFA was not entitled to deductions for patronage dividends and assessed deficiencies of $6,818 for 1970, and $1,202.31, for 1971.

The district court concluded that "[t]he question whether (CCFA) is entitled to the tax benefits available to organizations under Part I of Subchapter T of the Internal Revenue Code of 1954 depends on the interpretation of the term 'operating on a cooperative basis' in I.R.C. § 1381 (a)(2)."

The lower court concluded that CCFA, by conducting the majority of its business during fiscal years 1970 and 1971 with nonmembers, failed to qualify as a cooperative for federal income tax purposes and, therefore, the patronage dividends paid to its member-stockholders were not deductible under I.R.C. § 1382(b).

The dispositive question of law on appeal is whether CCFA was an organization "operating on a cooperative basis" within the meaning of Subchapter T.

We begin with the unquestioned congressional intent that admittedly true patronage dividends, such as those here involved, should be deductible by an organization "to which this part applies." The issue is whether that intent is broad enough to include such patronage dividends when an organization does more business in value with nonmembers than with members.

That CCFA is "organized" on a cooperative basis is unquestioned. That it is "operating" on a cooperative basis is unquestioned, except for the amount of business done with nonmembers. The sole basis for the government's contention that CCFA was not "operating on a cooperative basis," lies in CCFA's having conducted more than 50% of its business with nonmembers in fiscal years 1970 and 1971. Absent a contrary indication somewhere in the statute, the ordinary meaning of "operating on a cooperative basis" includes the conduct of some operations on a cooperative basis. In its dealings with its members, CCFA was necessarily "operating on a cooperative basis." That it was also operating on a for-profit basis, in its dealings with nonmembers, does not change the nature of its cooperative-type operations. The wording of § 1381(a)(2) is broad and comprehensive, reflecting a broad intent of Congress. It would do violence to that intent to read the statute, as the government would have us do, as though it contained words not present, i.e., as though it read "operating primarily on a cooperative basis." Congress having inserted no quantitative requirement in § 1381(a)(1) and in so many other acts dealing with cooperatives, neither we nor the IRS are at liberty to make that insertion in § 1381(a)(2).

The phrase "operating on a cooperative basis," though not specifically defined in the statute, is not ambiguous. Our task is not to substitute our judgment for that of the Commissioner, but to determine whether the Commissioner's rule "implements the congressional mandate in some reasonable manner."

The judgment is reversed and the case is remanded to the district court with instructions to enter judgment for plaintiff (CCFA). It is so ordered.

Reversed and Remanded.

16.4 NONPROFIT CORPORATIONS AND UNINCORPORATED ASSOCIATIONS

Nonprofit Corporations

A nonprofit corporation may engage in activities which produce income, but such activities must be in accord with its legal objectives and the income must be used in furtherance of the same objectives. It may not issue shares of stock or make loans to officers or directors. Payment of reasonable compensation for services is not regarded as a "distribution of income" and is permitted.

Such a corporation can usually "purchase, take, receive, lease as lessee, take by gift, demise or bequest, or otherwise acquire, own, hold, use, and otherwise deal in and with any real or personal property, or any interest therein, situated in or out of this state." It may also "sell, convey, mortgage, pledge, lease as lessor and otherwise dispose of all or any part of its property and assets." In addition, it may, for corporate purposes, "make contracts, borrow money, issue notes, bonds and other obligations, make investments and lend money."[39]

---

[39] ILL. REV. STAT. ch. 32, §163 *et seq.* The section of the statute quoted in the text is illustrative of the power granted to such corporations.

Suitable bylaws may be adopted and changed as frequently as the corporation desires, so long as they contain nothing inconsistent with law or the articles of the corporation. This means that the bylaws, besides providing for the usual procedural machinery, will be the source of policy and interpretation for the specific activities in which the corporation will engage.

A section or perhaps more than one section of the bylaws may list the major projects to be undertaken and the general plan under which each shall operate. The bylaws should require detailed project outlines, reports of work and progress, and other procedures which will tend to keep the functions of corporate officers and employees in line with objectives.

NOT-FOR-PROFIT CORPORATIONS

AMERICAN ABERDEEN-ANGUS BREEDERS' ASSOCIATION v. FULLERTON
Supreme Court of Illinois, 1927
325 Ill. 323, 156 N.E. 314

The American Aberdeen-Angus Breeders' Association is a corporation, not for profit, organized under the laws of Illinois for the purpose of collecting, verifying, preserving and publishing the pedigrees of the polled Aberdeen-Angus breed of cattle so as to maintain the purity of the breed and to do such other acts as will best promote the interests of the breed in America. The association was organized in 1883, and prior to 1923 had obtained a membership of between 5,000 and 6,000 breeders of Aberdeen-Angus cattle, residing in various states of the Union and in Canada. Its business affairs were managed by a board of nine directors, three of whom were elected annually for terms of three years at the annual meeting of the association held in Chicago in November or December, by the votes of the members present at the meeting or represented by proxies. The average attendance of members at such meetings for five years prior to 1923 had been about 100, with proxies numbering from 2,000 to 2,300.

The question of changing the government of the association by establishing a representative form of government instead of control through an annual meeting with proxy voting had been favored by some members of the association, and a resolution favoring this change was rejected at the annual meeting of 1922. At the annual meeting on December 5, 1923, 146 members were present in person and 2,787 proxies were presented, of which the proxy committee rejected 389.

Candidates were nominated for the offices of three directors which were to be filled. The printed ballots were distributed, and when the vote had been cast the tellers reported that John C. Mills had received 1,719 votes, J.M. Tudor 1,709, S.C. Fullerton 1,701, and A.C. Johnson 3,544, of which 3,496 were cumulative votes, and if each man had voted one-third of his votes for Johnson he would have had 1,218 votes. The president declared the three candidates receiving the highest votes elected.

A member of the association, Hartley, moved that the report of the tellers be rejected and Fullerton, Mills, and Tudor be declared elected. The president declared the motion out of order. An appeal was taken from his decision, and that was also declared out of order. Thereupon, Fullerton was nominated from the floor as chairman of the meeting. The maker of the motion put it, declared it carried, a number of the members came upon the platform where the president, secretary and treasurer were, ejected them from their positions and Fullerton assumed authority as chairman of the meeting. He appointed ten sergeants-at-arms, the ballots, proxies and other papers were taken from the treasurer but were returned to him.

When this occurred, a number of the members present withdrew from the meeting. Fullerton, acting as chairman, entertained the appeal which had been taken from the decision of the chair, it was sustained, and the motion to reject the report of the tellers and declare Fullerton elected was carried on a roll call by a unanimous affirmative vote of 1,724. The meeting then proceeded to adopt an amendment to the by-laws providing for the election of the president by the members by ballot at the annual meeting instead of by the directors, elected Fullerton president, and adopted other amendments to the charter and by-laws.

The by-laws provided that for the purpose of an election and the transaction of other business a quorum should consist of the members present either in person or by proxy. A majority of the members of the association present in person or by proxy at the annual meeting in 1923 voted for Fullerton, Mills and Tudor for directors, and they were elected unless the minority who voted for Johnson had the right to cumulate the three votes which each was entitled to cast for directors and cast them all for one person. If they had this right, Johnson was elected instead of Fullerton. This is the question which caused the revolt in the meeting, the deposition of the chairman, and the election of another in his place.

The right of the majority of the members to control the action of the meeting cannot be questioned. A presiding officer cannot arbitrarily defeat the will of the majority by refusing to entertain or put motions, by wrongfully declaring the result of a vote, or by refusing to permit the expression by the majority of its will. He is the representative of the body over which he presides. His will is not binding on it, but its will, legally expressed by a majority of its members, is binding. The body has authority to remove its presiding officer and choose another in his place. If the members were not authorized to cumulate their votes, the election of directors was to be determined by the number of individuals casting votes for the respective candidates, and the election could not be vitiated by an arbitrary refusal to declare the true result according to the number of members voting for each director and the meeting could not be legally terminated except by its own act.

Section 3 of Article 11 of the constitution provides:

The General Assembly shall provide, by law, that in all elections for directors or managers of incorporated companies, every stockholder shall have the right to vote, in person or by proxy, for the number of shares of stock owned by him, for as many persons as there are directors or managers to be elected, or to cumulate said shares and give one candidate as many votes as the number of directors multiplied by the number of his shares of stock shall equal, or to distribute them on the same principle among as many candidates as he shall think fit; and such directors or managers shall not be elected in any other manner.

In form this language is universal and applies to all elections of every incorporated company, but its substance is of such a character as to indicate that it was not intended to apply to corporations not having stockholders or shares of stock. Corporations organized not for profit, under the laws of this state, have no capital stock, no shares of stock and no stockholders.

The first legislature elected after the adoption of the new constitution passed an act providing for the organization of corporations for profit and corporations not for profit, providing that every stockholder of a corporation should have the right, in all elections for directors, to cast as many votes for one person as the number of directors multiplied by the number of his shares should equal, or divide that number of votes among as many candidates as he saw fit, but corporations, associations and societies not for pecuniary profit should elect trustees, directors, or managers not from the stockholders but from the members thereof at such times and places and for such period as might be provided for by the by-laws, who should have the control and management of the affairs and funds of the corporation, society or association.

Since the constitutional right of cumulative voting did not apply to the association the president was mistaken in announcing from the report of the tellers that Johnson was elected a director. He was also mistaken in declaring the motion to reject the report of the tellers out of order and refusing to entertain an appeal from his ruling, and the majority of the members present in person and by proxy were justified in exercising the power of the majority in the absence of any by-laws or rules of order contrary to such action, by deposing the chairman and proceeding with the business of the meeting. The fact that the president, secretary and treasurer all, or any of them, left the meeting or remained, or that others did either, did not affect the power of the majority who remained and constituted a quorum to do business or the legality of their action. The subsequent proceedings constituted a part of the action of the annual meeting of the association. The by-laws of the association provided for their amendment by a majority vote of the members represented in person or by proxy at an annual meeting or any adjournment thereof.

After the substitution of Fullerton as chairman an amendment to the by-laws providing a method of amending the charter was adopted—also an amendment of the charter increasing the number of directors from nine to fifteen.

Unincorporated Associations and Other Organizations

State legislatures have generally encouraged the organization of farmers' livestock, crop, soil, and home improvement associations as sound educational devices. In furtherance of such organizations, some states have enabled county boards or commissioners to appropriate funds for their use. There may be a limitation on the amount which can be so appropriated. Property held by such organizations and activities or events sponsored by them are usually held to be free from property taxation, but the exemption is not automatic. It has to be established after a review of purpose and activities by appropriate taxing authorities.

Unincorporated associations have many of the attributes of an incorporated organization, but legally they are not entities or "legal persons" in the sense that a corporation is. Hence, owning and transferring property, making and enforcing contracts, and employing services are covered by different legal rules. Generally, it is more difficult to do business and there is more uncertainty when an organization is not incorporated and when it engages in continuous and substantial activity. Smaller organizations with little or no property and no paid employees—such as 4-H clubs, local social and educational groups—are under no serious disadvantage by not being incorporated. Some questions regarding the tax status of such groups may be resolved by incorporation under nonprofit corporation statutes and by formal compliance with applicable tax provisions—such as filing for exemptions or proper reporting of income, for example.

Taxation of Nonprofit Corporations and Unincorporated Associations

A number of organizations qualify for tax exempt status under applicable federal and state law. Under federal Internal Revenue Code provisions, groups organized for charitable, religious, or scientific purposes; for prevention of cruelty to animals or children; or for other specified purposes can obtain exemption from income taxation.[40] This includes agricultural or horticultural organizations and certain farmers' and fruit growers' cooperatives.

In order to obtain exempt status, the organization must apply to the Internal Revenue Service and submit proof of exempt status. A determination is made by the IRS, and if exempt status is recognized, the organization files an annual informational tax return but pays no taxes unless they also operate a business enterprise not related to the purpose for which exempt status was granted.

Similar exemptions are often available from state income tax provisions and possibly state and local property taxation as well.[41]

---

[40] INT. REV. CODE § 501 *et seq.*
[41] *See, e.g.,* ILL. REV. STAT. ch. 120.

TAX EXEMPTIONS FOR CHARITABLE ORGANIZATIONS

PEOPLE ex rel. HELLYER v. MORTON
Supreme Court of Illinois, 1940
373 Ill. 72, 25 N.E. 2d 504

The county court of DuPage county sustained objections of the Morton Aboretum, one of appellees, to taxes levied for the year 1936 upon land held by it. The revenue being involved, this court has jurisdiction by direct appeal. The property is claimed to be exempt from taxation. The basis of the claimed exemption was that the real estate is held in trust for charitable purposes and, therefore, exempt under state statutes.

The trust was created by Joy Morton and Margaret Gray Morton, husband and wife, in 1922, when they conveyed a part of the real estate involved to certain trustees therein named and their successors in office for the purpose of

creating a foundation to be known as the Morton Aboretum, for practical scientific research work in horticulture and agriculture, particularly in the growth and culture of trees, shrubs, vines and grasses, by variety, and hybrid of the woody plants of the world able to support the climate of Illinois, such museum to be equipped with an herbarium, a reference library, and laboratories for the study of trees and other plants, with reference to their characters, relationships, economic value, geographical distribution and their improvement by selection and hybridization, and for the publication of the results obtained in these laboratories by the officials and students of the aboretum, in order to increase the general knowledge and love of trees and shrubs, and bring about an increase and improvement in their growth and culture.

The grantors reserved the right to serve as co-trustees with those named, thus providing for a board of nine trustees. The trust was to continue forever and vacancies occurring on the board were to be filled by a majority vote of the remaining trustees. The power of the trustees to convey or encumber any part of the land was limited and could be exercised only in the furthering of the interest of the arboretum. The grantors reserved the right to add other property to the trust by grant, transfer, devise or bequest, and the trustees were vested with power to accept property from other parties, subject, however, that it was to be devoted to the purposes expressed in the trust deed. Joy Morton reserved the right to change the provisions of the trust, but it does not appear that any change was made during his lifetime. Subsequent to the first conveyance, the grantors, by eight other instruments, conveyed other tracts to the trustees but each deed contained the same provisions as those expressed in the first instrument. The area of all the land conveyed by the several deeds was approximately 700 acres. It forms a tract one-half a mile wide and three miles long.

Appellant concedes these lands are being used by the trustees for the purposes of the trust but contends for a strict construction of the instrument creating the trust and urges that under such construction the property is not exempt from taxes.

The grantors prescribed the purposes of the trust in general terms and left the details of execution to the judgment and discretion of the trustees. Their interpretation of the trust deed, and what they considered as being the intent and purpose of the donors is fully disclosed by the evidence. The premises have been improved by the construction of artificial lakes. They maintain 18 miles of driveway and 15 miles of footpaths through the grounds. Since the foundation began there have been 428,000 plantings of various trees and wooded shrubbery. These plantings were gathered from a wide area, many of them coming from other States and some from foreign countries. The plantings are arranged for convenience of study, each plant family having a different locality, selected with a view as to its special characteristics. Many of the groupings are subdivided. A forest department is maintained and trees having an economical value are arranged in plots varying from one-half an acre to four acres. Trees and shrubs suitable for landscaping are planted and grown. The planting and propagation is done in a scientific way and a record is kept of every planting and, from time to time, the plantings are checked and the growth, development, and other characteristics are recorded in a permanent record. An administration building, plant nursery, library and other buildings, all used in the work of the arboretum, are located on these lands. An herbarium, containing 8500 mounted specimens is kept in the administration building. The library contains many volumes dealing with subjects on horticulture, arboriculture and illustrated landscaping. The library, the herbarium and the premises are open to the public for visitation and study. Lectures based upon the research work that is done are delivered to groups when requested. A bus is furnished to visitors and tours are conducted through the grounds accompanied by a staff representative, who explains the kind and character of the plantings. Large numbers of visitors from practically all the States in the union and from many foreign countries visit the grounds annually. No charge is made for the lectures or the transportation through the park or the privilege of visiting the place in the park. No seeds, plants, or scions are sold, but surplus stock of such is given to nurseries in various parts of the United States and foreign countries. This distribution is in the form of an exchange for other seeds and cuttings which are propagated and developed on these lands. Any one who desires to acquire any of the seeds or plants is furnished with the name or names of the nurseries that are growing them, and purchases may be made from such nurseries. The arboretum receives no commissions from such sales and has no income from the work that it is doing, except that it publishes a bulletin which is distributed to a small list of subscribers at a nominal fee which is less than the cost of printing. The trustees receive no compensation. They employ a superintendent and other persons, all of whom receive compensation. Three houses are maintained on the grounds as residences for the superintendent and other employees.

The state constitution requires that the General Assembly shall provide such revenue as may be needful for governmental purposes by levying a tax by valuation so that every person and group shall pay a tax in proportion to the value of his, her or its property.

Property of the State, county and other municipal groups, both real and personal, and such property as may be used exclusively for agricultural and horticultural societies, for schools, religious, cemetery and charitable purposes may be exempted from taxation by general law. This provision of the constitution is not self-executing and the General Assembly, in the exercise of its constitutional power, provided by state statute that all property of institutions of public charity, all property of beneficent and charitable organizations, whether incorporated in this or any other State of the United States and all property of old peoples' homes, when such property is actually and exclusively used for such charitable or beneficient purposes and not leased or otherwise used with a view to profit shall be exempt from taxation.

No fixed rule has been established by which it can be determined whether an organization is charitable and whether its property comes within the test established by statute. The principal and distinctive features of a charitable organization are that it has no capital, no provision for making dividends or profits but derives its funds mainly from public and private charity and holds them in trust for the objects and purposes expressed in the instrument creating such organization. It does not lose its charitable character, and consequent exemption from taxation, by reason of the fact that the recipients of some of its benefits who are able to pay are required to do so where no profit is made by the institution and the amounts so received are applied in furthering its charitable purposes. Another distinguishing feature upon which all exemptions in favor of charitable institutions are based is the benefits the public may receive from the institution and the consequent relief to some extent of the burden upon the State to render similar services to its citizens. A charitable use, where neither law nor public policy forbids, may be applied to almost anything that tends to promote the well-doing and well-being of society.

In the establishment of this foundation the express intent of the donors was to create a means whereby practical, scientific research work in horticulture and arboriculture could be carried on in an outdoor museum under natural conditions and the results obtained from such research recorded and preserved. It was considered that the scientific facts thus discovered would serve to increase the general knowledge and love of trees and shrubs and bring about an increase and improvement in their growth and culture. It is common knowledge that scientists engaged in the development and propagation of various species of plants, trees and shrubs have developed some that have proven to be of great benefit to man. The trustees in the present case have not limited their efforts to the study of one particular line but have extended it to include fruit trees, trees for forestation and trees and shrubs for landscaping. Such uses are a distinct contribution to the public welfare.

The object of the organization and the uses of its property are such as to create a charitable trust, and the property, having been devoted exclusively to such purposes, is exempt from general taxes.

The judgment is affirmed.

STUDY QUESTIONS

1. What must an agricultural cooperative do in order to qualify for federal antitrust exemptions?

2. Under what circumstance may an agricultural cooperative be found to be in violation of federal antitrust laws?

3. What is a "cooperative" as presently defined by federal law?

4. What is a "producer" as presently defined for federal law purposes?

5. Under what circumstances may a member of a cooperative bring a successful suit against the directors of that cooperative for their actions as directors?

6. How are patronage refunds (dividends) treated for tax purposes by the cooperative? By the patron-member?

7. May an unincorporated association of agricultural producers be exempt from federal income tax?

17
Estate Planning

Estate planning has received considerable attention in recent years—particularly in the agricultural sector.[1] This is due, in large part, to rapidly appreciating land values and increased values in non-real estate assets. Many farm families now realize that their estate is likely to be subject to substantial federal and state death taxes as well as other estate settlement costs. In addition, dramatic changes in federal estate and gift tax laws caused a focusing of attention on the problems of farm business and estate planning.

Estate planning is more than planning for the minimization of taxes and for the equitable disposition of assets at death. It involves planning for the *use* of assets during life and deals with providing security of income during retirement. Often, it involves planning for business continuity, since many farm families wish to see the farm ownership continue in the family through succeeding generations. Thus, estate planning not only involves tax planning and the development of a will to carry out the wishes of the family but also involves an evaluation of the business plans of the family and often some difficult decisions regarding the future of the business itself.

For farm families the process of estate planning is complicated by a number of factors. The major asset in the farm estate is normally land. If the business is to continue, land is essentially illiquid. It is possibly an indivisible asset as well. It is illiquid in the sense that there may be a disastrous impact on the business if the land must be used to pay taxes and estate settlement costs and to "buy-out" off-farm heirs. Likewise, the division of land into uneconomic units may severely hamper the business. Thus, much of the focus in farm estate planning is on avoiding the consequence of land division and on solving the liquidity problem.

Additional problems arise in the farm situation where some, but not all, of the children have remained on the farm and maintain an active role in the business. Frequently, such involvement starts with the younger family members in the role of employees. Later, informal sharing arrangements may develop—perhaps even a partnership. It is usually the desire of the older family members to have the younger members continue in the business. They may make oral promises concerning future rights in the farm property. However, if no appropriate plans are developed, the desires of the parents may be frustrated because the off-farm heirs will share in the estate to the same extent as the on-farm heirs. The failure to recognize the contribution of the on-farm heirs to the growth and development of the business can be frustrating to the younger family members and may result in their decisions to no longer participate in the business. On the other hand, off-farm heirs can feel frustrated if they are not treated equitably, so their interests must be considered in developing farm business and estate plans.

17.1 PROPERTY OWNERSHIP PROBLEMS

The form in which property is owned is the determining factor of how property will pass from one generation to the next. In addition, the form of property ownership is an important factor in determining the amount of tax liability at the time of death.

General Co-ownership Problems

Obviously, if a person owns property—real or personal—in his or her own name,

---

[1] *See* LOONEY, ESTATE PLANNING FOR FARMERS (1979) and HARL, FARM ESTATE AND BUSINESS PLANNING (1980).

that person can determine what will be done with the property both during lifetime and at death. Such property will pass by the terms of the owner's will or by state law if the person dies without a will. Planning for the disposition of solely owned property poses no special estate planning problems. The same cannot be said for co-owned property. As discussed in Chapter 5, there are several types of co-ownership and each has its own legal characteristics. From an estate planning perspective, joint tenancies and tenancies by the entirety are of major concern. These types of co-ownership are quite common with farm assets. They are of special interest in estate planning because they carry the right of survivorship. At the death of one co-owner, the entire interest in the property passes automatically to the surviving co-owner or co-owners. Such an interest cannot be conveyed by will nor does it pass according to state intestacy law.

A Closer Look at Joint Tenancy and Tenancy by the Entirety

The Advantage of Simplicity. Joint tenancy and tenancy by the entirety property automatically passes to the surviving co-owner, so no probate proceeding is necessary. This may be particularly important to the surviving spouse, so that the spouse can have immediate access to checking accounts and savings accounts and continued use of the family car and home. For those families holding relatively small estates, the delay and publicity surrounding a probate proceeding are avoided and some monetary savings may result as well.

Tax Disadvantages. From an estate planning perspective, the tax impact of holding property jointly is of crucial concern. Generally, the *full* value of the jointly owned property is included in the estate of the first co-owner to die for purposes of determining estate tax liability.[2] The amount included in the estate of the first co-owner to die will be reduced by the portion attributable to the contribution of the survivor. For example, assume a couple buys a parcel of land for $100,000, the husband pays $80,000 (four-fifths of total) and the wife pays $20,000 (one-fifth of total) from her own money, and title is taken in joint tenancy. If the husband dies first, four-fifths of the fair market value of the property will be included in his estate for tax purposes.

The Problem of Proving Contribution. Contribution is a matter of proof. To the extent that a surviving spouse can show an actual financial contribution to the purchase of the property, a reduction in the deceased spouse's estate will be allowed. The difficult questions are those involving a contribution of significant services to the business as opposed to direct financial contributions.[3]

This is a particular problem for farm couples, especially if the survivor is the wife, because of the rather stringent burden of proof in such cases.

---

[2] Treas. Reg. § 20-2040-1 (a) (2). This discussion focuses on joint tenancy and tenancy by the entirety. In eight states—Arizona, California, Idaho, Louisiana, Nevada, New Mexico, Texas, and Washington—couples may have their own separate property, property owned as joint tenants, or community property. Community property is included in the estate of the first spouse to die only to the extent of that spouse's interest— ordinarily one-half. No marital deduction is available for community property. For a discussion of community property and tax considerations, *see* KESS and WESTLIN, CCH ESTATE PLANNING GUIDE.

[3] *See* Estate of Everett Otte, 31 T.C.M. 301, PH TC Memo. ¶ 72,076 (1972).

PROOF OF CONTRIBUTION

CRAIG v. UNITED STATES
U.S. District Court, South Dakota, 1978
78-2 U.S.T.C. ¶13,252; 451 F. Supp 378

Plaintiff, Bessie Craig, was appointed Executrix of the estate of her husband, Clarence Craig, who died as the result of an automobile accident on November 22, 1968. His gross estate was listed as being $329,962.53 and his taxable estate was computed as being $135,010.95. His estate tax was reported at $29,515.11 and this was paid with the return.

This case involves plaintiff's attempt to recover from the Internal Revenue Service a deficiency in the amount of $40,206.67 plus interest which plaintiff paid while reserving the right to institute this action.

The alleged deficiency arose as a result of the claim by the Internal Revenue Service that 100 percent of the schedule F property (personal property) involved in the farming operation was a part of Clarence Craig's estate. Plaintiff contends that only 50 percent of that property should be included in her husband's estate because there existed a family partnership with respect to the farming operation and that, therefore, half of the personal property belonged to the plaintiff.

Clarence and Bessie Craig were married on October 25, 1925. At that time Clarence was 27 years old and Bessie was 22. This marriage continued until Clarence's death in 1968, a period of some 43 years. During this period of time, Clarence and Bessie Craig not only brought forth and raised a family of five children but also built a sizable farming operation in northeastern South Dakota. They built this profitable operation from scratch as neither Clarence nor Bessie owned any farmland at the time of the marriage. Clarence did have a small bank account at the time of their marriage and he also owned a little farm machinery and a few cows. The successful farm operation and the concomitant acquisition of agricultural land developed following the marriage of Clarence and Bessie Craig. The first real property purchased by the Craigs was not acquired until five years after their marriage.

All of the land owned by the Craigs was acquired subsequent to the marriage. With the exception of a small portion of land obtained through Clarence's inheritance, all of the land purchased by the Craigs was financed through loans, principally from the Federal Land Bank. Down-payments and the satisfaction of loan obligations were made possible from income derived from the land. Totally, at the time of the death of Clarence, Bessie owned 7 quarters of farmland, Clarence owned 5½ quarters of farmland and the Elm River pasture land was held in joint tenancy. The Internal Revenue Service did not dispute this division and made no attempt to include the land owned by Bessie Craig in the taxable estate of Clarence.

The IRS does dispute the exclusion of certain personal property from Clarence's estate. This property consists largely of grain, livestock and machinery and, with the possible exception of a minor portion of antiquated machinery, was all acquired by the Craigs during the tenure of their marriage. Plaintiff's contention that the excluded property is rightfully the property of Bessie Craig and not Clarence Craig, and, therefore, should properly be excluded from the estate of Clarence Craig is the basis of the controversy before this Court. Plaintiff raised the similar contention, that one-half the personal property in issue rightfully was Bessie's property in filing her state inheritance tax return. Her contention was accepted by the state department of revenue.

The Craig farming operation consisted principally of raising grain along with the hog and cattle feeding operation. Some chickens and horses were also raised on the farm. Most of the cattle were purchased at area sales and were raised on the farm, in part, from grain grown on the land. Bessie generally accompanied her husband on the buying trips to procure cattle. Moreover, it was usually her function to arrange for the shipping of the cattle back to the farm.

The entire operation was run out of a single checking account in the name of both Bessie and Clarence Craig at the First National Bank of Aberdeen. All income received by the Craigs during their 43 years of marriage that was deposited in a bank was deposited in this single account. All purchases and payments made by checks were made from this account. Deposits and checks drawn on this account were handled by Bessie Craig. Such was the case because she was the spouse in charge of the bookkeeping aspects of the farm operation. Also, she had the responsibility of writing the payroll checks and the maintenance of other business records. She also assisted in the preparation of the tax returns.

Grain raised on the Craig land was either used as feed in their cattle operaton or was sold. No records were kept showing the amount of grain obtained from the land owned by Bessie as distinguished from the land in Clarence's name. However, from 1958 to 1965 Bessie owned approximately half of the cultivated land and subsequent to 1965 she owned more than half. This is of even greater significance when it is considered that grain sales for the Craig operation in the years 1956 through 1968 amounted to over $325,000. This does not even consider the grain used in the Craig hog and cattle feeding operation. In any event, considering the respective division of land ownership, it appears indisputable that Bessie Craig made a very significant capital contribution to the operation; a contribution that, in comparison, rivals that of her husband, Clarence Craig.

Personal property sought to be excluded here represents the acquisitions of the Craigs together during the course of their 43-year marriage. These acquisitions were the direct result of income derived from the Craigs' farming operation; an operation in which, for a significant period of time, approximately half of the cultivated land was owned by the plaintiff, Bessie Craig. Not only did the income derived from the land owned by Bessie Craig contribute significantly to the development and growth of the Craig farming operation, but her individual labors represented a vital contribution to the operation as well.

In addition to shouldering a mother's share of the responsibility for raising a seven-member family, Bessie Craig contributed control and management, as well as other vital services toward the success of the family farm. Contrary to common practice in the farming community, Bessie Craig took an active role in providing the necessities and comforts of life for the hired help. She cooked all their meals, cleaned their sleeping rooms, and washed and patched their clothing. This extra non-monetary compensation probably provided an important asset in obtaining quality farm help. In addition, like all major decisions in the farm operation such as matters of land and machinery purchases, Bessie had an equal voice with Clarence in the selection of hired help.

Bessie was in total control of the egg marketing aspect of their chicken operation. For several years, this included her maintenance of a butter and egg route. In this regard, plaintiff put all the money made on their egg sales into the single checking account so that it could be used in the general farm operation. Altogether, Bessie deposited $19,886.23 in the account over a period of time spanning the years 1945 to 1963 from money made in the egg operation.

Plaintiff also raised a large garden. The vegetables raised in that garden formed part of the food stock for the Craig family and the hired men. Vegetables not eaten in the summer were canned by Bessie for winter consumption. She also canned meat.

Besides these duties and her contributions mentioned earlier, Bessie helped integrally in the harvest. This help included hauling grain from the fields to surrounding towns. She also, on occasion, hauled cattle to pasture and made frequent trips to surrounding towns to obtain repair parts for the farm machinery. All in all, the efforts of Bessie Craig in the operation of the family farm, as well as her capital contributions in terms of income derived from her land, can properly be characterized as those of a partner, in the fullest business sense of the word.

Internal Revenue Code Section 2033 provides that: "the value of the gross estate shall include the value of all property to the extent of the interest therein of the decedent at the time of his death."

This means that if there indeed existed a family farming partnership between Bessie and Clarence Craig at the time of Clarence's death, the IRS was in error to include the value of all the personal property in the taxable estate of Clarence Craig. After a careful consideration of the evidence presented to this court, I am convinced that Bessie and Clarence Craig did in fact pool their capital and labors with the intent to conduct a family partnership in the operation and growth of the family farm. Accordingly, plaintiff is entitled to the refund sought.

The critical issue for the court's determination in this case seeking a refund in taxes paid on the basis of a family partnership was noted in the United States Supreme Court in *Commissioner v. Culbertson*, 337 U.S. 733 (1949). There the court noted, at 742, that the determinative question is not whether the capital or services contributed by a partner are a certain quality to meet some objective standard but rather whether "the parties in good faith and acting with a business purpose intended to join together in the present conduct of the enterprise." That decision went on to note that a party's participation in control and management of the business is an important indicia of an intent to be a bona fide partner.

The evidence presented in this controversy convinces me that Bessie and Clarence Craig, in good faith, did intend to join their income and labors as equal partners in the establishment and growth of the family farm.

Reflective of that intent are the separate wills executed by Bessie and Clarence Craig in 1958. Those documents reveal that the Craigs, at that time, recognized that their personal property, the fruits of the labors of these two partners, was owned in common. Both wills contained the following statement: "if at my death we own personal property in common ownership (*as we do at this time*) I expressly authorize him (Executor) to divide all items of personal property that are divisible including cattle." [emphasis added.]

More importantly, however, in the establishment of the Craigs' intent to form a partnership is the evidence of the capital contributions of the parties, or the division of labor and arduous contributions of both parties in the operation of the farm, and the fact that all major decisions of the business were decided on the basis of equal participation by both Bessie and Clarence Craig. All this evidence leads to the conclusion that the Craigs intended to, and, in fact, did operate their farm as equal partners.

A similar conclusion as that reached by this Court is found in *United States v. Neel* [56-2 USTC 11,631], 235 F. 2d 395 (10th Cir. 1956). Following the authority established in *Culbertson, supra*, the Tenth Circuit Court of Appeals, in a similar fact situation as presented here, found for the plaintiff and held that a family partnership between husband and wife did exist. In doing so, the Court noted, at 400:

> In determining whether a husband and wife are bona fide business partners with respect to tax liability, the absence of a formal agreement and the failure to set up books as partners is not conclusive. Neither is it essential that written articles of partnership be prepared and executed. A partnership agreement may be oral and may result from the acts and conduct of the parties clearly manifesting an intention to engage in a bona fide business partnership....

Here, immediately after their marriage Alfred and Olive pooled their cash and other property. Thereafter, each made substantial contributions of labor and services to their joint undertakings of farming, business, and the practice of law. On occasions they engaged in separate activities, but always the earnings from such separate activities were placed in their joint bank accounts. Each exercised authority, control, and management over the various business endeavors in which they jointly engaged. Each contributed substantial vital services in carrying on their joint undertakings. Money that came to each of them through inheritance was placed in the joint bank accounts. Each had authority and in fact did draw checks on their several bank accounts.

I am convinced that the conclusion reached by the Court in *Neel, supra,* is warranted by the facts in this case. To hold otherwise would require this Court to ignore the reality of the wife's contribution to the family farm in this situation. To hold such the defendant here would also thwart the obvious intent of the Craigs, which was to operate the farm in partnership with each one contributing equally in the work and its control and management. The facts indicate that it was also agreed that the hard-earned rewards of that labor would be reinvested into the business rather than be kept by each spouse for his or her personal economic choices. Indicative of this is the fact that the household goods were valued at $400 on the estate tax return. Certainly Bessie Craig's indisputable hard work throughout the years was not directed toward her personal obtainment of a beautiful and well-furnished home. This Court will not ignore this farm wife's contribution to the success of the business as the Internal Revenue Service seeks to do.

The facts clearly indicate that Clarence and Bessie Craig intended to and did operate their farm as equal partners throughout their 43 years of marriage. The success they enjoyed in this endeavor was because of their joint efforts.

It is therefore the opinion of this Court that half of the personal property listed on Schedule F of the estate tax return of Clarence Craig was rightfully the property of Bessie Craig and that she, therefore is entitled to a refund to that extent plus interest.

Reforms of 1976 and 1978. A new rule was was created by the 1976 Tax Reform Act for real estate jointly owned between a husband and wife. If the joint tenancy was created after 1976 and if a gift tax return was properly filed electing to treat the creation of the joint tenancy as a gift, the property is treated as belonging 50 percent to each spouse for estate tax purposes.[4]

The Revenue Act of 1978 also addressed the issue of jointly owned property used in a farm or other trade or business if owned by a husband and wife.[5] A new "2 percent credit" rule was established, allowing the surviving spouse a credit of 2 percent per year of the value of jointly owned property for each year of marriage (up to a maximum of 25 years). This credit could be used to reduce the deceased's estate up to $500,000, but it only applies after the original contribution of the deceased has been adjusted by 6 percent simple interest for each year the property was owned. In addition, the credit can only be claimed for years in which the surviving spouse "materially participated" in the business. Material participation is to be interpreted in the social security sense.

The Inflexibility Problem. The second major estate planning problem created by the use of co-ownership arrangements is that flexi-

[4]Int. Rev. Code § 2040(b).
[5]Int. Rev. Code § 2040(c).

bility in the disposition of property at the time of death is eliminated. To reduce taxes, estate plans often call for the use of trust arrangements or life estates providing a life income interest to a surviving spouse. These arrangements are typically used so that the same property is not taxed in the estates of both the husband and the wife. If the property is held in joint tenancy or tenancy by the entirety, there is no opportunity to reduce taxes by using these methods unless the joint interest is severed.

In addition, the ultimate decision concerning disposition of the property is totally in the hands of the surviving co-owner. The first to die has no control over its disposition. The survivor can make whatever disposition he or she chooses during life or at death including a transfer to a new spouse or to some children to the exclusion of others, etc.

This review of joint interests in property should indicate that such arrangements are no panacea for family estate planning problems. There are situations where such arrangements can be successfully used, but it is well to understand the true meaning of jointly held property before such interests are created.

17.2 PROBATE AND ESTATE SETTLEMENT

Probate

Probate is not always necessary, but in many estates it is a procedure which is very important. Probate is governed by state law, but the following general discussion is fairly representative.

Among other things, probate bars the claims of creditors against the decedent's property if the claims are not filed within a specified period of time. This procedure, of course, tells the purchaser of the property that debts, expenses, and taxes have been

paid and that the property is being sold free of any such claims. If the property of the decedent is properly inventoried, the creditors have a statutory period to file claims from the date the executor or administrator is formally appointed.

Probate also officially determines the decedent's legal heirs and the beneficiaries of the decedent's last will. This step is important in clearly stating the kind and quality of ownership the heir or beneficiary has in the decedent's property.

There are many reasons for probating an estate, some of which are mentioned below. An attorney can help the family examine the necessity of probating the estate.

The usual steps in probating an estate are outlined below:

1. The will is filed with the clerk of the court. The place of probate is the county of the decedent's place of residence.

2. Proof of heirship and decree of heirship are established. The names of heirs must be determined so that the right persons are notified of the probate of the will. If there is no will, these heirs will receive the property.

3. A petition to probate the will and for Letters Testamentary is filed. If the will names an executor, then that person is entitled to Letters Testamentary, which give the executor or administrator the legal right to administer the estate of the decedent. A copy of this document is usually required before persons owing money to the decedent or holding property of the decedent will pay the money or transfer the property to the executor or administrator.

4. The personal representative (executor or administrator) files a personal bond and takes an oath that he or she will faithfully discharge the duties of the office according to the law. Surety on the bond is necessary unless the surety is made unnecessary by a provision of the decedent's will.

5. The will is admitted to probate. The admission of the will requires that at least two of the witnesses to the will testify that they saw the decedent sign the will and that they witnessed the will in the presence of the testator (person who made the will). They must also testify that the testator was of sound mind and memory when signing the will. Sometimes this testimony can be in the form of an affidavit of the witness, without the witness's having to testify in court.

6. After the executor or administrator is appointed, that person is required to file an inventory with the court describing the assets subject to probate.

7. Claims against the estate and costs of administration and federal estate, state inheritance, and fiduciary income taxes are paid.

8. The distribution of the decedent's property is approved by the court.

9. The personal representative files a Final Account, receives approval of the account, and the estate is closed.

There are many other aspects to probate. Guardians may have to be approved or appointed; court approval may be necessary before any sale, exchange, or mortgage of the estate's assets; if there is a will, contest litigation may be necessary; the surviving spouse's and child's awards may have to be determined and approved; and appraisals of property may have to be obtained.

It is obvious that the probate of a will and the administration and settlement of an estate require the technical skill of a lawyer. Involved in all settlements following death are rights, obligations, and common-law and statutory duties not apparent to

average citizens, who may think that they have a clear-cut notion of exactly what is involved in settling the estate when, in fact, they may not be aware of many elements. Generally, the executor or administrator makes the decision as to which attorney will represent the estate during probate.

The duration of the probate process varies. Probate may be as short as a few months or it may take up to 3 or more years in estates involving audits of the federal estate tax return and complicated distribution and notice requirements. If a longer period is required, portions or all of the property can sometimes be distributed and many items finalized even though the estate cannot be formally closed.

Many states have simpler procedures for small estates. In Illinois, for example, if the value of the personal property is less than $15,000, a small estates affidavit can be prepared which will permit any person or corporation indebted to or holding personal property of the decedent to transfer the property according to the requirements of the law without the necessity of the probate procedure.[6] Also, for estates of less than $150,000, a special probate proceeding involving less direct court supervision is available.[7]

17.3 INTESTATE DISTRIBUTION OF PROPERTY

Laws of descent (laws of intestate succession) govern the disposition of a deceased's property not disposed of by will or by some other method.[8] In effect, in cases where a person does not have a will, the state legislature has prepared a will. Generally, the

[6]ILL. REV. STAT. ch. 110 1/2, § 25-1 (Supp. 1978).
[7]ILL. REV. STAT. ch. 110 1/2, §28-1 (Supp. 1978).
[8]Joint tenancy and tenancy by the entirety property, for example, passes to the surviving joint tenants and is not disposed of by will or by the laws of descent.

laws of descent in a particular state distribute property to the closest relatives in a manner which the state legislature deems to be fair in most situations. In comparing the laws of descent for different states, many similarities will be found as well as some differences. Table 17.1 illustrates the rules of descent for Illinois, which has a fairly representative scheme. For example, the Illinois rules make no distinction between

Table 17.1   Descent of Property by Illinois Law When There Is No Will

Closest Surviving Relative	Distribution of Property
Wife or husband and descendants	1/2 to wife or husband; 1/2 to descendants[a]
Wife or husband, but no descendants	All to wife or husband
Descendants, but no wife or husband	All to children equally[b]
Parents, brothers, and sisters, but no surviving spouse or descendants	Parents, brothers, and sisters share equally[c]
Only grandparents or their descendants	(1) 1/2 to maternal grandparents, (2) 1/2 to paternal grandparents,[d] when there are no relatives in (1), then all goes to those in (2), and vice versa
Only great-grandparents or their descendants	(1) 1/2 to maternal great-grandparents, (2) 1/2 to paternal great-grandparents.[e] When there are no relatives in (1), then all goes to those in (2), and vice versa
Only collateral heirs[f]	Shared equally by nearest kindred of deceased
No relatives	All real property goes to the county in which the land is located; all personal property goes to the county in which the deceased resided[g]

[a] If one of the children has died, his or her children share that part. In some states, the fraction distribution is one-third to spouse, two-thirds to descendants. *See* VA. CODE § 64.1-1 *et seq.* (Supp. 1979). These shares can be affected by other statutory rules. The following are particularly important: (1) Homestead property. A homestead is exempt from the laws of descent. The spouse and minor children are entitled to an interest of $10,000 in the family home. Creditors cannot force sale of the homestead for debts incurred by the deceased, so long as the spouse lives on the homestead or so long as the youngest child is under 21 years of age and occupies the homestead. (2) Rights of an adopted child. A child who has been lawfully adopted has the same inheritance rights as a natural child. Similarly, the adopting parents inherit from the child as though the child were their own. There is one exception to this: Property received by the child from his or her natural parents or relatives goes back to them upon the child's death if he or she has not left a will. (3) Rights of a stepchild. A stepchild inherits from his or her natural parent (or parents, if divorced), but does not inherit from a stepparent unless the child is legally adopted by the stepparent.
[b] If one of the children has died, his or her children share that part.
[c] Descendants of a deceased brother or sister get the deceased's share. If one parent is deceased, the surviving parent gets a double share.
[d] For both maternal and paternal grandparents, if one has died the survivor gets a double share; if both have died, their descendants share equally.
[e] For both maternal and paternal great-grandparents, if one has died, the survivor gets a double share.
[f] Collateral heirs are relatives such as cousins, aunts, great-uncles, and great aunts. Persons in the same and nearest degree of relationship to the deceased get equal shares when only collateral heirs survive.
[g] If the deceased is not a resident of the state of Illinois, all the personal property goes to the Illinois county in which the property is located.

real and personal property, just as in most other states. Similarly, the fractional distribution in Illinois is quite typical.

Farmers and ranchers often find that the rules of descent are inadequate for their particular circumstances. For example, a retired farmer and his wife living in Illinois may find that their "nest egg" is sufficient to give them adequate security and income. But if the husband should pass away without a will, his spouse would be entitled to only one-half of his property if there were children. One-half of the "nest egg" would be insufficient to adequately provide for the surviving spouse. Fortunately, one can use a will to distribute property according to one's own wishes. If one distributes property by will, the laws of descent will not apply.

17.4 FEDERAL ESTATE AND GIFT TAXES

One of the most important objectives of most farm families is to minimize estate and gift taxes on the transfer of assets. Consideration must be given to all taxes that may be involved, but the federal estate tax and the federal gift tax are likely to have the greatest impact. Substantial changes were made in the federal estate and gift tax system in 1976. Many of these changes have direct application to the farm estate.

Unified Gift and Estate Tax Structure

The value of all property transferred by gift or through an estate is taxed according to a single unified rate structure. As later examples will show, the total transfer tax payable will be about the same whether property is transferred by gift or through an estate. This result is one goal of the unified system. Some savings possibilities for lifetime gifts still exist, and these will also be discussed later.

Amount Subject to Tax. The tax is based upon cumulative taxable transfers occurring after 1976. Taxable transfers may be in the form of taxable gifts or the taxable estate. Figure 17.1 illustrates how taxable gifts and the taxable estate add to the cumulative amount subject to tax.

Figure 17.1 The Cumulative Amount Subject to Tax

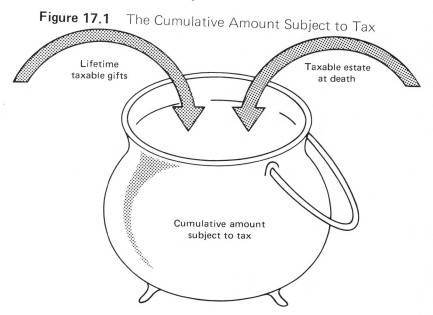

Lifetime taxable gifts

Taxable estate at death

Cumulative amount subject to tax

Table 17.2   New Single Unified Rate Schedule for Taxable Gifts and Taxable Estates

(1)		(3)	(4)
Cumulative Amount Subject to Tax, $		Cumulative Tax on Amount in Column 1, $	Tax Rate on Excess over Amount in Column 1, %
From	To		
—	10,000	—	18
20,000	40,000	1,800	20
40,000	60,000	8,200	24
60,000	80,000	13,000	26
80,000	100,000	18,200	28
150,000	250,000	38,800	32
250,000	500,000	70,800	34
500,000	750,000	155,800	37
750,000	1,000,000	248,300	39
1,000,000	1,250,000	345,800	41
1,250,000	1,500,000	448,300	43
1,500,000	2,000,000	555,800	45
2,000,000	2,500,000	780,800	49
2,500,000	3,000,000	1,025,800	53
3,000,000	3,500,000	1,290,800	57
3,500,000	4,000,000	1,575,800	61
4,000,000	4,500,000	1,880,800	65
4,500,000	5,000,000	2,205,800	69
5,000,000	—	2,550,800	70

Source: Derived from I.R.C. § 2001(c).

The new unified gift and estate tax system applies to both taxable gifts made after 1976 and the taxable estate. Both taxable gifts and the taxable estate add to the cumulative amount subject to tax. As the cumulative taxable transfers increase, progressively higher transfer tax rates will apply to each additional taxable transfer.

Unified Rate Structure and Unified Credit.   The transfer tax rate varies from 18 to 70 percent depending upon the value of cumulative taxable transfers occurring after 1976.[9]

The greater the value of total taxable transfers, the higher the tax rate on each additional taxable transfer. Table 17.2 illustrates the unified rate schedule for the federal transfer tax.

The amount found in column 1 of Table 17.2 is called a "tentative tax" in the new law. The tentative tax is offset dollar for dollar by the available tax credit. In effect, any unused tax credit is subtracted from the tentative tax when calculating the "tax payable." The Tax Reform Act provides a tax

[9]Taxable gifts made before 1977 will affect the tax rate applied to taxable gifts made after 1976, but the pre-1977 taxable gifts will not affect the tax rate applied to the taxable estate. For simpli-

city, the authors have assumed no pre-1977 taxable gifts in the general discussion of the 1976 changes.

Table 17.3 Phase-In of Unified Credit

Year of Death	Credit	"Equivalent Exemption"
1977	$30,000	$120,666
1978	34,000	134,000
1979	38,000	147,333
1980	42,500	161,563
1981 and thereafter	47,000	175,625

Source: I.R.C. § 2010.

credit of $30,000 in 1977 with a stepped increase to a $47,000 credit by 1981 as shown in Table 17.3.

The "equivalent exemption" in Table 17.3 is the amount of property that can be transferred "tax free" when the maximum credit is applied to the tentative tax.

Some Examples. The following examples illustrate how the tax credit and rate schedule apply to a series of taxable transfers, including taxable gifts and a taxable estate.

EXAMPLE 1

On July 1, 1977, Farmer Jones made a taxable gift of property worth $150,000. This was the first taxable gift made by Farmer Jones. According to the unified rate schedule, the tentative tax on this taxable gift would be $38,800 (see Table 17.2). The tax credit available in 1977 is $30,000 (see Table 17.3). Therefore, Farmer Jones must pay the remaining $8800 as a "tax payable."[10]

EXAMPLE 2

On January 1, 1979, Farmer Jones makes a taxable gift of $100,000. His cumulative taxable transfers have now increased from $150,000 to $250,000. This $100,000 gift will be taxed at 32 percent (see Table 17.2 for cumulative taxable transfers between $150,000 and $250,000). Therefore, the *additional* tentative tax will be $32,000 ($100,000 times 0.32 = $32,000). The maximum credit in 1979 is $38,000 (see Table 17.3), but Farmer Jones has already used $30,000 to offset tax on his gift in Example 1. The unused $8000 of credit can be applied against the additional $32,000 tentative tax. Farmer Jones must pay the remaining $24,000 as a "tax payable."

EXAMPLE 3

Farmer Jones dies on January 1, 1983, with a taxable estate of $250,000. His total taxable transfers have now increased from $250,000 (total of taxable gifts in Examples 1 and 2) to $500,000. This additional transfer of a $250,000 taxable estate will be taxed at 34 percent (see Table 17.2 for rate applying to cumulative taxable transfers from $250,000 to $500,000). Therefore, the *additional* tentative tax will be $85,000 (0.34 times $250,000 = $85,000). The maxi-

---

[10] The gift tax return would be filed before November 15, 1977 (15th day of the second month following the end of the calendar quarter). Generally, a gift tax return is due on April 15 of the year following the year in which the gifts are made *or* the 15th day of the second month following the calendar quarter in which aggregate taxable gifts for the year exceed $25,000. The latter rule applies in this case since the taxable gift exceeds $25,000.

mum credit in 1983 is $47,000 (see Table 17.3), but Farmer Jones has already used $38,000 for his taxable gifts in Examples 1 and 2. The unused $9000 of credit ($47,000 minus $38,000) can be applied against the additional $85,000 tentative tax, leaving an additional "estate tax" of $76,000.

Taxable and Nontaxable Gifts

Some gifts are taxable, while other gifts are nontaxable. Only the taxable gifts increase the cumulative amount subject to tax (see Figure 17.1). Nontaxable gifts now include the $3000 annual gift exclusion, split gift provisions for a husband and wife, and a marital deduction for gifts to a spouse. The old $30,000 lifetime exemption for gifts was eliminated by the Tax Reform Act of 1976 and is not available for gifts made after 1976.

The annual gift tax exclusion of $3000 per year per recipient was not changed by the Reform Act. Any person can give up to $3000 *per year* in cash or property to *each* of as many persons as he or she chooses.[11] Such gifts are nontaxable gifts and are not income to the recipient for income tax purposes. For example, if an annual $3000 gift was made to each of three children over a 10-year period, $90,000 in cash or property would be transferred tax-free. The $3000 annual gifts could be made to anyone, whether related or not.

The law also allows a husband and wife to combine their annual exclusions, even though only one spouse makes the gift of cash or property.[12] Thus a husband could make nontaxable gifts of $6000 to each recipient if his wife joined him in making the gifts. It would be necessary to file gift tax returns to elect this "split gift" treat-

ment, but the gift would not be taxable unless it exceeded $6000.

Nontaxable gifts can also be made between husband and wife. In fact, the new tax law offers increased opportunity for tax-free exchanges between spouses by increasing the maximum marital deduction in some cases. Under the new provisions, the first $100,000 of gifts to a spouse which exceed the $3000 annual exclusion is 100 percent exempt from the transfer tax. The next $100,000 of gifts to a spouse are fully taxable. Gifts to a spouse exceeding $200,000 are 50 percent exempt and 50 percent taxable.[13]

Table 17.4 shows the effect of the unified tax rates and the $47,000 tax credit. There is no "tax payable" in 1981 until cumulative taxable transfers exceed $175,625, because the $47,000 tax credit available in 1981 and later years will offset the "tentative tax" on that amount. The 32 percent rate is the lowest tax rate applying to taxable transfers exceeding the $175,625 "equivalent exemption." This table is presented for illustration purposes and should not be used to calculate the "tax payable."

EXAMPLE 4: Gifts to a Spouse

Between January 1, 1981, and March 31, 1981, H makes a series of gifts to his spouse totaling $357,250. Assuming H had made no previous taxable gifts, the calculation of "tax payable" would be as shown in Computation 17.1.

Example 4 illustrates that one spouse can transfer substantial assets to the other spouse through the use of the annual exclusion for gifts, marital deduction for gifts, and use of the tax credit. Of course, because H has used all of his credit to offset

[11] INT. REV. CODE § 2503(b).
[12] INT. REV. CODE § 2513.
[13] Use of the increased gift tax marital deduction for gifts up to $200,000 reduces the maximum

estate tax marital deduction. When gifts to a spouse reach $200,000, the estate tax marital deduction is not affected.

Table 17.4 Tax Payable and Rates after Subtraction of Unified Credit of $47,000 Available in 1981 and Later Years

Cumulative Amount Subject to Tax, $	Cumulative Tax Payable,* $	Rate on Excess, %	Cumulative Amount Subject to Tax, $	Cumulative Tax Payable,* $	Rate on Excess, %
25,000			1,100,000	339,800	41
50,000			1,200,000	380,800	41
75,000			1,300,000	422,800	43
100,000			1,400,000	465,800	43
125,000			1,500,000	508,800	45
150,000			1,600,000	553,800	45
175,625	0	32	1,700,000	598,800	45
200,000	7,800	32	1,800,000	643,800	45
250,000	23,800	34	1,900,000	688,800	45
300,000	40,800	34	2,000,000	733,800	49
350,000	57,800	34	2,100,000	782,800	49
400,000	74,800	34	2,200,000	831,800	49
450,000	91,800	34	2,300,000	880,800	49
500,000	108,800	37	2,400,000	929,800	49
550,000	127,300	37	2,500,000	978,800	53
600,000	145,800	37	2,600,000	1,031,800	53
650,000	164,300	37	2,700,000	1,084,800	53
700,000	182,800	37	2,800,000	1,137,800	53
750,000	201,300	39	2,900,000	1,190,800	53
800,000	220,800	39	3,000,000	1,243,800	57
850,000	240,300	39	3,500,000	1,528,800	61
900,000	259,800	39	4,000,000	1,833,800	65
950,000	279,300	39	4,500,000	2,158,800	69
1,000,000	298,800	41	5,000,000	2,503,800	70

Source: Derived from I.R.C. §§ 2001, 2010.
*After subtracting $47,000 credit.

gift tax, H will have no unified credit to offset any additional transfer tax generated by future taxable gifts or by his taxable estate.

The Taxable Estate at Death

It is important to understand how to arrive at the taxable estate. The calculation starts with the gross estate, subtracts certain items to arrive at the adjusted gross estate, and subtracts other deductions to arrive at the taxable estate. The first step in calculating the taxable estate is to determine the value of the gross estate. All property owned outright by the deceased at the time of death is included in the deceased's gross estate at fair market value.[14] Thus the fair market value of all land, machinery, grain, livestock, stocks and bonds, and deposits held in the deceased's name are included in the gross estate. A few items of special interest are mentioned below.

Life Insurance. Life insurance proceeds are

---

[14] Special valuation for agricultural land, discussed later, is an exception to the fair market value rule.

Computation 17.1 Gifts to a Spouse

Total gifts		$357,250
Less annual exclusion	($ 3,000)	
Less marital deduction for the first $100,000 exceeding the annual exclusion	(100,000)	
Less marital deduction for the next $100,000 exceeding the annual exclusion	(0)	
Less marital deduction for remaining $157,250 gifts (50% rule applies)	(78,625)	
Total deductions		(181,625)
Taxable gifts ($357,250–181,625)		175,625
Tentative tax (from Table 17.2)		47,000
Less unified credit available in 1981 and Later Years (Table 17.3)		(47,000)
Tax payable		$ 0

included in the decedent's gross estate if the decedent retained any of the "incidents of ownership" in the policy on his or her life (for example, the right to change beneficiaries, to surrender or cancel the policy, or to assign or borrow on the policy).[15] The proceeds are also included in the decedent's gross estate if they are payable to his or her "estate." Ownership of a life insurance policy can be transferred, but such transfer may be a taxable gift approximating the cash value of the policy at the time of transfer.

Retained Life Estate. If a person transfers property by gift and retains possession, enjoyment, or right to income from such property, the fair cash value of the property will be a part of the person's gross estate. A similar result will occur if the person retains the right to designate the persons who will possess the property or receive the income from it.[16]

Gifts within 3 Years of Death. Under the new law, gifts exceeding the $3000 annual exclusion which are made after 1976 and within 3 years of death are automatically included in the gross estate. Also, any gift tax paid on such a gift is included in the gross estate. The new rules are a departure from the old rule which stated that any gift made within 3 years of death was presumed to be included in the gross estate as a gift "in contemplation of death." The old presumption could be overcome if the deceased's executor could prove a lifetime motive. Such factual questions dealing with motive are removed by the new law which employs the simple 3-year test.[17]

Tenancy in Common Property. Property owned by the deceased and another person as tenants in common is included in the gross estate of the deceased only to the extent of the deceased's fractional interest. For example, if H and W own farmland as equal tenants in common, only one-half of the value of the farm is included in H's gross estate at the time of H's death.

Joint Tenancy Property.[18] Rules regarding joint tenancy property were altered by the Tax Reform Act of 1976 and the Revenue

[15] INT. REV. CODE § 2042.
[16] INT. REV. CODE § 2036.
[17] INT. REV. CODE § 2035.
[18] See INT. REV. CODE § 2040.

Act of 1978, but large joint tenancy holdings generally are still a disadvantage from an estate planning viewpoint. The disadvantage occurs because (1) there is no flexibility as to the disposition of the property—the surviving joint tenant automatically has outright ownership of the entire property, and (2) the law generally presumes that the *entire* value of the property will be included in the estate of the first joint tenant to die. The only way to remove all or part of the joint tenancy property value from the first estate is to *prove* that the surviving joint tenant was financially responsible for the acquisition of all or part of the property. This proof of contribution is very difficult to meet.

The Tax Reform act of 1976 did make one change regarding the taxation of joint tenancy property. For joint tenancies created between a husband and wife after 1976, one-half of the joint tenancy property is included in the estate of the first joint tenant to die *provided* creation of the joint tenancy was a gift for gift tax purposes. For real property, creation of a joint tenancy interest between husband and wife is a gift for gift tax purposes if a timely gift tax return is filed. The new provision is advantageous to the limited extent that it keeps the appreciation in value of one-half of the joint tenancy property out of the estate of the purchasing spouse, but it can have significant disadvantages if the spouse receiving the gift dies first.

The Revenue Act of 1978 also made a change regarding the amount of joint tenancy property that might be included in the gross estate of the first joint tenant to die. This change provides that an executor may elect to have "material participation"

by a surviving spouse taken into account in order to reduce the value of jointly owned real estate or tangible personal property included in the deceased joint tenant's gross estate. The new rule may offer some tax benefit in the estate of the first joint tenant, but does nothing to solve the greatest joint tenancy problem—the unnecessarily large gross estate of the surviving joint tenant.

Determining the Adjusted Gross Estate. Once the gross estate is determined, all debts of the decedent (including the expenses of last illness and burial paid by the executor) can be subtracted. Also, probate costs and estate administration expenses including attorney's fees and executor's fees are deductible. The remaining value is the adjusted gross estate.

Determining the Taxable Estate. The adjusted gross estate may be reduced by charitable contributions.[19] Thus, if a decedent bequeaths cash or property to a church, the United Fund, the 4-H Foundation, or some other charitable organization, the amount of these bequests is subtracted from the adjusted gross estate in determining the Taxable estate.

The Marital Deduction.[20] The value of property transferred to a surviving spouse at death is also subtracted from the adjusted gross estate if the property qualifies for the marital deduction. To qualify for the marital deduction, a surviving spouse must receive an outright interest in property which was included in the deceased's gross estate, or the surviving spouse must at least have a general power to determine who will enjoy the property after the death of the surviving spouse.[21] There is a limit to the marital deduction, however. The marital deduction cannot exceed the greater of $250,000 or

---

[19] INT. REV. CODE § 2055.
[20] INT. REV. CODE § 2056.
[21] It should be noted that property in which the surviving spouse receives only a life income interest does not qualify for the marital deduction. Although such property will be a part of the taxable estate of the first spouse, such property will not be included in the gross estate of the second spouse when the second spouse dies.

50 percent of the adjusted gross estate.[22] The old rule limited the marital deduction to 50 percent of the adjusted gross estate.

The following example illustrates the tax saving potential of the marital deduction. Suppose that A dies in 1981, with an adjusted gross estate of $425,625. If A leaves property worth at least $250,000 to A's spouse outright, there will be a marital deduction of $250,000. The taxable estate will be $175,625 ($425,625 adjusted gross estate minus $250,000 marital deduction equals $175,625 taxable estate). Assuming no prior taxable gifts, the tentative tax would be $47,000 (see Table 17.2). The "tax payable" would be zero since the unused $47,000 credit available in 1981 (see Table 17.3) would completely offset the tentative tax. Of course, there would be substantial taxes at the death of the second spouse, since no marital deduction would be available (unless the second spouse remarried and left qualifying property to the new spouse).

The Orphan's Deduction. The 1976 Tax Reform Act added a limited deduction available in those estates where the decedent had no surviving spouse but left minor children who have no surviving parent. This deduction for property passing to the minor child is equal to $5000 for each year that each child is under 21 years of age. For example, if a decedent had two minor children ages 11 and 16, the deduction would amount to $50,000 for property passing to the 11-year-old and $25,000 for property passing to the 16-year-old.

Agricultural Valuation for Certain Farmland[23]

As a general rule, property is included in the gross estate of an individual at its fair market value, regardless of its actual use. However, the Tax Reform Act of 1976 provides for an "actual use" valuation for certain qualifying real property, which may be elected by the executor or administrator. Where applicable, a special formula can be used to determine the "actual use" valuation. That formula is as follows:

$$
\text{"Actual use" valuation per acre} = \frac{\text{Average net cash rent}^{24} \text{ over the past 5 years for comparable property in the community}}{\text{Average interest rate for new Federal Land Bank loans over the past 5 years}}
$$

For example, assume that average net cash rent has averaged $100 per acre and that the interest rate on new Federal Land Bank loans has averaged 10 percent. The special valuation per acre would be:

$$
\frac{\$100}{0.10} = \$1000
$$

If appropriate data for the formula is not available, the new law provides for additional factors to be considered in determining the "actual use" valuation. These factors include capitalization of income over a reasonable period, capitalization of fair

---

[22] The maximum estate tax marital deduction may be somewhat less if a marital deduction for lifetime gifts has been used.

[23] See INT. REV. CODE § 2032A.

[24] Net cash rent equals gross cash rent minus real estate taxes.

rental value, assessed values if based upon current use, and comparable sales (for farming purposes) in the same area.

Qualifying for the "Actual Use" Valuation. A number of tests must be met in order for farmland to qualify for the special valuation:

1. Real and personal property used in farming that is passing to members of the decedent's family[25] must comprise at least 50 percent of the adjusted value of the gross estate.[26] For example, at least half of the adjusted value of a farmer's gross estate must be composed of land, buildings, machinery, livestock, grain, etc., used in farming *and* passing to a qualified family member.

2. *Real* property (buildings and land) used in farming and passing to a qualified family member must comprise at least 25 percent of the adjusted value of the gross estate.

3. The decedent or a member of the decedent's family must have owned the real property for 5 of the 8 years preceding the decedent's death and must have materially participated[27] in the management of the farming operation for at least 5 of the preceding 8 years.

Maximum Benefit Rule. Use of the special actual use valuation cannot reduce the value of the estate by more than $500,000.

Recapture Provisions. Any estate tax savings resulting from the use of the special valuation can be recaptured if certain conditions occur—for example, if a family member does not meet the material participation requirement of the new law during the 15-year period following death. In general, the potential for recapture will cease if the family member acquiring the property dies without having disposed of the property to nonfamily members or without having converted it to a nonfarming use, or if a period of 15 years passes after the decedent's death. A special federal lien is placed on real property for which the special valuation is used, to insure that the government will be able to recapture the tax savings if recapture is triggered.

Deferred Payment of Estate Tax

The Tax Reform Act of 1976 provides for a special deferred payment of some estate tax. A 15-year period for the payment of the estate tax attributable to the decedent's interest in a farm or other closely held business is allowed if the value of the closely held business in the decedent's estate comprises at least 65 percent of the adjusted gross estate.[28] An acceleration of the deferred tax payments will occur if all or a significant portion of the closely held business is disposed of or liquidated. Up to ten annual installment payments of the deferred tax can be made starting not later than the sixth year following decedent's death.

A special 4 percent interest rate is allowed on the deferred tax attributable to the first million dollars of closely held farm business property. Interest on the deferred tax ex-

---

[25] The definition of family member includes decedent's spouse, any ancestor or lineal descendant of the decedent, a lineal descendant of a grandparent, or the spouse of any lineal descendant. The definition includes, for example, the decedent's children, wife, parents, grandparents, aunts, uncles, nieces, and nephews.

[26] The adjusted value of the gross estate is the fair market value of property included in the gross estate less unpaid indebtedness on that property.

[27] Material participation will be determined in a manner similar to that used for purposes of determining self-employment tax liability on crop-share leases.

[28] INT. REV. CODE § 6166.

ceeding this amount will bear the regular rate of interest on deferred tax payments. The regular rate is subject to adjustment as market interest rates change. Interest payments must be paid annually, even during the first 5 years. The deferred payment provisions and the low interest rate should help solve some of the problems caused by insufficient liquidity in farm estates.

New Generation Skipping Tax

A "life interest" in property generally gives the holder of such interest the use, enjoyment, and income from the property for as long as he or she lives. For example, A might transfer a farm to B for life, and the remainder interest to C. B has a life estate which is a "life interest." Alternatively, A might transfer the farm to a trustee who was directed to pay the income from the trust property to B for B's lifetime. B is a life income beneficiary of the trust and has a "life interest" in the trust property. Generally, such a "life interest" is not subject to the estate tax when the life tenant or life income beneficiary dies.

Because a life interest is not generally subject to the estate tax, a series of life interests has been an effective way to "skip" the estate tax on some succeeding generations. For example, suppose A transfers his property to his child for life, then to his grandchild for life, then to his great-grandchildren. The child and grandchildren have the use, enjoyment, and income from the property during their respective lives, but the property is not taxed in their estates when they die. In effect, the estate tax has been "skipped" on these two generations.

The tax saving advantages of successive life interests were substantially limited by the Tax Reform Act of 1976, which created a "special generation skipping tax."[29] In effect, the new provision taxes the "skipped generation" as if the nonexempt portion of the property were a part of the income beneficiary's estate. However, $250,000 in income-producing property per child is exempt from the tax if the income is paid to a child of the grantor and a grandchild will receive the property after the child's death. For example, suppose X transfers the North Farm to son Y for life, remainder to Y's children, and transfers the South Farm in trust for the lifetime benefit of daughter Z, remainder interest in Z's children. When Y dies, the value of the North Farm exceeding the $250,000 exemption will be subject to the special generation skipping tax. Also, when Z dies, the value of the South Farm exceeding the $250,000 exemption will be subject to the special generation skipping tax.

There are many other complex rules applicable to the generation skipping tax. Some generation skipping plans enacted in trusts and wills prior to May 1, 1976 will not be affected by this new rule.

Income Tax Basis Considerations

An additional tax consideration in estate planning arises from application of income tax basis rules. The income tax basis of assets is, essentially, the amount a person has invested in a particular asset. This amount can be recovered upon sale of the asset without tax.

The tax basis for purchased assets is the original cost adjusted for any additional investment in the property such as improvements on real estate and for any recovery on tax investment such as depreciation claimed.

---

[29] INT. REV. CODE § 2601 *et seq.*

To illustrate, suppose a farmer purchases a parcel of land for $100,000 and adds $50,000 in improvements on which $20,000 has been claimed in depreciation. The income tax basis on this property is $130,000. Upon sale of the farm, the gain would be the amount by which the sales price exceeds the basis.

For gifted property, the donee's income tax basis is that of the donor at the time of the gift. In the above example if the farmer had given the farm to a daughter, her income tax basis would also be the $130,000.

A different rule applies to inherited property. The heir receives a new income tax basis on inherited property equal to the value for estate tax purposes, which is ordinarily the fair market value of the property as of the date of death. If the farm in the example above has a fair market value of $200,000 and is passed to the daughter by inheritance, she would receive a new "stepped-up" basis of $200,000 in the property.

One exception to the step-up to fair market value applies. If the estate elects to use actual use valuation for farmland, the basis for the inherited farmland in the hands of the heir is the value used for estate tax purposes, which will be a lower use value rather than the fair market value.

Considerable controversy has been generated by this rule. Congress, in fact, established a new rule in 1976—the so-called carryover basis for inherited property. The implementation of this rule, which involved an adjustment in basis so that existing owners would have a "fresh start," was postponed in 1978, then repealed in 1980, so that the old "stepped-up" basis rule applies to all estates of decedents, regardless of the date of death.

17.5 STATE DEATH TAXES

In addition to the federal taxes involved in the transfer of property by gift or at death, most of the individual states have also enacted some type of "death" tax. In some states, this tax has been coordinated with the federal tax so that it is also in the form of an "estate tax"—that is, payable out of the deceased's estate. For example, Virginia has an estate tax that is equal to the maximum amount of credit for state death taxes allowed under the federal estate tax laws.[30] Tables such as Table 17.5 are provided within the Internal Revenue Code for computing this credit. Thus, no state tax is due unless the estate owes federal tax.

In many states, the death tax takes the form of an inheritance tax payable by those who *receive* a share of the estate rather than payable directly out of estate assets. The person receiving the property is personally liable for the tax, and it is a lien on any property received. Frequently, state inheritance tax laws provide for deductions similar to those under federal law. Illinois, for example, allows deductions for funeral expenses of administration, debts of the decedent, federal income tax liabilities of the decedent, last illness expenses, real and personal property taxes which are a lien against the property on decedent's death, and the federal estate taxes.[31]

Under most inheritance tax schemes, higher rates of taxation are imposed as the degree of blood relationship decreases between the deceased and the deceased's beneficiaries. In addition, larger exemptions are frequently available for property left to closer relatives.

---

[30] VA. CODE § 58-238.1 *et seq.* (Supp. 1979).
[31] *See* regulations promulgated under ILL. REV. STAT. ch. 120 ¶ 375 *et seq.*

Kansas imposes a graduated inheritance tax on the respective shares received by a decedent's beneficiaries. An additional estate tax is assessed in the amount that the total inheritance tax due is less than the maximum credit allowed by the federal estate tax (see Table 17.6).

State laws also sometimes provide for gift taxes, or these may be unified into a single system similar to the federal one. Since state laws vary considerably and are subject to frequent revision, no set rules can be stated regarding taxes at the state level.

17.6 ESTATE PLANNING TOOLS TO REDUCE TAXES AND MEET OTHER OBJECTIVES

Reducing Taxes

Making Gifts of Property. Making gifts of property is one way to save transfer taxes. Gifts utilizing the $3000 annual exclusion, the "split gift" provisions up to $6000, and the marital deduction for gifts are not "taxable gifts," nor would they generally be a part of the "taxable estate" if made more than 3 years before death. The unified rate and credit structure of the new law has made the use of taxable gifts less beneficial than

Table 17.5 Maximum Credit for State Death Taxes

(1) Adjusted Taxable Estate,* $, Equal to or More Than	(2) Taxable Estate, $, Less Than	(3) Credit on Amount in Column 1, $	(4) Rate of Credit on Excess over Amount in Column 1, %
0	40,000	0	None
40,000	90,000	0	0.8
90,000	140,000	400	1.6
140,000	240,000	1,200	2.4
240,000	440,000	3,600	3.2
440,000	640,000	10,000	4.0
640,000	840,000	18,000	4.8
840,000	1,040,000	27,600	5.6
1,040,000	1,540,000	38,000	6.4
1,540,000	2,040,000	70,800	7.2
2,040,000	2,540,000	106,800	8.0
2,540,000	3,040,000	146,800	8.8
3,040,000	3,540,000	190,800	9.6
3,540,000	4,040,000	238,800	10.4
4,040,000	5,040,000	290,800	11.2
5,040,000	6,040,000	402,800	12.0
6,040,000	7,040,000	522,800	12.8
7,040,000	8,040,000	650,800	13.6
8,040,000	9,040,000	786,800	14.4
9,040,000	10,040,000	930,800	15.2
10,040,000		1,082,800	16.0

Source: Derived from the I.R.C. § 2011. Rates are those effective January, 1977.
*Adjusted taxable estate means the taxable estate reduced by $60,000.

under the prior law, where the separate lower rate schedule and the separate lifetime exemption for gifts were available. Nevertheless, making taxable gifts may still be beneficial. The current value of such gifts will be subject to gift tax, but future appreciation in value generally will not be taxed in the transferor's estate. For example, suppose a person makes a taxable gift more than 3 years before the person dies of property worth $100,000. If the person had not made the gift and dies when the property has appreciated in value to $300,000, that person would add $300,000 to his or her gross estate. By making the taxable gift of $100,000, the transferor avoids application of the transfer tax to the $200,000 appreciation in value.

Avoiding Large Joint Tenancy Holdings. Individuals should avoid most joint tenancy holdings in large estates. Even in relatively modest estates, joint tenancy can be disad-

Table 17.6 Kansas Inheritance Tax Rates and Exemptions

Exemptions*		
Class A1:	Surviving spouse	$250,000
Class A2:	Lineal ancestors, lineal descendants, legally adopted child or lineal descendants of legally adopted child, wife or widow of son, husband of daughter	30,000
Class B:	Brother or sister	5,000
Class C:	All others	None

		Rates+					
		Class A1		Class A2		Class B	
Share		Tax on Column 1	Rate on Excess, %	Tax on Column 1	Rate on Excess, %	Tax on Column 1	Rate on Excess, %
From	To						
$ 0	$ 25,000	$ 0	½	$ 0	1	$ 0	3
25,000	50,000	125	1	250	2	750	5
50,000	100,000	375	1½	750	3	2,000	7½
100,000	500,000	1,125	2	2,250	4	5,750	10
500,000	Balance	9,125	2½	18,250	5	45,750	12½

	Rates		
Share		Class C	
From	To	Tax on column 1	Rate on Excess, %
$ 0	$100,000	$ 0	10
100,000	200,000	10,000	12
200,000	Balance	22,000	15

Source: KAN. STAT. ANN. ¶ 79-1501. (1976).

*The share of any beneficiary is exempt if less than $200 in excess of the regular exemption (including Class C).

+Rates shown are those effective December 1, 1975.

vantageous. For estates exceeding $175,625 —the exemption equivalent of the unified credit—unnecessary taxes may be incurred. The lack of flexibility created by joint tenancy and the general presumption that the entire value of the joint tenancy property will be included in the estate of the first joint tenant to die can cause unnecessarily large gross estates for *both* spouses. The new rule regarding joint tenancies created between husband and wife after 1976 may help to reduce the gross estate of the first spouse to die, but it does not help to reduce the estate of the second spouse to die. The same can be said of the 1978 amendment. Thus, joint tenancy should be used with caution, even where the new joint tenancy rules could apply.

Qualifying for Actual Use Valuation of Farmland. Farmers who may benefit from the "actual use" valuation for farmland should consider steps to insure that their estates will meet the qualification tests. To qualify, farmers or members of their family should materially participate in the management of those farming businesses. They should insure that real and personal property used in farming comprises at least 50 percent of their assets, and that the real property used in farming comprises at least 25 percent of their assets. These rules may influence the kind of property that is transferred to others through a gift-giving program. Remember, a gross estate can be reduced up to $500,000 by use of the actual use valuation method.

Making Efficient Use of Deductions and Unified Tax Credit. It is important that an estate plan make *efficient* use of the marital deduction by examining the potential estate taxes in both the husband's and wife's estate. In some cases, the total taxes paid in both estates will be minimized if the maximum marital deduction is used. In other cases, total taxes will be minimized if no marital deduction is used. For example, suppose that both husband and wife own approximately $175,000 worth of property. If the first spouse dies in 1981, there is no tax advantage in using the marital deduction because the $47,000 unified credit available in 1981 would offset the entire tentative tax (assuming no earlier taxable gifts by the decedent). On the other hand, if the spouse left the property worth $175,000 outright to the surviving spouse, the entire amount would qualify for the marital deduction and the taxable estate of the first spouse would be zero. Thus, the $47,000 tax credit of the first spouse would be unused—an undesirable result from a tax standpoint.

Spouses Holding Approximately Equal Amounts of Property. As a general rule, there are potential estate tax savings if a husband and wife acquire property of their own in approximately equal amounts. Husbands and wives should keep this general rule in mind in discussing estate planning with their attorney. If this rule is followed, there will be greater opportunity to make efficient use of the marital deduction and unified tax credit, regardless of which spouse dies first.

Avoiding Double Tax. Generally, it is undesirable for a spouse to make outright bequests to the surviving spouse which exceed the maximum marital deduction. Such property will be a part of the taxable estate of the first spouse and will also be included in the gross estate of the second spouse. Double taxation of the property can result.

The double-tax problem can be eliminated through use of a life estate, or a life income interest in a trust, with the remainder interest in the children. These devices allow the income from property to be paid to the surviving spouse. However, the income-producing property would not be subject to the estate tax at the death of the second spouse because the estate tax law does not apply to such a life income interest.

Using the Special Generation Skipping Tax Exemption. By leaving a life interest to children with a remainder interest in grandchildren, one avoids inclusion of the income-producing property in the estates of the children when they die. The tax saving in the children's estates is limited, however, because of the new special generation skipping tax which taxes nonexempt life interests as if the income-producing property were included in the children's estates. Since the special generation skipping tax exempts the first $250,000 of income-producing property for each child, providing a life income interest to children does save some tax at the death of the child.

Providing Liquidity

The liquidity problem can often be resolved internally. In some estates, the assets may be more liquid than a first examination reveals. There may be substantial liquidity in crops, livestock, or other assets that can be readily sold. Even in those cases where few liquid assets are available, a number of techniques are available for solving the liquidity problem.

Exchanging Illiquid Assets for Liquid Forms. Since land—a relatively illiquid asset—makes up a major portion of the estate of most farmers, one method of providing liquidity is by exchanging land for other forms of assets. This might be accomplished through the use of installment sales contracts, debt instruments, annuities, etc., developed during the lifetime of older family members. Thus, upon the owner's death, the estate consists of assets that are more liquid and more easily divided. For example, the parents might be willing to transfer land to a child interested in continuing the business in exchange for promissory notes payable over several years. The notes that remain unpaid, rather than land itself, would be part of the parents' estate.

Use of Buy-Sell Agreements. Within partnerships and corporations some of the concern can be alleviated through the use of *buy-sell agreements.* These are contractual agreements between owners of interests in the business in which the heirs most interested in continuing the business can be per-

mitted to acquire the entire business by the purchase of the interests of family members who are not interested in the business. These can be built into a partnership agreement or can be part of the bylaws of the corporation. They can also be designed as separate contracts between the parties. Buy-sell agreements can provide for optional or mandatory buy-out and can include provisions for installment payments, interest rates, price, and other terms of sale.

Use of Installment Sales. The off-farm heirs may be willing to accept installment payments for their distributive share of business assets. These can be negotiated by the parties, but could result in an easing of the liquidity problem if payments can be arranged over a period of years rather than for immediate purchase.

Borrowing against Estate Assets. In some cases, it may be feasible for the heirs to borrow money to pay taxes and estate settlement costs and for on-farm heirs to purchase the interests of those who wish to sell. Obviously, consideration must be given to the total debt load of the business to determine whether this is the best course to follow.

Equalization Clause in Will. Some farm owners have left the arrangements open regarding the buy-out of the interest of some heirs by others. Some, however, have used an equalization clause within the will providing for installment payments to off-farm heirs by those who will continue the business. Such clauses typically leave property to certain heirs upon the condition that they pay to the off-farm heirs a set sum or an amount determined by a formula. In effect, such clauses give an option to on-farm heirs to purchase the property if they choose to do so.

Life Insurance for Illiquidity Relief. Not only is life insurance used to provide funds to surviving heirs for estate settlement costs and taxes, but it may serve as an important source of funds for funding buy-sell agreements in partnerships and the corporation or serve to preserve assets by providing cash for the buy-out of off-farm heirs.

Tax Provisions Providing Illiquidity Relief. Various provisions in the estate tax law provide some relief for farm estates. The special use valuation provisions[32] and the installment payment provisions[33] added by the 1976 tax law provide significant opportunities for asset preservation. In addition, redemptions of stock for the purpose of paying federal estate tax, inheritance taxes, and administrative expenses are permitted[34] and can benefit the family corporation.

17.7 WILLS

A *will* may be defined as a testamentary disposition of property. A will is only effective at the death of the maker or testator. Until the maker of a will dies, the maker generally can revoke or alter the will as he or she pleases. A will can be revoked in several ways. Perhaps the easiest way is by making a declaration to this effect in a new will—"I, John Doe, being of sound mind and memory, declare this to be my last will, hereby revoking all previous wills made by me." In most states, a will can also be revoked by burning or tearing, by obliterating the language entirely, or by physically destroying the will in any way with the intent to revoke the will.

Distribution of Property

A will can be an effective tool for accomplishing a variety of objectives. Perhaps the most important use of a will is to distribute property according to the personal desires of the deceased. Generally, an owner of property has the right to distribute that property at death to whomever the owner desires. This is one of the rights usually inherent in property ownership. There are some exceptions, however. State and federal death taxes (estate and inheritance taxes) may require that some of the property be used to pay taxes. Also, many states have laws that protect a surviving spouse from being disinherited. For example, Illinois law gives a surviving spouse the right to renounce the deceased spouse's will and take a statutory share of the property—one-half if there are no children, or one-third if there are children of the deceased.

WILLS—RENOUNCING

HENSON v. MOORE
Supreme Court of Illinois, 1882
104 Ill. 403

It appears from the record that Minerva A. Moore died testate, August 30, 1877, seized of fifty-six acres of land adjoining the city of Murphysboro, in Jackson County. She left surviving here a husband, James E. Moore, a brother, three sisters, and the son of one deceased sister and the daughter of

---

[32] INT. REV. CODE § 2032A.

[33] INT. REV. CODE § 6166 and INT. REV. CODE § 6166A.
[34] INT. REV. CODE § 303.

another deceased sister, but no children or descendants of children. About twenty acres of the east half of the land was in cultivation, where was situated a dwelling house, which was occupied by the testatrix and her husband at the time of her death. Moore was married to the testatrix on the 31st day of October, 1869, she being then the owner of the premises. The east half of the land Mrs. Moore devised to her brother, Benjamin F. Henson, for life, and at his death to his children. The west half of the tract of land she devised to her nephew, Benjamin F. Morgan, in fee. To her husband she devised one ton of hay, which was in a barn on the premises, but no other property whatever. The will was admitted to probate October 16, 1877, and on the 27th day of the following month James E. Moore filed in the probate court his written renunciation of the will, and his election to take under the statute.

On the trial of the cause the court held that James E. Moore was entitled to dower in the lands owned by the wife at the time of her death, and having renounced the provisions of the will, under section 12 of the Dower act he was entitled to one-half of the lands in fee. This decision is claimed to be erroneous. It is true that under the statute in force at the time of their marriage the husband was not entitled to dower in the wife's real estate, and had she died without any change in the statute he could not claim dower in her lands. But section 1 of the Dower act declares that the estate of curtesy is abolished, and the surviving husband and wife shall be endowed of the third part of all the lands whereof the deceased husband or wife was seized of an estate of inheritance at any time during the marriage, unless the same shall have been relinquished in a legal form. Section 12 of the same act declares: "If a husband or wife die testate, leaving no child or decendants of a child, the surviving husband or wife may, if he or she elect, have, in lieu of dower,...one-half of all the real and personal estate" which shall remain after the payment of debts.

Held for defendant.

Accomplishing Other Objectives

A will can be used to accomplish other objectives in addition to distributing property. The will can be used to designate the executor of the estate. Thus, a deceased can handpick the person who will act as the personal representative of the deceased while the estate is being administered. A will can be used to nominate guardians for minor children. Thus, a couple can be assured that a court will know their choice of guardian should both parents die. A will can be used to reduce the expense and time of probate.

For example, a will may grant the executor broader powers and greater discretion than would otherwise be available under state law. Thus, the estate can be administered with less red tape. A will can also be used to create trusts, to specify the property that will be used to pay federal and state death taxes, and to accomplish other objectives.

Formal Requirements

To be valid, a will must meet the formal legal requirements of appropriate state law.

Although the formal legal requirements vary somewhat from state to state, the following Illinois requirements are rather typical. The maker of a will must be of sound mind and memory and at least 18 years of age. The will must be written or typed and must be signed by the maker to be valid, although some states have recognized an oral will under particular circumstances. Also, a will must generally be witnessed by several persons (although some states, such as Nevada, recognize an unwitnessed handwritten will if the will was actually written and signed by the maker). An *attestation clause* (a statement by the witnesses that the will was executed in their presence and in the presence of each other) usually appears just before the signatures of the witnesses.

WILLS—INCOMPETENCY

QUELLMALZ v. FIRST NATIONAL BANK OF BELLEVILLE
Supreme Court of Illinois, 1959
16 Ill.2d 546, 158 N.E. 2d 591

Plaintiffs, three nephews and heirs-at-law of Lena Quellmalz, deceased, appeal from a decree of the circuit court of St. Clair County, in a will contest wherein the court declared the will to be a valid last will and testament of Lena Quellmalz.

The plaintiffs, sons of a predeceased brother of Lena Quellmalz, filed their complaint in the circuit court of St. Clair County praying that the instrument admitted to probate in the probate court of St. Clair County as the last will of Lena Quellmalz, be set aside and declared not to be the last will and testament of the deceased. The complaint alleged that at the time of making the instrument Lena Quellmalz was more than 86 years of age, was in her dotage and was physically weak and diseased, was incompetent and unable to make the instrument, and was then obsessed by and under the influence of insane delusions, rendering her incapable of making a will.

Plaintiffs presented numerous witnesses upon trial of the cause. Monroe Eckert testified that his wife operated a fruit store in Belleville in which he worked, that he knew Lena Quellmalz for many years but not well and that during the last few years of her life she came into his wife's store about twice a week. He said she would sit behind the counter complaining of her neighbors and of the firemen peeking in her windows, that she bought only a few stale, overripe vegetables and fruits, asserting she was too poor to buy anything else, that she would stare, and would have to be led out of the store.

Stella Eckert, wife of Monroe Eckert, said that from September, 1951, until April 10, 1954, she operated a fruit store which Lena Quellmalz visited, complaining she was too poor to buy anything, or to go to a doctor. She stated that Miss Quellmalz would sit and stare, never knew when to go home, would buy only trimmings and spoiled vegetables, and said people were peeping in her windows. Mrs. Eckert gave as her opinion, that Lena

Quellmalz was of unsound mind on April 22, 1953, but she continued to trade with her.

John Erlinger, a contractor, knew the deceased ten years and had last worked for her in 1952 when he did repairs on her house. She would only permit him to do essential repair, claiming she could not afford more and could not afford to fix a building on her property for rental.

Louis Ackerman knew her for many years and saw her once or twice a week. She wanted him to trim a tree for her but said she couldn't pay for it. The retired Belleville fire chief, Albert Nebgen, knew the deceased, as she lived next door to the No. 1 Fire Station. She frequently complained to him that the firemen were in her yard or were peeking in her windows.

Standlee I. Twitchell, a physician and surgeon, had known deceased many years and last treated her as a patient on March 18, 1950. He then found her weak and becoming feeble, with high blood pressure and loss of appetite. She became more feeble during the last two or three years as his patient, but always knew him.

William Handrich, trust officer of the First National Bank of Belleville, as an adverse witness, testified that the estate exceeded $120,000 in value, of which $89,410 was cash.

Numerous witnesses appeared in defense to the complaint. The attorney who prepared the will, Oscar Becherer, testified he had known the deceased many years, had represented her as the administratrix of her brother's estate in 1944, and prepared an earlier will for her in 1945. He said she asked him to come to her home in April of 1953 to prepare a new will, that she had written notes of what she wanted in her will, how she wished to be buried, who should officiate, that she discussed her relatives and made provisions for all of them, and wished to give the remainder to the named charities. He stated that she was of sound mind and memory on April 22, 1953.

The witnesses to the will, Edgar Baldus and Alfred Baldus, had known deceased many years and had talked with her often. They believed her to be of sound mind on April 22, 1953. Mr. and Mrs. Ed Vernier, who operated a grocery store and had deceased as a customer for about thirty years and saw her twice a week, said she was of sound mind and memory on April 22, 1953. Of like opinion were Dr. Charles Baumann, who treated her as a patient from August 7, 1946 to January 21, 1954; Edward Blaies, who did odd jobs for her from 1948 to the spring of 1953; Emma E. Kunz who visited with her at least once a week during the last five years of her life; Phroso B. Schmidt who saw and conversed with her once or twice a month from 1950 to 1954; Fred Schmidt who sold and delivered oil to her in 1952 and 1953; and Cleola Hartell who knew her all of his life and saw and conversed with her several times in 1953.

The manager of the safety deposit department of the First National Bank testified her records showed that deceased entered her deposit box twenty-five times in 1953, and made many visits each year.

None of these witnesses supplied any evidence of lack of testamentary capacity in Lena Quellmalz on April 22, 1953, except Stella Eckert. In fact, if anything, they tend to confirm that deceased was capable of executing a will on that date. All that is required of a testator in order to have testamentary capacity is that he have sufficient mental ability to know and remember who are the natural objects of his bounty, to comprehend the kind and character of his property and to make disposition of that property according to some plan formed in his mind. Where a person has sufficient mental capacity to transact ordinary business and act rationally in the ordinary affairs of life, he has sufficient mental capacity to dispose of his property by will.

The will itself established that Lena Quellmalz knew the natural objects of her bounty. She named her only surviving sister, all of her nieces and nephews, and several cousins as legatees. It is apparent from the will and the testimony of her attorney that she had a plan in mind for the disposition of her property, as she had made written notes of her desires and intentions. Moreover, the will and the testimony of Albert P. Nebgen show that Lena Quellmalz knew the character and extent of her property.

The plaintiff's witnesses thoroughly show that she had sufficient ability to transact ordinary business. That she lived frugally and miserly, was afraid and believed the firemen who came upon her property were looking in her windows is evidence of eccentricity, not uncommon to such an elderly woman, living alone. Eccentricity does not constitute unsoundness of mind. Old age brings on peculiarities, but peculiarities are a long way from unsoundness of mind. Neither old age and feebleness, nor miserly habits, of themselves, show a lack of testamentary capacity.

It appears that plaintiffs' attempt to show that the deceased suffered from insane delusions (1) when she stated she had no money, at a time when she had real estate, investments, and much cash, and (2) when she believed the firemen were looking into her windows. An insane delusion that will avoid a will must affect or enter into the execution of the will, and even if the testator does have an insane delusion on certain subjects, still if he had mental capacity to know his property and the objects of his bounty and to make a disposition of his property according to a plan formed by him, the will cannot be set aside on the ground of mental incapacity. Moreover, an insane delusion does not exist unless the fallacy of such belief can be demonstrated. There is no proof that the firemen were not looking in the windows or that they did not appear to do so. In addition, nothing presented in plaintiffs' evidence indicates that testator had any insane delusion which, in any way, affected or entered into the execution of this will.

The law presumes every man to be sane and of sound mind until the contrary is proved. Plaintiffs were confronted with that presumption, and only the opinion of Stella Eckert rebuts it. Stella Eckert's statement is the only matter appearing in plaintiffs' evidence, with all of its logical intendments, that indicates that Lena Quellmalz was lacking testamentary capacity on the date she executed this will, and amounts only to a bare scintilla of evidence in support of plaintiffs' cause.

The decree of the circuit court of St. Clair County is, therefore, affirmed.

WILLS—ATTESTING

IN RE ESTATE OF FISHER
Supreme Court of Illinois, 1951
409 Ill. 420, 100 N.E. 2d 564

Omer M. Fisher, a resident of Claremont, died September 29, 1948, leaving a widow, a sister, and a niece and a nephew as heirs. On November 29, 1948, the widow filed a complaint for partition of real estate left by decedent, alleging he died intestate. She thereafter filed a petition in the county court of Richland County, seeking probate of an alleged will of decedent dated September 2, 1948, in which he purported to bequeath five dollars each to the sister and the niece and nephew, and the residue of his property, real, personal and mixed, to his wife. (NOTE: In 1948 under the rules of descent a spouse received only half of the realty if there were no descendants.) The sister and the niece and nephew were made respondents. From an order denying probate, an appeal was taken to the circuit court where, after a hearing de novo, probate was again denied. As the instrument purports to dispose of real estate, the widow appeals directly to this court. The principal question presented is whether the evidence is sufficient to sustain the finding that the will was not signed by the testator in the presence of the attesting witnesses and was not attested by them in his presence as required by statute.

The instrument bears the usual attestation clause, reciting in part that it was signed, sealed, published and declared by the testator to be his last will and testament in the presence of the witnesses who, at his request, subscribed their names thereto in his presence and in the presence of each other. Both witnesses, however, testified in the county court that the testator was not present when they signed the will and that they did not see him sign it. They testified further that they did not read the instrument; that Mrs. Fisher, the testator's wife, requested them to sign it; and that they did so in her presence at the office of W.B. Roberts, a notary public in Marion, Illinois.

A transcript of this testimony was introduced in evidence on the appeal to the circuit court. In addition the court considered a deposition of Roberts, previously taken at the request of appellant, in which he testified that on September 2, 1948, the testator signed the will in his office in the presence of the attesting witnesses; that no women were present; and that, after seeing the testator and witnesses sign, he notarized their signatures. The respondents then produced several witnesses who contradicted Roberts concerning the physical appearance of the testator, and also an attorney who testified that on an occasion prior to the deposition he questioned Roberts concerning the transaction and that the latter at that time said he did not remember the name of the man who signed the will, did not know the testator and had no record of the transaction in his daily record book.

To support her contention that the evidence is sufficient to require admission of the will to probate, appellant argues that the attestation clause is prima facie proof of due execution and that the testimony of the subscribing witnesses, being in conflict with it, is entitled to little weight. It is further urged as improbable that the subscribing witnesses would sign and acknowledge the document before a notary public without knowing its nature or import; or that testator's wife would have filed a complaint for partition, alleging he had died intestate, if she had caused the will to be executed. We think, however, that the testimony of the subscribing witnesses clearly shows that the statutory requirements were not observed. The matters referred to, while tending to indicate some improbability that the will was signed at the request of appellant, cannot overcome the positive evidence provided by the subscribing witnesses, who were not shown to have had any motive for testifying falsely in the case. In *In Re Estate of Balicki*, 408 Ill. 84, we recently affirmed an order denying probate of a will where the attesting witnesses testified it was not signed or acknowledged by the testator in their presence. The weight of the evidence introduced in opposition to such testimony was not substantially different from that in the case at bar, and the same result must follow here.

It is extremely unfortunate that careless or unprincipled persons are so often selected as attesting witnesses. They cannot be too severely criticized for signed attestation statements such as those appearing in this will, and then swearing to the contrary when they are called as witnesses in court. Such conduct is doubtless responsible for defeating or nullifying many intended dispositions of property, and may have consequences far greater than those of ordinary carelessness. However, there can be no relief for proponent from their negligence. Persons desiring to make their wills should realize the importance of more carefully selecting the persons who are to act as attesting witnesses.

We have carefully considered the errors assigned, and find them to be without merit. The order of the circuit court must accordingly be affirmed.

Courts have held that the right to transfer property by will is not a natural or common-law right, but a right that must be created by the state legislature. Thus, the formal legal requirements of a will must be strictly followed. Also, the words used in a will must be chosen with great care because the deceased is not available to explain the meaning of the will when the will is offered for probate.

It is a cardinal rule that a lawyer should be used to draft a will. A lawyer will insure that all the formal legal requirements of a will are met and that the language of the will clearly expresses the intent of the maker. A "do-it-yourself" will should be avoided. It may not be valid because the formal legal requirements were not met, or it may use words that had one meaning to the deceased but an entirely different meaning to the court.

Generally, wills should not be secretive documents. The disposition of property should be based upon a plan that takes into account a number of factors including the wishes of the maker, the honest hopes and aspirations of other family members, various tax implications, etc. It is desirable that family members openly discuss the inevitable event of death and the alternative disposition possibilities.

Periodically reviewing a will is also extremely important. As time passes, circumstances change. A will that was prepared many years ago may not meet the current situation. If changes need to be made, the attorney will either prepare a new will or prepare an addition (called a *codicil*) to the existing will. In either case, one must follow the same legal requirements as were required for the first will.

As a general rule, whenever a person begins to acquire property and/or raise a family, a will should be executed. Most farmers, ranchers, and their spouses should have a will. If a person does not have a will, he or she would be wise to consult with an attorney about the advisability of having a will prepared.

WILLS—AMBIGUOUS LANGUAGE

WILLIAMS v. FULTON
Supreme Court of Illinois, 1954
4 Ill. 2d 524, 123 N.E. 2d 495

Plaintiffs-appellants appeal directly to this court from a decree of the circuit court of Moultrie County dismissing for want of equity a bill for partition and accounting. A freehold being involved, this appeal properly comes to this court.

Barnabas W. Fulton died testate in Moultrie County on January 10, 1895, leaving surviving him a widow and two sons, viz; Barney Fulton, a son by a former marriage, and the defendant, Issac W. Fulton, a son by his last marriage.

The will of Barnabas W. Fulton, which was duly admitted to probate in Moultrie County, by its first paragraph devised to the surviving widow, in fee simple, 160 acres in Shelby County. The second paragraph of said will, which is the paragraph here in issue, provided as follows:

I give and devise to my beloved son Barney Fulton the Southeast Quarter of Section 5 in Township 15 North of Range 6 East of the Third Principal Meridian in the County of Moultrie and State of Illinois, to have and to hold the said Quarter Section during his natural life with no power to sell or dispose of said life estate with the remainder in fee simple to the heirs of his body and in case he should die without children or descendants of children then said real estate to descend to his nearest of kin according to the rules of descent as declared by the Statute of the State of Illinois.

The third paragraph of said will made a devise of another quarter section of farm land in Moultrie County to the defendant Issac W. Fulton in identical language. The fourth paragraph of said will contained directions concerning the possession and rental of the testator's farm lands until certain mortgages were discharged, and the fifth paragraph appointed the surviving widow executor.

After the death of Barnabas W. Fulton, his son Barney Fulton went into possession of the quarter section of land described in the second paragraph of said will and continued in possession until he died intestate on January 21, 1930, leaving him surviving his widow, Lou Fulton, and the defendant, Issac W. Fulton, as his sole heirs-at-law. Since the death of Barney Fulton, the defendant Issac W. Fulton has collected all rentals from the quarter section of land described in paragraph 2 of the will of Barnabas W. Fulton and has paid all taxes thereon.

Lou Fulton, the surviving widow of Barney Fulton, died testate in 1942, and the plaintiff-appellants are the residuary beneficiaries under the terms of her will, or their alleged successors in title.

The bill for partition and accounting filed by plaintiffs-appellants alleges that an undivided one-half interest in the quarter section of land in question vested in Lou Fulton at the death of her husband, Barney Fulton, under the terms of the second paragraph of the last will of Barnabas W. Fulton, and that the other half vested in the defendant, Issac W. Fulton. The answer filed by defendants-appellees alleges that the widow of Barney Fulton is not within the meaning of the term "nearest of kin according to the rules of descent as declared by the Statute of the State of Illinois," as used in paragraph 2 of the last will of Barnabas W. Fulton, and also pleads the twenty-year Statute of Limitations as a bar to the claim of plaintiffs-appellants.

The trial court, in dismissing the complaint for want of equity, held that paragraph 2 of the will of Barnabas W. Fulton vested title to the quarter section of land in the defendant, Issac W. Fulton, as the nearest blood kin of Barney Fulton, on his death, to the exclusion of the surviving widow of Barney Fulton, and that the plaintiffs were further barred by the twenty-year Statute of Limitations.

The assignment of errors presents two issues for decision by this court. First, the proper legal construction of the will of Barnabas W. Fulton, deceased, and second, the application of the defense of the twenty-year Statute of Limitations.

Effect must be given to the whole will and the testator's intention cannot be determined from the language of any particular clause, phrase or sentence. Since wills are seldom exactly alike the precedents in other will cases are seldom of controlling importance in determining the intention of the testator as expressed in the particular will under consideration.

Under this controlling principle, what is the intention of the testator here as expressed in his will by the phrase "in case he should die without children or descendants of children then said real estate to descend to his nearest of kin according to the rules of descent as declared by the Statute of the State of Illinois."

There is no distinction between the phrase "nearest of kin" and the phrase "next of kin," and the same can be considered synonymous. The phrases "next of kin" and "nearest of kin," as shown by the English decisions, the decisions in other States, and the Illinois decisions, have been interpreted or construed in two ways, when unqualified by other words: first, as meaning the nearest blood relations according to the laws of consanguinity, and second, as those entitled to take under the statutory distribution of intestate estates. In Illinois the phrase "next of kin," when contained in a will simpliciter or unqualified by other words, has been held to mean the nearest blood relations according to the laws of consanguinity.

We have found no Illinois decision where the phrase "nearest of kin" or "next of kin," when used in connection with a reference to the statute of descent, has been construed.

Although this court has recognized and applied a technical legal meaning to the term "next of kin," when used alone, it has likewise recognized that in popular usage it has a broader meaning. In its practical use the term has come to mean, ordinarily, those persons who take the personal estate of the deceased under the statutes of distribution.

In determining the testator's intention in the instant case, it appears clear that if the testator had intended to restrict the devolution of his property to the nearest blood relations according to the laws of consanguinity he would have used the phrase "next of kin" alone and stopped, because such phrase, when used alone, had a fixed, established technical meaning. The additional phrase used has a definite fixed meaning also, and to construe the instant will as contended by appellees would completely disregard such phrase in violation of the rule of construction that no clause of a will can be rejected except from absolute necessity.

It is our opinion that in the instant case the testator, by use of the phrase "according to the rules of descent as declared by the Statute of the State of Illinois," negatives specifically any intention that the phrase "nearest of kin" was used in its strict technical sense but affirmatively disclosed an intention to use such phrase in its popular sense as meaning those who would take under the Descent Act of the State of Illinois.

Inasmuch as the testator's intention, as expressed in the will itself, was for the property to go according to the statute of descent upon the death of Barney Fulton, leaving no issue, the property here in question went to Issac W. Fulton, the defendant, and Lou Fulton, the surviving widow of Barney Fulton, as equal tenants in common.

The other issue for decision is the applicability of the affirmative defense of the twenty-year Statute of Limitations to the plaintiffs' claim of title.

We approach the determination of this question with the knowledge, as hereinabove determined, that Issac W. Fulton and the surviving widow of Barney Fulton were tenants in common at the time Issac W. Fulton went into possession. Before the possession of one tenant in common can be adverse to a cotenant, there must be a disseizin or ouster by outward acts of exclusive ownership of an unequivocal character, overt and notorious, and of such nature as to impart information and apprise the cotenant that an adverse possession and actual disseizin are intended to be asserted, and mere possession by one tenant in common who receives all rents and profits and pays taxes, no matter for how long, cannot be set up as a bar against a cotenant.

And in order to start the running of the Statute of Limitations against a cotenant it must be shown that the tenant in possession gave actual notice to the tenant out of possession that he was claiming adversely or that the tenant out of possession had received notice of such claim of the tenant in possession by some act of the tenant in possession which would amount to an ouster or disseizin.

The twenty-year Statute of Limitations being an affirmative defense in this case, the burden of proof was upon the defendants to prove disseizin or ouster of the cotenant not in possession by a positive, affirmative act. There is no competent evidence of such disseizin or ouster in the record, and the defense of the Statute of Limitations was not proved as a bar to the claims of the plaintiffs.

The decree of the lower court is reversed and this cause is remanded, with directions to enter a decree granting partition as prayed in the complaint, and to consider the issues with respect to the accounting.

Joint Wills.   A *joint will* is a single testamentary instrument which contains the wills of two or more persons, is executed jointly, and disposes of property owned jointly, in common, or in severalty by them. Such a will may be reciprocal or mutual, but it is not essential that it be so. There is no legal objection to uniting the wills of two or more persons in one instrument, provided the dispositions of the property of each maker are severable from those of the others, and provided the instrument can be given effect on the death of each testator as the will of that one. When such conditions exist, a joint will is held to be the will of each maker and subject to probate at the death of each. As a general rule, a joint will is not recommended even though it may be valid.

Wills—Charges against Gifts. In *Parsons v. Millar*, 189 Ill. 107 (1901), the court upheld a testamentary charge against certain bequests.

A paragraph in the will stated:

Eleventh—I give and bequeath to my son William E. Millar the following described land, to-wit: (here describing land in Coles County, Illinois) provided that my son William E. Millar pay, as before specified, to my daughter Hannah Vause, within two years after my death, the sum of $1,000, and to my daughter Mary Frances VanMeter, within three years after my death, the sum of $1,000, which amounts shall be the sums bequeathed to them in clauses 9 and 10 of this will.

The court held that:

It is evident from the language of paragraph 11 of the will that the title to the lands therein devised passed absolutely to William E. Millar, charged with the payment of the bequests of $1,000 each, contained in paragraphs 9 and 10, to Hannah D. Vause and Mary F. VanMeter.

17.8 TRUSTS

A *trust* is a fiduciary relationship between a trustee and beneficiaries whereby the trustee holds legal title to specific property under a duty to deal with the property for the benefit of the beneficiaries. The trust is a variation on the co-ownership forms of ownership discussed earlier. In tenancy in common, for example, legal title is held by several persons in undivided interests. In a trust the trustee is said to hold legal title and the beneficiaries are said to hold equitable title.[35]

Express Trusts

Although trusts are sometimes implied, most trusts are created by express written agreement in which an owner of property (the settlor, also called trustor) transfers title to a trustee for the benefit of the beneficiaries.[36] The trustee may be a person or persons, a corporation, or a combination of the two. If a person establishes a trust during lifetime (an *inter vivos* trust), it is possible to name anyone (including the settlor) as trustee and also as a beneficiary.

Many trusts are written into wills *(testamentary trusts)* and go into effect at death. In such cases, a person may change the provisions of the trust at any time simply by making a new will. Or, the trust may be canceled completely by leaving it out of a newly drafted will. Since a will-trust does not go into effect until the death of the owner, there is no tax saving in the estate. However, savings are usually made in the future estates of others who have an interest in the trust property. A will can also be used to add property to a trust that was established during the trustor's lifetime. For example, an owner can place a portion of the estate in trust and then have the balance of the estate (or any part of it) pass into trust upon death.

A trust can continue for any period of time set by the owner—for a lifetime, until a child reaches the age of 25, or until a spouse remarries, for example. The period is set out in the trust agreement or in a will. If the trust is to extend beyond a lifetime, certain legal limitations may apply.

Any kind of property can be placed in a trust, including both personal property and real estate. Usually only income-producing property or property that can be sold and the proceeds invested by the trustee is placed in trust. There is no minimum or maximum on the value of this property.

Beneficiaries do not hold title to the property (the trustee has title), and they may or may not have possession of the property, depending upon the terms of the trust. Beneficiaries have an equitable interest, however, and are entitled to the benefits of the trust.

The benefits are set out in the trust agreement, and the trustee must follow the directions for payment. For example, a trust for a grandchild might require that income be used only for the child's college education, with any extra accumulation of income to be paid by the trustee to the boy or girl at age 21. Or a will-trust could require that all income be paid to a surviving wife, that on her death the income be used for minor children, and that the trust be terminated when the youngest child reaches the age of 21.

An important advantage of the trust is its flexibility. The trustor can place any number of restrictions in a trust agreement or

---

[35] R. POWELL, THE LAW OF REAL PROPERTY §§ 2330–2337 (1979).
[36] *Id.* §§ 2345–2348.

give the trustee total discretion. For these reasons, a trust is a much more flexible device for transferring property than certain other legal devices such as a life estate or custodian agreement.

Lifetime trusts can be made revocable or irrevocable. This means that the trustor can reserve the power to terminate the trust anytime or can make it binding and irrevocable for the term of the trust.

The revocable trust will not reduce inheritance taxes for the trustor under current tax laws. These trusts are useful, however, to obtain professional investment guidance; to secure good management in case of illness, accident, or mental incapacity; to avoid probate costs; to provide flexibility in using insurance proceeds paid to the trust; and for other uses. A revocable trust can be drawn that will continue to operate after the death of the owner who placed property in trust, and there may be substantial tax savings in the estates of the beneficiaries.

The irrevocable trust (a trust that the owner cannot terminate) is most useful in estate planning because it can reduce death taxes. It can remove property from an estate and still insure that the property will be devoted to the benefit of persons selected by the owner. For example, an owner could transfer property in trust for a child with remainder to a grandchild. The property would not be included in the child's estate, and would pass automatically to the grandchild at the child's death. The gift tax law would apply, however, when the father placed the property in trust. Also, in certain of these situations a "generation skipping" transfer tax may be involved if large amounts are transferred in this fashion.

Irrevocable trusts cannot be substantially altered or amended and cannot be revoked. For this reason, an irrevocable trust must be drawn very carefully to anticipate all changes that may occur subsequent to its execution.

Common Situations Where a Trust May Be Helpful

Here is a list of situations in which a farmer or rancher should consider using a trust.

1. When relief from the burden of management is desired
2. When it is desirable to place title to several tracts in the hands of one person for ease of management, sale, or distribution at death and in order to avoid partition by heirs
3. When an heir (spouse or child, for example) has little or no management ability or no knowledge of farming
4. When heirs are minors
5. When the estate is subject to inheritance and estate taxes and a reduction in the tax burden is desired
6. When gifts of personal property are to be made to children or grandchildren (as, for example, for an educational fund)
7. When a person owns farmland in another state and wants to provide for its management and inheritance
8. When it is desired to avoid probate proceedings on a part or all of the estate
9. When there might be a conflict between a life tenant and remainderman (the person who takes the remainder interest after the death of the life tenant) if a life estate were used
10. When heirs live a considerable distance from the farm, making it difficult to give any personal attention to management
11. When a second marriage is contemplated and a present transfer to children of the first marriage is desired

Notice that the word "management" is used in describing almost half of these situations. If a trust is established to obtain or continue good management, it is important to select a trustee who can provide such management.

Under certain conditions, the trustor may want to retain management functions or allow the beneficiaries to manage the property. In fact, the trust agreement can provide that the trustee's only responsibility is to hold title and to mortgage or transfer title at the request of the trustor or the beneficiaries. When real estate is involved, this is sometimes called a "land trust."

Title is protected in the hands of the trustee. It cannot be splintered through inheritance or tied up for a time because some or all of the heirs are children. The trustee can be given the legal powers of an owner and can transfer title, mortgage the property, sign leases for farming or for drilling for oil, or assume any other power that the owner (trustor) chooses to give.

Establishing a Trust

Any trust, whether simple or complicated, should be drafted by an attorney. Setting up a trust also means selecting a trustee. The trustee is entitled to fees for the work involved. In some cases a member of the family may be willing to serve as trustee without compensation.

The trustee will usually earn the fee through expert management. For example, placing a farm in trust with a bank that has an outstanding farm management department may increase the farm's income to such an extent that it will more than pay the fee charge. Similarly, funds placed with a trust company for investment in securities may receive wise management and the trust receive more income. It should also be remembered that trustee fees are tax deductible.

A trust can be a very useful estate planning tool as well as a means of providing flexibility in carrying out the special wishes of a landowner. Trustee fees are a consideration, however, and there is the possibility that a trustee may not give as much personal attention to the trust as the trustor had hoped. But, in appropriate situations, the trust has many features that commend it to the farmer. In many cases it is possible to personalize a trust by naming a relative or friend as co-trustee, thus removing the objection that a trust is an impersonal relationship.

Land Trusts

Some states (Illinois, Indiana, Virginia, and Florida, for example) recognize a unique form of property interest that has been referred to as the Illinois land trust. It goes one step further than the typical trust and divorces the beneficiary not only from the legal interest in the land but also from the equitable interest. While common law accomplishes a split between the legal title in the trustee and equitable title in the beneficiary, in an Illinois land trust, the trustee has both legal and equitable titles. By placing the trustee in "full, complete and exclusive title to the real estate, both equitable and legal," the beneficiary in an Illinois land trust is left with a personal property interest only.

There are several commercially useful reasons for this arrangement. It helps to eliminate the cumbersome nature of real estate transactions when there are multiple owners, and it can simplify the management and financing of subdivisions and large-scale home or apartment building enterprises. It also avoids the delays involved when there is a death or disappearance of an owner of a fractional interest in land. The importance of this is also seen when creditors of the land trust beneficiaries are not allowed to affect the title of land in a land trust as they can when the equitable title is in the beneficiary in a common-law trust or when both equitable and legal title is in the hands of the owner of a fee simple interest.

Sometimes the question arises as to who are proper parties in suits against Illinois-type land trusts. In re *Application of County Treasurer*, 113 Ill. App. 2d 50 (1969), the treasurer of Cook County sold land in an Illinois land trust because its owner was delinquent in payment of property taxes. An Illinois statute required that all parties interested in the real estate sold for back taxes be given notice of the purchase of the land at a tax sale. Such parties entitled to notice are the owners, trustees of common-law trusts, and persons holding mortgages. The beneficiaries of the land trust objected to the purchase at the tax sale on the grounds that they did not receive notice as required by the statute. The court held that beneficiaries of an Illinois land trust are not entitled to notice under the statute as they only hold a personal property interest. The trustee is the only proper party in an action against a land trust, as only the trustee can accept an offer to purchase the real estate. The court concluded by saying that each form of property ownership has its peculiar advantages and disadvantages and the beneficiaries of a land trust give up all interest in the real estate for its many advantages. The court affirmed the trial court's validation of the tax sale.

17.9 TRANSFER BY GIFT OR SALE

Although the tax effect of transferring property by gift is essentially the same as transfers at death, there are still some tax advantages to be gained from the use of gifts. There are frequently nontax reasons for gifts as well. Gifts can be used to reduce the taxable estate by allowing one to take advantage of the $3000 annual exclusion and the gift tax marital deduction. Also, if gifts are made of property that is rapidly appreciating in value, some estate reduction may occur because items may be significantly higher in value if left in the estate for several more years as compared to the present value.

Gifts may be used as a method of balancing the estates of the two spouses. This can often result in some overall tax savings. Special problems may arise if joint tenancies are terminated in order to accomplish estate balancing, even in cases when use of the gift tax marital deduction permits significant gifts from one spouse to another. For example, for real property acquired after 1954 in which a joint tenancy was created, if the creation of the tenancy was treated as a gift and a gift tax return was filed, the joint tenancy can later be terminated without gift tax consequences so long as both spouses receive their proportional share of the property.[37] However, if no gift tax return was filed (i.e., no election to treat as a gift) when the joint tenancy is severed, a gift is involved to the extent that the non-contributing spouse receives a share of the property.

Gifts can be used for a number of nontax reasons as well. They may serve as an inducement to younger family members to become active in the business and may serve to provide timely assistance to heirs, to provide equitable treatment of heirs, and to provide security to a surviving spouse.

A potential problem area is the *sham sale* —that is, a gift of property disguised as a sale. This is sometimes attempted as a means of avoiding gift tax. However, even if a transfer is disguised as a sale, it will be considered to be a gift to the extent that the true market value of the property transfer-

---

[37] INT. REV. CODE § 2515.

red exceeds the amount of actual consideration received. Similar problems arise in the intrafamily transfer by installment sale. These transfers are sometimes used as a means of achieving a gift tax spread over a number of years. For example, parents might transfer assets to a daughter and son-in-law subject to a mortgage held by the parents. In succeeding years, the parents could make annual gifts by canceling part of the payments as they become due. While such techniques offer a number of potential advantages—inflationary increases in value eliminated from parents' estates, retirement income, incentive to younger family members, etc.—they are frequently challenged by the Internal Revenue Service and are the subject of continued congressional debate.

SALE OR GIFT

HAYGOOD v. COMMISSIONER
United States Tax Court, 1964
42 T.C. 936

Petitioner, an individual residing in Houston, Texas, filed a gift tax return for the calendar 1961 with the district director of internal revenue at Austin, Texas.

Sometime prior to 1961, petitioner owned certain property which was condemned and as a result of the condemnation she received approximately $147,000 which upon advice of an accountant and an attorney she reinvested in similar property.

Petitioner also owned certain property in 1961 which she had owned for many years and which had not been acquired with the proceeds which she received from the condemnation of certain of her property.

After purchasing the property with the proceeds received upon condemnation of other property, petitioner decided that she wished to share her property with her two sons, and with this in view consulted an accountant with respect to the manner in which she could transfer property to her sons with the least amount of tax resulting from the transfer.

Subsequent to petitioner's conversation with the accountant, she intended to make an outright gift of certain property of a total value of $28,180 to her two sons, which property petitioner has referred to as rural property, and to make a gift of an interest of $3,000 in certain other property located in Harris County, Texas, which petitioner has referred to as city property, to each of her two sons in the year 1961. Petitioner consulted an attorney and in accordance with what he believed to be petitioner's wishes and her accountant's advice to her, this attorney prepared deeds conveying a portion of the rural property outright to each of petitioner's sons. The deeds to the rural property so conveyed were delivered to petitioner's sons around December 19, 1961. Petitioner valued the rural property at $28,180 on her gift tax return for the year 1961. Respondent has accepted this valuation in his notice of deficiency and there is no issue in this case with respect to the conveyance of the rural property to petitioner's sons.

In accordance with what he likewise believed to be the advice petitioner received from her accountant and her intention of making an additional gift of a value of $3,000 to each of her sons for the year 1961 and for several years thereafter, the attorney also prepared the following documents: (1) Two deeds each containing a conveyance by petitioner of a portion of the city property to one of her sons subject to a vendor's lien; (2) two vendor's lien notes, one to be signed by each of the petitioner's sons; and (3) two deeds of trust, one to the property being conveyed to each son to be executed by that son. On December 30, 1961, petitioner executed the two deeds and her sons executed the notes and deeds of trust. The property conveyed on December 30, 1961, by petitioner to her son C. Gerald Haygood by warranty deed with vendor's lien had a fair market value on that date of $16,500, and the property conveyed on December 30, 1961, by petitioner to her son F. Donald Haygood by warranty deed with vendor's lien had a fair market value on that date of $16,000. The warranty deed whereby petitioner conveyed property to her son C. Gerald Haygood recited in part as follows:

for and in consideration of the sum of Ten ($10.00) Dollars, and other valuable considerations, CASH TO ME IN HAND PAID, BY C. GERALD HAYGOOD, Grantee herein, the receipt of which is hereby acknowledged, and the further consideration of the sum of Sixteen Thousand Five Hundred ($16,500.00) Dollars, secured to be paid and evidenced by one promissory Vendor's Lien note, of even date herewith executed by the Grantee herein, payable to the order of the Grantor herein, in annual installments of Three Thousand ($3,000.00) Dollars, said note being non-interest bearing, the first such installment being due and payable on or before the 31st day of December, 1961, and continuing annually thereafter until said note is paid in full, said note acknowledging the Vendor's Lien herein retained to secure the payment thereof, and being additionally secured by Deed of Trust of even date herewith,...

Following this statement in the deed were the general terms of conveyance and description of the property, followed by the statement of general warranties. The concluding paragraph of the deed stated:

But it is expressly agreed and stipulated that the Vendor's Lien is retained against the above described property, premises and improvements, until the above described note, and all interest thereon are fully paid according to its face and tenor, effect and reading, when this deed shall become absolute.

The warranty deed whereby petitioner conveyed property to her son F. Donald Haygood carried the same provisions except the amount of the note was $16,000. The non-interest-bearing vendor's lien note payable to petitioner executed by each of her sons on December 30, 1961, as specified in the deed, provided for payment of the principal in annual installments of $3,000 with the first installment due on or before December 31, 1961, as specified in the deed. The deed of trust covering the property transferred by petitioner to each of her sons named the lawyer who drafted the papers for petitioner as trustee. Each such deed of trust conveyed the property to the trustee in trust to secure the payment of the vendor's lien note and provided that if payments were made as due the conveyance was null and void, but in case of default in payment the property was to be sold to satisfy the debt. The deeds whereby petitioner conveyed the city property to her sons were recorded, but neither of these deeds of trust was ever recorded. No payments were ever made on the note of either C. Gerald Haygood or F. Donald Haygood to petitioner. Petitioner did not intend at the time she took the notes from her sons to collect on these notes, but intended to forgive each $3,000 payment as it became due, thus making a gift of $3,000 to each of her sons at the time of such forgiveness. Petitioner's sons understood at the time the notes were executed that it was not petitioner's intention to collect the payments provided for in the notes, but that petitioner was having them sign the notes and deeds of trust for the property as a means of being able to give each of them a gift of $3,000 each year as the payments became due under the terms of the notes.

It is respondent's position that in addition to the property of a value of $28,180 given by petitioner to her sons in December 1961 with respect to which no issue is here involved, petitioner made total gifts in the year 1961 of property to her sons of $32,500. Respondent takes the position that since the value of the pieces of city property which petitioner deeded to her sons taking back a non-interest-bearing vendor's lien note in the amount of $16,500 from one son and a similar note in the amount of $16,000 from the other was $32,500, this represents the amount of petitioner's gifts to her sons since the notes executed by her sons and the liens given as security therefor were without substance. It is respondent's position that petitioner's sons owed her nothing for the property in 1961 and were vested with ownership thereof and that such gifts constituted transfers subject to tax.

It is petitioner's position that she gave the rural property valued at $28,180 to her sons in 1961, and in addition gave them $6,000 of the value of the city property in that year. It is eminently clear from the testimony that it was petitioner's intent to give only a $3,000 interest to each of her sons in the city property deeded to them in the year 1961. Had petitioner in 1961 deeded only a 3/16.5 interest to C. Gerald Haygood in the portion of the city property which she intended to give to him and only a 3/16 interest to F. Donald Haygood in the portion of the city property she intended to give to him, which was apparently the procedure her accountant intended for her to follow, and in subsequent years deeded similar interest until the entire property was transferred, respondent apparently would not question the transaction as being a gift of a value of only $3,000 to each son in the year 1961.

It is respondent's position that petitioner transferred all of her interest in the property and in return therefor received nothing of value. Respondent does not consider there to be any substance to the notes and deeds of trust signed by petitioner's sons. Respondent states that his position is supported by provisions of the Internal Revenue Code of 1954 imposing a tax for years after 1954 on the transfer of property by gift, providing that the tax shall apply whether the transfer is in trust or otherwise and whether the gift is direct or indirect, and providing that where the gift is made in property the value of the property at the date of the gift shall be considered the amount of the gift and when property is transferred for less than an adequate and full consideration in money or money's worth, that the amount by which the value of the property exceeds the value of the consideration shall be deemed a gift. Respondent contends that it is immaterial whether petitioner intended to give the entire value of the property in 1961 since she in that year actually did part with dominion and control over the property without receiving any valuable consideration in return therefor.

Here the notes were vendor's lien notes given for the property. Clearly as a matter of law, they would have been enforceable and respondent does not contend otherwise. Respondent's position is, and the record shows, that it was not petitioner's intention to enforce payment of the notes. Respondent points out that petitioner's sons were not able to pay the $3,000 payments on the notes due on December 31, 1961, on that date since they did not have the funds with which to make the payments. There is a stipulated fact that the sons were not financially able to make the $3,000 payments due on December 31, 1961. This stipulation must imply without considering the rural property given to petitioner's sons the preceding day since this property had a value of $28,180. However, the ability of the sons to pay $3,000 on December 31, 1961, is academic since it was petitioner's intention to and she did forgive the payment due on that day. It is stipulated that at the time these notes were given, the fair market value of the properties conveyed was $16,000 and $16,500 respectively. In view of the agreed value of the properties, the deeds of trust to the properties further securing the vendor's lien notes would obviously have some value. Petitioner certainly did not retain title to the city property she conveyed to her sons by retaining a lien on the property. However, nothing in any of the cases cited by respondent questions the validity of a vendor's lien note provided for in a written instrument or the right to provide for a vendor's lien being retained as a guarantee of payment in a deed. Insofar as the cases cited by respondent deal with this question, they support the validity of such a written agreement irrespective of the construction placed by the parties on their obligations.

Respondent argues that since it was not petitioner's intent to collect the notes from her sons, there existed no debt and that without a debt there can be no lien.

If the notes of petitioner's sons were as a matter of law unenforceable, there might be validity to respondent's argument that there was no debt secured by the vendor's liens and deeds of trust which would be collectible. However, under the facts in this case where the very deeds conveying the properties recited that vendor's lien notes were being given in consideration therefor, the evidence certainly supports the fact that the notes did create enforceable indebtednesses even though petitioner had no intention of collecting the debts but did intend to forgive each payment as it became due.

In the instant case if donative intent were the criterion our question would be easily solved for the record is amply clear that petitioner intended to donate only $3,000 per year of the property here involved to each of her sons until such time as the full value had been given to them. However, since this is not the criterion, it is necessary to look to the property that passed to petitioner in return for the real property transferred to see if the amount of petitioner's gifts to her sons in 1961 of the city property exceeded the $6,000 she reported.

In the instant case we agree with respondent that the gift of the land, insofar as its value exceeded the consideration received by petitioner therefor, was completed in the year 1961. The existence of the vendor's lien notes and deeds of trust would not cause the transfer to be so incomplete as not to be a consummated gift at the time of the transfer to the extent the value of the property exceeded the value of the consideration received therefor.

We hold that the value of the property transferred by petitioner did not exceed the value of the vendor's lien notes and deeds of trust received in return therefor by more than the $3,000 in the case of each son, which amounts petitioner has reported as gifts in the year 1961. We do hold under the facts of this case that petitioner correctly reported the total gifts made by her to her sons in the year 1961.
Decision entered for petitioner.

17.10 LIFE INSURANCE

Life insurance can be used effectively in estate planning to accomplish a number of objectives. Obviously, it can serve as a means of providing liquidity in the estate to pay funeral expenses, estate settlement costs, and taxes. It can provide security for survivors—particularly the surviving spouse and minor children. It can provide an equitable inheritance for heirs who are not involved in the business and a means of funding buy-sell agreements so that those involved in the business will have the potential to buy out off-farm heirs. For example, assume that one son is actively involved in the business with his mother. He could purchase a life insurance policy on the life of the mother.

At the mother's death, he could use the life insurance proceeds to help purchase the interests of the other heirs. If a binding buy-sell agreement existed between the parties, he could be assured of being able to obtain the business assets. Similar arrangements can be made within partnerships or corporations for the protection of surviving partners and shareholders.

Life insurance has also played a major role in funding trusts. A typical arrangement is the life insurance trust, which may be used to achieve both tax and nontax estate planning objectives. The typical life insurance trust is set up during the lifetime of the insured but remains unfunded. The trust is then named beneficiary of life insurance policies. Upon the death of the insured, the proceeds are paid into the trust where they are invested, managed, and distributed according to the terms of the trust instrument.

When a family decides to use insurance as a part of an estate plan, their objectives in using the insurance should be clearly in mind. For example, if liquidity is the objective, they should compare the alternative of using life insurance to the other methods of achieving the same purpose, such as use of estate tax payment deferral. Installment sale options should be compared to the cost of insurance for business buy-sell arrangements. It should also be borne in mind that the cost of obtaining insurance rises as a person gets older, so the most cost-effective insurance plans are those obtained early.

17.11 BUSINESS ORGANIZATIONAL CONSIDERATIONS

One of the usual objectives of most farm families is to provide for the continuation of the farm business following the retirement and death of the parents. This is normally to be accomplished through the active participation of some younger family members in the business. Frequently, the younger family members will be first employed on a salary or share basis, with an informal partnership evolving as the next step. Some family members progress to a formalized partnership or corporate arrangement for purposes of operation of the business. At this point, attention should also be directed toward estate planning objectives in order to make the most appropriate choice of organizational structure. Both the partnership and the corporation offer some attraction as retirement and estate planning tools. The choice of entity will involve evaluation of the operational consid-

erations discussed Chapters 14 and 15 as well as estate planning objectives.

The Partnership in Estate Planning

Because of the flexibility of partnership agreements, this entity can be effectively used in estate planning if sufficient detail is included in the agreement regarding death or retirement of a partner. The agreement can provide a method for termination of an existing partnership and for continuation of the business itself upon death or retirement (or even incapacity) of any partner. Typically, such agreements take the form of buy-sell arrangements, whereby the remaining partners may continue the business and obtain a right to buy out the interest of any retiring or deceased partner. One commonly used technique is to provide for an installment sale of the interest to the remaining partners. This can provide an important source of retirement income for an older partner or income for the partner's surviving family members. An example of a typical arrangement illustrates how these agreements can work in a father-son partnership.

Example of Typical Clause Providing for Death or Dissolution

Death of Either Party

In the event of the death of either partner, this partnership shall terminate. In the event of the death of the son, the father shall have the option to buy the son's share of jointly-owned farm property at the inventory value as of the previous January 1. The father shall accept or reject said option within 60 days of the death of the son, and if he accepts, shall pay at least 25 percent down, and the remainder within 3 years. If he rejects the option to buy the son's share, the jointly-owned property shall be sold at private or public sale within *six* months.

In the event of the death of the father, the son shall have the option to rent the father's share of all farm property used in the farm business at 6 percent of the inventory value as of the previous January 1. The option to rent shall be on a year-to-year basis, to be renewed by the son at his discretion for a total period not to exceed *five* years from date of the father's death. At or before expiration of the *five* year rental period, the son may exercise an option to purchase the father's share of all farm property at the value listed on the farm inventory books the January 1 prior to the father's death. If he exercises the option to buy, he must pay at least *ten* percent down and at least *ten* percent additional each succeeding year until the debt is paid in full.

If the son fails to exercise his option to rent, or upon expiration of the rental option period, if he fails to purchase, then all jointly-owned farm property shall be sold at private or public sale.

Dissolution of Partnership for Reasons Other Than Death of a Partner

It is agreed that if the son wishes to dissolve the partnership, he shall be given the required *six* months notice, and he shall offer his share of all jointly-owned property to the father at the book value as of the previous January 1.

The father shall accept or reject this offer within 60 days, and if he accepts, shall pay the son a minimum of 25 percent down and the remainder within three years.

If he rejects the option, the jointly-owned property shall be sold at public or private sale within the period required for dissolution.

If the father wishes to dissolve the partnership at any date prior to January 1, 198_, the method and details of dissolution shall be decided by family conference, or if necessary, submitted to an arbitration committee. If the father wishes to dissolve the partnership at any time after January 1, 198_, he shall offer his share of jointly-owned property to the son at the inventory value as of the previous January 1. If the son accepts the option, he must pay at least ten percent down and the remainder in equal installments over a period of ten years. If he rejects the option, the property will be sold at public or private sale within the required period for dissolution.

One of the problems encountered in many family partnerships relates to the land used in the business. In many cases the land is owned by the parents and its use contributed to the partnership—perhaps through a lease. The younger family members may become full partners and acquire an interest in all partnership assets, but because the land is owned by the parents the younger partners acquire no interest in the land itself. As land values increase, the parents' estate grows, and it may become difficult for the younger family members to acquire the land at the retirement or death of the parents through a buy-sell arrangement. It is often more realistic to allow younger partners to gradually acquire assets, including land, over a period of years rather than at retirement or death of the parents. This allows the younger person to share in value increases in land. This can be accomplished through giving gifts of or selling parcels of land; by transferring the land to a partnership, limited partnership, corporation, or in some states a land trust; and by allowing the younger family members to acquire an interest in the land holding entity over time.

The Corporation in Estate Planning

The corporation can serve as a means of transferring assets from one generation to the next in much the same way as the partnership. Frequently, the bylaws of the corporation will contain restrictions on the transfer of stock which, in essence, give other shareholders the first option to purchase the stock. This concept can be extended by a buy-sell agreement between the parties to accomplish such a transfer upon the death or retirement of any shareholder. Provisions can be made for those family members who are active in the business to obtain operational control by acquiring enough shares to retain control after the death or retirement of the parents or by using separate classes of stock so that active members obtain voting stock and nonactive members receive stock without voting rights. The off-farm heirs may also be permitted to exchange their stock for notes, debentures, or other types of debt securities issued by the corporation, so that

operating members can continue the business.

The corporation is frequently used as a means of transferring fractional interests in the business by sale or gift. The transfer of shares of stock is less complicated than the transfer of fractional interests in land, livestock, machinery, or farm assets. The entire property can remain intact as an economic unit even when large interests are transferred. In addition, the parents can retain control of the business so long as they own over 50 percent of the voting stock.

By utilizing the $3000 per year per donee annual exclusion from gift tax (which can be doubled, since both parents can join in making gifts) over a period of years, the parents can reduce the size of their estate substantially while retaining control of the business. For example, assume a farm family has assets of $600,000 which they include in a corporation organized with 600 shares of stock valued at $1000 per share. Table 17.7 illustrates how a transfer might be accomplished where three children are involved.

In addition to providing a vehicle for gifts, the corporation may serve as a way of providing employee benefits to owners, such as

Table 17.7 Transfer Plan in a Family Corporation

Year	$ Value of Parents' Interest	% Parents Own	$ Value of Child A's Interest	% Child A Owns	$ Value of Child B's Interest	% Child B Owns	$ Value of Child C's Interest	% Child C Owns
1980	600,000	100	0	0	0	0	0	0
1981	582,000	97	6,000	1	6,000	1	6,000	1
1982	564,000	94	12,000	2	12,000	2	12,000	2
1983	546,000	91	18,000	3	18,000	3	18,000	3
1984	528,000	88	24,000	4	24,000	4	24,000	4
1985	510,000	85	30,000	5	30,000	5	30,000	5
1986	492,000	82	36,000	6	36,000	6	36,000	6
1987	474,000	79	42,000	7	42,000	7	42,000	7
1988	456,000	76	48,000	8	48,000	8	48,000	8
1989	438,000	73	54,000	9	54,000	9	54,000	9
1990	420,000	70	60,000	10	60,000	10	60,000	10

health and accident plans, deferred compensation plans, group life insurance plans, and possibly greater social security benefits upon retirement. Some of these programs may result in income tax advantages to the employee-owner as well.

17.12 RETIREMENT PLANNING

Generally

Retirement planning involves coordinating personal, financial, and estate planning objectives of the family. The personal decisions of when retirement is to occur, whether to sell the business, whether to stay active in the business, etc., often are based on financial and estate planning objectives. Most families hope to achieve a comfortable level of security for the retirement years. Living costs and expected income for the retirement years obviously determine the level of security. Thus, the decision of optimum retirement age is largely a financial decision.

Retirement Income

For most retired farmers, income will come from the farm business itself either from rental income, from corporate stock dividends, or from sale of the business. While these items may provide adequate income levels for some families, many will choose to supplement these from organized plans or programs.

Social Security Programs. Social security retirement benefits are the basic form of supplementary retirement income for most families. For some, these are the only source of retirement income.

Farmers, as self-employed individuals, make contributions to the social security system during income-producing years. Monthly benefits are then payable upon retirement or disability and to certain survivors of a deceased worker. The amount of

the benefits depends on the average earnings of the worker over a period years. Because the level of benefits is determined by the payment record maintained by the Social Security Administration, it is important that these records accurately reflect worker contributions. Because of the importance of these records, workers may want to check them on a periodic basis to make sure that proper credit is given for contributions.

A crucial decision for the retired farmer often is the trade-off between continued earnings from active participation in the business and full social security benefits. A reduction in social security benefits occurs when a person receives productive income above a certain limit. Income from rents, royalties, dividends, interests, annuities, and pension plans and from sale of property is investment income, so it does not serve to reduce social security benefits. Part of the strategy of retirement planning may be to plan productive activities, to take into account the possibility of benefit reduction arising out of such activities, and to the greatest extent possible provide for investment income so benefits will not be reduced.

Self-Employed Retirement Plans (Keogh). Under the Self-Employed Individuals' Tax Retirement Act, known as the Keogh Act, as modified by the Employment Retirement Income Security Act of 1974, farmers can establish individual retirement programs designed to achieve retirement benefits similar to those available to corporate employees. A certain amount of each year's income ($7500 or 15 percent of earned income, whichever is less) can be set aside in various types of investment programs. This amount of income is tax deductible, and any accumulations of interest or other income earned by the investment are not reported as income. Upon retirement, the individual can receive retirement benefits from the fund and at that time pay income taxes on the principal (contributions) and the earnings. Presumably, the retired individual will be in a lower income tax bracket at that time, resulting in less overall tax. Keogh plans are available to part-time farmers even if they are active participants in an employer's pension plan. A comparison of Keogh plans with other types is shown in Table 17.8.

Individual Retirement Accounts (IRA). The individual retirement account program was established to allow both the self-employed individual and those employees whose employer had no pension plan to establish retirement plans individually. Contributions to an IRA can be made up to the lesser of $1500 or 15 percent of earnings or up to $1750 if a separate account is established for a spouse who has no income from work outside the home. These plans, like the Keogh, provide for a current income tax deduction, with taxes due when retirement benefits are received. A comparison of IRA's with Keogh and corporate plans is outlined in Table 17.8.

Corporate Retirement Programs. For the farm business organized as a corporation additional options are available. Various types of pension plans may be established for employees which can sometimes result in current income tax savings to the corporation. In some cases, greater amounts can be set aside than through either Keogh plans or IRA's. A comparison follows in Table 17.8.

17.13 POSTMORTEM ESTATE PLANNING

While optimal estate planning results can be obtained only through actions taken during life there are some options available to the estate executor which may result in achieving some savings for the estate—particularly in taxes. Some options are also available to the surviving spouse and beneficiaries which can result in changes in estate distribution as well as changes in the tax picture. Each of these options will be considered briefly.

Options Involving the Decedent's Final Income Tax Return

The executor of the estate is required to file an income tax return that the decedent was required to file. If the decedent was married at his death and if his surviving spouse does not remarry before the end of the tax year a joint return may be filed for the surviving spouse and the decedent, an action which could result in split tax rates and some reduction in overall tax. The executor may elect to treat gifts as if each spouse gave one-half of the total. These, and other similar options, should be evaluated for possible tax savings.

Options Involving Decedent's Estate Tax Return

The federal estate tax return is normally due nine months following death, and the values used are the fair market values of estate assets on the date of death. The executor may elect to use an alternate valuation date—six months after death—for values used on the estate tax return. In some cases these values will be lower which could result in reduced tax liability.

The executor must determine whether the special use valuation procedure for farmland is to be utilized. Each person having an interest in the land to which special valuation is to be applied must consent to the election. A determination must be made as to whether this election will be used prior to the filing of the estate tax return.

Also, an election can be made in some estates to extend the time for payment of the estate tax—up to 15 years in appropriate cases. If the estate qualifies for extension, the executor must make the election within the time period for filing the estate tax return.

Table 17.8 Comparison of Corporate and Noncorporate Retirement Plans

Points Comparison	Self-Employed Plans (Keogh)*	Individual Plans (IRA)	Corporate Plans
Participation			
1. Who may participate	Self-employed persons and their employees; must have income from "personal services"	Persons not covered by a qualified corporate, self-employed or governmental plan; must receive compensation, except in special case of spouse	Employees
2. Coverage for employees	Required for full-time employees	Not applicable (contribution is really by the employee)	Required for certain "classes" of employees
3. Maximum waiting period	36 months for employees (less if employer has not been in business for 3 years)	Not applicable	1 year, or 3 years, if 100% immediate vesting is provided
4. Minimum age for participating	Not applicable	Not applicable	25 years
5. Vesting of benefits from employee contributions	100% immediately when eligible to participate	100% immediately upon establishing account	100% immediately when eligible to participate
6. Vesting of benefits from employer contributions	100% immediately when eligible to participate	Not applicable; really employee contribution	Graded over 5 to 15 years, or 100% after 10 years, or "rule of 45"
Contributions			
1. Limits on deductible contributions	Lesser of $7500 or 15% of self-employed person's earned income; $750 regardless, if AGI is less than $15,000; higher limit may apply under "defined benefit" plan	Lesser of $1,500 or 15% of compensation or earned income; in special case of employed person and unemployed spouse, limit is $1750 for both, or $875 for each beginning in 1977	(a) Lesser of $25,000+ or 25% of employee's compensation (b) 15% of aggregate compensation paid (25% for carry-over year)
2. Final date for deductible contribution	Final date for filing tax for year, including extensions	45 days after end of tax year, beginning in 1977	Final date for filing tax for year; including extensions; liability for the contribution must arise before the end of the tax year

Table 17.8 Comparison of Corporate and Noncorporate Retirement Plans (continued)

	Points Comparison	Self-Employed Plans (Keogh)*	Individual Plans (IRA)	Corporate Plans
3.	Penalties for excess contribution	6% cumulative, each year, on excess contribution left in account	6% cumulative, each year, on excess contribution left in account	Loss of tax deduction in current year
4.	Transfers of funds permitted:			
	Into plan	No	Yes	Yes, if plan allows
	Out of plan	Yes	Yes	Yes
		Within 60 days of distribution	Within 60 days of distribution, no more often than once in 3 years	

Distributions

	Points Comparison	Self-Employed Plans (Keogh)*	Individual Plans (IRA)	Corporate Plans
1.	Age for distribution	Not before 59½, nor after 70½	Not before 59½, nor after 70½	Determined by plan requirements (not later than 65, usually)
2.	Limits on benefits	Lesser of $75,000 or 100% of average of high 3 years' earnings (for defined benefit plans)	Not applicable	Lesser of $75,000+ or 100% of average high 3 years' pay
3.	Penalties:			
	Premature Distribution	10% of funds withdrawn (or pledged) plus income taxes on amount withdrawn in year of withdrawal (voluntary contributions excepted)	10% of funds in the account plus income taxes in year distributed or pledged	Doesn't apply
	Insufficient Distribution	Plan is terminated	50% of difference between what should have been withdrawn that year and what actually was	Doesn't apply
4.	Taxing of Benefits: Lump Sum	In year received; special 10-year averaging formula available; that portion attributable to years of participation before 1974 may be treated as capital gain	As ordinary income; can use standard 5-year income averaging	In year received, special 10-year averaging formula available; that portion attributable to years of participation before 1974 may be treated as capital gain

Table 17.8 Comparison of Corporate and Noncorporate Retirement Plans (continued)

Points Comparison	Self-Employed Plans (Keogh)*	Individual Plans (IRA)	Corporate Plans
Annuity	As ordinary income income in years received; standard (5-year) income averaging applicable	As ordinary income in years received; standard (5 year) income averaging applicable.	As ordinary income in years received; standard (5-year) income averaging applicable
5. Inclusion of balance of account in gross estate of decedent	Excluded to extent of income tax-deductible contributions if balance is not distributed as lump sum (within 1 year)	Excluded to extent of income tax-deductible contributions if balance is distributed as an annuity of at least 36 months.	Excluded to the extent attributable to employer contributions (i.e., tax deductible) and if balance is not payable to estate or distributed in lump sum (within 1 year)
Funding			
1. Alternatives	IRS-approved: trust with bank, trust company, building and loan; custodial account with bank or building and loan; mutual funds, life insurance contracts, annuities, endowments; special U.S. "retirement" bond; can design own plan	IRS-approved: Account—bank, savings and loan, credit union, others approved by IRS. Annuity—insurance company annuity or endowment contract. Special U.S. "retirement" bond; can design own plan	IRS-approved trusts are the usual method, but also certain annuities or face amount certificates or custodial accounts may be used

Source: "Tax Sheltered Retirement Plans of Farm Investments," North Central Regional Publication No. 55-1978.
*Applies to plans which cover at least one "owner-employee" (one who is a self-employed sole proprietor or who owns more than 10% of the capital interest or profit in a partnership).
+Modified by cost of living index.

Options Available to Spouses and Beneficiaries

The surviving spouse has the option, in most states, of taking the share designated in the will or renouncing the will and claiming a statutory share of the estate. The election must be made by renouncing the will after its admission to probate. In addition, any beneficiary has the option of disclaiming an interest in the estate under state disclaimer statutes. This is sometimes useful where property passing to a spouse exceeds the maximum marital deduction in order to prevent taxation again in the spouse's estate.

If a disclaimer is "qualified," the person making the disclaimer is not treated as having transferred the property for estate or gift tax purposes.[38] In order for the document to be treated as a qualified disclaimer, a number of specific requirements must be met. The disclaimer must be irrevocable, be in writing, and be made within 9 months of the date of transfer of the property interest.[39] The person making the disclaimer must not have accepted the property interest or any of the benefits therefrom prior to making the disclaimer. The property must then pass without direction on the part of the person making the disclaimer. Ordinarily, it will pass to another person, but it may pass to a trust in which the surviving spouse has an income interest even if he or she is the person making the disclaimer, so long as it passes without direction by the person disclaiming.[40]

Under the 1978 Revenue Act, an executor may elect to treat a portion of jointly owned property as belonging to the surviving spouse to reflect the material participation of the surviving spouse in the business —the so-called "2 percent credit" rule. If circumstances indicate use of the rule would be helpful, the election must be made no later than the time of filing of the estate tax return.[41]

STUDY QUESTIONS

1. What is estate planning, and why is it important to the farm family?

2. What are the major advantages and disadvantages of jointly owned or tenancy by the entirety property?

3. Assume a farm couple own substantial assets as joint tenants with a right of survivorship or as tenants by the entirety. What planning options are available to reduce potential estate taxes?

4. What are reasons for probate of an estate?

5. Under what circumstances do the state laws of intestacy (descent and distribution) control the disposition of a deceased's property?

6. What statutory distribution of assets is provided by the state law of intestacy in your state of residence?

7. Assume a married individual dies without a will, owning solely owned property valued at $930,000. What is the maximum estate tax marital deduction available to this estate assuming sufficient property passes to the surviving spouse to qualify for the maximum deduction?

8. In question 7, assume the deceased's will divides the property equally between the spouse, the son, and the daughter. What marital deduction is now available?

9. Assume a farmer dies owning real estate valued at $300,000, livestock valued at $200,000, machinery and equipment valued at $100,000, and $150,000 in stocks, bonds, and other nonfarm property. Will

[38] INT. REV. CODE § 2518.
[39] A minor may make such a disclosure within 9 months of attaining the age of 21. *See* INT. REV. CODE § 2518.
[40] INT. REV. CODE § 2518.
[41] INT. REV. CODE § 2040(c).

this estate qualify for special valuation of the farmland, assuming the farmer was active in farming in all years prior to death? Would it make any difference if all or part of this property was encumbered with debt?

10. Assume a mother wishes to make gifts to her three children and wants to take advantage of all exclusions and credits available to her. How much gift tax liability will she incur with the following gifts?

Child no.	Year 1 gifts	Year 2 gifts	Year 3 gifts
1	$50,000	50,000	0
2	25,000	50,000	25,000
3	75,000	25,000	0

11. If the children's mother, in question 10, dies within 3 years of the date of the gifts and if she has other assets (not counting the gifts) valued at $425,000 at the time of death, what estate tax liability will her estate have assuming she is a widow? What if she lives 5 years after the date of the gifts?

12. What state death taxes will be paid by each child, in questions 10 and 11, under the inheritance or estate tax law of the state in which you live?

13. Assume a farmer purchased land in 1965 for $50,000; has added $50,000 in improvements on the property; and has claimed $30,000 in depreciation on those improvements. If the property is now worth $250,000, what is the farmer's income tax basis on this property? If he gives the property to his children by lifetime gift, what basis will the property have in their hands? If the children inherit the property, what basis will it have in their hands?

14. What are the major limitations on the use of the will as an estate planning tool?

15. What are the formal requirements for a legal, valid will?

16. Under what circumstances may a will be declared invalid?

17. What is the tax effect of including a testamentary trust in a will?

18. What is the difference in tax effect of using an irrevocable *inter vivos* trust and one that is revocable?

19. How may a testamentary trust be used to reduce estate taxes?

20. What advantages are to be gained by the use of gifts in an estate plan?

21. Under what circumstances will a purported installment sale be treated as a gift of the property for tax purposes?

22. Under what circumstances may life insurance proceeds be free from taxation in the estate of the insured?

23. How may the partnership be used as an estate planning device?

24. What is the major reason farm corporations are used as an estate planning tool?

25. What is the income tax advantage of using a self-employed (Keogh) plan or an individual retirement account (IRA)?

18

Income Tax Planning

18.1 TAX PLANNING AS A MANAGEMENT TOOL

Tax planning has assumed an equal role with financial, marketing, and production decisions in the operation of a profitable farm enterprise.[1] Income tax minimization is but a part of the overall objective of maximizing profits over a period of time and requires day-to-day tax management. Although year-end adjustments may often improve a tax situation, poor planning during the remainder of the year can more than offset any reductions achieved at year's end. Once the year's business has been concluded, the taxpayer can do little to reduce the tax impact of poor tax management decisions made during the business year. These decisions must be made on a day-to-day basis.

The farm operator cannot be expected to become a tax specialist, because the maze of income tax laws and regulations is becoming thicker every year. The astute manager can, however, become aware of the importance of tax management in the overall farm profitability picture and be conscious of tax effects when reaching other management decisions. Such decisions as selecting or changing the form of operation, disposing of farm property for estate planning purposes, planning for retirement, planning for business expansions, purchasing new equipment, selling old equipment, selling livestock or crops, making major farm improvements, and a host of others all have significant in-

---

[1] For a general discussion of tax management as a financial tool, *see* O'BYRNE and DAVENPORT, TAX GUIDE FOR FARMERS (1979).

come tax implications. The successful operator develops a tax strategy to deal with the tax impact of management decisions.

The purpose of this chapter is to review the major income tax provisions that have an impact on management decisions. No attempt will be made to go into detail regarding tax laws and regulations. Tax laws are subject to change any time that Congress is in session. Interpretations by courts and by the Internal Revenue Service are continually evolving. Thus, only basic principles can be discussed. A general overview is intended.

18.2 FARM INCOME

The starting point in determining income tax liability is to determine the total income subject to taxation. The farm family may have income from wages or salaries, interest, and dividends or from other nonfarm investments. In addition, there are several sources of income directly related to the business operation. Income may have been generated from the sale of farm products, including livestock and crops; from custom work, breeding fees, rent, government benefits, and patronage dividends; and from commodity credit corporation loans. Sales of business assets, including land, livestock,

and machinery and equipment, result in reportable income. Sales of personal assets, such as the residence, the automobile, stocks and bonds, and similar items, can also result in reportable income. Income can also result from the condemnation of farm property, from exchanges of property, and from long-term contracts for the sale of property.

A number of special tax problems arise from attempts to manage income. The income tax rate structure is progressive—that is, as income increases the taxpayer is placed in increasingly higher tax brackets. A basic concept in managing income is to avoid year-to-year fluctuations in income to achieve the lowest possible rate of overall taxation. This objective may be achieved by several income management devices including deferred payment sales, installment sales, timing of sales, income splitting, and timing of losses.

Constructive Receipt of Income

Farmers sometimes try to defer taxable income into a succeeding tax year by contractual arrangements with purchasers of farm products—particularly at year's end. Such contracts can be effective if properly drafted and if the agreement clearly meets other IRS requirements.

CONSTRUCTIVE RECEIPT OF INCOME

HINEMAN v. BRODRICK
U.S. District Court, Kansas, 1951
99 F. Supp. 582

The above entitled case was tried before the Court without a jury, on January 22, 1951, and the parties were represented by counsel.

After hearing the evidence and the arguments of counsel and after due consideration thereof the Court makes the following findings of fact, conclusions of law and order for judgment.

Findings of Fact

1.   The plaintiff, a resident of Dighton, Kansas, is and, at all material times, was the duly qualified and acting executrix of the estate of J.A. Hineman, who died September 13, 1947.

2.   The Commissioner of Internal Revenue determined and assessed against the plaintiff for the year 1947 a deficiency tax in the amount of $11,075.33, including interest, which amount was duly paid by the plaintiff. The plaintiff's attorney was permitted to amend the complaint at the trial by increasing her claim from $10,451.25 to the correct amount of $11,072.45, the sum of $2.88 having been refunded prior to the commencement of the action, and the plaintiff seeks in this action to recover $11,072.45, with interest according to law. The deficiency in tax was attributable to the inclusion in plaintiff's 1947 income of the amount of $19,919.44 as proceeds from the sale by plaintiff in that year of 8,097 bushels, 20 pounds of wheat.

3.   Hineman, the plaintiff's testate, regularly reported income for tax purposes on the cash basis.

4.   In April 1947, Hineman, who was a wheat farmer, sold and delivered to the Farmers Cooperative Elevator and Mercantile Association, at Dighton, Kansas, herein referred to as the Elevator Association, 8,097 bushels, 20 pounds, of wheat for the agreed price of $19,919.44, and title to the wheat passed to the buyer at the time of the sale.

5.   Hineman had sold wheat to the Elevator Association many times before the transaction in question and had always been paid at the time of sale.

6.   It was customary in the grain elevator business, and it had long been the practice of the Elevator Association to pay the purchase price of wheat at the time of its purchase.

7.   The Elevator Association had available funds to pay Hineman in full for this wheat at the time it was purchased and Hineman could have received at that time the money due him, but at his request, because of his desire to effect a possible saving of federal taxes, the money was not paid to him until February 1, 1949.

8.   Hineman was entitled to receive the selling price of his wheat at the time of the sale and the Elevator Association was ready, able and willing to pay him in full at that time. Hineman's failure to receive the money was due entirely to his own volition.

Conclusions of Law

1.   The plaintiff was in constructive receipt of the selling price of his wheat in the sum of $19,919.44 and realized income from that source in that amount within the taxable year 1947.

2.   The tax and interest paid by the plaintiff for the year 1947 and which she seeks to recover in this action were not erroneously or illegally assessed or collected, and the defendant is entitled to judgment.

3.   Judgment for the defendant is hereby ordered accordingly.

The *Hineman* case is a good illustration of the "constructive receipt" doctrine.[2] If a cash-basis taxpayer has the right to draw upon proceeds of a sale or the right to receive possession of the money at will, then the taxpayer will be considered to have received income for tax purposes even if not actually in the person's physical possession. If the income is credited to the taxpayer's account, is set apart for the taxpayer, or is otherwise made available so that the taxpayer may draw upon it at any time, the income is taxable as "constructively received." It is for this reason that it is not enough just to instruct the operator of the elevator or the buyer of cattle to "hold the check" until after the first of the year.

Additional problems have been encountered in situations where the "buyer" was not really a buyer at all but was, in effect, an agent for a seller. For example, livestock marketing firms have been determined to be agents of the seller—not cattle buyers—so that deferred income contracts with such firms have not successfully deferred for income tax purposes.

To be effective, deferred payment contracts must be bona fide, arm's length transactions with the agreement for deferred payment clearly stated in writing. The contract should provide for a down payment—even a small one—and fix the date of payments in the following year. In addition, the contract must be nonassignable and should be binding on heirs, executors, and administrators of the parties. If the contract is assignable, IRS will consider it as a contract right which could be sold immediately to someone else for cash and therefore not a true deferral of income.

Income Splitting

Farmers sometimes attempt to lower taxes by shifting income from the taxpayer to other family members. This may be attempted by the payment of wages or through the transfer of income-producing property. If wages are paid to family members, these wages can serve as a farm business deduction if paid for work actually performed and if reasonable. If the income shift is attempted by the transfer of income-producing property as gifts, future income will, in fact, be taxable to the new owner. The transfer of growing crops or livestock avoids income tax upon sale for the donor, but the cost of producing the crop or raising the livestock cannot be claimed as a deduction. Gifts of the proceeds from the sale of harvested crops or of livestock do not result in an income shift for the donor. For example, if a farmer instructs an elevator operator to pay proceeds from a grain sale to the farmer's children, this is treated as a sale by the farmer and a gift of proceeds to the children. The income is still taxable to the donor, and a possible gift tax liability may also be incurred depending on the amount transferred.

18.3 BUSINESS DEDUCTIONS

Most expenses of the business are deductible—that is, they reduce the tax liability by directly offsetting income. Most purely personal expenses are not deductible, although a few are by specific statutory provisions—e.g., medical expenses, charitable contributions, interest, property taxes, etc. The usual business expenses, including those in connection with owning income-producing property, should be contrasted with capital expenditures which are deductible only by depreciation claimed over the life of the asset. For example, the deductible expenses include: hired labor, repairs and maintenance of equipment, machinery and buildings, cash rent, farm interest, taxes,

---

[2] *Contrast* J.D. Amend, 13 T.C. Memo. 178 (1949).

insurance, feed purchased, gasoline, oil, fuel, farm utilities, seed, fertilizers, lime, chemicals, veterinary fees, medicine, freight, trucking, advertising, farm organization dues, and miscellaneous supplies, etc. These should be contrasted with the nondeductible capital expenditures for the purchase of farm machinery, buildings, fences, breeding animals, or other property used in the farm business. For these items the cost is spread over the useful life and recovered as an annual depreciation deduction. A third category of items are those such as feeder calves, lambs, or pigs, which are held for sale and are not depreciable. The cost of these assets is deducted in the year of sale.

Major problem areas involving deductions center on distinguishing nondeductible personal expenses from deductible business expenses, prepayment of expenses, and land clearing and soil and water conservation expenses.

Personal Expenses versus Business Deductions

All ordinary and necessary expenses of a trade or business are deductible.[3]

PERSONAL EXPENSES

COBB v. COMMISSIONER
U.S. Tax Court, 1949
13 T.C. 495

In the spring of 1945 petitioner and his wife made their home at a tract owned by petitioner known as Maple Knoll Farm. There they kept their own riding horses. They employed a trainer and started to take in horses belonging to others for training, their purpose being to use the fees derived therefrom to offset the cost of training their own horses. They have purchased show horses from time to time and Ida Cobb has ridden practically every day. Petitioner rode very seldom. They opened a separate joint bank account for Maple Knoll Farm.

Ida Cobb prepared the 1946 partnership return for Maple Knoll Farm, in which fees charged others for boarding and training their horses were reported as gross receipts, and in arriving at the amount of gross profit or loss the cost of training, labor, feed, and other supplies were deducted, including costs of maintaining and training horses used by petitioner and wife. At the insistence of petitioner she also included therein an item of income as follows: "2 Horses used personally by partners at $100 per mo., 12 mos., $1,200.00."

The issue involves the question of the proper allocation of the expenses of the operation of Maple Knoll Farm for the years 1945 and 1946 between business and personal expenses. At this farm the petitioner maintained some horses for himself and his wife for their own pleasure. They also boarded and trained horses for others. The fees charged others for boarding and training their horses were reported as gross receipts of the business, and in arriving at the amount of gross profit or loss the costs of training, labor, feed and other supplies were deducted, including costs of maintaining and training

---

[3]Int. Rev. Code § 162.

horses used by petitioner and his wife. In the return for 1946 filed by the Maple Knoll Farm, $1,200 was included in gross income for maintenance of petitioner's horses. In the 1945 return of the Maple Knoll Farm, no amount was included for maintenance of their horses and the respondent, in determining the deficiency for that year, reduced the amount of a farm loss claimed by petitioner by $1,200.

The petitioner now contends that the respondent erred in reducing the loss from operation of Maple Knoll Farm claimed for 1945 by $1,200 and also erred in permitting $1,200 to be deducted from the expense of the farm as a personal expense for 1946.

The petitioner argues in support of his contention that Maple Knoll Farm was not a farm for pleasure; that it was strictly a business proposition; and that this is borne out by the fact that the respondent has so treated it in allowing the losses from its operation in 1945 and 1946 as deductions in computing petitioner's taxable income for those years. We do not agree with petitioner. The evidence indicates that the Maple Knoll Farm was purchased because both petitioner and his wife were fond of horses, and that the idea of boarding and training horses for others originated at the time Ida Cobb decided to learn how to show horses at horse shows and had as its objective the reduction or elimination of the cost of maintaining and training their own horses through profits realized from fees charged others for boarding and training horses. The farm was operated partly for profit and partly for pleasure. In so far as petitioner engaged in boarding and training horses for others, he was engaged in business for profit, but the cost of maintaining the horses owned by him and his wife was a personal expense. In reporting the income from the farm, petitioner was entitled to deduct from gross receipts only expenses attributable to operating it as a business for profit. In his 1946 return he accomplished this by deducting from gross receipts all of the expense of operation, whether business or personal, and then including in income as an offset the cost of maintaining horses owned by him and his wife. The respondent did substantially the same thing when he reduced the loss claimed from the operation of the stable for 1945 by the amount of $1,200. In the absence of any evidence that the expense of maintaining the horses owned by petitioner and his wife in 1945 and 1946 did not amount to $1,200, the petitioner's claim that respondent erred in his treatment of this expenditure in each year must be and is disallowed.

Reviewed by the Court.

Decision will be entered for the respondent.

In order to properly deduct farm business expenses, the farm must be operated with the intention of making a profit.[4] If there is no profit motive, then the deductions may be challenged, especially if used to offset substantial amounts of other income. If the challenge is successful and the operation is classified as a "hobby farm," deductions are limited to the amount of income generated by the operation.

---

[4] Int. Rev. Code § 183.

HOBBY FARMING

DEERMAN v. COMMISSIONER
U.S. Tax Court, 1974
33 T.C. Memo 440

The petitioners, Williard (or Willard) Deerman and Florence Deerman, are husband and wife. They filed joint Federal income tax returns for the calendar years 1964 and 1967.

In the years prior to 1966 petitioner Williard Deerman was engaged exclusively in the business of farming and raising cattle. Presently he farms approximately 1100 acres of land; 700 acres of his own land and 400 acres of land owned by other persons. In addition he sells between 800 and 2000 head of cattle each year.

Sometime during, or just prior to, 1966 petitioners decided that they could profitably expand their operations by raising and breeding quarter horses such as performance and halter horses. Before firmly committing themselves to this venture, petitioners consulted with knowledgeable horse breeders and trainers. These consultants confirmed petitioner's belief that horse raising and breeding, as they wished to do it, coincided well with their farming and cattle business and could be a very profitable operation. Additionally they were informed of the youth activities of the American Quarter Horse Association which provided a potentially large market for well trained quarter horses such as the types petitioners desired to raise.

In the years 1966 and 1967 petitioners acquired most of their horses. Due to their lack of knowledge and experience, a qualified trainer was hired to handle the horse operation. The initial trainer hired failed to control expenses to petitioners' expectations and a new trainer was subsequently employed. By the middle of 1968, petitioners' children John Fletcher Deerman and Deborah Deerman, had acquired sufficient experience and knowledge of the horse operation that they were deemed capable of taking full responsibility for the training of the horses, which subsequently they did. The children received no monetary compensation for their efforts.

Petitioner Florence Deerman (Florence) kept the records of the farm. A separate bank account distinguishing the horse operation from the farming and cattle business was not kept. However, complete and accurate records of the horse operation were readily available. Records were kept of deposits into the bank account indicating what each deposit represented. All expenses were recorded in a similar manner: the amount, what the money was spent for, and to whom it was paid. In addition, Florence kept income sheets on the horses. These sheets indicated which shows various horses were in and how the horses fared in them. Further, a book entitled "Horse Account" was maintained showing all pertinent information in regard to the horse venture.

On October 1, 1967, petitioners transferred their horse operations along with their farming and cattle raising operations to Deerman Farms, Inc., the stock of which is wholly owned by members of the Deerman family. The horse operation showed a continued record of losses from 1966 through 1971 reported in the initial years by petitioners as individuals and in later years by the corporation.

In 1969, due to unfortunate circumstances, petitioners realized that the horse operation would not become profitable. As a result, a decision to liquidate the horse operation was made. The circumstances which lead to this decision came about when two horses named Skip Fancy Pants and Bum's Barb could not be used for studs. At this time petitioners decided that they could not afford to purchase any other horses for breeding and the decision to liquidate was made.

Skip Fancy Pants was bought by petitioners when he was seven months old. He was first shown as a yearling, and later as a halter until he was over two years old. In 1969 petitioners decided to breed two mares to Skip Fancy Pants, and from this point on the horse became uncontrollable, trying to bite anyone near. On the advice of a qualified expert the horse was gelded and subsequently sold.

Bum's Barb, the other horse petitioners had originally expected to use for stud, became afflicted with bogged hocks (when the horse was used his hocks would swell) in 1969. The veterinarian consulted on this matter informed petitioners that this condition could be passed down in breeding and the horse should be gelded. Bum's Barb after one unsuccessful attempt to sell the horse, is still for sale and is presently used as a cow horse to work cattle.

For the taxable year 1967 petitioners claimed a loss attributable to the horse raising and breeding operation in the amount of $16,336.86, which petitioners carried back to their taxable year 1964 as a net operating loss under the provisions of section 172 of the Internal Revenue Code of 1954.

Respondent, in his statutory notice of deficiency dated August 12, 1971, determined a deficiency in petitioners' income tax for the taxable year 1964. This was based upon a determination that the above loss claimed by petitioners was not incurred in a trade or business, but rather constituted a nondeductible personal expenditure. Since the taxable year in issue is 1964, this determination has the effect of reducing the net operating loss claimed by petitioners for the year 1967 and thereby increasing the tax liability for the taxable year 1964.

OPINION

The sole question for decision is whether petitioners' horse operation constitutes a trade or business as that term is used in the appropriate sections of the Internal Revenue Code.

It is well established that breeding, racing, showing and raising horses for sale may constitute a trade or business. However, whether such activity constitutes a trade or business in the particular circumstances of each case is determined by whether the taxpayer engaged in the venture with the intention to operate for the purpose of making a profit. The expectation of making a profit need not be a reasonable one, but the taxpayer must show that the expectation was in fact genuine.

The issue presented is essentially one of fact and the burden of proof rests with petitioners. After closely reviewing all the facts and circumstances in the matter before us, we hold that petitioners have met this burden. They possessed the requisite genuine expectation of realizing a profit from their horse operations and were therefore engaged in the trade or business of raising and breeding horses.

We have made this determination on the basis of several factors which weigh in petitioners' favor. Initially we note that the petitioners conducted a thorough preliminary exploration of the type of horse they wished to raise and the potential markets available for this type of horse. We think this is indicative of a genuine profit motive.

Additionally, the petitioners hired qualified help during the initial years of the operation. Experienced trainers were maintained until the petitioners and their family were sufficiently experienced and knowledgeable in the operation to take over those duties previously undertaken by the hired help. We find this to be a further indication of the petitioners' expectation for an eventual profit.

Moreover, we have been swayed by the petitioners' businesslike concern for the economics of the horse venture and their method of accounting for income and expenses. The records of the operation were accurate and easily distinguishable from petitioners' farming and cattle business. Petitioner Florence was responsible for the record keeping of the farm. In regard to the horse operation she kept income sheets on the horses, indicating which shows various horses were in and how the horses placed. She kept a record of all deposits in the bank account, indicating what each deposit represented and also a record of expenses indicating what the money was spent for and to whom it went. Additionally a special book entitled "Horse Account" was kept showing all information pertinent to the horse operation. Although no separate bank account was kept, an accurate and complete reconstruction of the income and expenses of the horse operation was easily attainable. Furthermore, as indicative of their concern for the economics of this venture, petitioners began liquidating the horse operation when it became apparent that it would not prove to be profitable.

Respondent's position is that the venture did not constitute a trade or business. As indicative of this he points to the record of losses by petitioners. Although we recognize that a history of losses over a period may be an important factor bearing on a taxpayer's true intentions, the presence of losses in the formative years of a business, particularly one involving the breeding of horses, is not inconsistent with the intention to achieve a later profitable level of operation. We are convinced that had it not been for unfortunate circumstances outlined in the facts of this case, petitioners may well have made a profitable enterprise out of horse raising and breeding. We, therefore, do not consider their record of losses indicative of a lack of intent to realize a profit.

Therefore, for all the reasons above, we hold petitioners' horse operation to constitute a trade or business for purposes of the appropriate sections of the Internal Revenue Code of 1954.

Decision will be entered for Petitioners.

Prepayment of Expenses

Generally, expenditures for feed, fertilizer, seed, and similar farm supplies are deductible business expenses. Many farmers, particularly at year's end, will purchase these items for use during the following year. If properly handled, prepayments for these items can be properly deductible in the year purchased even if delivery is not made until the following year.[5] This strategy can reduce the tax impact in a "good" year.

PREPAID FEED DEDUCTION

HEINHOLD v. COMMISSIONER
U.S. Tax Court, 1979
39 T.C. Memo 496

The sole issue is whether petitioner, a cash method taxpayer, is entitled to deduct in the year of purchase and payment the cost of cattle feed which was not completely consumed until the following taxable year.

Petitioner realized a large capital gain from the sale of stock in the last quarter of 1972. About that time he acquired a 50 percent interest in a cattle feedlot in Minatare, Nebraska, and purchased 4,936 head of cattle to feed at Minatare for approximately $2,000,000. In November and December of 1972, he made three feed purchases totaling $568,957 for his cattle feeding operation at Minatare. Although the feed was paid for and delivered in 1972, it was not completely consumed until July 31, 1973.

Petitioner maintains that the cost of the cattle feed is deductible as an ordinary and necessary business expense for which he had a valid business purpose. He argues that, as a cash method farmer, he is entitled to deduct in 1972 the full amount he paid for cattle feed in that year.

---

[5] Revised Rev. Rul. 75-152 states the IRS position on prepaid expenses. This was restated and amplified in Rev. Rul. 79-229, I.R.B. 1979-31.

Respondent conceded that the amount petitioner deducted in 1972 for feed consumed by March 31, 1973, was proper. Respondent maintains, however, that the amount petitioner deducted for feed consumed from March 31, 1973, through July 31, 1973, should be disallowed. Respondent's disallowance is based on essentially two arguments: (1) petitioner was motivated by tax avoidance rather than a valid business purpose when purchasing the feed, and (2) the purchase of the feed consumed after March 31, 1973, created an asset having a useful life extending substantially beyond the close of the taxable year of deduction making it nondeductible in such year in that the deduction caused a material distortion of petitioner's 1972 income. Since our decision in this case is controlled by *Van Raden v. Commissioner* [Dec. 35,964], 71 T.C. 1083, on appeal—F. 2d—(1979), we hold for petitioner.

In *Van Raden v. Commissioner, supra,* the taxpayers, as limited partners, invested in a cash basis partnership cattle-feeding operation in mid-December 1972. During the last few days of 1972, the partnership purchased a one year supply of feed and some cattle. The Commissioner disallowed the deduction for the feed expense on the grounds that there was no business purpose for the prepayment of feed expense and that the deduction of the cost of the feed caused a material distortion of income in the year of purchase. On the basis of all the evidence, this Court found that there was a business purpose for the feed purchases and rejected the argument that the purchases caused a material distortion of income.

Business purpose for the timing of a business expense deduction is a question of fact. The factor that generally distinguishes the court decisions allowing a deduction for prepaid feed costs from those disallowing the deduction is the reasonable expectation by the taxpayer of receiving some business benefit as a result of the prepayment. If an expenditure is appropriate and helpful to the taxpayer's business, the courts are reluctant to override a taxpayer's judgment.

Respondent contends that there was no business purpose for petitioner's purchase of shelled corn in November and December of 1972 because the prices for shelled corn were lower during the first quarter of 1973 than at the time of purchase in 1972. Although there was a slight decline in price in the first quarter of 1973 as compared to December 1972, we disagree with respondent's contention.

Petitioner testified that shelled corn prices are usually lower at harvest time and that he expected the price to rise in 1973 due to bullish market trends causing most commercial cattle feeders to acquire more cattle for feeding than they had in previous years. Petitioner is a knowledgeable businessman and his testimony was forthright and credible. We believe that he had a business purpose in protecting himself from a speculative rise in the market price of shelled corn. Moreover, respondent conceded that the feed purchased for consumption during the first quarter of 1973 was proper. After the first quarter of 1973, however, the price of shelled corn did increase significantly compared to the price at the time of petitioner's purchase.

Therefore, if in 1972 petitioner had purchased only the amount of feed respondent conceded he was entitled to deduct in that year, and after the first quarter in 1973 had purchased shelled corn for the remainder of 1973, the cost of shelled corn would have been substantially higher not only due to a rise in market price, but also due to the additional costs of storage, handling, and transportation resulting from making the purchase outside the harvest season. For these reasons we find that petitioner derived a substantial business benefit from making the bulk purchase of shelled corn during the 1972 harvest season.

As to the roughage feed items, we also find that the testimony of petitioner and his experts established a business purpose for the purchase of those items. Certain roughage feed items can only be acquired at harvest time. Furthermore, one of petitioner's experts testified that there are preservational and nutritional benefits in acquiring roughage feeds at harvest and allowing them to properly ferment prior to their actual use. He further testified that bulk purchases of feed are preferable because changing feeds upsets the dietary habits of cattle causing them to reject the new feed for a short period of time. Another expert testified that although the feed purchases in dispute were insufficient to feed out the number of cattle petitioner originally intended to purchase, the amount of feed was not excessive for the cattle on hand at the end of 1972 and those purchased in early 1973.

Due to our finding that petitioner had a business purpose for making the feed purchases in dispute, we find respondent's arguments for tax avoidance without merit. Petitioner is a successful farmer who has many years of experience in the business of feeding livestock. By making bulk purchases of feed he was able to fix the cost of feed which enabled him to ascertain the potential profitability of his feeding operation at Minatare. Moreover, his primary consideration in making the feed purchases was based on the number of cattle to be fed, not on the income tax deduction such purchases would generate.

In relying on *Van Raden*, we also note that the feed purchased in that case was not completely consumed until early in the second taxable year following the year of deduction. Here, the feed was completely consumed by July 31, 1973, six months after the taxable year in which the deduction was taken. Not only did petitioner have a valid business purpose, but the amount of the deduction for feed purchased was not nearly as great as that permitted in *Van Raden*. Finally, unlike *Van Raden* where the taxpayers were limited partners in a cattle feeding partnership formed in the last few days of their taxable year, petitioner had been engaged in the business of feeding cattle for many years. In sum, we find that petitioner has shown he had a valid business purpose for making the three purchases of feed in November and December 1972.

Respondent next argues that the feed purchased in 1972 but consumed after March 31, 1973, was a capital asset the deduction for which, under the principles of section 263, must be prorated over the period during which the feed is used. Section 1.461-(a)(1), Income Tax Regs., the argument goes, provides that "If an expenditure results in the creation of an asset having a useful life which extends substantially beyond the close of the taxable year," such an expenditure may not be deductible, or may be deductible only in part, for the taxable year in which made. Relying upon section 446(b), which gives the Commissioner discretionary power to require a recomputation of income if the method used by the taxpayer does not clearly reflect income, respondent argues that allowing a deduction for the full amount of feed purchased in 1972 distorts petitioner's income.

This Court rejected that argument in *Van Raden*, and we reject it here. Petitioner's income in 1972 was not distorted because he failed to use all the cattle feed purchased in that year. The distortion is due to petitioner's failure to sell the cattle for which he purchased the feed so that income would be available to match the cost of the feed purchases. Such distortions can be prevented only by requiring farmers to employ a method of accounting which requires a matching of income with expenses. As set out above, however, the regulations expressly permit farmers to use the cash method of accounting.

In *Van Raden*, this Court refused to capitalize the taxpayers' feed costs by distinguishing "period" costs from "product" costs. Period costs are costs that arise with respect to time intervals rather than the creation of products or rendition of services. They are similar to overhead costs which are ongoing regardless of the size of the business. Unlike period costs which tend to be keyed to more than one taxable period, feed or "product" costs do not depend upon the mere passage of time but upon the size of the production process. Moreover, period costs are easily allocable to more than one accounting period, whereas product costs are not so easily allocable because their rate of consumption does not rest solely upon the passage of time.

Furthermore, in *Haynes v. Commissioner* [Dec. 36,145(M)], T.C. Memo. 1979–240 respondent's argument for capitalizing the cost of cattle feed was rejected as follows:

> Cattle feed is not an asset having a "useful life" which extends substantially beyond the close of the taxable year within the meaning of the quoted language from section 1.461-(a) (1), Income Tax Regs. The term "useful life" refers to an asset which is gradually exhausted through use or the passage of time. Cattle feed does not deteriorate with the passage of time or become exhausted through use over an extended period. It is merely an inventory item which is consumed in the production of cattle for slaughter, and the inventory is reduced in a taxable period by the amount fed to cattle during that period. It is part of the cost of goods—the cattle—ultimately sold. [Footnote omitted.]

Respondent's position must also be rejected because farmers would be forced to maintain consumption records which would in effect require them to use the inventory method of accounting and deny them the option of using the cash method of accounting.

Cash method farmers have historically been accorded special treatment due to the nature of the business including the effects of weather, seasonal nature of farming, the cyclical nature of feed prices, and, most important, the practical difficulties of using the inventory method of accounting. As explained by the Supreme Court in *Catto v. United States* [66-1 USTC ¶ 9376], 384 U.S. 102, 116 (1966):

> The sacrifice in accounting accuracy under the cash method represents an historical concession by the Secretary and the Commissioner to provide a unitary and expedient bookkeeping system for farmers and ranchers in need of a simplified accounting procedure.

Over a period of time, consistent utilization of the cash method will produce a fair result. A "distortion" in one year will be offset by a "distortion" in another year so that over a period of time the taxpayer's income will be clearly reflected.

To reflect the foregoing.

Decision will be entered for petitioner.

In order for one to claim a deduction for prepaid farm expenses, three tests must be met.

1. The expenditure must be a payment—not a deposit.
2. The payment must be made for a valid business purpose—not merely to avoid taxes.
3. The payment must not materially distort the farmer's income.

If the payment fails to meet any one of these tests, the deduction will be available only in the year in which the item is used or consumed.

To determine if the expenditure is actually a payment and not a deposit, the courts look to see if the purchase is pursuant to a written contract for a fixed quantity at a fixed price. If the buyer is not entitled to a refund of any part of the payment and the seller treats the transaction as a sale on the seller's records and sets aside or delivers the item, then the transaction is much more likely to be treated as a payment rather than a deposit. However, if the buyer is not obligated to accept a specific quantity, is allowed to substitute delivery of other goods, or is entitled to a refund if all the supplies contracted for are not required, or if the buyer obtains the benefit of market prices prevailing at the date of delivery if lower than the contract price, the expenditure may be treated as a deposit rather than a payment. In cases involving advance payments for feed, the courts have looked to see if the farmer was "irretrievably out-of-pocket the amount paid for" the supplies.

To determine if the payment is for a valid business purpose, the courts look to see if the expenses are ordinary and necessary. "Ordinary" is determined by looking at the farming business community to see if the expense is a common and accepted kind of expense in the commercial context. "Necessary" refers to the specific business and whether the expenditures are appropriate and helpful. Examples of valid business purposes include offering price discounts, pegging a price for needed supplies, assuring a source of supplies, or obtaining preferential treatment in case of shortages in supply.

The material distortion of income test has become the chief ground for challenge by the IRS in advance payment cases. If the amount of the payment is a sizable portion of the farmer's income for the year, the payment may be challenged. A number of factors will be considered in determining if distortion in income has occurred, including prior prepayment practices, amount of expenses for that item, etc. No hard and fast rules exist regarding what is considered to be material distortion of income, and the rule has not been clarified by the courts to date.

While a majority of the cases dealing with prepayment of expenses have involved feed purchases, the same rules apply for advance payment for seed, fertilizer, chemicals, and other supply items. However, some items clearly do not qualify for a deduction upon prepayment. For example, if the prepayment is for services to be performed in the subsequent tax year, the deduction will be disallowed. The final and binding expense has not been incurred until the services have been performed. The same can be said for prepayment of interest, insurance, and taxes if paid before the year in which they are actually due.

Land Clearing Expenses and Soil and Water Conservation Expenses

For a taxpayer engaged in the business of farming, elections exist for the handling of land preparation expenses. For both land clearing expenses[6] and soil and water conservation expenses[7] immediate deductions, within defined limits, are available, although

these might usually be considered the types of items that should be capitalized.[8]

Land Clearing Expenses. Expenses for land clearing operations to prepare the land for farming may be considered as a current deduction, but the amount in any one year is limited to $5000 or 25 percent of the *taxable* income (not gross income) derived from farming. Land clearing includes the removal of rocks, trees, stumps, and brush; the moving of earth; the diversion of watercourses; and mineral removal. Taxable income is gross income from all farming operations of the taxpayer reduced by all proper deductions except land clearing expenses. The deductions include the 60 percent capital gains deduction for gain resulting from the sale of draft, breeding, dairy, or sporting livestock.

Expenditures above the $5000 or 25 percent of taxable income limits may not be carried over to subsequent years, and recapture rules apply if the land is sold within 10 years of acquisition.

Soil and Water Conservation Expenses. When a farmer incurs expenses for the purpose of soil and water conservation on land used in farming or for the prevention of soil erosion on land used in farming, these expenses may be capitalized into the value of the farm. If so, they are not deductible. The farmer may, however, elect to treat qualified expenditures as currently deductible expenses up to 25 percent of gross income from *farming* in any one year. Gross income from farming includes income from the sale of farm products and from livestock but not gains from the sale of machinery, land, or similar business assets. The expenses exceeding 25 percent of gross income from farming may be carried forward to succeeding tax years within the 25 percent limit each year. This

---

[6] INT. REV. CODE § 182.
[7] INT. REV. CODE § 175.
[8] Fertilizer, lime, and soil conditioners may be de-

ducted without limits under I.R.C. § 180, whereas limits apply to both land clearing and soil and water conservation expenses.

carry-over can be for an indefinite number of years—until the full expenditure has been deducted. Qualified expenditures include amounts spent for water detention or control activities such as filling gullies, collecting water, retarding runoff, and preventing flood damage; leveling, grading, terracing, and contour furrowing of soil; constructing earthen dams, diversion channels, and drainage ditches; eradication of brush; and planting of windbreaks.

A special rule applies if the farm is sold at a gain within 10 years of acquisition. A portion of the soil and water conservation expenses claimed as deductions will be recaptured as ordinary income—that is, this is added to the year's income for calculation of tax liability. If the farm is sold within 5 years of acquisition, all the soil and water conservation expense deductions are recap-

tured. If the land is disposed of within the sixth year, 80 percent of the deductions are recaptured; within the seventh year, 60 percent; within the eighth year, 40 percent; and within the ninth year, 20 percent. If the land is owned 10 years or more before it is sold, the deduction is not recaptured no matter in which year the expenses were incurred and the deduction claimed.

In order to be eligible for either the land clearing expenditure deduction or the soil and water conservation expenditure deduction, the taxpayer must be engaged in the trade or business of farming. The land involved must be used in farming for the soil and water conservation deduction to be available and must be cleared for farming purposes for the land clearing deduction to apply.

BUSINESS OF FARMING

A.W. PETERSON v. COMMISSIONER
U.S. Tax Court, 1970
29 T.C. Memo 802

During the years in issue, petitioners owned and operated a commercial apple orchard at Manson, Washington, that had produced its first commercial crop in 1945. The orchard consisted of two separate parcels of land, totaling 35 acres, with 48 trees per acre.

The operation of the orchard is a year-round affair, requiring the permanent employment of five people and the hiring of at least twelve additional men during the harvest season, which extends from about September 25 to November 1 of each year.

Both Arthur and his son, Dale Peterson (hereinafter sometimes referred to as Dale), managed the orchard. Dale was almost entirely in charge of the orchard business and paid most of its expenses during the spring, summer and fall of each year, when Arthur was away managing the operation of his other property at Stehekin, Washington.

As noted above, during significant periods of the years in issue Arthur was not present at the orchard. At such times he was at petitioners' property at Stehekin, Washington, a 110 acre tract of land which was purchased in 1943 for $3,700. The property is approximately 45 miles from Manson, at the northwest end of Lake Chelan, borders on the Stehekin River, and is accessible only by boat or airplane.

When the property was purchased, all but eight to ten acres were covered with timber. Arthur began cutting the timber in 1945 and continued to do so up to and including the years in issue. In 1945 Arthur also began construction of a sawmill on the Stehekin property that commenced operation in 1947 but was not entirely completed till 1948. Electricity for the operation of the mill and for other electrical needs at Stehekin was supplied by a hydroelectric generating plant. During the years in issue, the plant consisted of two hydroelectric generators (one installed in 1945 and the other in 1955), and the attendant foundations, footings and water transmission facilities.

When the timber was cut, it was either processed into lumber in the sawmill and sold, or stored on the property for future processing. Timber was cut during the years in issue, but none was processed at the sawmill because of a lack of available power from the generating plant.

Despite his inability to process the timber, Arthur continued to cut and store it during this period with the intention to resume the mill operation as soon as the electric power was restored. Approximately 200,000 board feet of timber was cut during this period when the mill was not in operation.

During the years in issue and prior thereto, tree stumps were blasted and removed from the soil; the holes filled in with soil from the surrounding area and grass seed planted at the Stehekin property. Arthur's primary purpose for planting the grass seed was to enrich the soil. He also intended to produce and market both bluegrass seed and the stalks of bluegrass as hay, however, he never sold any hay because the grass crop was too dense for his mowing equipment. He did not sell any grass seed because its weed seed content had not yet been reduced to a level which met the requirements for sale of Washington State's Agricultural Department.

Other than timber cutting and clearing and grass planting, the only activities carried on at Stehekin during the years in issue were river protection work to prevent erosion and flooding of the land which consisted primarily of diversion of water routes; brush burning to comply with forestry regulations; mowing grass and "repairing" equipment.

By the time of trial herein, 60 acres of the Stehekin property had been cleared, and about 50 acres were planted in bluegrass. The cleared land, however, is not sufficiently extensive to justify the costs of a farming operation, which is Arthur's intent once sufficient land has been cleared. An underground sprinkler system is installed on the entire acreage, installation of which occurred prior to the years in issue, though some minor finishing work was done in 1962.

Petitioners deducted numerous expenses relating to the operation of their properties at Stehekin and Manson, Washington. They argue that they were engaged in two businesses on the Stehekin property during the years in issue, that of logging and sawmilling (hereinafter sometimes referred to as logging) and grass seed farming (hereinafter sometimes referred to as grass farming); and that therefore, their expenses relating to such activities are deductible business expenses. Moreover, petitioners contend that any Stehekin expenditures which are not deductible as business expenditures are capital expenditures for clearing the land to farm and deductible for the years 1963 and 1964 under the section allowing a deduction for land clearing expenses.

Respondent, on the other hand, argues that all expenses relating to the Stehekin property are nondeductible personal expenditures because petitioners were not engaged in any trade or business there. Alternatively, respondent contends that the expenditures were nondeductible capital expenditures. Moreover, respondent argues that the expenditures are not deductible because petitioners were not "engaged in the business of farming" under the provisions allowing a deduction for land clearing expenses.

A taxpayer may be engaged in more than one business simultaneously. Petitioners, therefore, may have been engaged in both a logging and a grass farming business at Stehekin while, concededly, they were engaged in an apple farming business at Manson.

For almost 20 years, petitioners were engaged in cutting timber and sawmilling the timber into lumber at Stehekin. They built a sawmill, employed laborers to cut and process timber and sold timber. During the years in issue, over 200,000 board feet of timber was cut. Though no timber was processed into lumber in 1962, 1963, or 1964, petitioners intended to process their timber and sell it as lumber as soon as they regained electric power to run their sawmill. We hold this activity, carried on for such an extensive length of time, is a trade or business and the expenses which are substantiated as relating thereto are deductible. To be sure, the expenses would not only produce a benefit from the profits of the sale of timber, but also a long-term benefit in that the land became *partially* cleared for farming. But the latter benefit, which required many more steps before its fruition—namely, blasting of the stumps, enriching the soil, etc.—does not detract from the fact that petitioners were independently engaged in a trade or business and the expenses attributable thereto, paid in the operation of that business, were deductible. Since petitioners were cash basis taxpayers they are entitled to a deduction for those expenses substantiated as relating to logging in the years in which the expenses were paid.

The activities, other than the logging, conducted on the Stehekin property, such as grass planting, stump blasting, brush clearing and river protection, are a different matter. We do not believe that petitioners' intent in engaging in these activities was to grass farm and reap a profit therefrom. Rather, the primary purpose was to replenish the soil in order to bring it into a productive capacity for the eventual operation of the property as a farm. No seed was ever sold, nor any attempt made to get approval for its sale from Washington State's Agricultural Department. This aspect of the operation at Stehekin was not a trade or business but rather preparation of the land for future farming. The *entire* benefit from the expenditures in these activities is to accrue in the future when the property is farmed. As such these are capital expenditures. Thus these expenditures are nondeductible unless some other provision of the Internal Revenue Code allows a deduction.

Petitioners contend that any expenses in the years 1963 and 1964, which are not deductible as business expenses may be deducted pursuant to the section allowing a land clearing deduction ("section 182"). This section provides that a person who is engaged in the business of farming may elect to deduct land-clearing expenses, incurred for the purpose of making land suitable for use in farming, in the lesser amount of $5,000 or 25 percent of his taxable income from farming during the taxable year.

Respondent contends first that petitioners were not engaged in a trade or business of farming at Stehekin and, therefore, that section 182 is not applicable. However, section 182's requirement that the taxpayer must be engaged in the business of farming makes no indication that the farming operation must be part of or contiguous to the very property which is being prepared for farming, nor do the committee reports indicate that this is the case. In the absence of any contrary language in the statute or the legislative history, we give the ordinary meaning to this requirement, and construe the section's provision that the taxpayer be engaged in farming to mean that he may be so engaged on any property.

Petitioners also meet the requirement that their purpose be to make the land suitable for farming. Their intent was to farm once a sufficient acreage on the land was clear. Their preparation activity was to enrich soil, clear brush and otherwise put the land in a suitable condition so that it could be farmed. While it is true that they were engaging in their activity over an extended period of time, the section places no time limit within which the property must be ready for farming.

Finally, it is clear that many of the expenses, such as stump blasting, grass planting, and river protection, are "land clearing" expenses. Many of petitioner's activities fall within the terms of the applicable regulations. [The court held that the taxpayer had made a proper election for the year 1963 and allowed a deduction for that year but held that for 1964 the petitioners did not elect according to the applicable provisions so no deduction was allowed for that year. The court then dealt separately with the specific expenses and allowed those which were substantiated by petitioners. Some were disallowed due to inadequate records.]

18.4 CAPITAL GAIN VERSUS ORDINARY INCOME

Ordinarily, a gain from the sale of property is included as income and taxed at ordinary income rates. However, gains on the sale of property used in the business often qualify for treatment as long-term capital gains which receive favored tax treatment.[9] A 60 percent capital gain deduction is avail-

---

[9] INT. REV. CODE § 1221.

able, which means that only 40 percent of long-term gain is subject to tax.[10] For example, assume an asset used in the business—perhaps a breeding bull—is purchased for $1500, kept for over 2 years, then sold for $4500. The gain on the sale is $3000 (assuming no depreciation had been claimed). This $3000 of gain is not fully taxed. Rather, only $1200 is subject to tax because of the 60 percent capital gain deduction. Generally, to qualify as long-term capital gain the asset must have been held for more than 1 year (24 months for cattle and horses used for draft, dairy, breeding, or sporting purposes), if the asset has been held less than the prescribed period, the gain upon sale is treated as ordinary income and is subject to tax at regular rates with no benefit of the capital gains deduction.

The special capital gain treatment is available for what is called "Section 1231" property.[11] This is property used in the business, held for the prescribed period, subject to depreciation, and not included in inventory or held primarily for sale to customers. It specifically includes livestock held for draft, dairy, breeding, or sporting purposes. Cattle and horses have a 24-month holding period, whereas other livestock are eligible after 12 months from the date of acquisition. Also included are unharvested crops sold with the land and timber, coal, and iron royalties or timber contracts treated as a sale in the year in which the timber is cut. In addition, the special capital gain treatment is available upon the sale or exchange of capital assets, such as land, if held for more than 1 year.

In using the capital gain deduction, one caution must be borne in mind. The capital gain deduction is subject to an alternative minimum tax. In some cases the actual taxes due may be higher than regular tax calculation methods would reflect because of the effect of capital gain on this alternative minimum tax.

18.5 DEPRECIATION METHODS

The depreciation deduction serves as the major technique for recovering the cost of depreciable property by charging the cost of property against income generated by the property. The taxpayer has a choice of methods to use in deducting depreciation. Also, an additional part of the cost can be deducted during the year of purchase if an election to claim this extra depreciation is made. Special problems arise when real estate is involved and when depreciable assets are sold.

Straight-Line Method

The straight-line method is the most widely used and the easiest method of taking depreciation. The cost of the property is recovered over the entire useful life of the property.[12] For example, a farmer buys a $30,000 tractor with a useful life of 10 years. The annual depreciation is $3000 ($30,000 ÷ 10). This assumes the salvage value of the asset at the end of the useful life is less than 10 percent of the original cost and that no additional depreciation is claimed for the year of purchase.

Declining-Balance Method

Several declining-balance methods of depreciation are available. The double-declining-balance method is the most rapid.[13] It is allowed only for tangible property with a useful life of 3 years or more for which the "original use" began with the

---

[10] INT. REV. CODE § 1202.
[11] INT. REV. CODE § 1231.

[12] Treas. Reg. § 1.167 (b) (1).
[13] Treas. Reg. § 1.167 (b)-2.

taxpayer—i.e., new property only. This method cannot be used for buildings or structural components of a building. The impact of this method is to allow higher amounts of the cost of an item to be recovered in the early years.

The procedure for using the method is to (1) determine the rate under the straight-line method, (2) double that rate, (3) apply the rate against the adjusted balance each year.

In the example used above, a $30,000 tractor had a useful life of 10 years. This is a rate of 10 percent per year under the straight-line method. Under the double-declining-balance method, the rate would be 20 percent applied as shown in Computation 18.1.

Computation 18.1   Declining-Balance Method of Depreciation

First year:	20%	x	30,000	=	$6000 depreciation
Second year:	20%	x	24,000	=	$4800 depreciation
Third year:	20%	x	19,200	=	$3840 depreciation
Fourth year:	20%	x	15,360	=	$3072 depreciation

Depreciation each year following would be 20 percent of the remaining balance.

Other declining-balance methods may also be used. For example 150 percent declining-balance method is like the double-declining-balance method, except that the rate used is 1½ times the straight-line rate. This method is available for new depreciable property including buildings and their structural components and is allowed for used property other than buildings.

Sum-of-the-Digits Method

The sum-of-the-digits method is another form of rapid depreciation.[14] The depreciation allowed each year is computed by applying a different fraction each year to the amount to be depreciated. The numerator is the remaining years of useful life and the denominator is the sum of the digits of each of the years of useful life.

For a 10-year useful life, the sum of the digits is:

$$1 + 2 + 3 + 4 + 5 + 6 + 7 + 8 + 9 + 10 = 55$$

The depreciation each year is the appropriate fraction times the cost. For example, using the same $30,000 tractor with a 10-year useful life, the depreciation each year is as shown in Computation 18.2.

Computation 18.2   Sum-of-the-Digits Method of Depreciation

First year:	10/55	x	$30,000	=	$5454.54 depreciation
Second year:	9/55	x	$30,000	=	$4909.05 depreciation
Third year:	8/55	x	$30,000	=	$4363.60 depreciation
Fourth year:	7/55	x	$30,000	=	$3818.15 depreciation

[14] Treas. Reg. § 1.167 (b)-3.

Each of the following years' depreciation is calculated in the same manner.

This method, like the declining-balance method, applies only to the original user of the property and only to property having a useful life of 3 or more years and is not available for buildings or their structural components.

In the long run, the amount of depreciation recovered is essentially the same for all the methods. The difference is the amount recovered early in the life of the asset. The taxpayer is permitted to change from one of the rapid methods to the straight-line method during the life of the asset, and the same factors must be evaluated in considering such a change.

Additional First-Year Depreciation

Additional first-year depreciation is extra depreciation allowed in the year of acquisition of a depreciable item.[15] It amounts to up to 20 percent of the cost of the property and applies to new or used property with a useful life of at least 6 years. It is not available for buildings, structures, or improvements to real estate.

In the year the property is purchased, a deduction of up to 20 percent of the cost of the asset can be made in addition to any regular depreciation allowed on the item. It serves to reduce the undepreciated balance on which regular depreciation can be claimed. The amount of the deduction is limited to $2000 on a separate return or $4000 on a joint return.

For example, the $30,000 tractor with a 10-year useful life can be depreciated as shown in Computation 18.3 (assuming a separate return).

Computation 18.3   Additional First-Year Depreciation

$30,000	original cost
2,000	additional first-year depreciation (20% x $30,000 = $6000 but is limited to $2000)
$28,000	÷ 10 years = $2800 regular depreciation per year on the straight-line method

In some cases it will be appropriate to use one of the rapid depreciation methods even after taking the additional first-year depreciation allowance.

Real Estate Depreciation

Depreciation on real estate applies only to buildings, structural components, and other improvements attached to land.[16] Land itself is permanent so it has no measurable life; thus, no depreciation can be claimed for investment in the land itself. Depreciable real estate does not include the personal residence since it is not used in the trade or business.

For real property used in the trade or business, the amount of depreciation allowed is limited. It does not qualify for additional first-year depreciation, and most rapid methods of calculating ordinary depreciation cannot be used if the real estate was acquired after July 24, 1969. New property is the exception in that the 150 percent

---

[15] Treas. Reg. § 1.179-1.   [16] INT. REV. CODE § 167(j).

Table 18.1 Asset Guideline Classes and Periods; Asset Depreciation Ranges; Asset Guideline Repair Allowance Percentages; (Rev. Proc. 77-10, 1977 IRB No. 12 at 4)

Asset Guideline Class	Description of Assets Included	Asset Depreciation Range (in years)			Annual Asset Guideline Repair Allowance Percentage
		Lower Limit	Asset Guideline Period	Upper Limit	
	Depreciable assets used in the following activities:				
01.1	Agriculture: Includes machinery and equipment, grain bins, and fences but no other land improvements, that are used in the production of crops or plants, vines, and trees; livestock; the operation of farm dairies, nurseries; greenhouses, sod farms, mushroom cellars, cranberry bogs, apiaries, and fur farms; the performance of agricultural, animal husbandry, and horticultural services.	8	10	12	11
01.11	Cotton Ginning Assets	9.5	12	14.5	5.5
01.21	Cattle, Breeding or Dairy	5.5	7	8.5	
01.22	Horses, Breeding or Work	8	10	12	
01.23	Hogs, Breeding	2.5	3	3.5	
01.24	Sheep and Goats, Breeding	4	5	6	
01.3	Farm Buildings	20	25	30	5

declining balance method is available. Also, residential rental property can qualify for the double declining balance method if there is more than one rental unit in the building.

If depreciable real estate is sold, some or all of the depreciation claimed may be recaptured—that is, may be treated as income in the year of sale.[17] It is treated as ordinary income with no capital gain deduction applicable. It is recaptured only to the extent of gain. For property owned in 1979 or thereafter, the recapture rules apply only to excess depreciation claimed after 1969, but the excess is fully recaptured as ordinary income when the property is sold.

Slightly different recapture rules apply to depreciable real property (not buildings and their structural components) used as an integral part of the business for the production of income, such as fences, water installations, outside light and power systems, depreciable parts of dams and ponds, pavements, etc., as well as farm storage facilities which are not buildings such as grain bins, corn cribs, silos, etc. For these items recapture of depreciation applies for deductions

---

[17] INT. REV. CODE §§ 1245, 1250.

taken after 1961, and the amount of gain which represents the recovery of depreciation is treated as ordinary income.

Useful Life of Depreciable Property

The rate of depreciation, the fast methods of depreciation, and the 20 percent first-year depreciation (as well as investment credit) are all related to the useful life of the depreciable assets. Useful life, for these purposes, can be determined by the past experience of the taxpayer and the actual expected life the asset has in that particular taxpayer's hands based on facts and circumstances.

An alternative method of determining useful life is to use guideline lives determined for broad classes of assets known as the Asset Depreciation Range (ADR). The ADR system allows a taxpayer to choose a useful life 20 percent below or 20 percent above the established guideline life. Use of the ADR system to establish useful life is optional. The asset classes and ranges are published periodically by the Internal Revenue Service. The most recent guidelines applicable to agriculture are outlined in Table 18.1. It should be noted that many farmers do not use these guidelines and that much agricultural equipment is set up on a 7 year depreciation schedule.

DEPRECIABLE PROPERTY

WOLFSEN LAND & CATTLE CO. v. COMMISSIONER
U.S. Tax Court, 1979
72 T.C. 1

Petitioner Wolfsen Land & Cattle Company is a California corporation. Petitioner accounts for its income on a cash basis and, as mentioned above, utilizes a fiscal year ending July 31 as its tax accounting period. Timely Federal Corporate income tax returns were filed by petitioner for its taxable years ended July 31, 1971, 1972, 1973 and 1974.

The amount of net operating loss originally determined by petitioner for its taxable year ended July 31, 1974 was $596,124. This operating loss was in part attributable to certain depreciation deductions taken by a partnership Wolfsen M.C. Ranch (partnership), in which petitioner is a limited partner, for the depreciation of the earthwork components of an extensive irrigation system on the partnership's ranch, the M.C. Ranch (hereinafter M.C. or Ranch). Prior to the trial herein the parties reached agreement with respect to the allowability of all the deductions constituting the net operating loss except these depreciation deductions. It is, thus, the propriety of these deductions and if the deductions are proper, the correct basis for depreciation and the period over which the system must be depreciated, that is at issue in this case.

The farming operations of the Ranch are dependent upon an irrigation system. All the Ranch's crops are grown on irrigated land. The system contains approximately 90 miles of man-made earthen ditches, canals, and levees for conveying and containing water. Approximately 95 percent of these ditches are used for both irrigation supply and drainage.

Most of the irrigation system is composed of earthwork interspersed with "hardware" components such as dams, valves, pumps, etc. The parties have stipulated that the system's hardware components have a useful life of 20 years. The system's earthworks themselves are differently named according to their size and function. On the Ranch, 95 percent of the earthen water-moving structures are used both for water delivery and drainage. These combination structures are referred to herein as "ditches".

The proper maintenance of these various structures is essential to the Ranch's efficient operation. It is important that the supply and drainage ditches in the irrigation system be kept clear of sediment and water plants so that water can be quickly and efficiently delivered to and drained from the fields. The main method of ditch maintenance is the use of a machine called a "dragline". A "dragline" is a mobile platform onto which is attached a motor driven "boom" or arm. On the end of the boom is a "bucket" which is designed to scoop, hold, and then empty itself of dirt. The booms and buckets of these machines vary in length and carrying capacity (the latter being measured in cubic yards).

A combination of factors requires that the ditches be worked on with a dragline periodically to prevent dysfunction. Although petitioner performs spot or emergency repairs on the system, it does not have a plan of annual repair and maintenance. Rather, petitioner had adopted a plan whereby it delays repair until a particular stretch of ditch or levee absolutely requires draglining or other work in order to avoid dysfunction. The Ranch's combination ditches become dysfunctional (i.e., unable to perform efficiently the tasks for which they were designed) and require cleaning at the end of 10 years. The Ranch's large levees and canals can withstand 30 years between maintenance procedures. The Ranch's field checks require maintenance to prevent dysfunction every 5 years. Thus, under petitioner's plan it needs to dragline any one ditch, for example, only once every approximately 10 years. At the end of this time the hydraulic capacity of the supply and drainage ditches is so reduced that they can neither supply nor drain water efficiently.

The purpose and effect of draglining a ditch is to restore it to its original, or near original, hydraulic capacity. Once a ditch is draglined it is left unattended until such time as it needs to be redraglined or requires emergency repair. It can cost as much to clean a ditch as it costs to build one *ab initio*, disregarding inflation.

In arguing whether or not the earthen components of the Ranch's irrigation system are depreciable the parties have raised the issue of the character of certain dragline and related system maintenance expenditures. Petitioner has argued that these activities and expenditures are capital in nature as they are for the reconstruction of parts of the system. Respondent has argued that the activities and expenditures are not capital and implies that they are currently deductible.

The partnership's irrigation system will qualify for a depreciation deduction if it is property described in section 167. That section says in relevant part:

SEC. 167. DEPRECIATION.

(a)   General Rule—There shall be allowed as a depreciation deduction a reasonable allowance for the exhaustion, wear and tear (including a reasonable allowance for obsolescence)—

(1) of property used in the trade or business...

Without question the irrigation system is a vital integral part of the economic value of the Ranch. Absent the system the Ranch would be a bog of little or no worth.

While it is obvious from the fact that the dragline expenses at issue were incurred and that the system was subject to wear and tear, it does not follow that the system was going to expire at some predictable time. In fact, while petitioner indicated that the Ranch had not been maintained adequately by its previous owner, it made no effort to describe the condition of the system in terms of its longevity when the Ranch was purchased. Furthermore, the evidence affirmatively shows the indeterminability of the system's useful life.

We hold that the petitioner has failed to prove that the system or any of its non-hardware components had a definite life viewed from a perspective of the date of purchase. Thus such items are not entitled to an allowance for depreciation.

A much more difficult question concerns the treatment of the amounts spent by petitioner to keep the system operable, the so-called dragline expenses.

We have noted that the partnership elected to operate the system according to a plan under which any particular system component was allowed to deteriorate until it was almost dysfunctional, at which time it was draglined. In this way the present system will be maintained at generally its original hydraulic capacity for the foreseeable future.

The partnership had no intention, and never has had any intention, to alter the ultimate hydraulic capacity of any of the system's canals, lateral drains, or other ditches. It had no plans to increase, beyond current design limits, the strength of the Ranch's levees and checks, or to relocate a canal, lateral, drain, ditch, levee, or check.

Petitioner claims that the partnership should be allowed to depreciate all its ditches on their cost basis over 10 years and then capitalize and depreciate the costs of draglining the ditch to reopen it.

While respondent does not precisely spell out his position, he states his view on brief that "the depreciation issue...should be disposed of by the Court's finding...that the earthwork at issue, given adequate maintenance would have an indefinite useful life." Presumably he is taking the uncharacteristic position that the petitioner should deduct currently the expenses incurred to maintain the system.

Thus, we are faced with something of a conundrum, how do we treat a maintenance-type expense substantial in amount, which only restores a subject to its original operating condition, yet need be repeated only on the average of every 10 years and is performed on a subject of indefinite life.

To permit a current deduction of such a large expenditure with a beneficial effect lasting on the average of 10 years would surely distort that year's income. Yet to deny even an amortization deduction for an expenditure with a specific demonstrable beneficial life on the grounds that its deductibility is contaminated by its relationship to an asset of indefinite life, i.e., the land, would similarly require an uneven reporting of income.

Since a basic premise of the income tax laws is to relate expenses to the income which they helped earn, a reasonable solution to our conundrum is to hold that the expenses in issue should be written off over their useful life. In short we would subscribe independent status to those expenditures on the basis that they create a free-standing intangible asset with an amortizable 10-year life.

The cases in this area have focused on both value and useful life and whether the particular expenditure at issue was made pursuant to a larger plan the purpose and effect of which was to increase the value or extend the useful life of the item involved. Those cases which have held an expense currently deductible have also found that the expense did not substantially increase the repaired item's value or original useful life.

Applying the principles of these cases to the peculiar facts before us we consider several points to be important: The subject expenditures are part of a systematic plan under which most of the earthworks on the Ranch will be draglined. Thus the dragline expenditures have significant impact on the value of the system. A cleaned ditch or reworked levee is of more value than is one in need of repair. A more efficient system renders the Ranch more productive and valuable. We also believe that to the extent that the expenditures have the effect of replacing the previously wasted intangible created by the last draglining of the subject ditch or levee, they have a substantial impact on the value of the system, as well as produce a separate item of value. Related to this point is the magnitude of the expenditures themselves. Petitioner indicates that it can cost as much to dragline a ditch as it did to construct one originally.

Secondly, we consider important the fact that the expenditures in issue produce an item of value which is not used up by the end of the taxable year in which made. Indeed, many of these expenditures produce value which is used up only gradually over the course of up to 30 years. Thirdly, these expenditures will affect the Ranch's production of income over a course of many years. In the case of, for example, general field ditches these expenditures will have an effect on the ditch's efficiency and hence on the Ranch's production of income for up to 10 years. Finally, we note that the item of value produced wastes over a predeterminable useful life. Any particular ditch, levee, or canal is less efficient and more clogged with sediment and tule growth at the end of any year than it was the year before. Each year part of the value and effect of the last draglining operation on that part of the system is used up—until at the end of 10 years the whole value has been used up and the ditch again needs to be draglined. In sum, these expenditures are more than merely "incidental." They are, rather, in the nature of capital "replacement" expenditures which must be capitalized and amortized over their appropriate useful lives, i.e., 5 years for field checks, 10 years for ditches, 30 years for large levees and canals.

18.6 INVESTMENT CREDIT

A tax credit reduces tax liability as a direct offset against taxes due. The credit of most interest to farm operators is the investment credit which is allowed in an amount equal to 10 percent of the investment in most depreciable property (except most buildings and their structural components).[18]

To qualify for the credit, the eligible property must have a useful life of at least 3 years. If the useful life is 3 years or more but less than 5, the amount of the investment which qualifies for the credit is 33 1/3 percent. If the useful life is 5 years or more but less than 7, the amount which qualifies is 66 2/3 percent. If the useful life is 7 years or more, the full amount qualifies. The amount of credit used in any one year cannot exceed $25,000 plus a fixed percentage of the excess over $25,000. (The percentage is 70 percent in 1980, 80 percent in 1981, and 90 percent thereafter.) If the amount of credit available in any one year exceeds these limits, it may be carried back to 3 prior years and forward to future years.

Most depreciable property is eligible for application of the investment credit. Depreciable machinery, equipment, and livestock with a useful life of 3 years or more qualifies. Single-purpose livestock or horticultural structures, such as hog and cattle feeding facilities, greenhouses, poultry houses, milking parlors, etc., qualify. Rehabilitation expenditures on farm buildings made after October 31, 1978, may be eligible if the building has been in use at least 20 years. Otherwise, investments in farm buildings or structural components do not qualify.

The investment credit is subject to recapture upon early disposition of the asset for which it was claimed. The amount of tax for the year of disposition is increased by the amount of credit not earned—that is, the excess over the amount that would have been allowed if the actual useful life had been used in determining the amount of credit originally claimed. For example, if a full credit of $1000 on a $10,000 item with a useful life of 7 years is claimed as an investment tax credit and then the item is sold after only 3 years, the credit actually earned was $333 (10 percent x 33 1/3 percent x $10,000). The excess of $667 must be recaptured and paid in the year of disposition of the item.

INVESTMENT CREDIT

LESHER v. COMMISSIONER
U.S. Tax Court, No. 32 1979
73 T.C.

From 1960 to 1967 petitioners leased 320 acres of land in Iowa and farmed it. On November 2, 1967, petitioners purchased the 320 acres pursuant to a sales contract. During the subsequent years, including the years in

---

[18] INT. REV. CODE § 46-48.

issue, petitioners have continued to farm this land and have raised cattle and pigs. Petitioners made a number of improvements to the property, including a quonset-type machine shed, corn bins, hog raising facilities and the facility with respect to which they claimed the investment credit here in issue.

During the summer of 1974 petitioners purchased and constructed a "Morton Building," which was designated by Morton Buildings as a "general purpose livestock barn." Since the facility's construction, petitioners have stored hay therein. During the winter months, at which time the cattle are unable to forage for themselves, petitioners feed that hay to their cattle.

The total cost of constructing the facility was $9,324.79, of which $7,923 constituted payment for the structural portions of the facility. The structural components include a roof, roof trusses, three exterior walls, siding, doors and cement foundation for each six-inch post supporting the facility. Petitioners paid $1,401.79 for the cement floor.

The structure is 81 feet in length and 53 feet in width (including a 3 foot overhang of the roof on the open south side). Doors are located on the east and west sides and are 10 feet 6 inches in height and 15 feet 5 inches in width. Facing the structure's south side, which is the only side completely open to the weather, the first 5 feet has a cement floor over which hangs the roof, and the height from the floor to the roof is 8 feet. The next 15 feet is separated from the first 5 feet by gates erected by petitioners after the initial construction of the building. Those gates can be swung open, and the 15 feet located immediately thereafter has a concrete floor covered by a roof, sloping up to a maximum height of 12 feet. The next 30 feet of the structure, which extends to the north side of the facility and is separated from the prior 20 feet by planking installed by Mr. Lesher to restrain cattle movement, has a dirt floor and is covered by a roof having a minimum height of 17 feet 6 inches. Thus, the roof peaks near its north side and drops to its lowest point on the south side.

The facility is petitioners' sole structure for hay storage. Hay is stored in the facility from the north wall to the south side, there being no interior solid walls. When filled, the structure holds in excess of 5,000 bales of hay.

To protect the hay from debasement the cattle are restrained from entering the structure past the gates until all hay previously stored in the 20-foot cement floored area has been consumed. Thereafter, the gates are opened, and the cattle are allowed to roam into the entire concrete floored area. The planking installed by petitioners subsequent to the structure's initial construction restrains the cattle from entering the 30–foot dirt floored portion. That 30-by-81 foot area is used solely for the storage of hay. To feed the cattle, on a regular basis Mr. Lesher rotates forward several bales previously stored in the latter area, placing them in the cement floored area for the cattle to eat. Thus, when hay is harvested and baled from the fields each season, it is moved into petitioners' structure and placed in the positions of bales previously eaten.

After Morton Buildings erected the facility petitioners added the 20–foot concrete flooring on a slope away from the dirt area to further insure against quality deterioration of the hay. That construction directs all cattle excretions away from the hay storage area.

The final issue is whether the facility constructed by petitioners in 1974 qualifies for investment credit by virtue of being "section 38 property" as defined in the Internal Revenue Code. In pertinent part, section 38 property is defined as follows:

SEC. 48. DEFINITIONS; SPECIAL RULES.

(*a*)   Section 38 Property—
   (1) In general—Except as provided in this subsection, the term "section 38 property" means—
      (*A*) tangible personal property, or
      (*B*) other tangible property (not including a building and its structural components) but only if such property—
         (*i*) is used as an integral part of manufacturing, production, or extraction or of furnishing transportation, communications, electrical energy, gas, water, or sewage disposal services, or...
         (*iii*) constitutes a facility used in connection with any of the activities referred to in clause (*i*) for the bulk storage of fungible commodities (including commodities in a liquid or gaseous state), or...
      (*D*) single purpose agricultural or horticultural structures,...

The Revenue Act of 1978 amended section 48(*a*)(1) to include subsection (*D*), which is entitled "single purpose agricultural or horticultural structures" and is given meaning by section 48(*p*)(2). Section 48(*p*)(2) states:

(2) Single purpose livestock structure—The term "single purpose livestock structure" means any enclosure or structure specifically designed, constructed, and used—
      (*A*) for housing, raising, and feeding a particular type of livestock and their produce, and
      (*B*) for housing the equipment (including any replacements) necessary for the housing, raising, and feeding referred to in subparagraph (*A*).

Respondent argues that petitioners' facility does not qualify as a single purpose agricultural or horticultural structure because it is a multipurpose structure.

H. Rept. No. 95–1800, 95th Cong., 2d Sess. (1978), 1978–3 C.B. 523,561, states:

In order to be included under this provision, a livestock structure must be specifically designed, constructed, and used for the housing, raising and feeding of livestock and their produce.... The full range of livestock breeding, raising and production activities is intended to be included so that special purpose structures will qualify for credit if used, for example, to breed chickens or hogs, to produce milk from dairy cattle, or to produce feeder cattle or pigs, broiler chickens, or eggs. In addition, the structure or enclosure must be designed and used to house equipment necessary to feed and care for the livestock. As a result, such facilities must include, as an integral part of the structure or enclosure, equipment to contain the livestock and to provide water, feed and temperature control, if necessary....

It should be emphasized that the structure must be used exclusively for the purpose for which it was specifically designed and constructed. As a result of this requirement, a hog structure will not be eligible property, for example, if it is used for the housing and feeding of poultry or cattle or if more than incidental use of a structure is made to store feed or machinery....

S. Rept. No. 95-1263, 95th Cong., 2d Sess. (1978), 1978-3 C.B. 315, 415, highlights the application proposed for section 48(a)(1)(D):

Also, a structure ceases to be a qualifying structure if it used for a purpose (such as for storage of feed or equipment) which does not qualify it for the investment credit under this or other definitions of qualifying property.

It is intended that this provision be broadly construed to apply to all types of special purpose structures and enclosures used to breed, raise and feed livestock and poultry....Thus this provision will cover unitary hog, poultry, and cattle raising systems,...

In applying the Senate and House Reports to this case, we are of the opinion that the structure does qualify as a single purpose agriculture structure. We earlier determined that petitioners specifically designed, constructed, and have used the facility for the raising and feeding of livestock. Although petitioners have stressed their use of the structure for storage of hay, the facts show that the building was laid out specifically to accommodate the convenient feeding of the cattle with this stored hay. The hay was not stored in the structure to be sold or to be carried to another location to feed the cattle. Considering all the facts in this record, we conclude that the storage of the feed (hay) was incidental to the use of the structure as a feeding facility. Mr. Lesher testified that the structure is not used to house the cattle, but rather to feed them. However, he stated that cattle infrequently have sought shelter there when protection from the weather is necessary. There was no other shelter provided on the farm for the cattle since generally they need no shelter.

Considering these facts, in our view the facility provides the full range of livestock raising activities necessary in petitioners' operations and is the only structure used by petitioners for "housing, raising, and feeding" cattle. In broadly constructing section 48(a)(1)(D) as intended by Congress, we hold that petitioners are entitled to an investment credit on the Morton structure as a single purpose livestock structure.

18.7 TAX EFFECT OF BUYING AND SELLING LAND

The sale of real estate usually results in gain. This gain can receive the favored capital gain treatment if the property has been held for more than 1 year. The amount of gain in such transactions is the difference between the sales price and the tax basis in the real estate.[19] The tax basis in land is essentially the original cost plus the cost of any improvements added, less any depreciation previously claimed on property subject to depreciation. Land is nondepreciable; thus the tax basis for unimproved land is the acquisition cost. If any improvements are added and are not claimed as deductible expenses, the undepreciated portion adds to the tax basis of the property. The tax basis in property received by gift is the same tax basis that the property had in the hands of the donor. For inherited property, the tax basis is the fair market value of the property at the date of death of the previous owner.

Installment Sales

When property is sold, any gain on the sale is normally reported in the year of sale. If it is a major transaction—land, for example—the amount of gain may be substantial. If the total amount of gain is taxed in the year of sale, the impact on tax liability can be great because the taxpayer is forced into a higher tax bracket.

One method of avoiding high-bracket tax liability is by use of an installment sale contract in which payment of the purchase price is made over a period of years. A special provision is available for the installment sale by which the taxpayer may report a pro rata part of the gain as each installment payment is received rather than all in the year of sale.[20] The installment sale provision allows tax deferral and permits the postponing of recognition of gain until the year in which payments are received.

To qualify as an installment sale, the contract must provide for interest at a rate of no less than 9 percent. If this is not provided for in the contract, the IRS will presume interest at 10 percent compounded semi-annually. This can affect the amount of the payment that is considered as interest for tax purposes.

If the sale qualifies for the installment sale election, the amount of income to be reported each year is a pro rata share of the gain in the transaction. For example, assume a farm is sold for $150,000 with a $30,000 down payment, with the balance payable on a 6-year contract at $20,000 per year with interest of at least 9 percent. Assume that the seller's basis in the property is $105,000. This would mean that $45,000 or 30 percent of the total sales price is gain. Thus 30 percent of the first year's $30,000 payment and of each succeeding year's $20,000 payment is gain. By spreading the gain over a period of years, the taxpayer would have a lower tax bracket with less total tax liability.

If the buyer takes over an existing mortgage on the property the amount of income to be reported each year will be determined by comparing the gain ("gross profit") to the selling price reduced by the mortgage ("contract price"). For example, assume a

---

[19] INT. REV. CODE § 1011.

[20] Treas. Reg. § 1.453-1. Proposed regulations have been issued which if adopted, could alter some of the provisions significantly. In late 1980 Congress passed a new provision (H.R. 6833—Installment Sales Revision Act) which modified the installment sales provisions significantly. Under the new provisions no limit is placed on the amount of down payment nor is it required that payments be received in more than one year.

buyer purchases a farm for $200,000, with $50,000 paid in the year of sale; takes on a mortgage of $75,000; and agrees to pay the balance at $7500 per year for 10 years with interest of at least 9 percent. If the seller's basis in the property is $105,000, this would mean that $95,000 is gain, or "gross profit." The selling price ($200,000) less the mortgage ($75,000) leaves a "contract price" of $125,000. The "gross profit" ($95,000) bears the relation to the "contract price" ($125,000) of 76 percent. Thus 76 percent of the $50,000 payment in the first year and 76 percent of each $7500 annual payment is gain.

Like-Kind Exchanges

There are special rules that apply in the exchange of farms which can allow for tax deferral. If one farm is traded for another (or for "like-kind" property as defined in the tax law), any recognition of gain is postponed if the trade is, in effect, a continuation of the original property.[21] The new property takes over the basis of the old, which is adjusted upward for any cash boot paid. However, if cash boot or other property is received in the transaction, gain must be recognized to the extent of the boot or the fair market value of the other property. For example, if a farmer trades one farm for another and receives $10,000 in cash plus farm equipment valued at $5000, the farmer would have to recognize $15,000 in gain.

Sale of Residence

Tax deferral is possible on the gain resulting from the sale of a residence if another residence is acquired within 18 months before or after the sale of the old residence.[22] If the cost of the new residence equals or exceeds the sale price of the old, then tax on the gain can be deferred. Regarding the sale of a residence by persons 55 years of age or older, special rules apply which allow the first $100,000 of gain on the sale of a personal residence to be excluded from income.[23] This provision does not apply to the sale of real estate other than the residence.

18.8 FILING THE TAX RETURN/ TAX AUDITS

Most taxpayers rely on professional preparers in filing of the income tax return. However, much of the tax planning must occur prior to the end of the year, and an increasing number of farmers are finding that they must obtain the services of competent tax advisers to assist in the day-to-day tax planning. By such planning, good records, and a properly completed and filed tax return one can avoid most questions concerning the return.

Farmers (those whose gross income from farming exceeds two-thirds of their gross income from all sources) are allowed to file a declaration of estimated tax on or before January 15 rather than quarterly.[24] Or if the farmer files the income tax return before March 1, no declaration of estimated taxes is required.[25]

Once the return is filed, it is scanned by computer for questionable entries. It may then be checked by IRS personnel for irregularities. If these reviews indicate that a challenge is necessary, the taxpayer is notified. This notice may consist of a request for additional information or for a meeting

---

[21] INT. REV. CODE § 1031.
[22] INT. REV. CODE § 1034.
[23] INT. REV. CODE § 121.

[24] INT. REV. CODE § 6073 (b).
[25] INT. REV. CODE § 6015 (f).

with an IRS examiner. At this point the taxpayer often can provide the additional information requested or sufficiently answer the examiner's questions to resolve any problems. If adjustments in the amount of tax due are made by the auditor, the taxpayer can agree and pay the additional tax or can request an appeal. Usually an immediate conference can be held with supervisory personnel of the IRS or a request for conference can be filed. If no satisfactory agreement is reached at the appeals conference concerning tax due, the taxpayer can either pay the tax, file a claim for refund and then file suit in federal court if the refund is denied, or refuse to pay the tax and file a petition in the U.S. Tax Courts. In tax cases, the burden is on the taxpayer to prove matters in dispute, so the outcome of the case will depend on how effectively the taxpayer can present the case.

TAX RETURNS

UNITED STATES v. TAYLOR
U.S. Court of Appeals, 5th Circuit, 1978
574 F. 2d 232

Appellant, Moody Aubrey Taylor, was convicted on three counts of willfully making and subscribing false personal income tax returns in violation of 26 U.S.C. § 7206(a).[26] The district court sentenced him to imprisonment for concurrent terms of two years each on Counts 1 and 2, relating to the tax years 1969 and 1970, and three years on Count 3, relating to the tax year 1972.

Taylor challenges his conviction on several grounds, relying primarily upon his assertion that proof of unreported gross receipts is not sufficient to support a conviction for violating Section 7206(1). We affirm.

Defendant Taylor was employed by Producers Grain Corporation (P.G.C.), a regional grain cooperative headquartered in Amarillo, Texas. In 1969, P.G.C. entered the custom cattle feeding business, feeding cattle P.G.C. feed for a fee plus the cost of feed. Defendant managed P.G.C.'s feeding operation from its inception and became vice president in charge of the livestock division.

P.G.C. encouraged its employees purchase cattle to be fed in P.G.C.'s feed lots. In the three tax years in question herein defendant bought and sold cattle on his own account and in partnerships and joint ventures with others, feeding the cattle in P.G.C.'s feed lots.

---

[26] U.S.C. § 7206 (1977) provides that: "Any person who—

(1)   "Declaration under penalties of perjury. Willfully makes and subscribes any return, statement, or other document, which contains or is verified by a written declaration that it is made under the penalties of perjury, and which he does not believe to be true and correct as to every material matter;...shall be fined not more than $5,000, or imprisoned not more than 3 years, or both, together with the costs of prosecution."

Defendant did not report any livestock receipts on his 1970 or 1971 income tax returns and did not file Schedules E or F with either return. On his 1972 return defendant filed both schedules and reported some, but not all, of his livestock receipts for the year.

In essence, Taylor's defense to the allegations was that his unreported income was offset by unreported losses. He testified that he did not know that he was required to report losses. Defendant kept no systematic written records of his cattle transactions, relying upon periodic mental calculations to determine that his losses exceeded profits.

We do not consider it oversimplification to assert that inherent in the scheme of self-assessment of income taxes is the imperative that a return by a taxpayer must be truthful as to every material matter.

The only questions at issue in this case were whether the return was not true and correct as to every material matter and whether defendant possessed the requisite *mens rea*.

The trial court charged the jury thus on the issue of materiality:

I also rule as a matter of law that if you find that a substantial amount of partnership income, livestock receipts, commissions, or other income was omitted from one or more of the federal income tax returns in issue here, such omission is of a material matter as contemplated by Section 7206, Subsection 1, of Title 26 of the United States Code.

Counsel for defendant objected to the charge that the omission of livestock receipts is material as a matter of law.

This appeal raises squarely the question of whether a taxpayer's failure to report substantial amounts of gross livestock receipts on Schedule F renders the return materially false. We hold that it does.

The trial judge did not err in deciding the question of materiality as a matter of law rather than submitting it to the jury. We have long held that in a prosecution for perjury the materiality of the alleged false statement is a question of law. The rule applies to prosecutions under section 7206(1).

The test for materiality in this case is whether the information is essential in order to permit the Internal Revenue Service to verify and monitor the reporting of income.

In the instant case the information required by Schedule F was vitally necessary for the IRS to verify defendant's claim that he realized a net loss from his livestock transactions. Without such information the IRS was compelled to conduct an extensive investigation of bank deposit records in an attempt to reconstruct defendant's income. Here the taxpayer conducted dozens of transactions involving over one hundred thousand dollars in receipts in each tax year and kept no written records. In such a case the burden imposed upon the IRS to verify the taxpayer's return is so extreme that it verges upon impossibility.

In sum, we hold that the jury was correctly instructed that the omission of substantial amounts of livestock receipts from Taylor's income tax returns in 1970, 1971 and 1972 would, as a matter of law, constitute the omission of a material matter. Taylor was permitted to present as a defense that he did not believe the omission was material because offsetting expenses rendered it without tax consequences. The existence of such offsets, however, does not go to materiality of the omitted receipts but to the lack of *mens rea* in the omission.

We also reject defendant's contention that because the schedules were not expressly promulgated by any regulation, section 7206(1) does not require truthful reporting on Schedules E and F.

While there is no explicit requirement in the regulations for the completion and filing of Schedules E and F, it is implicit in required Form 1040 that such schedules, when appropriate, become integral parts of such form and are incorporated therein by reference. Each Form 1040 filed by this defendant included lines reading "Pensions and annuities, rents and royalties, partnerships, estates or trusts, etc. (attach Schedule E)," and "Farm income (or loss) (attach Schedule F)." Therefore, we conclude that section 7206(1) requires the same duty of honest reporting on schedules as it requires for entries on the Form proper.

Thus, defendant's understatement of his receipts on his 1972 return rendered the return untrue and incorrect. Likewise, defendant's omission of schedules reporting his receipts for 1970 and 1971 rendered those returns false.

The judgment is affirmed.

STUDY QUESTIONS

1. What is the most important concept in managing income to minimize tax liability?

2. What is "constructive receipt" of income? What rules apply to determine whether constructive receipt of income rules apply?

3. What factors are used to determine whether a person is "hobby farming"? What is the effect of a finding that a person is hobby farming?

4. What tests must be met in order to claim a deduction for prepaid farm expenses?

5. What is the difference in the tax treatment of a land clearing expense and a soil and water conservation expense?

6. Compare and contrast the various methods of calculating depreciation.

7. When may additional first-year depreciation be claimed, and how is it calculated?

8. What property qualifies for investment credit, and how is it calculated?

9. What is the advantage of the installment sale reporting option for gain from the sale of real estate?

10. Under what circumstances does the sale of a residence allow for deferral of gain or for the exclusion of gain from income?

Index